PROGRAMMING MICROSOFT'S CLOUDS

Programming Microsoft's Clouds

Programming Microsoft's Clouds

WINDOWS AZURE™ AND OFFICE 365

Thomas Rizzo
Razi bin Rais
Michiel van Otegem
Darrin Bishop
George Durzi
Zoiner Tejada
David Mann

WILEY

John Wiley & Sons, Inc.

Programming Microsoft's Clouds: Windows Azure™ and Office 365

Published by
John Wiley & Sons, Inc.
10475 Crosspoint Boulevard
Indianapolis, IN 46256
www.wiley.com

Copyright © 2012 by John Wiley & Sons, Inc., Indianapolis, Indiana

Published simultaneously in Canada

ISBN: 978-0-470-07656-9
ISBN: 978-1-118-22264-5 (ebk)
ISBN: 978-1-118-23655-0 (ebk)
ISBN: 978-1-118-26148-4 (ebk)

Manufactured in the United States of America

10 9 8 7 6 5 4 3 2 1

For general information on our other products and services please contact our Customer Care Department within the United States at (877) 762-2974, outside the United States at (317) 572-3993 or fax (317) 572-4002.

Wiley publishes in a variety of print and electronic formats and by print-on-demand. Some material included with standard print versions of this book may not be included in e-books or in print-on-demand. If this book refers to media such as a CD or DVD that is not included in the version you purchased, you may download this material at http://booksupport .wiley.com. For more information about Wiley products, visit www.wiley.com.

Library of Congress Control Number: 2012934990

For Lexi, Leila, and Stacy, I will love you forever.

—THOMAS RIZZO

I would like to dedicate my work to my mother Zahida Rais and sister Khaizran Siddiqui—they provide me amazing confidence and support regardless of the circumstances. You are the best in the world!

—RAZI BIN RAIS

To Annette, Jarod, and B'Elanna

—MICHIEL VAN OTEGEM

To my sweet Maxie.

—GEORGE DURZI

I would like to dedicate this book to my wife Ashley as we start our lives as a married couple together. Your patience and support during the long nights spent researching, working, and perfecting is love in its purest form.

—ZOINER TEJADA

To my family.

—DAVID MANN

ABOUT THE AUTHORS

THOMAS RIZZO is a senior director in the Microsoft Office 365 team. Before working in Office 365, Tom worked in the SharePoint, SQL Server, and Exchange businesses at Microsoft. You can reach Tom at thomriz@microsoft.com.

RAZI BIN RAIS is a Microsoft Most Valuable Professional (MVP) for SharePoint Server and currently based in New York. For over eight years, he has been a SharePoint SME and helped companies like Microsoft and Avanade to successfully implement SharePoint Server for their enterprise customers. He is also a Microsoft Certified Trainer (MCT) and enjoys conducting trainings and informal chalk talks. As an active speaker for INETA since 2004, he's presented in conferences and events including the SharePoint Conference SEA, Microsoft TechDays, Microsoft ISV innovation Days and SharePoint Saturdays. He holds a master's degree in Computer Science and passionately works on emerging technologies. He is a founder and leader for New York Office 365 User Group www.meetup.com/off365. In his spare time he likes watching cricket and writing for his blog at http://razirais.wordpress.com. He tweets @razibinrais and can be reached at razibinrais@live.com.

MICHIEL VAN OTEGEM is senior software architect at Sogeti Netherlands. He has a broad expertise on the Microsoft platform and beyond, with a focus on cloud computing, integration, and security. Michiel was a pioneer on the .NET platform and founded the Dutch .NET Usergroup dotNED in 2002. He is the author of numerous articles and several books, and a speaker at development conferences. For his work in the Microsoft community, he has received the Microsoft MVP Award many times since 2002. Michiel lives in The Netherlands with his wife, son, and daughter.

DARRIN BISHOP is a speaker, author, and developer focusing on Microsoft SharePoint Technologies since the release of SharePoint Portal Server 2001. Lately he has focused on mobile and cloud development. He has authored chapters in various SharePoint–related books. As an international speaker, Darrin presents at many conferences, at SharePoint Saturdays, at MOSS Camps and to user groups. Contact Darrin via his blog at www.darrinbishop.com/blog or via www.aptillon.com.

GEORGE DURZI is a principal consultant at Clarity Consulting, where he works with clients to implement solutions based on various Microsoft tools and technologies. George started working with Lync as part of a project for the Microsoft Developer and Platform Evangelism team to build and deliver developer training content for early adopters of Lync and Exchange. George was born in Lebanon, raised in the United Arab Emirates, and moved to the United States to attend college. To this day, some American pop-culture references completely elude him.

ZOINER TEJADA (zoinertejada@tejadanet.com) is the president and chief problem solver at TejadaNET, providing strategic guidance to enterprises and startups leveraging cutting-edge technologies from Microsoft. He is passionate about leveraging cloud technologies and Windows Azure services to build web-based solutions that run at scale. He is an advisor to Microsoft and enjoys engaging the greater community by speaking at conferences and user group meetings, authoring a column on cloud for *DevProConnections* magazine, and teaching at UCSD. He has a degree in computer science from Stanford University.

DAVID MANN is a co-founder of Aptillon (www.aptillon.com), a leading SharePoint-focused consulting company, a part-time trainer for Critical Path Training (www.criticalpathtraining.com) and a five-time SharePoint MVP. As a developer, software architect, author, and trainer, he has focused on Microsoft's Information Worker and Collaboration stack, working with portal, collaboration, and content management technologies for more than 15 years. Dave is the founder of the Tri-State SharePoint User Group, focused on developer, administrator, and end-user topics covering SharePoint and the entire Office System. He is an author of *Workflow in the 2007 Microsoft Office System* (Apress, 2007) and has written whitepapers for MSDN and articles for magazines and online sites. He presents regularly at SharePoint and Office user groups and code camps, and has presented or moderated sessions at major conferences, including Tech Ed, Microsoft's SharePoint Conference, the Microsoft Office Developer's Conference, and the SharePoint Best Practices Conference. Dave has also done MSDN webcasts on topics related to SharePoint development.

ABOUT THE TECHNICAL EDITORS

KAYODE DADA is the principal at TwistEdge, Inc., a technology consulting company focused on Microsoft technologies. At TwistEdge, he architects and develops solutions leveraging SharePoint 2010 and Window Azure platform. He has worked with SharePoint beginning with the first version, and has helped many clients to migrate their on-premises line of business application to the cloud. Prior to founding TwistEdge, Inc., he was responsible for the engineering of a technology platform that integrates SharePoint with enterprise content-management platforms as well as a framework for developing enterprise portal solutions based on SharePoint. He blogs at www.twistedge.com.

HILTON GIESENOW is based out of beautiful Cape Town, South Africa, where he is a software development professional and consultant, these days working primarily with SharePoint and the Office 365 and the Azure family of products. His experience includes development, architecture, team leadership, consulting, and project management roles. He is a lead for the local .NET and information-worker communities, an internationally recognized author, speaker, podcaster, and webcaster, and a long-standing Microsoft MVP. You can find his SharePoint podcast at www.TheMossShow.com and a more detailed bio at http://hilton.giesenow.com/.

CREDITS

ACKNOWLEDGMENTS

I'D LIKE TO THANK PAUL REESE for getting me involved in this book; Maureen Spears and San Dee Phillips for their wonderful editing; and my employer Sogeti Netherlands (specifically my manager Toine de Laet) for giving me the freedom to work on this book.

—Michiel van Otegem

THANKS TO MY PEERS AND COWORKERS for inspiring me to be the best I can be. I couldn't take on all these extracurricular projects and activities if it weren't for the never-ending patience and understanding of my beautiful wife Amy. I love you honey.

—George Durzi

A FEW INCREDIBLE PEOPLE HAVE HELPED ME along in this process, and to them specifically I wish to give my sincerest thanks. I would like to thank Michele Leroux Bustamante for challenging me to reach ever higher and higher, and actually put it down on paper while I did so. Suren Machiraju at Microsoft, whose creativity in exploring the unexplored to help the customer uniquely solidified my expertise in the technology and business of software.

For my work in this book, I owe my gratitude to Jora Khodagholian for his patient review and testing of every draft and code sample. Thanks go to my editor at Wiley, Maureen Spears, whose guidance helped make this book something I would want to read. Finally, a big thank you goes to my parents, who always said I would be a teacher. You were right.

—Zoiner Tejada

CONTENTS

INTRODUCTION

THIS BOOK IS INTENDED for developers interested in learning more about how to develop against the set of Microsoft cloud services: Windows Azure and Office 365. In some cases, you can combine the two technologies to build your solution, but in other cases you will use only one of the cloud solutions, so understanding what each has to offer enables you to decide on which cloud technology to build your solution.

WHO THIS BOOK IS FOR

This book is for the professional developer who understands the Microsoft development platform and web-development technologies. To get the most value from the book, you need to read it sequentially, and then after you have decided which technologies you want to use, refresh your knowledge with that particular chapter. We assume you have knowledge of .NET and web programming such as JavaScript in the chapters. Although some content requires some IT professional knowledge, you are not overburdened with understanding these IT pro-centric topics deeply.

WHAT THIS BOOK COVERS

This book covers Windows Azure and Office 365. Although cloud-centric technologies are primarily discussed, the book also mentions on-premises software because it is the primary software deployed today. However, over time, more and more of you will need to support hybrid cloud and on-premises deployments until finally the majority of your applications and application development are cloud-based.

HOW THIS BOOK IS STRUCTURED

This book is divided logically so that you can get a deep understanding of one cloud technology, such as Office 365, before diving deeply into another cloud technology. Each section introduces the technologies so that you have a good grounding in the overview before jumping into the development topics. The following sections summarize each chapter's content.

PART I

This gives an introduction to Microsoft's Cloud and includes the following

> ➤ **Chapter 1, "Welcome to the Cloud":** This chapter discusses various approaches for clouds, an overview of what both the Microsoft Azure Platform and Office 365 have to offer, and what challenges you may encounter.

➤ **Chapter 2, "Getting Your Environment Ready for the Office 365":** This covers setting up the Office 365 environment and the various approaches to build that environment as well as how to set up a development environment in Office 365. You also see how to develop your first applications for SharePoint Online, Exchange Online, and Lync Online using Visual Studio and discover the various Office 365 development challenges you may face.

Part II

This part gives you an overview of Office 365. Individual chapters include:

➤ **Chapter 3, "Office 365 Identity Services":** This chapter has an overview of identity in Office 365 (Online IDs, Password Policy Controls for Microsoft Online ID's, Directory Synchronization, and Federated Authentication and Identity) as well as a discussion of Role Based Administration.

➤ **Chapter 4, "Introducing SharePoint Online":** Discusses SharePoint Online versus On-Premises, what is possible for application developers, and what isn't supported by SharePoint Online.

PART III

This part discusses how to develop various Office 365 solutions and includes:

➤ **Chapter 5, "SharePoint Online Development":** You are introduced to SharePoint Online, exploring your development options, and gain an understanding of authentication and authorization

➤ **Chapter 6, "Exchange Online Development":** In this chapter, you learn various Developing Solutions for Exchange Online using the Exchange Web Services Managed API and how to connect to Exchange Online. You also learn how to administer Exchange Online using Remote PowerShell as well as how to work with Exchange data and services using the Exchange Web Services Managed API.

➤ **Chapter 7, "Lync Online Development":** This chapter shows you how to develop solutions for Lync Online using the Microsoft Lync 2010 SDK as well as how to work with the Lync Controls in WPF and Silverlight, Conversations, and Extensibility Applications.

PART IV

This part shows how to work with Azure and includes the following chapters:

➤ **Chapter 8, "Setting Up Azure":** You learn how to set up your Windows Azure account and development environment as well as how to create and deploy your first Windows Azure application.

➤ **Chapter 9, "Identity in Azure":** This chapter covers federated identity and claims-based identity, and how to work with federation and claims with Windows Identity Foundation. You also see how to create a website and WCG service with Windows Identity Foundation.

➤ **Chapter 10, "Leveraging Blob Storage":** This chapter covers how to work with blobs and blob storage as well as how to program that storage.

PART V

In this part, you learn how to program Azure. Content includes:

➤ **Chapter 11, "SQL Azure":** The chapter starts with a comparison between SQL Azure and SQL Server, then shows how to manage SQL Azure Servers and Databases with the Azure Portal. You learn how to use SQL Server Management Studio with SQL Azure, how to querying SQL Azure and how to troubleshooting connectivity issues.

➤ **Chapter 12, "An Azure Datamarket Overview":** This chapter covers the Windows Azure Datamarket including how to build the Datamarket.

➤ **Chapter 13, "Service Bus":** You learn how to program Service Bus Brokered Messaging, how to select between REST and managed clients and how to choose between Service Bus Brokered Messaging and Windows Azure Queues.

➤ **Chapter 14, "AppFabric: Access Control Service":** You see how to use the Access Control Service to secure Web applications with Windows Live ID and Google ID. You then learn how to integrate the Access Control Service login page into your application. Finally, you set up Single Sign-On from the local network to the cloud.

➤ **Chapter 15, "Azure Connect":** This chapter shows you how to define Windows Azure Connect as well as explores the differences between it and Service Bus. You also see how to set up Azure Connect, test if your SQL Server is connect and how to troubleshoot Windows Azure Connect.

➤ **Chapter 16, "Azure Diagnostics and Debugging":** This covers how to define Windows Azure diagnostics, the differences between local and cloud debugging and how to use Intellitrace and profiling. You also see how to use Windows Azure Diagnostics and Windows Azure MMC.

➤ **Chapter 17, "When to Use Azure Versus Office 365":** This chapter shows how flexibility, identity federation, productivity features, cross platform challenges, Service Level Agreements, and develop tools differ between these to services.

WHAT YOU NEED TO USE THIS BOOK

You need the following:

➤ A copy of Visual Studio.

➤ An Office 365 account that can be a 30-day trial.

➤ A Windows Azure account.

➤ (Optional) Windows Server installed locally with trial copies of SQL Server, Exchange Server, Lync Server, and SharePoint Server if you want to try developing against on-premises software and integrating that into Azure and Office 365.

CONVENTIONS

To help you get the most from the text and keep track of what's happening, you see a number of conventions throughout the book.

> *Boxes with a warning icon like this one hold important, not-to-be forgotten information directly relevant to the surrounding text.*

> *The Pencil icon indicates notes, tips, hints, tricks, and asides to the current discussion.*

As for styles in the text:

➤ We *italicize* new terms and important words when we introduce them.

➤ We show keyboard strokes like this: Ctrl+A.

➤ We show filenames, URLs, and code within the text like so: `persistence.properties`.

➤ We present code in two different ways:

```
We use a monofont type with no highlighting for most code examples.
We use bold to emphasize code that's particularly important in the present context.
```

SOURCE CODE

As you work through the examples in this book, you may choose either to type in all the code manually or to use the source code files that accompany the book. All the source code used in this book is available for download at `www.wrox.com`. The code snippets from the source code are accompanied by a download icon and note indicating the name of the program so that you know it's available for download and can easily locate it in the download file. When at the site, simply locate the book's title (either by using the Search box or by using one of the title lists) and click the Download Code link on the book's detail page to obtain all the source code for the book.

> *Because many books have similar titles, you may find it easiest to search by ISBN; this book's ISBN is 978-0-470-07656-9.*

After you download the code, decompress it with your favorite compression tool. Alternatively, you can go to the main Wrox code download page at www.wrox.com/dynamic/books/download.aspx to see the code available for this book and all other Wrox books.

ERRATA

We make every effort to ensure that there are no errors in the text or in the code. However, no one is perfect, and mistakes do occur. If you find an error in one of our books, such as a spelling mistake or faulty piece of code, we would be grateful for your feedback. By sending in errata you may save another reader hours of frustration and at the same time you can help us provide even higher quality information.

To find the errata page for this book, go to www.wrox.com and locate the title using the Search box or one of the title lists. Then, on the book details page, click the Book Errata link. On this page you can view all errata that has been submitted for this book and posted by Wrox editors. A complete book list including links to each book's errata is also available at www.wrox.com/misc-pages/booklist.shtml.

If you don't spot "your" error on the Book Errata page, go to www.wrox.com/contact/techsupport.shtml and complete the form there to send us the error you have found. We'll check the information and, if appropriate, post a message to the book's errata page and fix the problem in subsequent editions of the book.

P2P.WROX.COM

For author and peer discussion, join the P2P forums at p2p.wrox.com. The forums are a web-based system for you to post messages relating to Wrox books and related technologies and interact with other readers and technology users. The forums offer a subscription feature to e-mail you topics of interest of your choosing when new posts are made to the forums. Wrox authors, editors, other industry experts, and your fellow readers are present on these forums.

At http://p2p.wrox.com you can find a number of different forums to help you not only as you read this book, but also as you develop your own applications. To join the forums, follow these steps:

1. Go to p2p.wrox.com and click the Register link.

2. Read the terms of use and click Agree.

3. Complete the required information to join and any optional information you want to provide, and click Submit.

4. You will receive an e-mail with information describing how to verify your account and complete the joining process.

You can read messages in the forums without joining P2P, but to post your own messages, you must join.

After you join, you can post new messages and respond to messages other users post. You can read messages at any time on the web. If you would like to have new messages from a particular forum e-mailed to you, click the Subscribe to this Forum icon by the forum name in the forum listing.

For more information about how to use the Wrox P2P, be sure to read the P2P FAQs for answers to questions about how the forum software works and many common questions specific to P2P and Wrox books. To read the FAQs, click the FAQ link on any P2P page.

PART I
An Introduction to Microsoft's Cloud

1

Welcome to the Cloud

WHAT'S IN THIS CHAPTER

➤ Learning the various approaches for cloud computing

➤ Learning about factors that impact moving to the cloud

➤ Understanding the Microsoft Azure Platform

➤ Understanding the Office 365 offering

This chapter helps you gain a better understanding of Microsoft's two primary cloud technologies—Office 365 and Microsoft Azure. You also learn about various approaches towards cloud computing and how Microsoft aligns its strategy with these approaches. Toward the end, this chapter touches on the various challenges and risks that are associated with cloud computing in general.

AN OVERVIEW OF THE CLOUD

The word *cloud*, without any doubt, is one of the most ambiguous words out there in the information technology industry today. You ask ten people about how they define the cloud and you will get ten different replies—what constitutes the cloud is rather complex question. However, there is one common factor that most replies share: Cloud is anything that can be offered as a service for which you don't need to bother about how it's implemented and maintained. Also, it's generally agreed that to utilize the cloud you must have Internet access, without which the concept of cloud does not exist. For the purpose of this book, cloud computing refers to a varied range of scalable services that are available to you on-demand. In order to utilize these services, you need an Internet connection, preferably one with higher bandwidth and low latency. Vendors like Microsoft, IBM, Oracle, and others provide various cloud-based services for which businesses pay as they consume the services.

The concept of service offerings in the Internet world is nothing new. Take, for example, well known e-mail providers (such as AOL, Yahoo, and Microsoft). They offer free services (like POP, IMAP, and so on) as well as other services (like e-mail forwarding and advance spam filters), and additional storage at extra cost. This means consumers are intrinsically comfortable these days with the dynamics behind this service model. What is missing, however, is a detailed view of various approaches that most commercial vendors follow when they offer their cloud services. Later in this chapter you learn more about these approaches.

Why Use the Cloud Now?

You may be wondering why the cloud has gained so much attention in recent years. Perhaps the biggest factor is that it offloads the cost of hardware and software ownership to vendors and allows you to use the cost savings to grow your business. Because information technology is mainly an enabler, cloud carries serious weight as a proposition for many businesses. If you find it difficult to keep up with the hardware and software updates, moving to the cloud makes perfect sense—you avoid upgrades and let someone else handle that work for you.

Another motivation makes the cloud more relevant now than ever before—the low barrier to entry. As more and more Internet-based businesses start up and grow at a greater pace, their growth demands a working model where businesses can pay and expand as they grow rather than making investments up front for capacity that they may not need. For medium and large businesses cloud services offer even more varied solutions. For example, businesses can use cloud services mainly for SDLC and QA purposes and still keep their production environment on-premises. Conversely, if high availability and fault tolerance is desired, cloud services provide an excellent way to mitigate risks in the case of a disaster. Figure 1-1 illustrates these concepts.

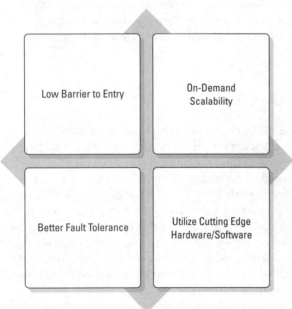

FIGURE 1-1

Understanding the Cloud Approach to Services

Today, there is a wide spectrum of services available in the cloud, including messaging solutions, collaborative solutions, identity management solutions, storage solutions, customer relationship management, and many more. Major vendors have also released cloud services based on their widely used on-premises software products. For example, Microsoft has released Office 365, which provides an online version of SharePoint Server, Exchange Server, and Lync Server. Microsoft also provides the Windows Azure platform, which makes the Windows Server operating system and other features available as services.

> **HOW PIXAR PRODUCED *TOY STORY 3 IN 3D* IN THE CLOUD**
>
> When Pixar produced *Toy Story 3 in 3D*, it faced a real computation challenge. *Toy Story 3* is a three-hour movie with approximately 290,000 frames (for 3D) with every frame taking roughly eight hours to completely render. Even with some of the fastest servers in the market it was a real computational challenge for Pixar to process the movie's visual effects within a reasonable time frame and to keep the cost minimal. This was where cloud computing perfectly fit Pixar's needs and rescued the project. Pixar chose the Windows Azure Platform to run the rendering software in the cloud, which allows the user to easily increase and decrease the number of servers required for rendering. In fact, Pixar went a step further and offered its rending software as a service to smaller studios that would otherwise have been unable to afford the hardware and software required to render visual effects.

Notice how the Windows operating system (which the Azure Platform offers) and Microsoft Office server and client products (which Office 365 offers) are fundamentally different. An operating system provides a core set of functionality (hence the term *platform*) and what actually sits on top of it can be practically anything—from an e-commerce website to complex video processing software. However, products such as Microsoft Exchange, which is a messaging solution, provide a well-defined set of features that target specific needs. This leads to an important observation: The number of ways and degrees to which a service is consumed and utilized can vary broadly. To address this in the world of cloud computing there are three different approaches to cloud-based services:

➤ Infrastructure as a Service (IaaS)

➤ Platform as a Service (PaaS)

➤ Software as a Service (SaaS)

Infrastructure as a Service (IaaS)

With *Infrastructure as a Service (IaaS)*, you can basically outsource typical elements of infrastructure like virtualization, storage, networking, load balancers and so on, to a vendor of choice. The vendor offering IaaS bills you for the infrastructure services usage as per its *service level agreement (SLA)*. One of the biggest benefits of IaaS is that it provides granular control, in which you can choose the core components for your infrastructure. With the launch of the VM Role on Azure, Microsoft has entered into the IaaS space along with vendors such as Amazon EC2, GoGrid, and OpSource, which already are key players in the IaaS market. For more information on the Azure VM Role, visit `www.windowsazure.com/en-us/home/tour/compute`.

Platform as a Service (PaaS)

Platform as a Service (PasS) provides a core platform from which custom applications can deploy. With PaaS, you don't have to work with infrastructure level elements and low level configuration of networking, security, and load balancers; all this is done for you by the vendor. The vendor provides you with a fully functional operating system with major platform software. For example, the Microsoft Azure platform provides support for the latest version of the .NET framework. This type of service offering means you can focus on deploying your custom applications on the platform and can easily configure your applications to scale up or down as demands change.

One of the key advantages of PaaS is that you don't have to worry about performing operating system or application platform updates (for example, service packs) and hardware upgrades. The vendor regularly patches your operating system, whatever platform features are being offered (such as the core .NET platform or SQL database engine) and updates hardware on demand to meet your needs. Microsoft offers the Azure platform as a PaaS because it supports various types of Worker Roles and different types of applications. For example, you can run web applications with the Web Role, as well as host middle tier applications, such as Workflow, in the Worker Role. Similarly, SQL Azure provides Microsoft's core relational database engine as a platform service. For more information about the Windows Azure Platform, visit `www.windowsazure.com/en-us/home/tour/overview`.

Software as a Service (SaaS)

With *Software as a Service (SaaS)*, the vendor manages everything from infrastructure, including load balancers and firewalls, to platforms, such as operating systems and virtual runtime environments like .NET and Java, all the way up to a complete line of business applications and services, such as e-mail or a Customer Relationship Management product. SaaS provides you with fully provisioned and finished services with a well-defined feature set, which you can potentially later customize to a certain degree. Vendors usually provide browser-based interfaces so users can easily access and customize these services. APIs are also usually made available for developers. Microsoft Office 365 also offers these types of services, which currently include SharePoint Online, Exchange Online, Lync Online, and Office Professional Plus. Most of these online services have subset of the features of their on-premises counterparts. For more detailed information on various services and plans for Office 365 visit `www.microsoft.com/en-us/office365/online-services.aspx`.

DECIDING TO MOVE INTO THE CLOUD

The cloud is neither a panacea nor a silver bullet that magically solves your business' IT problems. So how easy it is to move to and/or embrace the cloud? The answer is "it depends." It's clear that the cloud has major benefits but every organization should look at other factors to determine if the cloud is the way to go. The advantages of cost savings and on-demand scalability are obvious temptations to move to the cloud, but an organization should also consider the disadvantages of the cloud, such as poor network connectivity issues and lack of global Information Protection laws.

Although it's impossible to cover every aspect that goes into the process of deciding whether to move to the cloud, the following list points out some key items you need to consider:

> ➤ **Are network connectivity issues tolerable?** This involves such problems as poor bandwidth and low latency.

➤ **Will moving to the cloud impact your company's organizational IP (information protection) policies?** Not every country/region follows the same practices and policies; the information stored in the cloud (stored at the vendors' data center) may be subject to government audits or other policies. In addition, if the cloud provider hosts your data in datacenters outside of your country, you may run afoul of legislation.

➤ **What if the service becomes unavailable?** How will this impact overall business productivity?

➤ **How will you handle information leaks?** You need an action plan in case critical information is intentionally/accidentally leaked from the cloud. Leaked information can, for instance, include e-mail addresses and your company's financial forecast.

➤ **How will moving to the cloud impact your processes, policies, and procedures?** The vendor's Service Level Agreement must always fully align with your organization's operational needs and legal policies.

WINDOWS AZURE PLATFORM

Microsoft first revealed the Windows Azure Platform to the attendees of the Microsoft Developers Conference (PDC) in 2008. At the same conference, Microsoft released a Community Technology Preview (CTP) version of Windows Azure, meant only for testing and early feedback purposes. At that time, all Windows Azure services were offered free of charge.

At the 2009 PDC, Microsoft announced that it was transitioning Azure from the CTP stage to a major release for businesses. Initially, it released a pricing model, SLA details, and a mandatory signup process for new Windows Azure Platform customers, but it waived the fees for the month of January, 2010. Starting in February 2010, Microsoft released a version of the Windows Azure Platform that charged customers for their usage per its agreement. Since then, Microsoft has occasionally added to and updated various sets of the Azure Platform components as well as the pricing. These updates primarily keep up with technological changes occurring in the world of cloud computing.

This book covers the Windows Azure Platform in detail. Specific chapters are dedicated to individual components of the platform. The following is a list of those chapters with a brief description of what is covered.

➤ **Chapter 9, "Identity in Azure":** Describes how the identity system works in Azure. Walkthroughs are provided on how to develop, test, and deploy a service project using WIF as well as how to build a local custom STS.

➤ **Chapter 10, "Leveraging Blob Storage":** Provides an understanding of Azure BLOB storage. It also demonstrates how to programmatically access BLOBs using the REST API, setting permissions on BLOBs, copying and downloading BLOBs, and optimizing BLOB storage.

➤ **Chapter 11, "SQL Azure":** Discusses SQL Azure service and how it works. This chapter provides a walkthrough on how to create and work with the SQL Azure service, as well as on how to manage users and logins. This chapter also has sections on SQL Azure troubleshooting, which covers firewalls, sessions, transactions, latency, and so on.

➤ **Chapter 12, "An Azure Datamarket Overview":** Provides an overview of the Azure Datamarket and how to sign up for it and register to get an account key. A walkthrough demonstrates various programming techniques that you can use to work with and access Datamarket data.

➤ **Chapter 13: "Service Bus":** In this chapter, you dive into the concept of a Service Bus. The chapter describes the Service Bus architecture fundamentals and includes hands-on exercises that cover various programming techniques, including programming relays and queues.

➤ **Chapter 14, "AppFabric: Access Control Service":** Provides an understanding of the Access Control Services architecture and how to work with it using various APIs. The walkthrough shows how to create a service namespace, work with service tokens, modify client applications to use Access Control Services, and work with SAML and ADFS 2.0.

➤ **Chapter 15, "Azure: Connect":** Discusses the concept behind Connect and its core fundamentals. It also dives into programming WF and WCF with Connect, including how map to your legacy Line of Business (LOB) systems.

➤ **Chapter 16, "Azure Diagnostics and Debugging":** Covers the key aspects of debugging Azure projects, including the challenges of local versus cloud debugging, using Intellitrace, Azure Diagnostics, and common gotchas that you might encounter together with how to avoid them.

➤ **Chapter 17, "When to Use Azure Versus Office 365":** Discusses important aspects of decision-making related topics that you need to know about when deciding when to use Azure and when to use Office 365.

Figure 1-2 illustrates the major components of Windows Azure Platform. The rest of this section briefly covers some of the key components. If you are already familiar with them, you can skip to the next section, "Office 365."

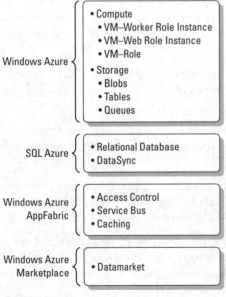

FIGURE 1-2

Web Role

Windows Azure Web Role essentially provides features and functionality to host front end web applications in the cloud. This role comes with a dedicated IIS (Internet Information Services) web server which allows you to deploy web-based applications on this role. As with other roles, you can easily scale up and down the resources using the configuration file. Microsoft Azure SDK comes with tools that integrate with Microsoft Visual Studio, which let developers build, test, and deploy web-based applications on Web Role. For more information on the Web Role please visit `https://www.windowsazure.com/en-us/home/features/compute`.

Worker Role

Although Web Role is ideal for hosting web-based applications, it does not provide features to execute long running tasks like business workflows or complex calculations that require lengthy processing. To decouple back-end operations from the front end, the Worker Role was introduced. The core function of the Worker Role is to process tasks that are considered too costly for the Web Role. Commonly, Web Role delegates processing to a Worker Role and focuses only on front end–related activities, like hosting web sites that provide a user interface. Azure allows you to scale up and down both Worker Roles and Web Roles independently. This means you can increase or decrease the number of roles based on your specific needs rather than consuming resources that you don't need. To see more, visit `https://www.windowsazure.com/en-us/home/features/compute`.

VM Role

Recently added to the Windows Azure platform, the VM Role enables you to run a *virtual hard disk (VHD)* image of Windows Server on the Windows Azure Platform. You can create a VHD file on premises and then upload it to the Windows Azure Platform. The VM Role is unique in a sense that it allows you to perform a great number of customizations at the operating system level. It also provides you with the flexibility to migrate existing applications to the cloud. Administrators can remotely log in into the VHD and perform administrative tasks as needed. However, unlike Web and Worker Roles, operating system patches are not automatically applied to the VM Role; it's your responsibility to keep the operating system updated with the desired patches. In a nutshell, the VM Role brings you the ability to perform customizations at the operating system level, which is absent from the other roles. For more information on the VM Role please visit `www.windowsazure.com/en-us/home/features/virtual-machines`.

AppFabric

Windows AppFabric acts as a cloud middleware service stack that has services like caching, access control, identity management, and more. These services help developers to develop, deploy, and manage robust Azure applications in the cloud. Because developers can decouple the application development pieces into logical components, the application development itself is rather simplified. For example, rather than worry about providing access control features, developers can rely on the Access Control Service for that.

Access Control

Windows Azure decouples management of identities and access control from the rest of the application development process. This offloads the plumbing that developers usually need to integrate their applications and replaces it with a variety of prebuilt identity providers. Access control is also provided as a feature of Windows Azure and it takes care of integrating your application with commonly used identity providers like Active Directory, Windows Live ID, Google, Yahoo, and Facebook. Access control also enables developers to create authorization rules to manage permissions using claims. For more information on access control visit `https://www.windowsazure.com/en-us/home/features/access-control`.

Content Delivery Network (CDN)

Users consuming Microsoft Azure data from various geographical locations other than where Microsoft data centers are located may end up paying considerable high latency costs as they download data. To overcome this challenge, Microsoft provides a *Content Delivery Network (CDN)*, which caches data in various geographic locations across the globe. This helps reduce the number of hops that a user request goes through before the data is finally delivered to a user. For more information on CDN please read `https://www.windowsazure.com/en-us/home/features/cdn`.

Caching

Microsoft Azure Caching service provides a distributed in-memory cache for Azure applications. This gives developers an alternative to the disk based caching, which is slower in nature and does not scale very well. Developers can utilize the caching service to store data based on an individual user session or to store and share data across the applications. As with other Azure services, this service comes with 99.9 percent SLA, with a pricing model based on the Caching service usage. For more information on Microsoft Azure Caching visit `https://www.windowsazure.com/en-us/home/features/caching`.

Storage

Windows Azure Storage provides storage services as part of the Windows Azure Platform. These services include Blob storage, Tables, and Queues. Blob (Binary Large Object) storage specifically stores unstructured digital assets like audio, video, and images. Tables provide containers for more structured data; however, they do not allow you to create relationships between the data (this is often referred as NoSQL storage), but this allows it to scale to extremely high volumes. For traditional relational database features, you should use SQL Azure (described in the next section) and not Azure Table storage. Queues allow you to perform messaging between applications in a consistent and reliable fashion. Essentially with queues you can easily decouple the communication and dependencies between application components, where one component places messages in a queue and another component pulls them later when it is ready to process the data.

Azure storage is exposed via HTTP, REST, and OData endpoints, making it easily consumable by various platforms and devices. The storage products provide various levels of permissions support though, meaning these multiple endpoints don't translate into poor security. This design choice by the Windows Azure team provides greater flexibility in the way you access the Azure storage. For example, your on-premise applications can use the Azure storage for storing data on the cloud and thus remove the need of on-premises storage. On the other hand, cross platform applications can easily consume data by using REST style queries to access the Azure Storage. For more information on Azure Storage visit www.windowsazure.com/en-us/home/features/storage.

SQL Azure

SQL Azure provides cloud based relational database service based on Microsoft SQL Server technologies. You can utilize SQL Azure relational database features both from on-premises and online solutions. As with other Azure Platform services, you receive high availability, fault tolerance, and scalability as part of Windows Azure SLA. From a developer's perspective, you can use existing development and management tools to work with SQL Azure, which means that you'll have a small learning curve. For more information on SQL Azure visit www.windowsazure.com/en-us/home/features/sql-azure.

Windows Azure Appliance

Microsoft Azure Appliance enables large enterprises, service providers, and government institutions to deploy Windows Azure and SQL Azure in their own datacenters using a Microsoft recommended infrastructure, which is provided through various Microsoft partners including Dell, Fujitsu, eBay, and HP. Windows Azure Appliance helps organizations to meet their unique security, availability, scalability and information protection policy needs while letting them enjoy the benefits of private, and public cloud computing. You can learn more about Azure Appliance by visiting www.windowsazure.com/en-us/community/partners/windows-azure-appliance.

Windows Azure Marketplace

Microsoft Azure is a powerful IaaS and PaaS cloud platform but there are times when businesses require off the shelf and ready to be consumed SaaS applications that are built and tested specifically for the Windows Azure Platform. Similarly, there are times when you need data from certain knowledge domains (for example, financial, governmental, and so on) without going through the hassle of arranging it yourself. To meet these requirements, Microsoft launched Windows Azure Marketplace, an online marketplace where you can purchase or sell software as a service (SaaS) applications and datasets. Figure 1-3 shows an applications listing page from Microsoft Azure Marketplace. Note that by using the filters on the left side of this screen, you can filter applications based on price, category, and publisher. Figure 1-4 shows the datasets page for Azure Marketplace; it has the same filters as Figure 1-3.

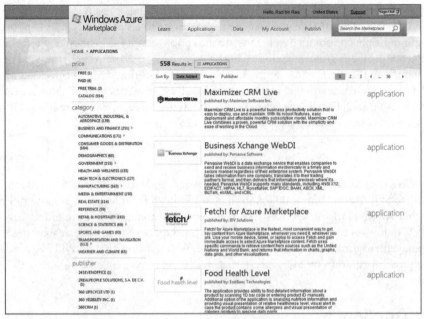

FIGURE 1-3

FIGURE 1-4

Registration on Microsoft Azure Marketplace is free of charge and rather simple. Go to `https://datamarket.azure.com/account/info` and follow the instructions. For more details on Microsoft Azure Marketplace please visit `https://datamarket.azure.com/about`.

Developer Story

From the first day it launched Windows Azure, Microsoft has provided excellent developer support in the form of the Azure SDK, which allows developers to use Visual Studio to develop, test, and deploy Windows Azure–based applications. From a developer's standpoint, this essentially means using already familiar tools with a focus on leveraging Azure services. Figure 1-5 displays a snapshot of the Visual Studio 2010 template for Windows Azure projects that developers can use to develop Azure-based cloud solutions.

FIGURE 1-5

Microsoft understands that developers around the globe have capitalized on a variety of software platforms, frameworks, and tools. Limiting Azure development to only Microsoft-based frameworks and tools is rather restrictive for developer. As a result, Azure supports various runtimes and frameworks. Table 1-1 shows a current list of these that Windows Azure supports.

TABLE 1-1: Windows Azure SDK's

PLATFORM	URL
.NET	www.windowsazure.com/en-us/develop/net
Java	www.windowsazure.com/en-us/develop/java
PHP	www.windowsazure.com/en-us/develop/php
Node.js	www.windowsazure.com/en-us/develop/nodejs
Miscellaneous	www.windowsazure.com/en-us/develop/other

OFFICE 365

Office 365 is a SaaS offering from Microsoft that offers online versions of SharePoint 2010, Exchange 2010, and Lync 2010—all hosted and maintained by Microsoft at their data centers. Office 365 also includes Microsoft Office Professional Plus, a desktop application, and Office Web Apps, a browser-based online version of Word 2010, Excel 2010, and PowerPoint 2010.

Microsoft launched Office 365 private beta (to the limited audience) in November 2010 and finally released it to the public on June 28, 2011. Office 365 is the next version of Business Productivity Online Services (BPOS), which provided online versions of Exchange 2007 and SharePoint 2007.

This book covers all major services that Office 365 has to offer. The following list gives which chapters cover Office 365, including what they discuss.

➤ **Chapter 3, "Office 365 Identity Services":** This chapter drills into the Office 365 identity architecture and management. You will learn about authenticated mechanisms, working with DirSync, and planning and configuring identity federation.

➤ **Chapter 4, "Introducing SharePoint Online":** Provides an overview and discussion of the key components of SharePoint Online. You will learn about SharePoint Online development options, authentication and authorization, SharePoint Web Services, declarative workflows, InfoPath Forms, BCS, and ways to debug your SharePoint solutions.

➤ **Chapter 5, "SharePoint Online Development":** This discusses various approaches to integrate Azure and Office 365. It also covers how to share the identity between the two platforms, model of communication, and connecting from on-premises to Azure to Office 365.

➤ **Chapter 6, "Exchange Online Development":** In this chapter you learn about building applications for Exchange Online using Exchange Web Services (EWS). Sample applications include building an Email application, Tasks application, and Contacts application. You also learn about administration of Exchange Online through PowerShell.

➤ **Chapter 7, "Lync Online Development":** Provides details on Lync architecture, programming Conversations in Lync, and using Lync Silverlight Controls and WPF Controls to develop custom applications.

➤ **Chapter 17, "When to Use Azure Versus Office 365":** Discusses important aspects of the decision-making related topics that you need to know when deciding when to use Azure and when to use Office 365.

Figure 1-6 gives a quick overview of what is covered under the umbrella of Office 365.

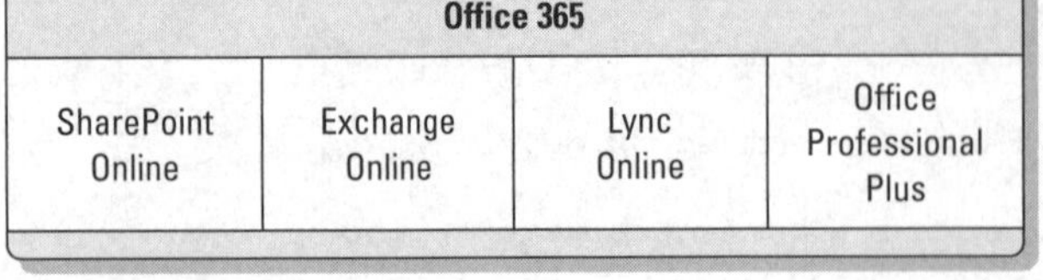

Office 365			
SharePoint Online	Exchange Online	Lync Online	Office Professional Plus

FIGURE 1-6

SharePoint Online

SharePoint Online is one of the key services that Office 365 offers. With its origins in SharePoint 2010 Enterprise Edition, SharePoint Online brings the benefits of SharePoint for small, medium, and large organizations without them needing to invest in infrastructure and maintain SharePoint 2010 on-premises. SharePoint Online comes in two flavors: SharePoint Online and SharePoint Online - D (where *D* represents dedicated). Microsoft hosts both flavors of SharePoint Online on its data centers, but the dedicated version allows organizations to have SharePoint Online hosted on physical hardware exclusively dedicated to them. For non-dedicated packages, SharePoint Online takes a multi-tenancy route and organizations have to share the SharePoint instance with other tenants. For more information on the SharePoint Online service visit `www.microsoft.com/download/en/details.aspx?id=13602`.

Developers can easily build and deploy their custom solutions based on the standard SharePoint Solutions Framework (WSP). Microsoft only allows deployment of Sandbox solutions on SharePoint Online (the dedicated version does support full-trust solutions but it requires approval from Microsoft before deployment). One of the benefits that developers have is to leverage their existing knowledge of SharePoint 2010 development and start building the solutions for SharePoint Online immediately without any major learning curve. For more information on developing SharePoint Online solutions visit `http://msdn.microsoft.com/en-us/sharepoint/gg153540`.

Exchange Online

Office 365 offers Exchange Online as a service based on Microsoft Exchange Server 2010 hosted on Microsoft data centers. With Exchange Online, organizations can offload (either fully or partially) their messaging needs to the cloud, eliminating the need to invest in the IT infrastructure. Exchange Online provides typical Exchange features such as e-mail, archiving, retention, the calendar, contacts, distribution groups, and so on. With an SLA of 99.9 percent, Microsoft takes care of managing, upgrading, and performing the security and service patches. For more information on the Exchange Online service visit `www.microsoft.com/download/en/details.aspx?id=13602`.

Microsoft provides developers with a powerful managed API to program against Exchange Online. Under the hood, this API uses web services calls to Exchange Online, which means developers can easily develop robust and highly decoupled applications. For more information on the Exchange Managed API visit `http://msdn.microsoft.com/en-us/exchange/aa731543`.

> *Many organizations leverage Exchange Online and SharePoint Online together to enhance their productivity. A good walkthrough titled "Office 365 – Enhance Productivity through SharePoint Online & Exchange Online" is provided on the MSDN MVP blog at* `http://tiny.cc/n6loj`.

Lync Online

Lync Online brings unified communication features to Office 365. Lync Online is based on Lync 2010 Server, which Microsoft hosts at its data centers. Unlike Exchange Online and SharePoint

Online, in order to fully leverage Lync Online you must install the Lync Client on your machine. The Lync Client essentially performs all the communication to Lync Online so its presence is mandatory on the client. For more information on Lync Online service visit www.microsoft.com/download/en/details.aspx?id=13602.

Developers can reuse and extend Lync 2010 Silverlight controls to develop custom communication solutions. For more information on Lync 2010 development visit http://msdn.microsoft.com/en-us/hh181578.

Office Professional Plus and Office Web Apps

Microsoft offers Microsoft Office Professional Plus as part of Office 365 (currently available with Plan E3 and E4). This version of Office is the same as Office Professional Plus 2010 Retail, which is one of the most common productivity suites in the market today. When you register for Office 365's monthly plan, you can install and use Office Professional Plus on five devices. The following is a list of products that are available as part of Office Professional Plus.

- ➤ Microsoft Word 2010
- ➤ Microsoft Excel 2010
- ➤ Microsoft PowerPoint 2010
- ➤ Microsoft Outlook 2010
- ➤ Microsoft InfoPath 2010
- ➤ Microsoft SharePoint Workspace 2010
- ➤ Microsoft Access 2010
- ➤ Microsoft OneNote 2010

With Office 365, you can also leverage Office Web Apps, which provides a web-based subset of the features and functionality of Office Professional Plus. With Office Web Apps, you can save your files on SharePoint Online and then read and work with them online without the need of any client side application (e.g., Word) to be installed on your machine. Office Web Apps contain online versions of the following desktop applications. For more information on Office Web Apps visit http://office.microsoft.com/en-us/web-apps.

- ➤ Microsoft Word 2010
- ➤ Microsoft Excel 2010
- ➤ Microsoft PowerPoint 2010
- ➤ Microsoft OneNote 2010

Developer Story

Office 365 offers a range of services, based on existing Microsoft products, that give developers a rather diverse landscape. At the time of this writing, there is no single SDK that developers can download and start developing for Office 365. However this fact should not deter developers from building applications and solutions for Office 365 because Microsoft provides excellent APIs and SDKs for each of the Office 365 services. Table 1-2 lists the available SDKs for each service offering along with the download URL.

TABLE 1-2: Office 365 Services Development SDK's

TITLE	URL
SharePoint 2010 SDK	http://msdn.microsoft.com/en-us/library/ee557253.aspx
Lync 2010 SDK	http://www.microsoft.com/download/en/details.aspx?id=18898
Exchange Web Services Managed API	http://www.microsoft.com/download/en/details.aspx?id=13480

For example, developers with a background in SharePoint 2010 on-premises development can easily start SharePoint Online development using the SharePoint Server 2010 SDK. The same is true for Exchange Online and Lync Online. In a nutshell, as a developer, you can reuse the current skills, tools, and APIs with which you're already familiar to build Office 365 applications. This means you can:

➤ Utilize a broad range of collaboration, messaging, and communication services to develop business solutions for Office 365.

➤ Leverage Office 365 Martketplace to publish your applications to a wide range of audiences.

➤ Reuse your existing development skills to develop high productivity applications with Office 365.

➤ Build highly federated solutions and integrate LOB (Line of Business) applications using SharePoint BCS (Business Connectivity Services).

➤ Develop custom communication solutions leveraging Lync Client APIs.

➤ Build custom applications using Exchange Online and using messaging features like e-mail, calendar, and tasks items.

➤ Create add-ins to connect with cloud services using Office Development with VSTO (Visual Studio Tool for Office) for Word 2010, Excel 2010, and PowerPoint 2010.

SUMMARY

This chapter introduces two major Microsoft cloud technologies—Microsoft Azure and Office 365. The chapter explains basic types of cloud services that exist in the market today. You also learn about building blocks of Microsoft Azure and Office 365 services. Later sections briefly cover key components of both of these cloud services.

This chapter also set the roadmap for all the chapters in this book by providing a brief description of what each chapter will cover. Lastly, you learn about the developer story for Microsoft Azure and Office 365 and what kind of tooling and SDK support is provided by Microsoft.

2

Getting Your Environment Ready for Office 365

This chapter helps you set up a development environment for Office 365. At the time of this writing, Microsoft does not provide Office 365 SDK as a single download. This means that you must do a bit more work to get everything set up and running before you kick-start the development. Separate sections cover SharePoint Online, Exchange Online, and Lync Online. Later in the chapter you learn about common challenges associated with Office 365 development and various resources that Microsoft makes available for Office 365 developers.

YOUR OFFICE 365 CLOUD ENVIRONMENT

Before you start setting up your development environment, the first thing to do is to register for Office 365. For testing purposes you can create a trial account with Office 365, which is available free of charge for 30 days. If your business already has an existing Office 365 account, you can use this existing account. However its highly recommended that you set up a new account with Office 365 because Microsoft does not provide separate test environments, so any changes that you make to the existing one are against a production (or live) environment and are reflected immediately to business users.

Office 365 is offered through different plans targeting professionals, small businesses, midsize businesses, enterprises, and education. Table 2-1 describes various plans available to you.

TABLE 2-1: Office 365 Plans

CATEGORY	DESCRIPTION	TRIAL AVAILABILITY
Office 365 for professionals and small businesses (Plan P)	Supports up to 25 users	Yes
Office 365 for midsize businesses and enterprises (Plan E1, E2, E3, E4)	Supports 25+ users	Only Plan E3
Microsoft Office 365 for education	Supports only academic and education institutions	No

For most development scenarios, plan E3 is a good choice because it includes all the key features of Exchange Online, SharePoint Online, and Lync Online (except full enterprise voice capabilities with on-premises Lync Server). Not every plan is available for trial; however, in most cases as mentioned earlier, plan E3 is sufficient.

Registering for Office 365 (Trial)

To register for Office 365 trial, visit `www.microsoft.com/en-us/office365/free-office365-trial.aspx`. You can choose to register either with Plan P or Plan E. For this exercise you will register with plan E3, but the registration process is identical for other plans.

> *It's a common practice for businesses to begin with the Office 365 trial offering for development and testing purposes but later to upgrade to a licensed version for the production usage. However, you cannot migrate between the Plan P and E plans, so you need to be careful when deciding on a plan that it is best suited to your needs for both the short and long term. The only way to switch, should you really need to, is to cancel your account with an existing plan and then register for a different one. This can seriously impact your business continuity as content, configurations, customizations, and users are not automatically migrated between plans. Also the visual interface for an administration console differs slightly among plans, because not all service features are available with all plans. To avoid this situation, it's recommended that you communicate this issue as a potential risk to the project stakeholders. Please note that the stakeholders also understand that there is no easy way to fix this. However to mitigate this risk you can propose a well-defined proof of concept (PoC) for Office 365 targeting a subset of users and limiting its scope to the basic feature set of Office 365.*

Figure 2-1 shows the trial sign-up page for Plan E3 and mentions that the free trial period will expire in 30 days. To sign up for a trial, follow these steps:

1. You start by filling in your contact details.

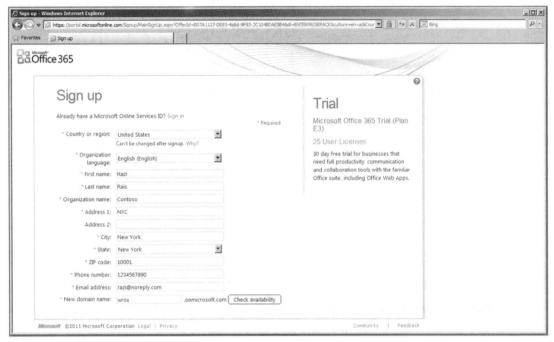

FIGURE 2-1

2. Choose your domain name and Microsoft Online Services ID carefully because you cannot change them later. Also the e-mail address you provide here will be used for all the communication related to your trial account.

3. Accept the conditions to finish the registration process, as shown in Figure 2-2.

4. You may need to wait a moment or two before your account is provisioned with Office 365. When it is, you can click the Continue button to land on the Office 365 Admin Home Page.

 It's a good idea to add the link `https://portal.microsoftonline.com` *to your favorites list; this way you can easily access the Admin Home Page.*

Notice that an alert displays on top of the page, as shown in Figure 2-3. Here, you see the number of days left in your trial account.

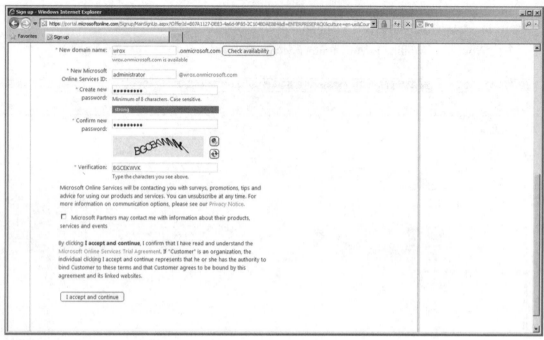

FIGURE 2-2

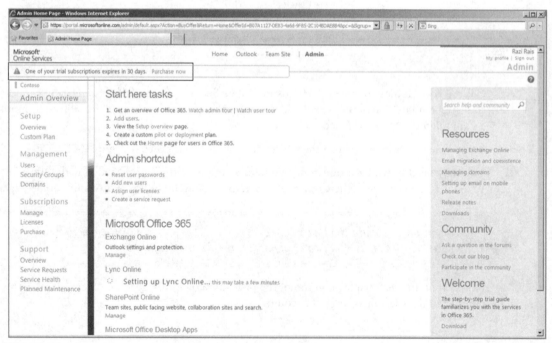

FIGURE 2-3

When your trial expires, you have an additional 30 days to convert your account to the paid subscription after which your account will be completely deleted along with all content, customizations, configurations, and users. You can easily convert to a paid subscription by clicking the Purchase Now link, as shown in Figure 2-3. You can also do it any time during your trial period and additional 30 days of grace period.

Your trial account is now ready. In the next section, you see how to add a few users to it, so that you can later use them during development.

Adding Users

On the Admin Home Page, under the Management section on the left, click the Users link, as shown in Figure 2-4.

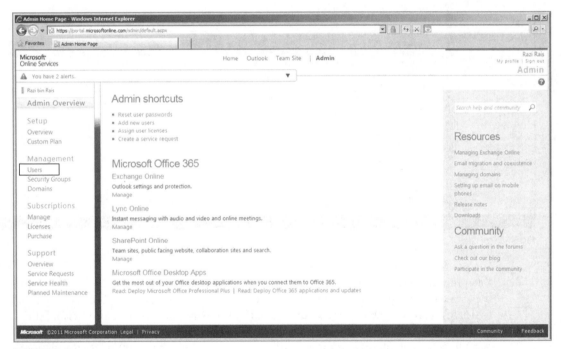

FIGURE 2-4

You have two options available for adding users: You can add them manually—one user at a time using the user interface, or add them in bulk by uploading a CSV file containing a list of users in an Office 365–preferred format. The advantage of the latter approach is an obvious gain in productivity; imagine hundreds of users and the time it takes to add them manually. However if you have only a few users, you can add them easily using the user interface. Now look at both of these approaches to add users.

Adding Users Manually

To add users manually, follow these steps:

1. On the Users page, click the New menu item, and select User from the drop-down that appears, as shown in Figure 2-5. The New User page displays:

FIGURE 2-5

2. Enter the user details, as shown in Figure 2-6. The username field is also the login name that the user will enter to access Office 365, so be sure you enter it correctly, because you need to delete and recreate the user account again if it is misspelled. You can also expand the Additional Properties section, which enables you to add additional details for the user, such as address, e-mail, physical address, and so on. For the user, this is optional information; for now leave it empty. Click the Next button to continue.

3. The Assign Role settings page, as shown in Figure 2-7, enables you to assign various types of roles to the user. It also enables you to set the user's geographic location. Keep the default value of No for Assign Role, and for the Set User Location option provide the appropriate country value. Note that the Set User Location value is a required field. Once you are done, click the Next button.

4. The Assign Licenses pages (shown in Figure 2-8) enable you to assign specific functionality and associated license costs to the users. If you assign no licenses to the account, that user cannot access any of the Office 365 services. You can select from different license types; for development purposes you may want to create multiple users and assign them different licenses so that your test matrices remain wider. For now, select Microsoft Office 365 Plan E3, which

automatically selects all the suboptions below it, and click the Next button. If for some reason you don't want to assign this user a license now, simply don't select options. You can assign licenses to the user and modify your existing licenses later by using the Licenses link under Subscriptions Panel from the Admin home page.

FIGURE 2-6

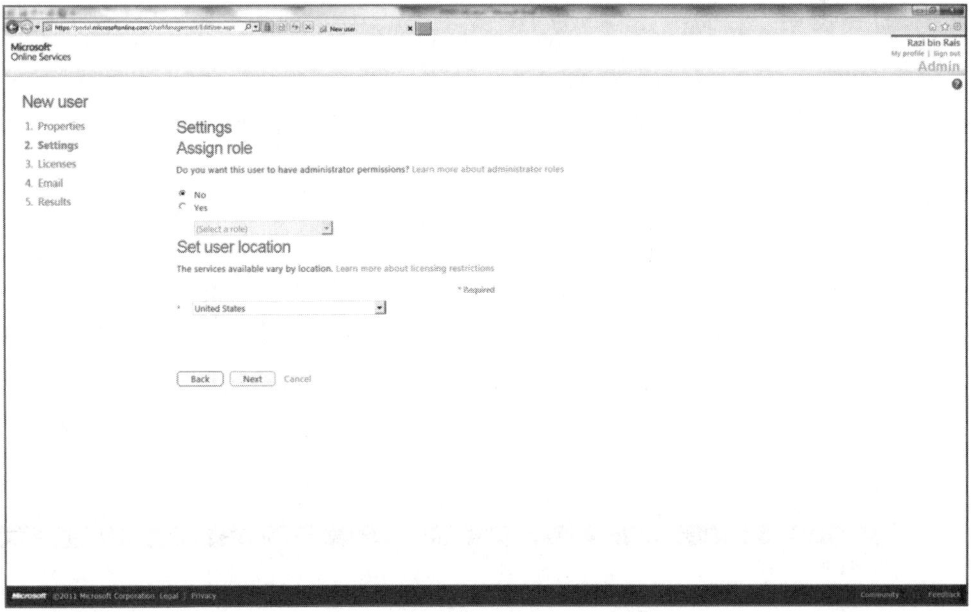

FIGURE 2-7

5. On the Email page, keep the default settings and click the Create button. The page displays user details along with temporary passwords, as shown in Figure 2-9.

FIGURE 2-8

FIGURE 2-9

6. Click the Finish button. The new user now has been created and is able to access Office 365.

Adding Users in Bulk

To add multiple new users in bulk, follow these steps:

1. One the main Users screen, select the Bulk Add Users option from the New menu, as shown in Figure 2-10.

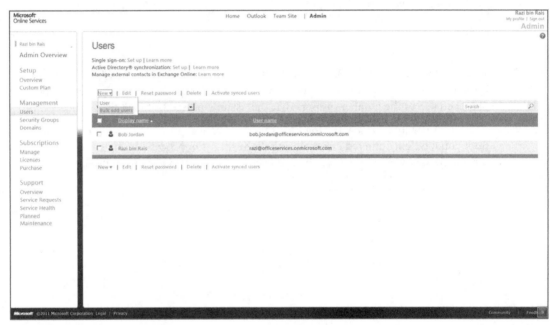

FIGURE 2-10

2. Download the supported CSV file format by clicking the Download a Blank CSV File link. You can also download a sample CSV file by clicking Download Sample CSV file; this file resembles the template file, but it also contains sample users along with their contact details. In the CSV file, the Username and Display name columns are mandatory but all other user details are optional. If you already have user details in another external system—for example, PeopleSoft or another internal HR system, you may want to extract user contact details from the system directly into a CSV file, either one matching the available template or one that you easily can convert over. Figure 2-11 shows a CSV file after three users have been added to it.

3. When you finish adding users to the CSV file, save it locally on your computer. If you use Microsoft Excel, make sure that the file is saved as a comma-delimited (CSV) format; otherwise you may get an error while uploading it back to Office 365.

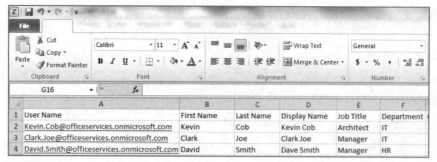

FIGURE 2-11

4. To upload the file to Office 365, click the Browse button and select the CSV file containing users; then click the Next button. As shown in Figure 2-12, the Verification results page displays and shows the number of users that successfully passed or failed the verification process.

5. Click the View link to view the log file of the verification process. This log is especially helpful if you have encountered errors during the verification process. In Figure 2-12, note that all three users that were in the CSV file earlier have passed the verification process.

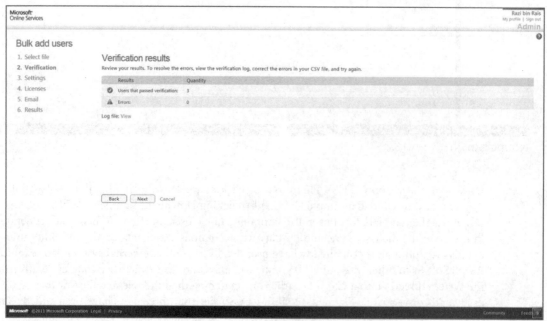

FIGURE 2-12

6. On the Settings page, click the Next button. Keep the default value of Allowed for Sign-In Status; you should only block the users if you don't want them to access the Office 365 services. Set the user location and click the Next button. As the users are added in bulk, these settings are applied uniformly to all users.

7. On the Assign licenses page, select Plan E3 and click the Next button.

8. On the Email page, keep the default settings and click the Create button. Office 365 now provisions the users; depending on the quantity of users, this may take a moment or two. The results page displays the usernames along with their temporary passwords, as shown in Figure 2-13. The passwords for your users will be different from what is shown in this figure because these are randomly generated.

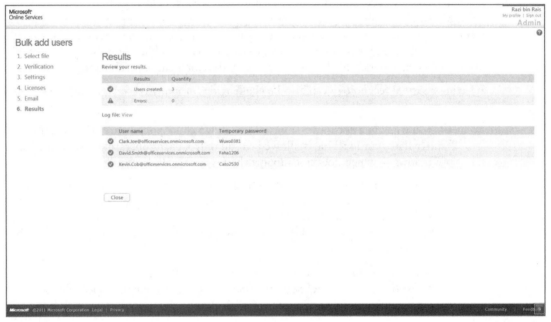

FIGURE 2-13

9. To return to the Admin Home Page, click the Close button.

YOUR OFFICE 365 DEVELOPMENT ENVIRONMENT

In this section, you learn various approaches that you can use to build an Office 365 development environment. Later in this section, a step-by-step walkthrough is provided so you can set up the Office 365 environment.

Using Virtualization for Your Development Environment

Virtualization is a powerful technology, and in recent years it has become an integral part of any IT infrastructure. For developers, it provides flexibility and ease of development while providing them the ability to develop on multiple disparate environments and platforms hosted in the same physical workstation. In addition, by taking snapshots of the current state of the virtual machine, you can easily revert back to any earlier state at a later stage in case your changes do not work the way you intend them to. Also, it's relatively easier to copy and move virtual machines around than physical ones, which gives you freedom to use different physical machines during the course of your development cycle.

Virtualization does have its shortcomings, and depending on your specific scenario, you should determine whether it's feasible to use:

➤ **You must give your virtual machine sufficient memory and hard disk space on the host machine.** This is in addition to what your host operating system already consumes on the physical machine. For example, to have a responsive virtual machine for Office 365 development that typically runs products such as Visual Studio 2010 and SharePoint Server 2010, you should allocate at least 5 GB of memory to the guest machine. Otherwise, the virtual machine will have noticeable lag as you perform development and debugging tasks.

➤ **Selecting a virtual technology can also be challenging for many reasons.** Examples of this are as follows:

  ➤ If you work in a corporate environment in which IT policies are enforced, it's likely that your machine is allowed to run only a client operating system such as Windows 7, which does not support the Hyper-V role on Windows 7.

  ➤ You may install Virtual PC 2007, but it does not support x64-bit virtualization, which is required to install most of the Microsoft server-side products, including Microsoft SharePoint Server 2010. However, you can use virtualization products like VMware, Virtual Box, and the like to fill the need of x64 bit virtualization on the client operating system.

  ➤ If you run Windows 2008 SP2 or Windows 2008 R2 or above, then Hyper-V is available to you, but Windows Server 2008 resource requirements (especially the memory requirement) are higher than that of a client operating system such as Windows 7.

  ➤ You may face compatibility issues with drivers for all the hardware components for your workstation and with certain software products your organization requires you to install on your workstation.

With Microsoft Windows 8 on the horizon, the good news is that it is scheduled to support the Hyper-V role even on the workstation version, which is a good reason for developers to adopt Windows 8 as early as possible.

Using Microsoft Trial Virtual Machines

In recent years, Microsoft has released virtual machines that have trial versions of various Microsoft products and technologies installed and configured on them, thus allowing you to save considerable time getting started with these products. This is especially true for server-side products such as Microsoft SharePoint Server 2010, which can take a while to set up because it requires you to install a set of prerequisites followed by a multi-stage process for the actual SharePoint Server 2010 product installation. To download these virtual machines, visit `www.microsoft.com/download/en/details.aspx?id=27417`.

For Office 365 development, you only need trial virtual machine "a." Virtual machines "b" and "c" have Microsoft Exchange Server 2010 and Lync Server 2010, respectively, installed on them. Although you'll use these technologies in this book, you need only certain APIs for programming against Lync Online and Exchange Online and they are downloaded separately. You learn more about them later in the chapter. Figure 2-14 shows a more detailed breakdown of what is available on each of these virtual machines.

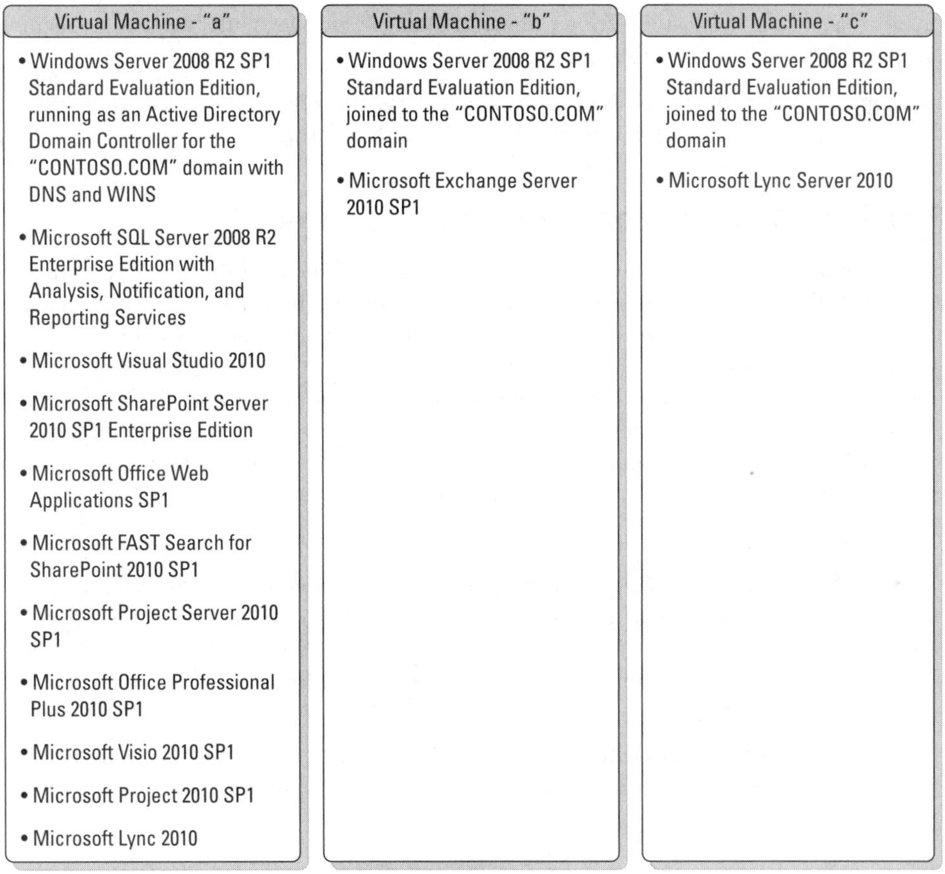

Virtual Machine - "a"	Virtual Machine - "b"	Virtual Machine - "c"
• Windows Server 2008 R2 SP1 Standard Evaluation Edition, running as an Active Directory Domain Controller for the "CONTOSO.COM" domain with DNS and WINS • Microsoft SQL Server 2008 R2 Enterprise Edition with Analysis, Notification, and Reporting Services • Microsoft Visual Studio 2010 • Microsoft SharePoint Server 2010 SP1 Enterprise Edition • Microsoft Office Web Applications SP1 • Microsoft FAST Search for SharePoint 2010 SP1 • Microsoft Project Server 2010 SP1 • Microsoft Office Professional Plus 2010 SP1 • Microsoft Visio 2010 SP1 • Microsoft Project 2010 SP1 • Microsoft Lync 2010	• Windows Server 2008 R2 SP1 Standard Evaluation Edition, joined to the "CONTOSO.COM" domain • Microsoft Exchange Server 2010 SP1	• Windows Server 2008 R2 SP1 Standard Evaluation Edition, joined to the "CONTOSO.COM" domain • Microsoft Lync Server 2010

FIGURE 2-14

After your download for the trial virtual machine "a" is complete, follow the instructions from the download center site to set up the virtual machine using Hyper-V.

Using the Microsoft trial virtual machine is often the easiest option to kick-start Office 365 development; however a few drawbacks exist with this approach:

➤ **The trial virtual machines have products installed on them that are not required for Office 365 development.** For example, Microsoft FAST Search for SharePoint 2010 and Microsoft Project Server 2010 are installed and configured but not required for Office 365 development.

➤ **To use the trial virtual machines, you need to run Windows Server 2008 SP2 or R2 as a host operating system.** As mentioned earlier, this is needed because virtual machines require Microsoft Hyper-V, which is only available as part of Windows Server 2008 SP2 and Windows Server R2. As stated in the previous section, this limitation will be removed with the launch of Windows 8, which supports Hyper-V: however, at the time of this writing, Windows 8 is in beta, and running trial virtual machines on the beta is not recommend.

➤ **The trial virtual machine has a 180-day evaluation period.** In addition, it requires activation, or re-arming, which if not done during the first 10 days of usage, shuts the virtual machine down after 2 hours of continuous operation.

➤ **Microsoft does not provide any support for trial virtual machines.** The best option you have is to post your questions on relevant MSDN and TechNet forums.

Using a Physical Machine for Your Development

Depending on your situation, you may want to use a physical machine for Office 365 development and may not have policy restrictions in your organization against doing so. This approach has certain benefits over a virtual machine running on your workstation. For example, you may not have sufficient physical memory and storage resources available to store and run a virtual machine. And even if you do manage to run the virtual machine with limited memory, the virtual machine performance is extremely poor and may hinder your development productivity. Another common limitation is licensing, which may require you (or your organization) to purchase separate licenses for the operating systems running on the virtual and the physical machines.

 Microsoft provides an MSDN developer's license which enables you to install and use the Microsoft software on as many machines as you want for development purposes. For more information on MSDN subscriptions, visit http:// msdn.microsoft.com/en-us/subscriptions/aa718661.aspx.

Regardless of the reason, it's not always feasible to use a virtualized environment for development. The following sections discuss the pros and cons of using a physical machine for development.

Pros

The advantages of using a physical machine include:

➤ When limited by the memory and storage, using a physical machine is the most viable option.

➤ Because everything runs on bare metal, generally the performance is better overall than in a virtual environment.

➤ Organizations can deploy patches and updates uniformly to all the machines, whereas virtual machines are often not patched and updated, and can introduce security vulnerabilities to the organization.

Cons

The disadvantages of using a physical machine include:

➤ Your host operating system is a single point of failure. Virtual machines can easily be copied and shared.

➤ Reverting back to a previous state on the host operating system, although possible, is not as easy as taking snapshots on virtual machines. You may want to get back quickly to a certain snapshot without consuming too much time configuring your system.

➤ Performing updates to a host operating system used for development tasks can be challenging and may even have unexpected negative side effects. The development software APIs may be sensitive to certain Windows updates, and there is always a risk of a potential conflict. For example, you may want to limit Windows updates for Microsoft Silverlight but allow updates for Microsoft Lync. However, it's tedious to monitor all the updates, and it takes substantial effort; sometimes updates are dependent on one another, and it's just not possible to control them.

➤ Using the same host operating system for development as well as for office-related tasks can lead to unnecessary complications. For example, when you develop a Lync component, you may need to close all the chat windows to facilitate debugging, but these may be required for communication within the team or wider organization. These types of annoyances may quickly accumulate and impact your productivity.

CREATING AN OFFICE 365 DEVELOPMENT ENVIRONMENT

The previous section covered various approaches available for hosting an Office 365 development environment. In this section, you put the boxing gloves on and build a fully-functional Office 365 development environment. It's recommended that you choose the virtualization route and download Microsoft trial virtual machine "a," as mentioned in the previous section.

Figure 2-15 captures the necessary software required for an Office 365 development environment. When you use the Microsoft trial virtual machine "a," it already includes a number of the required components, so you need to install and configure only the additional software highlighted in the gray boxes; otherwise, you need to install and configure all of the software, which can take substantial effort on your part. For completeness, the following section covers all of them.

"Step 1: Installing Mandatory Software" walks through the installation of all the mandatory software. You should complete this step before continuing to "Step 2: Installing Service-Specific Software."

Depending on your needs, you may want to skip the installation of service-specific software that you don't require. However, if you start with Office 365 development and are not sure which services you want to use, install all the software.

If you use a Microsoft trial virtual machine (recommended), you need to install only the software listed in Step 2, as shown in Figure 2-15.

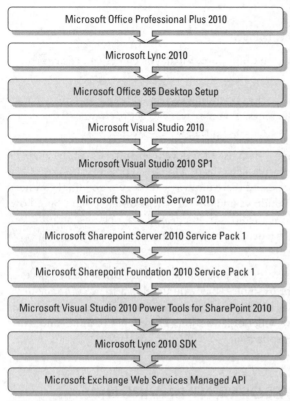

FIGURE 2-15

System Requirements

The following are the system requirements for an Office 365 development environment:

- ➤ Windows 7 x64-bit Professional | Ultimate | Enterprise.
- ➤ Windows 2008 SP2 Standard | Enterprise.
- ➤ Windows 2008 R2 SP1 Standard | Enterprise.
- ➤ Visual Studio 2010 x86 with SP1 Professional | Premium | Ultimate.
- ➤ IE 7 or above.
- ➤ Microsoft Office 2010 Professional Plus.
- ➤ Windows Update Agent (WUA) service must be started.

Step 1: Installing Mandatory Software

Before you begin the installation, make sure that the account used (preferably a domain account) has administrator rights on the system. Also, you need a reasonable Internet connection for downloading software from the Internet.

1. **Go to the downloads page.** Browse the Office 365 downloads page at `https://portal` `.microsoftonline.com/download/default.aspx` and choose to install the following software:

   ➤ **Microsoft Office Professional Plus:** Select the language of your choice and keep the default option to the 32-bit version. Click the Install button, as shown in the upper portion of Figure 2-16.

   ➤ **Microsoft Lync 2010:** Select the language of your choice and keep the default option to the 64-bit version. Click the Install button, as shown in the lower portion of Figure 2-16.

Installing Microsoft Office Professional Plus

Installing Microsoft Lync 2010

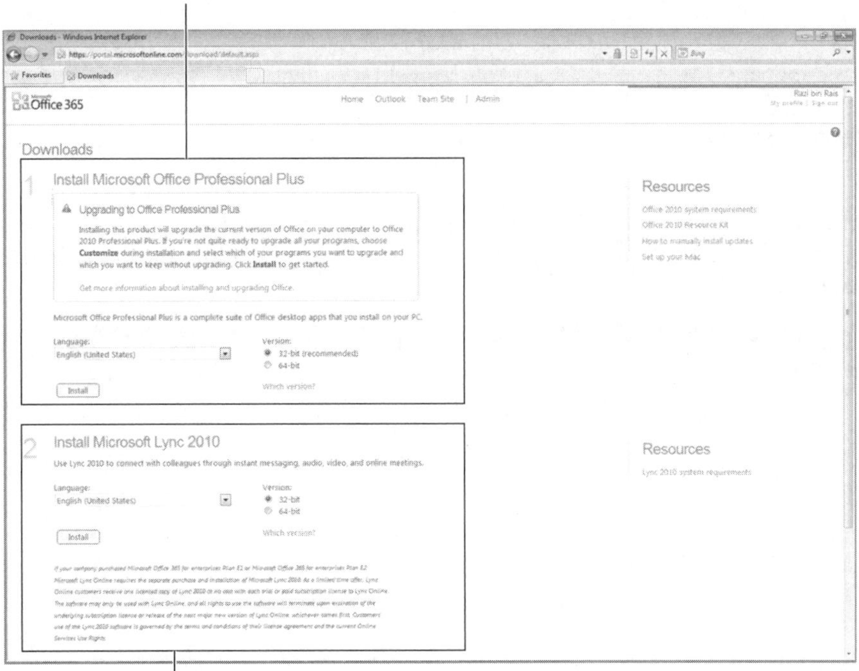

FIGURE 2-16

A dialog appears asking you to save or run `LyncSetup.exe` on your machine.

2. **Save the setup file on your machine.** Do this if you want to reuse it for a future install. Otherwise, click the Run button to let the setup download it on the Windows temporary directory: the setup starts automatically after the download.

3. **Click Install.** On the Microsoft Lync 2010 Setup dialog, click the Install button to begin Lync 2010 installation, as shown in Figure 2-17. Installation may take a few moments to complete. This is because setup verifies that all the required software prerequisites are installed correctly, and if they are not, it will try to download them and then install them before installing Lync 2010. It is recommended to let the setup download the prerequisite software, even though it may take some extra time; this way it is guaranteed that all the prerequisites are installed automatically with the correct version.

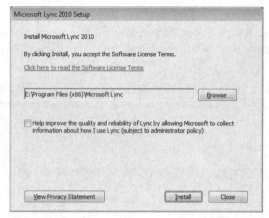

FIGURE 2-17

4. **Set up and configure your Office desktop apps.** Click the Set Up button, as shown at the bottom of Figure 2-18. You may need to wait a few moments before the Office365DesktopSetup dialog launches.

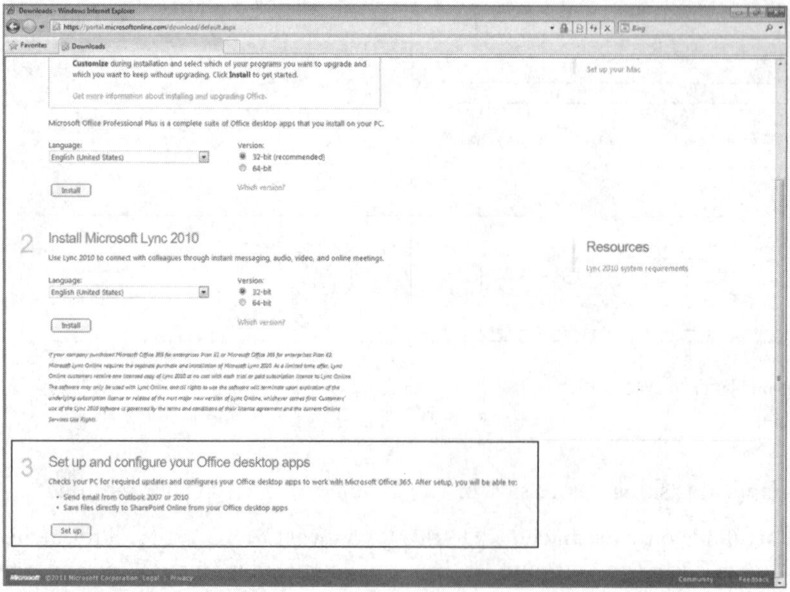

FIGURE 2-18

5. **Run the installation.** On the Office365DesktopSetup Launch Application dialog, click the Run button, as shown in Figure 2-19.

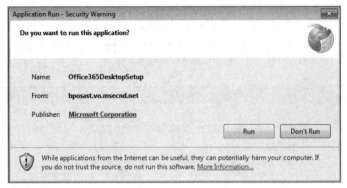

FIGURE 2-19

6. **Sign in to Office 365.** On the Microsoft Office 365 desktop Setup dialog, sign in using your Microsoft Online Services ID, as shown in Figure 2-20. Your Microsoft Online Services ID is created when you registered for Office 365 earlier in the section "Registering for Office 365 (Trial)" Microsoft Online Services ID. Please note that your Microsoft Online Services ID will be different from the one shown in the Figure 2-20, which is used for demonstration purpose only.

FIGURE 2-20

7. **Configure your desktop.** After you successfully sign in, the desktop setup displays the Install Updates dialog. Keep the default options for the Select Applications To Configure section and click the Continue button, as shown in Figure 2-21. This is an important step, and these updates are necessary for the client applications to function properly. For example, if you uncheck the Microsoft Lync option, the required updates do not install for Lync 2010, and you cannot sign in using the Lync 2010 client unless you manually download and install the required updates or run the Office 365 desktop setup again.

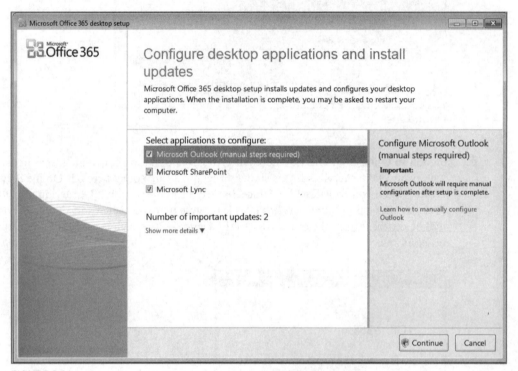

FIGURE 2-21

8. **Accept the Service agreement.** Do this by clicking the I Agree button. Wait until all the updates install. Finally, click the Finish button to close the Setup dialog.

9. **Download and install Microsoft Visual Studio 2010 x86 version.** You can download it from MSDN subscribers' download at `https://msdn.microsoft.com/en-us/subscriptions/securedownloads/default.aspx`. If you don't have an MSDN membership and want to use the trial version of Visual Studio 2010, you can download the Visual Studio 2010 Ultimate Edition Trial ISO image from `www.microsoft.com/download/en/details.aspx?id=12187`.

To mount an ISO file, you need a virtual CD/DVD ROM emulator. Many free tools are available online that provide this functionality, including: Virtual CD ROM Control Panel by Microsoft, although not officially supported by them (http://download.microsoft.com/download/7/b/6/7b6abd84-7841-4978-96f5-bd58df02efa2/winxpvirtualcdcontrolpanel_21.exe), *MagicDisk by MagicISO Maker* (www.magiciso.com/download.htm), *and Daemon Tools* (www.daemon-tools.cc/eng/downloads). *As a good practice before downloading and installing any third-party tool on your machine, you should seek advice from your IT administrator.*

10. **Download and install Microsoft Visual Studio 2010 SP1.** You can download it from http://go.microsoft.com/fwlink/?LinkId=210710.

Your Office 365 development environment now has base software installed on it. If you opt for a virtual environment, you can take a snapshot and label it **After - Office 365 Base Software Installed.**

Step 2: Installing Service-Specific Software

In this section, you will learn about specific software that you need to install for following Office 365 services:

➤ Microsoft SharePoint Online

➤ Microsoft Exchange Online

➤ Microsoft Lync Online

Software Setup for SharePoint Online Development

To develop and test solutions for SharePoint 2010 Online, you must install and configure SharePoint Server 2010 locally on your development machine. Visual Studio 2010 Templates for SharePoint 2010 cannot be used with SharePoint Online or a remote SharePoint server web application. You need the following software for a SharePoint Online development environment:

➤ **Microsoft SharePoint Server 2010 Enterprise Edition:** Download it from the MSDN subscription website at https://msdn.microsoft.com/en-us/subscriptions/securedownloads/default.aspx.

➤ **Language Packs for SharePoint Foundation 2010 (optional):** Download it from www.microsoft.com/download/en/details.aspx?id=4731.

➤ **2010 Server Language Packs for SharePoint Server 2010, Project Server 2010, Search Server 2010** and **Office Web Apps 2010 (optional):** Download them from www.microsoft.com/download/en/details.aspx?id=3411.

➤ **Microsoft SharePoint Foundation 2010 Service Pack 1:** Download it from `www.microsoft.com/download/en/details.aspx?id=26640`.

➤ **Microsoft SharePoint Server 2010 Service Pack 1:** Download it from `www.microsoft.com/download/en/details.aspx?id=26623`.

➤ **Microsoft SharePoint Foundation 2010 Language Pack Service Pack 1 (optional):** Download it from `www.microsoft.com/download/en/details.aspx?id=26629`.

➤ **Microsoft 2010 Server Language Pack Service Pack 1 (optional):** Download it from `www.microsoft.com/download/en/details.aspx?id=26621`.

➤ **SharePoint Designer 2010:** Download the 32-bit version from `www.microsoft.com/download/en/details.aspx?id=16573`.

➤ **Visual Studio 2010 SharePoint Power Tools:** Download it from `http://visualstudiogallery.msdn.microsoft.com/8e602a8c-6714-4549-9e95-f3700344b0d9/`.

The following are steps for installation. Please make sure that Step 1 is completed successfully before you move to next steps. Please note that these steps are optional:

1. **Follow the full instructions.** The step-by-step installation and configuration of SharePoint Server 2010 in a development environment is covered in the MSDN article, "Setting Up the Development Environment for SharePoint 2010 on Windows Vista, Windows 7, and Windows Server 2008" at `http://msdn.microsoft.com/en-us/library/ee554869.aspx`.

2. **After SharePoint Server 2010 is successfully installed and configured, you need to install Service Pack 1 for SharePoint Foundation 2010 and SharePoint Server 2010.** You may also need to install the Service Pack 1 for SharePoint Foundation 2010 and SharePoint Server 2010 language packs. For more details on installing Service Pack 1, follow the instructions from Microsoft's blog at `http://sharepoint.microsoft.com/blog/Pages/BlogPost.aspx?pID=984`. The language packs are optional because you need them only if you target multilingual scenarios in which the default language of SharePoint Foundation and SharePoint Server 2010 is not enough.

3. **Install Microsoft SharePoint Designer 2010.** It is highly recommended that you use the 32-bit version instead of the 64-bit version because a few Office 2010 components (SharePoint Designer 2010 is considered part of the Office 2010 product line) won't work as expected with the 64-bit version, and SharePoint Designer 2010 is considered part of the Office 2010 product line and therefore needs to match the edition of the base Office suite. For more details on this topic, visit `http://office.microsoft.com/en-us/word-help/choose-the-32-bit-or-64-bit-version-of-microsoft-office-HA010369476.aspx` and `http://blogs.technet.com/b/office2010/archive/2010/02/23/understanding-64-bit-office.aspx`.

4. **Install Visual Studio 2010 SharePoint Power Tools.** These are additions to the out-of-the-box Visual Studio 2010 templates for SharePoint. One of the key features included as part of power tools is the template for Sandboxed-compatible Visual Web Part, which enables you to use a Visual Designer to create SharePoint web parts that can be deployed in a Sandbox Solution. You learn more about Sandbox Solutions in Chapter 4 and Chapter 5.

At this point, you should have your machine equipped with the software required for SharePoint Online development.

Software Setup for Exchange Online Development

The Exchange Online development requires Microsoft Exchange Web Services (EWS) Managed API 1.1. Download the 64-bit version (recommended) or the 32-bit version from `www.microsoft.com/download/en/details.aspx?id=13480`. The Managed API utilizes Exchange Web Services SOAP protocol and Autodiscover features. Also pay attention to the overview section on the download page, because Microsoft lists any KB articles that need be installed before/after the install of this software. The step-by-step installation instructions are available on the download page.

Software Setup for Lync Online Development

Lync Online development requires both the Lync 2010 client and Lync 2010 SDK to be installed on the development machine. You have already installed the Lync 2010 client as part of installing mandatory software in the section "Step 1: Installing Mandatory Software." Download Lync 2010 SDK from `www.microsoft.com/download/en/details.aspx?id=18898` and run the setup to install it. The Lync 2010 client is a prerequisite for Lync 2010 SDK, and if it is not already installed you must install it now before proceeding any further.

Also pay attention to the overview section on the download page, because Microsoft lists any KB articles that need be installed before/after the install of this software. The step-by-step installation instructions are available on the download page.

Other Development Tools (Optional)

The following software is a great addition to your development tools; none is mandatory for Office 365, but all are highly recommended.

➤ **Fiddler:** The most famous tool for web debugging. Fiddler is a web debugging proxy that logs all HTTP(s) traffic between your computer and the Internet. It enables you to inspect traffic, set breakpoints, and inspect incoming or outgoing data. It also includes a powerful event-based scripting subsystem and can be extended using any .NET language. Fiddler is available as freeware and can debug traffic from virtually any application that supports a proxy, including Internet Explorer, Google Chrome, Apple Safari, Mozilla Firefox, Opera, and more. You can download it from `www.fiddler2.com/Fiddler2/version.asp`.

➤ **HttpWatch:** HttpWatch is another common HTTP(S) sniffing tool that integrates with Internet Explorer and Firefox browsers to show you which HTTP traffic is triggered when you access a web page. If you access a site that uses secure HTTPS connections, HttpWatch automatically displays the decrypted form of the network traffic. One advantage to using HttpWatch is that it is available as an add-on, which integrates with supported browsers rather than acting as a proxy, so you don't run into any limitations of a proxy. You can download a free version of HttpWatch from `www.httpwatch.com/download/`.

➤ **NET Reflector:** If you work with Microsoft .NET technologies, you may already be aware of the .NET Reflector tool. Reflector is a decompiler that can examine a .NET assembly. It shows you all the components inside each assembly including classes, resources, and so on. The tool is flexible and can disassemble assemblies written in any version of Microsoft.NET. You can download the .NET Reflector from `http://shop.reflector.net/download`.

Step 3: Finalizing Installation

As a last step, restart the development machine. This ensures that any pending changes to the operating system are committed properly. If you use a virtual machine, wait for the operating system to restart; because you reach the login screen before you login, take the snapshot of the virtual machine. Label this snapshot **Office 365 Development Ready** or something similar.

YOUR FIRST OFFICE 365 APPLICATION

With the development environment finally ready, you are all set to fire up Visual Studio 2010 and start building applications for Office 365. This section demonstrates how to build simple, yet fully functional, solutions for SharePoint Online, Exchange Online, and Lync Online. The section ends with a discussion of the development challenges you may encounter with Office 365. The idea is to give you a head start before you move to later chapters, which dive more deeply into each service offering of Office 365.

The following is the breakdown of chapters and service offerings they cover.

➤ Chapter 4: "introducing SharePoint Online"

➤ Chapter 6: "Exchange Online Development"

➤ Chapter 7: "Lync Online Development"

Your First SharePoint Online Solution

In this section, you will build a basic Hello World Web Part for SharePoint Online and then deploy it to the SharePoint Online site using a WSP file.

SharePoint Online is one of the most feature-enriched services among the whole stack of Office 365 service offerings. It provides a broad set of features ranging from collaboration, content management, business intelligence, workflows, and more. By developing custom solutions for SharePoint Online, developers can extend and add new features and functionally to SharePoint Online. Imagine the possibility of building a Recruitment or Supply Chain Management system that an entire organization can use and reuse. Even better, you can sell your custom solutions based on Office 365 offerings on the Microsoft Marketplace, which you learn more about later in the chapter.

If you already have development experience with the SharePoint 2010 on-premises version, there is a little learning curve involved. You must understand the few key differences as noted here.

If this is your first time with SharePoint development, don't worry because Chapter 4 covers the basics of SharePoint Online, and Chapter 5 digs deeper into SharePoint Online development and customization.

➤ **Microsoft hosts SharePoint Online as part of its Office 365 offering on its datacenters.** This means that you have no control over the physical hosting and no direct access to the environment. For example, you cannot remotely log in to the servers hosting SharePoint Online for any debugging or testing.

➤ **Office 365 provides SharePoint Online as both a multitenant and dedicated offering.** From a development prospective, the major difference is that you can develop and deploy only Sandbox Solutions (you learn more about them in Chapters 4 and 5) in a multitenant environment. The SharePoint Online dedicated environment supports both Sandbox and Farm Solutions; however, before solutions are deployed into a dedicated environment, they must go through a thorough submission process, which can take anywhere from a few days to a few weeks before your solutions are approved for deployment. This is done to ensure that the quality of the solutions deployed in the dedicated environment do not degrade the server performance in any way.

➤ **Microsoft Visual Studio 2010 does not enable you to use a SharePoint Online site (or any other remote SharePoint Server 2010 site, for that matter) for development and debugging.** This does not mean that you cannot develop client applications (for example, WinForm, WPF, and so on) that push/pull data to/from SharePoint Online remotely but rather that you are limited to using a local SharePoint site when using Visual Studio 2010 templates for SharePoint development. This is something that is likely to change in a future version of Office 365.

Developing a SharePoint Online Solution

In this section, you will develop a Visual Web Part that displays "Hello World" on the page where it is placed. Perhaps not the most impressive web part, but it gives you insight on how to develop and deploy a custom Sandbox Solution on SharePoint Online.

Also, unless explicitly mentioned, all the SharePoint solutions discussed throughout this book are Sandbox Solutions and targeted toward a SharePoint Online multitenant environment. The dedicated environment is available only to large organizations that have 5,000 or more users registered to them.

1. From the Start menu, launch Microsoft Visual Studio 2010.

2. Click File ➪ New ➪ Project, as shown in Figure 2-22.

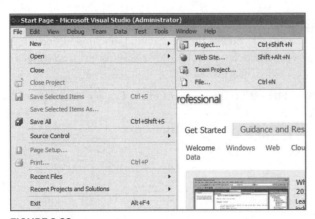

FIGURE 2-22

3. On the New Project dialog, expand Visual C# ➪ SharePoint and select 2010. For the Project Template, select Empty SharePoint Project. Use the following details and click OK, as shown in Figure 2-23:

➤ Name: **HelloWorldSharePointOnline**

➤ Location: Keep default or change it as required

➤ Solution name: **MyFirstSharePointSolution**

➤ Deselect: Create directory for solution option

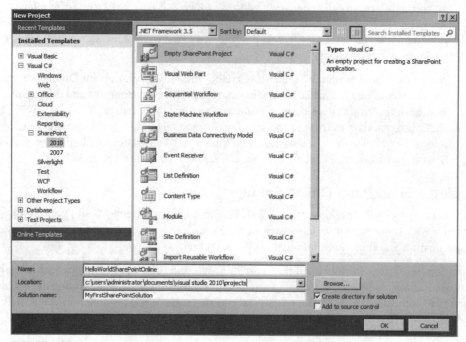

FIGURE 2-23

4. On the SharePoint Customization Wizard dialog, enter the site collection URL in the format `http[s]://SiteCollectionUrl`. If you use the trial virtual machine, you can use `http://intranet.contoso.com/`. Keep the default choice of the solution to Deploy as a Sandbox Solution, as shown in Figure 2-24. Click Finish.

5. Right-click the newly-created HelloWorldSharePointOnline Project, and select Add ➪ New Item, as shown in Figure 2-25.

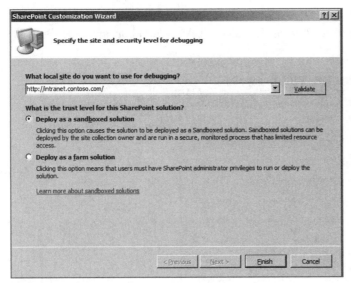

FIGURE 2-24

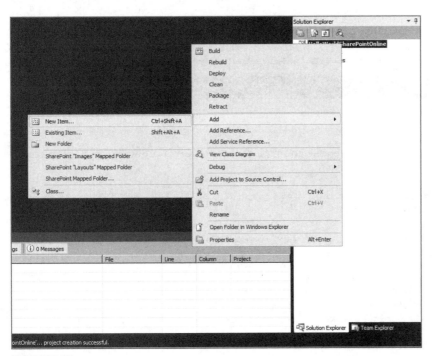

FIGURE 2-25

6. On the Add New Item dialog, as shown in Figure 2-26, select the Visual Web Part (Sandboxed), and type **HelloWebPart** for the name. Click the Add button to add this web part to the project.

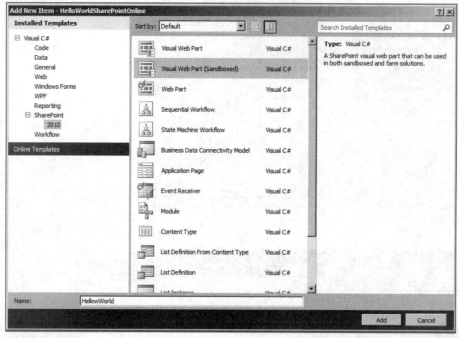

FIGURE 2-26

7. Open the HelloWebPart.ascx file and replace the ASPX markup with the markup shown in Listing 2-1.

LISTING 2-1: HelloWebPart.ascx

```
<%@ Assembly Name="$SharePoint.Project.AssemblyFullName$" %>
<%@ Assembly Name="Microsoft.Web.CommandUI, Version=14.0.0.0,
Culture=neutral, PublicKeyToken=71e9bce111e9429c" %>
<%@ Register Tagprefix="SharePoint"
Namespace="Microsoft.SharePoint.WebControls"
Assembly="Microsoft.SharePoint, Version=14.0.0.0,
Culture=neutral, PublicKeyToken=71e9bce111e9429c" %>
<%@ Register Tagprefix="Utilities"
Namespace="Microsoft.SharePoint.Utilities"
Assembly="Microsoft.SharePoint, Version=14.0.0.0,
Culture=neutral, PublicKeyToken=71e9bce111e9429c" %>
<%@ Import Namespace="Microsoft.SharePoint" %>
<%@ Register Tagprefix="WebPartPages"
Namespace="Microsoft.SharePoint.WebPartPages"
Assembly="Microsoft.SharePoint, Version=14.0.0.0,
Culture=neutral, PublicKeyToken=71e9bce111e9429c" %>
<%@ Control Language="C#" AutoEventWireup="true"
```

```
CodeBehind="HelloWebPart.ascx.cs"
Inherits="HelloWorldSharePointOnline.HelloWebPart.HelloWebPart" %>
<asp:Label ID="lblMsg" runat="server" Text="">
</asp:Label>
```

8. Open the `HelloWebPart.ascx.cs` file and replace the ASPX markup with the markup shown in Listing 2-2.

LISTING 2-2: HelloWebPart.ascx.cs

```csharp
using System;
using System.ComponentModel;
using System.Web.UI;
using System.Web.UI.WebControls;
using System.Web.UI.WebControls.WebParts;
using Microsoft.SharePoint;
using Microsoft.SharePoint.WebControls;

namespace HelloWorldSharePointOnline.HelloWebPart
{
    [ToolboxItem(false)]
    public partial class HelloWebPart : System.Web.UI.WebControls.WebParts.WebPart
    {
        protected override void OnInit(EventArgs e)
        {
            base.OnInit(e);
            InitializeControl();
        }

        protected void Page_Load(object sender, EventArgs e)
        {
            this.lblMsg.Text =
            String.Format("Hello World, the time on the server is {0}",
            DateTime.Now.ToShortTimeString());
        }
    }
}
```

9. To set the Title and Description of the web part, open the `HelloWebPart.webpart` file and replace its content with the Listing 2-3.

LISTING 2-3: HelloWebPart.webpart

```xml
<?xml version="1.0" encoding="utf-8"?>
<webParts>
  <webPart xmlns="http://schemas.microsoft.com/WebPart/v3">
    <metaData>
      <type name="HelloWorldSharePointOnline.HelloWebPart.HelloWebPart,
          $SharePoint.Project.AssemblyFullName$" />
      <importErrorMessage>$Resources:core,ImportErrorMessage;</importErrorMessage>
    </metaData>
    <data>
      <properties>
```

continues

LISTING 2-3 *(continued)*

```
            <property name="Title" type="string">Hello WebPart</property>
            <property name="Description" type="string">
              This is my first sandboxed web part for SharePoint Online
            </property>
          </properties>
        </data>
      </webPart>
  </webParts>
```

Testing the SharePoint Online Solution

To test the SharePoint Online solution that you developed in the previous section, perform the following steps:

1. Press F5 in Visual Studio so that your solution builds and automatically deploys and activates on the SharePoint site that you chose for your project. Visual Studio opens a new browser instance with a SharePoint site that you choose for the solution.

2. To actually add your web part on the page, click the Site Actions menu and select Edit Page, as shown in Figure 2-27.

FIGURE 2-27

3. When the page is in Edit mode, click the Insert tab and select WebPart. From the Categories select Custom. Your Hello WebPart displays along with a brief description, as shown in Figure 2-28. The title and description of the web part is read from the `HelloWebPart.web-part` file. Click the Add button to insert this web part on the page.

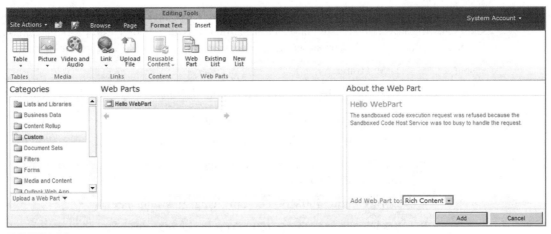

FIGURE 2-28

Deploying a Solution to SharePoint Online

In the previous section, you developed a simple HelloWebPart, which displays "Hello World" and shows the time on the server. You also built and deployed it locally on your development machine. This section shows you how to upload your solution to the SharePoint Online site and activate it for usage. However, before you do this, you must create a site collection on SharePoint Online. The following steps show how to create a new site collection and add and activate a solution on it. Finally, it shows how to add the web part on the newly created site collection home page.

1. From the Office 365 Admin Home Page, locate the SharePoint Online section and click the Manage link under it.

2. On the SharePoint Online Administration Center, click the Manage Site Collections link, as shown in Figure 2-29.

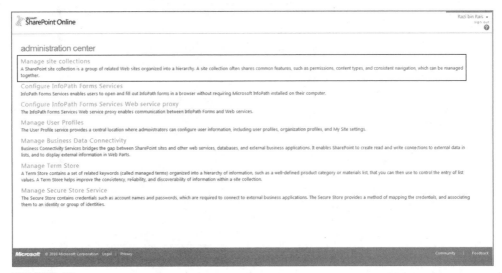

FIGURE 2-29

3. On the Manage Site Collection page, click New and select Private Site Collection. Figure 2-30 shows how the screen looks after all the information is provided. Don't worry too much about the details, which you will learn about in later chapters. Enter the following information:

> ➤ Title: **Home**

> ➤ Web Site Address: **Home** (Keep other defaults)

> ➤ Template Selection: Team Site (default)

> ➤ Time Zone: UTC - 800 Pacific Time (U.S. and Canada)

> ➤ User Name: Enter the same username you used for registering for Office 365 earlier in this chapter

> ➤ Storage Limit: **500MB** (You can change this value later.)

> ➤ Resource Usage Quota: **4000** (You can change this value later.)

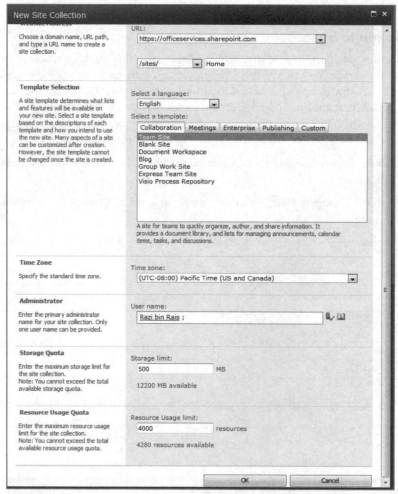

FIGURE 2-30

4. Click the OK button. SharePoint provisions the new site collection; wait until it appears in the list of the site collection.

5. Now browse to the newly-created site collection. From Site Actions, select Site Settings. Click the Solutions link present under the Galleries section, as shown in Figure 2-31.

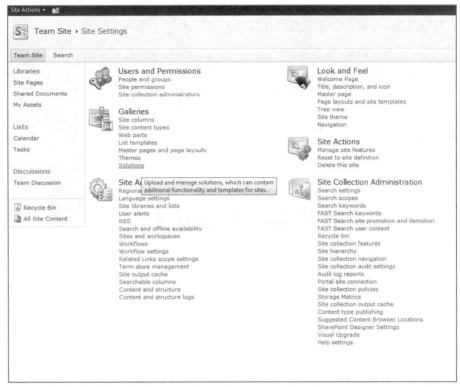

FIGURE 2-31

6. Figure 2-32 displays the Solutions Gallery Page. Click the Upload Solution button on the Solutions tab.

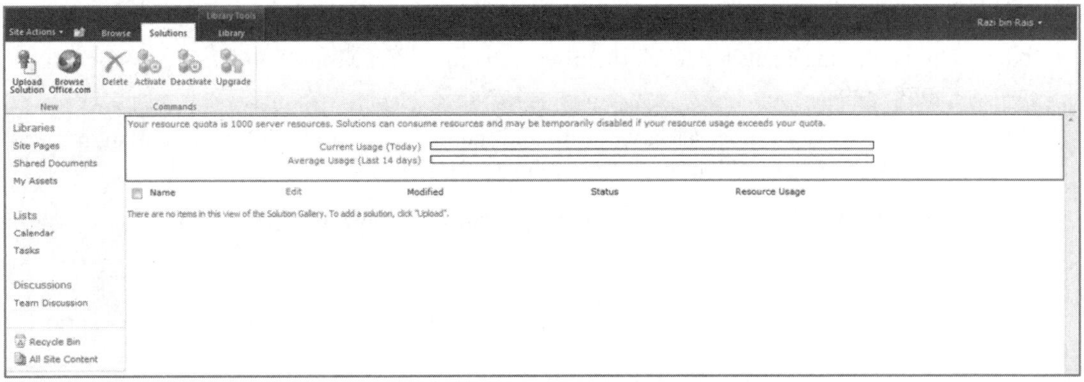

FIGURE 2-32

7. On the Upload Document dialog (shown in Figure 2-33), click the Browse button and locate the `HelloWorldSharePointOnline.wsp` solution file. The default location of the solution is as follows. The Drive and Folder structure depend on where you created the solution in the previous section. You should build your solutions in release mode rather than debug mode when deploying to SharePoint Online because `web.config` files cannot be changed to cater for Debug mode. Because you cannot attach the debugger to the SharePoint Online site, there is no point having solutions build for debug mode.

> *Replace the placeholder* <<DRIVE>> *with the actual drive letter where solution was created. The default is the* c: *drive.*
>
> ➤ `<<DRIVE>>:\[Folder]\MyFirstSharePointSolution\`
> `HelloWorldSharePointOnline\bin\Release\`
>
> ➤ `<<DRIVE>>:\[Folders]\MyFirstSharePointSolution\`
> `HelloWorldSharePointOnline\bin\Debug\`

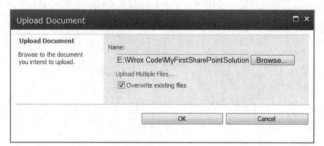

FIGURE 2-33

8. After the solution uploads successfully, the Solution Gallery - Activate Solution Page displays, as shown in Figure 2-34. Click the Activate button to activate the solution. This is required to have your web part available for use throughout the site collection. The HelloWorldSharePointOnline solution is now activated, as shown in Figure 2-35.

9. Browse to the site collection home page, click Site Actions, and then select Edit Page.

10. On the Editing Tools tab, click the Insert tab, and select More Web Parts, as shown in Figure 2-36.

11. From the Create dialog, select Custom, and then select Hello WebPart, as shown in Figure 2-37. Click Add to insert this web part on the page.

12. The Hello WebPart is now available on the page, as shown in Figure 2-38.

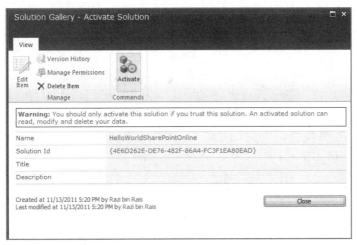

FIGURE 2-34

FIGURE 2-35

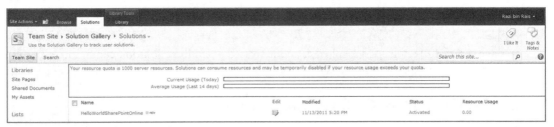

FIGURE 2-36

FIGURE 2-37

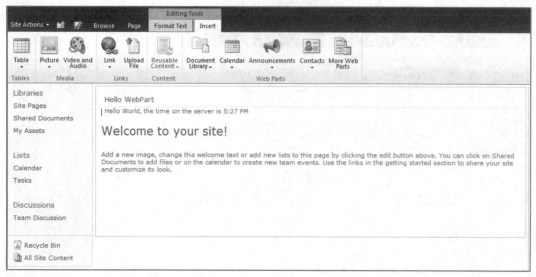

FIGURE 2-38

You have successfully uploaded, deployed, and activated a Sandbox Solution containing a simple web part on your SharePoint Online site collection.

Your First Exchange Online Application

Microsoft provides the Exchange EWS Managed API (MA) 1.1 to build solutions for Exchange Online. Under the hood, the MA uses the Exchange Web Services to interact with the server, but you don't need to worry about it, because it shields you from the details of this interaction and provides a higher-level API against which to work. One of the primary objectives of Managed API is to keep things simple for developers by exposing them to Exchange objects such as Inbox, Send Items, Attachments, and so on. You can easily perform CRUD operations for the following items using the Managed API:

- ➤ E-mails
- ➤ Contacts
- ➤ Attachments
- ➤ Calendar
- ➤ Tasks
- ➤ Public Folders

One the biggest advantages of MA is that Autodiscovery MA uses this feature, so you don't need to provide the URL of EWS for your target Exchange Online service. Autodiscovery can find the most efficient Client Access Server (CAS) available for a given mailbox. From a development prospective, this gives you great flexibility because you don't need to hardcode the EWS URL.

You learn more about Exchange Online Development in Chapter 6. In this next section, you will create your first application targeting Exchange Online using MA 1.1. Your application is a simple

Windows Console application that you can use as part of the IT support tools. It reads the list of the running process on your machine and e-mails it to a designated e-mail address; it also saves the copy of the e-mail to your Sent Items folder for future reference. Before you continue, make sure that you have more than one user account registered and activated on Office 365. User account creation is covered earlier in this chapter.

Developing Exchange Online Application

The following steps demonstrate how to develop a basic Exchange Online application using Visual Studio 2010.

1. From the Start menu, launch Microsoft Visual Studio 2010.

2. Click File ➪ New ➪ Project, as shown in Figure 2-39.

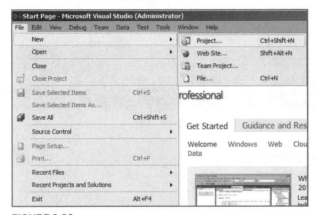

FIGURE 2-39

3. On the New Project dialog, expand Visual C# ➪ Windows. For the Project Template select Console Application. Use the following details and click OK, as shown in Figure 2-40:

➤ Name: **EmailProcessListing**

➤ Location: Keep default or change it as required

➤ Solution Name: **EmailProcessListing**

4. From the Solution Explorer, right-click References and click Add Reference. On the Add Reference dialog, select the Browse tab and locate the `Microsoft.Exchange.WebServices.dll` assembly. The default location is `<<DRIVE>>:\Program Files\Microsoft\Exchange\Web Services\1.1\Microsoft.Exchange.WebServices.dll`. You need to replace `<<DRIVE>>` with the correct drive letter on your machine. Click OK to add the assembly reference to your project, as shown in Figure 2-41.

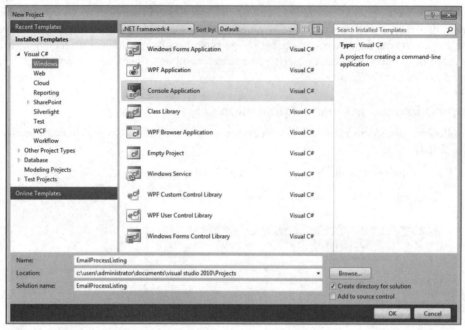

FIGURE 2-40

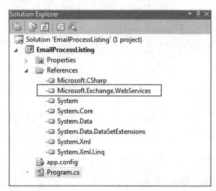

FIGURE 2-41

5. Open the `Program.cs` file and replace its code with the code in Listing 2-4. Make sure you replace the `[USER1]` and `[USER2]` token names with actual user Microsoft Online Services IDs. You created users earlier in the section titled "Adding Users."

Available for download on Wrox.com

LISTING 2-4: Program.cs

```csharp
using System;
using System.Collections.Generic;
using System.Configuration;
using System.Linq;
```

```csharp
using System.Text;

using Microsoft.Exchange.WebServices.Data;
using System.Diagnostics;

namespace ExchangeOnlineSample
{

    class Program
    {
        static void Main(string[] args)
        {
            SendEmail("[USER1]@officeservices.onmicrosoft.com", "pwd",
                GetProcessesListing(),
                "List of running processes",
                "[USER2]@officeservices.onmicrosoft.com");

        }
        private static string GetProcessesListing()
        {
            string processList = string.Empty;

            Process[] runningProcesses = Process.GetProcesses();

            foreach (Process theprocess in runningProcesses)
            {
                processList += (string.Format("Process: {0} ID: {1}</br>",
                    theprocess.ProcessName, theprocess.Id));
            }
            return processList;
        }

        private static void SendEmail(string userID, string userPassword,
            string emailMsg, string emailSubject,
            string toAddress)
        {
            ExchangeService service;

            service = new ExchangeService(ExchangeVersion.Exchange2010_SP1);

            service.Credentials = new System.Net.NetworkCredential(userID,
                userPassword);

            service.AutodiscoverUrl(userID, UrlValidationCallback);

            EmailMessage msg = new EmailMessage(service);
            msg.ToRecipients.Add(new EmailAddress(toAddress));
            msg.Subject = emailSubject;
            msg.Body = new MessageBody(BodyType.HTML, emailMsg);
            msg.SendAndSaveCopy();
        }

        private static bool UrlValidationCallback(string redirectionUrl)
```

continues

LISTING 2-4 *(continued)*

```
        {
            return true;
        }
    }
}
```

Testing the Exchange Online Application

Your application is now available for testing. To test it, follow these steps:

1. Press F5 to run the application. Wait a few moments until it executes the code; when the execution finishes, Visual Studio terminates the application.

2. Open a browser and navigate to the Office 365 Home Page available at `https://portal .microsoftonline.com/Default.aspx`.

3. Sign in using the actual login ID for `[USER1]`. After you successfully sign in, click the Outlook link from the top of the page, as shown in Figure 2-42. The Mail page displays the e-mails of `[USER1]`.

FIGURE 2-42

4. Click the Sent Items folder to view e-mails sent by your application. Notice the e-mail with the subject "List of running processes" in the Sent Items folder, as shown in Figure 2-43.

5. Now check the `[USER2]` account for the e-mail. If you have multiple browsers, you can simply sign in using a different browser. Otherwise, you must sign out and then sign in using

the [USER2] account. The [USER2] inbox displays the e-mail from [USER1] with the subject "List of running processes," and the body contains the details of those processes, as shown in Figure 2-44.

FIGURE 2-43

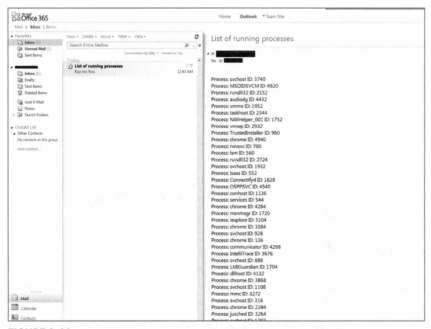

FIGURE 2-44

Your First Lync Online Application

Microsoft provides developers with Lync SDK, which contains MA API targeting Lync 2010 Object Model (OM). You can use this SDK to build custom applications that leverage Lync 2010 features, such as Audio and Video conferencing, File Sharing, Desktop Sharing, and so on.

Microsoft has used Lync MA API to develop controls for the Lync 2010 client. You can also develop your custom Lync controls using the MA API, and these controls can integrate easily with the Lync 2010 client. Alternatively, you can use the Lync 2010 controls that Microsoft ships as part of SDK, because these controls are thoroughly tested, and you can reuse them easily without worrying about their performance and quality. Figure 2-45 shows the Lync Controls in Visual Studio 2010.

FIGURE 2-45

One important point to remember while working with the MA API is that it requires running an instance of a Lync 2010 client on the same machine where you plan your application to run.

Now, create a simple WPF application that places an audio call for you. The call is made to an account that you specify in the code. This user must be available on Office 365 and, to receive the call, must be signed in to Lync 2010 client.

Developing Lync Online Application

In this section, you will create a simple Lync Online application that will place an audio call to a specific Microsoft Online User account. The following steps demonstrate how to build a Lync Online application using Visual Studio 2010.

1. From the Start menu, launch Microsoft Visual Studio 2010.
2. Click File ➪ New ➪ Project, as shown in Figure 2-46.

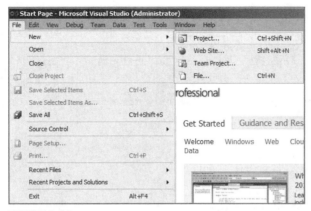

FIGURE 2-46

3. On the New Project dialog, expand Visual C# ⇨ Windows. For the Project Template select the Lync WPF Application. Use the following details and click OK, as shown in Figure 2-47.

➤ Name: **LyncOnlineAudioCall**

➤ Location: Keep default or change it as required

➤ Solution: Create a new solution (default)

➤ Solution Name: **LyncOnlineAudioCall**

4. From the Solution Explorer, open `Window1.xaml` and replace its markup with the code in Listing 2-5. Your `Window.xaml` design view should resemble Figure 2-48.

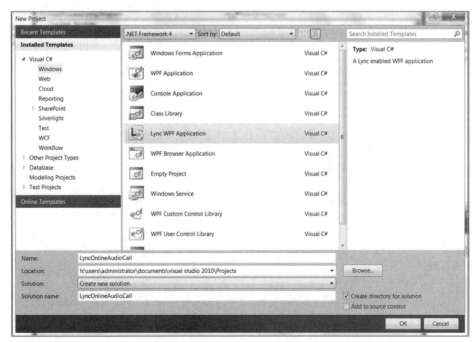

FIGURE 2-47

LISTING 2-5: Window1.xaml

```xaml
<Window x:Class="LyncOnlineAudioCall.Window1"
    xmlns="http://schemas.microsoft.com/winfx/2006/xaml/presentation"
    xmlns:x="http://schemas.microsoft.com/winfx/2006/xaml"
    xmlns:controls=
    "clr-namespace:Microsoft.Lync.Controls;assembly=Microsoft.Lync.Controls"
    Title="Home" Height="79" Width="153">
    <Grid>
        <StackPanel Orientation="Horizontal"
                    HorizontalAlignment="Center"
                    VerticalAlignment="Center">
        </StackPanel>
        <Button Content="Start Audio Call" Height="35"
                HorizontalAlignment="Left"
                Margin="8,2,0,0" Name="btnStartAudioCall"
                VerticalAlignment="Top" Width="114"
                Click="btnSendIM_Click" />
    </Grid>
</Window>
```

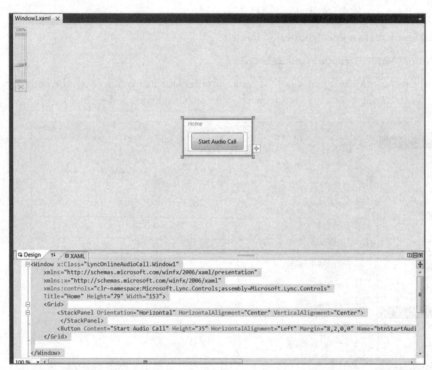

FIGURE 2-48

5. From the Solution Explorer, click `window1.xaml.cs` and replace its code with the code from Listing 2-6. Make sure you replace the [USER] token with actual Microsoft Online Services user ID. You created users earlier in the section titled "Adding Users."

LISTING 2-6: Making an Audio Call Using Lync Online API (Window1.xaml.cs)

```csharp
using System.Windows.Data;
using System.Windows.Documents;
using System.Windows.Input;
using System.Windows.Media;
using System.Windows.Media.Imaging;
using System.Windows.Navigation;
using System.Windows.Shapes;
using System.Diagnostics;
using Microsoft.Lync.Model.Extensibility;

namespace LyncOnlineAudioCall
{
    public partial class Window1 : Window
    {
        public Window1()
        {
            InitializeComponent();
        }

        private void btnSendIM_Click(object sender, RoutedEventArgs e)
        {

                List<string> participants = new  List<string>();
                participants.Add("user@officeservices.onmicrosoft.com");

                Automation automation =
                  Microsoft.Lync.Model.LyncClient.GetAutomation();

                automation.BeginStartConversation(
                    AutomationModalities.Audio,
                    participants,
                    null,
                    null,
                    automation);
        }
    }
}
```

Testing the Lync Online Application

To test your Lync online application, follow these steps:

1. Before you test your application, make sure you are signed in to your local Lync Client.

2. Press F5 to build and run your application. The application shows a WPF Form with a single button labeled Start Audio Call.

3. Press the Start Audio Call button and the call will be made using the Lync Managed API. Depending on the user on the receiving end, you may need to wait before you can start the conversation, as shown in Figure 2-49.

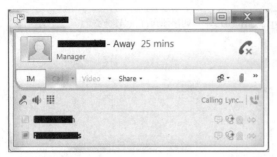

FIGURE 2-49

Office 365 Development Challenges

This section discusses a few common challenges that you may encounter while developing Office 365 solutions. It's better to take them into consideration earlier rather than later in your development life cycle.

Error Logging

Office 365 provides little support when it comes to working with the error logs. If you get an error, you must rely on the technical support for troubleshooting. This makes troubleshooting for developers, especially regarding SharePoint Online, challenging. Office 365 does not provide you any way to access the SharePoint Online logs, which are located on the server file system. This restriction exists because you share hardware and software with other tenants, and logs are not separated based on tenancy. As error logs may contain business-critical or users' personal information, providing access to a log file may lead to serious legal consequences. The dedicated version of the SharePoint Online has the same limitation on accessing error logs.

Lync and Exchange Online products impose the same restrictions as SharePoint Online and do not allow access to error logs. However, this is less of an issue because you won't be deploying custom server-side solutions to either Lync Online or Exchange Online in an Office 365 environment.

Bandwidth and Network Latency

You can access Office 365 through the Internet. Having a high bandwidth and low latency connection is extremely important to get consistent performance from custom solutions that consume Office 365 services. You should test your solutions under different bandwidths and network latencies. For example, users with a cable Internet connection usually have latencies of less than 100 ms; on the other hand, users with satellite Internet connection experience latencies of 500 ms or more. Your solutions should be responsive and function correctly under different bandwidths and network latencies.

Cross-Browser Support

While developing custom web-based solutions for Office 365, you should consider cross-browser support as a high priority. Office 365 supports a wide range of browsers, from Microsoft Internet Explorer to Google Chrome. Determine browser support for your solutions before you begin development. You should also develop your solutions to degrade gracefully when users access them with an unsupported browser. Users may simply assume that your web solution supports all the browsers that Office 365 supports, especially if they are available through the Office 365 Marketplace. It's always a good idea to provide details to your users about which browsers are supported and which are not.

OFFICE 365 DEVELOPER RESOURCES

This section discusses Office 365 resources available to developers including wikis, forums, learning resources, and so on.

Quick Start Office 365 Development

The following section provides details to help you quickly start development for Office 365.

Minimize Your Learning Curve

You can minimize your learning curve for Office 365 development by leveraging technical skillsets that you already possess. For example, if you already have an ASP.NET development background, developing custom web-based solutions for Office 365 will be easier than developing a WPF application. Office 365 service offerings are based on already-released products from Microsoft, so if you have experience with either one of them, you can leverage that development experience because it's highly likely that you will pick up the differences rather quickly.

When compared to on-premises solutions, developing cloud-based solutions does require a certain discipline. A good example of this is when you build sandbox solutions for SharePoint Online. When you develop SharePoint solutions on-premise, sandbox solutions only expose a subset of the available APIs. In addition, every piece of code that you execute in the sandbox counts toward the resource threshold that SharePoint administration allocates. If your code consumes more resources than what SharePoint administration allocates, your code will be penalized. For example, a web part on the home page of your corporate portal may suddenly stop working because it consumes too many resources. In short, good coding practices are mandatory when you build applications for the cloud services, and this may add to the learning curve for developers.

Learning Resources from Microsoft

You can also use learning resources provided by Microsoft, as listed in Table 2-2; these resources are available online and free of charge. Microsoft performs frequent updates to these resources as changes are made to Office 365.

TABLE 2-2: Office 365 Learning Resources

TITLE	DESCRIPTION	URL
Office 365 Developer Training Course	Developer-focused presentations, self-paced labs, and links to key resources to help you build solutions that leverage SharePoint Online, Exchange Online, and Lync Online	`http://msdn.microsoft` `.com/en-us/` `Office365TrainingCourse`
Exchange Online Development Center	Developer Center for Microsoft Exchange Online as part of Microsoft Office 365	`http://msdn.microsoft` `.com/exchange/gg490662`
SharePoint Online Developer Resource Center	Developer Center for Microsoft SharePoint Online as part of Microsoft Office 365	`http://msdn.microsoft` `.com/sharepoint/gg153540`
Exploring the Office Developer Story in Microsoft Office 365	Session recording from TechEd 2011 covering topics such as client-side add-ins accessing Microsoft SharePoint data, client object model, cloud programmability with Microsoft Excel, and Visio Services	`http://channel9.msdn` `.com/Events/TechEd/` `NorthAmerica/2011/OSP206`

Office 365 Community

Microsoft has established a proactive community for Office 365. The community is built around consumers of Office 365, including developers, IT professionals, end users, project managers, and others. Table 2-3 provides details about the Office 365 forums, blog, and wikis.

TABLE 2-3: Office 365 Community

TITLE	DESCRIPTION	URL
Forums	Forums where your platform can post questions and start discussions about topics related to Office 365	`http://community.office365` `.com/en-us/f/default.aspx`
Blogs	Office 365 engineering team blog	`http://community.office365` `.com/en-us/b/office_365_` `technical_blog/default.aspx`
Wiki	Office 365 team wiki	`http://community.office365` `.com/en-us/w/default.aspx`

Office 365 Marketplace

Office 365 Marketplace is a platform that enables Office 365 consumers to locate applications, professional services, and subject-matter experts for Microsoft Office 365. To enroll your application or professional services with Office 365 Marketplace, you must meet certain requirements. You can get more details on requirements and how to apply them from `http://office365.pinpoint.microsoft.com/`.

Office 365 Marketplace is mostly directed toward business users that usually have a different set of needs and expectations. For example, developing an Angry Birds game as a SharePoint Online solution may not give the same return on investment as it does on the Windows Phone Marketplace.

SUMMARY

This chapter provides the foundation to start developing applications for Office 365. It starts by providing the walkthrough of the Office 365 registration process. It then discusses the two major approaches available to you for building development environments. It also explains the pros and cons of using a virtualized development environment versus physical machines. The walkthrough later in the chapter demonstrates how to build a development environment for Office 365 and add software to it as required. The sections on SharePoint Online, Exchange Online, and Lync Online development demonstrate how to quickly build and test your application using Visual Studio 2010. You also learn how to provision a new Site Collection on SharePoint Online and upload and activate you custom solution on it. Later in the chapter, you learn about a few common development challenges associated with Office 365 development and some important Office 365 community and learning resources available to you.

PART II
Office 365

3

Office 365 Identity Services

WHAT'S IN THIS CHAPTER?

➤   What is identity?

➤   An overview of identity in Office 365

➤   Working with role-based administration

When you work with any application, identity is important because it provides who the users are, what permissions they have, and whether they can access the resources they attempt to access. In cloud computing, identity becomes even more critical because you have a single user wanting to access resources and applications stretching beyond the premises and into the cloud, and because you want to provide a single set of login credentials and as seamless an experience as possible.

In this chapter, you learn some of the important concerns and issues with identity in this context and what Microsoft provides in the Office 365 space to help resolve them.

UNDERSTANDING IDENTITY

Before diving into the identity system in Office 365, it is worthwhile to look at some key concepts concerning the identity management space (referred to as *Identify Lifecycle Management*, or *ILM*) and to see how cloud services impact identity management.

When you hear people talking about *identity management*, they're referring to a system that identifies individuals in the system and controls access to the resources in that system. An identity management system does this through the two fundamental capabilities of authentication and authorization:

➤   **Authentication (or AuthN):** The ability to verify that a user, device, or service is the entity it claims to be. This can be done in a number of ways: through a username and password, certificates, or other mechanisms.

➤ **Authorization (or AuthZ):** This determines what actions an authenticated entity is authorized to perform on resources in the system. For example, you can authorize an entity to access files, services, or other resources contained in your system.

These days, even within the enterprise, you may find it quite a challenge to have multiple client-facing and back-end systems that you need to integrate together in order to reduce the management and administrative overhead. However, the cloud introduces a whole range of additional complexities, because you now must deal with remote, cloud-based resources, further security concerns, and interacting with potentially quite disparate systems as business partners. However, providing users with only a single identity to worry about that can span across both environments is worth the complexity; it significantly reduces the hassle, the overhead, and the security risk of having multiple disparate identities, one for each environment or system.

Getting identity in the cloud working requires several important components:

➤ **Enhanced access controls:** The ubiquity of the cloud requires that you provide controlled access to services with an IP-based access control. In addition, it may require that you have a two-factor-based authentication.

➤ **Directory management:** This management is between on-premises and cloud-based identities because customers may want to store their identities in both places and require directory synchronization to ensure that both places are always kept synchronized.

➤ **Single sign-on:** This is a big feature of cloud services. Whether users' identities are hosted in the cloud or on-premises, they only want to use a single identity to log on and access resources.

UNDERSTANDING IDENTITY IN OFFICE 365

Office 365 provides two ways to master identities using a purely Office 365–based identity system:

➤ Mastering on-premises and synchronizing with Office 365 using directory synchronization

➤ Mastering on-premises and synchronizing to the cloud and providing a federated identity between the environments by leveraging *Active Directory Federation Services* (*ADFS*) and your on-premises *Active Directory* (*AD*) infrastructure

This section explores these options and the pros and cons associated with each.

Establishing Identity Using Only Office 365 Identities

The built-in identity system in Office 365 is the easiest means to deploy, manage, and support identity because you do not have the complexity of directory synchronization; you do not configure single sign-on; and you don't require any additional on-premises servers. In addition, the Office 365 online identities work seamlessly with the Office desktop client, web clients, and mobile clients without any other configuration.

However, using only the online identity has its downside:

➤ **You may need to require your users to remember two sets of credentials.** One set would be for their on-premises login and the other for their Office 365 login.

➤ **You may end up with two sets of password policies.** This is because the on-premises password policies may differ from the Office 365 password policies.

➤ **You cannot use two-factor authentication or single sign-on in this scenario.** This is because both require that you deploy ADFS on-premises.

The Office 365 password policy depends on which edition of Office 365 you purchase. For example, with the Professional SKU version, passwords are never set to expire. With the Enterprise SKU, passwords expire every 90 days, and this is not configurable. Using PowerShell, however, you can set your password to never expire as you'll see later in this chapter. In addition, irrespective of the edition, Enterprise or Professional, strong passwords are required, which means having a password between 8 to 16 characters with a mix of lowercase, uppercase, numbers, or symbols. Also, you cannot use a password again in Office 365. Finally, after 10 unsuccessful logon attempts, the user needs to solve a CAPTCHA dialog as part of the log-on. After another 10 unsuccessful log-on attempts, the user is locked out for an unspecified amount of time. Further incorrect passwords cause this timeout to grow exponentially.

When you use test accounts, you may find that the 90-day password expiry makes working with the service more difficult. With a little PowerShell, you can make your password permanent; however, you should understand that doing so makes your account weaker and more vulnerable. The following PowerShell script uses the `Set-MsolUser` cmdlet with the `-PasswordNeverExpires` boolean option to turn off password expiry. You can also use the `-StrongPasswordRequired` boolean option to turn off strong passwords. Make sure to run this PowerShell script with the Microsoft Online Services cmdlets loaded. Figure 3-1 shows an Online Identity managed in the Office 365 Portal.

```
Connect-MsolService
Set-MsolUser -UserPrincipalName user@domain.com -PasswordNeverExpires $true
```

 For more information on setting up user accounts in Office 365, refer to Chapter 2.

Using Office 365 with On-Premises Active Directory

With this Office 365 option, you can integrate with an on-premises AD using either directory synchronization or federated identities and single sign-on. The benefits for integrating with an on-premises AD are as follows:

➤ **You have a single place for your identity management through your on-premises technology.** This means that you have one place in which to manage your users and groups and all your passwords.

➤ **You can control your password policies.** This means you don't have to rely on the password policies in Office 365.

➤ **You can leverage single sign-on.** This means your users have to log on to your on-premises domain only once, and they can use that identity with both on-premises applications and services and the Office 365 services.

➤ **You can support strong authentication.** You can do this using technologies such as two-factor authentication and smartcards in addition to usernames and passwords.

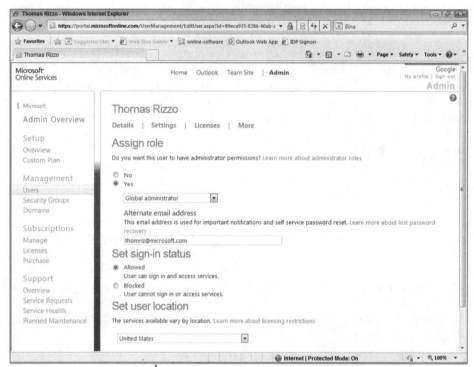

FIGURE 3-1

General Requirements

When working with an on-premises AD, your infrastructure needs to meet some general requirements:

➤ **Your AD Forest must be at least the 2003 functional level.** For this reason, you cannot have a Windows 2000 level of functionality for your AD forest.

➤ **You can have only a single AD forest deployed.** Your forest can have multiple domains, but Office 365 currently does not support multiforest deployments. For example, you can have one forest with user accounts and another forest with resources but you must synchronize both to Office 365. To do this, you must consolidate your multiple forests into a single forest.

➤ **To support ADFS 2.0, you need Windows Server 2008 or above for ADFS 2.0.**

➤ **To use directory synchronization, you must have Windows Server 2003 or above.** Directory synchronization ships for both 32-bit and 64-bit, so you must decide which version you want depending on your server infrastructure.

➤ **A hybrid deployment of Exchange Server requires Exchange 2010 Service Pack 1 Client Access Server and the associated schema applied to your AD infrastructure.** As you'll see in the next section, with Exchange SP1, you can manage a hybrid Exchange deployment from a single Exchange management console.

Directory Synchronization with Office 365

If you want to master your accounts on-premises and synchronize those accounts to Office 365, you must use the Office 365 directory synchronization tool to synchronize your on-premises accounts to the cloud. When you use the tool, it synchronizes your on-premises users, groups, and contacts into Office 365.

You can install either a 32-bit or 64-bit version of the directory synchronization tool. The tool is the same regardless of what version you install, but the underlying SQL Schema is different, so you need to stick with one edition of the synchronization tool. In addition, the tool installs SQL Server Express as part of its installation. This is fine for smaller directories, but if you have a large directory—over 20,000 objects—you need a full version of SQL Server, and you need the directory synchronization tool to use that full version.

Figure 3-2 shows the directory synchronization tool. The tool is easy to set up, and with a few clicks, you can have your on-premises AD synchronizing to the cloud.

FIGURE 3-2

The tool just asks for your Office 365 user name, your AD credentials, and whether you want to set up a hybrid Exchange environment. A *hybrid Exchange environment* is an Exchange environment that has some mailboxes hosted in on-premises servers and some mailboxes hosted in Exchange Online. Some of the benefits of an Exchange hybrid environment are that you can:

➤ Archive your on-premises mailboxes to the cloud.

➤ Off-board mailboxes from the cloud to on-premises.

➤ Maintain on-premises mail filtering, which determines how a user makes changes to safe and blocked senders in the cloud.

➤ Know when a user has voice mail in the cloud.

To run an Exchange hybrid environment with directory synchronization, you need to grant write access to your AD for the directory synchronization account.

Directory synchronization provides on-going synchronization of your user accounts, mail-enabled contacts, and mail-enabled groups. Without directory synchronization, you can't have a single Global Address List (GAL) because your on-premises accounts will be unknown to Exchange Online. For those of you newer to Exchange, the *Global Address List* is what Exchange provides for users to look up other users, distribution groups, conference rooms, and other resources in a central-ized address book.

Besides having a unified GAL, by using directory synchronization, you can manage a hybrid Exchange environment from the Exchange management console. In the console, you can work with your on-premises deployed Exchange servers and your Exchange Online services. Figure 3-3 shows how you manage both Exchange on-premises and Exchange Online in a single console.

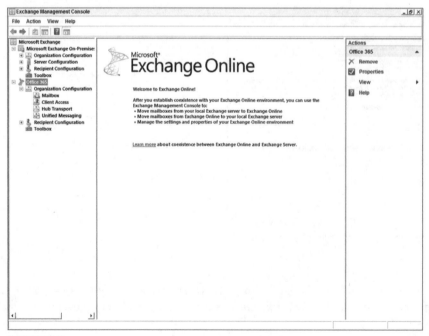

FIGURE 3-3

The following are the caveats you should consider when you work with directory synchronization:

➤ **Online objects aren't editable:** You cannot edit the online objects after synchronizing them to the cloud.

➤ **On-premises accounts synchronized and then accessed through the online portal are read-only:** Any changes to accounts, besides licensing changes, must be made in your on-premises AD and synchronized to the cloud. Figure 3-4 shows a synchronized account. Notice how the fields are grayed out so that you cannot edit them.

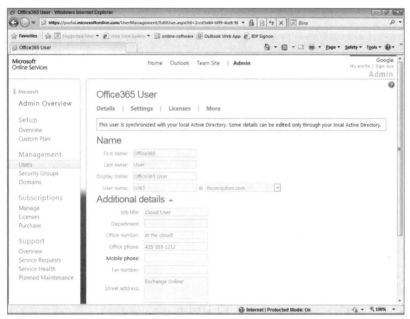

FIGURE 3-4

➤ **You can't customize filters:** One question users always ask about Office 365 directory synchronization concerns how you customize the filters that the dirsync tool uses. Unfortunately, you cannot customize the filters. Instead, you must work within the limitations of the default filters, which are shown in Table 3-1.

➤ **Synchronized users are deactivated by default.** You either need to use PowerShell or the administration portal to activate the users. Until you do this, the users cannot use the online service.

➤ **Passwords are not synchronized between on-premises and online with the directory synchronization tool.** When the administrator activates the synchronized accounts, a new password is created for the account. If users change their passwords in either location, those passwords aren't synchronized to the other location. There are third-party tools that provide password synchronization for Office 365, or you can use single sign-on so as not to require passwords beyond the on-premises passwords used by your AD accounts.

TABLE 3-1: DirSync Filters

AD OBJECT	DIRSYNC FILTER TO REMOVE
Contact	MSOL in DisplayName msExchHideFromAddressLists = TRUE
SecurityEnabledGroup	isCriticalSystemObject = TRUE
MailEnabledGroupsMailEnabledContacts	The proxy address does not have a primary SMTP address, and the mail attribute is not present.
iNetOrgPerson	sAMAccountName is not present. isCriticalSystemObject is present.
User	mailNickName starts with "SystemMailbox{" mailNickName contains "{" mailNickName starts with "CAS_" sAMAccountName starts with "CAS_" sAMAccountName has "}" sAMAccountName equals "SUPPORT_388945a0" sAMAccountName equals "MSOL_AD_Sync" sAMAccountName is not present isCriticalSystemObject is present

Using Single Sign-on with Office 365

Single sign-on enables your users to enter their AD credentials to access Office 365 resources via Active Directory Federation Services (ADFS) 2.0. Your users just click to access certain services without entering their local domain credentials. One word of caution with SSO: The experience depends on whether the client machines are domain-joined as well as the services the users on these machines are accessing such as Exchange Online, SharePoint Online or others. Table 3-2 shows different scenarios and what SSO supports.

TABLE 3-2: SSO Scenarios

SCENARIO NAME	SSO DETAILS
Computer domain-joined	Requires no additional sign-in
Roaming with domain-joined machine	Requires no additional sign-in
Nondomain-joined machine off network	Requires additional sign-in with ADFS proxy

SCENARIO NAME	SSO DETAILS
Nondomain-joined machine on corporate network	Requires additional sign-in without ADFS proxy
Office Client Applications	Requires additional sign-in

SSO provides a number of benefits that include controlling the account policies, such as password policies, workstation restrictions, lockouts, and other policies. In addition, you can implement 2-factor authentication if you implement SSO.

Please note that the 2-factor authentication supports only web clients. Figure 3-5 shows how to log into the Office 365 portal using SSO. Notice the link to log on to the domain.

FIGURE 3-5

When working with rich clients and SSO, you must log on to Office 365 with your domain credentials because the Office client cannot pass the Windows credentials from your machine to the service. You can use your domain credentials, but this requires an extra click. Figure 3-6 shows the Office client asking for credentials for Office 365.

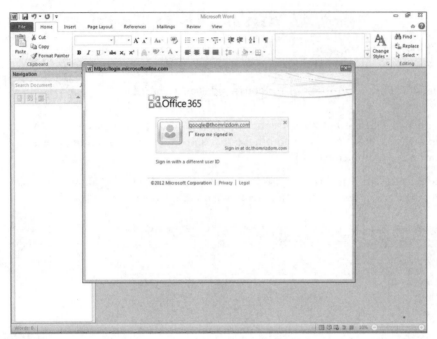

FIGURE 3-6

Smart Linking

Another feature of ADFS and Office 365 is the capability to perform smart linking or identity provider-initiated linking. These are fancy ways to say that you can create links that have the authentication endpoint in the URL and that bypass the Office 365 logon page. This is accomplished by passing the authentication realm for the user so that the endpoint can decide where to redirect the user.

In particular, deep links send the browser to the authoritative ADFS 2.0 server passive login endpoint. The endpoint encodes any SAML token as well as the relying party service that the user attempts to reach, such as the URL for Exchange Online or the Office 365 portal. All these steps prevent the user from manually going to the portal and logging on to the service.

Currently, constructing a smart link is a manual process, with the exception of Outlook Web Access, which requires you to put only `http://outlook.com/domainname` or `http://outlook.com/owa/domainname`. For other services, you must http trace the service you want to log on to using something like Fiddler and the web address such as `https://portal.microsoftonline.com/`.

Then, follow these steps:

1. Do a federated logon with the tracing tool running.

2. Use your tracing tool to find the call to your ADFS logon URL such as `https://YOURADFSSERVER/adfs/ls`.

3. Find the line in the text that has your `sts` such as the following:

```
https://sts.YOURDOMAIN.com/adfs/ls/?cbcxt=&vv=&username=johndoe%40cont
oso.com&mkt=&lc=1033&wa=wsignin1.0&wtrealm=urn:federation:MicrosoftOnl
ine&wctx=MEST%3D0%26LoginOptions%3D2%26wa%3Dwsignin1.0%26rpsnv%3D2%26ct
%3D1292977249%26rver%3D6.1.6206.0%26wp%3DMCMBI%26wreply%3Dhttps:%252F%252F
portal.microsoftonline.com%252FDefault.aspx%261c%3D1033%26id%3D271345%26bk
%3D1292977249
```

4. Remove everything up to the `wa` `querystring` parameter, and remove the last query string parameter `bk`. Your final URL will look like the following:

```
https://sts.YOURDOMAIN.com/adfs/ls/?wa=wsignin1.0&wtrealm=urn:federation:Mi
crosoftOnline&wctx=MEST%3D0%26LoginOptions%3D2%26wa%3Dwsignin1.0%26rpsnv%3D
2%26ct%3D1292977249%26rver%3D6.1.6206.0%26wp%3DMCMBI%26wreply%3Dhttps:%252F
%252Fportal.microsoftonline.com%252FDefault.aspx%261c%3D1033%26id%3D271345
```

The following link shows how to log on to SharePoint Online by setting the `wreply` to the SharePoint Online page.

```
https://dc.thomrizdom.com/adfs/ls/?wa=wsignin1.0&wtrealm=urn:federation:Microsoft
Online&wctx=MEST%3D0%26LoginOptions%3D2%26wa%3Dwsignin1.0%26rpsnv%3D2%26ct%3D1323
123053%26rver%3D6.1.6206.0%26wp%3DMCMBI%26wreply%3Dhttps:%252F%252Fthomrizdom
.sharepoint.com%252Fsitepages%252Fhome.aspx%253Ftarget%253D%25252fDefault.aspx%26
1c%3D1033%26id%3D271346
```

ROLE-BASED ADMINISTRATION

The last area to explore is role-based administration in Office 365. Role-based administration is offered in the different products in Office 365 as well as at the all-up Office 365 administration level. At the service level, you can set up five different roles:

➤ Billing Administrator

➤ Global Administrator

➤ Password Administrator

➤ Service Administrator

➤ User Management Administrator

Assigning these roles does not allow the user to manage other resources by default. For example, you must set SharePoint permissions for the user. Figure 3-7 shows setting role-based administration for Office 365.

In Exchange Online, you can create roles that allow you to customize the types of activities that administrators can do—from resetting passwords to viewing audit logs. Figure 3-8 shows setting roles in Exchange Online.

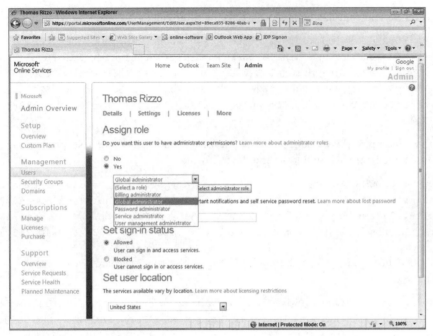

FIGURE 3-7

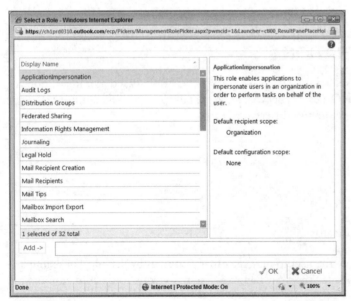

FIGURE 3-8

In SharePoint Online, you can create groups and assign permissions to the group and then assign users in the group to give them those permissions. Figure 3-9 shows setting permissions for groups in SharePoint Online.

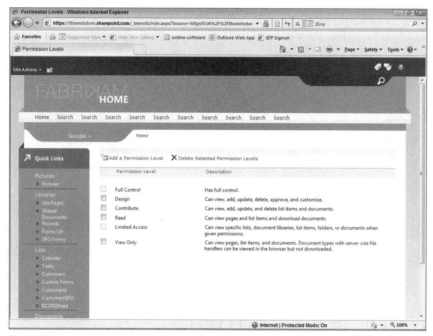

FIGURE 3-9

SUMMARY

In this chapter, you learned about identity management and integrating Office 365 with your on-premises identity infrastructure. In addition, you learned about how to configure deep linking to make logging onto the service easier for your users without having to enter credentials. You also saw how to configure user permissions within Office 365 as a whole as well as within the individual service offerings.

Introducing SharePoint Online

WHAT'S IN THIS CHAPTER?

➤ What is SharePoint Online?

➤ A brief technical overview of SharePoint Online

➤ Comparing SharePoint Online and SharePoint On-premises

➤ Developing for SharePoint Online

A discussion of a locally installable product such as SharePoint may seem out of place in a book on programming for the cloud. SharePoint has, after all, historically been an application that a company installed in its datacenter and managed itself. True, there have been various incarnations of *hosted SharePoint*, ranging from Microsoft's massive Business Productivity Online Services (BPOS) instance to many smaller hosting or service companies providing instances of shared SharePoint. However, prior to the 2010 release, these shared instances have been largely static out-of-the-box installations with little support for custom development.

With the 2010 release of SharePoint, Microsoft changed this game entirely. One of the primary drivers for the changes introduced with SharePoint 2010 was a need for large scale multitenancy, that is, multiple companies coexisting within a single SharePoint farm. Another driver was support for enhanced options for customization via server-side code without breaking security or impacting performance across tenants.

This chapter provides an overview of SharePoint Online, mostly from a developer's perspective, contrasting it with SharePoint on-premises. The goal is to help you to understand what is and is not possible in SharePoint Online.

SHAREPOINT ONLINE 101

SharePoint Online (SPO) is the evolution of the portal and collaboration aspects of Microsoft's Business Productivity Online Services, bringing the hosted SharePoint portions of that offering into the 2010 product release, including most of the rich capabilities offered by the latest release of SharePoint. Much of SPO should be immediately familiar to anyone with some experience with SharePoint 2010. There are, however, some important items of which you must be aware.

The first point may be obvious but it bears mentioning—SPO *is* SharePoint. Many, if not most, end users would never know that they are interacting with a hosted service if they weren't told. All the distinctions discussed in this chapter are technical details of interest only to those who peel back the covers and take a peek at what occurs underneath. End users could, and likely should, live their lives blissfully unaware of the messy technical details of multitenancy, Sandboxes, globally distributed datacenters, and so on. End users have a job to do that touch only upon the technical details of SPO tangentially. They need to create and collaborate on content, search for existing content, share content, and so on. They don't care how those services are provided. They care only that they *are* provided.

SPO is an instance of SharePoint 2010 hosted in the cloud by Microsoft. Other hosting providers offer their own version of *hosted SharePoint*, and each differs depending on what features and functionality are made available and how the hosting company configures the environment. This book is concerned only with SPO. Although other hosting providers' offerings are almost certainly similar—they are all SharePoint-based—there are important differences with which you must familiarize yourself if you want to operate effectively in other hosted SharePoint environments.

Any discussion of SPO must begin with a cursory review of the larger differences between it and its on-premises sibling that frames the rest of the conversation. You must understand the changes to the game board if you have any hope of following along. At a high level, SPO is SharePoint, except for the following:

➤ All server-side code runs in the Sandbox (see the next section "SharePoint Online—A Brief Technical Overview," which discusses the Sandbox).

➤ Not all features of SharePoint are available (see the section "Licensing").

➤ Central Administration is not available. Rather, in this multitenant version, you have access to "Tenant Administration." a slimmed down, focused counterpart to Central Administration.

➤ Multiple companies (tenants) coexist on the same SharePoint farm.

➤ Each tenant is allocated one or more site collections, depending upon the plan purchased.

➤ The tenant has NO access to the underlying hardware or servers via any type of remote desktop or similar capability. In other words, all administrative or customization interaction with SPO happens via the browser or tools such as SharePoint Designer.

Other than those six things, SPO is effectively identical to an on-premises installation.

SHAREPOINT ONLINE—A BRIEF TECHNICAL OVERVIEW

Development in SPO is all about the Sandbox. This is the single most important aspect of SPO for developers to understand. The Sandbox has been mentioned a couple of times so far, so now let's take a moment to ensure you understand it. In SharePoint 2010, the *Sandbox* is a controlled, monitored execution environment operating inside the SharePoint application. It is responsible for ensuring the security of content, as well as the stability and performance of the SharePoint farm. To say that code is "running in the Sandbox" means that this special execution environment manages the code's execution to ensure that it does not perform actions that have been blocked, and that it doesn't use too many server resources, such as processor time or memory, with the ultimate goal of ensuring that no single tenant can destabilize any other.

As part of this controlled execution model, SPO has a few important aspects:

➤ **Deployment options:** SPO supports only the Sandbox deployment model for custom solutions. You cannot deploy Farm solutions to SPO.

➤ **Resource Monitoring:** SPO tracks the work done by custom code and shuts it down if too much strain is placed on the server environment.

➤ **Code Restrictions:** SPO allows only programmatic access to those elements accessible from the Sandbox or via the client object model. For the most part, this means access to the site collection level and below. Web Application and Farm elements are not available in SPO via custom code, server-side or client-side. This also means there is no access to external components, such as remote WCF services, e-mail services, or similar external systems.

➤ **Solution Validation:** SPO layers additional validation requirements upon those enforced by the Sandbox.

Deployment Options

In SPO, unlike SharePoint on-premises, the only deployment option is the Sandbox. Farm solutions cannot be installed in SPO.

Resource Monitoring

The Sandbox environment tracks the number of cumulative total server resources used and can temporarily shut down to prevent poorly written or malicious code from consuming so many resources that they impact other tenants or the server. Table 4-1 shows the various resources that the Sandbox tracks as well as details on what each means and the cost of usage.

TABLE 4-1: Resources That the Sandbox Tracks

RESOURCE NAME	DESCRIPTION	UNITS	RESOURCES PER POINT	LIMIT
AbnormalProcessTerminationCount	Process gets abnormally terminated	Count	1	1
CPUExecutionTime	CPU exception time for site	Seconds	3,600	60

continues

TABLE 4-1 *(continued)*

RESOURCE NAME	DESCRIPTION	UNITS	RESOURCES PER POINT	LIMIT
CriticalExceptionCount	Critical exception fired	Number	10	3
InvocationCount	Number of times the solution has been invoked	Count	N/A	N/A
PercentProcessorTime	Percentage of processor time used	%	85	100
ProcessCPUCycles	CPU cycles consumed by the solution	CPU Cycles	1×10^{11}	1×10^{11}
ProcessHandleCount	Windows handles created	Handle item	10,000	1,000
ProcessIOBytes	(Hard Limit Only) Bytes written to IO	Bytes	0	1×10^{8}
ProcessThreadCount	Number of Threads in Overall Process	Threads	10,000	200
ProcessVirtualBytes	(Hard Limit Only) Memory consumed	Bytes	0	1×10^{9}
SharePointDatabaseQueryCount	# of SP database queries	Count	20	100
SharePointDatabaseQueryTime	Elapsed query time	Seconds	120	60
UnhandledExceptionCount	Unhanded Exception count	Exception instance	50	3
UnresponsiveprocessCount	Count of unresponsive processes	Number	2	1

The easiest way to understand this table is with an example. If you have a web part on a page that requires 20 calls into the SharePoint database to deliver its content, this costs one "point" every time that page loads. If you have 50 people in your company and each person views that page twice per day, that page costs 100 points (1 point per page load × 50 people × 2 page loads per person).

By default, each Sandbox (that is, each site collection) has 300 "points" available before it shuts down and stops processing additional requests for Sandboxed solution items. This 300-point quota is configurable on a site collection-by-site collection basis through the SPO administration pages. When the Sandbox for a given site collection shuts down, users see the message shown in Figure 4-1 until either the next day (usage is reset at midnight, datacenter time, or an administrator increases the quota allocation for that site collection.

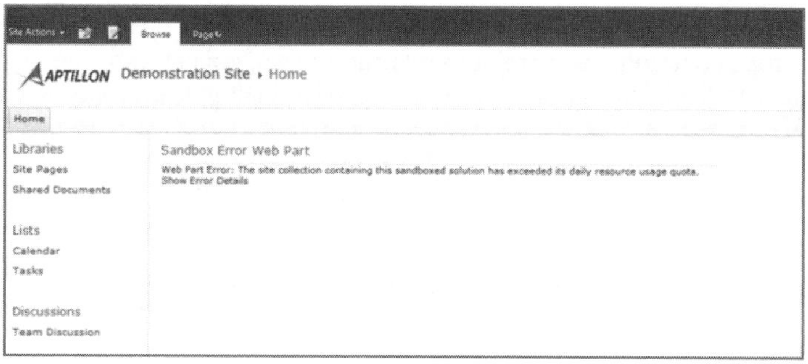

FIGURE 4-1

Code Restrictions

In addition to resource monitoring, the Sandbox also restricts access to elements in the SharePoint object model. Sandboxed Solutions are not allowed to access every object in the SharePoint server-side object model. Instead, they have access to the *subset object model*. The subset object model is just what the name implies—limited portions of the full server-side object model. While not an exhaustive list, some important items not in the subset object model include:

➤ The SPSite constructor

➤ SPSecurity

➤ SPWebApplication

➤ SPFarm

Solution Validation

In addition to the code restrictions previously covered, SPO implements validation logic when custom Sandboxed Solutions are activated. This logic prevents custom code deployed to SPO from accessing other resources that could present security or performance problems. For details on how to work within the scope of this additional validation logic, see the information on the FxCopRules project in the "Tooling" section later in this chapter.

Programmable Scope

As might be expected in a multitenant environment in which each tenant must be totally isolated from each other tenant, all custom code in SPO is restricted to accessing the current site collection. You cannot reach across site collection boundaries to access content, users, configuration details, and so on from another site collection. Furthermore, you cannot reach outside SPO, except through Business Connectivity Services. This restriction is enforced regardless of where the code executes—managed code in a Sandboxed Solution running on the server, JavaScript running in a client browser, managed code running in a Silverlight application on the client, managed code running in a .NET application on a client, or any code running anywhere using the REST APIs. While it's true that some access mechanisms (notably the managed code client object model and the REST APIs) can access multiple site collections, they must authenticate with valid credentials to each site collection they connect to. They cannot hop from one site collection to another without authenticating. Because these approaches do not operate within the context of a site collection, they are not violating the site collection boundaries. For JavaScript code and Sandboxed Solutions, the site collection boundary is still paramount.

The end result of all these elements is allowing tenants to add server-side code to their custom solutions with no fear that it can impact or interact with the resources or content of another tenant in any way.

SHAREPOINT ONLINE VERSUS SHAREPOINT ON-PREMISES

Looking at SPO more closely, the biggest benefit may not be immediately obvious. Quite simply, this is the effort required to set up servers, install the application, patch the application, create the farm, and all the other myriad of details required to build a SharePoint environment from scratch. When you use SPO, the time from when you decide to use the tool to the time users browse your SharePoint environment can be measured in hours or days, not weeks or months. Naturally, this is not always the case, and large-scale adoptions of SPO can involve a significant effort, especially if migration of existing content is involved. However, at a bare minimum, that effort does not need to include the establishment of a datacenter and the building out of a server infrastructure, which can often run into months of effort.

The rest of this section delves more deeply into some key differences between SPO and SharePoint on-premises.

Licensing

When installed in your (self-hosted or rented) datacenter, the functionality of SharePoint is governed by its license selection. The license choices:

➤ **Foundation:** The free core product. Provides basic SharePoint functionality for content creation, sharing, collaboration, and social interaction.

➤ **Standard:** Built on top of Foundation, it introduces additional functionality, such as enhanced Search and Social capabilities, content rating and tagging, managed metadata, and web analytics.

➤ **Enterprise:** The whole enchilada—all SharePoint functionality.

For a detailed breakdown of features and functionality by on-premises SKU, see the chart published at: `http://sharepoint.microsoft.com/en-us/buy/Pages/Editions-Comparison.aspx`.

Features and Functionality

The feature set of SPO is most closely analogous to the feature set of SharePoint Server Enterprise, with a few notable exceptions:

➤ **Claims-based security:** Available in all SKUs of SharePoint on-premises but not available in SPO

➤ **Custom Timer jobs:** Available in all SKUs of SharePoint on-premises but not available in SPO

➤ **FAST Search:** Available in SharePoint Server Enterprise but not available in SPO

➤ **Secure Store Service:** Available in SharePoint Server on-premises but not available in SPO

➤ **Web Analytics:** Available in SharePoint Server on-premises but not available in SPO

➤ **PowerPivot for SharePoint:** Available in SharePoint Server Enterprise on-premises but not available in SPO

➤ **PerformancePoint Services:** Available in SharePoint Server Enterprise on-premises but not available in SPO

➤ **Specific enhancements to search, social, business intelligence, security, and so on:** Available in SharePoint Server Enterprise on premises but not in SPO.

Cost

The cost for SPO is an obvious benefit for the bean-counters in the room. If you can fit your requirements into the capabilities of SPO, you can gain significant cost-savings.

SPO is a hosted service for which you pay a monthly fee per user. SharePoint on-premises is a per-server and per-user license-based model. The difference can be considerable. At the time of this writing, the per-user fee for SPO as part of the full Office 365 Suite can cost as little as $72 per user per year for typical small business functionality—e-mail, content sharing and collaboration, social networking, instant messaging, online meetings, and web-based versions of the Office client applications. For larger enterprises that need licenses for the desktop Office applications, enhanced capabilities for content sharing, collaboration, and so on as well as full phone system integration, the cost can go up as high as $264 per user per year—depending on which options you choose.

Contrast this with a typical on-premises installation that could cost tens of thousands of dollars in licensing and services to hundreds of thousands of dollars; the cost benefit of SPO is immediately apparent.

Availability

Related to cost is the question of availability. Highly available environments simply cost more to set up and maintain. Without insulting the IT Pros who maintain an on-premises environment, keeping an environment always-on is a difficult prospect, and most SharePoint environments do not come close to the availability of SPO. Microsoft guarantees 99.9 percent uptime for Office 365 with financially backed service agreements. This means that if it does not meet that agreement, you get a credit against future billing; 99.9 percent availability translates to just under 9 hours per year (or 1 minute, 26 seconds per day) of down time. Although initially that may seem like a lot, realize that this includes scheduled downtime for patches and updates, which are typically scheduled for off-hours to minimize the impact on users.

IT Professional Requirements

Maintaining a SharePoint environment on-premises is not a feat to be undertaken lightly. There are a *LOT* of moving parts—Windows Server, SQL, IIS, Active Directory, antivirus software, firewalls, monitoring, SharePoint, and so on. To maintain the environment, all the components that make up a SharePoint environment require resources from a variety of disciplines to work in concert.

Maintaining an SPO environment is almost a nonevent. For smaller businesses there are no requirements for these types of resources—it is all handled by Microsoft. For larger enterprises the need might be there, but it is greatly reduced to just maintaining connectivity and interactions between on-premises services and SPO as required by your particular usage scenario.

Administrative Requirements

The day-to day administrative tasks to manage users, security, lists/libraries, and so on are not significantly different between SPO and SharePoint on-premises. In either environment, site collection administrators use the same (or similar) web pages to perform their tasks. These can range from adding users to security groups to controlling resource access to creating and managing lists and libraries. There are some minor differences in screens and steps between the two environments but nothing significant.

Developer Requirements

Although identifying the exact skills necessary to be an effective SharePoint developer is a highly subjective exercise, any list would likely include the following:

- Managed code—either C# or VB.NET
- ASP.NET
- JavaScript
- The SharePoint server-side object model
- CAML
- SharePoint administration (yes, even for a developer)
- Web services
- The SharePoint client-side object model (managed code, Silverlight, and JavaScript)
- REST

Depending on your environment and the task at hand, you'll use some of those more than others.

When you move into SPO development, however, your skill level in most of those areas needs to improve. For example, it is far more likely that you need to use JavaScript in SPO development than in SharePoint on-premises development because resource restrictions are in place as part of the Sandbox. JavaScript does not count against your resource quotas. Therefore, you'll to need to upgrade basic JavaScript skills to more advanced skills.

Similarly, you must write efficient, managed code in an SPO environment because *every line of custom server-side code that executes counts against your resource quota.* A deeper understanding of how your custom managed code operates and how to make it as efficient as possible is likely the most important aspect in becoming an effective SPO developer. Tweaking your CAML query to be as efficient as possible, returning only the necessary rows and columns and nothing else is more important than ever before. Understanding the importance of efficient looping, proper disposal of objects, minimizing processing time and bandwidth all come to the forefront of what it means to be an SPO developer. Although not technically correct, it was often possible to get away with somewhat sloppy code and processing when your code had the full horsepower of the servers available to it and direct access for an administrator to clean up any fallout. As covered in the previous section, this is no longer true, and every processor cycle you waste or every byte of additional RAM you consume is counted against you—use too much and you run into trouble.

Finally, you must be far more familiar with the features and functionality of native SharePoint to know the most efficient way to meet a business requirement. Sometimes fulfilling a requirement means a unique combination of out-of-the-box capabilities augmented with a smattering of custom server- or client-side code. SharePoint, even SPO, gives you an amazing toolkit with which to build your application, and knowing everything in that toolkit is more important than ever when you operate in a resource-controlled environment such as SPO.

In addition to enhancing your overall developer skills, a few new skills are necessary to be an effective SPO developer:

➤ **Load/performance testing and tuning:** The aforementioned resource restrictions of the Sandbox make it far more important that your code is as optimized as possible to avoid potential problems. The only way to validate this is to test for it.

➤ **JavaScript:** This was mentioned previously but bears repeating. By its nature, SPO lends toward more client-side development. In practice, this is doubly true. You're almost certainly going to do more JavaScript coding in SPO than in SharePoint on-premises. Period. Just accept it. This likely means that you must be comfortable with native JavaScript as well as one of several popular extension libraries—JQuery, MooTools, Dojo, and so on. JQuery is currently the market leader de jour, but is by no means the only option.

➤ **SharePoint Designer:** Often seen as the bane of a SharePoint developer's existence, SPD is no longer a tool that can safely be ignored, relegated to an "end user tool." For a variety of reasons, SPD is more often going to be the right answer to get SharePoint to do what you need in SPO. Whether this is workflows, DataView web parts, or another SPD capability, it plays a role in your solution. The trick is maintaining good application development discipline while still taking advantage of what SPD has to offer, but that's a discussion for another time.

DEVELOPING FOR SHAREPOINT ONLINE

Other than the things mentioned previously, writing code for SPO is identical to writing code for any other SharePoint 2010 installation. Solutions still consist of Features; Features are deployed in WSPs, and Features consist of declarative and programmatic elements to define Lists, web parts, workflows, and branding.

Capabilities

This is not to say that everything that can be built in SharePoint can be built for SPO. There are still some restrictions around the actual artifacts available for SPO. For SPO deployment, the Solutions are limited to the following:

- List Definitions and Instances
- WebTemplate Feature elements
- Site Columns and Content Types
- Modules
- Feature Receivers
- Web Parts
- Event Receivers (item, list, and Web receivers)
- Custom Actions
- Declarative workflows

Each of these elements can be deployed to a specific site collection and will execute within the confines of that boundary.

Tooling

As might be expected, the primary tool for SPO development is the same as the primary tool for SharePoint on-premises development: Visual Studio. In addition, SharePoint Designer plays a larger role in SPO development than it typically does in SharePoint on-premises development. Finally, there are several additional tools, some of which are also useful for SharePoint on-premises, which are particularly useful for SPO development. The following sections discuss these tools.

Fiddler

Fiddler (or a similar HTTP inspector) enables you to inspect browser requests sent to SPO (or any website, it is not SPO-specific) at a low level to get a better understanding of what is happening in your application. Fiddler is freeware. Detailed help on using Fiddler is available on its website (www.fiddler2.com).

FXCop Rules for Office 365

You can find this at `www.fxcoprules.codeplex.com`. This tool is a code analysis plug-in for Visual Studio that can help you use only those aspects of the SharePoint object model enabled in SPO. As of October 2011, the following items are checked by this tool.:

Assembly References

Referencing the following assemblies is not allowed:

- `Microsoft.AnalysisServices`
- `Microsoft.BusinessData`
- `Microsoft.Office.Excel.Server.Udf`
- `Microsoft.Office.SecureStoreService`
- `Microsoft.Office.SecureStoreService.Server.Security`
- `Microsoft.Office.Server`
- `Microsoft.Office.Server.Diagnostics`
- `Microsoft.Office.Server.Search`
- `Microsoft.Office.Server.UserProfiles`
- `Microsoft.SharePoint.Portal`
- `Microsoft.SharePoint.Publishing`
- `Microsoft.SharePoint.Search`
- `Microsoft.SharePoint.Search.Extended.Administration.Common`
- `Microsoft.SharePoint.Search.Extended.Administration.dll`
- `Microsoft.SharePoint.Search.Extended.Administration.ResourceStorage.dll`
- `Microsoft.SharePoint.SubsetProxy.dll`
- `Microsoft.SqlServer`
- `Microsoft.Win32`
- `System.Data.Sql`
- `System.Data.SqlClient`
- `System.Data.SqlTypes`
- `System.IO.Pipes`
- `System.IO.Ports`
- `System.Runtime.Remoting`

Method Calls

Calling any of the following is not allowed:

➤ `System.Array.CreateInstance (System.Type, System.Int32)`

➤ `System.Type.GetType`

➤ `System.Type.InvokeMember`

➤ `System.Threading.Monitor.Enter`

➤ `System.Threading.Monitor.Exit`

➤ `System.Threading.Interlocked.CompareExchange`

➤ `System.Threading.Thread.get_CurrentThread`

➤ `System.Threading.Thread.get_ManagedThreadId`

➤ `System.Reflection.FieldInfo.GetFieldFromHandle`

➤ `System.Reflection.MethodBase.GetMethodFromHandle`

➤ `System.Reflection.FieldInfo.GetValue`

➤ `System.Reflection.ConstructorInfo`

➤ `System.Reflection.MemberInfo.get_Name`

➤ `System.Reflection.MemberInfo.GetCustomAttributes`

➤ `System.Reflection.PropertyInfo.get_PropertyType`

➤ `System.Reflection.PropertyInfo.GetValue`

➤ `System.Reflection.PropertyInfo.SetValue`

➤ `System.Reflection.MethodInfo`

Object Creation

Creating any objects whose full class name begins with the following is not allowed:

➤ `Microsoft.SqlServer`

➤ `Microsoft.Win32`

➤ `System.Data.Sql`

➤ `System.Data.SqlClient`

➤ `System.Data.SqlTypes`

➤ `System.IO.Pipes`

➤ `System.IO.Ports`

➤ `System.Runtime.Remoting`

➤ `System.Threading`

➤ `System.Reflection`

Miscellaneous

The following other rules are enforced as well:

➤ Including a finalizer is not allowed.

JavaScript Debugger

The IE Developer Tools (included with Internet Explorer), Firebug (`www.getfirebug.com`), or a similar JavaScript debugger tool enables you to work much more closely with your JavaScript code. With the enhanced focus on JavaScript development, these tools enable you to debug, test, and work more closely with your JavaScript code in the client browser.

SUMMARY

SPO is an exciting new opportunity for SharePoint developers to flex their development muscles and offer new solutions to business problems. This chapter provided an overview of SPO ranging from available features and functionality to an introduction to the controlled and monitored execution model of SPO development. If you want to dive further into SPO, read on. Chapter 5 gives you more detail.

PART III
Developing Office 365

5

SharePoint Online Development

If you have not heard about public or private clouds, you must not be reading the news or blogs, or looking at what the different vendors are doing. *Software as a service (SAAS)* is all the rage in the computing world. Although it has many merits, including ease of deployment, anywhere access, and quick upgrades, at the same time it has a number of obstacles, such as limited offline support, fewer mature development tools, and less control of customization. Regardless of these limitations, many people are looking to the cloud as the next major shift in the computing world. If you have not tried to build applications against a cloud service such as Microsoft Azure or SharePoint Online, start today.

SHAREPOINT ONLINE OVERVIEW

SharePoint Online is, as the name implies, a Microsoft-hosted version of SharePoint. One of the major differences between your on-premises deployment of SharePoint and SharePoint Online is that SharePoint Online does not support the full range of customizations or functionality that you can host on-premises. The reason for this is that your SharePoint deployment is hosted in a multitenant environment, so your SharePoint deployment is shared with other customer deployments. When building solutions on SharePoint Online, you must build nonfarm solutions rather than solutions that require full-trust or farm-level permissions because you do not own the farm in SharePoint Online. Table 5-1 shows examples of no-code solutions versus farm solutions.

TABLE 5-1: No-Code Versus Farm Solutions

NO-CODE SOLUTION	FARM SOLUTION
Custom Markup (HTML, ASP.NET, XSLT)	Custom Server Components (coded workflows, timer jobs, and Window Services)
SharePoint Designer solutions	Visual Studio Solutions (except for Sandboxed Solutions)
Client-side code, such as Client OMs, including JavaScript and Silverlight	Application pages
Coding against SharePoint Web Services, and REST Services	Visual Web Parts without VS Power Tools

One other major difference between online and on-premises is that the cloud version is currently a subset of the full feature. In particular, SharePoint Online does not support PerformancePoint or FAST in the cloud. In addition, when dealing with search technologies, architecture and deployment become more critical as you deploying in the cloud. For example, if you have a hybrid environment in which you want to have SharePoint sites split between on-premises and online, where do you put which site? The answer is that it depends, but either place that you decide to place it, you deal with access across WANs.

DEVELOPING IN THE CLOUD

As you can see by the previous summary, some of the ways you are used to developing on-premises do not translate to the multitenant cloud. Using server-side code is a no-no when it comes to building applications on which you run SharePoint with other tenants on the server. However, when developing for online use, you have a number of choices for development, including Sandboxed Solutions, SharePoint Designer (SPD), InfoPath, Access, or the SharePoint client object, REST and Web Services models in ASP.NET, Windows Form applications, or Silverlight applications.

Deploying and Debugging Your Solutions

Before diving into development on SharePoint Online, first consider deploying and debugging. Sometimes you might find deployment and debugging painful when developing for SharePoint Online, which provides a limited set of capabilities for these two functions as opposed to SharePoint on-premises. For example, because you cannot run Visual Studio on your SharePoint Online server and because SharePoint Online, today, does not support PowerShell, you must to manually copy your WSP files to SharePoint Online and activate them.

In addition, you cannot attach the debugger directly to your processes because VS is not running on your server, and you cannot set up remote debugging on SharePoint Online. Your only options for debugging are to use a local SharePoint Server, write to a list as a log file, or use the Developer Dashboard.

WSP Files and the Solution Gallery

To deploy solutions to SharePoint Online, you need to manually copy your WSP files, which you can have Visual Studio package up for you. Then, you need to activate the solution contained in the WSP file using the SharePoint user interface, as shown in Figure 5-1. From there, you can use your web part, workflow action, or whatever other component it contains that you have created for SharePoint Online.

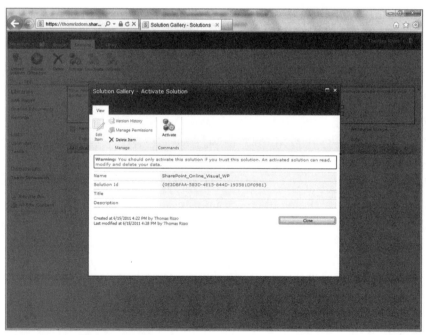

FIGURE 5-1

Developer Dashboard

One feature that helps with debugging in SharePoint Online is that the Developer Dashboard is enabled by default. By clicking the Developer Dashboard icon in the upper-right corner of the SharePoint user interface, you can quickly see what's happening. However, Sandboxed Solutions do not support SPMonitoredScope, which enables you to add richer tracking of your solution in the sandbox. Figure 5-2 shows the Developer Dashboard running in SharePoint.

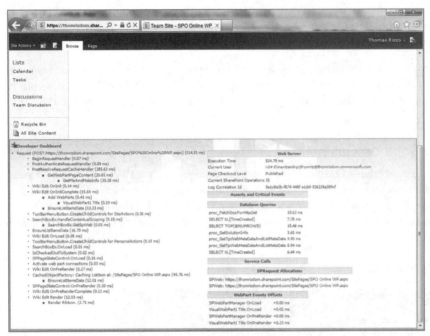

FIGURE 5-2

Fiddler

Because you are dealing with an online service, you need to become adept at looking at HTTP packets when you debug. For this reason, you need to install Fiddler (or an equivalent tool) on your machines because Fiddler can help you understand the traffic between your client machine and SharePoint Online. When you can look at the traffic, you can discover what happens between the instances and also determine whether your problems are authentication- or identity-related, or are caused by other issues.

Client-side Code

For Silverlight or client-side code, your choices for debugging are better because you can use the tools built into Internet Explorer or Firefox to debug your solution.

Debugging Using Logging

The following Sandbox web part shows how to log on to a SharePoint list for debugging purposes:

```
using System;
using System.ComponentModel;
using System.Runtime.InteropServices;
using System.Web.UI;
using System.Web.UI.WebControls;
using System.Web.UI.WebControls.WebParts;
using Microsoft.SharePoint;
using Microsoft.SharePoint.WebControls;

namespace SharePointOnlineLogging.WebPart1
```

```
{
    [ToolboxItemAttribute(false)]
    public class WebPart1 : WebPart
    {

        private Button logResultsButton = new Button() { Text = "Log Results" };
        private Label lbl = new Label();

        public WebPart1()
        {
        }

        protected override void CreateChildControls()
        {
            logResultsButton.Click += (object sender, EventArgs e) =>
            {

                SPContext context = SPContext.Current;

                SPWeb web = context.Web;

                SPList list = web.GetList("/Lists/
                 SharePointOnlineLogging-ListInstance1");

                string logResults = DateTime.Now.ToShortDateString() + " " +
                 DateTime.Now.ToShortTimeString()
                   + ": Logged from Sandbox Web Part!";

                SPListItem newItem = list.AddItem();


                newItem["Title"] = "New Log Result - " +
                DateTime.Now.ToShortTimeString();
                newItem["LoggingResult"] = logResults;

                newItem.Update();


                lbl.Text = "Logged Result: " + logResults;
            };
            Controls.Add(logResultsButton);

            Controls.Add(lbl);

            //base.CreateChildControls();
        }

        protected override void RenderContents(HtmlTextWriter writer)
        {
            base.RenderContents(writer);
        }
    }
}
```

code snippet WebPart1.cs

EXAMPLE CLOUD SCENARIOS

As you will find, for out-of-the-box (OOB) functionality, SharePoint Online is a viable solution. The areas to watch out for include custom code and unsupported features in the cloud or features that require administrative access to the server. To help understand areas in which using SharePoint in the cloud makes sense, the following scenarios describe where you can use the cloud and where you can't:

- ➤ **An Extranet site:** SharePoint Online in Office 365 has an offering for building extranets because the security for extranets is different than Intranet sites. Plus, sharing and invitations with external parties makes it easy for end users to invite their business partners from other companies. Extranets may be the first scenario that you undertake with SharePoint Online as a complement to your on-premises deployment of SharePoint. You may get a quick win by making it easy to share information with your business partners without worrying about access to your internal corporate networks. Make sure that the online service-level agreements (SLA) for availability and recovery meet your corporate standards and that the security in place for SharePoint Online meets your security guidelines for your company.

- ➤ **A typical team collaboration:** In this scenario, you are creating a team site, sharing documents, and performing simple customization of the site. Because this case does not require high-end development or administrative access, this scenario is easily supported in the cloud. The only gotchas are to make sure that users who use Office on their desktop understand how to authenticate against SharePoint Online and how to determine the address for their sites because the address will be fully qualified domain names rather than Intranet-style short names.

- ➤ **A company portal:** This is where it gets more complex because many portals require rich customization and publishing infrastructure. This is one scenario in which you must evaluate your needs versus what SharePoint Online provides from a development standpoint. If you find that your existing portal makes use of a lot of custom code (such as custom field controls or complex workflows), you may not want to run your solution in SharePoint Online or rewrite these solutions to use Sandboxed Solutions, which are supported in the Online environment.

OFFICE 365 OVERVIEW

Office 365 is the next generation of the BPOS suite and is the latest offering in Microsoft's cloud services infrastructure. With Office 365, you get Exchange, SharePoint, Lync, and Office Professional Plus as part of the bundle. Microsoft runs the infrastructure for you by providing you with hosting, billing, backup, antivirus, and anti-spam services, as well as a host of other services that an IT department would normally run on-premises.

Differences Between SharePoint On-Premises and Online

So, what's the difference between SharePoint Online and SharePoint on-premises from a developer perspective? There are a number of differences, with the majority falling into the level of control and the extensibility scenario. For example, because SharePoint Online runs in a multitenant environment, you do not have the same level of access that you do when you run on-premises on your own server. You do not have access to SharePoint Central Administration. You cannot run full-trust solutions, and any pieces of SharePoint that require full server configuration changes, Central Administration access, or full-trust access will not work in SharePoint Online. So, if you find that you need full control of your environment or the ability to write code that accesses all the resources on the SharePoint Server, you may need to continue to deploy SharePoint on-premises or look at implementation options for those components, including possibly migration these to Azure-hosted solutions.

For example, Figure 5-3 shows the tenant administration page in SharePoint Online. This administration page is different and less functional than what you can do in SharePoint's Central Administration site.

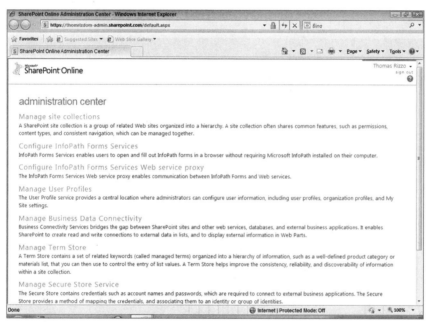

FIGURE 5-3

What's in SharePoint Online in Office 365?

Because SharePoint Online is not an exact replica of SharePoint on-premises, you may be wondering what is supported in SharePoint Online. Table 5-2 shows the developer features available in SharePoint Online. There are also IT and end user features not available in SharePoint Online, so you need to check the SharePoint website for more information about which features are available in SharePoint Online.

TABLE 5-2: Developer Differences Between Online and On-Premises

AREA	SHAREPOINT ONLINE	SHAREPOINT ON-PREMISES
Browser-only customization (for example, CQWP and CEWP)	Supported	Supported
SharePoint Designer	Supported but limited BCS support	Supported
SharePoint Solutions	Sandbox only	SandboxFarm/full trust
Client object models	Supported	Supported
Silverlight web part	Supported	Supported
Web Services	Subset of Web ServicesREST APIExcel services REST API	All Web ServicesREST APIExcel services REST API
InfoPath forms	Sandbox only	SandboxFull trust
Workflow and Workflow Activities	DeclarativeSandbox workflow activities only	DeclarativeSandbox and full-trust workflow activities
Anonymous access	Not supported	Supported
Mobile control adapters	Not supported	Supported
Visual Studio	Supported	Supported
Developer Dashboard	Supported	Supported
Business Connectivity Services	Supported against WCF Services only	Supported
Custom authentication	Office 365 IDADFS	Custom authentication supported

What About Hybrid Solutions?

Given the limitations of SharePoint Online, there may be times when you need to build a hybrid solution that encompasses both SharePoint Online and SharePoint on-premises. For example, given that SharePoint Online supports only a limited subset of the Business Connectivity Services (BCS) functionality found on-premises, bridging this gap is not as easy when it comes to data connectivity. However, for applications that need to span across the two environments when writing client-side code, such as Silverlight and JavaScript applications, hybrid solutions can make sense as long as you can overcome the connectivity and identity issues. Another very useful type of hybrid solution involves leveraging both Office 365 and Windows Azure. By combining the two clouds, you can build richer solutions that span the two environments. The rest of this chapter covers integrating SharePoint, both on-premises and online, with the Microsoft Azure technologies.

WRITING SHAREPOINT ONLINE APPLICATIONS

The rest of this chapter deals with writing SharePoint Online applications. Because SharePoint Online is the same software as SharePoint on-premises, except with some functionality and platform differences, many of the techniques you'll learn throughout this book work with SharePoint Online. The main hurdle that you run into when writing SharePoint Online applications is in understanding the limitations of SharePoint Online and making sure you understand how to authenticate and authorize using SharePoint Online. Looking at some sample scenarios can help make this clear, so dive in.

Identity and Authentication in Office 365

One of the major components of Office 365 is the authentication system as we saw in Chapter 3. Office 365 supports direct authentication via a username and password. The Office 365 security system is known as OrgID, which is based off the LiveID technologies. Although it's similar, you cannot use LiveID in the same way you can use OrgID. The following steps outline where OrgID differs:

1. When you log into the system, you request a token from the Office 365 STS, which is located at `https://login.microsoftonline.com/extSTS.srf`.

2. You pass your username and password using the SAML 1.1 protocol and, if successful, the STS returns a security token.

3. That security token is sent to the service you are trying to use, in this case SharePoint Online, and if validated, SharePoint Online returns two cookies that act as tokens. One is called `FedAuth` and the other is `rtFa`.

4. From that point, you must pass these two tokens with every call to SharePoint Online.

When writing SharePoint Online applications, you need to grab the two cookies that represent your tokens and add them to your calls as part of your `CookieContainer`.

Rather than writing your own code to do all this work, you have two choices.

➤ Use a Microsoft sample, which utilizes a web browser control to have the user log in and then retrieves the cookies if there is a successful login.

➤ Use a sample that Wictor Wilen wrote at `http://www.wictorwilen.se/Post/How-to-do-active-authentication-to-Office-365-and-SharePoint-Online.aspx`.

Both samples are included in the sample applications of this chapter. The main difference is that the Microsoft sample does display a web browser control, as shown in Figure 5-4, and the other sample does not.

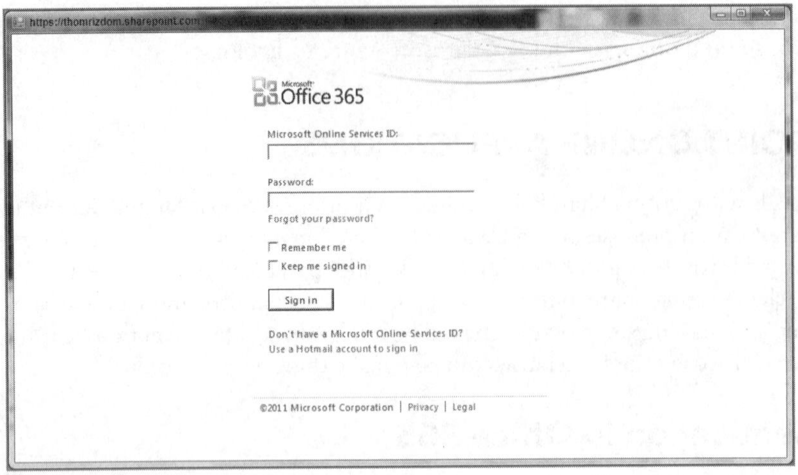

FIGURE 5-4

Developing for SharePoint Online

You may think you can just fire up Visual Studio and start working directly against SharePoint Online. Unfortunately, there is a limitation in the current SharePoint tools for Visual Studio such that it requires a locally-deployed SharePoint instance for development so that you can't point your VS projects at your SharePoint Online tenant. Instead, you must develop and debug locally and then deploy your applications to SharePoint Online. With the next release of Visual Studio, Visual Studio 11 (currently in beta), you will be able to deploy SharePoint solutions to a remote SharePoint server.

Calling the Client Object Model

To make the authentication concepts clear, we will write a sample application that calls the client object model using both sets of samples for performing authentication. The sample can retrieve the title of the website and all the lists in the site, and display them on the screen.

Microsoft Authentication Sample

The Microsoft authentication sample can be compiled and referenced in your projects. The only issue with the Microsoft sample is that it does display its own form so you can run into issues trying to use the sample in Windows Forms applications. The following sample references the Microsoft sample and displays the name of the site and all the lists using the client object model:

```
using System;
using System.Collections.Generic;
using System.Linq;
using System.Text;
using Microsoft.SharePoint.Client;
using MSDN.Samples.ClaimsAuth;

namespace SharePoint_Online_MSFT_Authentication
{
```

```
class Program
{
    [STAThread]
    static void Main(string[] args)
    {

        if (args.Length < 1) { Console.WriteLine
    ("Please enter a URL for SharePoint Online"); return; }

        string targetSite = args[0];
        using (ClientContext ctx = ClaimClientContext.GetAuthenticatedContext
          (targetSite))
        {
            if (ctx != null)
            {
                ctx.Load(ctx.Web);
                ctx.ExecuteQuery();

                Console.WriteLine ("Your site name is:
                    " + ctx.Web.Title.ToString());

                Console.WriteLine("Your lists are: ");
                ListCollection listCollection = ctx.Web.Lists;
                ctx.Load(
                    listCollection,
                    lists => lists
                        .Include(
                            list => list.Title,
                            list => list.Hidden)
                        .Where(list => !list.Hidden)
                    );
                ctx.ExecuteQuery();
                foreach (var list in listCollection)
                    Console.WriteLine(list.Title);




            }
        }
        Console.ReadLine();
    }
}
}
```

Wictor Authentication Sample

Rather than using a web browser control to capture the username and password, Wictor's sample takes the username and password as inputs and then uses the cookies to authenticate against the service. The following sample uses the same client object model code but with a different authentication code:

```
using System;
using System.Collections.Generic;
using System.Linq;
```

```
using System.Text;
using Microsoft.SharePoint.Client;

namespace Wictor.Office365.ClaimsDemo {
    class Program {
        static void Main(string[] args) {
            if (args.Count() != 3) {
                Console.WriteLine("Syntax: Wictor.Office365.ClaimsDemo.exe
                                  url username password");
            }
            MsOnlineClaimsHelper claimsHelper = new MsOnlineClaimsHelper
                      (args[0], args[1], args[2]);
            using (ClientContext context = new ClientContext(args[0])) {
                context.ExecutingWebRequest +=
                    claimsHelper.clientContext_ExecutingWebRequest;

                context.Load(context.Web);

                context.ExecuteQuery();

                Console.WriteLine("Name of the web is: " + context.Web.Title);

                Console.WriteLine("Your lists are: ");
                ListCollection listCollection = context.Web.Lists;
                context.Load(
                    listCollection,
                    lists => lists
                        .Include(
                            list => list.Title,
                            list => list.Hidden)
                        .Where(list => !list.Hidden)
                );
                context.ExecuteQuery();
                foreach (var list in listCollection)
                    Console.WriteLine(list.Title);



            }
        }
    }
}
```

LIST, VIEW, AND EVENT ENHANCEMENTS

SharePoint 2010 offers a number of new list, view, and event enhancements that translates into developer enhancements for SharePoint Online. For example, there is support for referential integrity and formula validation in lists. In addition, all views of lists are now based on the XsltListViewWebPart, which makes customization easier. Finally, you can take advantage of new events with SharePoint—for example, when new sites and lists are added. Now dive into these new enhancements.

List Enhancements

Lists are the backbone of SharePoint. They're where you create your data models and your data instances. They're what your users understand are their documents or tasks. Without lists, your SharePoint site would cease to function because SharePoint uses lists for its own functionality and capability to run. With 2010, you can take advantage of new list enhancements and even new tools to work with your custom lists.

SharePoint Designer and Visual Studio Support

Before diving into the new enhancements in lists, you need to first look at the tools you can use to create your lists. The tools of choice are SharePoint Designer (SPD) and Visual Studio (VS). Both are good options, depending on what you want to do. If you want barebones, down to the metal, XML-style creation of lists, Visual Studio is your best bet. If you would rather work with a GUI, SPD provides a nice interface to work with your lists, whether it is creating columns or views, or customizing your list settings. Of course, you can use the built-in list settings in SharePoint to work with your lists, but SPD is a better choice if you are interested in a GUI editor.

SPD makes it easy to work with your lists, whether it's creating new lists or modifying existing ones. SPD can make working with your columns, views, forms, content types, workflows, and even custom actions for your list easier. If you need to rapidly create a list or list definition, SPD is going to be the fastest and easiest way to work with your SharePoint lists. You must give up some control because SPD does not enable you to get down to the same level of customization that Visual Studio does, but you trade customizability for speed when you work with SPD. Figure 5-5 shows the List Settings user interface for SPD.

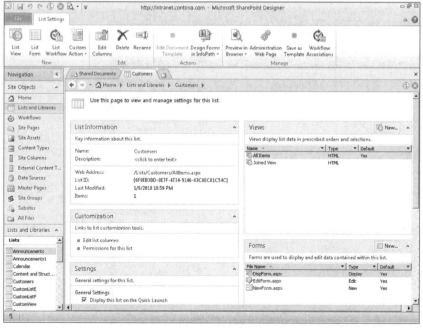

FIGURE 5-5

Also with SharePoint Designer, you can edit your list columns and permissions using a graphical interface. Figure 5-6 shows editing SharePoint columns using SharePoint Designer.

With Visual Studio, you can create list definitions and list instances. List definitions are a built-in project type for Visual Studio. Figure 5-7 shows the List definition project in Visual Studio.

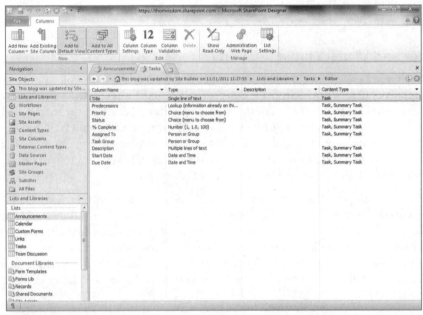

FIGURE 5-6

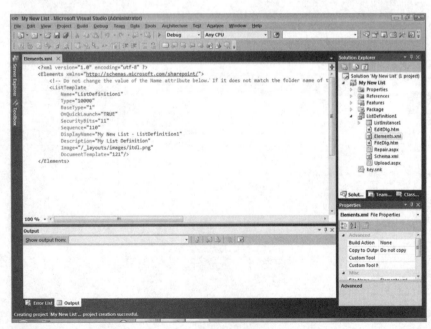

FIGURE 5-7

Don't expect nice designers when you create a list definition in Visual Studio 2010, but Visual Studio vNext may have them. Instead, with Visual Studio 2010, get ready to work with some XML. The nice thing about the list definition project in Visual Studio is that it enables you to create a list instance at the same time. Plus, your application is deployed as a feature, so you can reuse the list definition and instance in many sites. If you need ultimate flexibility, VS is your tool of choice for creating list definitions and customizing lists.

List Relationships with Cascade or Block

One common complaint about SharePoint is that it doesn't behave like a relational database. For example, if you have a lookup between two lists and you want to have some referential integrity, SharePoint previously would not block or cascade your deletes between your lists. With 2010, SharePoint can now block or cascade your deletes between lists automatically. Now, don't think SharePoint is going to become your replacement for SQL Server with this functionality. It is implemented more to make simple relationships work, and if you have a complex data model, you want to use SQL Server and surface its data through SharePoint using BCS and external lists.

The way that list relationships work is through the creation of a lookup between your lists. One new thing about lookups is that you can retrieve more than just the identifier, including additional properties from the list such as built-in or custom fields. On the list where you create your lookup, you can enforce the relationship behavior to either restrict deleting parent list items (if items exist in the list) related to the parent item, or cascade the delete from the parent list to the child list. Figure 5-8 shows the user interface for setting the properties of the lookup column to enforce relationship behaviors.

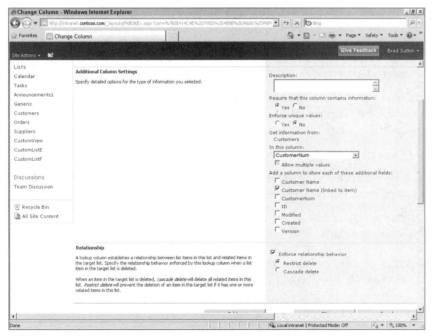

FIGURE 5-8

If you restrict the delete, SharePoint throws an error telling the user that an item is in the related list that exists and cancels deleting the error, as shown in Figure 5-9.

FIGURE 5-9

If you cascade the delete, SharePoint performs a transacted delete of the related items in the related list.

Through the user interface you cannot create cross-web lookups, but through the object model and by using site columns, you can. Cross-web lookups don't support the referential integrity features such as cascading deletes. Also, referential integrity won't be enforced for a lookup that has multiple values.

When working with the object model, you want to use the RelationshipDeleteBehavior property on your SPFieldLookup object. This property takes a value from the SPRelationshipDeleteBehavior enumerator of which the possible values are None, Cascade, or Restrict.

Two Properties affect relationships when you use them with the SPWebApplication class:

➤ CascadeDeleteMaximumItemLimit: This enables you to specify as an integer the maximum number of cascaded items that SharePoint deletes. By default, this value is 1,000 items.

➤ CascadeDeleteTimeoutMultiplier: This enables you to specify as an integer the timeout, which is 120 seconds by default.

To find lookup fields, you can use the GetRelatedFields method of your list, which returns an SPRelatedFieldCollection collection. From this collection, you can iterate through each related field. From there, you can retrieve properties, such as the `LookupList` that the field is related to, the `ListID`, the `FieldID`, or the relationship behavior when something is deleted from the list.

```
using (SPSite site = new SPSite("http://intranet.contoso.com"))
{

    SPList list = site.AllWebs[""].Lists["Orders"];
    SPRelatedFieldCollection relatedFields = list.GetRelatedFields();
    foreach (SPRelatedField relatedField in relatedFields)
    {
        //Lookup the list for each

        SPList relatedList = relatedField.LookupList;
        MessageBox.Show(relatedField.ListId + " " +
          relatedField.FieldId);
        //MessageBox.Show("List Name: " +
          relatedList.Title + " Relationship Behavior: " +
          relatedField.RelationshipDeleteBehavior.ToString());


    }
}
```

Validation with Excel-Like Formulas

Another new list feature gives you the capability to do list validation using formulas. This is more of an end-user or power-user feature, but for simple validation scenarios, developers find this feature easy to use because it is quicker to write formulas than to write code. You can write validation at either the list level or the column level, depending on your needs. SharePoint also supports this approach for site columns that you add to your content types. Figure 5-10 shows setting the formula, and Figure 5-11 shows the custom error message that appears when the formula does not validate.

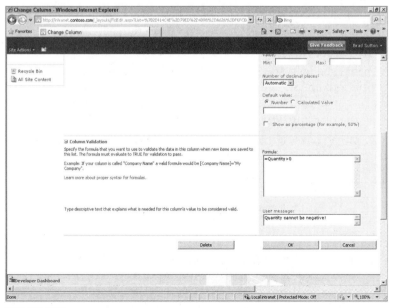

FIGURE 5-10

One of the easiest ways to understand which formulas you can enter into the validation rules is to connect Microsoft Access to your SharePoint list and use the formula editor in Access. SharePoint supports the same formula functions as Access, so you can use string manipulation, logic, financial, conversion, and date/time functionality. In the API, you can use the `SPList.ValidationFormula` and `SPField.ValidationFormula` properties to get and set your formulas.

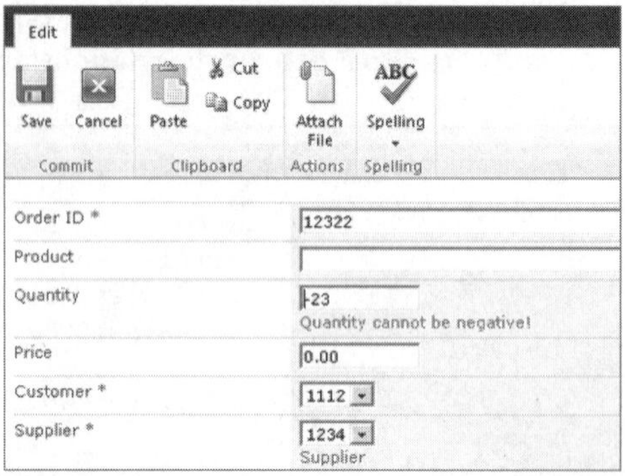

FIGURE 5-11

Ensuring Uniqueness

Another new feature of lists is the capability to ensure uniqueness for the values in your columns. Previously, SharePoint didn't require unique values so that multiple items could have the same value for a field. With uniqueness, SharePoint can use the field as an index to make lookups faster because the field is guaranteed to have a unique value.

List Joins

Just like a database, SharePoint supports list joins. Again, SharePoint won't provide as much functionality as a relational database because its data model sits above the bare-metal database, but compared to 2007 the join functionality is a welcome addition. SharePoint can perform left and inner joins but not right joins. An inner join is where you combine the values from the data sources based on the join predicate, such as "show me all employees who are in a particular department based on their department ID," which joins an employee list and a department list, both of which have department IDs in them. A left join or left outer join just means that anything that appears in the leftmost list, even if it does not have matching entries in the other list, is returned in the result set.

The following code performs a join across two lists on a lookup field. You need to set the `Joins` property on your `SPQuery` object with the join you want to perform. In the code, you join on the Customers list, where the customer is the same as the Customer in the Orders list.

Beyond setting the `Joins` property, you must specify a value for the `ProjectedFields` property. This property gets fields from the lookup list. You can alias the field by using the `Name` attribute and tell SharePoint the field name by using the `ShowField` attribute. When you get your results, you must use the `SPFieldLookupValue` object to display the values for your projected fields.

```
SPList OrderList = web.Lists["Orders"];
        SPQuery CustomerQuery = new SPQuery();
        CustomerQuery.Joins =
            "<Join Type='INNER' ListAlias='Customers'>" +
                "<Eq>" +
                    "<FieldRef Name='Customer' RefType='Id' />" +
                    "<FieldRef List='Customers' Name='ID' />" +
                "</Eq>" +
            "</Join>";
        StringBuilder ProjectedFields = new StringBuilder();
        ProjectedFields.Append("<Field Name='CustomerTitle'
          Type='Lookup' List='Customers' ShowField='Title' />");
```

```
ProjectedFields.Append("<Field Name='CustomerAddress'
  Type='Lookup' List='Customers' ShowField='CustomerNum' />");
CustomerQuery.ProjectedFields = ProjectedFields.ToString();
SPListItemCollection Results = OrderList.GetItems(CustomerQuery);
foreach (SPListItem Result in Results)
    {
    SPFieldLookupValue CustomerTitle = new
      SPFieldLookupValue(Result["CustomerTitle"].ToString());
    SPFieldLookupValue CustomerAddress = new
      SPFieldLookupValue(Result["CustomerAddress"].ToString());

    MessageBox.Show(Result.Title + " " + CustomerTitle.LookupValue + "
      " + CustomerAddress.LookupValue);

    }
```

Customize Default Forms Using Web Parts or InfoPath

One of the new features of lists is that you can customize the default forms for your list items. SharePoint 2010 moved to using web part pages for the default forms, so your customization can be as easy as adding new web parts to the existing default forms, or you can even replace the default forms with your own custom InfoPath forms. With SharePoint 2010, you can modify the New, Display, and Edit forms.

When you use the Ribbon option to edit the form in InfoPath, InfoPath automatically launches. Connect to your list and display your form, as shown in Figure 5-12.

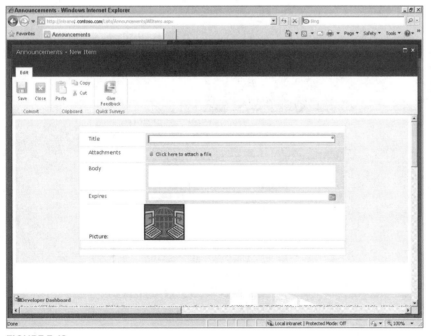

FIGURE 5-12

View Enhancements

The biggest change with views in 2010 is the technology used to display them. 2010 uses the SharePoint Designer `XsltListViewWebPart` as the default web part for viewing lists. This is much better than 2007 for a number of reasons:

➤ XSLT views enables you to replace your use of CAML to create views. You can also use standards-based XSLT to define your view.

➤ With the addition of the new XSLT view, performance is better than 2007.

➤ Editing with SPD is easier because the XSLT view technology is originally an SPD technology so SPD has extensive capabilities to edit it.

➤ The same view technology is used for all SharePoint lists, including standard SharePoint lists and external lists.

The easiest way to understand, prototype, and get sample code is to use SPD to design your views and then view the code that SPD creates to work with your XSLT views. For example, you may want to create a view that makes any numbers that meet or exceed a limit turn red, yellow, or green and implements a custom mouseover event. With SPD, this is as easy as using the conditional formatting functionality and the IntelliSense built-in to modify the view. Figure 5-13 shows the editing of the view in SPD.

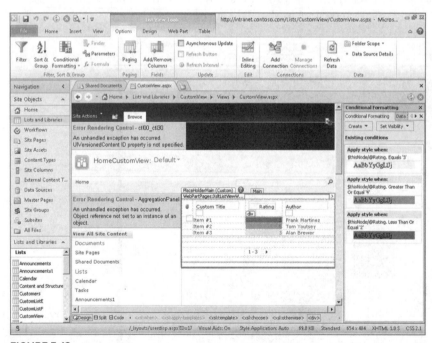

FIGURE 5-13

The following code shows the conditional formatting XSLT that SPD generates for you:

```
<div align="right" onmouseover="javascript:alert('You moused over!');">
        <xsl:attribute name="style">
                <xsl:if test="$thisNode/@Rating. = 3"
                        xmlns:ddwrt="http://schemas.microsoft.com
/WebParts/v2/DataView/runtime" ddwrt:cf_explicit="1">background-color:
#FFFF00;</xsl:if>
                        <xsl:if test="$thisNode/@Rating. &gt;= 4"
        xmlsn:ddwrt="http://schemas.microsoft.
        com/WebParts/v2/DataView/runtime" ddwrt:cf_explicit="1">
        background-color:#71B84F;</xsl:if>
                        <xsl:if test="$thisNode/@Rating. &lt;= 2"
                        ddwrt:cf_explicit="1" xmlns:ddwrt="
        http://schemas.microsoft.com/WebParts/v2/DataView/runtime">
                background-color:#FF0000;</xsl:if>

                </xsl:attribute>
```

To work with views programmatically, use the SPView object and SPViewCollection. You can add new views, modify existing views, or delete views. The following are a few properties in which you should be interested:

➤ **DefaultView** off the **SPList** object: This property returns an SPView object, which is the default view for your list.

➤ **RenderAsHTML:** This method returns the HTML that your view renders.

➤ **PropertiesXml, Query, SchemaXml,** and **Xsl:** These return the properties, query, schema, and XSL used in your list, respectively.

Events Enhancements

With 2010, you can take advantage of six new events, including WebAdding, WebProvisioned, ListAdding, ListAdded, ListDeleting, and ListDeleted. This is in addition to the events that were introduced in SharePoint 2007, such as ItemAdding, ItemUpdating, and ItemUpdated. There are also other enhancements beyond new events, including new registration scopes to support the new events, new tools support in Visual Studio, support for post-synchronous events, and custom error pages and redirection.

New Events

As part of SharePoint 2010, you can take advantage of ten new events. These events enable you to capture creation and provisioning of new webs, and the creation and deletion of lists. Table 5-3 goes through each of the events and what you can use them for.

TABLE 5-3: New 2010 Events

NAME	DESCRIPTION
WebAdding	A synchronous event that happens before the web is added. Some URL properties may not exist yet for the new site because the new site does not exist yet.
WebProvisioned	A synchronous or asynchronous after-event that occurs after the web is created. You make the event synchronous or asynchronous by using the `Synchronization` property and setting it to `Asynchronous` or `Synchronous`. This is located under the `Receiver` node in the `elements.xml` file for your feature.
ListAdding	A synchronous event that happens before a list is created.
ListAdded	A synchronous or asynchronous after-event that happens after a list is created but before it is presented to the user.
ListDeleting	A synchronous event that happens before a list is deleted.
ListDeleted	A synchronous or asynchronous after-event that happens after a list is deleted.
WorkflowStarting	An event that occurs before a workflow starts. All Workflow events get `SPWorkflowEventProperties` object that contains information about the workflow.
WorkflowStarted	An event that occurs after a workflow has started.
WorkflowPostponed	An event that occurs if a workflow is postponed.
WorkflowCompleted	An event that occurs after a workflow is completed.

Using these events is the same as writing event receivers for any other type of events in SharePoint. The nice thing about writing event receivers with SharePoint 2010 is that you have Visual Studio 2010 support for writing and deploying your event receivers. Figure 5-14 shows the new event receiver template in Visual Studio, where you can select the type of event receiver you want to create and the events you want to listen for in your receiver. After you finish the wizard inside of Visual Studio, you can modify your feature definition or your code using the standard Visual Studio SharePoint tools. Plus, with on-click deployment and debugging, it's a lot easier to get your receiver deployed and start debugging it.

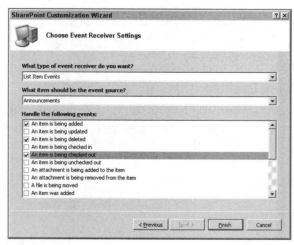

FIGURE 5-14

The code that follows shows you how to use the new web events in SharePoint. The code writes the properties for the event to an event log list. The sample applications with this book include the same sample for the new list events, but for brevity only the web event sample code is shown. If you wanted to, you could cancel the `before-events`, such as `WebAdding`, `ListDeleting`, or `ListAdding`, by setting the `Cancel` property to `false`. These events fire even in the Recycle Bin, so if you restore a list or delete a list, you get an event for those actions.

```csharp
namespace WebEventReceiver.EventReceiver1
{
    /// <summary>
    /// Web Events
    /// </summary>
    public class EventReceiver1 : SPWebEventReceiver
    {
        /// <summary>
        /// A site is being provisioned.
        /// </summary>
        public override void WebAdding(SPWebEventProperties properties)
        {
            LogWebEventProperties(properties);

            base.WebAdding(properties);
        }

        /// <summary>
        /// A site was provisioned.
        /// </summary>
        public override void WebProvisioned(SPWebEventProperties properties)
        {
            LogWebEventProperties(properties);
            base.WebProvisioned(properties);
        }


        private void LogWebEventProperties(SPWebEventProperties properties)
        {

            StringBuilder sb = new StringBuilder();

            try
            {
                sb.AppendFormat("{0} at {1}\n\n", properties.EventType,
                  DateTime.Now);
                sb.AppendFormat("Cancel: {0}\n", properties.Cancel);
                sb.AppendFormat("ErrorMessage: {0}\n", properties.ErrorMessage);
                sb.AppendFormat("EventType: {0}\n", properties.EventType);
                sb.AppendFormat("FullUrl: {0}\n", properties.FullUrl);
                sb.AppendFormat("NewServerRelativeUrl: {0}\n",
                  properties.NewServerRelativeUrl);
                sb.AppendFormat("ParentWebId: {0}\n", properties.ParentWebId);
                sb.AppendFormat("ReceiverData: {0}\n", properties.ReceiverData);
                sb.AppendFormat("RedirectUrl: {0}\n", properties.RedirectUrl);
                sb.AppendFormat("ServerRelativeUrl: {0}\n",
                  properties.ServerRelativeUrl);
```

```
            sb.AppendFormat("SiteId: {0}\n", properties.SiteId);
            sb.AppendFormat("Status: {0}\n", properties.Status);
            sb.AppendFormat("UserDisplayName: {0}\n",
               properties.UserDisplayName);
            sb.AppendFormat("UserLoginName: {0}\n", properties.UserLoginName);
            sb.AppendFormat("Web: {0}\n", properties.Web);
            sb.AppendFormat("WebId: {0}\n", properties.WebId);
        }
        catch (Exception e)
        {
            sb.AppendFormat("Exception accessing Web Event Properties: {0}\n",
               e);

        }


    }
  }
}
```

code snippet WebEventReceiver/Receiver1.cs

One quick comment regarding this code is that with the AfterProperties property, which you can use to determine if the item has been modified during an update, you must decode the column name because SharePoint encodes spaces and other special characters in column name, for example a Hello World column having an internal column name of Hello_x0020_World. You need to use the System.XML.XmlConvert.DecodeName to decode and System.XML.XmlConvert.EncodeName to encode these names.

New Event Registration Feature

To support the new events, SharePoint now provides a new mechanism for registering your event receivers, using the <Receivers> XML block. This new feature enables you to register your event receiver at the site collection level by using the new Scope attribute and to set the receiver either to Site or Web, depending on the scope that you want for your event receiver. If you set it to Web, your event receiver works across all sites in your site collection, as long as your feature is registered across all these sites as well. You can tell SharePoint to have the receiver work on only the root site by using the RootWebOnly attribute on the <Receivers> node. The last new enhancement is the ListUrl attribute, which enables you to scope your receiver to a particular list by passing in the relative URL.

Post-Synchronous Events

With SharePoint 2007, all your after-events were asynchronous, so if you wanted to perform some operations after the target—such as an item—was created but before it was presented to the user, you couldn't. Your event receiver would fire asynchronously, so the user might already see the target, and then if you modified properties or added values, the user experience might not be ideal. With SharePoint 2010, there is support for synchronous after-events, such as listadded, itemadded, or webprovisioned. To make the events synchronous, you need to set the Synchronization property either through the SPEventReceiverDefinition object model if you are registering your events programmatically or by creating a node in your <Receiver> XML that sets the value to synchronous or asynchronous. That's it if you run SharePoint on-premises. Unfortunately, post-synchronous events are not supported by SharePoint Online and Sandboxed Solutions.

Custom Error Pages

With SharePoint 2007, you could only cancel events and return an error message to the user, but that provided limited interactivity and not much help to the user beyond what your error message said. With 2010 events, you can cancel the event on your synchronous events and redirect the user to a custom error page that you create. This enables you to have more control over what users see, and you can try to help them figure out why their action is failing. The custom error pages and redirection work only for presynchronous events, so you cannot do this for post-synchronous events such as `ListAdded`. Plus, this works only with browser clients. Office clients show an error message if you cancel the event.

The way to implement custom error pages is to set the `Status` property on your property bag for your event receiver to `SPEventReceiverStatus.CancelWithRedirectUrl`, set the `RedirectUrl` property to a relative URL for your error page, and set the `Cancel` property to `true`, as shown in the following code:

```
properties.Cancel = true;
properties.Status = SPEventReceiverStatus.CancelWithRedirectUrl;
properties.RedirectUrl = "/_layouts/mycustomerror.aspx";
```

The Ribbon

In SharePoint, one of the major changes to which you must acclimate yourself is the new Ribbon user interface. The Ribbon provides a contextual tab model and a fixed location at the top of the page so that it never scrolls out of view. In terms of controls, if you have worked with the Office client Ribbon, the SharePoint Ribbon has near parity with the client. The areas missing between the client and the server are controls that provide more complex functionality. The best example of a control that is on the client but not on the server is the in-Ribbon gallery control. This gallery is used, for example, when you click Styles button on the Home tab in Word and you can see all the styles in the document, or in Excel, when you click the Cell Styles button in the Home tab right from the gallery control.

The Ribbon does support the majority of controls that you need, and the main unit of organization for these controls is tabs. You can build custom tabs that contain your custom controls. Even though the server can support up to 100 tabs, it is recommended that you try to limit the tabs to 4–7 to avoid confusing your users. Table 5-4 lists the different controls supported by SharePoint with a description of each.

TABLE 5-4: SharePoint Ribbon Controls

NAME	DESCRIPTION
Button	A simple button that a user can click.
Checkbox	A check box that can either have a label or not.
ColorPicker	A grid of colors/styles that the user can use to choose a color.

continues

TABLE 5-4 *(continued)*

NAME	DESCRIPTION
ComboBox	A menu of selections that the user can type or select.
DropDown	A menu of selections that the user can click to select.
FlyoutAnchor	An anchor button that includes a button that triggers a drop-down menu.
InsertTable	A 10 x 10 grid of boxes where a user can specify dimensions for a table.
Label	A line of text.
Menu	A container for showing pop-ups. You can place it inside other controls that show menus, such as the FlyoutAnchor.
MenuSection	A section of a menu. You can give the menu a title and controls.
MRUSplitButton	A split button control that remembers the last item that a user most recently used out of its submenu with that item bubbling up into the "button" part.
Spinner	Enables the user to enter values and "spin" through them using the up and down arrows.
SplitButton	A control with a button and a menu.
Textbox	A box where a user can enter text.
ToggleButton	A button with an on/off state.

If you look at the architecture for the Ribbon in SharePoint, you find that SharePoint uses Ajax, on-demand JavaScript, caching, and CSS layout to implement the Ribbon. In addition, the Ribbon uses no tables, so it is all constructed from CSS styling and hover effects that make the Ribbon function. For this reason, you should investigate the CSS classes that the Ribbon uses, especially corev4.css. Look through the styles beginning with ms-cui, which is the namespace for the Ribbon in the CSS file.

Ribbon Extensibility

The Ribbon is completely extensible in that you can add new tabs or controls, or you can remove the OOB controls on existing tabs. You can entirely replace the Ribbon just by using your own custom Master Page. The Ribbon does support backward compatibility, so any custom actions you created for 2007 toolbars appear in a custom commands tab in the Ribbon.

To understand how to customize the Ribbon, look through the different actions you normally want to perform and the way to achieve those actions. Before diving in, though, you need to get a little bit of grounding in how the architecture of the Ribbon works.

The architecture of the Ribbon enables you to perform your customizations by creating XML definition files. At run time, the Ribbon merges your XML definitions with its own to add your custom Ribbon elements and code to handle interactions. For more complex customizations, such as writing more complex code, consider using a JavaScript page component. The next section looks at both options.

If you want to understand how SharePoint implements its Ribbon XML elements, go to %Program Files%\Common Files\Microsoft Shared\Web Server Extensions\14\TEMPLATE\GLOBAL\XML on your local SharePoint Server and find the file `cmdui.xml`. In that file, you see the SharePoint default Ribbon implementation, and it is a good template to look at as you implement your own Ribbon controls because it can help you to understand how certain controls work inside the SharePoint environment.

If all the different types, elements, and attributes are confusing, take a look at the XSD for the Ribbon by browsing to `%Program Files%\Common Files\Microsoft Shared\Web Server Extensions\14\TEMPLATE\XML` and look at `cui.xsd` and `wss.xsd`. These XSD files can help you understand what SharePoint expects for structure and content to make your custom user interface.

XML-Only Operations

When you write your custom XML to define your Ribbon, SharePoint combines your XML changes with its own definitions in `cmdui.xml`, and the merged version displays the new Ribbon interface. Even though you use XML, you want to deploy your custom Ribbon XML with a SharePoint feature. The easiest way to create a feature is using Visual Studio 2010. To do so, follow these steps:

1. Create an empty SharePoint project and customize the feature name and deployment path. Ribbon extensions can be Sandboxed Solutions, which you learn about later in this chapter, so they can run in a restricted environment like SharePoint Online.

2. Create a new feature. You do this by adding a new file to your project and by creating an empty elements file. This is where you place the XML for your new Ribbon interface. To understand the XML, break it down piece by piece.

The snippet that follows shows some XML from a custom Ribbon:

Available for download on Wrox.com

```xml
<?xml version="1.0" encoding="utf-8"?>

<Elements xmlns="http://schemas.microsoft.com/sharepoint/">

  <CustomAction

    Id="CustomRibbonTab"

    Location="CommandUI.Ribbon.ListView"

    RegistrationId="101"

    RegistrationType="List"

    Title="My Custom UI"

    Sequence="5"

  >


  </CustomAction>

</Elements>
```

code snippet Elements.xml

First, all XML for the Ribbon will be wrapped in a `CustomAction` node. This tells SharePoint that you want to perform customization of the user interface. For the node, you can set attributes to give the specifics for your customization. One key node is the `Location` attribute, which tells SharePoint where your customization should appear, such as on a list view, a form, or everywhere. The pattern match for the `Location` attribute is `Ribbon.[Tab].[Group].Controls._children`. Table 5-5 outlines the options for the `Location` attribute.

TABLE 5-5: Location Attribute Settings

NAME	DESCRIPTION
`CommandUI.Ribbon`	Customization appears everywhere.
`CommandUI.Ribbon.ListView`	Customization appears when `ListView` is available.
`CommandUI.Ribbon.EditForm`	Customization appears on the edit form.
`CommandUI.Ribbon.NewForm`	Customization appears on the new form.
`CommandUI.Ribbon.DisplayForm`	Customization appears on the display form.

One other piece to notice in the XML is the `RegistrationID`. When combined, the registration ID and the registration type define the set of content you want your custom UI to appear for. The registration type can be a list, content type, file type, or a `progID`. The registration ID is mostly used with the content type registration type, and it's where you specify the name of your content type. This enables you to customize even further when your custom UI appears, depending on what displays in SharePoint.

The `Sequence` attribute, which is optional, enables extensions to be placed in a particular order within a set of subnodes of a node. The built-in tab controls use a sequence of 100, so you want to avoid using any multiples of 100 for your sequence in tabs. Groups use a sequence in multiples of 10, so you should avoid multiples of 10. For example, if you had a Ribbon tab with the following groups—Clipboard, Font, Paragraph—you could set their sequence attributes to 10, 20, and 30, respectively. Then, you could insert a new group between the Clipboard and the Font groups via the feature framework by setting its sequence attribute to 15. A node without a `Sequence` attribute is sorted last.

Because the current XML does nothing (you haven't added any new commands to the user interface), you can expand your XML. To add commands, you create a `CommandUIExtension` element. This `CommandUIExtension` is a wrapper for a `CommandUIDefinitions` element, which is a container for a `CommandUIDefinition`.

The `CommandUIDefinition` element has an attribute that enables you to set the location for your UI. In the example, you add a new button to the new set of controls in a document library. You can see `_children` as part of the location that tells SharePoint not to replace a control, but instead add this as a child control on that user interface element.

The CommandUIDefinition element is where you create your user interface elements, whether they are tabs, groups, or individual controls. In this simple example, you create a button that has the label Click me! which has two images. The image that is used depends on whether the button is rendered in 16 × 16 or 32 × 32 size (because the Ribbon has the ability to scale based on the screen resolution), and SharePoint calls JavaScript code to perform the action when the button is pressed. The attributes are self-explanatory, except for one — TemplateAlias. TemplateAlias controls whether your control is displayed in 16 × 16 or 32 × 32. If you set it to o1, you get a 32 × 32 icon, and o2 makes it 16 × 16. You can define your own template, but most times you use the built-in values of o1 or o2.

So, how do you call code from your Ribbon code? You wrap your code in a CommandUIHandler, where you can put in the CommandAction attribute, which is inline JavaScript that handles the action for your button. If you do not want to place your JavaScript inline, you can use the ScriptSrc attribute and pass a URL to your JavaScript file. Figure 5-15 shows the new custom button on the top-left of the Documents Ribbon.

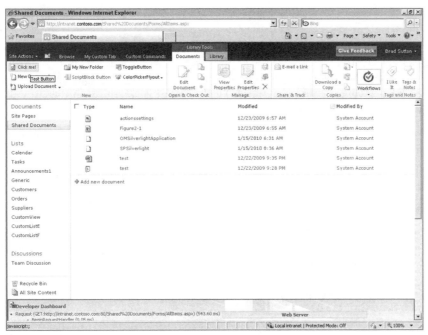

FIGURE 5-15

```
<CommandUIExtension>
    <CommandUIDefinitions>
        <CommandUIDefinition Location="Ribbon.Documents.New.Controls._children">
            <Button
                Id="Ribbon.Documents.New.RibbonTest"
                Alt="Test Button"
                Sequence="5"
```

```
            Command="Test_Button"
            LabelText="Click me!"
            Image32by32="/_layouts/images/ribbon_blog_32.png"
            Image16by16="/_layouts/images/ribbon_blog_16.png"
            TemplateAlias="o1" />
    </CommandUIDefinition>
  </CommandUIDefinitions>

  <CommandUIHandlers>
    <CommandUIHandler
      Command="Test_Button"
      CommandAction="javascript:alert('I am a test!');" />
  </CommandUIHandlers>

</CommandUIExtension>
```

code snippet Elements.xml

Replacing Existing Controls

At times you may want to replace existing, built-in controls from your SharePoint deployment and put your own controls in place. You can replace the entire Ribbon if you want. The way to replace an existing control is to insert your own custom control that overwrites the ID of the control you want to replace and also has a lower sequence number. The key point is you must get the Location attribute set to the same ID as the control ID you want to replace.

The following code replaces the new folder button for a document library. There are a couple of things to highlight in this code:

➤ Notice the **Location** attribute in the **CommandUIDefinition** element. It maps exactly to an ID in the cmdUI.XML file. SharePoint parses both files, and if it finds the same ID, it places the one with the lower sequence into the final XML that is parsed and used to create the Ribbon layout.

➤ Notice the use of the **$Resources** for globalization and pulling from a compressed image. The format map on your server contains lots of icons, and the XML code contains the coordinates to pull the new folder icon from the larger image.

Available for download on Wrox.com

```
<CustomAction Id="Ribbon.Documents.New.NewFolder.ReplaceButton"
    Location="CommandUI.Ribbon"
    RegistrationId="101"
    RegistrationType="List"
    Title="Replace Ribbon Button"
>
  <CommandUIExtension>
    <CommandUIDefinitions>
      <CommandUIDefinition
        Location="Ribbon.Documents.New.NewFolder">
        <Button Id="Ribbon.Documents.New.NewFolder.ReplacementButton"
          Command="MyNewButtonCommand"
          Image16by16="/_layouts/$Resources:core,Language;/images/
          formatmap16x16.png?vk=4536"
          Image16by16Top="-240" Image16by16Left="-80"
          Image32by32="/_layouts/$Resources:core,Language;/images/
```

```
               formatmap32x32.png?vk=4536"
               Image32by32Top="-352" Image32by32Left="-448"
               ToolTipTitle="Create a New Folder"
               ToolTipDescription="Replaced by XML Custom Action"
               LabelText="My New Folder"
               TemplateAlias="o1" />
          </CommandUIDefinition>
        </CommandUIDefinitions>
        <CommandUIHandlers>
          <CommandUIHandler
            Command="MyNewButtonCommand"
            CommandAction="javascript:alert('New Folder Replaced.');" />
        </CommandUIHandlers>
      </CommandUIExtension>
    </CustomAction>
```

code snippet Elements.xml

Figure 5-16 shows the replaced button. Even though the icon image is the same, the action performed when the user clicks the icon is the custom code.

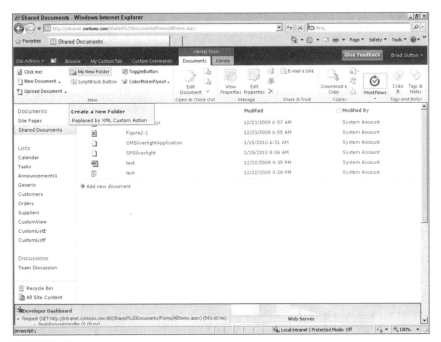

FIGURE 5-16

Using URL Actions

You may be wondering how you use just URLs with token replacements, rather than having to write JavaScript as the payload for your controls. To do this, you use the URLAction node in your CustomAction node. Your URL actions can be simple URLs, or you can use token replacement, such as ListID or ItemID. You can also place inline JavaScript if you want. When you use URL actions, you can make a simple CustomAction node to handle your changes, as shown in the following listing, which adds a new toolbar item to the new announcements form:

```
<CustomAction
        Id="SimpleAction"
        RegistrationType="List"
        RegistrationId="104"
        ImageUrl="/_layouts/images/saveas32.png"
        Location="NewFormToolbar"
        Sequence="10"
        Title="Custom Button"
        Description="This is an announcement button."
                    >
    <UrlAction Url="javascript:alert('Itemid={ItemId} and Listid={ListId}');"/>

</CustomAction>
```

code snippet Elements.xml

Why Doesn't Your Button Show Up?

Troubleshooting your custom Ribbon user interface is not as easy as you would think. If you get something wrong, your customizations just do not appear. Even though this can be frustrating, there are a couple of places to start looking to troubleshoot your issues:

➤ **Fire up your JavaScript debugger and set a breakpoint.** Because the Ribbon is implemented in JavaScript, you can set breakpoints in the code in SP.Ribbon.debug.js. Also, make sure to look at the XML in cmdui.xml to see if there is a pattern your code resembles so you can model your code on that pattern.

➤ **Check that the sequence is set correctly and does not collide with other controls.** SharePoint uses sequences in multiples of 10 or 100, so make sure that you are not using those multiples.

➤ **Check that the name of your function is the same as your command attribute on your control definition and your CommandUIHandler.** If you get the name wrong, even with the same spelling but different cases, your commands don't fire.

➤ **Check the registration for your CustomAction.** Did you register your UI on a document library? When you test your code, are you in a document library? Or did you register on an edit form for announcements?

➤ **Check the toolbar type property.** This ties in with the previous tip and applies when you are wondering why your user interface does not appear if you select your list instance as a web part in another page. For example, suppose that you are on your home page and you added your Shared Documents library as a web part on that page. When you select the document library as the web part, your button does not appear on the menu. The culprit behind this is the toolbar type property for the web part under web part properties. By default, this property is set to summary toolbar, and you want it to be set to full toolbar because the summary toolbar doesn't load any of the customizations for the toolbar.

Rights and Site Administrators

As part of the definition of your CustomAction, you can also specify the rights required to view your custom interface. You can specify a Rights attribute, which takes a permissions mask that SharePoint will logically AND together, so the user must have all the permissions to view the new user interface. Permissions can be any from SPBasePermissions, such as ViewListItems or ManageLists.

Beyond permissions, you can also specify whether a person must be a site administrator to view the new user interface. To do this, create a Boolean RequireSiteAdministrator attribute, and set it to true to require the user to be a site administrator. This is useful for an administration-style UI that you do not want every user to see.

Hiding Existing Controls

Sometimes you want to hide controls rather than replace them. For example, the control may not make sense in the context of your application. To hide UI controls, use the HideCustomAction element and set the attributes to the nodes you want to hide, as shown in the following code:

```
<HideCustomAction
    Id="HideNewMenu"
    Location="Microsoft.SharePoint.StandardMenu"
    GroupId="NewMenu"
    HideActionId="NewMenu">
</HideCustomAction>
```

Writing Code to Control Menu Commands

If you prefer to write code instead of XML, you can use the SharePoint object model to make changes to menu items. This hasn't changed from the EditControlBlock (ECB) technologies in 2007 and is shown here for completeness:

```
using (SPSite site = new SPSite("http://intranet.contoso.com"))
        {
        using (SPWeb web = site.RootWeb)
            {
            SPUserCustomAction action = web.UserCustomActions.Add();
            action.Location = "EditControlBlock";
            action.RegistrationType =
            SPUserCustomActionRegistrationType.FileType;
            action.RegistrationId = "docx";
            action.Title = "Custom Edit Command For Documents";
            action.Description = "Custom Edit Command for Documents";
            action.Url = "{ListUrlDir}/forms/editform.aspx?Source={Source}";
            action.Update();
            web.Update();
            site.Close();
            }
        }
```

Creating New Tabs and Groups

Beyond just creating buttons, you may want to add new tabs and groups. To do this, you just need to create Tab and Group elements in your code. The process is close to the same as adding a button with some minor tweaks. Figure 5-17 shows a custom tab and group with three controls: two buttons and a combo box.

FIGURE 5-17

The following code shows the beginning of the new tab and group. As you can see, the XML looks similar to the earlier XML when you create a button. This code also defines a tab:

```
<!~DHCreate new Tab and Group~DH>
  <CustomAction
  Id="MyCustomRibbonTab"
  Location="CommandUI.Ribbon.ListView"
  RegistrationId="101"
  RegistrationType="List">
    <CommandUIExtension>
      <CommandUIDefinitions>
        <CommandUIDefinition
          Location="Ribbon.Tabs._children">
          <Tab
            Id="Ribbon.CustomTabExample"
            Title="My Custom Tab"
            Description="This holds my custom commands!"
            Sequence="501">
            <Scaling
              Id="Ribbon.CustomTabExample.Scaling">
```

```
<MaxSize
  Id="Ribbon.CustomTabExample.MaxSize"
  GroupId="Ribbon.CustomTabExample.CustomGroupExample"
  Size="OneLargeTwoMedium"/>
<Scale
  Id="Ribbon.CustomTabExample.Scaling.CustomTabScaling"
  GroupId="Ribbon.CustomTabExample.CustomGroupExample"
  Size="OneLargeTwoMedium" />
</Scaling>
  . . .
```

Some things to note about this code:

➤ **Tabs support scaling, so if the page is resized, you can control how your buttons look.** Scaling has a MaxSize node that is the maximum size your buttons will be and a Scaling node that's used if the page is resized. You need to know a couple of things about the Scaling node.

  ➤ It has a GroupID attribute, which should point to the group that the scaling affects.

  ➤ It has a Size attribute, which has a descriptor of the style of your group. For example, you can have LargeLarge if you have two buttons and want both to be large buttons, or LargeMedium if you want a large and a medium button.

➤ **After creating the tab, the code then creates the group.** A group can have commands, descriptions, and all the standard attributes that other controls have. A group is a logical container for your controls and physically lays out the controls in your group with your description at the bottom of the group user interface. Your Group node contains the definition of your controls that live within that group.

```
<Groups Id="Ribbon.CustomTabExample.Groups">
        <Group
          Id="Ribbon.CustomTabExample.CustomGroupExample"
          Description="This is a custom group!"
          Title="Custom Group"
          Sequence="52"
          Template="Ribbon.Templates.CustomTemplateExample">
        <Controls>
  . . .
```

After you have your tab and group, you create your controls just as you would if the control were an extension of an existing group.

A combo box has more commands than a button has because users can interact more with a combo box by selecting options from its list. Also, you can populate a combo box either statically, as the code does, by creating menu options in the XML, or by passing a function that SharePoint calls to populate the combo box dynamically. Look at the PopulateDynamically, PopulateOnlyOnce, and PopulateQueryCommand sections of the code because these operate the combo box options.

In addition, you can set attributes, such as AllowFreeForm and InitialItem, to control whether users can type values into the combo box and select the initial item in the combo box.

The code earlier showed you how to create a button, so the following code shows you how to create a combo box as a control in your group:

```
<ComboBox
 Id="Ribbon.CustomTabExample.CustomGroupExample.
 Combobox"  Sequence="18"
 Alt="Ribbon.CustomTabExample.CustomGroupExample.
 Combobox_Alt"
 Command="Ribbon.CustomTabExample.CustomGroupExample.
  Combobox_CMD"
 CommandMenuOpen="Ribbon.CustomTabExample.
  CustomGroupExample.Combobox_Open_CMD"
 CommandMenuClose="Ribbon.CustomTabExample.
  CustomGroupExample.Combobox_MenuClose_CMD"
 CommandPreview="Ribbon.CustomTabExample.
  CustomGroupExample.Combobox_Preview_CMD"
 CommandPreviewRevert="Ribbon.CustomTabExample.
  CustomGroupExample.Combobox_PreviewRevert_CMD"
                            InitialItem="StaticComboButton1"
                            AllowFreeForm="true"
                            PopulateDynamically="false"
                            PopulateOnlyOnce="true"
                            PopulateQueryCommand="Ribbon.CustomTabExample.
                            CustomGroupExample.Combobox_PopQuery_CMD"
                            Width="125px"
                            TemplateAlias="cust3">
                    <Menu Id="Ribbon.CustomTabExample.CustomGroupExample.
                      Combobox.Menu">
                      <MenuSection
                        Id="Ribbon.CustomTabExample.CustomGroupExample.Combobox.
                         Menu.MenuSection"
                        Sequence="10"
                        DisplayMode="Menu32">
                        <Controls Id="Ribbon.CustomTabExample.CustomGroupExample.
                          Combobox.Menu.MenuSection.Controls">
                          <Button
                            Id="Ribbon.CustomTabExample.CustomGroupExample.
                            Combobox.Menu.MenuSection.Button1"
                            Sequence="10"
                            Command="Ribbon.CustomTabExample.CustomGroupExample.
                             Combobox.Menu.MenuSection.Button1_CMD"
                            CommandType="OptionSelection"
                            Image16by16="/_layouts/$Resources:core,Language;
                            /images/formatmap16x16.png?vk=4536"
                            Image16by16Top="-48" Image16by16Left="-112"
                            Image32by32="/_layouts/$Resources:core,Language;
                            /images/formatmap32x32.png?vk=4536"
                            Image32by32Top="-192" Image32by32Left="-32"
                            LabelText="StaticComboButton1"
                            MenuItemId="StaticComboButton1"/>
                          <Button
```

```
                    Id="Ribbon.CustomTabExample.CustomGroupExample.
                    Combobox.Menu.MenuSection.Button2"
                    Sequence="20"
                    Command="Ribbon.CustomTabExample.CustomGroupExample.
                    Combobox.Menu.MenuSection.Button2_CMD"
                    CommandType="OptionSelection"
                    Image16by16="/_layouts/$Resources:core,Language;
                    /images/formatmap16x16.png?vk=4536"
                  Image16by16Top="-32" Image16by16Left="-112"
                    Image32by32="/_layouts/$Resources:core,Language;
                    /images/formatmap32x32.png?vk=4536"
                    Image32by32Top="-384" Image32by32Left="-352"
                    LabelText="StaticComboButton2"
                    MenuItemId="StaticComboButton2"/>
              </Controls>
            </MenuSection>
          </Menu>
        </ComboBox>
```

code snippet Elements.xml

After your controls, you can handle the commands to which your controls need to respond in the CommandUIHandlers node. For the complete listing for all the code for the commands, tab, and group, refer to the sample code for this chapter on www.wrox.com.

ToolTips and Help

Your user interface should guide the user on how to use your controls. To aid in this, the Ribbon supports ToolTips and also linking to help topics. Both of these are set using the ToolTip* set of commands such as ToolTipTitle and ToolTipDescription. The following code sets the title, description, help topic, and shows the keyboard shortcut for your control:

```
ToolTipTitle="Tooltip Title"

ToolTipDescription="Tooltip Description"

ToolTipShortcutKey="Ctr-V, P"

ToolTipImage32by32="/_layouts/images/PasteHH.png"

ToolTipHelpKeyWord="WSSEndUser"
```

Writing a Page Component

So far, you have been writing code inline in your XML to handle your control commands. However, SharePoint does enable you to write more complex handlers for your user interface if you need to. You should try to keep your code in the XML definition if you create simple buttons with simple code. However, if you create Ribbon extensions dynamically populated via code; if your Ribbon requires variables beyond the default ones you can get with {SiteUrl}, {ItemId}, or other similar placeholders; or if your code is so long that it makes sense from a manageability standpoint to break it out separately, you should consider creating a page component.

A *page component* is a set of JavaScript code that can handle commands from your user interface customizations. Your JavaScript must derive from the `CUI.Page.PageComponent` and implement the functions in the prototype definition of the `RibbonAppPageComponent`. As part of this code, you can define the global commands that your page component works with. These are the tabs, groups, and commands, such as buttons, that you handle in your page component. In addition, you can define whether your global commands should be enabled through the `canHandleCommand` function. This is the function you use to enable or disable your control. For example, you may want to enable your control only if the context is correct for your control to work, such as when an item is selected in the user interface or when the right variables are set. If you return `false` to this function, your user interface is grayed out.

In addition, the page component enables you to handle the command, so if someone clicks your button, you can run code to handle that click.

After you define all this JavaScript, you need to register your script with the `PageManager` that SharePoint creates so that SharePoint knows to call the script when actions are performed on the user interface.

Notice a couple of points about the following code:

➤ **You can get the selected items by using the `SP.ListOperation.Selection.getSelected-Items()` method.** This is a good way to determine whether any items are selected in the user interface so that you can enable or disable your control. You can go a step further and look for particular properties or item types by writing some more code.

➤ **You can write more functions to do things such as populate your drop-downs dynamically or change the buttons on your user interface.** You can write your Ribbon component to perform a postback to the server that a custom .NET program can handle so that you can avoid writing JavaScript. If you do this, you want the command action to be a postback command such as `CommandAction="javascript:__doPostBack('CustomButton', '{ItemUrl}')"`. Then, on the backend that captures the postback, you can handle the postback in two ways:

  ➤ You can look at the `__EVENTTARGET` variable in the page request variables to see if your custom command caused the postback.

  ➤ You can spin up a Ribbon object—make sure to reference `Microsoft.SharePoint.WebControls`—and implement the `IPostBackHandler` interface. You can then check if your custom button generated the postback by deserializing the postback event using the `SPRibbonPostBackCommand.DeserializePostBackEvent` method, and then checking the ID of the control that generated the event with the ID of the control you were looking for. If they match, handle the event.

  The first method is simpler and requires less code than the second method.

Figure 5-18 shows the custom button on the Ribbon. Also, the figure has a custom color picker and other buttons. You can see the code to implement these other buttons in the sample code for this chapter.

FIGURE 5-18

```xml
<CustomAction
  Id="SharedDocAction"
  RegistrationType="List"
  RegistrationId="101"
  Location="CommandUI.Ribbon.ListView">
    <CommandUIExtension>
      <CommandUIDefinitions>
        <CommandUIDefinition
          Location="Ribbon.Documents.New.Controls._children">
          <Button
            Id="CustomContextualButton"
            Alt="MyDocumentsNew Alt"
            Command="MyDocumentsNewButton"
            LabelText="ScriptBlock Button"
            ToolTipTitle="Tooltip Title"
            Image16by16="/_layouts/$Resources:core,Language;
            /images/formatmap16x16.png?vk=4536" Image16by16Top="-80"
            Image16by16Left="0"
            Image32by32="/_layouts/$Resources:core,Language;
            /images/formatmap32x32.png?vk=4536"
            Image32by32Top="-96" Image32by32Left="-64"
            ToolTipDescription="Tooltip Description"
            TemplateAlias="o1"/>
        </CommandUIDefinition>
```

```xml
      </CommandUIDefinitions>
    </CommandUIExtension>
  </CustomAction>

  <CustomAction
   Id="MyScriptBlock"
   Location="ScriptLink"
   ScriptBlock="
ExecuteOrDelayUntilScriptLoaded(_registerMyScriptBlockPageComponent,
                                'sp.ribbon.js');

function _registerMyScriptBlockPageComponent()
{
    Type.registerNamespace('MyScriptBlock');

    MyScriptBlock.MyScriptBlockPageComponent =
function MyScriptBlockPageComponent_Ctr() {
        MyScriptBlock.MyScriptBlockPageComponent.initializeBase(this);
    };

    MyScriptBlock.MyScriptBlockPageComponent.prototype = {

        init: function MyScriptBlockPageComponent_init() {
        },

        _globalCommands: null,


        buildGlobalCommands:
function MyScriptBlockPageComponent_buildGlobalCommands() {
            if (SP.ScriptUtility.isNullOrUndefined(this._globalCommands)) {
                this._globalCommands = [];
                this._globalCommands[this._globalCommands.length] = 'DocumentTab';
                this._globalCommands[this._globalCommands.length]
                 = 'DocumentNewGroup';
                this._globalCommands[this._globalCommands.length]
                 = 'MyDocumentsNewButton';
            }
            return this._globalCommands;
        },

        getGlobalCommands: function MyScriptBlockPageComponent_getGlobalCommands()
        {
            return this.buildGlobalCommands();
        },

        canHandleCommand: function
MyScriptBlockPageComponent_canHandleCommand(commandId) {
            var items = SP.ListOperation.Selection.getSelectedItems();
            if (SP.ScriptUtility.isNullOrUndefined(items))
                return false;
            if (0 == items.length)
                return false;
            if (commandId === 'DocumentNewTab'){
```

```
                    return true;
                }
                if (commandId === 'DocumentNewGroup'){
                    return true;
                }
                if (commandId === 'MyDocumentsNewButton'){
                    return true;
                }
                return false;
            },

            handleCommand: function
            MyScriptBlockPageComponent_handleCommand(commandId, properties, sequence) {
                alert('You hit my button!');
                return true;
            }
        }

    MyScriptBlock.MyScriptBlockPageComponent.get_instance =
     function MyScriptBlockPageComponent_get_instance() {
        if (SP.ScriptUtility.isNullOrUndefined(MyScriptBlock.
          MyScriptBlockPageComponent._singletonPageComponent)) {
            MyScriptBlock.MyScriptBlockPageComponent._singletonPageComponent
              = new MyScriptBlock.MyScriptBlockPageComponent();
        }
        return MyScriptBlock.MyScriptBlockPageComponent._singletonPageComponent;
    }
    MyScriptBlock.MyScriptBlockPageComponent.registerWithPageManager
        = function MyScriptBlockPageComponent_registerWithPageManager() {
        SP.Ribbon.PageManager.get_instance().addPageComponent
            (MyScriptBlock.MyScriptBlockPageComponent.get_instance());
    }
    MyScriptBlock.MyScriptBlockPageComponent.unregisterWithPageManager =
    function MyScriptBlockPageComponent_unregisterWithPageManager() {
        if (false == SP.ScriptUtility.isNullOrUndefined(
          MyScriptBlock.MyScriptBlockPageComponent._singletonPageComponent)) {
            SP.Ribbon.PageManager.get_instance().removePageComponent(
          MyScriptBlock.MyScriptBlockPageComponent.get_instance());
        }
    }

    MyScriptBlock.MyScriptBlockPageComponent.registerClass(
    'MyScriptBlock.MyScriptBlockPageComponent', CUI.Page.PageComponent);
    MyScriptBlock.MyScriptBlockPageComponent.registerWithPageManager();
}">
  </CustomAction>
```

code snippet Elements.xml

Adding Buttons with SPD

The easiest way to add a button to the Ribbon or your items is to use SharePoint Designer. Built
right into SPD is the ability to add custom actions to your list. SPD can create these actions on the
Ribbon forms, such as the display, edit, or new form for a list item, and also on a list item drop-
down menu. You can customize the action performed by the button, for example, navigating to a
form such as the edit form for the item, initiating a workflow, or launching a URL. In addition, you

can use SPD to assign graphics to your icons, set your sequence number, and even set your Ribbon location in the same way you set the `Location` attribute in the Ribbon XML you saw earlier. Figure 5-19 shows the form used to tell SPD how to customize the Ribbon for your list.

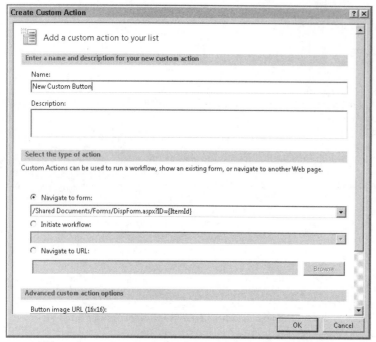

FIGURE 5-19

Contextual Tabs and Groups with Web Parts

You may want to build a Ribbon user interface and have it automatically appear when a user selects a web part. This is the way the media-player web part works; it displays a new tab in the Ribbon when you select the web part in the user interface. To perform this functionality, you need to add a contextual tab and contextual group to the Ribbon interface through code. You do not use the declarative XML file, but instead place the XML in code and add it programmatically to the Ribbon.

To build a contextual web part, you create your web part as you normally do, but you want your web part to inherit from the `IWebPartPageComponentProvider` interface. You need to implement the `WebPartContextualInfo` method of the interface. This method tells the Ribbon which group and tab to activate when the web part is selected.

Available for download on Wrox.com

```
public WebPartContextualInfo WebPartContextualInfo
        {
            get
            {
                WebPartContextualInfo info = new WebPartContextualInfo();
                info.ContextualGroups.Add(
```

```
                          new WebPartRibbonContextualGroup
                          {
                              Id = "Ribbon.MyContextualGroup",
                              VisibilityContext = "WebPartSelectionTest",
                              Command = "MyContextualGroupCMD"
                          }
                      );
                      info.Tabs.Add(
                          new WebPartRibbonTab
                          {
                              Id = "Ribbon.MyContextualGroup.MyTab",
                              VisibilityContext = "WebPartSelectionTest"
                          }
                      );

                      info.PageComponentId = SPRibbon.GetWebPartPageComponentId(this);
                      return info;
                  }
              }
```

code snippet CustomWebPart.cs

Then you need to implement a custom page component using JavaScript. This is similar to the code you saw earlier in the chapter where you added and registered the custom page component. The code that follows uses the executeOrDelayUntilScriptLoaded command, which is part of the SharePoint infrastructure, to load and run the script on-demand.

Available for download on Wrox.com

```
      private string DelayScript
              {
                  get
                  {
                      string wppPcId = SPRibbon.GetWebPartPageComponentId(this);
                      return @"
                      <script type=""text/javascript"">
          //<![CDATA[

                      function _addCustomPageComponent()
                      {
                          SP.Ribbon.PageManager.get_instance().addPageComponent(new
                          CustomPageComponent.TestPageComponent(" + wppPcId + @"));
                      }

                      function _registerCustomPageComponent()
                      {
                          RegisterSod(""testpagecomponent.js"",
                          ""\/_layouts\/TestPageComponent.js"");
                          var isDefined = ""undefined"";
                          try
                          {
                              isDefined = typeof(CustomPageComponent.TestPageComponent);
                          }
                          catch(e)
                          {
```

```
                        }
                        EnsureScript(""testpagecomponent.js"",isDefined,
                            addCustomPageComponent);
                    }
                    ExecuteOrDelayUntilScriptLoaded(_registerCustomPageComponent,
                        ""sp.ribbon.js"");
        //]]>
        </script>";
                }
            }
```

code snippet CustomWebPart.cs

Contextual tabs always exist on the Ribbon but are hidden. To add your tabs and groups to the Ribbon, you need to use the server-side Ribbon API to get the Ribbon and add your custom Ribbon elements, as shown in the following code.

```
private void AddCustomTab()
    {

        Microsoft.Web.CommandUI.Ribbon ribbon = SPRibbon.GetCurrent(this.Page);
        XmlDocument xmlDoc = new XmlDocument();

        //Contextual Tab
        xmlDoc.LoadXml(this.CuiDefinitionCtxTab);
        ribbon.RegisterDataExtension(xmlDoc.FirstChild,
          "Ribbon.ContextualTabs._children");
        xmlDoc.LoadXml(this.CuiDefinitionScaling);
        ribbon.RegisterDataExtension(xmlDoc.FirstChild,
          "Ribbon.Templates._children");
        exists = true;

    }
```

code snippet CustomWebPart.cs

To tie it all together, you need to implement the `OnPreRender` method, which allows the code to add the new Ribbon elements to the page before the page renders. The following code calls the `AddCustomTab` method to do this; this method also registers the script block that implements the custom page component with the SharePoint client script manager:

```
protected override void OnPreRender(EventArgs e)
    {
        base.OnPreRender(e);

        //RegisterDataExtensions; add Ribbon XML for buttons
        this.AddCustomTab();

        ClientScriptManager csm = this.Page.ClientScript;
        csm.RegisterClientScriptBlock(this.GetType(),
          "custompagecomponent", this.DelayScript);
    }
```

The last piece to look at is the custom page component, which implements the functionality to tell SharePoint which commands the page component implements, as well as when to focus on the contextual tab, and when to yield focus depending on whether the web part is selected.

```
Type.registerNamespace('CustomPageComponent');

//////////////////////////////////////////////////////////////////////////////
// CustomPageComponent.TestPageComponent
var _myWpPcId;
CustomPageComponent.TestPageComponent = function
CustomPageComponent._TestPageComponent(webPartPcId) {
    this._myWpPcId = webPartPcId.innerText;
    CustomPageComponent.TestPageComponent.initializeBase(this);
}
CustomPageComponent.TestPageComponent.prototype = {

    init: function CustomPageComponent_TestPageComponent$init() {
    },

    getFocusedCommands: function
CustomPageComponent_TestPageComponent$getFocusedCommands() {
        return ['MyTabCMD', 'MyGroupCMD', 'CommandMyJscriptButton'];
    },

    getGlobalCommands: function
CustomPageComponent_TestPageComponent$getGlobalCommands() {
        return [];
    },

    isFocusable: function CustomPageComponent_TestPageComponent$isFocusable() {
        return true;
    },

    receiveFocus: function CustomPageComponent_TestPageComponent$receiveFocus() {
        return true;
    },

    yieldFocus: function CustomPageComponent_TestPageComponent$yieldFocus() {
        return true;
    },

    canHandleCommand: function
CustomPageComponent_TestPageComponent$canHandleCommand(commandId) {
        //Contextual Tab commands
        if ((commandId === 'MyTabCMD') || (commandId === 'MyGroupCMD') ||
            (commandId === 'CommandMyButton') ||
        (commandId === 'CommandMyJscriptButton')) {
            return true;
        }
    },

    handleCommand: function CustomPageComponent_TestPageComponent$handleCommand
```

```
      (commandId, properties, sequence) {

        if (commandId === 'CommandMyJscriptButton') {
            alert('Event: CommandMyJscriptButton');
        }
      },

      getId: function CustomPageComponent_TestPageComponent$getId() {
          return this._myWpPcId;
      }
    }


CustomPageComponent.TestPageComponent.registerClass(
'CustomPageComponent.TestPageComponent', CUI.Page.PageComponent);
if(typeof(NotifyScriptLoadedAndExecuteWaitingJobs)!="undefined")
NotifyScriptLoadedAndExecuteWaitingJobs("testpagecomponent.js");
```

code snippet CustomWebPart.cs

Status Bar and Notification Area

Two new additions to the user interface for 2010 are the status bar, which appears right below the Ribbon tab; and the notification area, which is transient in nature, that appears below and to the right of the Ribbon tab. You should use both to give your users contextual information so long as it's not distracting. For example, if you are editing a page and have not checked it in or published it, the status bar tells you that only you can see the page. The status bar is for more permanent information, whereas the notification area is similar to instant message pop-ups or Windows system tray notifications because notifications pop up and then disappear after a certain amount of time. Notification area messages are inherently more transient in nature than status bar messages.

Customizing the Status Bar

The status bar is extensible through client- and server-side code. The message you can deliver in the bar is HTML, so it can be styled and contain links and images. In addition, the bar can have four preset colors, depending on the importance of the message. To work with the status bar, you use the SP.UI.Status class, which is a simple client-side API because it contains only six methods, and you can find their definitions in SP.debug.js. On the server side, you should use the SPPageStatusSetter class, which is part of the Microsoft.SharePoint.WebControls namespace. That API is even simpler because you call one method—addStatus. You can also use the SPPageStateControl class to work with the status bar on the server side. Table 5-6 outlines the methods for the client side.

TABLE 5-6: SP.UI.Status Methods

NAME	DESCRIPTION
addStatus	Enables you to pass a title, the HTML payload, and a Boolean specifying whether to render the message at the beginning of the status bar. This function returns a status ID that you can use with other methods.

NAME	DESCRIPTION
appendStatus	Appends status to an existing status. You need to pass the status ID for the existing status being updated, and the title, and HTML you want appended.
updateStatus	Updates an existing status message. You need to pass the status ID and the HTML payload for the new status message.
setStatusPriColor	Enables you to set the priority color to give a user a visual indication of the status messages' meanings, such as green for good or red for bad. You need to pass the status ID of the status you want to change color and one of four color choices: red, blue, green, or yellow.
removeStatus	Removes the status specified by the status ID you pass to this method from the status bar.
removeAllStatus	Removes all status messages from the status bar. You can pass a Boolean that specifies whether to hide the bar. Most times, you want this Boolean to be true.

Programming the status bar is straightforward. The sample code with this chapter includes a snippet that you can add to the HTML source for a Content Editor web part. When you do this, you can see what appears in Figure 5-20.

FIGURE 5-20

```
<script type="text/javascript">

var sid;
var color="";

function AppendStatusMethod()
{
    SP.UI.Status.appendStatus(sid, "Appended:", "<HTML><i>My Status Append to "
        + sid + " using appendStatus</i></HTML>");
}

function UpdateStatus()
{
    SP.UI.Status.updateStatus(sid, "Updated: HTML updated for " + sid +
        " using updateStatus");
}

function RemoveStatus()
{
    SP.UI.Status.removeStatus(sid);
}

function RemoveAllStatus()
{
    SP.UI.Status.removeAllStatus(true);
}


function SetStatusColor()
{
    if (color=="")
    {
      color="red";
    }
    else if (color=="red")
    {
      color="green";
    }
    else if (color=="green")
    {
      color="yellow";
    }
    else if (color=="yellow")
    {
      color="blue";
    }
    else if (color=="blue")
    {
      color="red";
    }

    SP.UI.Status.setStatusPriColor(sid, color);
}

function AppendStatus()
```

```
{
    SP.UI.Status.addStatus("Appended:", "<HTML><i>
       My Status Message Append using atBeginning</i></HTML>", false);
}


function CreateStatus()
{
     return SP.UI.Status.addStatus(SP.Utilities.HttpUtility.htmlEncode(
       "My Status Bar Title"), "<HTML><i>My Status Message</i></HTML>", true);
}

}
</script>
<input onclick="sid=CreateStatus();alert(sid);" type="button" value="
   Create Status"/> <br/>
<input onclick="AppendStatus()" type="button"
   value="Append Status using atBeginning"/> <br/>
<input onclick="AppendStatusMethod()" type="button"
   value="Append Status using appendStatus"/> <br/>
<input onclick="UpdateStatus()" type="button"
   value="Update Status using updateStatus"/> <br/>
<input onclick="SetStatusColor()" type="button" value="Cycle Colors"/> <br/>
<input onclick="RemoveStatus()" type="button" value="Remove Single Status"/> <br/>
<input onclick="RemoveAllStatus()" type="button" value="Remove All Status"/> <br/>
```

code snippet CustomDialogandNotifications.txt

Customizing the Notification Area

Beyond working with status information, you can also customize the notification area on the upper-right side of the screen below the Ribbon. Given that SharePoint is now leveraging a lot of Ajax, there is a need to give users feedback that their pages and actions are completed. The notification area does this by telling the user that the page is loading or that a save was successful, for example, which used to be indicated by a postback and page refresh.

The notification API is limited in that you can create and remove only notifications. Table 5-7 describes the methods for SP.UI.Notify that work with notifications, with sample code following the table.

TABLE 5-7: SP.UI.Notify

NAME	DESCRIPTION
addNotification	Enables you to pass your HTML payload, whether the notification is sticky (which when set to false means the notification disappears after 5 seconds), your ToolTip text, and the name of a function to handle the onclick event. The last two parameters are optional. This function returns an ID that you can use with the removeNotification method to remove your notification.
removeNotification	Removes the notification specified by the notification ID that you pass to this method.

```
<script type="text/javascript">

var notifyid;
function CreateNotification()
{
    notifyid = SP.UI.Notify.addNotification("My HTML Notification", true,
      "My Tooltip", "HelloWorld");
    alert("Notification id: " + notifyid);
}

function RemoveNotification()
{
    SP.UI.Notify.removeNotification(notifyid);
}
</script>
<input onclick="CreateNotification()" type="button"
    value="Create Notification"/><br/>
<input onclick="RemoveNotification()" type="button" value="Remove Notification"/>
```

code snippet CustomDialogandNotifications.txt

Working with Dialogs

Beyond working with notifications and status bars, SharePoint now also offers a dialog framework that you can write code to. The purpose of the new dialog framework is to keep the user in context and focus the user on the dialog rather than all the surrounding user interface elements. With the new dialog framework, dialogs are modal and gray out the screen, except for the dialog that is displayed. Figure 5-21 shows a custom dialog in SharePoint 2010.

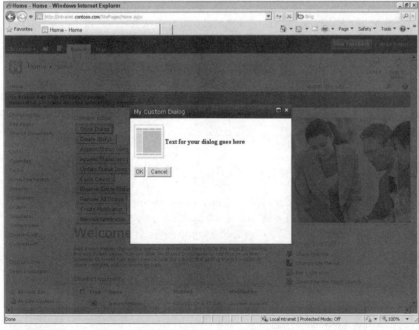

FIGURE 5-21

The implementation of the dialog takes the form of your contents being loaded into an iframe in a floating `div`. The dialog is modal, so the user can't get to other parts of SharePoint from it. Plus, the dialog can be dragged to other parts of the browser window and can be maximized to the size of the browser window.

If you look in `SP.UI.Dialog.debug.js`, you see the implementation for the dialog framework. The framework has a JavaScript API against which you can program to have SharePoint launch and load your own dialogs. You do this by calling the `SP.UI.showModalDialog` method and passing in the options you want for your dialog, such as height, width, page to load, and other options. You can see the full set of options in Table 5-8.

TABLE 5-8: Parameters for the SP.UI.showModalDialog method

NAME	DESCRIPTION
Width	The width of the dialog box as an integer. If you don't specify a width, SharePoint autosizes the dialog.
Height	The height of the dialog box as an integer. If you don't specify a height, SharePoint autosizes the dialog.
autoSize	A Boolean that specifies whether to have SharePoint autosize the dialog.
X	The x coordinate for your dialog.
Y	The y coordinate for your dialog.
allowMaximize	A Boolean that specifies whether to allow the Maximize button in your dialog.
showMaximized	A Boolean that specifies whether to show your dialog maximized by default.
showClose	A Boolean that specifies whether to show the Close button in the toolbar for the dialog.
url	A URL for SharePoint to load as the contents for your dialog.
Html	A `DOMElement` that contains the HTML you want SharePoint to load as the contents for your dialog. This `DOMElement` is destroyed after use, so make a copy before passing it to SharePoint if you need it after the dialog is destroyed.
Title	The title of your dialog.
dialogReturn-ValueCallback	The function SharePoint calls back to when the dialog is closed. You create a delegate to this function for this option with the `createDelegate` function in JavaScript.

Now that you know the options you can pass to the `showModalDialog` function, programming a dialog is straightforward. A couple of tips before you look at the code:

➤ **If you use URLs, take a look at the `SP.Utilities.Utility` namespace.** This namespace has a number of utilities to help you find the right places from which to grab your URLs no matter where your code is running. For example, one utility you will see in the code is

`SP.Utilities.Utility.getLayoutsPageUrl('customdialog.htm')`, which gets the URL to the `_layouts` folder so that the custom dialog HTML file can be retrieved.

➤ **Dialogs support the `Source=url querystring` variable like the rest of SharePoint.** So, if you want to have SharePoint redirect to another page, you can specify the source along the query string, and SharePoint respects that.

The following code contains the `OpenDialog` function. As part of this function, a variable called `options` is created, which uses the `SP.UI.$create_DialogOptions` method. This method returns a `DialogOptions` object that you can utilize to specify your options. In the code, all the options are specified, including the creation of the delegate that points to the function—`CloseCallback`—that is called after the dialog is called. Then, the code calls the `SP.UI.ModalDialog.showModalDialog` with the `options` object that contains the specified options for the dialog.

The `CloseCallback` function gets the result and any return value. The result is the button the user clicked. SharePoint has an enumeration for the common buttons OK and Cancel that you can check against with the result value—for example, `SP.UI.DialogResult.OK` or `SP.UI.DialogResult.cancel`.

```
function OpenDialog()
{
  var options = SP.UI.$create_DialogOptions();

  options.url = SP.Utilities.Utility.getLayoutsPageUrl('customdialog.htm');
  options.url += "?Source=" + document.URL;
  alert('Navigating to dialog at: ' + options.url);
  options.width = 400;
  options.height = 300;
  options.title = "My Custom Dialog";

  options.dialogReturnValueCallback = Function.createDelegate(null, CloseCallback);
  SP.UI.ModalDialog.showModalDialog(options);
}

function CloseCallback(result, returnValue)
{
  alert('Result from dialog was: '+ result);
  if(result === SP.UI.DialogResult.OK)
  {
    alert('You clicked OK');
  }
  else if (result == SP.UI.DialogResult.cancel)
  {
    alert('You clicked Cancel');
  }
}
```

code snippet CustomDialogandNotifications.txt

Now that you have seen the code for calling the dialog and evaluating the result, look at what the HTML for the dialog body looks like. The code that follows is for SharePoint to load the dialog. The code contains two buttons for OK and Cancel. The `onclick` event handlers for the buttons use methods from the `window.frameElement` object. By using this object, you can get methods from the dialog framework. `commitPopup` returns `OK`, and `cancelPopUp` returns `Cancel` as the result of your dialog. Table 5-9 shows the methods you want to use from the `frameElement`.

```
<p>
<img src="/_layouts/1033/images/DefaultPageLayout.tif" alt="Default Page"
    style="vertical-align: middle"/>
<B>Text for your dialog goes here</B>
</p>

<input type="button" name="OK" value="OK"
    onclick="window.frameElement.commitPopup();
    return false;" accesskey="O" class="ms-ButtonHeightWidth" target="_self" />

<input type="button" name="Cancel" value="Cancel"
    onclick="window.frameElement.cancelPopUp();
    return false;" accesskey="C" class="ms-ButtonHeightWidth" target="_self" />
```

code snippet CustomDialogandNotifications.txt

TABLE 5-9: Methods for frameElement for Dialogs

NAME	DESCRIPTION
commitPopup	Returns OK as the result of your dialog
cancelPopUp	Returns Cancel as a result of your dialog
navigateParent	Navigates to the parent of the dialog

CALLING SHAREPOINT WEB SERVICES

SharePoint's Web Services have been around for a number of releases of SharePoint and continue to work with SharePoint Online, with the caveat that you need to pass the correct cookies for authentication. Also, you want to make sure that when you add a reference to the SharePoint Online Web Services, such as `lists.asmx`, that you add them as a web reference and not a service reference. You can add a web reference by using the Advanced dialog as part of the Add Service Reference dialog. By using the older-style web references, you can access the cookie container, and add the authentication cookies to your calls to SharePoint Online. The following code shows how to add the cookie container and call a SharePoint web service. Whenever possible you should use the SharePoint Client Object Model rather than the legacy SharePoint Web Services. Please remember that the Client Object Model is a subset of the full functionality of the SharePoint API.

```
//Call Lists Web Service
listWS.Lists spList = new listWS.Lists();
spList.Url = "https://thomrizdom.sharepoint.com/_vti_bin/lists.asmx";
spList.CookieContainer = claimsHelper.CookieContainer;
XmlNode spLists = spList.GetList("Announcements");
```

OVERVIEW OF DATA TECHNOLOGIES

When it comes to SharePoint, working with, manipulating, and displaying data are the important tasks you do as a developer. If you break SharePoint down to its simplest form, it is just an application that sits on top of a database. Because SharePoint can reveal its data in so many ways—whether through the browser, inside Office, in applications running on the SharePoint server, or in applications running off the SharePoint server—there are a number of data technologies you can take advantage of when working with SharePoint. Which one you use depends on your comfort level with the technology required and also whether you write your application to run on or off the SharePoint server. Your choices in 2010 are:

- ➤ LINQ
- ➤ Server Object Model
- ➤ Client Object Model
- ➤ REST-style services

Of course, you can continue to use the Web Services APIs of SharePoint, but for the bulk of your operation you should look at moving to the Client OM or the SharePoint Data Services (an OData service) rather than using that technology. Table 5-10 goes shows the pros and cons of each data-access technology.

TABLE 5-10: Data Access Technologies

NAME	PROS	CONS
LINQ to SharePoint	Entity-based programming Strongly typed Supports joins and projections Good tools support and IntelliSense	Server-side only New API, so new skills required Pre-processing of list structure required, so changing list could break application
Server OM	Familiar API Works with more than just list data	Server-side only Strongly typed
Client OM	Works off the server Easier than Web Services API Works in Silverlight, JavaScript, and .NET More than just list data	New API Weakly typed
SharePoint Data Service	Standards-based URL-based commands Strongly typed	Only works with lists and Excel
Web Services	Simple to program Standards-based	Weakly typed Legacy API

SharePoint LINQ Support

With SharePoint 2007, you had to use CAML queries to write queries against the server, using the `SPQuery` or `SPSiteDataQuery` objects. You would write your CAML as a string and pass it to those objects, so there were no strongly-typed objects or syntax checking as part of the API. Instead, you would either have to cross your fingers that you got the query right, or use a third-party tool to try to generate your CAML queries. To make this easier, SharePoint 2010 introduces SharePoint LINQ (SPLINQ). By having a LINQ provider, 2010 enables you to use LINQ to write your queries against SharePoint in a strongly typed way with IntelliSense and compile-time checking. Under the covers, the SharePoint LINQ provider translates your LINQ query into a CAML query and executes it against the server. As you will see, you can retrieve the CAML query that the LINQ provider generated to understand what is passed back to the server.

Getting Started with SharePoint LINQ: SPMetal

The first step in starting with SPLINQ is generating the entity classes and properties for your lists. Rather than writing these by hand, you can use the command-line tool that ships with SharePoint, called SPMetal. SPMetal parses your lists and generates the necessary classes that you can import into your Visual Studio projects. You can find SPMetal in the `%ProgramFiles%\Common Files\ Microsoft Shared\web server extensions\14\BIN` directory. You can run SPMetal from the command prompt, but if you prefer, you can write a batch file that you have Visual Studio run as part of your prebuild for your project so that the latest version of your entity classes are always included.

Using SPMetal is straightforward for performing common tasks that you want to do. It does support XML customization, but most of the time you don't need to customize the default code generation. Table 5-11 shows the SPMetal command-line parameters that you can pass.

TABLE 5-11: SPMetal Command-Line Parameters

NAME	DESCRIPTION
Web	Absolute URL of the website you want SPMetal to generate entity classes for.
Code	The relative or absolute path and filename of the location where you want the outputted code to be placed.
Language	The programming language you want for the generated code. The value for this can be either `csharp` or `vb`. SPMetal can look at your code parameter and infer the language you want by the extension of the filename you specify.
Namespace	The namespace you want to use for the generated code. If you do not specify this property, SPMetal uses the default namespace of your VS project.
Useremoteapi	SPMetal uses the client object model if you specify this parameter.

continues

TABLE 5-11 *(continued)*

NAME	DESCRIPTION
User	Enables you to specify the *DOMAIN\username*, such as */user:DOMAIN\username*, that SPMetal runs as.
Password	The password that SPMetal uses to log on as the user specified in the /user parameter.
Serialization	Specifies whether you want your objects to be serializable. By default, this parameter is none, so they are not. If you specify unidirectional, SPMetal puts in the appropriate markup to make the objects serializable.
Parameters	Specifies the XML file used to override the parameters for your SPMetal settings. This is for advanced changes.

The following code snippet shows you some of the generated code, but to give you an idea of the work SPMetal does for you, the complete code for even a simple SharePoint site is more than 3,000 lines! You definitely want to use SPMetal to generate this code and tweak SPMetal to meet your requirements.

```
/// <summary>
/// Use the Announcements list to post messages on the home page of your
/// site.
/// </summary>
[Microsoft.SharePoint.Linq.ListAttribute(Name="Announcements")]
public Microsoft.SharePoint.Linq.
  EntityList<AnnouncementsAnnouncement> Announcements {
      get {
              return this.
                GetList<AnnouncementsAnnouncement>("Announcements");
      }
  }

/// <summary>
/// Create a new news item, status or other short piece of information.
/// </summary>
[Microsoft.SharePoint.Linq.ContentTypeAttribute(Name="Announcement", Id="0x0104")]
[Microsoft.SharePoint.Linq.DerivedEntityClassAttribute
(Type=typeof(AnnouncementsAnnouncement))]
public partial class Announcement : Item {

    private string _body;

    private System.Nullable<System.DateTime> _expires;

    #region Extensibility Method Definitions
    partial void OnLoaded();
    partial void OnValidate();
    partial void OnCreated();
```

```
        #endregion

        public Announcement() {
                this.OnCreated();
        }

        [Microsoft.SharePoint.Linq.ColumnAttribute(Name="Body",
          Storage="_body", FieldType="Note")]
        public string Body {
                get {
                        return this._body;
                }
                set {
                    if ((value != this._body)) {
                            this.OnPropertyChanging("Body", this._body);
                            this._body = value;
                            this.OnPropertyChanged("Body");
                    }
                }
        }

        [Microsoft.SharePoint.Linq.ColumnAttribute(Name="Expires",
            Storage="_expires",FieldType="DateTime")]
        public System.Nullable<System.DateTime> Expires {
                get {
                        return this._expires;
                }
                set {
                    if ((value != this._expires)) {
                            this.OnPropertyChanging("Expires", this._expires);
                            this._expires = value;
                            this.OnPropertyChanged("Expires");
                    }
                }
        }
    }
}
```

What About Default Fields?

One thing you may realize is that SPMetal, by default, does not generate all the fields for your content types. So, you may find that fields such as Created or ModifiedBy do not appear in the types created by SPMetal. To add these fields, you can specify them in a Parameters.XML. The example that follows adds some new fields to the contact content type:

```xml
<?xml version="1.0" encoding="utf-8"?>
<Web xmlns="http://schemas.microsoft.com/SharePoint/2009/spmetal">
  <ContentType Name="Contact" >
    <Column Name="CreatedBy" />
    <Column Name="ModifiedBy"/>
  </ContentType>
</Web>
```

Adding References in VS

After you generate SPMetal code imported into VS, it's time to make sure you have the right references set up to use that code. You want to add two references at a minimum:

➤ A reference to `Microsoft.SharePoint`, which is the general SharePoint namespace.

➤ A reference to the specific SharePoint LINQ assembly using `Microsoft.SharePoint.Linq`.

This adds all the necessary dependent LINQ assemblies to your project.

Working with the DataContext Object

The `DataContext` object provides the heart of your LINQ programming. Your `DataContext` object is named after whatever you named the beginning of your generated file from SPMetal. For example, if you had SPMetal create a `LINQDemo.cs` file for your generated code, your `DataContext` object becomes `LINQDemoDataContext`, but you can override this in your `parameter.xml` file. To create your `DataContext` object, you can pass along the URL of the SharePoint site to which you want to connect.

When you have your `DataContext` object, you can start working with that object's methods and properties. The `DataContext` contains all your lists and libraries as `EntityList` properties. You can retrieve these lists and libraries and then work with them. Table 5-12 lists the other methods and properties you can use from the `DataContext` object.

TABLE 5-12: Common Methods and Properties of the DataContext Object

NAME	DESCRIPTION
GetList<T>	Returns the list of the specified type, for example, GetList<AnnouncementsItems>("Announcements").
Refresh	Refreshes the datasource.
RegisterList	Enables you to register a list by registering a new name and new URL (if needed) as a replacement for the old name. This is helpful if a list has been renamed or moved and you do not want to rewrite your code.
ChangeConflicts	Returns a ChangeConflictCollection, which is a list of conflicts from your transactions.
DeferredLoadingEnabled	A Boolean that gets or sets whether LINQ should defer loading your objects until they are needed.
Log	Gets the CAML query generated by LINQ. This is a good way to view what LINQ is generating on your behalf.
ObjectTrackingEnabled	Gets or sets whether changes to objects are tracked. If you are just querying your site, for performance reasons, you should set this to false.
Web	Gets the full URL of the SharePoint website the DataContext object is connected to.

Typed Data Classes and Relationships

As part of SPMetal, you get autogenerated typed data classes and relationships using the `Association` attribute. This enables you to use strongly typed objects for your lists and also to do queries across multiple lists that are related by lookup fields. This makes programming much cleaner and also enables you to catch compile-time errors when working with your objects, rather than runtime errors.

Querying and Enumerating Data and Inefficient Queries

To query and enumerate your data, you need to write LINQ queries. When you write your queries, you need to understand that LINQ translates the query into CAML, so if you try to perform LINQ queries that cannot be translated into CAML, SharePoint throws an error. SharePoint considers these inefficient queries, and the only way to work around them is to use LINQ to Objects and perform the work yourself. The following is a list of the unsupported operators that cause errors in SharePoint:

➤ `Aggregate`

➤ `All`

➤ `Any`

➤ `Average`

➤ `Distinct`

➤ `ElementAt`

➤ `ElementAtOrDefault`

➤ `Except`

➤ `Intersect`

➤ `Join` (in complex instances)

➤ `Max`

➤ `Min`

➤ `Reverse`

➤ `SequenceEqual`

➤ `Skip`

➤ `SkipWhile`

➤ `Sum`

The simplest query you can write is a `select` from your list. The following code performs a `select` from a list and then enumerates the results:

```
var context = new LinqDemoDataContext("http://intranet.contoso.com");
var orderresults = from orders in context.Orders
```

```
                                        select orders;

               foreach (var order in orderresults)
               {
                   MessageBox.Show(order.Title + " " + order.Customer);
               }
```

From the following in the code, you can see that you need to:

➤ Get your `DataContext` object.

➤ Define your LINQ query as you do against any other datasource.

➤ Enumerate the results, once you have them, using a `foreach` loop.

➤ Use the `ToList` method to return a generic list that you can perform LINQ to Object operations on, if you want to.

➤ Add `where` clauses to your queries to perform selection. For example, if in the previous query you wanted to select only orders that were more than $1,000 dollars, you would change the query to the following one:

```
               var orderresults = from orders in context.Orders
                                        where orders.Total > 1000
                                        select orders;
```

For the next example, the query performs a simple inner join between two lists that share a lookup field. Because CAML now supports joins, this is supported in LINQ as well. In the code that follows, you'll notice:

➤ You get the `EntityList` objects for the two lists that you will join, so you can use them in the query.

➤ In the query, you just use the `join` operator to join the two lists together on a lookup field.

➤ The code then uses the `ToList` method on the query results so that you can get back a LINQ to Object collection that you can iterate over.

```
               var context = new LinqDemoDataContext("http://intranet.contoso.com");


               EntityList<OrdersItem> Orders = context.GetList<OrdersItem>("Orders");
               EntityList<CustomersItem> Customers = context.GetList<CustomersItem>
                ("Customers");

               var QueryResults = from Order in Orders
                                  join Customer in Customers on Order.Customer.Id
                                  equals Customer.Id
                                  select new { CustomerName = Customer.Title,
                                  Order.Title, Order.Product };

               var Results = QueryResults.ToList();
               if (Results.Count > 0)
```

```
        {

            Results.ForEach(result => MessageBox.Show(result.Title + " " +
                result.CustomerName + " " + result.Product));
        }
        else
        {
            MessageBox.Show("No results");
        }

    }
```

Adding, Updating, and Deleting Data and Dealing with Conflicts

LINQ enables you to add, delete, and update your data in SharePoint and even send items to the recycle bin. Because LINQ is strongly typed, you can just create new objects that map to the type of the new objects you want to add. After the new object is created, you can call the `InsertOnSubmit` method and pass the new object or the `InsertAllOnSubmit` method and pass a collection of new objects. Because LINQ works asynchronously from the server with a local cache, you need to call `SubmitChanges` after all modifications to data through LINQ to actually have the changes propagated back to SharePoint.

Updating items involves updating the properties on your objects and then calling `SubmitChanges`. For deleting, you need to call `DeleteOnSubmit` or `DeleteAllOnSubmit`, passing either the object or a collection of objects, and then call `SubmitChanges`. Recycling works much the same as deleting.

Because LINQ does not directly work against the SharePoint store, changes could be made to the backend while your code is running. To handle this, SharePoint LINQ provides the ability to catch exceptions if duplicates are present, if conflicts are detected, or if general exceptions occur. The code that follows shows how to code for all these cases.

One thing to note is that the code uses the `ChangeConflict` exception and then enumerates all the `ObjectChangeConflict` objects. Then, it looks through the `MemberConflict` objects, which contain the differences between the database fields and the LINQ object fields. After you decide what to do about the discrepancies, you can resolve the changes with the `ResolveAll` method. The `ResolveAll` method takes a `RefreshMode` enumeration, which can contain one of three values:

➤ `KeepChanges`: Keeps the new values since retrieval, even if they are different than the database values, and keeps other values the same as the database.

➤ `KeepCurrentValues`: Keeps the new values since retrieval, even if they are different from the database values, and keeps other values the same as they were retrieved, even if they conflict with the database values.

➤ `OverwriteCurrentValues`: Keeps the values from the database and discards any changes since retrieval.

 You need to call `SubmitChanges` *after resolving any conflicts to save changes.*

```
try
    {
        EntityList<OrdersItem> Orders =
          context.GetList<OrdersItem>("Orders");
        OrdersItem order = new OrdersItem();
        order.Title = "My LINQ new Order";
        order.Product = "Chai";

        //Add a lookup to Customers
        EntityList<CustomersItem> Customers =
          context.GetList<CustomersItem>("Customers");
        var CustomerTempItem = from Customer in Customers
                    where Customer.Title == "Contoso"
                    select Customer;

        CustomersItem CustomerItem = null;
        foreach (var Cust in CustomerTempItem)
            CustomerItem = Cust;

        order.Customer = CustomerItem;

        Orders.InsertOnSubmit(order);
        context.SubmitChanges();

        //Delete the item
        Orders.DeleteOnSubmit(order);
        context.SubmitChanges();

    }
catch (ChangeConflictException conflictException)
    {
        MessageBox.Show("A conflict occurred: " +
          conflictException.Message);
        foreach (ObjectChangeConflict Items in context.ChangeConflicts)
        {
            foreach (MemberChangeConflict Fields in Items.MemberConflicts)
            {
                StringBuilder sb = new StringBuilder();
                sb.AppendLine("Item Name: " + Fields.Member.Name);
                sb.AppendLine("Original Value: " + Fields.OriginalValue);
                sb.AppendLine("Database Value: " + Fields.DatabaseValue);
                sb.AppendLine("Current Value: " + Fields.CurrentValue);
                MessageBox.Show(sb.ToString());
            }
        }

        //Force all changes
        context.ChangeConflicts.ResolveAll(RefreshMode.KeepChanges);
        context.SubmitChanges();

    }
catch (SPDuplicateValuesFoundException duplicateException)
    {
        MessageBox.Show("Duplicate value found: " +
          duplicateException.Message);
    }
```

```
catch (SPException SharePointException)
{
    MessageBox.Show("SharePoint Exception: " +
        SharePointException.Message);
}
catch (Exception ex)
{
    MessageBox.Show("Exception: " + ex.Message);
}

}
```

Inspecting the CAML Query

If you want to inspect the CAML query that LINQ is generating, you can use the Log property and set that to a TextWriter or an object that derives from the TextWriter object, such as a StreamWriter object. If you are writing a console application, the easiest way to set the Log property is to set it to the Console.Out property. From there, you can retrieve the CAML query that SharePoint LINQ executes on your behalf. The following code shows how to write a log file for your LINQ query using the Log property and then shows the CAML query generated by LINQ:

```
var context = new LinqDemoDataContext("http://intranet.contoso.com");

        context.Log = new StreamWriter(File.Open("C:\\SPLINQLog.txt",
          FileMode.Create));



        EntityList<OrdersItem> Orders = context.GetList<OrdersItem>("Orders");
        EntityList<CustomersItem> Customers =
          context.GetList<CustomersItem>("Customers");

        var QueryResults = from Order in Orders
                           join Customer in Customers on Order.Customer.Id
                           equals Customer.Id
                           select new { CustomerName = Customer.Title,
                           Order.Title, Order.Product };

        context.Log.WriteLine("Results :");

        var Results = QueryResults.ToList();
        if (Results.Count > 0)
        {

            Results.ForEach(result => context.Log.WriteLine(result.Title
              + " " + result.CustomerName + " " + result.Product));
        }
        else
        {
            context.Log.WriteLine("No results");
        }

        context.Log.Close();
        context.Log = null;
```

Please note that the log will only work for queries and not for inserts, updates, or deletes. The output for the previous code is as follows:

```
<View><Query><Where><And><BeginsWith><FieldRef Name="ContentTypeId" /><Value
Type="ContentTypeId">0x0100</Value></BeginsWith><BeginsWith><FieldRef
Name="CustomerContentTypeId" /><Value
Type="Lookup">0x0100</Value></BeginsWith></And></Where><OrderBy
Override="TRUE" /></Query><ViewFields><FieldRef Name="CustomerTitle"
 /><FieldRef Name="Title" /><FieldRef Name="Product"
/></ViewFields><ProjectedFields><Field Name="CustomerTitle" Type="Lookup"
List="Customer" ShowField="Title" /><Field Name="CustomerContentTypeId"
Type="Lookup" List="Customer" ShowField="ContentTypeId"
/></ProjectedFields><Joins><Join Type="INNER" ListAlias="Customer"><!~DHList
Name: Customers~DH><Eq><FieldRef Name="Customer" RefType="ID" /><FieldRef
List="Customer" Name="ID" /></Eq></Join></Joins><RowLimit
Paged="TRUE">2147483647</RowLimit></View>
```

Best Practice: Turning Off Object Change Tracking

One best practice is to turn off object tracking if you just query the list and do not plan to add, delete, or update items in the list. This makes your queries perform better because LINQ doesn't have the overhead of trying to track changes to the SharePoint objects. The way to turn off object tracking is to set the `ObjectTrackingEnabled` property to `false` on your `DataContext` object.

If you do need to make changes to the list, you can open another `DataContext` object to the same list with object change tracking enabled. LINQ allows two `DataContext` objects to point at the same website and list, so you can have one `DataContext` object for querying and another for writing to the list.

WHEN TO USE CAML AND LINQ

You'll still have times when you should revert to using CAML directly. One scenario is when performance is paramount. LINQ makes CAML programming much easier, but no matter how LINQ is optimized, it adds some overhead to your code. Another example is if you have large amounts of adds, deletes, or updates that you need to perform. CAML provides better performance in this scenario.

TOOLS: LINQPAD

If you do not want to write your LINQ queries by hand, give the tool LINQPad a try. It makes writing your queries easier by giving you a graphical designer. You can find it at http://www.linqpad.net.

Managed Client OM

With SharePoint 2007, if you wanted to program on the client side, in reality you had only one API choice—the ASMX Web Services API. Although functional, the Web Services API was not the easiest API to program against, and although it was easy to program from managed code, programming against it from JavaScript or Silverlight was difficult at best. With the growth of client-side technologies, such as .NET CLR–based clients (for example, Windows Presentation Framework [WPF] or Silverlight); new technologies for programming in JavaScript, such as JSON; and the introduction of REST, moving from the Web Services API to a richer API was sorely needed in SharePoint. Welcome the managed client object model, which this chapter refers to as the Client Object Model (Client OM).

The Client OM is actually two object models:

➤ One works with .NET-based clients, such as Windows Forms, WPF, or Silverlight because these clients can handle the results in .NET objects

➤ The other works with ECMAScript/JavaScript clients to get back the JSON response.

Figure 5-22 shows the way the Client OM works.

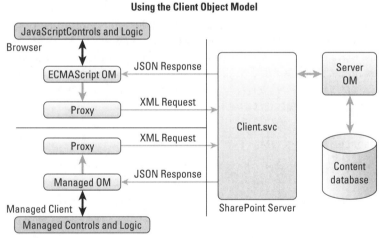

FIGURE 5-22

One principle of the Client OM is to minimize network chatter. So Fiddler is a key tool for helping you troubleshoot any issues because the Client OM batches its commands and sends them all at once to the server at your request. This minimizes the round-trips and network bandwidth used by the object model and makes your application perform better. In addition, you should write asynchronous code with callbacks so that your user interface doesn't block when users perform actions.

In terms of API support, the Client OM supports a subset of the server OM, so access to lists, libraries, views, content types, web parts, and users/groups is part of the OM. However, the OM does not provide coverage of all features, such as the taxonomy store or BI data. Figure 5-23 shows the major objects in the Client OM.

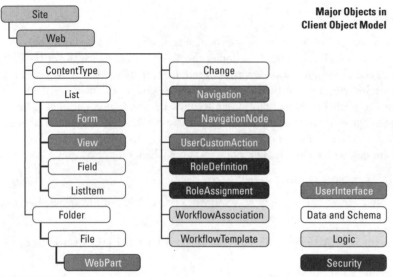

FIGURE 5-23

There is also a difference in the namespaces provided by the .NET and ECMAScript OMs. Because you extend the Ribbon using script, the ECMAScript OM has a Ribbon namespace, while the managed Client OM does not. Plus, there is a difference in naming conventions for the foundational part of the namespaces. For example, if you wanted to access a site, in the .NET API you would use the `Microsoft.SharePoint.Client.Site` object, but in ECMAScript you would use `SP.Site`. Table 5-13 shows the different namespaces for the two Client OMs.

TABLE 5-13: Supported Namespaces in Client OMs

.NET MANAGED	ECMASCRIPT
`Microsoft.SharePoint.Client.Application`	N/A
N/A	`SP.Application.UI`
N/A	`SP.Ribbon`
N/A	`SP.Ribbon.PageState`
N/A	`SP.Ribbon.TenantAdmin`
N/A	`SP.UI`
N/A	`SP.UI.ApplicationPages`
N/A	`SP.UI.ApplicationPages.Calendar`
`Microosft.SharePoint.Client.Utilities`	`SP.Utilities`

.NET MANAGED	ECMASCRIPT
`Microsoft.SharePoint.Client.WebParts`	`SP.WebParts`
`Microsoft.SharePoint.Client.Workflow`	`SP.Workflow`

To convert your understanding of server objects to the client, Table 5-14 shows how server objects would be named in the Client OMs.

TABLE 5-14: Equivalent Objects in Server and Client OMs

SERVER OM	.NET MANAGED	ECMASCRIPT
`Microsoft.SharePoint.SPContext`	`Microsoft.SharePoint.Client.ClientContext`	`SP.ClientContext`
`Microsoft.SharePoint.SPSite`	`Microsoft.SharePoint.Client.Site`	`SP.Site`
`Microsoft.SharePoint.SPWeb`	`Microsoft.SharePoint.Client.Web`	`SP.Web`
`Microsoft.SharePoint.SPList`	`Microsoft.SharePoint.Client.List`	`SP.List`
`Microsoft.SharePoint.SPListItem`	`Microsoft.SharePoint.Client.ListItem`	`SP.ListItem`
`Microsoft.SharePoint.SPField`	`Microsoft.SharePoint.Client.Field`	`SP.Field`

Which DLLs Implement the Client OM?

Before you dive into writing code with the Client OM and adding references in VS, you first need to understand where these DLLs are located and what some of the advantages of the DLLs, especially size. As with other SharePoint .NET DLLs, you can find the .NET DLLs for the Client OM located under `%Program Files%\Common Files\Microsoft Shared\Web Server Extensions\14\ISAPI`. There are two DLLs for the managed OM, `Microsoft.SharePoint.Client` and `Microsoft.SharePoint.Client.Runtime`. If you look at these DLLs in terms of size, combined they are under 1MB. Compare that with `Microsoft.SharePoint`, which weighs in at more than a hefty 15 MB.

Because the ECMAScript implementation is different from the .NET one and needs to live closer to the web-based code for SharePoint, this DLL is located in `%Program Files%\Common Files\Microsoft Shared\Web Server Extensions\14\TEMPLATE\LAYOUTS`. There, you can find four relevant JS files: `SP.js`, `SP.Core.js`, `SP.Ribbon.js`, and `SP.Runtime.js`. Of course, when you debug your code, you use the debug versions of these files, such as `SP.debug.js`, because the main versions are crunched to save on size and bandwidth. Also, you can set your SharePoint deployment to use the debug versions of these files automatically by changing the `web.config` file for your deployment located at `%inetpub%\wwwroot\wss\VirtualDirectories\80` and adding to the `system.web` section the following line `<deployment retail="false" />`. Again, these files are less than 1 MB.

Lastly, Silverlight is a little bit different in that it has its own specific implementation of the Client OM for Silverlight. You can find the Silverlight DLLs at `%Program Files%\Common Files\ Microsoft Shared\Web Server Extensions\14\TEMPLATE\LAYOUTS\ClientBin`. You can find two files, `Microsoft.SharePoint.Client.Silverlight` and `Microsoft.SharePoint.Client .Silverlight.Runtime`. Combined, the files also come under 1 MB in size.

Microsoft has redistributable versions of the .NET and Silverlight object models to install on your client machines. If you have Office 2010 installed on your machine, you don't need the redistributable version, but if you don't, you can retrieve the 32-bit and 64-bit versions of the redistributable object model at `www.microsoft.com/downloads/en/details.aspx?FamilyID=b4579045-b183-4ed4-bf61- dc2f0deabe47`. Given the long URL, it is probably easier to search for SharePoint Client Object Model redistributable.

Adding References Inside VS

Depending on the type of application you write, the way you reference the different Client OMs varies. With WPF or WinForms, you use the VS Add Reference user interface to add a reference to the DLLs discussed earlier. From there, you can use the proper statements to leverage the namespaces in your code. The same process is true for Silverlight. Figure 5-24 shows how to add a reference inside of Visual Studio for a regular managed code project.

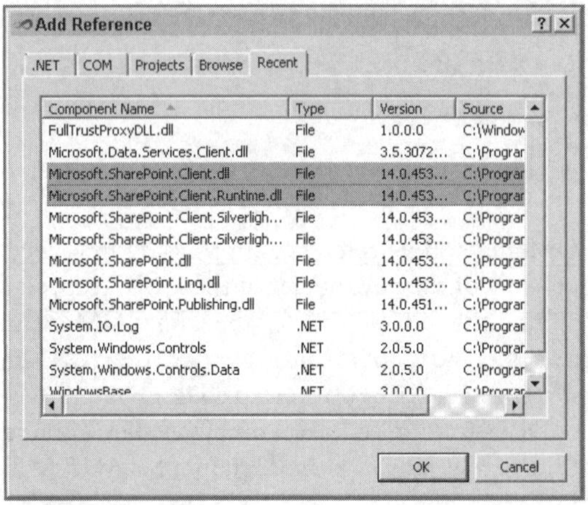

FIGURE 5-24

When it comes to referencing the ECMAScript OM, you use the `ScriptLink` control, which is part of the `Microsoft.SharePoint.WebControls` namespace. The following code snippet shows you how to do this:

```
<SharePoint:ScriptLink ID="ScriptLinkSPDebug" Name="sp.debug.js"
LoadAfterUI="true" Localizable="false" runat="server" />
```

Authentication

Before you write your first line of code, you need to understand the context that your code will run in. With the Client OM, by default, your code runs in the context of the currently logged-on user. Because many web applications support forms-based authentication, the Client OM supports this as well. You must provide the username and password for the Client OM to use and also set the authentication mode to forms-based authentication on your `ClientContext` object. The following code shows you how to set the Client OM to use forms-based authentication and set the correct properties to send a username and password:

```
clientContext.AuthenticationMode = ClientAuthenticationMode.FormsAuthentication;
FormsAuthenticationLoginInfo formsAuthInfo = new
FormsAuthenticationLoginInfo("User", "Password");
clientContext.FormsAuthenticationLoginInfo = formsAuthInfo;
```

Remember that SharePoint Online requires that you pass the custom authentication cookies with your Client OM requests so that you cannot use the forms authentication in the previous code to log on to SharePoint Online. Instead, you must use the methods described earlier in this chapter.

ClientContext Object

At the heart of all your code is the `ClientContext` object. This is the object that you instantiate first to tell SharePoint what site you want to connect to in order to perform your operations. With the .NET API, you must pass an absolute URL to the client context to open your site, but with the ECMAScript API, you can pass a relative or blank URL in your constructor and SharePoint finds the relative site or uses the current site as the site you want to open.

One quick note on `ClientContext` is that in managed code, it inherits from `IDisposable`, which you can tell by looking at the implementation. This means that you must properly dispose of your `ClientContext` objects by wrapping your code with `using` statements or by calling `Dispose` explicitly. If you don't dispose correctly, you may run into memory leaks and issues. One tool you should use to make sure you dispose of your objects correctly is `SPDisposeCheck`, which you can find at `http://archive.msdn.microsoft.com/SPDisposeCheck`.

When working with the constructor for the `ClientContext`, you can pass in either a string that is the URL to your site or a URI object that contains the URL to your site.

Table 5-15 shows the important methods and properties for the `ClientContext` class.

TABLE 5-15: Methods and Properties for the ClientContext Class

NAME	DESCRIPTION
Dispose	Call this method to dispose of your object after you finish using it.
ExecuteQuery	After loading all the operations for your site, such as queries, call this method to send the commands to the server.

continues

TABLE 5-15 *(continued)*

NAME	DESCRIPTION
executeQueryAsync	Available in the ECMAScript object model, this enables you to call a query and pass two delegates to call back to. One is for when the query succeeds, and the other is used when the query fails.
Load	Enables you to load your query using the method syntax of LINQ and fills the object you pass. You can also pass an object without a query to return just the object, such as Site.
LoadQuery	Use this to return a collection of objects as an IQueryable collection. This supports both the method and query syntax for LINQ.
AuthenticationMode	Gets or sets the authentication mode for your object. The values can be Default, FormsAuthentication, or Anonymous. FormsAuthentication is not applicable for SharePoint Online development.
FormsAuthenticationLoginInfo	Use this property to set the username and password for your forms authentication to authenticate against your site. This property is not applicable for SharePoint Online development.
RequestTimeout	Gets or sets the timeout for your requests.
Site	Gets the site collection associated with the ClientContext.
URL	Gets the URL of the site that the ClientContext is associated with.
Web	Gets the website that the ClientContext is associated with.

As demonstrated in the sample code throughout this section, you use the Load or LoadQuery method on the ClientContext object and then call the ExecuteQuery or executeQueryAsync method to execute your query. The rest of this section goes through the different programming tasks you perform with the Client OM to show you how to use it.

Retrieving Items from SharePoint

To retrieve your list items from SharePoint, you use the Load method to load the object into the Client OM. For example, if you want to load a Web object into the Client OM and then access the properties from it, you would use the following code:

```
ClientContext context = new Microsoft.SharePoint.Client.ClientContext(
        "http://intranet.contoso.com");
            Web site = context.Web;
```

```
context.Load(site);
context.ExecuteQuery();
MessageBox.Show("Title: " + site.Title + " Relative URL: " +
  site.ServerRelativeUrl);
context.Dispose();
```

If you try to use any of the other objects below the requested site, you get an error message saying that the collection is not initialized. For example, if you try to retrieve the lists in the site, an error occurs. With the Client OM, you need to be explicit about what you want to load. The following modified sample shows you how to load the list collection and then iterate over the objects in the collection:

```
//Load the List Collection
            ListCollection lists = context.Web.Lists;
            context.Load(lists);
            context.ExecuteQuery();

            MessageBox.Show(lists.Count.ToString());

            foreach (Microsoft.SharePoint.Client.List list in lists)
            {
                MessageBox.Show("List: " + list.Title);
            }
```

Properties Returned and Requesting Properties

By default, SharePoint returns a large set of properties and hydrates your objects with these properties. For performance reasons, you may not want to have it do that if you are using only a subset of the properties. Plus, certain properties are not returned by default, such as permission properties for your objects. As a best practice, you should request the properties that you need rather than let SharePoint retrieve all properties for you. This is similar to the best practice of not doing a SELECT * in SQL Server.

The way to request properties is in your load method. As part of this method, you need to request the properties you want to use in your LINQ code. The following example changes the previous site request code to retrieve only the Title and ServerRelativeURL properties, and for the lists only the Title property, because that is all that's used in the code:

```
ClientContext context = new Microsoft.SharePoint.Client.ClientContext(
    "http://intranet.contoso.com");

            Web site = context.Web;
            context.Load(site, s => s.Title, s => s.ServerRelativeUrl);
            ListCollection lists = site.Lists;
            context.Load(lists, ls => ls.Include(l => l.Title));

            context.ExecuteQuery();



            MessageBox.Show("Title: " + site.Title + " Relative URL: " +
```

```
        site.ServerRelativeUrl);


    MessageBox.Show(lists.Count.ToString());

    foreach (Microsoft.SharePoint.Client.List list in lists)
    {
        MessageBox.Show("List: " + list.Title);
    }


    context.Dispose();
```

Load Versus LoadQuery

You may wonder what the difference is between `Load` and `LoadQuery`.

➤ `Load` hydrates the objects in-context, so if you pass a `Web` object to your `Load` method, SharePoint fills in that object with the properties of your SharePoint web. With the `Load` method, the objects are tied to the client context, so they are destroyed and are eligible for garbage collection only when the client context is destroyed.

➤ `LoadQuery` does not fill in the objects in-context, so it returns an entirely new collection. This method is more complex, but it's also more flexible. In certain cases, it enables the server to be more effective in processing your queries. Plus, you can query the same object collection multiple times and have different result sets for each query. For example, you can have one query that returns all lists with a certain title, whereas another collection returns lists with a certain number of items. You can also destroy these objects out of context.

The `LoadQuery` method is similar to the `Load` method, except that it returns a new collection. The other key difference is that the properties for objects off the client context are not populated with `LoadQuery` after your `LoadQuery` call. You need to call `Load` method to populate these. The following code shows you a good example of this:

```
ClientContext context = new Microsoft.SharePoint.Client.ClientContext(
    "http://intranet.contoso.com");

        Web site = context.Web;
        ListCollection lists = site.Lists;


        IEnumerable<List> newLists = context.LoadQuery(lists.Include(
          list => list.Title));
        context.ExecuteQuery();

        foreach (List list in newLists)
        {
            MessageBox.Show("Title: " + list.Title);
        }

        //This will error out because lists is not populated
        MessageBox.Show(lists.Count.ToString());

        context.Dispose();
```

Nesting Includes in Your LoadQuery

In your `LoadQuery` calls, you can nest `Include` statements so that you can load fields from multiple objects in the hierarchy without making multiple calls to the server. The following code shows how to do this:

```
ClientContext context = new Microsoft.SharePoint.Client.ClientContext(
    "http://intranet.contoso.com");

            Web site = context.Web;
            ListCollection lists = site.Lists;


            IEnumerable<List> newLists = context.LoadQuery(lists.Include(
              list => list.Title, list => list.Fields.Include(Field
              => Field.Title)));
            context.ExecuteQuery();

            foreach (List list in newLists)
            {
                MessageBox.Show(" List Title: " + list.Title);
                foreach (Field field in list.Fields)
                {
                    MessageBox.Show("Field Title: " + field.Title);
                }
            }

            context.Dispose();
```

Using CAML to Query Lists

In the Client OM, you can use CAML to query the server as part of the `GetItems` method. As you see in the code that follows, you create a new `CamlQuery` object and pass the CAML query that you want to perform into the the `ViewXml` property. From there, you call the `GetItems` on your `ListCollection` object and pass in your `CamlQuery` object. You still need to call the `Load` and `ExecuteQuery` methods to have the client object model perform your query. Also, CAML does support row limits, so you can also pass a `<RowLimit>` element in your CAML query and page over your results. In the OM, on the `ListItemCollection` object, there is a property `ListItemCollectionPosition`. You need to set your `CAMLQuery` object's `ListItemCollectionPosition` to your own `ListItemCollectionPosition` object to keep track of your paging, and then you can position your query starting point before querying the list and iterate through the pages until there are no pages of content left, as shown here:

```
ClientContext context = new Microsoft.SharePoint.Client.ClientContext(
    "http://intranet.contoso.com");


List list = context.Web.Lists.GetByTitle("Announcements");

ListItemCollectionPosition itemPosition = null;
while (true)
{
    CamlQuery camlQuery = new CamlQuery();
    camlQuery.ListItemCollectionPosition = itemPosition;
```

```
        camlQuery.ViewXml = @"
            <View>
                <Query>
                    <Where>
                        <IsNotNull>
                            <FieldRef Name='Title' />
                        </IsNotNull>
                    </Where>
                </Query>
                <RowLimit>1000</RowLimit>
            </View>";
        ListItemCollection listItems = list.GetItems(camlQuery);
        context.Load(listItems);
        context.ExecuteQuery();

        itemPosition = listItems.ListItemCollectionPosition;

        foreach (ListItem listItem in listItems.ToList())
        {
            MessageBox.Show("Title: " + listItem["Title"]);
        }


        if (itemPosition == null)
        {
            break;
        }

        MessageBox.Show("Position: " + itemPosition.PagingInfo);

    }
```

Using LINQ with Queries

If you don't want to use CAML to query your lists, you can use LINQ. To do this:

1. Create your query and put it in a variable.

2. Use the `LoadQuery` method you pass your LINQ query.

3. Call the `ExecuteQuery` method to execute your query and iterate through the results.

```
ClientContext context = new Microsoft.SharePoint.Client.ClientContext(
    "http://intranet.contoso.com");

        var query = from list
                    in context.Web.Lists
                    where list.Title != null
                    select list;

        var result = context.LoadQuery(query);
        context.ExecuteQuery();

        foreach (List list in result)
        {
```

```
            MessageBox.Show("Title: " + list.Title);
    }

    context.Dispose();
```

Creating Lists, Fields, and Items

Using the Client OM, you can create lists and items. To do this, you need to use the `ListCreationInformation` object and set the properties, such as the title and the type, for your list. Your `ListCollection` object has an `Add` method that you can call and pass your `ListCreationInformation` object to in order to create your list.

To create a field, follow these steps:

1. Use the `Fields` collection for your list and define the XML in the `AddFieldAsXml` property. This property takes your XML, a Boolean value that specifies whether to add the field to the default view, and `AddFieldOptions`, such as adding the field to the default content type.

2. Create list items by creating a `ListItemCreationInformation` object, and passing it to the `AddItem` method, which returns a `ListItem` object representing your new item. Using this object, you can set the properties for your item. Make sure to call the `Update` method when you finish modifying your properties.

3. Make sure to call the `ExecuteQuery` method to have the Client OM send your changes back to the server.

```
ClientContext context = new Microsoft.SharePoint.Client.ClientContext
    ("http://intranet.contoso.com");
            Web site = context.Web;

            ListCreationInformation listCreationInfo = new
    ListCreationInformation();

            listCreationInfo.Title = "New List";
            listCreationInfo.TemplateType = (int)ListTemplateType.GenericList;
            List list = site.Lists.Add(listCreationInfo);

            Field newField = list.Fields.AddFieldAsXml(@"
                <Field Type='Text'
                    DisplayName='NewTextField'>
                </Field>", true, AddFieldOptions.AddToDefaultContentType);

            ListItemCreationInformation itemCreationinfo = new
    ListItemCreationInformation();
            ListItem item = list.AddItem(itemCreationinfo);
            item["Title"] = "My New Item";
            item["NewTextField"] = "My Text";
            item.Update();


            context.ExecuteQuery();

    context.Dispose();
```

Deleting Lists and Items

To delete lists and items, you can use the `DeleteObject` method. One caveat to remember is that when you delete items from a collection, you should materialize your collection into a `List<T>` object, using the `ToList` method, so you can iterate through the list and delete without errors.

```
ClientContext context = new Microsoft.SharePoint.Client.ClientContext(
    "http://intranet.contoso.com");


        List list = context.Web.Lists.GetByTitle("New List");

        CamlQuery camlQuery = new CamlQuery();

        camlQuery.ViewXml = @"
            <View>
                <Query>
                    <Where>
                        <IsNotNull>
                            <FieldRef Name='Title' />
                        </IsNotNull>
                    </Where>
                </Query>
            </View>";
        ListItemCollection listItems = list.GetItems(camlQuery);

        context.Load(listItems, items => items.Include(item => item["Title"]));
        context.ExecuteQuery();
        foreach (ListItem listItem in listItems.ToList())
        {
            listItem.DeleteObject();
        }

        context.ExecuteQuery();
        context.Dispose();
```

Working with Users and Groups

Another feature of the Client OM, beyond enabling you to work with lists, libraries, and items, is that it gives you the ability to work with users and groups. The Client OM includes the `GroupCollection`, `Group`, `UserCollection`, and `User` objects to make working with users and groups easier. Just as you iterate on lists and items, you can iterate on users and groups using these collections. The Client OM also has access to built-in groups such as the Owners, Members, and Visitors groups. You can access these from your context object using the `AssociatedOwnerGroup`, `AssociatedMemberGroup`, and `AssociatedVisitorGroup` properties, which return a `Group` object. Remember to hydrate these objects before trying to access properties or `User` collections on the objects.

To add a user to a group:

1. Use the `UserCreationInformation` object and set the properties, such as `Title`, `LoginName`, and others, on that object.

2. Call the `Add` method on your `UserCollection` object to add the user and `ExecuteQuery` to submit the changes.

Because this is similar to the steps used to create items, the sample code that follows shows you how to query users and groups but not create users:

```
ClientContext context = new Microsoft.SharePoint.Client.ClientContext(
    "http://intranet.contoso.com");

            GroupCollection groupCollection = context.Web.SiteGroups;

            context.Load(groupCollection,
                groups => groups.Include(
                    group => group.Users));

            context.ExecuteQuery();

            foreach (Group group in groupCollection)
            {

                UserCollection userCollection = group.Users;

                foreach (User user in userCollection)
                {
                    MessageBox.Show("User Name: " + user.Title + " Email: " +
                        user.Email + " Login: " + user.LoginName);

                }
            }
            //Iterate the owners group
            Group ownerGroup = context.Web.AssociatedOwnerGroup;

            context.Load(ownerGroup);
            context.Load(ownerGroup.Users);
            context.ExecuteQuery();
            foreach (User ownerUser in ownerGroup.Users)
            {
                MessageBox.Show("User Name: " + ownerUser.Title + " Email: " +
                    ownerUser.Email + " Login: " + ownerUser.LoginName);
            }

            context.Dispose();
```

Working Asynchronously

All the code shown so far is synchronous code running in a .NET client, such as a WPF, console, or Windows Forms application. You may not want to write synchronous code, even in your .NET clients, so your application can be more responsive to your users, rather than having them wait for operations to complete before continuing to use your application. ECMAScript and Silverlight are asynchronous by default, so you can program them separately, but for .NET clients, you need to do a little bit of work to make your code asynchronous. The main change is that you need to use the `BeginInvoke` method to execute your code and pass a delegate to that method, which .NET calls when your code is done executing asynchronously. Then, you can do other work while you are polling to see if the asynchronous call is complete. When it's complete, call the `EndInvoke` method to get back the result.

```
public delegate string AsyncDelegate();

        public string TestMethod()
        {
            string titleReturn = "";
            using (ClientContext context = new
             Microsoft.SharePoint.Client.ClientContext
             ("http://intranet.contoso.com"))
            {

                List list = context.Web.Lists.GetByTitle("Announcements");
                context.Load(list);
                context.ExecuteQuery();
                titleReturn = list.Title;
            }
            return titleReturn;
        }

        private void button1_Click(object sender, EventArgs e)
        {

            // Create the delegate.
            AsyncDelegate dlgt = new AsyncDelegate(TestMethod);

            // Initiate the asychronous call.
            IAsyncResult ar = dlgt.BeginInvoke(null, null);

            // Poll while simulating work.
            while (ar.IsCompleted == false)
            {
                //Do work
            }

            // Call EndInvoke to retrieve the results.
            string listTitle = dlgt.EndInvoke(ar);

            //Print out the title of the list
            MessageBox.Show(listTitle);
```

Working with ECMAScript

Using ECMAScript with the client object model is similar to using the .NET object model. The main differences are that you use server-relative URLs for your `ClientContext` constructor, and the `ECMAScript` object model does not accept LINQ syntax for retrieving items from SharePoint. Instead, you use string expressions to define your basic queries. Also, ECMAScript is always asynchronous, so you need to use delegates and create callback functions for the success and failure of your call into the Client OM. The final piece, as shown in the code that follows, is that you need to:

➤ Reference the `WebControls` namespace from the `Microsoft.SharePoint` assembly

➤ Reference the ECMAScript Client OM in `SP.js` or `SP.debug.js` using a `SharePoint:ScriptLink` control

➤ Put a `SharePoint:FormDigest` on your page for security reasons, if you want to write or update to the SharePoint database

```
<%@ Page Language="C#" %>
<%@ Register Tagprefix="SharePoint"
    Namespace="Microsoft.SharePoint.WebControls"
    Assembly="Microsoft.SharePoint, Version=14.0.0.0, Culture=neutral,
    PublicKeyToken=71e9bce111e9429c" %>

<!DOCTYPE html PUBLIC "-//W3C//DTD XHTML 1.0 Transitional//EN"
"http://www.w3.org/TR/xhtml1/DTD/xhtml1-transitional.dtd">
<html xmlns="http://www.w3.org/1999/xhtml">
  <head>
    <title>ECMAScript Client OM</title>
      <script type="text/javascript">


        function CallClientOM() {
            var context = new SP.ClientContext.get_current();
            this.website = context.get_web();
            this.listCollection = website.get_lists();

            context.load(this.listCollection, 'Include(Title, Id)');
            context.executeQueryAsync(Function.createDelegate(this,
             this.onQuerySucceeded),
             Function.createDelegate(this, this.onQueryFailed));
        }


        function onQuerySucceeded(sender, args) {

        var listInfo = '';

        var listEnumerator = listCollection.getEnumerator();

        while (listEnumerator.moveNext())
        {
            var list = listEnumerator.get_current();
            listInfo += 'List Title: ' + list.get_title() + ' ID: ' +
             list.get_id() + '\n';
        }
    alert(listInfo);

        }

        function onQueryFailed(sender, args) {
            alert('request failed ' + args.get_message() + '\n' +
             args.get_stackTrace());
        }

    </script>
  </head>
  <body>
    <form id="form1" runat="server">
```

```
        <SharePoint:ScriptLink ID="ScriptLink1" Name="sp.debug.js" LoadAfterUI="true"
            Localizable="false" runat="server" />

    <a href="#" onclick="CallClientOM()">Click here to Execute</a>

        <SharePoint:FormDigest runat="server" />
      </form>
    </body>
</html>
```

code snippet ClientOM.aspx

Working in Silverlight

You must use the right Client OM DLLs. Silverlight has special DLLs in the `%Program Files%\`
`Common Files\Microsoft Shared\Web Server Extensions\14\TEMPLATE\LAYOUTS\ClientBin`
directory for the core OM and the run time.

To deploy your Silverlight application, the application needs to run in a trusted area of SharePoint,
which could be in a SharePoint library or in the `ClientBin` directory. The easiest way to get your
code into the `ClientBin` directory is to make the output of your project go to this directory. For
deploying to SharePoint document libraries, you could manually upload your XAP file to SharePoint
and point the Silverlight web part at your manually uploaded XAP. Another way is to use a Sandbox
Solution, which you learn about later in this chapter, to create a feature that copies the file to your
SharePoint site using a `Module` with a `File` reference in your `Elements` manifest.

Watch out for the caching of your Silverlight application while you develop it. Update the
`AssemblyVersion` and `FileVersion` in your `AssemblyInfo` file in VS to ensure that an old version
is not loaded. You may also have to clear your browser cache. Another recommendation is to change
something in the UI so you can recognize visually that your application is the latest version.

If you use anonymous access and Silverlight, you must modify the `SPClientCallableSettings`
`.AnonymousRestrictedTypes` property. For example, if you attempt to retrieve list items as an
anonymous user, you get an error message stating that the `GetItems` method has been disabled by
the administrator. To enable this method or other methods, you can use the following PowerShell
command.

```
$webapp = Get-SPWebApplication -Identity "http://sharepointsite"
$webapp.ClientCallableSettings.AnonymousRestrictedTypes.Remove
    ([Microsoft.SharePoint.SPList], "GetItems")
$webapp.Update()
```

Also, if you work across domains, you need to understand how to create cross-domain policies
using a `ClientAccessPolicy.XML` file that you host at the root of your website. If you work
in the same domain, you do not need to write this policy file, but if you go across domains
(for example, if your Silverlight application runs in your domain but calls a service in another
domain) you must use the `ClientAccessPolicy.XML` file to allow those calls. Figure 5-25 shows
the Silverlight application in action.

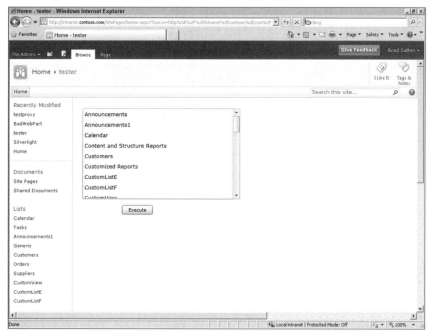

FIGURE 5-25

```csharp
using SP = Microsoft.SharePoint.Client;

namespace SPSilverlight
{
    public partial class MainPage : UserControl
    {

        IEnumerable<SP.List> listItems = null;
        public MainPage()
        {
            InitializeComponent();
        }

        private void getItemsSucceeded(object sender,
         Microsoft.SharePoint.Client.ClientRequestSucceededEventArgs e)
        {
            Dispatcher.BeginInvoke(() =>
            {
                //Code to display items
                //Databind the List of Lists to the listbox

                listBox1.ItemsSource = listItems;
                listBox1.DisplayMemberPath = "Title";
            });
```

```csharp
    }

    private void getItemsRequestFailed(object sender,
     Microsoft.SharePoint.Client.ClientRequestFailedEventArgs e)
    {
        Dispatcher.BeginInvoke(() =>
        {
            MessageBox.Show("Error:  " + e.ErrorCode + " " + e.ErrorDetails + "
             " + e.Message + " " + e.StackTrace.ToString());
        });
    }

    private void button1_Click(object sender, RoutedEventArgs e)
    {

        ClientContext context = null;

        if (App.Current.IsRunningOutOfBrowser)
        {
            context = new ClientContext(
                "http://intranet.contoso.com");
        }
        else
        {
            context = ClientContext.Current;
        }

        var query = from listCollection
in context.Web.Lists
                    where listCollection.Title != null
                    select listCollection;

        listItems = context.LoadQuery(query);


            ClientRequestSucceededEventHandler success = new
             ClientRequestSucceededEventHandler(getItemsSucceeded);
            ClientRequestFailedEventHandler failure = new
             ClientRequestFailedEventHandler(getItemsRequestFailed);
            context.ExecuteQueryAsync(success, failure);


        }

    }
}
```

code snippet MainPage.xaml.cs

Programming Using REST

With SharePoint 2010, you can program against SharePoint and Excel Services using
Representational State Transfer (REST). This section covers the core SharePoint REST Services.

SharePoint REST services are implemented using the WCF Data Services, formerly known as the
ADO.NET Data Services, and formerly known as Astoria. The easiest way to think about REST

is that it provides URL-accessible functionality, so you can query, create, and delete lists and items using just the standard HTTP protocol.

Here are a couple of best practices before getting started with REST in SharePoint 2010:

➤ REST is implemented in your _vti_bin directory by accessing `http://yourserver/_vti_bin/ListData.svc`, so if you connect to that URL and get a 404 error, you do not have the WCF Data Services technologies installed.

➤ If you connect to your REST services for SharePoint from Internet Explorer (IE), turn off Feed Reading View in IE so that you get the raw XML returned from SharePoint. You can find this under Tools ⇨ Internet Options ⇨ Content ⇨ Feeds and Web Slices.

The easiest way to start with REST in SharePoint is to look at what is returned when you connect to `http://yourserver/yoursite/_vti_bin/ListData.svc`, as shown in Figure 5-26. You see the XML returned for all your lists in your site.

FIGURE 5-26

REST offers two ways to return your data in SharePoint:

➤ Using ATOM, an XML format and a recognized standard.

➤ Using JavaScript Object Notation (JSON), which returns your data using JSON markup so that you can parse that data using JavaScript objects.

JSON is especially good if you want to turn the returned data into JavaScript objects, but it can be useful in other situations as well. You can specify the type of data you want returned by using the `Content-Type` header in your request. The tools that work with REST, such as Visual Studio, use ATOM, not JSON, so you need to request JSON specifically if you want your results in that format.

Because REST uses a standard URL-addressable format and standard HTTP methods, such as `GET`, `POST`, `PUT`, and `DELETE`, you get a predictable way to retrieve or write items in your SharePoint deployment. Table 5-16 lists some examples of URL addresses.

TABLE 5-16: Methods and Properties for the ClientContext Class

TYPE	EXAMPLE
List of lists	`../_vti_bin/listdata.svc`
List	`listdata.svc/Listname`
Item	`listdata.svc/Listname(ItemID)`
Single column	`listdata.svc/Listname(ItemID)/Column`
Lookup traversal	`listdata.svc/Listname(ItemID)/LookupColumn`
Raw value access (no markup)	`listdata.svc/Listname(ItemID)/Column/$value`
Sorting	`listdata.svc/Listname?$orderby=Column`
Filtering	`listdata.svc/Listname?$filter=Title eq 'Value'`
Projection	`listdata.svc/Listname?$select=Title,Created`
Paging	`listdata.svc/Listname?$top=10&$skip=30`
Inline expansion (lookups)	`listdata.svc/Listname?$expand=Item`

Using REST in Visual Studio

Because Visual Studio has built-in support for using WCF Data Services, programming with REST starts with adding a service reference in your code. Follow these steps to use REST in Visual Studio:

1. Add the service reference. In this reference, point to your `ListData.svc` URL in `_vti_bin`.

2. Create new proxy classes by running in a command prompt `DataSvcUtil.exe /uri:"http://URL/_vti_bin/ListData.svc" /out:Reference.cs`. This creates a C# file that you use to replace the existing `Reference.cs` in your project. You can find `Reference.cs` in the file directory for your project, not in the user interface, unless you turn on Show All Files in Solution Explorer.

3. You should see your lists in the Data Sources window inside of Visual Studio, as shown in Figure 5-27. If you do not see your datasource in the window, right-click your service reference and select Update Service Reference.

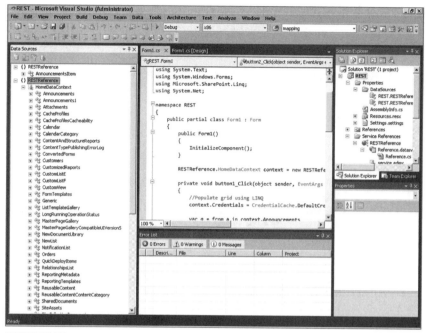

FIGURE 5-27

4. Add a new `Object` datasource to your project, so you can work with a subset of the lists, such as binding the datasource to a data grid in your code. You can do this by creating a new `Object` datasource and selecting the lists you are interested in, as shown in Figure 5-28.

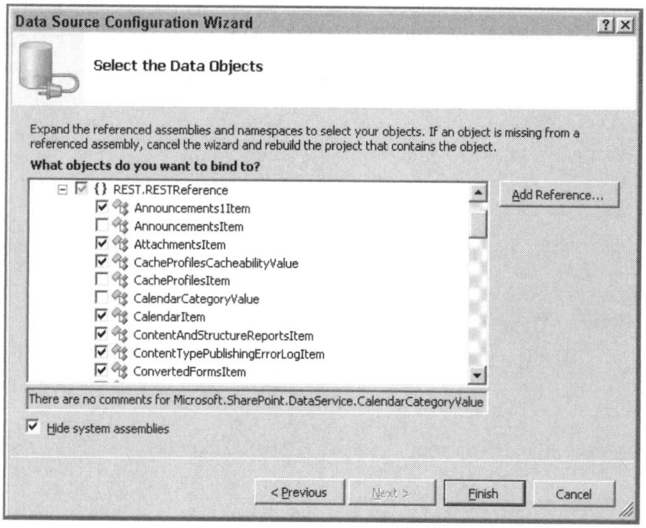

FIGURE 5-28

5. Drag and drop your datasource onto your form. Visual Studio creates and binds a grid to your datasource. You can also use LINQ to program against your REST datasource. Figure 5-29 shows a databound grid against a SharePoint REST datasource.

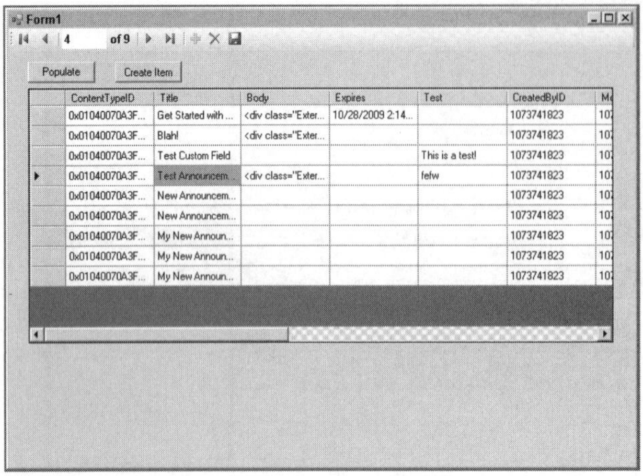

FIGURE 5-29

Because the code for programming using REST is similar to programming using the Client OM, a quick example of adding an item to your SharePoint list using REST follows. Notice that it uses a call to generate a context for the rest of your calls to leverage so that you can batch commands and send them to server when you need to.

For adding, you call the specific `AddTo` method for your list, such as `AddToAnnouncements`. For updating and deleting, you use the `UpdateObject` and `DeleteObject` methods and pass in the object you want to delete, which is derived from your item type, such as `AnnouncementItem`.

```
RESTReference.HomeDataContext context = new RESTReference.HomeDataContext(
    new Uri("http://intranet.contoso.com/_vti_bin/listdata.svc"));

        private void button1_Click(object sender, EventArgs e)
        {
            //Populate grid using LINQ
            context.Credentials = CredentialCache.DefaultCredentials;

            var q = from a in context.Announcements
                    select a;

            this.announcementsItemBindingSource.DataSource = q;
        }

        private void button2_Click(object sender, EventArgs e)
        {
            //Add a new Announcement
            RESTReference.AnnouncementsItem newAnnounce = new
             RESTReference.AnnouncementsItem();
```

```
        newAnnounce.Title = "My New Announcement! " + DateTime.Now.ToString();

        context.AddToAnnouncements(newAnnounce);
        context.SaveChanges();
    }
```

> **EXTERNAL LIST SUPPORT AND REST**
>
> *Unfortunately, external lists are not supported with the WCF Data Services and REST. If you look at your lists using REST, you find that your external lists do not appear in your list results. This is a deficiency that you must work around by using other methods, such as the Client OM, to access external lists.*

jQuery and SharePoint

You may also be wondering about jQuery support in SharePoint because REST supports putting out JSON objects that you can load with jQuery, as do other parts of SharePoint. Although SharePoint does not include a jQuery library, you can easily link to jQuery in your SharePoint solutions. This linking does require connectivity to the Internet. Microsoft has made jQuery and a number of other libraries available via the Microsoft Ajax Content Delivery Network. To get the jQuery library from the CDN, use the following statement in your code:

```
<script src="http://ajax.microsoft.com/ajax/jquery/jquery-1.5.2.js"
type="text/javascript"></script>
```

Deploying Your jQuery Applications

One of the big complaints about script-based applications is that deployment and maintenance is difficult. This is where the power of SharePoint comes into play. You can create a central script library in SharePoint and use the native functionality of SharePoint to maintain your scripts, such as versioning and meta data. Because SharePoint is URL accessible, you can then link to your script using the URL.

If you would rather store your scripts in the file system, you can use solution packages to deploy your scripts. Where you store your scripts is up to you, but the SharePoint option is most likely easier.

When it comes to leveraging your script, there are a number of options to link to your script. You could add the script link to your Master Page definition so that you know jQuery is referenced on every page, but that presents issues if you have lots of pages that don't use jQuery. You pay the cost of loading the script without using the script.

jQuery Basics

If you have never used jQuery before, you are missing out. It is a library that makes programming in JavaScript a lot easier, especially when it comes to manipulating your HTML objects. When executing your jQuery methods, you can use `JQuery()` or the shorthand `$()`. Most people use the shorthand `$()` in their code.

To interact with elements, place the element in parentheses. For example, if you want to append some HTML to an element, you would use the ID of the element with the jQuery `Append` function, such as `$('#elementid').append('HTML to Append');`.

Table 5-17 lists some other examples of jQuery functions. This is not the exhaustive list of jQuery functionality, so pick up a resource on jQuery to learn more.

TABLE 5-17: Basic jQuery Methods

EXAMPLE	DESCRIPTION
`$('#elementID')`	Accesses any element.
`$('#elementID').append('value');`	Appends text to the element.
`$('#elementID').html();`	Gets or retrieves the HTML within an element.
`$('#elementID').val();`	Gets the value of inputs.
`$('#elementID').hide();`	Hides the element.
`$('#elementID').show();`	Shows the element.
`var divs = $('div');`	Returns all instances of element specified, in this case all `divs`.
`$('#elementID').addClass('className');`	Adds a CSS class to the element.
`$('#elementID').removeClass('className');`	Removes the specified class.
`$('#elementID').attr('attribute');`	Retrieves the attribute.
`$('table[class="className"]').each( function () { $('#' + this.id).show(); } );`	Performs an action on multiple elements of the same class.

jQueryUI

After you start using jQuery, you can expand your repertoire of jQuery libraries. One key library to learn more about is jQueryUI, which adds visual elements that you can program using jQuery, such as accordions, datepickers, dialogs, and progress bars. It also includes interactions such as drag and drop and sorting.

Bringing It All Together

Rather than talk about programming with jQuery, this section presents an example. The first example combines jQuery and jQueryUI to add an accordion visual element that turns SharePoint announcements into a nicer visual representation. Notice from this example that you can leverage the SharePoint Client OM with jQuery so all your knowledge of the Client OM moves easily into your jQuery solutions. Figure 5-30 shows the final solution hosted in SharePoint.

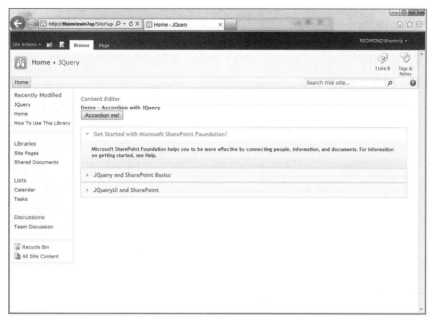

FIGURE 5-30

The following listing contains the sample code for the application. jQueryUI does most of the heavy lifting so that you do not need to write a lot of code. The key point is to look at how the scripts are linked into the application via the `<script>` tags. Rather than going to the Internet for the scripts, the application pulls the script from a central script library under the `SiteAssets` folder.

```
<!~DH Load JQuery ~DH>
<script src= "/SiteAssets/jquery/jquery-1.5.2.js" type= "text/javascript"></script>

<!~DH Load JQuery UI ~DH>

<link type="text/css" href="/SiteAssets/jQueryUI/css/ui-lightness/
jquery-ui-1.8.11.custom.css" rel="stylesheet" />
<script type="text/javascript" src="/SiteAssets/jQueryUI/js/
jquery-1.5.1.min.jss"></script>/>
<script type="text/javascript" src="/SiteAssets/jQueryUI/js/
jquery-ui-1.8.11.custom.min.js"></script>/>

    <B>Demo - Accordion with JQuery</B>
            <div class="demoControls">
                <button id="btnDemo2" type="button">Accordion me!</button>
            </div>
            <div id="accordion">
            </div>


<script type="text/javascript">
```

```javascript
var allDocs;

$('#btnDemo2').click(function () {

    var ctx = new SP.ClientContext.get_current();

    var targetList = ctx.get_web().get_lists().getByTitle('Announcements');

    var query = SP.CamlQuery.createAllItemsQuery();

    allDocs = targetList.getItems(query);

    ctx.load(allDocs);

    ctx.executeQueryAsync(Function.createDelegate(this, getAllItemsSuccess),

    Function.createDelegate(this, getAllItemsFailure));

});


function getAllItemsSuccess(sender, args) {

    var listEnumerator = allDocs.getEnumerator();

    while (listEnumerator.moveNext()) {

        $('#accordion').append('<div><h3><a href="#">' +
          listEnumerator.get_current().get_item("Title")
          + '</a></h3><div>' + listEnumerator.get_current().
          get_item("Body") + '</div></div>');


    }


    accordionContent();


}

function accordionContent() {

    $("#accordion").accordion({ header: "h3" });

}


function getAllItemsFailure(sender, args) {

    alert('Failed to get list items. \nError: ' + args.get_message() +
```

```
                     '\nStackTrace: ' + args.get_stackTrace());

    }

</script>
```

What About CSS3 and HTML5?

With all the excitement around CSS3 and HTML5, you may wonder how either one plays in the SharePoint environment. Because both are browser-dependent, a lot of the answer depends on your browser, especially for HTML5. SharePoint 2010 does not leverage HTML5, but if you create content using HTML5 and place it in a SharePoint site, as long as you browse that content with an HTML5-compatible browser, your content should work seamlessly. To see some CSS3 working inside of SharePoint, Figure 5-31 shows a Polaroid sample that takes images from a SharePoint picture library and turns them into dragable Polaroid images. The image URLs are retrieved using the Client OM. Manipulating the images leverages CSS3 and jQuery.

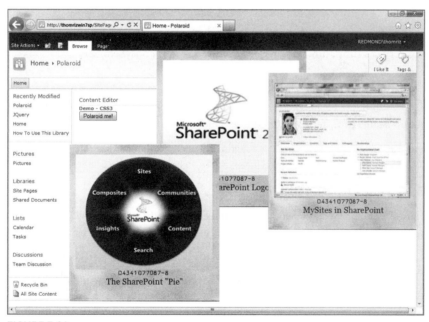

FIGURE 5-31

SANDBOXED SOLUTIONS

Often developers who want to build solutions for SharePoint can't because they require access to the SharePoint server directly, and their solutions must be deployed as full-trust solutions, which could affect the stability of the server if there are bugs in the code. For these reasons, IT administrators may not allow developers to deploy their solutions against SharePoint 2007. With Sandboxed

Solutions in SharePoint 2010, the server administrator can allow site administrators to deploy solutions while still maintaining the integrity of the server. Sandboxed Solutions are self-regulating because there are quotas for resource usage, and the server shuts down any solutions that exceed their quota.

Types of Solutions You Can Build

With Sandboxed Solutions, you can build a subset of the solutions you can build in SharePoint. Solutions that require extensive privileges are not allowed in the sandbox because of its limited nature. The following list gives you the types of solutions you can build with Sandboxed Solutions.

➤ Content types

➤ Site columns

➤ Custom actions

➤ Declarative workflows

➤ Event receivers

➤ Feature receivers

➤ InfoPath forms services (not admin-approved, that is, without code-behind)

➤ JavaScript, Ajax, jQuery, REST, or Silverlight applications

➤ List definitions

➤ Site pages (but no application pages with code-behind)

➤ Web parts (but not visual web parts without the VS Power Tools installed)

Executing Code in the Sandbox

Before a Sandbox Solution can run, a site administrator must upload the solution and activate it in the site. When you upload a Sandbox Solution, you upload it to the Solution gallery.

The Solution gallery contains all your Sandboxed Solutions and displays the resource quota that your solutions are taking both for the current day and averaged over the past 14 days. The Solution gallery is located in `_catalogs/solutions`.

The Sandboxed Solutions architecture provides three main components to use when executing your solution. Please note that this is for on-premises SharePoint deployments since SharePoint Online does not provide access to this functionality or architecture.

➤ **User Code Service (`SPUCHostService.exe`):** This service decides whether the server where this service is running will participate in Sandboxed Solutions. SharePoint has a modular architecture for Sandboxed Solutions where you can run them on your WFEs or dedicate separate servers for executing your sandbox code. If the User Code Service runs on a machine, Sandboxed Solutions can run on that machine. When you troubleshoot your Sandboxed Solutions, the first thing to check is that this service runs on a SharePoint server in your farm.

From an architectural standpoint, SharePoint enables you to pin the execution of the Sandbox Solution to the server that received the web request. This means that the User Code Service must run on all your WFEs in your farm. Although this provides for easy administration, because you don't need to create separate servers for Sandboxed Solutions or remember which servers the service runs on, it does limit your scalability because the WFEs must process other web requests while running the Sandboxed Solutions.Your other option is to run requests by solution affinity. You set up application servers in your SharePoint farm that run the User Code Service and are not processing web requests. SharePoint routes Sandboxed Solutions to these servers rather than have the solution run on your WFE.

➤ **Sandbox Worker Process (`SPUCWorkerProcess.exe`):** This is the process in which your code executes. As you can tell, it is not part of `w3wp.exe`, which is one reason you don't need to reset your entire site when you deploy a Sandbox Solution. If debugging does not work for your sandbox, you can always manually attach the debugger to this process, but be forewarned that SharePoint may kill your debugging session in the middle if you take too long or exceed one of the quotas set on the sandbox.

➤ **Sandbox Worker Proxy (`SPUCWorkerProcessProxy.exe`):** Given that SharePoint has the service application architecture, this proxy enables Sandboxed Solutions to tie into that infrastructure.

Subset Object Model

The Sandbox implements only a subset of the `Microsoft.SharePoint` namespace. Sandboxed Solutions enable you to use full trust proxies to access other APIs or capabilities, for example, accessing network resources. However, out-of-the-box (OOB) the following capabilities from the `Microsoft.SharePoint` namespace are supported:

➤ `Microsoft.SharePoint`, except

    ➤ `SPSite` constructor

    ➤ `SPSecurity` object

    ➤ `SPWorkItem` and `SPWorkItemCollection` objects

    ➤ `SPAlertCollection.Add` method

    ➤ `SPAlertTemplateCollection.Add` method

    ➤ `SPUserSolution` and `SPUserSolutionCollection` objects

    ➤ `SPTransformUtilities`

➤ `Microsoft.SharePoint.Navigation`

➤ `Microsoft.SharePoint.Utilities`, except

    ➤ `SPUtility.SendEmail` method

    ➤ `SPUtility.GetNTFullNameandEmailFromLogin` method

➤ `Microsoft.SharePoint.Workflow`

➤ `Microsoft.SharePoint.WebPartPages`, except

    ➤ `SPWebPartManager` object

    ➤ `SPWebPartConnection` object

    ➤ `WebPartZone` object

    ➤ `WebPartPage` object

    ➤ `ToolPane` object

    ➤ `ToolPart` object

What About Accessing External Data?

One question people commonly ask is, "If I can't access local resources (such as the hard drive on the server or network resources except for SharePoint), how can I access external data (such as a database, Twitter, or some other external datasource)?" Well, you can use external lists and BCS in SharePoint to access external data because Sandboxed Solutions can access external lists. Of course, you need to have permissions to set up BCS and external lists, but if there are already BCS solutions set up with access to the external datasources that you need, you can use the external lists in your Sandboxed Solutions to read and write quickly to that external data.

What About iframes?

Sandboxed Solutions do support iframes, so you can add a literal control to your nonvisual web part and make the text the iframe that you want to display in the control. This enables you to connect to many solutions on the Internet, such as Silverlight or web pages that expose information that you want to display in your environment. Using Sandboxed Solutions for this, rather than content editor web parts, makes the control reusable and easier to distribute.

Visual Studio Support

VS 2010 supports Sandboxed Solutions. When you create a new SharePoint project, for project types that support Sandboxed Solutions, VS gives you the option to create and deploy your solution as a Sandbox Solution. In addition, VS limits the API set in IntelliSense to only those APIs that work for Sandboxed Solutions. VS does not do a compile-time check to determine if you are using restricted APIs because you program against the full SharePoint namespace, and it's only at run time that your code is limited. So, if you ignore IntelliSense and write to APIs not supported in the sandbox, you don't get a compile-time error but instead get a run-time error. One tip to avoid this is to reference the `Microsoft.SharePoint.dll` under the `Assemblies` folder, under the `UserCode` folder in the SharePoint hive. That limits the APIs you can use. You *must* remember to change the reference back to the full `Microsoft.SharePoint.dll` before deployment.

Visual Studio 2010 SharePoint Power Tools

One of the deficiencies of Visual Studio 2010 OOB is that it doesn't enable you to use the visual design capabilities to create web parts in the sandbox. Instead, you must hand code all the components of your user interface. The Visual Studio 2010 SharePoint Power Tools add this capability and provide pre-compilation support so that you can view any errors for types or members not allowed in a SharePoint sandbox environment. Figure 5-32 shows how to create a sandboxed visual web part in Visual Studio.

FIGURE 5-32

BUILDING DECLARATIVE WORKFLOWS

Another option for SharePoint Online development is building declarative workflows in SharePoint Designer. SharePoint Designer enables you to build workflows that you can associate with a list, a site, or a content type. In addition, you can have globally-reusable workflows that allow you to share the workflow to many lists or content types.

Beyond using SharePoint Designer to build your workflow, you can also use Visio to prototype your workflow. Then import that prototype into SharePoint Designer to add your business logic to implement the workflow. Because SharePoint Online supports Visio Services, the Visio representation of the workflow is used on the status page to visualize where the workflow is in process. Figure 5-33 shows prototyping a workflow in Visio and Figure 5-34 shows the Visio visualization status page.

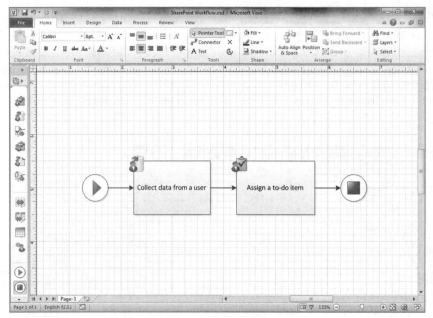

FIGURE 5-33

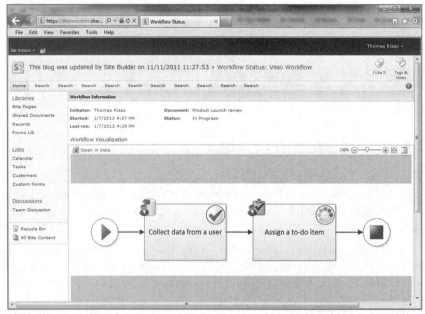

FIGURE 5-34

SharePoint Designer Workflow Designer

Using the SharePoint Designer workflow designer is straightforward. SharePoint Designer provides a graphical user interface designer to build your workflow. This designer enables you to create your steps in your workflow, set the conditions and actions for the workflow, and pass parameters and initialization variables to your workflow.

The SharePoint Designer workflow designer also enables you to have parallel blocks and embedded steps in your workflow. The only deficiency you will find with the workflow designer is that you cannot have looping inside of your workflow.

In addition, the SharePoint Designer workflow designer enables you to use InfoPath to customize your workflow forms. This means you can customize your input parameters and the forms that appear for your workflow. Figure 5-35 shows the SPD workflow designer.

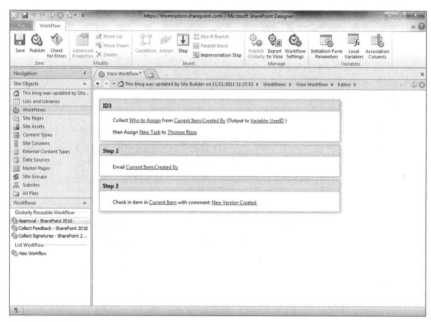

FIGURE 5-35

Building Workflow Actions in the Sandbox

Although the SharePoint Designer workflow designer comes with a large set of workflow actions OOB, such as sending e-mails, checking in and out documents, setting permissions, looking up users, and other actions, you may still want to extend the designer with your own custom workflow activities that you implement as a Sandbox Solution. Your workflow activities are limited to what Sandboxed Solutions can do, so you cannot access networking, disk, or any other highly elevated tasks.

When creating sandbox workflow actions, you must create a class with a method that accepts a `SPUserCodeWorkflowContext` as the first parameter. This method must return back a `Hashtable` object. This hashtable contains the return parameters that you want the workflow to receive from your action. One parameter should be success or failure, and the other parameters can be customized to your business scenario. If you add custom parameters, you need to define these in the `WorkflowActions` element of your feature's `elements.xml` file. The following XML shows how to pass in the workflow context and return back a success or failure string:

```xml
<Parameters>
  <Parameter Name="__Context"
             Type="Microsoft.SharePoint.WorkflowActions.WorkflowContext,
                 Microsoft.SharePoint.WorkflowActions"
             Direction="In"
             DesignerType="Hide"/>
  <Parameter Name="Result"
             Type="System.String, mscorlib"
             Direction="Out"
             DesignerType="ParameterNames"
             Description="Success or failure result"/>
</Parameters>
```

BUILDING INFOPATH FORMS

SharePoint Online supports InfoPath forms so that you can design the forms that run either in the InfoPath client, in the web browser, or in both. You can use InfoPath forms in SharePoint Online as a standalone form or in a web part using the InfoPath Forms web part. A key change from previous versions of SharePoint is that you can customize the OOB list forms directly in InfoPath.

> *Describing all the capabilities of InfoPath Forms development is beyond the scope of this book, but you should review the InfoPath Forms chapter in the Professional SharePoint 2010 Development Wrox book for more information.*

InfoPath does include a compatibility checker, so you can check your InfoPath forms before you convert them to web-based forms. This checks to make sure that you do not use any capabilities that do not translate to the web-based version of InfoPath.

To give you a taste of what InfoPath can do, Figure 5-36 shows an InfoPath form running in SharePoint Online and Figure 5-37 shows an InfoPath form running as a web part in SharePoint Online.

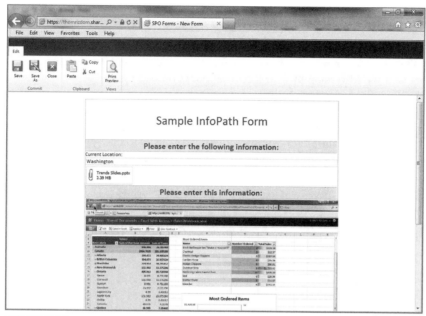

FIGURE 5-36

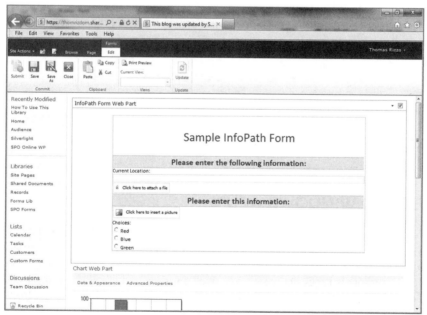

FIGURE 5-37

USING ACCESS SERVICES

Another option for application development is using Access and Access Services. If you are already a proficient Access database developer, you can save your Access applications to SharePoint and, similar to InfoPath, have a web-based version of your Access application. Access includes a compatibility checker to see which pieces of your application can convert to Access Services, and which pieces need to continue to run inside of the Access client. Most times, the issues you run into are VBA macros and reporting because Access Services does not support VBA, and SharePoint Online has not enabled Access Services reporting. Figure 5-38 shows a sample Access Services application running in SharePoint Online.

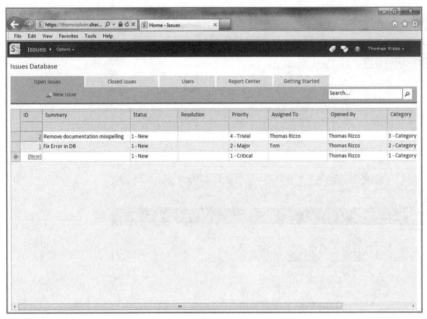

FIGURE 5-38

CONNECTING BCS TO WINDOWS AZURE

One of the newest features to Office 365, and one that was added after the initial launch of the services, was the ability to connect BCS to external datasources using WCF endpoints. These endpoints can exist in Windows Azure or other locations. The endpoints do not need to connect solely to databases, but can also connect to other types of data such as Web Services and REST datasources. This section shows you the steps necessary to leverage this capability in SharePoint Online.

CREATING THE WCF SERVICE

The first step is to create your WCF service for BCS to connect to. Your endpoint needs to implement methods for SharePoint to call in order to, at a minimum, to read from your datasource, but you can also provide capabilities to write to your datasource.

To create the WCF service, follow these steps:

1. Create a new WCF Service Web Role in Azure using Visual Studio. Figure 5-39 shows this project type.

2. After you create your project, you need to connect to your datasource. Although this example connects to a SQL Azure datasource, you can connect to any datasource that you want. To connect to SQL Azure, you need to add a new datasource to the project and use the Entity Data Model Wizard to configure your datasource, as shown in Figure 5-40.

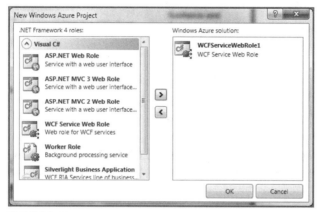

FIGURE 5-39

FIGURE 5-40

Make sure that you set your Build Action to Entity Deploy for your Entity Model and the Copy to Output Directory to Copy Always so that it is always deployed to Azure with your project.

3. Write code that represents your dataset that you want returned. To do this, add a new class to your service project that will be a customer record. The following code implements the customer record class called `SharePointBCSRecord`:

```
using System;
using System.Collections.Generic;
using System.Linq;
using System.Web;

namespace WCFServiceWebRole1
{
    public class SharePointBCSRecord
    {
        public string CustomerID { get; set; }
        public string CompanyName { get; set; }
        public string ContactName { get; set; }
        public string City { get; set; }


    }
}
```

4. Add code to your WCF service that will read a single item and also read all items so that the BCS service can call these methods to return both all items and a single item by its unique identifier. The following code implements this functionality:

```
using System;
using System.Collections.Generic;
using System.Linq;
using System.Runtime.Serialization;
using System.ServiceModel;
using System.ServiceModel.Web;
using System.Text;


namespace WCFServiceWebRole1
{


    public class Service1 : IService1
    {

        public SharePointBCSRecord[] GetCustomers()
        {
            using (CustomerEntities customerRecords = new CustomerEntities())
            {
                var customerRecordItems = (from c
                in customerRecords.Customers
                select c);

                SharePointBCSRecord[] customerArray =
                new SharePointBCSRecord[customerRecordItems.Count()];

                int i = 0;

                foreach (Customer item in customerRecordItems)
```

```
                    {
                        customerArray[i] = new SharePointBCSRecord();
                        customerArray[i].CustomerID = item.CustomerID;
                        customerArray[i].CompanyName = item.CompanyName;
                        customerArray[i].City = item.City;
                        customerArray[i].ContactName = item.ContactName;

                        i++;
                    }

                    return customerArray;
                }

            }

            public SharePointBCSRecord GetCustomer(string customerID)
            {
                using (CustomerEntities customerRecords = new CustomerEntities())
                {
                    var customerRecord = (from c in customerRecords.Customers
where c.CustomerID == customerID
select c).FirstOrDefault();


                    SharePointBCSRecord returnCustomerRecord =
new SharePointBCSRecord();
                    returnCustomerRecord.CustomerID = customerRecord.CustomerID;
                    returnCustomerRecord.ContactName =
customerRecord.ContactName;
                    returnCustomerRecord.CompanyName =
customerRecord.CompanyName;
                    returnCustomerRecord.City = customerRecord.City;


                    return returnCustomerRecord;
                }
            }
        }
    }
}
```

5. After this code is added, modify the default interface contract for your service so that WCF knows what you implemented as methods as well as the required parameters to those methods. You can find the contract in the ISevice1.cs file in your project.

```
using System;
using System.Collections.Generic;
using System.Linq;
using System.Runtime.Serialization;
using System.ServiceModel;
using System.ServiceModel.Web;
using System.Text;

namespace WCFServiceWebRole1
{
    [ServiceContract]
```

```
public interface IService1
{

    [OperationContract]
    SharePointBCSRecord[] GetCustomers();

    [OperationContract]
    SharePointBCSRecord GetCustomer(string customerID);

    }
}
```

6.   Save the project and deploy it to Azure. When deployed, browse to our site to see the service running, as shown in Figure 5-41.

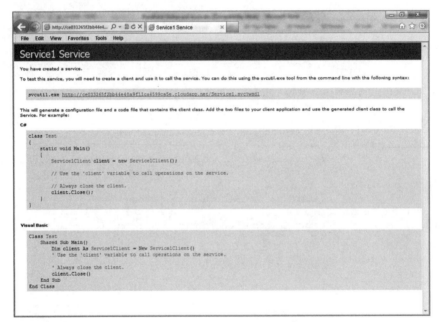

FIGURE 5-41

7.   Move to SharePoint Online to configure SharePoint Online to use your service and call your methods. The first step is to set the permissions for your external content type meta data so that you can modify the meta data using SharePoint Designer. You can do this through the Office 365 administration console, as shown in Figure 5-42. You must add an account so that it can edit the metadata models.

8.   Use SharePoint Designer to create your external content type just like you would if you were connecting to an on-premises SharePoint Server.

9.   In SharePoint Designer, connect to your SharePoint Online team site.

10.   Click the External Content Types option in the left navigation pane, and click External Content Type in the new menu.

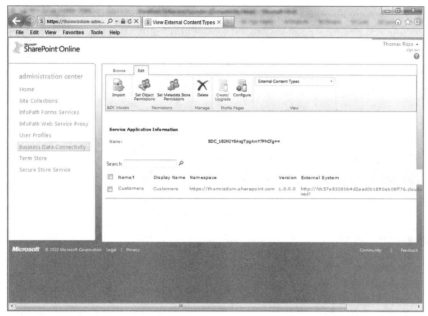

FIGURE 5-42

11. Give your external content type a name, and then click to navigate datasources.

12. Select WCF as the type of connection, and in the connection properties, under the Service Metadata URL, put in the URL to your service but end it with **?wsdl**.

13. In the Service Endpoint URL, put in the URL to your service, as shown in Figure 5-43.

14. Navigate the methods available from your WCF service and map them to SharePoint's BCS methods.

15. Right-click your read item method.

16. Select New Read Item Operation and follow the wizard.

17. Do the same thing for your read items operation and map that to the new Read List Operation, as shown in Figure 5-44.

18. You must map the unique identifier from your backend system as part of the wizard for creating your operations, so you need to make sure you return that unique ID as part of your dataset from your WCF service. Figure 5-45 shows this mapping using the read item operation.

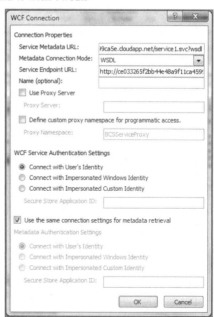

FIGURE 5-43

19. Now, you can create your external list by clicking the Create Lists & Forms button on the top menu, and you now have connected SharePoint Online to your datasource using WCF.

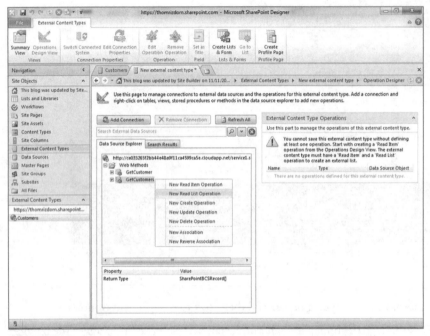

FIGURE 5-44

FIGURE 5-45

SUMMARY

In this chapter, you learned how to build solutions with SharePoint Designer, Visual Studio, and SharePoint Online. SharePoint Online provides a robust development platform with a few limitations because you run in a multitenant environment. However, the possibilities of what you can build on SharePoint Online far outweigh the limitations that you will run into.

Exchange Online Development

WHAT'S IN THIS CHAPTER?

➤ Understanding Exchange Online in Office 365

➤ Developing solutions for Exchange Online using the Exchange Web Services Managed API

In this chapter, you learn how to build solutions that integrate with Microsoft Exchange Online data and services. Using the Exchange Web Services Managed API, you can create and manage mailbox items such as email messages, contacts, tasks, and appointments. You can also leverage Exchange services, such as the Free Busy service, to replicate the functionality in Microsoft Outlook that finds the best meeting times for a set of attendees. Finally, you learn how to build notification solutions in which your application subscribes to streaming notifications in a mailbox, enabling you to listen for and handle specific events in the mailbox.

INTRODUCING EXCHANGE ONLINE IN OFFICE 365

Exchange Online provides a cloud-hosted mail and calendar solution based on Microsoft Exchange Server. Users access their mailbox using Microsoft Outlook 2010 or in their browser using Outlook Web Access. The fact that their mailbox is in the cloud is invisible to the user.

In this section, you learn about the tools for developing solutions for Exchange Online—specifically the Exchange Web Services Managed API. You learn how to use Remote PowerShell to administer Exchange Online, and also how your applications use Autodiscover to connect to Exchange Online.

Exchange On-Premises Versus Exchange Online

From a development perspective, there isn't much difference between Exchange Online and Exchange on-premises. With only minor tweaks, applications written to run against Exchange Service on-premises can work against Exchange Online.

However, compared to other products that are part of Office 365, Exchange Online is relatively mature, having been previously available as a hosted version in *Business Productivity Online Services* (*BPOS*). Microsoft's experience in providing a hosted Exchange offering gives a tremendous benefit to Exchange developers and administrators; Microsoft has worked through the challenges to enable the product to run in a multitenant, cloud-hosted environment without limiting its functionality. As a developer, you are not limited in the type of solutions you can build for Exchange Online.

So be sure to thumb your nose at SharePoint developers who are limited to building Sandboxed Solutions and can't yet use PowerShell to remotely administer SharePoint Online.

Introducing the Exchange Web Services Managed API

Exchange Server exposes a set of web services that applications can use to access Exchange services and mailbox data; these web services are known as Exchange Web Services (EWS). Application such as Microsoft Outlook use EWS to configure a user's mailbox and access services, such as the Exchange Free Busy service.

The *Exchange Web Services Managed API* (*EWS Managed API*) is a managed API built on top of EWS; it abstracts the complexity of working directly with EWS by wrapping the functionality in an easy-to-use, managed API.

When to Use the Exchange Web Services Managed API

The EWS Managed API greatly simplifies the development experience of working with EWS. Before the release of the EWS Managed API, the only way for developers to work with EWS from managed code was to add a service reference from their Visual Studio project and code against the generated proxy classes.

The EWS Managed API abstracts the complexity of working with EWS; for example, by eliminating the need to manually construct and send the EWS web request and handle the asynchronous response. However, you need to give up the convenience of working with the EWS Managed API in some development scenarios:

- ➤ The current version of the EWS Managed API is not compiled for Silverlight; you cannot reference and use it from a Silverlight application. You can work around this limitation by creating a service that wraps the necessary functionality from the EWS Managed API and calling it from Silverlight.

- ➤ HTML5/JavaScript development is quickly becoming more prevalent; in this development model you need to interact directly with EWS through JavaScript.

- ➤ You must work with EWS directly if you need to access it from a non-.NET platform.

- ➤ Some of the less frequently used, more obscure features of EWS have not been exposed in the EWS Managed API.

- ➤ Updates to the EWS Managed API tend to lag behind updates to Exchange Server. If you need to leverage the latest and greatest EWS features before an updated version of the EWS Managed API is released, you need to work directly with EWS.

The EWS Managed API makes EWS development easy using a discoverable and easy-to-use, managed API. However, you must work with EWS directly in some development scenarios.

Setting Up Your Development Environment

The EWS Managed API installer is available as a 32- or 64-bit download. Download and install the appropriate version for your development and environment that you'll deploy your application into.

The API is installed by default to `C:\Program Files\Microsoft\Exchange\Web Services\1.1` (or `Program Files (x86)` for the 32-bit version). In the above install path, 1.1 indicates the version of the EWS Managed API that is installed. You can reference `Microsoft.Exchange.WebServices.dll` from this location, or you can copy it to a folder in your source code and reference it from there.

You can download the EWS Managed API (and other Exchange Server developer downloads) from the Exchange Server Developer Center at `http://msdn.microsoft.com/en-us/exchange/aa731546.aspx`.

Administering Exchange Online Using PowerShell

When administering an on-premises Exchange Server deployment using PowerShell, the Exchange Server Management Shell connects using the identity of the logged-in user. To administer Exchange Online using PowerShell, you need to establish a Remote PowerShell connection to the Exchange Online environment. However, you first must set the credentials to authenticate with Exchange Online. You can capture the credentials by running the `Get-Credential` PowerShell cmdlet; this pops up a window into which you can enter Live ID credentials.

Next, use the `New-PSSession` cmdlet to establish a connection with the generic Remote PowerShell endpoint at `http://ps.outlook.com/powershell`. Office 365 is a multitenant environment, so you must connect to a Remote PowerShell endpoint specific to your Office 365 tenancy. You don't need to know the address of the endpoint for your Office 365 tenancy; after you authenticate with the Remote PowerShell endpoint at `http://ps.outlook.com/powershell`, it uses the provided credentials to find and connect to an appropriate endpoint.

Available for download on Wrox.com

```
$LiveCred = Get-Credential

$Session = New-PSSession
        -ConfigurationName Microsoft.Exchange
        -ConnectionUri https://ps.outlook.com/powershell/
        -Credential $LiveCred
        -Authentication Basic
        -AllowRedirection

Import-PSSession $Session -ea SilentlyContinue
```

code snippet ConnectToExchangeOnline.ps1

As you can see in Figure 6-1, the connection is redirected until it connects to the Remote PowerShell endpoint specific to your Office 365 tenancy.

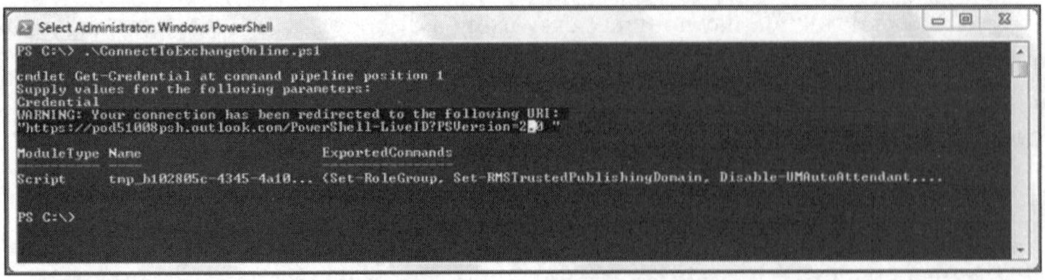

FIGURE 6-1

Now that you are connected to Exchange Online via Remote PowerShell, you can execute other PowerShell management cmdlets as you would on-premises using the Exchange Server Management Shell.

BUILDING APPLICATIONS FOR EXCHANGE ONLINE

Before your EWS Managed API-based application can leverage Exchange Online data and services, it must connect to Exchange Online. In this section, you learn how to connect to Exchange Online using the `ExchangeService` class and how to use the Autodiscover service to configure the instance of `ExchangeService` to connect to EWS at the most efficient URL for a certain user's mailbox.

You then learn how to work with Exchange data such as emails, conversations, tasks, and appointments. You see how the EWS Managed API can enable your application to impersonate another user or perform mailbox operations using their credentials. You also learn how to use the new streaming notification functionality to subscribe to notifications on a user's mailbox.

The ExchangeService Object

The `ExchangeService` class is the primary class through which your application connects to Exchange Online to interact with a user's mailbox or access an Exchange service such as the Autodiscover service or Free Busy service.

To use the `ExchangeService` class in your code, make sure you add the appropriate `using` directive:

```
using Microsoft.Exchange.WebServices.Data;
```

Create an instance of the `ExchangeService` class, using an overload of the constructor to specify the version of the Exchange Server that you target:

```
var exchangeService
    = new ExchangeService(ExchangeVersion.Exchange2010_SP1);
```

The `ExchangeVersion` enum includes the following values:

➤ `Exchange2007_SP1`

➤ `Exchange2010`

➤ `Exchange2010_SP1`

You can use the EWS Managed API to connect to different types of Exchange Server deployments, not just Exchange Online. The `ExchangeService` class enables you to target a specific version of Exchange Server to take full advantage of the features in that version. If you don't specify an `ExchangeVersion`, you can access only the least common denominator of features available across all the versions.

At the time of this writing, Exchange Online is based on Exchange Server 2010 Service Pack 2; however, the EWS Managed API is still at version 1.1. Specify `ExchangeVersion.Exchange2010_SP1` *when creating an instance of the* `ExchangeService` *class to take advantage of the latest Exchange Server features available to the EWS Managed API.*

The `ExchangeService` class also requires a set of credentials that it uses to connect to Exchange Online; set these using an instance of `System.Net.NetworkCredential`:

```
var credentials = new NetworkCredential()
{
    UserName = userName,
    Password = password
};
```

Now that you have created an instance of the `ExchangeService` class and specified the credentials to use to connect to Exchange Online, you must use the Autodiscover service to find the EWS URL that the application needs to connect to for the specific user.

Working with the Autodiscover Service

In a typical Exchange Server deployment, EWS is available at a URL such as `https://exchange .mycompany.com/EWS/Exchange.asmx`.

EWS is only available at an https endpoint.

However, in a large deployment that may be geographically dispersed, EWS is available at multiple URLs hosted on servers around the globe—the application must connect to the URL most convenient to the signed-in user. For example, if a user's mailbox is on a server in Japan, connecting to an EWS URL hosted on a server in the United States can cause performance issues due to network latency.

An application should always connect to the EWS URL most convenient to the user's mailbox, but how do you find the EWS URL to connect to? Enter the Autodiscover service, which uses a set of credentials to find the most efficient EWS URL with which to connect.

You should never hardcode the EWS URL in your application. The most efficient EWS URL for a given user's mailbox may vary in a large and globally distributed environment. Always use the Autodiscover service to locate the most efficient EWS URL for the user's mailbox.

Autodiscover isn't intended just for use by custom applications using the EWS Managed API. Microsoft Outlook also uses Autodiscover to configure users' mailboxes and their connection to the Exchange environment.

The simplest way to use the Autodiscover service is to call the `AutodiscoverUrl` method on the instance of `ExchangeService` and specify the SMTP address of the user:

```
exchangeService.AutodiscoverUrl("user@domain.com");
```

You can then access the EWS URL using the `Url` property of the `ExchangeService` class:

```
var ewsUrl = exchangeService.Url;
```

The Autodiscover process is optimized for an Exchange Server on-premises deployment. However, you can tweak the process slightly to make it go faster when executing your code against Exchange Online. To better understand these optimizations, it is beneficial to first explore how the Autodiscover works against Exchange Server on-premises.

Autodiscover in an Exchange On-Premises Deployment

Before exploring how to use Autodiscover in Exchange Online, it is helpful to understand how Autodiscover works in an Exchange on-premises deployment.

An Exchange Server on-premises deployment includes one or more servers running the Client Access role. The Client Access servers expose an Autodiscover virtual directory responsible for handling Autodiscover requests from EWS Managed API applications, or applications such as Microsoft Outlook.

The Client Access servers also contain an Active Directory object called the Service Connection Point (SCP). The SCP contains a list of all the URLs for the Autodiscover service in the Exchange Service deployment.

When your application calls `ExchangeService.AutodiscoverUrl`, the EWS Managed API queries the SCP for the Autodiscover service URL to use. The Autodiscover URL then returns the EWS URL to use for the particular users' credentials/mailboxes.

Autodiscover in Exchange Online

Now that you have a basic understanding of how the Autodiscover process works in an Exchange Server on-premises deployment, you can learn how to optimize the process for Exchange Online.

In Exchange Online, there is no SCP that contains a list of all the Autodiscover service URLs in the environment. However, when you call `ExchangeService.AutodiscoverUrl` against Exchange Online, the EWS Managed API still tries to find the SCP to query it for that list. Several seconds are wasted until the operation times out and throws an exception, and the EWS Managed API tries another way to locate the Autodiscover service URL—this can be a frustrating experience for the user because it appears that the application is hanging.

If you set the `TraceEnabled` property of the `ExchangeService` class to `true` and call `ExchangeService.AutodiscoverUrl`, you see the exception that is thrown when the EWS Managed API can't find the SCP, as shown in Figure 6-2.

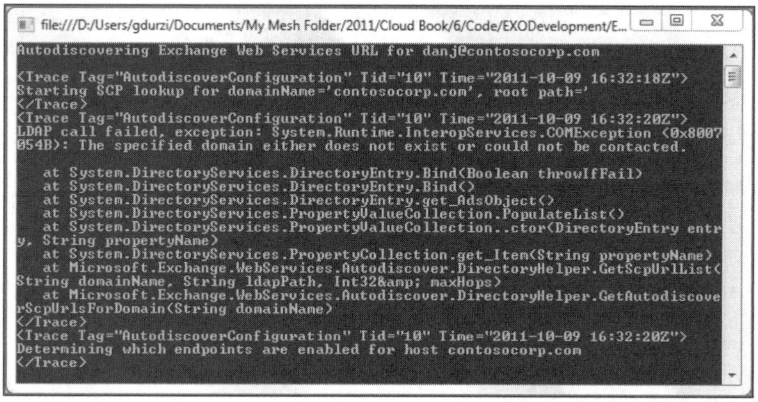

```
file:///D:/Users/gdurzi/Documents/My Mesh Folder/2011/Cloud Book/6/Code/EXODevelopment/E...
Autodiscovering Exchange Web Services URL for danj@contosocorp.com

<Trace Tag="AutodiscoverConfiguration" Tid="10" Time="2011-10-09 16:32:18Z">
Starting SCP lookup for domainName='contosocorp.com', root path='
</Trace>
<Trace Tag="AutodiscoverConfiguration" Tid="10" Time="2011-10-09 16:32:20Z">
LDAP call failed, exception: System.Runtime.InteropServices.COMException (0x8007
054B): The specified domain either does not exist or could not be contacted.

   at System.DirectoryServices.DirectoryEntry.Bind(Boolean throwIfFail)
   at System.DirectoryServices.DirectoryEntry.Bind()
   at System.DirectoryServices.DirectoryEntry.get_AdsObject()
   at System.DirectoryServices.PropertyValueCollection.PopulateList()
   at System.DirectoryServices.PropertyValueCollection..ctor(DirectoryEntry entr
y, String propertyName)
   at System.DirectoryServices.PropertyCollection.get_Item(String propertyName)
   at Microsoft.Exchange.WebServices.Autodiscover.DirectoryHelper.GetScpUrlList(
String domainName, String ldapPath, Int32&amp; maxHops)
   at Microsoft.Exchange.WebServices.Autodiscover.DirectoryHelper.GetAutodiscove
rScpUrlsForDomain(String domainName)
</Trace>
<Trace Tag="AutodiscoverConfiguration" Tid="10" Time="2011-10-09 16:32:20Z">
Determining which endpoints are enabled for host contosocorp.com
</Trace>
```

FIGURE 6-2

Instead of relying on the shortcut to simply call ExchangeService.AutodiscoverUrl, you can work with the Autodiscover service directly and control the steps that it goes through to find the EWS URL with which to connect.

To work with the Autodiscover service directly, make sure you add the appropriate using directive to your code:

```
using Microsoft.Exchange.WebServices.Autodiscover;
```

The following code snippet goes through the following steps to get the EWS URL:

1. Specify the credentials to use by creating an instance of NetworkCredentials.

2. Create an instance of the ExchangeService class.

3. Set the credentials to use for the ExchangeService.

4. Create an instance of the AutodiscoverService class.

5. Set the credentials to use for the AutodiscoverService.

6. Set the EnableScpLookup property of the AutodiscoverService instance to false to bypass querying the Active Directory SCP.

7. Define a RedirectionUrlValidationCallback delegate on the AutodiscoverService instance. The Autodiscover service may redirect the request several times until it finds the URL. The delegate returns true, indicating that it is OK for the EWS Managed API to redirect the request.

8. Call GetUserSettings on the AutodiscoverService instance to extract specific user settings into an instance of GetUserSettingsResponse.

9. Extract the ExternalEwsUrl property from the GetUserSettingsResponse instance. This property is the EWS URL for the specified user.

10. Set the Url property of the ExchangeService instance to the value of ExternalEwsUrl.

That's a lot of work for what you could previously achieve with one line of code, but it greatly improves the performance of the Autodiscover process.

The code snippet also enables tracing on both the `ExchangeService` and `AutodiscoverService` class instances, so you can see the requests and responses directly in the console application.

```csharp
// Set the credentials to user to connect to Exchange Online
var credentials = new NetworkCredential()
{
    UserName = userName,
    Password = password
};

Console.WriteLine("Autodiscovering Exchange Web Services URL for {0}{1}",
    _userName,
    Environment.NewLine);

// Create an instance of ExchangeService
_exchangeService = new ExchangeService(ExchangeVersion.Exchange2010_SP1);

// Enable tracing
_exchangeService.TraceEnabled = true;

// Set the credentials
_exchangeService.Credentials = credentials;

// Create an instance of the AutodiscoverService
_autodiscoverService
    = new Microsoft.Exchange.WebServices.Autodiscover.AutodiscoverService();

// Enable Autodiscover tracing
_autodiscoverService.TraceEnabled = true;

// Set the credentials
_autodiscoverService.Credentials = credentials;

// Prevent the AutodiscoverService from querying the Active Directory SCP
_autodiscoverService.EnableScpLookup = false;

// Specify a redirection Url validation callback that returns true
_autodiscoverService.RedirectionUrlValidationCallback
    = delegate { return true; };

// Use the AutodiscoverService to get the EWS Url for the user's mailbox
GetUserSettingsResponse response =
    _autodiscoverService.GetUserSettings(
        _userName,
        UserSettingName.ExternalEwsUrl);

// Extract the Exchange Web Services Url for the user's mailbox
var externalEwsUrl =
    new Uri(response.Settings[UserSettingName.ExternalEwsUrl].ToString());

// Set the Url of the ExchangeService object
_exchangeService.Url = externalEwsUrl;
```

code snippet EXODevelopment\Program.cs

Take a look at the trace generated by the Autodiscover process.

As you recall, there is no Active Directory SCP in Exchange Online that lists all the available Autodiscover endpoints. In this case, the Autodiscover process relies instead on convention to locate an Autodiscover endpoint. Autodiscover endpoints are typically located at URLs such as the following:

➤ `https://mydomain/autodiscover/autodiscover.xml`

➤ `https://autodiscover.mydomain/autodiscover/autodiscover.xml`

You can see in the trace that the Autodiscover process tries to locate an Autodiscover endpoint at several URLs before being finally redirected to `https://autodiscover-s.outlook.com/autodiscover/autodiscover.xml`.

```
<Trace Tag="AutodiscoverConfiguration"
        Tid="10" Time="2011-10-01 20:27:22Z">
   Determining which endpoints are enabled for host
   mydomain.com
</Trace>

<Trace Tag="AutodiscoverConfiguration"
        Tid="10" Time="2011-10-01 20:27:44Z">
   No Autodiscover endpoints are available for host
   mydomain.com
</Trace>

<Trace Tag="AutodiscoverConfiguration"
        Tid="10" Time="2011-10-01 20:27:44Z">
   Determining which endpoints are enabled for host
   autodiscover.mydomain.com
</Trace>

<Trace Tag="AutodiscoverConfiguration"
        Tid="10" Time="2011-10-01 20:27:44Z">
   No Autodiscover endpoints are available for host
   autodiscover.mydomain.com
</Trace>

<Trace Tag="AutodiscoverConfiguration"
        Tid="10" Time="2011-10-01 20:27:44Z">
   Trying to get Autodiscover redirection URL from
   http://autodiscover.mydomain.com/autodiscover/autodiscover.xml.
</Trace>

<Trace Tag="AutodiscoverConfiguration"
        Tid="10" Time="2011-10-01 20:27:44Z">
   Redirection URL found:
   'https://autodiscover-s.outlook.com/autodiscover/autodiscover.xml'
</Trace>

<Trace Tag="AutodiscoverConfiguration"
        Tid="10" Time="2011-10-01 20:27:44Z">
   Determining which endpoints are enabled for host
   autodiscover-s.outlook.com
</Trace>

<Trace Tag="AutodiscoverConfiguration"
        Tid="10" Time="2011-10-01 20:27:44Z">
```

```
        Host returned enabled endpoint flags: Legacy, Soap, WsSecurity
    </Trace>
```

Next, you see the HTTP POST made to the Autodiscover endpoint as a result of calling
`AutodiscoverService.GetUserSettings` to get the value of `ExternalEwsUrl`.

```
    <Trace Tag="AutodiscoverRequestHttpHeaders"
           Tid="10" Time="2011-10-01 20:27:44Z">
     POST /autodiscover/autodiscover.svc HTTP/1.1
     Content-Type: text/xml; charset=utf-8
     Accept: text/xml
     User-Agent: ExchangeServicesClient/14.02.0051.000
    </Trace>

    <Trace Tag="AutodiscoverRequest"
           Tid="10" Time="2011-10-01 20:27:44Z"
           Version="14.02.0051.000">
     <?xml version="1.0" encoding="utf-8"?>
     <soap:Envelope
            xmlns:a="http://schemas.microsoft.com/exchange/2010/Autodiscover"
            xmlns:wsa="http://www.w3.org/2005/08/addressing"
            xmlns:xsi="http://www.w3.org/2001/XMLSchema-instance"
            xmlns:soap="http://schemas.xmlsoap.org/soap/envelope/">
       <soap:Header>
         <a:RequestedServerVersion>Exchange2010</a:RequestedServerVersion>
         <wsa:Action>
           http://schemas.microsoft.com/exchange/2010/Autodiscover
                 /Autodiscover/GetUserSettings
         </wsa:Action>
         <wsa:To>
           https://autodiscover-s.outlook.com/autodiscover/autodiscover.svc
         </wsa:To>
         </soap:Header>
       <soap:Body>
         <a:GetUserSettingsRequestMessage
           xmlns:a="http://schemas.microsoft.com/exchange/2010/Autodiscover">
           <a:Request>
             <a:Users>
               <a:User>
                 <a:Mailbox>george@mydomain.com</a:Mailbox>
               </a:User>
             </a:Users>
             <a:RequestedSettings>
               <a:Setting>ExternalEwsUrl</a:Setting>
             </a:RequestedSettings>
           </a:Request>
         </a:GetUserSettingsRequestMessage>
       </soap:Body>
     </soap:Envelope>
    </Trace>
```

And finally, the response containing the value of `ExternalEwsUrl`, the EWS URL for the specified user.

```
    <Trace Tag="AutodiscoverResponseHttpHeaders"
           Tid="10" Time="2011-10-01 20:27:44Z">
     200 OK
     Transfer-Encoding: chunked
```

```
    RequestId: 205e5b8f-21f4-47d5-868c-560ae408a3d8
    X-DiagInfo: CH1PRD0302CA003
    Cache-Control: private
    Content-Type: text/xml; charset=utf-8
    Date: Sat, 01 Oct 2011 20:26:29 GMT
    Server: Microsoft-IIS/7.5
    X-AspNet-Version: 2.0.50727
    X-Powered-By: ASP.NET
</Trace>

<Trace Tag="AutodiscoverResponse"
      Tid="10" Time="2011-10-01 20:27:44Z" Version="14.02.0051.000">
  <s:Envelope xmlns:s="http://schemas.xmlsoap.org/soap/envelope/"
              xmlns:a="http://www.w3.org/2005/08/addressing">
    <s:Header>
      <a:Action s:mustUnderstand="1">
        http://schemas.microsoft.com/exchange/2010/Autodiscover
              /Autodiscover/GetUserSettingsResponse
      </a:Action>
      <h:ServerVersionInfo
          xmlns:h="http://schemas.microsoft.com/exchange/2010/Autodiscover"
          xmlns:i="http://www.w3.org/2001/XMLSchema-instance">
        <h:MajorVersion>14</h:MajorVersion>
        <h:MinorVersion>1</h:MinorVersion>
        <h:MajorBuildNumber>225</h:MajorBuildNumber>
        <h:MinorBuildNumber>71</h:MinorBuildNumber>
        <h:Version>Exchange2010_SP2</h:Version>
      </h:ServerVersionInfo>
    </s:Header>
    <s:Body>
      <GetUserSettingsResponseMessage
        xmlns="http://schemas.microsoft.com/exchange/2010/Autodiscover">
        <Response xmlns:i="http://www.w3.org/2001/XMLSchema-instance">
          <ErrorCode>NoError</ErrorCode>
          <ErrorMessage />
          <UserResponses>
            <UserResponse>
              <ErrorCode>NoError</ErrorCode>
              <ErrorMessage>No error.</ErrorMessage>
              <RedirectTarget i:nil="true" />
              <UserSettingErrors />
              <UserSettings>
                <UserSetting i:type="StringSetting">
                  <Name>ExternalEwsUrl</Name>
                  <Value>
                  https://sn2prd0302.outlook.com/EWS/Exchange.asmx
                  </Value>
                </UserSetting>
              </UserSettings>
            </UserResponse>
          </UserResponses>
        </Response>
      </GetUserSettingsResponseMessage>
    </s:Body>
  </s:Envelope>
</Trace>
```

Working with Mailbox Items

The EWS Managed API makes it easy to work with mailbox items such as email messages, tasks, and appointments. In this section, you learn how to create and send an email message, how to create and update a task, and how to create a contact.

Working with Email

The ability to send email messages is a common feature of line-of-business applications; for example, to send a confirmation email after submitting a form or completing a workflow.

Fortunately, it is easy to send an email using the EWS Managed API:

1. Create a new email message by creating an instance of the `EmailMessage` class and specifying the instance of `ExchangeService` to use.

2. Set properties of the email message such as `Subject`.

3. Set the email message recipients using the `ToRecipients`, `CcRecipients`, and `BccRecipients` properties—these are all collections of strings that you can simply add recipients to.

4. Set the body of the message using an instance of the `MessageBody` class, which allows you to either specify that the body text is either `BodyType.HTML` or `BodyType.Text`.

5. Send the email message by calling `EmailMessage.Send` or `EmailMessage.SendAndSaveCopy` (which saves a copy of the email message in the user's Sent Items folder).

Available for download on Wrox.com

```
// Create an EmailMessage
var emailMessage = new EmailMessage(_exchangeService);

// Set message properties
emailMessage.Subject = "Hello from the cloud!";
emailMessage.ToRecipients.Add(recipient);

// Set message body
emailMessage.Body = new MessageBody()
    {
        BodyType = BodyType.HTML,
        Text = "<p>I sent this using Exchange Web Services.</p>"
    };

// Send the message and save a copy in Sent Items
emailMessage.SendAndSaveCopy();
```

code snippet EXODevelopment\EXOMailboxItems.cs

The constructor for most mailbox item classes in the EWS Managed API requires an instance of the `ExchangeService` class. Recall that the `ExchangeService` class has a `Url` property, which is the EWS URL that the `ExchangeService` instance is connected to. This is how the EWS Managed API knows to connect to the user's mailbox to send email, create a task, and so on.

You can also add file attachments to an email message by specifying the path to the file or loading it from a byte array or stream.

```
emailMessage.Attachments.AddFileAttachment("C:\\Invoice.docx");
```

You can even add other mailbox items as attachments to an email message. For example, you can attach a task or contact item to the message—handy if you like to include your contact card with every email. You can use the ItemAttachment<T> class, where T indicates the type of attachment; for example, ItemAttachment<Task>.

```
ItemAttachment<Task> taskAttachment =
    emailMessage.Attachments.AddItemAttachment<Task>();
```

You should of course set the minimum required properties of the mailbox item you are attaching to the email message, such as the task subject.

Working with Tasks

The ability to create and assign a task in code can come in handy. For example, a CRM application can use the EWS Managed API to create a task to remind a sales representative to call a client.

To create a simple task, create an instance of the Task class, set its Subject, StartDate, and DueDate properties, and save it.

```
// Create a Task
var task = new Task(_exchangeService);

// Set the Task subject
task.Subject = "Finish writing Chapter 6";

// Set the Start and Due dates
task.StartDate = DateTime.Now;
task.DueDate = DateTime.Now.AddMonths(1);

// Create the Task
task.Save();
```

code snippet EXODevelopment\EXOMailboxItems.cs

You can also define a recurrence pattern for a task to repeat daily, weekly, monthly, or yearly; recurrence patterns are defined by the Recurrence enum. The following code snippet defines a simple weekly recurrence pattern to repeat the task every 1 week on a specific day of the week.

```
// Create a recurrence pattern for the Task
var dayOfTheWeek = (DayOfTheWeek)Enum.Parse(
    typeof(DayOfWeek),
    task.StartDate.Value.DayOfWeek.ToString());

// Repeat every 1 week
task.Recurrence = new Recurrence.WeeklyPattern(
    startDate: task.StartDate.Value,
    interval: 1,
    daysOfTheWeek: dayOfTheWeek);
```

Working with Contacts

The EWS Managed API enables you to easily create contacts just as you would in Microsoft Outlook. To create a contact, create an instance of the Contact class, and set some of its basic properties such as Give Name, Surname, and CompanyName. You can also set the FileAs property to control how the contact name displays; for example as First Name Last Name (Company Name).

```
// Create a Contact
var contact = new Contact(_exchangeService);

// Set Contact properties
contact.GivenName = "Rebecca";
contact.Surname = "Laszlo";
contact.CompanyName = "Big Company, Inc.";
contact.FileAs = String.Format("{0}, {1}, ({2})",
    contact.Surname,
    contact.GivenName,
    contact.CompanyName);

// Set the Contact's email address
contact.EmailAddresses[EmailAddressKey.EmailAddress1]
    = "becky@notreallymyemail.com";

// Set the Contact's physical address
var workAddress = new PhysicalAddressEntry()
{
    Street = "2525 N. Long St.",
    City = "Megalopolis",
    State = "CA",
    CountryOrRegion = "United States of America",
    PostalCode = "90055"
};
contact.PhysicalAddresses[PhysicalAddressKey.Business]
    = workAddress;

// Create the Contact
contact.Save();
```

code snippet EXODevelopment\EXOMailboxItems.cs

Email addresses and physical addresses work differently in contacts because a contact record can have several of each. The EmailAddresses and PhysicalAddresses properties of the Contact class are dictionaries, not collections, so you set them differently. For example, you can set contact.EmailAddresses[EmailAddressKey.EmailAddress1] to a string representing an email address, or contact.PhysicalAddresses[PhysicalAddressKey.Business] to an instance of PhysicalAddressEntry. This allows a contact record to have multiple email addresses and multiple physical addresses, such as a home or business address.

Working with Calendar Items

The EWS Managed API includes functionality that makes it easy to work with meeting appointments. In this section, you learn how to create a recurring meeting appointment, how to get a user's upcoming appointments, and how to use the Free Busy service to find a suitable meeting time for a set of attendees.

Working with Meeting Appointments

To create a meeting appointment, create an instance of the `Appointment` class and set properties such as the `Subject` of the appointment, add required and optional attendees, optionally set a recurrence pattern, and send the meeting invite to the invitees.

```
// Create an Appointment
var appointment = new Appointment(_exchangeService);

// Set properties of the Appointment
appointment.Subject = "Weekly Status Meeting";
appointment.RequiredAttendees.Add("user@mydomain.com");
appointment.Start = new DateTime(
    DateTime.Now.Year,
    DateTime.Now.Month,
    DateTime.Now.Day,
    DateTime.Now.AddHours(1).Hour,
    0,
    0);
appointment.End = appointment.Start.AddHours(1);

// Create a recurrence pattern for the Appointment
var dayOfTheWeek = (DayOfTheWeek) Enum.Parse(
    typeof(DayOfWeek), appointment.Start.DayOfWeek.ToString());

// Repeat every 1 week
appointment.Recurrence = new Recurrence.WeeklyPattern(
    appointment.Start.Date,
    1,
    dayOfTheWeek);

// Save the appointment and send an invitation to the attendees
appointment.Save(SendInvitationsMode.SendToAllAndSaveCopy);
```

code snippet EXODevelopment\EXOCalendarItems.cs

You can use the `RequiredAttendees` and `OptionalAttendees` properties of the `Appointment` to invite people, resources, and rooms to an appointment. These are simple collections that you can add attendees to; you can define an attendee using a string representing an SMTP address or with an instance of the `AttendeeInfo` class. The `AttendeeInfo` class is useful because it allows you to add different types of attendees such as meeting organizers, optional attendees, resources (such as a projector), and conference rooms.

```
// Specify the meeting organizer
appointment.RequiredAttendees.Add(new AttendeeInfo()
{
    SmtpAddress = "organizer@mydomain.com",
    AttendeeType = MeetingAttendeeType.Organizer
});

// Invite someone else
appointment.RequiredAttendees.Add(new AttendeeInfo()
{
    SmtpAddress = "user@mydomain.com",
```

```
        AttendeeType = MeetingAttendeeType.Required
});

// Add a resource
appointment.RequiredAttendees.Add(new AttendeeInfo()
{
    SmtpAddress = "projector@mydomain.com",
    AttendeeType = MeetingAttendeeType.Resource
});

// Set a room
appointment.RequiredAttendees.Add(new AttendeeInfo()
{
    SmtpAddress = "ConferenceRoom1@mydomain.com",
    AttendeeType = MeetingAttendeeType.Room
});
```

Getting Upcoming Appointments

You can use the EWS Managed API to get a list of upcoming meeting appointments from your calendar and integrate the data into your application; for example, a CRM application can use the EWS Managed API to retrieve and display an account manager's upcoming client meetings.

To retrieve a user's meeting appointments from their calendar, start by defining a `CalendarView`; this class allows you to define a date range view of appointments in the user's Calendar folder. To retrieve the list of meeting appointments, call `ExchangeService.FindAppointments` and specify the folder to search in, and the instance of `CalendarView` that you created. You need to define the folder to search in because meeting appointment items can technically exist in any mailbox folder.

```
// Create a CalendarView
var calendarView = new CalendarView(
    DateTime.Now,
    DateTime.Now.AddDays(numberOfDays));

// Search for Appointments in the Calendar folder
//    during the time range specified by the CalendarView
FindItemsResults<Appointment> appointments =
    _exchangeService.FindAppointments(
        WellKnownFolderName.Calendar,
        calendarView);

// Display Appointments
foreach (var appointment in appointments)
{
    Console.WriteLine("Subject:\t"
        + appointment.Subject);
    Console.WriteLine("Date:\t\t"
        + appointment.Start.ToString("dd MMMM yyyy"));
    Console.WriteLine("Start Time:\t"
        + appointment.Start.ToString("hh:mm tt"));
    Console.WriteLine("End Time:\t"
        + appointment.End.ToString("hh:mm tt"));
    Console.WriteLine();
}
```

code snippet EXODevelopment\EXOCalendarItems.cs

Working with the Free Busy Service

The calendar in Microsoft Outlook provides functionality that helps you find suitable meeting times for a set of attendees, resources, and rooms, as shown in Figure 6-3.

After you choose the people to invite to the meeting, and optionally choose a room to have the meeting in, Microsoft Outlook displays a list of meeting times that work for all the attendees and the rooms that are available during those times. Each meeting suggested is also rated as Good, Fair, or Poor. Any conflicts are also highlighted. To enable this functionality, Microsoft Outlook uses the Exchange Free Busy service. You can use the EWS Managed API to interact with the Free Busy service directly from your application.

FIGURE 6-3

Here's how to use the EWS Managed API to interact with the Free Busy service to find a set of suitable meeting times:

1. Define a list of attendees. This could include a meeting organizer, required attendees, optional attendees, resources, and rooms.

2. Create an instance of the `AvailabilityOptions` class to define the criteria that the Free Busy service can use to recommend meeting times.

3. Call `ExchangeService.GetUserAvailability` to make a request to the Free Busy service for suggestions for the defined list of attendees, during a specified time window, using the specified options.

4. Iterate through the provided suggestions and choose one.

5. Schedule the appointment.

Available for download on Wrox.com

```
// Specify the meeting organizer
appointment.RequiredAttendees.Add(new AttendeeInfo()
{
    SmtpAddress = "organizer@mydomain.com",
    AttendeeType = MeetingAttendeeType.Organizer
});

// Invite someone else
appointment.RequiredAttendees.Add(new AttendeeInfo()
{
    SmtpAddress = "user@mydomain.com",
    AttendeeType = MeetingAttendeeType.Required
});

// Set a room
appointment.RequiredAttendees.Add(new AttendeeInfo()
{
    SmtpAddress = "ConferenceRoom1@mydomain.com",
    AttendeeType = MeetingAttendeeType.Room
});

// Set the AvailabilityOptions of the meeting
var options = new AvailabilityOptions();
```

```csharp
        options.MeetingDuration = 60;
        options.MaximumNonWorkHoursSuggestionsPerDay = 4;
        options.MinimumSuggestionQuality = SuggestionQuality.Good;
        options.RequestedFreeBusyView = FreeBusyViewType.FreeBusy;

        // Call the service to get a collection of meeting suggestions
        GetUserAvailabilityResults results =
            _exchangeService.GetUserAvailability(
                attendees,
                new TimeWindow(DateTime.Now, DateTime.Now.AddDays(1)),
                AvailabilityData.FreeBusyAndSuggestions,
                options);

    var availableTimes = new List<DateTime>();
    int option = 1;

    foreach (var suggestion in results.Suggestions)
    {
        Console.WriteLine("Please select an available appointment time for "
            + suggestion.Date.ToString("dddd, dd MMMM yyyy") + ":");
        Console.WriteLine();

        Console.WriteLine("#\tSuggestion\tQuality");
        Console.WriteLine();

        foreach (var timeSuggestion in suggestion.TimeSuggestions)
        {
            availableTimes.Add(timeSuggestion.MeetingTime);
            Console.WriteLine(option.ToString() +
                "\t" + timeSuggestion.MeetingTime.ToString("hh:mm tt") +
                "\t" + timeSuggestion.Quality);
            option++;
        }
    }
```

code snippet EXODevelopment\EXOCalendarItems.cs

The `AvailabilityOptions` class controls the types of meeting suggestions and data returned by the Free Busy service. For example, the `MeetingDuration` property denotes the duration in minutes of the meeting suggestions. The `MinimumSuggestionQuality` defines the quality of the suggestions. The `RequestedFreeBusyView` indicates the level of detail in the returned meeting suggestions; for example `FreeBusyViewType.Details` includes all the detail about appointments in the users' calendar that the requesting user has permissions to view, whereas `FreeBusyViewType.FreeBusy` includes only start and end times of appointments in the users' calendar.

The results returned by the Free Busy service are in the form of `Suggestion` objects. You can access properties of each suggestion, such as its quality, start, and end time.

Impersonating Other Users

Applications often need to perform mailbox operations that appear to have been created by another user. For example, if a CRM application creates a meeting appointment for a user, it shouldn't appear to have been created by a service account. Email messages must also come from the actual sender, not the service account.

The EWS Managed API allows an account with the appropriate permissions to impersonate another account. In this section, you learn how to configure application impersonation, and see how to impersonate other users to create a meeting appointment using their rights.

Configuring Application Impersonation

To grant a service account permission to impersonate other users, you need to grant it the `ApplicationImpersonation` role over a set of users. The set of users can be an Active Directory Organizational Unit (OU), a security group, or a Microsoft Exchange management scope role filter that defines a set of users using some search criteria.

Use the `New-ManagementRoleAssignment` PowerShell cmdlet to configure impersonation. The following example grants the `ApplicationImpersonation` role to the `serviceaccount@mydomain.com` account over all the users in the organization—obviously not something you'd want to do, but a good, simple example to start with.

```
New-ManagementRoleAssignment
    -Name "Impersonation-MyApp"
    -Role "ApplicationImpersonation"
    -User serviceaccount@mydomain.com
```

You can also grant the permission to impersonate users to a group of accounts; the following example grants the `ApplicationImpersonation` role to all the accounts in the Service Accounts group.

```
New-ManagementRoleAssignment
    -Name "Impersonation-MyApp-Group"
    -Role "ApplicationImpersonation"
    -SecurityGroup "Service Accounts"
```

The previous examples granted a service account—or group of service accounts—permission to impersonate all the users in the organization. A more realistic scenario is to grant this permission only for a smaller set of users. You can create a management scope filter that defines the set of users, for example, based on their membership in a specific department.

Create the management scope filter using the `New-ManagementScope` PowerShell cmdlet, and set the `RecipientRestrictionFilter` to define the condition for membership in this management scope filter.

```
New-ManagementScope
    -Name "Sales Users"
    -RecipientRestrictionFilter { Department -Eq "Sales" }
```

You can then create the management role assignment and specify the management scope filter to apply it to. In the following example, `serviceaccount@mydomain.com` has permission to impersonate members of the Sales department.

```
New-ManagementRoleAssignment
    -Name "Impersonation-MyApp-Scope"
    -Role "ApplicationImpersonation"
    -User serviceaccount@mydomain.com
    -CustomRecipientWriteScope "Sales Users"
```

Impersonating a User Account

Now that you have configured impersonation using PowerShell, you can use the EWS Managed API to impersonate other users and perform mailbox operations using their rights.

To impersonate an account, set the `ImpersonatedUserId` property of the `ExchangeService` instance to an instance of the `ImpersonatedUserId` class. Any mailbox operations that you perform after setting the `ImpersonatedUserId` are executed using that account's rights.

```
// Set the user to impersonate
_exchangeService.ImpersonatedUserId =
    new ImpersonatedUserId(
        ConnectingIdType.SmtpAddress,
        "user1@mydomain.com");

// Create the Appointment
var appointment = new Appointment(_exchangeService);
appointment.Subject = "Review Proposal";
appointment.Start = DateTime.Now;
appointment.End = appointment.Start.AddHours(1);
appointment.RequiredAttendees.Add("user2@mydomain.com");

// Handle the ServiceResponseException
try
{
    appointment.Save(
        SendInvitationsMode.SendToAllAndSaveCopy);
}
catch (Microsoft.Exchange.WebServices.Data.ServiceResponseException ex)
{
    throw ex;
}

// Set ImpersonatedUserId to null
_exchangeService.ImpersonatedUserId = null;
```

code snippet EXODevelopment\EXOCalendarItems.cs

If the service account doesn't have the permission to impersonate the specified account, calls to perform any impersonated mailbox operations can throw a `Microsoft.Exchange.WebServices .Data.ServiceResponseException` exception.

> *When performing mailbox operations using impersonation, it's as if you connect to EWS using the impersonated account's credentials. Therefore, when running Autodiscover to get the EWS URL to connect to, you should specify the impersonated account's SMTP address instead of that of the service account.*

Recall that any operations that you perform after setting `ExchangeService.ImpersonatedUserId` will be created using the impersonated user's rights—and will appear to have been created by them. You should set `ExchangeService.ImpersonatedUserId` back to `null` when you finish impersonating the account.

Working with Conversations

Microsoft Outlook—and other email clients—include the ability to organize email messages into conversations. You can then perform actions on all the messages in a conversation; such as moving them to a different folder or categorizing them.

In this section, you learn how to use the EWS Managed API to work with conversations, including how to retrieve conversations from a user's mailbox, move the messages in the conversation and categorize the messages in the conversation.

Retrieving Conversations from a Mailbox

Email messages in a conversation are typically spread out across multiple folders in a user's mailbox; for example, the latest messages would be in the inbox folder, and the user might have already moved other messages in the conversation to a different folder.

The EWS Managed API provides functionality to retrieve conversations from the user's mailbox and examine their contents. The first step is to define a ConversationIndexedItemView and specify how many conversations the operation should retrieve. You can then call ExchangeService .FindConversation to find conversations in the user's mailbox; the FindConversation method accepts an instance of ConversationIndexedItemView and the folder to search in.

Available for download on Wrox.com

```
var conversationView = new ConversationIndexedItemView(
    pageSize: Int32.MaxValue,
    offset: 0,
    offsetBasePoint: OffsetBasePoint.Beginning);

var conversations = _exchangeService.FindConversation(
    view: conversationView,
    folderId: WellKnownFolderName.Inbox);

foreach (var conversation in conversations)
{
    Console.WriteLine("Conversation Id: {0}", conversation.Id);
    Console.WriteLine("Conversation Topic: {0}", conversation.Topic);
    Console.WriteLine("Number of Messages in Conversation: {0}",
        conversation.GlobalMessageCount);

    Console.WriteLine("Messages:");
    var messageIdsInConversation = conversation.GlobalItemIds;

    foreach (var itemId in messageIdsInConversation)
    {
        var item = Item.Bind(_exchangeService, itemId);
        Console.WriteLine("Received: {0}", item.DateTimeReceived);
        Console.WriteLine("Contained in Folder: {0}", item.ParentFolderId);
    }
}
```

code snippet EXODevelopment\EXOConversations.cs

You can then iterate through all the conversations in the search results and the messages contained in them.

This example specifically looks for conversations in the Inbox folder, however, as you know, the email messages in a conversation can be spread out across multiple folders in a user's mailbox. The `Conversation` class exposes properties such as `MessageCount` and `ItemIds` that apply only to messages in the folder specified in the instance of `ConversationIndexedItemView`. For example, the `conversation.MessageCount` property indicates the number of email messages in the conversation in the Inbox folder.

These properties have "global" counterparts; for example the `GlobalMessageCount` and `GlobalItemIds` apply to all the messages in a conversation regardless of the folder they are in. The `conversation.GlobalMessageCount` property indicates the number of email messages in the conversation across the user's entire mailbox.

Table 6-1 shows a list of conversation properties and their global equivalents.

TABLE 6-1: Conversation Properties

PROPERTY	GLOBAL PROPERTY	PURPOSE
Categories	GlobalCategories	The categories that have been applied to the conversation
FlagStatus	GlobalFlagStatus	Whether the conversation is flagged as important
HasAttachments	GlobalHasAttachments	Indicates if any of the messages in the conversation have attachments
Importance	GlobalImportance	The importance of the conversation
ItemClasses	GlobalItemClasses	The different types of mailbox items contained in the conversation
ItemIds	GlobalItemIds	The unique IDs of the messages in the conversation
LastDeliveryTime	GlobalLastDeliveryTime	The delivery time of the last message received in the conversation
MessageCount	GlobalMessageCount	The number of messages in the conversation
Size	GlobalSize	The total size of all the messages

PROPERTY	GLOBAL PROPERTY	PURPOSE
UniqueRecipients	GlobalUniqueRecipients	All the recipients of the messages in the conversation
UniqueSenders	GlobalUniqueSenders	All the senders of the messages in the conversation
UniqueUnreadSenders	GlobalUniqueUnreadSenders	List of people who have sent messages that are still unread
UnreadCount	GlobalUnreadCount	Number of unread messages in the conversation

SOURCE: EWS MANAGED API 1.1 DOCUMENTATION

Performing Actions on Messages in a Conversation

After getting a handle to a particular conversation, you can perform actions that apply to all the email messages in the conversation. You can delete the conversation and all the email messages in it; move or copy the conversation to another folder; or mark the conversation as read or unread.

To delete a conversation, call Conversation.DeleteItems, and specify the folder to delete items from and the delete mode. The following example deletes the conversation from the Inbox folder; the messages are hard-deleted—they are permanently deleted and not copied to the Deleted Items folder.

```
conversation.DeleteItems(
    WellKnownFolderName.Inbox,
    DeleteMode.HardDelete);
```

The DeleteMode enum contains the following values:

➤   HardDelete: Permanently delete the email messages in the conversation.

➤   MoveToDeletedItems: Move the email messages in the conversation to the Deleted Items folder.

➤   SoftDelete: Move the email messages in the conversation to the dumpster; you can later retrieve them from the dumpster using the Recover Deleted Items feature accessible in the Ribbon in Microsoft Outlook.

If you don't specify a folder to delete from, the email messages in the conversation are deleted from all the folders in the user's mailbox.

You can also move the email messages in a conversation to another folder by using Conversation.MoveItemsInConversation, or copy them to another folder by using Conversation.CopyItemsInConversation.

Categorizing Conversations

Microsoft Outlook allows you to apply categories to email messages in a conversation to make them easier to manage. Categories are also used in the Quick Steps feature of Microsoft Outlook, which allows you to perform multiple actions on a conversation using a keyboard shortcut; for example, apply a category and move the email messages in the conversation to a specific folder.

The following example applies multiple categories to the email messages in a conversation. You can define the categories in a `List<string>` and call `Conversation.EnableAlwaysCategorizeItems` to apply them to the conversation.

```
var conversationView = new ConversationIndexedItemView(
    pageSize: Int32.MaxValue,
    offset: 0,
    offsetBasePoint: OffsetBasePoint.Beginning);

var conversations = _exchangeSevice.FindConversation(
    view: conversationView,
    folderId: WellKnownFolderName.Inbox);

foreach (var conversation in conversations)
{
    var categories = new List<string>()
        {
            "2011",
            "Projects"
        };
    conversation.EnableAlwaysCategorizeItems(categories, false);
}
```

code snippet EXODevelopment\EXOConversations.cs

`Conversation.EnableAlwaysCategorizeItems` indicates that all future email messages in the conversation should be automatically tagged with those categories. You can disable that by calling `Conversation.DisableAlwaysCategorizeItems`.

Alternatively, you can access the `Conversation.Categories` collection directly to add and remove items from it.

Working with Streaming Notifications

Notifications allow you handle certain events on a user's mailbox and run custom actions when those events occur. For example, you can monitor a customer service mailbox for new emails, and when a new message arrives, parse its contents and create a record in a customer service ticketing system. In this section, you learn how to work with the new Streaming Notification functionality in the EWS Managed API 1.1.

Version 1.0 of the EWS Managed API provided functionality to create subscriptions for both pull and push notifications. When subscribing to pull notifications, you specify the mailbox events to subscribe to and then manually check for any notifications; for example, using a timer to check for new notifications every 30 seconds. Push notifications work as you would expect; they automatically push notifications about events that your application is subscribed to. Using the EWS Managed API to develop pull subscription functionality is easy to do; however, it requires you to continuously poll Exchange for new notifications. Push subscriptions get around this issue, but they are complex to develop by comparison—you have to implement your own push notification listener for Exchange or Exchange Online to send notifications to.

The EWS Managed API 1.1 introduces Streaming Notifications, which replicate the functionality in push notifications but remove the need to build your own notification listener—making it a lot easier to implement in your application.

Creating a Streaming Notification Subscription

To subscribe to Streaming Notifications and handle notification events, your application should:

1. Call `ExchangeService.SubscribeToStreamingNotifications` and specify the folders and events to subscribe to.

2. Create a new `StreamingSubscriptionConnection` that specifies the lifetime of the subscription.

3. Add the Streaming Notification subscription to the subscription connection.

4. Define handlers for the different events raised by the subscription connection.

5. Implement the events handlers to handle the specific events.

When calling `ExchangeService.SubscribeToStreamingNotifications` to create a subscription for Streaming Notifications, provide an array of mailbox folder IDs to subscribe to events in, and an array of the types of events to subscribe to. The `EventType` enum defines the types of mailbox that can occur; its values include the following:

➤ `Status`

➤ `NewMail`

➤ `Deleted`

➤ `Modified`

➤ `Moved`

➤ `Copied`

➤ `Created`

➤ `FreeBusyChanged`

After creating a `StreamingSubscriptionConnection`, you can add multiple subscriptions to it. This gives you the flexibility to create subscriptions for different events in different mailbox folders and add them all to the same subscription connection.

The `SubscriptionConnection` class exposes three events:

➤ `OnNotificationEvent`: Indicates that a mailbox event has occurred

➤ `OnSubscriptionError`: Indicates that an error has happened in the subscription

➤ `OnDisconnect`: Indicates that the subscription has expired or been disconnected

```
// Subscribe to events on the user's Inbox
var subscription =
    _exchangeService.SubscribeToStreamingNotifications(
        folderIds: new FolderId[] {WellKnownFolderName.Inbox},
        eventTypes: new EventType[]
        {
            EventType.NewMail,
            EventType.Created,
            EventType.Deleted
        });

// Define a connection for the subscription
var subscriptionConnection = new StreamingSubscriptionConnection(
    service: _exchangeService,
    lifetime: 30);

// Add the subscription
subscriptionConnection.AddSubscription(subscription);

// Define handlers for notification events
subscriptionConnection.OnNotificationEvent +=
    new StreamingSubscriptionConnection.NotificationEventDelegate(
        subscriptionConnection_OnNotificationEvent);

// Define handler for subscription errors
subscriptionConnection.OnSubscriptionError +=
    new StreamingSubscriptionConnection.SubscriptionErrorDelegate(
        subscriptionConnection_OnSubscriptionError);

// Define handler for when the subscription disconnects or expires
subscriptionConnection.OnDisconnect +=
    new StreamingSubscriptionConnection.SubscriptionErrorDelegate(
        subscriptionConnection_OnDisconnect);

// Open the subscription connection
subscriptionConnection.Open();

Console.WriteLine("Created streaming notification subscription.");
Console.WriteLine("Waiting for notifications...");
Console.ReadLine();
```

code snippet EXODevelopment\EXONotifications.cs

You can use `SubscribeToStreamingNotificationsOnAllFolders` *to subscribe to Streaming Notifications on all the folders in a user's mailbox instead of having to list them all.*

Handling Notification Events

In this section, you learn how to implement the handlers for the different events raised by the SubscriptionConnection class:

➤ OnNotificationEvent

➤ OnSubscriptionError

➤ OnDisconnect

The SubscriptionConnection.OnNotificationEvent event is raised when an event defined in the Streaming Notification subscriptions occurs. The NotificationEventArgs exposes an Events collection; you can iterate through each event, examine it, and take appropriate action.

Notification events can occur on either mailbox items or folders; you can examine the type of notification event by checking if it is an ItemEvent or FolderEvent. This gives you the flexibility to take different action based on the type of notification event.

Available for download on Wrox.com

```
void subscriptionConnection_OnNotificationEvent
    (object sender, NotificationEventArgs args)
{
    // Get a handle to the subscription
    var subscription = args.Subscription;

    // Iterate through the events
    foreach (var notificationEvent in args.Events)
    {
        if (notificationEvent is ItemEvent)
        {
            switch (notificationEvent.EventType)
            {
                case EventType.Created:
                    Console.WriteLine("Notification: message created.");
                    break;
                case EventType.Deleted:
                    Console.WriteLine("Notification: message deleted.");
                    break;
                case EventType.NewMail:
                    Console.WriteLine("Notification: new email message.");
                    break;
                default:
                    break;
            }

            var itemEvent = notificationEvent as ItemEvent;
            Console.WriteLine("ItemId: {0}", itemEvent.ItemId.UniqueId);
            Console.WriteLine("Subject: {0}",
                Item.Bind(_exchangeService, itemEvent.ItemId.UniqueId).Subject);
        }
    }
}
```

code snippet EXODevelopment\EXONotifications.cs

The `SubscriptionConnection.OnSubscriptionError` event is raised when an error occurs in the subscription connection. The underlying `Exception` object is accessible through the instance of `SubscriptionErrorEventArgs`.

```
void subscriptionConnection_OnSubscriptionError
    (object sender, SubscriptionErrorEventArgs args)
{
    Console.WriteLine(
        "An error has occurred: {0}",
        args.Exception.Message);
}
```

code snippet EXODevelopment\EXONotifications.cs

The `SubscriptionConnection.OnDisconnect` event is raised when the subscription expires or is disconnected. You can choose to automatically reconnect to the subscription or present a choice to the user. You can access the subscription connection by casting the sender parameter as an instance of `StreamingSubscriptionConnection` and then call the `Open` method to reopen it.

```
void subscriptionConnection_OnDisconnect(
    object sender, SubscriptionErrorEventArgs args)
{
    var subscriptionConnection =
        sender as StreamingSubscriptionConnection;

    ConsoleKeyInfo cki;
    Console.WriteLine("The connection has expired or been disconnected.");
    Console.WriteLine("Do you want to reconnect? Y/N");
    while (true)
    {
        cki = Console.ReadKey(true);
        {
            if (cki.Key == ConsoleKey.Y)
            {
                subscriptionConnection.Open();
                Console.WriteLine("Reopened subscription connection.");
                break;
            }
        }
    }
}
```

code snippet EXODevelopment\EXONotifications.cs

Streaming Notifications in the EWS Managed API 1.1 provide a much easier way to work with notifications; they leverage the best features of push notifications but are easier to implement.

SUMMARY

The EWS Managed API is an easy-to-use, managed API that makes it easier to work with EWS to connect to Exchange Online, work with mailbox items, and interact with Exchange services such as the Free Busy service.

In the next chapter, you learn about working with the Lync API to build communications solutions for Lync Online.

7

Lync Online Development

WHAT'S IN THIS CHAPTER?

➤ Developing solutions for Lync Online using the Microsoft Lync 2010 SDK

➤ Working with the Lync Controls in WPF and Silverlight

➤ Working with conversations

➤ Working with extensibility applications

In this chapter, you learn how to build solutions for Lync Online in Office 365. Using the Lync 2010 SDK, you see how to integrate presence and click-to-communicate functionality into WPF and Silverlight applications, and also in Silverlight Web Parts in SharePoint Online. You also learn how to use the Lync 2010 Managed API to interact with conversations and program against the Lync object model. Finally, you build extensibility applications that run inside a Lync conversation window.

INTRODUCING LYNC ONLINE IN OFFICE 365

Lync Online provides a cloud-hosted instant messaging, presence, and peer-to-peer voice solution. Users can connect to Lync Online using the Lync 2010 client for Windows or Mac.

In this section, you learn about the different types of solutions that you can build for Lync Online, and how they differ from the solutions that you can build for Lync on-premises. You also learn about the tools for developing solutions for Lync Online—specifically the Microsoft Lync 2010 SDK, which includes the Lync Controls for WPF and Silverlight, and the Lync 2010 API.

Lync On-Premises Versus Lync Online

Microsoft Lync Server 2010 is an enterprise presence, instant messaging, online meeting, and voice solution. When taking full advantage of the voice features available in Lync, a company can use it to completely replace its phone system, allowing people to use their computers and other Lync-supported phone devices to make and receive calls.

From a functionality point of view, Lync Online includes only a subset of the functionality available in Lync on-premises—this includes presence, instant messaging, online meetings, and peer-to-peer voice. Peer-to-peer voice is only a subset of the full voice capabilities of Microsoft Lync Server 2010. In an on-premises deployment, you can use Lync to dial any phone number, for example +1 (425) 555-1212, and also to place a peer-to-peer Lync call to somebody else who runs the Lync client. In Lync Online, you can make peer-to-peer Lync calls only to other people in your organization (or organizations that yours is federated with).

From a development point of view, Lync solutions are typically divided into client-side and server-side solutions. In a client-side solution, code runs in a client application such as a custom WPF application, a Silverlight Web Part in SharePoint, or directly in a Lync conversation window. Client-side solutions reuse the connection that the Lync client has with the underlying Lync Server infrastructure—you are not responsible for programming the connectivity of these applications back to the Lync server.

In server-side solutions, the application code runs directly on the Lync server. Examples of server-side solutions include call centers and Interactive Voice Response (IVR) solutions. In a Lync-based call center, callers are greeted, put through an IVR to gather some information such as the purpose of their call, possibly placed on hold, and finally connected with an available customer service agent with the appropriate skills to assist them. The call center software can include functionality that enables supervisors in the call center to monitor these calls and provide coaching to agents when necessary. To build such applications, developers use the Unified Communications Managed API 3.0 (UCMA), which is a server-side API that interacts closely with the underlying Lync Server infrastructure. UCMA-based applications are not supported in Lync Online.

Other SDKs such as the Lync Server 2010 SDK allow you to interact directly with the Lync Server—these SDKs are not supported in Lync Online.

A good rule of thumb is that, in Lync Online, you can build only client-side applications. Lync Online is a multitenant environment, so applications that interact directly with the Lync Server infrastructure are not supported. In the next section, you learn about building client-side solutions for Lync Online using the Lync 2010 SDK.

Introducing the Lync 2010 SDK

The Lync 2010 SDK includes the Lync controls and the Lync API. The Lync controls enable you to easily integrate presence and click-to-communicate functionality into Silverlight and WPF applications. The Lync API enables you to program directly against the Lync object model, which means you can programmatically interact with the user's running instance of the Lync client.

In this section, you learn how to set up your development environment to work with the Lync SDK. You also learn about the different type of client-side Lync solutions that you can build using the Lync controls and Lync API. Before you install the Microsoft Lync 2010 SDK, take a moment to ensure that you have the right prerequisites installed and configured in your development environment.

Microsoft Lync 2010

The user's machine must have the Lync client installed and running to use the Lync controls and Lync API in your applications. Lync acts as an *endpoint* that provides a communication channel back to the Microsoft Lync Server 2010 infrastructure. You can use the Lync API to programmatically sign the user into Lync; however, the Lync controls appear grayed out if the user is not signed in.

Visual Studio 2010

Visual Studio 2008 SP1 and Visual Studio 2010 are supported for developing applications with the WPF Lync controls. You can use the WPF controls in both C# and Visual Basic .NET applications targeting either .NET Framework 3.5 SP1 or .NET Framework 4. The Silverlight Lync controls are supported only in Visual Studio 2010 and Silverlight 4. You can use the Silverlight controls in both C# and Visual Basic .NET applications targeting .NET Framework 4.

Visual Studio 2008 SP1 and Visual Studio 2010 are supported for developing applications with the Lync API. You can use the Lync API in .NET applications targeting either .NET Framework 3.5 SP1 or .NET Framework 4. The Lync API for Silverlight is supported only in Visual Studio 2010 and Silverlight 4. You can use the Lync API in Silverlight applications targeting .NET Framework 4.

Silverlight Support

The Lync controls are supported only in Silverlight 4. Be sure to install the Silverlight 4 Tools for Visual Studio before beginning development. If the appropriate Silverlight tools are not installed in your development environment, you cannot use the Visual Studio Silverlight project templates available with the Lync SDK.

When building Silverlight applications using the Lync SDK—leveraging either the Lync controls or Lync API—be sure to add the website that hosts the Silverlight application to the user's Trusted Sites collection in the security settings in Internet Explorer. Because of this requirement, the Lync SDK is not supported in Silverlight applications running out of browser.

Installing the Lync SDK

In a default installation, the Lync SDK is installed at `C:\Program Files (x86)\Microsoft Lync\ SDK`. The installer deploys the necessary assemblies for Silverlight and WPF, some sample applications, and Visual Studio project templates.

Referencing the Lync SDK Assemblies

The Microsoft Lync 2010 SDK installation directory contains an Assemblies folder where you can find assemblies compiled for Silverlight and WPF. If you do not use the Visual Studio project templates available with the SDK, you should reference the assemblies from this location.

A good practice is to include the necessary assemblies in a lib folder in your Visual Studio solution and reference them directly from there. This is particularly useful if you use Microsoft Team Foundation

Server — or any other build automation software — to perform automated builds of your application, because you don't need to install the Microsoft Lync 2010 SDK directly on the build server.

DEVELOPING APPLICATIONS FOR LYNC ONLINE

Now that you have installed the Lync SDK and configured your development environment for Lync development, it's time to build your first application for Lync Online.

This section introduces you to the types of applications that you can build for Lync Online, which include the following:

➤ WPF and Silverlight applications that leverage the Lync controls to integrate presence and click-to-communicate functionality.

➤ WPF and Silverlight applications that use the Lync API to interact directly with the Lync object model and the running instance of the Lync client.

➤ Extensibility applications that run directly in the Lync conversation window.

In this section, you learn how to build these types of applications for Lync Online. Learning how to build each of these types of applications warrants its own chapter; each section covers the basics.

Working with the Lync Controls

The Lync controls enable you to replicate functionality found in the Lync client using little to no code. Controls are available to show the presence of contacts, group them into lists, and search for contacts and display the results. Other controls allow you to easily start instant message and audio or video applications directly from your WPF and Silverlight applications.

 When you use the Lync controls in a Silverlight application, an ActiveX control provides an automation bridge between the controls and Lync. ActiveX is obviously supported only in Internet Explorer. Unfortunately, this means that the Lync controls are currently supported only in Silverlight applications running in Internet Explorer.

The Lync controls are easy to integrate into your applications; in this section, you walk through building a simple Silverlight application that displays the current user's presence and contact list. After building the Silverlight application, you create a SharePoint solution and integrate the Lync controls Silverlight application into a SharePoint Silverlight Web Part. Finally, you upload the SharePoint solution to SharePoint Online to see the Lync controls working in SharePoint Online and Lync Online.

Creating a Lync Silverlight Project

The first step is to create a Silverlight project that uses the Lync controls. After installing the Lync SDK, you can see some new project templates in Visual Studio, as shown in Figure 7-1. The Lync

WPF Application and Lync Silverlight Application project templates take care of adding the appropriate Lync SDK assembly references and get you started building Lync applications.

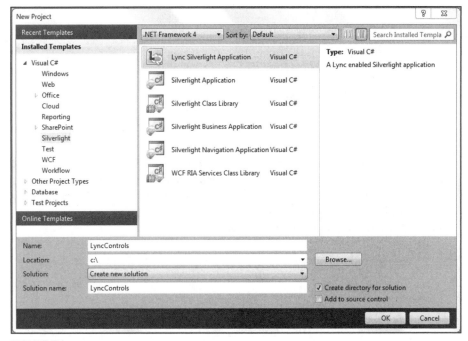

FIGURE 7-1

Choose the option for Visual Studio 2010 to create an ASP.NET Web Application to host your application; this is useful for testing before you integrate the Silverlight application into a SharePoint solution.

 A web application hosting a Silverlight application that uses the Lync SDK needs to be placed in the user's Trusted Sites collection in Internet Explorer. For this walkthrough, add `http://localhost` *to your Trusted Sites collection.*

As you can see in Figure 7-2, the necessary assembly references for the Lync SDK were created by the Lync Silverlight Application project template in Visual Studio.

These assembly references include the following:

➤ `Microsoft.Lync.Controls`

➤ `Microsoft.Lync.Controls.Framework`

➤ `Microsoft.Lync.Model`

➤ `Microsoft.Lync.Utilities`

The project template also creates a default XAML page, defines the appropriate XAML namespaces for the Lync controls, and places a sample control on the page. The `controls` XAML prefix is used to integrate the Lync controls in the XAML on the page in the Silverlight application.

```
<UserControl x:Class="LyncContactList.Page"
    xmlns="http://schemas.microsoft.com/winfx/2006/xaml/presentation"
    xmlns:x="http://schemas.microsoft.com/winfx/2006/xaml"
    xmlns:d="http://schemas.microsoft.com/expression/blend/2008"
    xmlns:mc="http://schemas.openxmlformats.org/markup-compatibility/2006"
    xmlns:controls="clr-namespace:Microsoft.Lync.Controls;
                    assembly=Microsoft.Lync.Controls">
```

code snippet LyncControls\LyncContactList\Page.xaml

Finally, the project template adds a `PresenceIndicator` control to the page to demonstrate how to use the Lync controls in XAML. To run the project, first change the `Source` property of the `PresenceIndicator` control to your Lync Online address; for example, `sip:george.durzi@ myoffice365domain.com`. Run the project; you see the `PresenceIndicator` control showing the signed-in user's current presence, as shown in Figure 7-3.

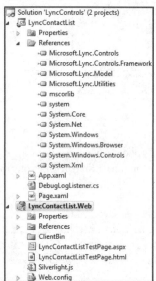

FIGURE 7-2

FIGURE 7-3

Adding Lync Controls to the Silverlight Application

Now that you have a simple Silverlight application that uses the Lync controls, you can add some additional controls to the application and explore their functionality.

1. Add a `MyStatusArea` control to the page. If you have `Page.xaml` in Design view, you can drag the controls from the Visual Studio Toolbox onto the design surface. The `MyStatusArea` control is handy because it bundles several features available in other controls: It shows the signed-in user's personal note and allows him or her to change the personal note, photo, and display name. It also shows a drop-down list allowing him or her to change their presence. The functionality in the `MyStatusArea` is available separately in the following Lync controls:

> `MyNoteBox`: Allows the signed-in user to set a personal note

> `MyPresenceChooser`: Provides a drop-down list that the signed-in user can use to change his or her presence

> `PresenceIndicator`: Shows the presence of a specific user

2. Add a `ContactList` control to the page; this control integrates the current user's Lync contact list directly into the Silverlight application. It includes properties such as `ContactLayoutView`, `ShowFriendlyName`, `ShowFrequentContacts`, `GroupViewBySettings`, and `ShowPivotBar` to customize how it appears in the application.

Available for download on Wrox.com

```xml
<Grid x:Name="LayoutRoot" HorizontalAlignment="Left">
    <StackPanel Orientation="Vertical"
                HorizontalAlignment="Left"
                VerticalAlignment="Top">
        <controls:MyStatusArea />
        <controls:ContactList
            ShowFrequentContacts="False"
            ShowFriendlyName="True"
            GroupViewBySetting="Status"
            ContactLayoutView="TwoLines"/>
    </StackPanel>
</Grid>
```

code snippet LyncControls\LyncContactList\Page.xaml

3. Run the application; as shown in Figure 7-4, you can view the current user's personal note and presence. You can also change the current user's Lync presence directly from the application—the changes are reflected immediately in the Lync client. You also see the user's contact list; you can interact with the contact list just as you would in the Lync client.

Packaging the Silverlight Application XAP into a SharePoint Solution

Now that you have a simple working Silverlight application that uses the Lync controls, create a SharePoint solution that integrates your Lync controls Silverlight application into a SharePoint Silverlight Web Part.

1. In Visual Studio, add an Empty SharePoint Project to the project solution.

2. Because you will later deploy this solution to SharePoint Online, specify that it should be a Sandboxed Solution.

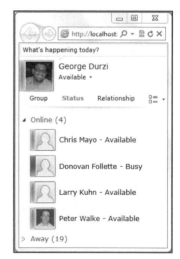

FIGURE 7-4

3. Add a blank Module item to the SharePoint project and name it: **Silverlight**.

4. Delete the `sample.txt` file that was automatically created with the module. The SharePoint project should include the output of the Lync controls Silverlight project, so that it can be automatically deployed with it. You can use Visual Studio to package the Silverlight application XAP with the SharePoint solution.

5. Right-click the new Silverlight module and select Properties.

6. As shown in Figure 7-5, highlight the Project Output References section and click the Ellipsis button to open the dialog shown in Figure 7-6.

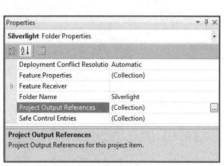

FIGURE 7-5

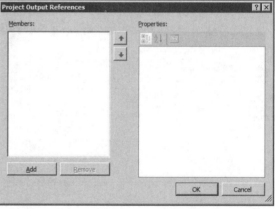

FIGURE 7-6

7. Click the Add button in the Project Output References dialog.

8. Change the Project Name property to the name of the Lync Silverlight application.

9. Change the Deployment Type property to **Element File**.

10. Expand the Deployment Location section and clear the value of path. The Project Output References dialog should look like Figure 7-7.

11. Click OK and save your changes.

12. Examine the `Elements.xml` file in the Silverlight module of your SharePoint project. You can see how the file `LyncContactList.xap` is included in the module, ensuring that it will be packaged with the SharePoint project when you deploy it to SharePoint Online.

13. Add the text **Url="SLXAPs"** to the `Module` element; this ensures that the XAP file is deployed to a folder on the SharePoint site called `SLXAPs`.

```xml
<?xml version="1.0" encoding="utf-8"?>
<Elements xmlns="http://schemas.microsoft.com/sharepoint/">
  <Module Name="Silverlight" Url="SLXAPs">
    <File Path="LyncContactList.xap" Url="LyncContactList.xap" />
  </Module>
</Elements>
```

code snippet LyncControls\LyncContactList.WebPart\Silverlight\Elements.xml

If you deploy the SharePoint project as-is to your on-premises SharePoint 2010 development environment, you can download `LyncContactList.xap` at `http://yoursite/SLXAPs/LyncContactList.xap`.

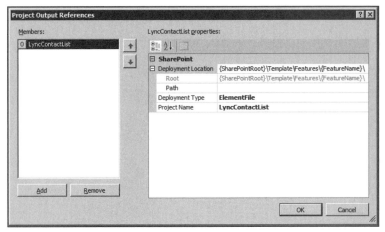

FIGURE 7-7

Creating a Page to Host the Silverlight Application

You can manually upload the Silverlight application XAP into a SharePoint Document Library, create a page, and add a Silverlight Web Part to it. However, it's more fun to automate this as part of your solution. In this section, you create a site page that automatically provisions a Silverlight Web Part containing the Lync controls Silverlight application.

1. Add a blank Module item to the SharePoint project and name it: **CustomPages**. Delete the `sample.txt` file that was automatically created with the module. The SharePoint tools in Visual Studio 2010 don't contain a project item for a simple site page; however, SharePoint development Visual Studio add-ins such as CKSDev provide this functionality. This is actually just a simple page that applies the content placeholders defined in the default master page.

2. After creating the site page in the module, open the `Elements.xml` file for the module, and set the `Url` property of the `Module` element to `SitePages`—this deploys the page to the Site Pages document library in the SharePoint site.

```xml
<?xml version="1.0" encoding="utf-8"?>
<Elements xmlns="http://schemas.microsoft.com/sharepoint/">
  <Module Name="CustomPages" Url="SitePages">
    <File Url="LyncContactList.aspx"
          Path="CustomPages/LyncContactList.aspx"
          Type="Ghostable" />
  </Module>
</Elements>
```

3. The site page contains two `WebPartZone` controls; you can include syntax in the `Elements.xml` file to provision a Silverlight Web Part in one of the web part zones and automatically load the `LyncContactList.xap` Silverlight application in it.

Of particular interest is the `AllUsersWebPart` item under the `File` element. This syntax provisions a web part of the specified type—a Silverlight Web Part—into the specified web part zone. The `Url` property of the web part points to the XAP file at `~site/SLXAPs/LyncContactList.xap`.

```xml
<?xml version="1.0" encoding="utf-8"?>
<Elements xmlns="http://schemas.microsoft.com/sharepoint/">
 <Module Name="CustomPages" Url="SitePages">
 <File Url="LyncContactList.aspx"
  Path="CustomPages/LyncContactList.aspx"
  Type="Ghostable">
 <AllUsersWebPart WebPartOrder="1"
  WebPartZoneID="Left"
  ID="LyncContactListSLWP">
 <![CDATA[ <webParts>
   <webPart xmlns="http://schemas.microsoft.com/WebPart/v3">
    <metaData>
     <type name="
     Microsoft.SharePoint.WebPartPages.SilverlightWebPart,
     Microsoft.SharePoint, Version=14.0.0.0,
     Culture=neutral, PublicKeyToken=71e9bce111e9429c" />
     <importErrorMessage>
     Cannot import this Web Part.
     </importErrorMessage>
    </metaData>
    <data>
     <properties>
     <property name="HelpUrl" type="string" />
     <property name="AllowClose" type="bool">True</property>
     <property name="ExportMode" type="exportmode">All</property>
     <property name="Hidden" type="bool">False</property>
     <property name="AllowEdit" type="bool">True</property>
     <property name="Direction" type="direction">NotSet</property>
     <property name="TitleIconImageUrl" type="string" />
     <property name="AllowConnect" type="bool">True</property>
     <property name="HelpMode" type="helpmode">Modal</property>
     <property name="CustomProperties" type="string" null="true" />
     <property name="AllowHide" type="bool">True</property>
     <property name="Description" type="string">
      A web part to display a Silverlight application.
     </property>
     <property name="CatalogIconImageUrl" type="string" />
     <property name="MinRuntimeVersion" type="string" null="true" />
     <property name="ApplicationXml" type="string" />
     <property name="AllowMinimize" type="bool">True</property>
     <property name="AllowZoneChange" type="bool">True</property>
     <property name="CustomInitParameters" type="string" null="true" />
     <property name="Height" type="unit">400px</property>
     <property name="ChromeType" type="chrometype">Default</property>
```

```
      <property name="Width" type="unit">350px</property>
      <property name="Title" type="string">Lync Contact List</property>
      <property name="ChromeState" type="chromestate">Normal</property>
      <property name="TitleUrl" type="string" />
      <property name="Url" type="string">
        ~site/SLXAPs/LyncContactList.xap
      </property>
      <property name="WindowlessMode" type="bool">True</property>
    </properties>
   </data>
  </webPart>
 </webParts> ]]>
 </AllUsersWebPart>
</File>
</Module>
</Elements>
```

code snippet LyncControls\LyncContactList.WebPart\CustomPages\Elements.xml

Packaging and Testing the Solution

After testing the SharePoint solution in your SharePoint 2010 on-premises SharePoint deployment, package it and upload it to the Solution Gallery of your SharePoint Online site. Browse to the site's feature management screen, and activate the Lync Contact List Web Part feature, as shown in Figure 7-8.

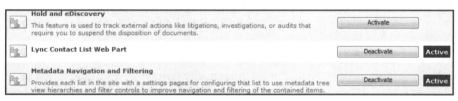

FIGURE 7-8

Browse to `https://yoursite.sharepoint.com/SitePages/ LyncContactList.aspx`. You can see that the `LyncContactList.aspx` was provisioned into the Site Pages library as specified by the SharePoint solution. The Lync Contact List Silverlight application was also automatically provisioned into a Silverlight Web Part on the page, as shown in Figure 7-9.

 Don't forget to add `https://*.sharepoint.com` *to your Trusted Sites collection in Internet Explorer.*

Working with Conversations

The Lync 2010 Managed API (Lync API) is part of the Lync SDK; it provides functionality for developers to interact with and automate the running instance of the Lync client. Like the Lync controls, any code that uses the Lync API requires that the Lync client is installed and running, because it reuses the connection that the Lync client has with the underlying Lync Server infrastructure.

The Lync API provides an easy-to-use, managed API that you can work with in your WPF, Windows Forms, and Silverlight applications. Using the Lync API, you can programmatically sign in to Lync, subscribe to and handle presence events for contacts and groups, and start conversations in different modalities.

FIGURE 7-9

In this section, you learn how to use the Lync API to sign in to the running instance of the Lync client. You also learn how to easily start conversations from your application.

Signing in to Lync

Because the Lync API relies on the Lync client running on the user's machine, your application should check if the Lync client is running and programmatically sign the user in if he or she isn't signed in already. The status of the Lync client can change; for example, the user may sign out of Lync—your application should gracefully react to these state changes.

The `LyncClient` class in the `Microsoft.Lync.Model` namespace is what you use to interact with the Lync client. Create a module-level variable of this type.

```
private Microsoft.Lync.Model.LyncClient _lyncClient;
```

code snippet LyncEventsLogger\Window1.xaml.cs

When your application starts, call the static `GetClient` method of the `LyncClient` class to get a handle to the Lync client. Wrap this code in a try/catch block; the method call throws an exception if the Lync client is not running.

```
try
{
    _lyncClient =
        Microsoft.Lync.Model.LyncClient.GetClient();
}
catch
{
```

```
MessageBox.Show(
    "Microsoft Lync is not running.",
    "Error",
    MessageBoxButton.OK,
    MessageBoxImage.Error);
Close();
}
```

code snippet LyncEventsLogger\Window1.xaml.cs

Now that you have a handle to the running instance of the Lync client, you can programmatically sign the user in. However, you should first check if the user is already signed in—do this by checking the State property of the LyncClient object. The State property is an enum called ClientState that has the following values:

➤ Invalid

➤ Uninitialized

➤ SignedOut

➤ SigningIn

➤ SignedIn

➤ SigningOut

➤ ShuttingDown

➤ Initializing

To sign the user in, call the BeginSignIn method of the LyncClient class. The first three parameters of the BeginSignIn method are the user's URI, domain name, username, and password. Leaving these as null signs the current user in using the credentials with which he or she logged into Windows.

The BeginSignIn method is asynchronous; you need to define an asynchronous callback function that executes when the operation completes. You can also use a lamba expression and handle the asynchronous callback directly within the method call.

Available for download on Wrox.com

```
if (_lyncClient.State != ClientState.SignedIn)
{
    _lyncClient.BeginSignIn(
        null,
        null,
        null,
        result =>
        {
            if (result.IsCompleted)
            {
                _lyncClient.EndSignIn(result);

                // Setup application logic here
            }
            else
```

```
              {
                  // Count not sign in to Lync
              }
          },
          "Local user signing in" as object);
    }
```

code snippet LyncEventsLogger\Window1.xaml.cs

The asynchronous callback in the lamba expression checks to see if the operation has completed and then calls `EndSignIn` to complete the sign in process. Because the user may sign in and out of Lync while your application is running, this is a good place to set up some application-specific logic that the application should execute when the user signs in to Lync.

Now that your application has signed the current user in to Lync, it also needs to monitor the state of the Lync client and react accordingly. In the next section, you learn how to monitor changes in the state of the Lync client.

Handling Changes in the State of the Lync Client

If your application includes functionality that depends on the state of the Lync client, it needs to monitor it and enable/disable features as necessary. For example, users shouldn't be able to start a conversation from the application if they are not signed in to Lync.

Use the `StateChanged` event of the `LyncClient` class to subscribe to events that fire when the status of the Lync client changes.

Available for download on Wrox.com

```
lyncClient.StateChanged +=
    new EventHandler<ClientStateChangedEventArgs>
        (LyncClient_StateChanged);
```

code snippet LyncEventsLogger\Window1.xaml.cs

The instance of `ClientStateChangedEventArgs` in the `StateChanged` event handler exposes `OldState` and `NewState` properties that tell you about the previous and current state of the Lync client. Your application can perform specific logic based on the state of the Lync client; for example, clean up any Lync API resources if the user is signing out.

Available for download on Wrox.com

```
void LyncClient_StateChanged
    (object sender, ClientStateChangedEventArgs e)
{
    switch (e.NewState)
    {
        case ClientState.SigningOut:
            Cleanup();
            break;
    };
}
```

code snippet LyncEventsLogger\Window1.xaml.cs

Starting Conversations Using Automation

Automation, a feature of the Lync API, enables you to quickly and easily start conversations in different modalities such as an instant message or video call. Automation automates the running instance of the Lync client, hence the name.

In this section, you learn how to handle Automation, how to start instant message and video calls, and how to get a handle to the conversation after starting it.

Getting a Handle to Automation

The Automation functionality is exposed by the `Microsoft.Lync.Model.Extensibility` `.Automation` class. Create a module level variable of this type so you can leverage the functionality throughout your application.

To initialize Automation in your application, call `LyncClient.GetAutomation()`.

```
_automation = LyncClient.GetAutomation();
```

code snippet LyncEventsLogger\Window1.xaml.cs

You can now use your `_automation` module-level variable to start conversations throughout your application.

Starting conversations using Lync Automation follows a simple pattern:

1. Create a list of participants to invite to the conversation.

2. Create a set of automation modality settings to attach to the conversation. These settings can vary, depending on whether you deal with instant messaging, desktop sharing, transferring files, using video, and so on.

3. Start the conversation.

4. Handle the callback.

Starting an Instant Message Conversation

To start a conversation using Automation, call `Automation.BeginStartConversation` and specify the conversation modality, participants, and any context data to embed into the conversation. You also need to specify a callback function that can run when the asynchronous operation completes.

```
var contextData =
    new Dictionary<AutomationModalitySettings, object>();
contextData.Add(
    AutomationModalitySettings.FirstInstantMessage,
    imText.Text);
contextData.Add(
    AutomationModalitySettings.SendFirstInstantMessageImmediately,
```

```
        true);

    _automation.BeginStartConversation(
        AutomationModalities.InstantMessage,
        myContactList.SelectedContactUris,
        contextData,
        StartConversationCallback,
        _automation);
```

code snippet LyncEventsLogger\Window1.xaml.cs

You don't need to specify any context to start an instant message conversation; however, it can be useful to accomplish something such as automatically embedding the first instant message to send. To do so, follow these steps:

1. Define the context data as a `Dictionary<AutomationModalitySettings, object>`.

2. Start adding context data items to it; for example, specify the first instant message, including that it should automatically be sent to all participants after the conversation is started.

3. Use the `AutomationModalities` enum to indicate the modality of the conversation to start; for example, `AutomationModalities.InstantMessage` indicates that the conversation contains the instant message modality.

When the conversation starts, you can see in Figure 7-10 how the first instant message is immediately sent to all the participants in the conversation.

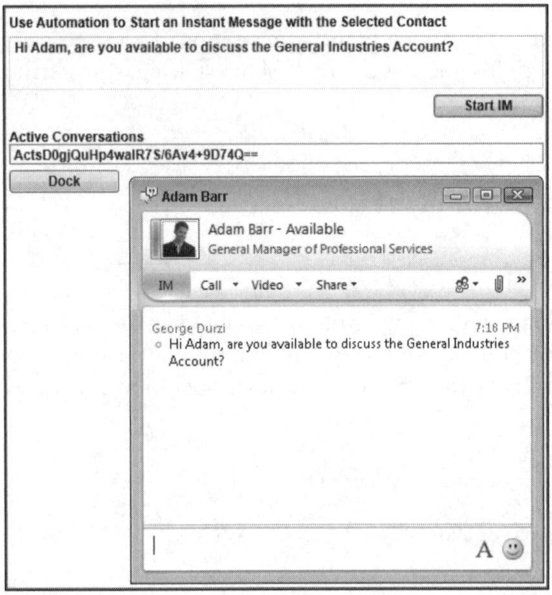

FIGURE 7-10

Starting an Audio or Video Call

You don't need to set any specific `AutomationModalitySettings` to start a simple audio or video conversation; you can simply pass `null` to the `contextData` parameter of the `BeginStartConversation` function.

```
_automation.BeginStartConversation(
    AutomationModalities.Video,    •
    myContactList.SelectedContactUris,
    null,
    StartConversationCallback,
    _automation);
```

code snippet LyncEventsLogger\Window1.xaml.cs

Getting a Handle to the Conversation

You may have noticed `_automation` being passed as the last parameter of the `BeginStartConversation` method. This parameter represents the asynchronous state of the operation; you can reference it in the start conversation callback to get a handle to the conversation window (and conversation) started as a result of the method call.

```
void StartConversationCallback(IAsyncResult ar)
{
    ConversationWindow conversationWindow = null;

    if (ar.IsCompleted)
    {
        conversationWindow =
            ((Automation)ar.AsyncState).EndStartConversation(ar);
        var conversation = conversationWindow.Conversation;

        // do something with the conversation
    }
}
```

code snippet LyncEventsLogger\Window1.xaml.cs

After you get a handle to the conversation window, you can dock it into your WPF or Windows Forms application. You can also access the underlying conversation using the `Conversation` property of the conversation window, allowing you to subscribe to events on the conversation.

Working with Extensibility Applications

A Lync extensibility application is an application that runs directly in the Lync conversation window. An example of a Lync extensibility application is a conversation translator application that translates instant message text from one language to another before injecting it into the conversation flow. In a Lync-based call center where agents field calls using Lync, an extensibility application can perform a reverse-lookup on customers and load their customer profile data from CRM into the Lync conversation window. Injecting the context of the conversation into an extensibility application running in the Lync conversation window can reduce unnecessary switching between applications because the participants already have all the data they need in the Lync conversation window.

In this section you learn how to build a Silverlight application that runs in the Lync extensibility application. The companion code to this section includes a WPF application shown in Figure 7-11 that allows you to browse a list of Fabrikam's customers and sales information and start a conversation with the account manager for a particular account. When the account manager picks up the incoming conversation, a Silverlight version of the application opens directly in the Lync conversation window and displays a chart of the account's recent sales.

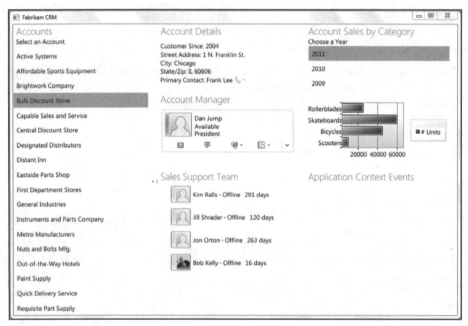

FIGURE 7-11

A Lync extensibility application is a type of contextual application in that it contains data related to the context of the conversation—in the case of the Fabrikam CRM application, the selected account.

To start an extensibility application and pass it the necessary context data, you need to:

➤   Install a contextual application package to register the extensibility application with the Lync Server infrastructure.

➤   Attach context to the Lync controls to start a conversation that includes context.

➤   Extract the application context data and load the extensibility application.

Registering a Contextual Application Package Using Install Registration

A contextual application package is a Windows Registry file that contains the information necessary to run the Lync extensibility application. To run the Lync extensibility application, a user must run the Windows Registry file on their machine. This registers the application with the Lync Server infrastructure, allowing Lync to run the extensibility window in the user's Lync conversation window.

Running a Windows Registry file to register a contextual application package with Lync Server is referred to as *Install Registration*. There are other techniques to register contextual application packages; however, this section focuses on Install Registration.

Available for download on Wrox.com

```
Windows Registry Editor Version 5.00

[HKEY_CURRENT_USER\Software\Microsoft\Communicator\ContextPackages]
[HKEY_CURRENT_USER\Software\Microsoft\Communicator\ContextPackages\
    {6B7BACE8-3968-4A1E-9BB5-F4BD666E36FB}]
"Name"="Fabrikam CRM"
"Parameters"="%AppData%"
"InternalURL"="http://crm.fabrikam.com/Default.aspx"
"ExternalURL"="https://crm.fabrikam.com/Default.aspx"
"ExtensibilityWindowSize"=dword:00000000
```

code snippet LyncExtensibilityApplication\Fabrikam.CRM.WPF\PackageRegistration_FabrikamCRM.reg

The contextual application package includes the following elements:

➤ A GUID: Represents a unique identifier for the package

➤ `Name`: The name of the application

➤ `Parameters`: A mechanism to pass application data to the extensibility application

➤ `InternalURL`: The internally accessible URL to launch the extensibility application from

➤ `ExternalURL`: The externally accessible URL

➤ `ExtensibilityWindowSize`: The size of the extensibility window in the Lync conversation window

Now that you have registered the contextual application package, you can attach context to the Lync controls to start contextual conversations.

Attaching Context to Lync Controls and Starting a Contextual Conversation

After running the Windows Registry file to register the contextual application package with the Lync Server infrastructure, your application can start a contextual conversation that launches the extensibility application in the Lync conversation window. A contextual conversation is a Lync conversation that has application context attached to it; in this section you learn how to attach context to a conversation so that the recipient can process it.

To specify the context to attach to a conversation, follow these steps:

1. Create an instance of `ConversationContextualInfo` and set its `ApplicationId` property to the GUID specified in the contextual application package. The `Subject` property of `ConversationContextualInfo` sets the text that appears in the toast (the incoming conversation notification).

2. Use the `ApplicationData` property to package data into the contextual conversation; for example, the ID of the account selected in the CRM system.

3. To attach the context to a Lync control, set the control's `ContextualInformation` property to the instance of `ConversationContextualInfo`.

```
// Create application context
var context = new ConversationContextualInfo();
context.Subject = account.AccountName;
context.ApplicationId = _applicationGuid;
context.ApplicationData =
    String.Concat("AccountId:", account.Id.ToString());

// Attach context
accountManager.ContextualInformation = context;
```

code snippet LyncExtensibilityApplication\Fabrikam.CRM.WPF\MainWindow.xaml.xs

4. To anticipate a user selecting an account in the Fabrikam CRM application, create an instance of `ConversationContextualInfo` and set its `Subject` property to the name of the selected account. Set the `ApplicationData` property to a string containing the `Id` of the selected account; the Silverlight extensibility application in the Lync conversation window parses this string to extract the account ID to display a chart of the recent sales for that account.

After you set the `ContextualInformation` property of the `ContactCard` Lync control to the instance of `ConversationContextualInfo`, any conversation you start from the `ContactCard` control includes the context. When the account manager receives the conversation, the Silverlight extensibility application is automatically loaded into the Lync conversation window.

Retrieving Application Context Data from an Extensibility Application

A Silverlight extensibility application running in the Lync conversation window can access the conversation it is hosted in and extract any data that was passed in with the conversation. When an account manager receives a conversation initiated from the Fabrikam CRM application, you can retrieve the account ID from the context provided in the conversation and use that to load the sales data for the account.

```
Conversation conversation = null;
conversation = LyncClient.GetHostingConversation() as Conversation;

if (conversation != null)
{
    _appData = conversation.GetApplicationData(_applicationGuid);

    this.Dispatcher.BeginInvoke(
```

```
new Action(() =>
{
    int accountId =
        Convert.ToInt32(_appData.Split(new char[] { ':' })[1]);
    Account account = _accounts.Where(a => a.Id == accountId).First();
    this.accountName.Text = account.AccountName;

    ((BarSeries)accountSalesChart.Series[0]).ItemsSource =
        account.GetSalesByYear(DateTime.Now.Year);
}));
}
```

code snippet LyncExtensibilityApplication\Fabrikam.CRM.Silverlight\Page.xaml.xs

You can call `LyncClient.GetHostingConversation` to access the conversation that the Silverlight extensibility application runs in. If the returned value is not null, you can confirm that the Silverlight extensibility application is actually running in the Lync conversation window.

You can then extract the application data from the conversation by calling `Conversation .GetApplicationData` and providing the GUID of the contextual application. Finally, you can use the application data to take the appropriate action in the Silverlight extensibility application; for example, to display a chart of the account's sales as shown in Figure 7-12.

FIGURE 7-12

SUMMARY

When developing communications solutions for Lync Online, you are limited to developing client-side applications using the Lync SDK. You can integrate the Lync controls into Silverlight Web Parts that run in SharePoint Online, build applications that interact with the running instance of the Lync client via the Lync API, and build extensibility applications that run in the Lync conversation window.

In the next chapter, you start learning about Windows Azure—Microsoft's foray into cloud computing.

PART IV
Working with Azure

8

Setting Up Azure

WHAT'S IN THIS CHAPTER?

➤ Setting up your Windows Azure account

➤ Getting your development environment set up for Windows Azure

➤ Making your first Windows Azure application

➤ Deploying your first Windows Azure application

➤ Controlling your Service by programming it

To host a working application on Windows Azure, you need to have a Windows Azure subscription and set it up for your application. In this chapter you learn how to do this, and you learn about the management portal through which you can manage subscriptions and hosted applications. But before you can even think about deploying an application, you need to develop it, and that means you need a development environment. You don't just need a development tool; you need an environment that emulates Windows Azure as it works in the cloud. Apart from setting up the environments, in this chapter you learn about the components that make up the Windows Azure hosting environment and the development environment. You also learn about the role of each component, and how to work with the core components, by creating a simple application and deploying it to the Windows Azure production environment.

GETTING WINDOWS AZURE

Getting Windows Azure isn't about downloading and installing software. It's an online service, so you need to register to gain access; after this, you can view a management portal through which you can control the different components of Windows Azure. You also gain access to a subscription portal to manage billing.

The following sections walk you through everything you need to start working with Windows Azure.

Registering for a Windows Azure Account

To register for Windows Azure, go to www.windowsazure.com. There you can find information about Windows Azure, and how you can "buy" it. At its core, Windows Azure uses a Pay-As-You-Go model; you pay for what you consume of the services it offers. If you don't use Azure at all, you pay nothing, so you can safely set up an account without being charged. Although Microsoft does offer invoiced use of Windows Azure, by default you pay for it through a credit card. The following purchase options are available for Azure:

➤ **Free trial:** You can sign up for a free trial, which gives you free use up to a certain quota for a fixed period of time after which you're charged the going rate.

➤ **Plan:** If you know upfront how much you will consume, you can also purchase a Plan, which gives you a monthly prepaid quota at a discount instead of the Pay-As-You-Go model. Anything you consume beyond the quota is billed afterwards.

 MSDN Subscribers, Microsoft Partners, and BizSpark program members can use Windows Azure at no charge up to a certain quota so before you register, it makes sense to determine if you qualify for free service under one of these memberships.

To start you must set up a *subscription*. A subscription is basically a container for services you want to consume under a single invoice. You can set up a subscription in a few simple steps:

1. Select one of the purchase options.

2. Sign up with your Windows Live ID.

3. Verify your account with your mobile phone.

4. Enter your credit card and billing information and accept the Subscription Agreement and Rate Plan.

After you enter all the information, your subscription will be *provisioned*, meaning that when the subscription is set up, the subscription details are available in the Microsoft Online Services Customer Portal, and you can manage the environment through the Windows Azure Platform Management Portal. You get e-mails that guide you to both portals when your subscription is provisioned, and the browser can automatically switch to the Management Portal when everything is set up.

A Tour of the Azure Portal

You use the Windows Azure Platform Management Portal to manage everything for your Windows Azure environment. The Management Portal is a Silverlight application, so you must have a browser capable of running Silverlight installed. You can access the Management Portal at https://windows.azure.com. After you log in with your Windows Live ID, you see the screen in Figure 8-1.

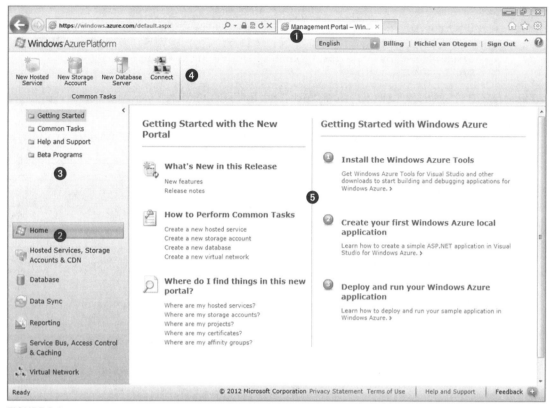

FIGURE 8-1

The Management Portal screen consists of several elements (refer to Figure 8-1).

1. **Navigation bar:** This is at the top and you can change the portal language here, as well as navigate to the Microsoft Online Services Customer Portal to see your billing information, and sign out of the portal.

2. **Main menu:** Located at the bottom left, you use this menu to manage the different components of the platform.

3. **Submenus:** Above the main menu is the submenu, where you can access information and tasks related to the chosen menu item.

4. **Taskbar:** You can also start common tasks from the taskbar. These tasks are applicable to the current context (that is, the chosen menu and submenu items). The tasks shown here differ as you navigate through the portal.

5. **Main screen:** This is where you get an overview of what you've selected in the menu and where you can take action. In some situations there is a properties window on the right of the main screen.

WHAT'S IN THE MAIN MENU?

Besides Home, the main menu contains items for the key components of the Windows Azure Platform:

➤ **Hosted Services, Storage Accounts & CDN:** In this chapter you mainly deal with this section.

➤ **Database:** This section manages SQL Azure and is covered in Chapter 11.

➤ **Data Sync and Reporting:** These sections are related to the Data Database section. With Data Sync, you can manage data synchronization between on-premises SQL Server databases and SQL Azure databases or between SQL Azure databases. In the Reporting section, you can manage SQL Azure Reporting Services.

➤ **Service Bus, Access Control & Caching:** In this section, you can manage the AppFabric Service Bus covered in Chapter 13, the AppFabric Access Control Service covered in Chapter 14, and the AppFabric Cache.

➤ **Virtual Network:** This section manages AppFabric Connect, which is covered in Chapter 15.

Some of the features available in the Windows Azure platform may still be offered in beta or Community Technology Preview (CTP). In that case you can sign up for the beta or CTP under Beta Programs in the submenu of Home.

System administrators may prefer to manage applications using the Windows Azure Platform PowerShell Cmdlets available at `http://wappowershell.codeplex.com/`. *Another option is the Windows Azure Platform Management Tool, a Microsoft Management Console Snap-in available at* `http://wapmmc.codeplex.com/`.

Managing the Windows Azure Environment

The opening screen of Hosted Services, Storage Accounts & CDN section shows the Deployment Health overview. This is basically a dashboard that shows you the health of everything you run. Although this is not clear from the overview, there is a hierarchy you should be aware of. The top level is the subscription, of which you can have multiple. Under a subscription you can have multiple hosted services, which in turn can contain different deployments.

A *hosted service* is basically an application that you host in Windows Azure. You can have a *production deployment* and/or a *staging deployment* of a hosted service. These are two identical deployments of your application. However, the production deployment is meant to run your live application, whereas the staging deployment is meant for final testing before you go into production. A staging environment basically gives you the opportunity to install and test your application as if it were in production. The next step is then to make the staging environment the production environment and vice versa. This way, you can deploy an application with minimum risk. If the staged application fails in production, you can switch back to the original production deployment.

In a deployment you can have multiple *roles*. For now, you can think of a role as a single part of your application, running in its own environment. As an example, you can have a website talking to web services. The website would be in one role, and the web services in another. Roles are discussed in more detail in the section "Understanding Azure Roles" later in this chapter.

A role can be run on multiple instances. An *instance* is comparable to a (virtual) machine. To facilitate load balancing and failover, you typically run your application on at least two instances. Microsoft gives uptime guarantees only if you run at least two instances per role. If your uptime requirements aren't that stringent, you can, of course, run on a single instance. You can also add more instances if the load on your application increases.

Affinity Groups

Windows Azure is hosted from quite a few datacenters around the world. When you deploy an application, you can tell Windows Azure in which region or subregion you want your application hosted. Examples of regions are Anywhere US and Anywhere Europe. A subregion is more specific, for instance South Central US or West Europe. This location can be significant because the farther users are from the datacenter an application is hosted, the higher the latency. This may result in significant performance degradation.

Now, a subregion can consist of multiple datacenters, and datacenters are so huge that there can be several switches and routers between two different applications in the same datacenter. So, if you have two applications that communicate with each other, latency may be a factor. This is where affinity groups come in. You can view an *affinity group* as a directive to Windows Azure to host two applications as close to each other within the same datacenter as possible. You can also include Windows Azure Storage in an affinity group. This doesn't increase only performance, but it can also lower cost because network traffic within a datacenter is free. Network traffic between datacenters on the other hand is charged.

Management Certificates

You can manage most of your applications using the Management Portal. However, there is also a Management API through which Windows Azure subscriptions can be managed. When you deploy applications through Visual Studio, this API is used. You can imagine that the security of this Management API is critical. After all, you don't want some unauthorized person to play with your application settings, or worse, deploy another application that does harmful things to your users. To avoid this, the Management API is secured with certificates and you need to upload at least one to use the Management API. You don't have to, but it makes some operations much simpler. This is discussed in more detail in the section "Deploying from Visual Studio."

User Management

If you plan to have administrators manage applications in the Management Portal, just having a single Windows Live ID that you can use isn't handy. The owner of the subscription, which is the Windows Live ID to which the subscription is tied, can create one or more Co-Admin accounts under User Management. A Co-Admin can do the same as the owner, except create new subscriptions.

Hosted Services

Under Hosted Services you can find detailed information about all the hosted services you have and the active deployments of these hosted services. As you can see in Figure 8-2, the subscription-hosted services-deployment-roles hierarchy discussed is shown.

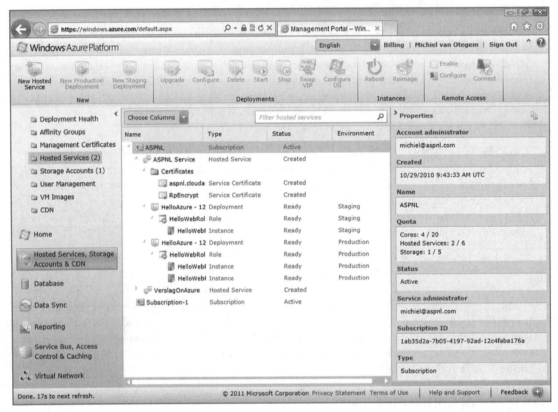

FIGURE 8-2

In Figure 8-2 you also see a Certificates folder under each hosted service. Here you configure certificates used by your application, either for a secure SSL connection or for other purposes, such as signing and encryption.

 The certificates in the Certificates folder are not the same as the certificates used for the management API. You learn more about this in Chapter 9.

Under a hosted service you can have one production deployment and one staging deployment. This is reflected in the taskbar, which does not enable you to add a production deployment to a hosted service already containing a production deployment. If you have a running deployment, you can fold it open to see all the roles and the instances running those roles. Clicking any of the nodes in the hierarchy displays detailed information in the Properties window on the right. A deployment is selected (refer to Figure 8-2), and among others the URL to access the application is shown, as well information regarding the public IP address and when the application was deployed.

Storage Accounts

Under Storage Accounts you manage your accounts on Azure Storage. These accounts are separate from hosted services because Azure Storage is in a sense one big data store managed by Microsoft. It isn't hosted on distinguishable instances but on a huge farm. You can create multiple storage accounts. These don't need to correspond with hosted services, but if there is a relationship, you may want to consider placing it in the same affinity group as explained earlier. You can have multiple applications share the same storage or create a single storage account for any application requiring storage. You can also use storage without using hosted services. Having multiple accounts makes sense to keep applications separated, especially if some of your storage accounts are also used by applications outside your control, such as a partner or client.

To access a storage account you need a key, and each storage account has a unique key, so you can ensure only applications that have the key can access the application. You can regenerate a key in case it is compromised in some way. This does take time however, so to avoid downtime, each storage account has two keys generated. You get a primary key and a secondary key. It doesn't matter which key you use, so if the primary key gets compromised, you can use the secondary key and then regenerate the primary key. To maintain a high level of security, you should refresh keys every once in a while. You can do this round-robin, so that refreshing keys does not cause downtime.

Content Delivery Network

The Windows Azure Content Delivery Network (CDN) enables you to make content in your hosted service or in Azure Storage available in other regions than where it is hosted. From the Management Portal you can set up one CDN endpoint for each hosted service or storage account. An endpoint exposes the content of the particular hosted service or storage account it is attached to by caching the content around the world. Clients accessing content through the CDN are routed to a copy geographically close to their location to get the best response time. Because the CDN caches content, it is only suitable for static content. You should not expose content that dynamically changes due to user interaction. Content that differs by querystring can be made available through the CDN however, but you should be aware that it takes a while to propagate changes, so users can get outdated copies.

> *If it is not just static content you want to make available in geographic locations close to the user, you have to deploy your hosted services to different data centers around the world. You then use Azure Traffic Manager to route clients to the closest data center. You may then also need some synchronization strategy to keep the different deployments synchronized. Azure Traffic Manager is beyond the scope of this book.*

Figure 8-3 shows the management interface for CDN endpoints. An endpoint is shown under the hosted service or storage account to which it applies, as is the case for the CDN under the `aspnl` storage account. When you add a new endpoint, you need to select what the endpoint applies to. You can tell Windows Azure to enforce a secure connection and whether it should accept querystring parameters to differentiate between content. You can also add a domain (refer to Figure 8-3). By default, a URL is assigned to your CDN. For storage accounts this is some random identifier followed by the domain of the CDN. If you don't like this, you can use the Add Domain function to add a custom domain name. This domain name needs to be verified, so you do need control over the DNS of that domain. When you add a domain, you will be instructed to add a record to the DNS.

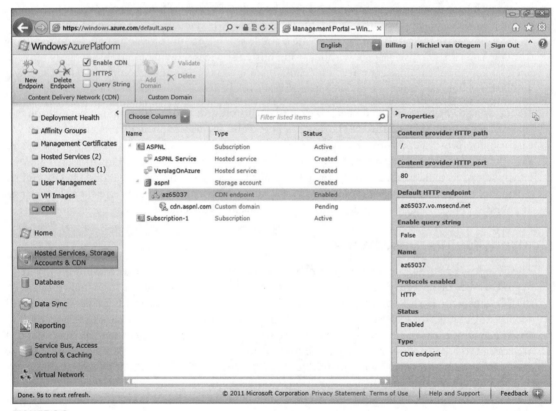

FIGURE 8-3

A Tour of the Customer Portal

If you want to see how much you've used of the Windows Azure platform, you must go to the Microsoft Online Services Customer Portal. This is where you can manage subscriptions and several services Microsoft offers online, not just Windows Azure. You can go there via the Billing link at the top of the Management Portal, or navigate directly to `https://mocp.microsoftonline.com/site/default.aspx`. Even if you come from the Management Portal, you are not automatically signed in, so before you can do anything, you need to make sure you are.

The Customer Portal serves two purposes: managing your existing subscriptions and buying new subscriptions. Most interesting about managing your subscriptions is your usage, and consequently what you're being billed. You can view all that by clicking View My Bills on the homepage. This shows you a list with one item for each subscription. If you click one of those links, you can see a screen, as shown in Figure 8-4. Each item with an Arrow icon is expandable to show the detailed charges. You can view any invoice by switching the billing period, but by default you see the current period up until today. Be aware that this is not real time, so it may not be entirely accurate.

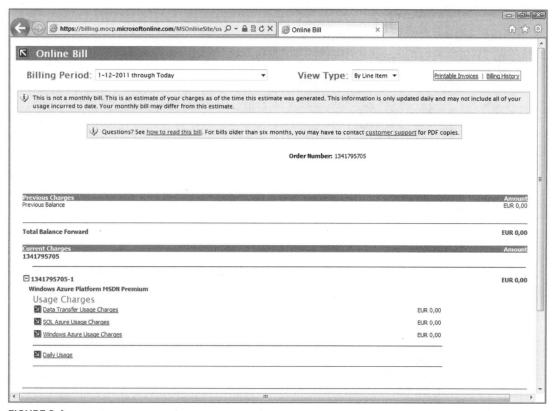

FIGURE 8-4

UNDERSTANDING AZURE ROLES

Earlier you were briefly introduced to the concept of a role in Windows Azure. The best way to understand roles in more depth is to look at large scale multitier applications, as shown in Figure 8-5, which is divided in four major blocks of servers, each with a different function.

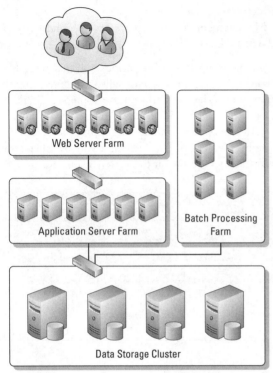

FIGURE 8-5

A typical action by a user comes in at the web front end. The web front end takes care of only the user interface, so it forwards the real work to the application servers. The application servers talk with the data servers to retrieve and store data for the business operations it performs. A separate set of servers is responsible for batch processing not directly related to user requests. For each block of servers, also known as a *farm*, the other block of servers looks like a single server because they sit behind a load balancer. The load balancer is responsible for routing a request to the server that has the least load on it at that time.

The reason you would want to run applications in such an environment is twofold (refer to Figure 8-5): availability and scaling. Should a server in the farm fail, the other server(s) can take over. This redundancy ensures that an application stays available to users. With multiple servers active at the same time, user requests can be sent to the different servers to balance the load and ensure quick response times. When more users use the application, more servers can be added to the farm, as long as the server runs the same software and is configured in the same way as the other servers in the farm. Also, dividing the different functions over different servers prevents the functions from working against each other.

Of course, there is one major drawback to the setup in Figure 8-5: It's expensive, especially if you need all the capacity only at peak hours. In addition, this environment is difficult and thus expensive to maintain. Managing a server farm is an order of magnitude more complex than managing a single server. If you've ever worked on an application that runs on more than a single server, you probably know that it takes a complex hardware and network configuration. It is also hard to ensure that the software runs properly on all servers. Installing a new version of the application without down time complicates matters even further, and the same is true when you want to add additional servers to meet the demand.

When you use Windows Azure, management of the hardware and network configuration is taken care of for you. Management is highly automated, so adding additional instances (or removing them) is something you can do without the need for a systems engineer. In a sense, you can think of Windows Azure as a giant warehouse of servers waiting to become part of a farm running (part of) an application. Basically the only difference between an instance in your application and an instance in another application is the software components running on the instance and its configuration. The operating system, server software, and runtime framework are the same on each instance. If you must add a new instance to the farm running your application because you require additional capacity or because a running instance fails, all that you need is the software you built and some configuration to join the farm. This brings you back to what a role is. You can think of a *role* as a functional unit of your application, but you can also think of it as a unit of configuration for a farm of instances. For a role, you determine which software will run on the instances, how many instances the software will run on, and so on.

For the most part, the one-size-fits-all approach works fine. However, servers performing one function may not run as well on a server configured for another function. For instance, running a batch process on a web server is not a particularly good idea. This is why Windows Azure offers different types of roles: the Web Role, the Worker Role, and the VM Role. Each of these roles is discussed in more detail in the following sections.

Web Role

You're likely to use the *Web Role* the most. It has the setup of a web server and is mainly intended to host web applications and web services. It has Internet Information Services (IIS) preconfigured, so that all you need to do is deploy the web application and it's good to go. This is also the main benefit of using a Web Role. It requires the least amount of setup, so when a new instance is provisioned, it is up and running in no time.

In Visual Studio, you can find several types of Web Role projects. The common denominator between them is that they are hosted in IIS. Three of those are ASP.NET Web Role projects, each for a slightly different technology stack (that is, WebForms, MVC 2, and MVC 3). These only differ in how you create the user interface. The other Web Role project is for Windows Communication Foundation (WCF), so you can host web services. There is nothing preventing you from using WCF in one of the ASP.NET Web Roles, so if your application consists of both a web interface and web services, you can choose one of the ASP.NET Web Roles and add WCF services to it.

Although a Web Role is hosted in IIS, you can still have some custom work done before the role becomes active using a *startup task*. This enables you to install and configure components you need. You can upload these as part of the setup package, but you can also acquire them from an Internet-based source. Using NuGet (see `http://NuGet.org`) that is integrated to Visual Studio to get packages into your project is one good way to retrieve packages and keep them up to date in your Web Role. Maarten Balliauw explains how to do this in a blog post you can find at `http://bit.ly/azurenuget`.

Worker Role

A *Worker Role* is similar to a Web Role but it doesn't come with a preconfigured instance of IIS, although you could run IIS on it if you need it. The Worker Role is essentially a clean Windows Server with no running services. This means your application can benefit from the machine's resources as much as possible. The primary reasons to use a Worker Role are as follows:

> ➤ **Running background processes:** Some processes need to run periodically to perform some task. This can be done efficiently on a Worker Role.

> ➤ **Running long running processes:** Long-running processes run outside of a web server because they can't be limited by timeouts imposed by the web server and should not rely on an active connection with the client. Web applications can offload requests that take a long time to a Worker Role process.

In addition to the preceding reasons, you can use a *startup task* to install and configure application components and services your application may need, just like you can in a Web Role. This makes the Worker Role suitable for a few more scenarios:

> ➤ **Use a web server other than IIS:** For instance, if you have an application that runs on Apache, rather than IIS, you can install Apache in the Worker Role and use that to serve the application instead.

> ➤ **Use a framework other than .NET:** Windows Azure applications aren't restricted to the .NET Framework, but it is the only framework available by default.

The Worker Role works by virtue of the `RoleEntryPoint` class, which a Web Role and Worker Role both implement. The `RoleEntryPoint` class contains three methods, which are fired at appropriate points in the life cycle of a role. These methods are as follows:

> ➤ `OnStart`: Used to do anything needed before the application can be used, such as installing components.

> ➤ `Run`: Used to run the application. By default the implementation never returns.

> ➤ `OnStop`: Runs when the `Run`-method returns.

The `Run`-method is the key to the Worker Role. You can see it as the `Main`-method. As long as it doesn't return, the application is running.

VM Role

The Web Role and the Worker Role provide a predefined environment on which you can deploy applications specifically created for those environments. So what must you do when you need something that's not available in either role? This is what the *VM Role* is for. A VM Role enables you to create a complete custom environment and upload it to Windows Azure. It is called a VM Role because the custom environment is a Virtual Machine image based on Windows Server 2008 R2. When you use a VM Role, you must create a disk image and upload it to Windows Azure Blob Storage. That disk image, known as the *base image*, is then used as a template for instances deployed because the stored image is immutable. This is logical because you can't run multiple instances from one disk because of concurrency. Therefore each instance is imaged from the base image. An obvious side effect is that each instance runs on its own disk image, so changes to the disk of one image are not available to other instances. And to make matters worse, if an instance fails, regardless of whether this is due to software or hardware failure, the disk image is thrown away, and a new instance is spawned with a fresh image. This is also the case if the AppFabric Controller decides to move an instance to another physical server within the datacenter. This is by design because Windows Azure assumes that failure is inevitable.

If you are familiar with virtual machines, you may have thought that you could install just about anything and run it in on Windows Azure. By now you probably realize that this is not the case. Although you can install any software that runs on Windows Server 2008 R2, there is no guarantee that it will work as expected. If the software writes data to the disk other than temporary data just needed while the instance runs, you're out of luck. The software essentially needs to be *stateless*. This is twofold; it can't maintain state within an image because instances can be recycled at any time, and it can't maintain state across client requests because there is no guarantee that the next request from the same client will be handled by the same instance because of the load-balancing infrastructure.

So with the preceding information in mind, when does it make sense to use a VM Role? Following are two main scenarios in which this makes sense:

➤ **Setup takes a long time:** If the startup task of the role takes a long time, adding new instances may take too long for it to be effective.

➤ **Automated installation is not possible:** This mainly happens when you have a setup package that requires manual interaction or configuration, or when the installation has a high probability of running into problems you have to correct.

A final thing you need to be aware of if you decide to use a VM Role is that you are responsible for keeping it updated. Windows Azure automatically updates and patches Web Roles and Worker Roles, but if a VM Role needs an update, you must upload a new base image.

 Creating a VM Role application is beyond the scope of this book, but you can find a walkthrough at http://bit.ly/createvmrole.

GETTING YOUR DEVELOPMENT ENVIRONMENT READY

Developing for Windows Azure is somewhat different from developing other types of applications. Your local machine is not the same as a Windows Azure instance, let alone multiple instances in different roles. So to properly develop Windows Azure applications, you need to emulate the Windows Azure environment locally. Therefore getting your development environment ready involves more than just installing you code editor of choice. The following sections walk you through which components you need and how to install these.

System Requirements

Windows Azure essentially runs on top of Windows Server 2008 or Windows Server 2008 R2, and you can set up a good development environment on either. If you want to develop on a desktop machine, Windows 7 and Windows Vista SP2 are also capable of running the needed components for Windows Azure.

What Language Should You Choose?

If you're already a .NET developer, you're used to choosing between different programming languages. Windows Azure is no different because it is built on top of Windows and has the .NET Runtime installed. This means that you can develop applications in C#, F#, and VB.NET. These are all first-class citizens that can run out of the box, as you would expect. But the story doesn't end there. Windows Azure is a Windows Server under the hood, so it's a fair assumption that anything that can run on Windows Server could run on Windows Azure. This isn't entirely true because Windows Azure has some restrictions to ensure performance, scalability, security, and so on. But a lot of things can run on Windows Azure, including application platforms not natively supported on Windows Azure. This means you can also host Java, PHP, Python, and Ruby applications on Windows Azure although you must install and kick-start the runtime required for those languages. This isn't incredibly hard, and Microsoft contributes to several (open source) initiatives that help you leverage Windows Azure with other platforms.

Windows Azure works best with Microsoft's languages and tools. Microsoft is definitely committed to making other platforms work on Windows Azure, but most effort goes into tuning the .NET Framework for Windows Azure and making development easy for developers preferring Visual Studio.

Regardless of the language you choose, running an application on Windows Azure isn't quite the same as running it on a server (farm) under your control. You need to take the restrictions mentioned earlier into account. For example, writing to the Windows Azure file system is recommended only for temporary data because files are not persisted across restarts of you application.

Getting the Developer Tools

To develop Windows Azure applications, you at least need the Windows Azure SDK. What else you need depends on the language you intend to use. If you're going to use C#, F#, or VB.NET, using Visual Studio is a no-brainer. You could develop without Visual Studio, but there's no good reason not to use it. If you don't have Visual Studio, don't worry. If you intend to use C# or VB.NET, you can use Visual Web Developer Express, which is available for free.

You can install the needed developer tools in several ways, depending on what you already have, what you need, and how much you want to do manually. You can find information about several ways to do the installation in the following section.

Installing from Visual Studio

If you already have Visual Studio 2010 Professional or better installed, you can start the installation from there. All you need to do is open the dialog to create a new project, and select the Cloud section, as shown in Figure 8-6.

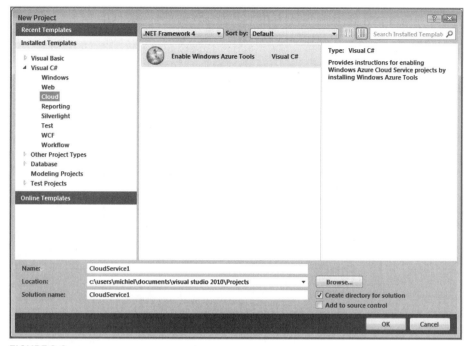

FIGURE 8-6

When you double-click Enable Windows Azure Tools, another screen opens where you need to click Install Now. That initiates the download of the Web Platform Installer. From here the installation is almost the same as when you don't have Visual Studio, so read on.

Installation with the Web Platform Installer

If you don't have Visual Studio 2010, you can use a development environment known as Visual Web Developer Express (VWDE), which is a free entry-level version of Visual Studio just for web development. You could install that separately, but if you go to http://bit.ly/windowsazuresdk you can install it together with the Windows Azure tools you need at once, using the Web Platform Installer. This is a tool that checks what's already on your machine, downloads and installs all the necessary updates and components, and configures them. This is even the case for needed Windows components such as Internet Information Services 7.x (IIS). For Windows Azure, it also installs SQL Server Express (if not installed already) so the Windows Azure emulator can also emulate Windows Azure Storage. This makes installation with the Web Platform Installer a no-brainer. When it is done, you're ready to go.

The Web Platform Installer you download is preconfigured with a scenario to install the Windows Azure SDK, the Windows Azure AppFabric SDK, Visual Studio (if not installed already), and the Windows Azure Tools for Visual Studio, so after it's installed it automatically shows a screen like in Figure 8-7, indicating you are going to install both Visual Studio and Windows Azure tooling.

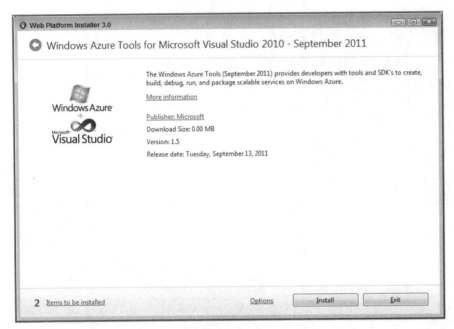

FIGURE 8-7

When you click Install, you're asked to accept the license agreement. Because you're installing a whole bunch of software, you're accepting the license agreement of all the software. You can scroll through the list to see what's being installed and configured on your system. After you accept the license agreement, you still need to determine the security settings for SQL Server Express. You can choose between the following:

➤ **Windows Integrated Security:** Enables access to SQL Server only through a Windows account. This is more secure, but is also somewhat harder to get working properly because an application runs under the account configured in IIS.

➤ **Mixed Mode Authentication:** Enables access to SQL Server through a Windows account as above, but also through a username and password only known to SQL Server. This makes it easier to set up, especially with a SQL Server not running in the same Windows domain. This option is the best choice for Windows Azure development.

Now you can sit back and relax. You can easily have a cup of coffee because not only does the download take a while, but the installation also takes its fair share of time. Also, because the Web Platform Installer installs everything you need, it may need to restart Windows. After the restart the Web Platform Installer continues automatically. When installation finishes, you are notified of everything that installed. When you click Finish, the Web Platform Installer returns to an overview screen, showing other software you can install. This includes the latest Visual Studio service pack, which you should also install for good measure. In Chapter 9, "Identity in Azure," you also work with Visual C# 2010 Express (VCSE). It makes sense to install that before installing the service pack because the service pack applies to both products. You can install VCSE from `http://bit.ly/vcse2010`. If you need to run the Web Platform Installer again, you can find it in All Programs.

Both VWDE and VCSE are free, but if you want to use them for longer than 30 days, you need to register. If you are not prompted to do so automatically, you can start it from the menu under Help ⇨ Register Product.

 In this book, Visual Studio and Visual Web Developer Express are mostly synonymous. VWDE is named explicitly only when the distinction is important.

Installing Windows Identity Foundation

In the next chapter you work with Windows Identity Foundation (WIF) to secure applications. This means you need WIF and the WIF SDK. These are not installed by the Web Platform Installer when you install Windows Azure Tools because you don't need them. However, as you learn in the next chapter, WIF is a key component for modern user authentication, so it is a good idea to install it. You can download WIF from the accompanying Knowledgebase article at `http://bit.ly/wifinstall`. This installs the WIF runtime components. This is installed as a Windows Update and not as a separate installation, so it won't show up in the installed programs list by default. You can find the WIF SDK download in the Related Resources at the bottom of the WIF download page. Be sure to install the 4.0 version of the SDK. The SDK contains some tools, samples, and documentation, and several Visual Studio templates. You learn about these in the next chapter when WIF is discussed in detail.

If you use VWDE, the Visual Studio templates are not installed properly because the WIF SDK doesn't recognize VWDE as Visual Studio. To ensure the templates show up in VWDE, you need to add them to VWDE manually by doing the following:

1. Open Windows Explorer.

2. Navigate to `C:\Program Files\Windows Identity Foundation SDK\v4.0\Visual Studio Extensions\10.0`.

3. Copy all files in the folder.

4. Navigate to `C:\Program Files\Microsoft Visual Studio 10.0\Common7\IDE\VWDExpress\ProjectTemplates\Web\CSharp\1033`.

5. Paste the copied files.

6. Open the command prompt as Administrator.

7. Change directory to `C:\Program Files\Microsoft Visual Studio 10.0\Common7\IDE`.

8. Type **VWDExpress /InstallVSTemplates**.

If your machine runs 64-bit Windows, you need to replace Program Files with Program Files (x86) in the steps above.

Installing the Windows SDK

If you don't have Visual Studio, then you are missing the makecert tool you use in the next chapter. This is a tool to create certificates used for encryption and signing. Fortunately, this tool is also available in the Microsoft Windows SDK for Windows 7 and .NET Framework 4, which you can install from `http://bit.ly/windows7sdk`. You need only a small portion of the SDK, and because this is a web installer, only the selected bits are downloaded. What you need to select is shown in Figure 8-8.

FIGURE 8-8

Installing the SDK Only

If you plan to develop applications using a different tool than Visual Studio you can just install the SDK. At `http://bit.ly/windowsazuresdk` you can perform a manual installation.

You should also install the Windows Azure Libraries for .NET. You use these libraries to work with services in the Azure platform for access control, caching, and communication between applications.

The Azure services addressed by the Windows Azure Libraries for .NET are discussed in detail in Chapters 13, 14, and 15.

Installing Other Language Tools

As explained earlier, you can develop for Windows Azure with languages not supported natively by the Windows Azure platform. For the following languages tools are available through `http://bit.ly/windowsazuresdk`:

➤ **Java:** Consists of client libraries to work with various Azure APIs and tools for the Eclipse development environment. These tools include a Project Creation Wizard and project templates, utility scripts, and an Ant-based builder.

➤ **Node.js:** Consists of client libraries and PowerShell tools. These are also available from github at `http://bit.ly/gitazurenodejs`.

➤ **PHP:** Consists of client libraries, command line tools, and scaffolding templates.

If you want to develop in another language, you can still download the Windows Azure SDK to develop applications with, but you need to do everything that the client libraries provide yourself. In the next section you learn more about what is in the Windows Azure SDK, and why you need it.

WINDOWS AZURE SDK

The Windows Azure SDK is the only requirement when you want to make applications for Windows Azure. Apart from documentation and samples, the SDK contains two sets of tools: the Windows Azure SDK Tools and the Windows Azure Tools for Visual Studio.

The documentation and samples that go with the SDK are all online and linked to from the SDK. The advantage of that is that the documentation and samples are up to date. The disadvantage, however, is that developing without an Internet connection is not a good idea.

Windows Azure SDK Tools

There are several important tools in the SDK. Most important is the Windows Azure Compute Emulator and the Windows Azure Storage Emulator, also referred to as the *Development Fabric* or *DevFabric*. Without these, developing applications for Windows Azure would be almost impossible because the Azure environment has some unique characteristics your local computer does not. Most obvious, of course, is that Windows Azure theoretically scales out infinitely. The Compute Emulator is a virtualized environment capable of running multiple roles simultaneously and multiple instances within a single role. That said, it can become excruciatingly slow if you fire up too many roles and instances, so you should do so wisely. Only test with multiple instances if you intend to test whether your application runs well on multiple instances. You can deploy and start applications using the command line tools in the SDK. When you use Visual Studio or some of the other development environments that support Windows Azure development, these command-line tools are run under the covers, so you are not crippled in any way if you decide just to use the command line. The Windows Azure SDK comes with the following command-line tools:

➤ **CSEncrypt:** Encrypts a password for use with a Remote Desktop Connection to a running instance

➤ **CSPack:** Builds and packages applications for deployment to Windows Azure or the DevFabric

➤ **CSRun:** Runs a package on the compute emulator

➤ **CSUpload:** Uploads VHD images for a VM Role and certificates to connect to an instance via a Remote Desktop Connection

➤ **DSInit:** Initializes the local storage environment

 It is beyond the scope of this book to demonstrate how to use the command-line tools without a development environment, but at `http://bit.ly/azurecmdline` *you can find a great blog post by Steve Marx of the Windows Azure team with details.*

Of the preceding tools, DSInit is the only one you need to remember. You need to run it when the local storage environment has not been set up (correctly) or if the local storage environment is corrupt. If you want to use the command-line tools, you can go to Start ➪ All Programs ➪ Windows Azure SDK vX.X and open the Windows Azure SDK Command Prompt.

Windows Azure Tools for Visual Studio

The Windows Azure Tools for Visual Studio enable you to develop and deploy applications from within a single environment. After you install the tools, you have a template for a Windows Azure Project in the Cloud section that creates a solution with all the necessary content. The tools also come with several context menus applicable to Windows Azure projects in the Solution Explorer. With these, you can package or publish the application, add a new Role to the project, or go directly to the Management Portal. In addition there's a context menu for existing projects that aids you in turning a project into a Windows Azure application.

A key aspect for most developers is that the Windows Azure Tools for Visual Studio enable you to debug applications by setting breakpoints in code, just as in any other C# or VB.NET application. This works fine in Visual Web Developer Express, so there is no reason why you shouldn't use Visual Studio to develop .NET-based Windows Azure applications. Visual Studio can save you an enormous amount of time with just the debugging support.

Another benefit of the tools is the configuration editor that is installed with them. This prevents you from making mistakes in the XML file governing the Role configurations in a Windows Azure application.

To develop a Windows Azure application in Visual Studio, you need to run Visual Studio under elevated rights, so it has administrator privileges. You can do so by right-clicking Visual Studio in the Start menu and selecting Run as Administrator. Alternatively, you can turn off User Account Control (UAC), but this is not recommended on a computer you also use to read e-mail and browse the Internet.

DEVELOPING A WINDOWS AZURE APPLICATION

The best way to get a feel for the Windows Azure development environment and the Visual Studio tools supporting it is by creating a simple application. Assuming you already have some experience with developing .NET applications, the focus is on what is specific to Windows Azure.

Starting with Hello World

One of the advantages of Visual Studio is that several templates are available that provide you with a fully functional application. This means you can get up and running quickly with a working demo application. Follow these steps:

1. Run Visual Studio as Administrator.

2. Create a new project by clicking File ➪ New Project.

3. In the left box in the New Project dialog, go to Installed Templates ➪ Visual C# ➪ Cloud.

4. There is only one project type: Windows Azure Project. Under Name, enter **HelloAzure** and click OK.

5. In the New Windows Azure Project, add an ASP.NET Web Role to the Window Azure solution.

6. Right-click the added Web Role, and click Rename.

7. Rename the Web Role to **HelloWebRole** and click OK.

After Visual Studio sets up the solution, the Solution Explorer should show a solution with two projects in it, as shown in Figure 8-9. The HelloWebRole project is just like a regular ASP.NET Web Application, except that it contains `packages.config` with the NuGet configuration and `WebRole.cs` implementing the `RoleEntryPoint` class discussed earlier. The HelloAzure project contains the configuration needed to run the ASP.NET application in HelloWebRole on Windows Azure (or on the DevFabric).

You can now build and run the application by pressing F5 (with debugging) or Ctrl+F5 (without debugging). This results in the Compute Emulator starting and HelloWebRole deploying to the DevFabric. The browser opens automatically to show the home page of the web application running at `http://127.0.0.1:81/`.

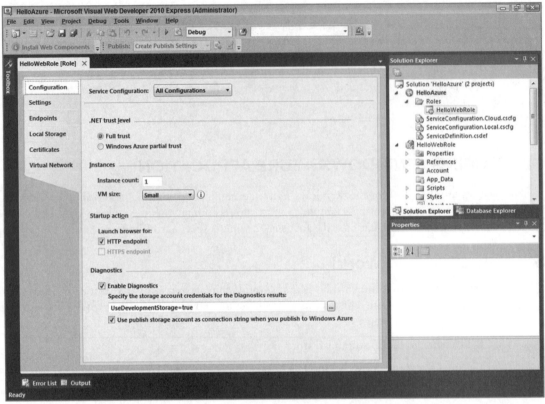

FIGURE 8-9

When you start a Windows Azure project for the first time, DSInit automatically executes to set up the Storage Emulator. On subsequent starts, DSInit does not run again, but you can run it manually if you have problems with as explained earlier.

You can change the web application you created just like any other ASP.NET application, although the configured Membership, Role, and Profile providers all point at a local SQL Server Express database. This can definitely cause problems when you deploy to Windows Azure. If you need these providers, the following are three ways to solve this:

➤ **Use SQL Azure with the existing providers:** To do this, you need to run the scripts that create the needed tables in SQL Azure. The scripts installed with the .NET Framework do not work, but you can find correct scripts and instructions at `http://bit.ly/aspnetsqlazurescript`. When you finish this, you need to change the connection string to point to SQL Azure and configure SQL Azure to allow the application to connect. In Chapter 11 you learn more about using SQL Azure.

➤ **Use providers that store the data in table storage:** You can download code for providers using table storage from `http://bit.ly/tablestorageproviders`.

➤ **Use Windows Identity Foundation instead of the providers:** You learn about this in Chapter 9.

There's a similar problem with the session state provider, which is configured to use the `DefaultSessionStateProvider`, which stores session state in process. As soon as you run your application on multiple instances, this can cause problems because the session state isn't shared between instances. Again, if the application requires session state, you must store it in some shared source. This could be SQL Azure, but officially that isn't supported by Microsoft. The best solution here is to use table storage for session state. You can find code for that as well at `http://bit.ly/tablestorageproviders`.

Using Azure Table Storage

The problems described in the previous paragraphs amply demonstrate the problems you can face because of load balancing and statelessness of the Windows Azure platform. The solution in almost all cases is the same: use Azure Table Storage. It provides persistent storage available across instances with a single, shared configuration. Also, using affinity groups you can ensure that the data is stored close to your instances to benefit from optimal performance.

Azure Table Storage is a data store for structured data. Because of its name, most people are quick to associate Azure Table Storage with relational databases. But although the name suggests otherwise, Azure Table Storage is different from relational databases. If you need a relational database, you should use SQL Azure (discussed in Chapter 11). However, in many cases another data storage mechanism can work just as well.

 A detailed discussion of the Azure Table Storage API is beyond the scope of this book, but if you want to know more, you can find a whitepaper with all the ins and outs at `http://bit.ly/watablewhitepaper`.

Understanding Azure Tables

The data model of Azure Table Storage is a fairly simple hierarchy. At the top level is the storage account. A storage account can contain an unlimited number of *tables*, and there is also no limit to the size of a table. Although it is called a table, it is not the same as a table in a relational database. A table is a container for *entities*. An entity is a collection of typed name-value pairs, referred to as *properties*. Because a table has no fixed schema, two different entities in a table can have different properties. Also, properties are typed per entity. This means that you can have the same property name in another entity, but with a different data type. Table 8-1 shows all the supported data types.

TABLE 8-1: Supported Data Types for Azure Table Storage

DATA TYPE	DESCRIPTION
Binary	Array of bytes up to 64 KB in size
Bool	Boolean value

continues

TABLE 8-1 *(continued)*

DATA TYPE	DESCRIPTION
DateTime	UTC time value in the range 1/1/1601 to 12/31/9999 (64 bit)
Double	64-bit floating point number
GUID	Globally Unique Identifier (128-bit)
Int	32-bit integer
Int64	64-bit integer
String	UTF-16 string of up to 64 KB in size

An entity can be no larger than 1 MB. Beyond 1 MB, you should consider using Page or Blog Storage. An entity can also have at most 255 properties, including some mandatory properties. These properties are as follows:

➤ `PartitionKey`: A string of at most 1 KB, identifying the partition the entity belongs in

➤ `RowKey`: A string of at most 1 KB, a unique identifier of an entity within a partition

➤ `Timestamp`: A read only value maintained by the system for versioning

The `PartitionKey` and `RowKey` together uniquely identify an entity within a table. What you choose as a `PartitionKey` is important. Entities with the same `PartitionKey` are stored close together, and hence have good query performance when queried together. Entities with a different `PartitionKey` are stored separately, so they don't benefit from the query performance. However, entities with a different `PartitionKey` can be handed by different servers, which can increase scalability. This is a trade-off that requires you to carefully determine how you want to partition your data, providing you have a large enough data set that partitioning makes sense.

The Azure Tables Storage REST API

Azure Table Storage uses a REST API. This means that you can access and manipulate the data store using HTTP requests. The URL determines what data structure you work with, and the HTTP verb (GET, POST, and so on) determines the operation you perform. Because Azure Table Storage uses a REST API, any platform that supports the HTTP protocol and understands XML can talk to Azure Table Storage. You don't need a library of sorts to work with Azure Table Storage. In .NET applications you can use ADO.NET Data Services, which abstract away the REST operations from developers using Language Integrated Query (LINQ).

Before diving into using ADO.NET Services with Azure Table Storage, it is insightful to look at the REST API because that gives you a better understanding of what works (well) and what doesn't when you work with Azure Table Storage. The API consists of two sets of operations: Table operations and Entity operations. With the Table operations, as shown in Table 8-2, you can manage the tables in your storage account. With the Entity operations in Table 8-3, you can manipulate data in the tables.

TABLE 8-2: REST API Table Operations

HTTP VERB	OPERATION
GET	Lists the tables in the storage account, or a subset if a filter is specified
POST	Creates a new table in the storage account
DELETE	Deletes a table in the storage account

TABLE 8-3: REST API Entity Operations

HTTP VERB	OPERATION
GET	Returns all the entities in the specified table, or a subset if a filter was specified
PUT	Updates the given entity by replacing the entire entity
MERGE	Updates values of an entity
POST	Inserts a new entity into the specified table
DELETE	Deletes the specified entity from the table

The Table operations are fairly simple. Creating a table is easy because there is no fixed schema. That means you have to create only the table. After you do that you can use the Entity operations to manipulate data. A simple example is getting a single record by querying on `PartitionKey` and `RowKey`, as shown in the following URL:

```
http://yourstorage.windows.core.net/Cars(PartitionKey="BMW",RowKey="320i")
```

The path part of the URL (after the last slash) can't exceed 260 characters, which goes for any operation. You can get around this limitation by using a so-called *Entity Group Transaction*, not listed in Table 8-3. This operation also uses POST, but this can be used for multiple types of operations. With an Entity Group Transaction, you can save multiple entities in a single table and with the same partition key within a single transaction. You can also use it to query entities in a table.

As you can see from the URL, you always operate within the context of a table. As a consequence, you can't combine data from multiple tables as you would with a SQL join-statement for instance. To do something like that, you must query both tables and process the data in your application. Because tables don't have a fixed schema, you can also solve this by adding entities with different properties to a table, and use the partition key to relate them, so you only have to do one query. That still leaves you with some processing in the application, but chances are that retrieving the data takes more time than processing it. Whichever way you solve this problem, the key take away is that Azure Table Storage uses a different paradigm from relational databases. You must adapt your data access strategy and data model to work well with this paradigm.

Working with Azure Storage Tables

When you want to use Azure Storage Tables in .NET applications, the REST API just discussed is abstracted away. Instead, you can use the classes in the `Microsoft.WindowsAzure.StorageClient` namespace to create objects that hook into LINQ. This makes using tables a lot easier because it feels similar to technologies such as LINQ-to-SQL and LINQ-to-Entities, although the capabilities of Azure Storage Tables are much more limited.

The first thing you need to do is create entities to work with. An entity is a class that inherits from the `TableServiceEntity` class, as shown in Listing 8-1. As you can see in Listing 8-1, an entity class is nothing more than a data container. Because it inherits from the `TableServiceEntity` class, it already has properties for the PartitionKey, RowKey, and Timestamp.

LISTING 8-1: HelloEntity

```
using System;
using Microsoft.WindowsAzure.StorageClient;

namespace HelloWebRole
{
    public class HelloEntity : TableServiceEntity
    {
        public HelloEntity()
        {
        }

        public string Name { get; set; }
        public string Message { get; set; }
        public DateTime PostDate { get; set; }
    }
}
```

To work with Azure Table Storage, you need a `TableServiceContext` object. The `TableServiceContext` object is basically an in-memory cache between the application and the storage table. You can add objects to the context, query for objects, and manipulate these, and save the changes when you finish. You can get a `TableServiceContext` object from a `CloudTableClient` object, and to get it you need to have a `CloudStorageAccount` object that works against the table storage you want to use. The constructor in Listing 8-2 goes through the motions to create the needed objects to get a `TableServiceContext` object.

LISTING 8-2: HelloTableManager

```
using System;
using System.Collections.Generic;
using System.Linq;
using Microsoft.WindowsAzure;
using Microsoft.WindowsAzure.StorageClient;
using Microsoft.WindowsAzure.ServiceRuntime;

namespace HelloWebRole
```

```
    {
        public class HelloTableManager
        {
            public const string HelloTableName = "HelloTable";

            TableServiceContext _context;

            public HelloTableClient() : this(RoleEnvironment.
    GetConfigurationSettingValue(
                "StorageConnectionString"))
            {
            }

            public HelloTableClient(string connectionString)
            {
                var account = CloudStorageAccount.Parse(connectionString);
                var tableClient = account.CreateCloudTableClient();
                tableClient.CreateTableIfNotExist(HelloTableName);
                _context = tableClient.GetDataServiceContext();
            }

            public void AddHello(string name, string message)
            {
                _context.AddObject(HelloTableName, new HelloEntity()
                {
                    Name = name,
                    Message = message,
                    PostDate = DateTime.Now,
                    PartitionKey = DateTime.Today.ToString("yyyyMMdd"),
                    RowKey = Guid.NewGuid().ToString()
                });
                _context.SaveChanges();
            }

            public List<HelloEntity> GetMessagesByDay(DateTime day)
            {
                var query = _context.CreateQuery<HelloEntity>(HelloTableName);
                query = query.Where(c =>
                        c.PartitionKey == day.ToString("YYYYMMDD"));
                var list = query.AsTableServiceQuery().ToList();
                return list.OrderByDescending(e => e.PostDate).ToList();
            }
        }
    }
```

The AddHello method in Listing 8-2 just adds a HelloEntity object to the table, by adding it to the context and then having the context save the changes. To update an entity you would get the entity from table storage first, manipulate it, and then call SaveChanges.

The GetMessagesByDay method demonstrates how to get entities from the table. It first creates a query object for the table. If you were to use that immediately, it would be an unfiltered query, yielding all entities in the table. You can imagine that if this wouldn't be limited somehow, this could potentially cause a huge data transfer if there are many entities. Fortunately, Azure Storage Tables does not return more than 1,000 entities. If more entities satisfy the query, a continuation token is provided, so you can query the next set of up to 1,000 entities. In the GetMessagesByDay method, a where-clause is added to the query to filter by day. The `PartitionKey` is used to make this possible. Using the `PartitionKey` that way foregoes the need to post-process the queried data.

The call to `AsTableServiceQuery` converts the `DataServiceQuery` query to a `CloudTableQuery`. At that point the query is not yet executed, so you could set properties on the query, such as the `RetryPolicy`. The `ToList` method triggers the query and gets the data. You can post-process the results if needed, such as the sorting done in the `GetMessagesByDay` method.

The code in Listing 8-2 is enough to implement a guestbook with Azure Table Storage. Listing 8-3 demonstrates using the `HelloTableManager` in an `ObjectDataSource` used with a `FormView`-control for adding new messages, and a `DataList`-control to list messages.

LISTING 8-3: ASP.NET Azure Table Storage Guestbook

```
<asp:ObjectDataSource ID="ObjectDataSource1" runat="server"
                      InsertMethod="AddHello"
                      SelectMethod="GetMessagesByDay"
                      TypeName="HelloWebRole.HelloTableManager"
                      Onselecting="ObjectDataSource1_Selecting">
    <InsertParameters>
        <asp:Parameter Name="name" Type="String" />
        <asp:Parameter Name="message" Type="String" />
    </InsertParameters>
    <SelectParameters>
        <asp:Parameter Name="day" Type="DateTime" />
    </SelectParameters>
</asp:ObjectDataSource>

<asp:FormView ID="FormView1" runat="server" DefaultMode="Insert"
              DataSourceID="ObjectDataSource1">
    <InsertItemTemplate>
        Name:
        <asp:TextBox ID="NameTextBox" runat="server"
                     Text='<%# Bind("Name") %>' />
        <br />
        Message:
        <asp:TextBox ID="MessageTextBox" runat="server"
                     Text='<%# Bind("Message") %>' />
        <br />
        <asp:LinkButton ID="InsertButton" runat="server" Text="Insert"
                        CommandName="Insert" CausesValidation="True" />
    </InsertItemTemplate>
</asp:FormView>

<asp:DataList ID="DataList1" runat="server"
              DataSourceID="ObjectDataSource1">
    <ItemTemplate>
        Name:
        <asp:Label ID="NameLabel" runat="server"
                   Text='<%# Eval("Name") %>' />
        <br />
        Message:
        <asp:Label ID="MessageLabel" runat="server"
                   Text='<%# Eval("Message") %>' />
```

```
        <br />
        PostDate:
        <asp:Label ID="PostDateLabel" runat="server"
                Text='<%# Eval("PostDate") %>' />
            <hr />
    </ItemTemplate>
</asp:DataList>
```

To get a working guestbook based on the code shown in the previous listings, you need to add the code to your project and configure table storage, as follows:

1. Add `HelloEntity` to the HelloWebRole project.

2. Add `HelloTableManager` to the HelloWebRole project.

3. Replace the main content in `Default.aspx` of the HelloWebRole project with Listing 8-3.

4. Add the following code to Default.aspx.cs:

Available for download on Wrox.com

```
protected void ObjectDataSource1_Selecting(object sender,
    ObjectDataSourceSelectingEventArgs e)
{
    e.InputParameters["day"] = DateTime.Today;
}
```

code snippet 01_ObjectDataSource1_Selecting.txt

5. In the Roles folder of the HelloAzure project, double-click the HelloWebRole item so that the configuration is shown.

6. In the configuration navigate to the Settings tab.

7. Click Add Setting.

8. Name the new setting **StorageConnectionString**.

9. Choose Connection String as type.

10. In the value type **UseDevelopmentStorage=true**, so all entities are saved in the local development store instead of in an actual storage account. You can also do this by clicking the Ellipsis button in the Value column and clicking OK to default to Use the Windows Azure Storage Emulator.

11. Save all files and run the project.

 If you want to know more about how you can work with Azure Table Storage, check out the How To at `http://bit.ly/tablestoragehowto`.

 So far everything uses the local DevFabric and local storage. You learn how to change this later in this chapter in the sections "Configuring Your Application" and "Deploying Your Application."

CONFIGURING YOUR APPLICATION

The configuration of your application consists of two parts:

➤ **Service Definition:** You can think of this as the configuration of your overall infrastructure. It contains information about the roles in your application, the endpoints at which these are available, and the IIS configuration for virtual directories.

➤ **Service Configuration:** By contrast, this contains a configuration more specific to the roles within the application, such as the number of instances and application settings.

Service Definition

The Service Definition is an XML file that you can edit with any text editor. You can also configure portions of it through the Visual Studio dialogs that come with the Windows Azure SDK, but those don't cover everything. You can find the entire schema for the service definition at `http://bit.ly/servicedefinition`.

At the highest level the service definition consists of the following sections:

➤ `WebRole`: Settings for the Web Roles in the application.

➤ `WorkerRole`: Settings for the Worker Roles in the application.

➤ `VirtualMachineRole`: Settings for the VM Roles in the application.

➤ `NetworkTrafficRules`: Rules to determine which roles have access to which internal endpoints on other roles. With these routing rules you can tighten the security of the infrastructure.

Each section is optional but needs at least one of the first three to work. The first three are also similar. One of the most important settings on the role element is the `vmsize` attribute, which determines the size of the instances used for the role in terms of CPU power and memory size. Table 8-4 describes the sections you can find for each of the role elements.

TABLE 8-4: Service Definition Role Configuration

ELEMENT	DESCRIPTION
Certificates	The definition of the certificates available in the role. These can be used for SSL, encryption, and signing. The actual certificate references are stored in the service configuration. You learn more about using certificates in Chapter 9.
ConfigurationSettings	The definition of configuration settings available to a role. The values of these settings are stored in the service configuration.
Endpoints	The endpoints through which the role can be accessed. Input Endpoints are available to clients; Internal Endpoints are only available to other roles.

ELEMENT	DESCRIPTION
Imports	The Windows Azure modules made available to the role.
LocalResources	Defines folders on disk that can be used to store temporary data.
Runtime	Settings for the Windows Azure runtime environment. Does not apply to VM Role.
Sites	The collection of websites and web applications hosted in a Web Role. This enables you to host multiple sites and applications in a single role. Only applies to Web Role.
Startup	The tasks that need to be run when a role starts. Does not apply to VM Role.
Contents	Defines locations for content in the role and external locations to copy the content from. Does not apply to VM Role.

Service Configuration

Like the Service Definition, the Service Configuration is an XML file. Its schema is much less elaborate than the Service Definition. You can find the entire schema at `http://bit.ly/serviceconfiguration`. At the top level the Service Configuration defines attributes for the family and version of the operating system running a role. The family can be either Windows Server 2008 SP2 or Windows Server 2008 R2, which defaults to the former. The version relates to the Windows Azure Guest OS, which is based on the chosen OS family. By default, the latest version is used and instances are automatically upgraded when a new version is released. You can however specify a specific version if you have compatibility issues.

The Service Configuration contains a role configuration for each role in the Service Definition. This configuration can contain the following:

➤ The number of instances used to run the role

➤ The values for the configuration settings defined in the service definition

➤ The certificate references corresponding to the certificate definitions in the service definition

For a VM Role the configuration can also contain a reference to the VM Role image.

The configuration settings in the service configuration compare to the application settings in `app.config` or `web.config`. If you currently have values in there that are subject to change, you may want to consider moving them to the service configuration. You can then read them with the following line of code:

```
string setting = RoleEnvironment.GetConfigurationSettingValue("mySetting");
```

Using the Configuration Dialogs

A full discussion of everything in the service definition and the service configuration is beyond the scope of this book. The main settings you need to know about are configured through the Visual Studio dialogs installed with the Windows Azure SDK. These dialogs actually operate on both the service definition and the service configuration simultaneously. In Figure 8-10 for instance, you can see settings for the number instances and size of these instances. Although edited together, the size is stored in the service definition, whereas the number of instances is part of the service configuration. You can open the Visual Studio configuration dialogs by clicking the role you want to configure in the Roles folder of the cloud project. Figure 8-10 shows this for the HelloAzure project you created earlier.

FIGURE 8-10

A few more tabs exist (refer to Figure 8-10) through which you can configure a role. The Settings tab corresponds to the ConfigurationSettings sections in the service definition and service configuration. The other tabs correspond to the sections with the same names, except Virtual Network. The latter is used for Windows Azure Connect, which is discussed in detail in Chapter 15.

> *To get a better understanding of the Service Definition and Service Configuration, and the dialogs that manage them, you can change settings and look in the different configuration files to see what has been changed.*

In the configuration dialogs you can differentiate between the local environment and the cloud (production) environment. If you do nothing, all settings are used in both environments. But at the top of the dialog, you can change the settings for a specific environment by selecting it from the Service Configuration drop-down list. In the Azure project you can see service configurations corresponding to the configurations you have defined. By default these are Local and Cloud.

Running Multiple Instances

As discussed earlier, Microsoft gives uptime guarantees if you run a role on at least two instances. This is easy to configure (refer to Figure 8-10). Just increase the instance count and redeploy. In your local development environment, press Ctrl+F5 again, and the application redeploys with the new instance count. You can see it running on multiple instances with the Compute Emulator UI. You can find a Windows Azure icon in the notification area of the taskbar. When you right-click the icon, you can select Show Compute Emulator UI to show the console. Figure 8-11 shows the Compute Emulator UI with two running instances for the HelloWebRole.

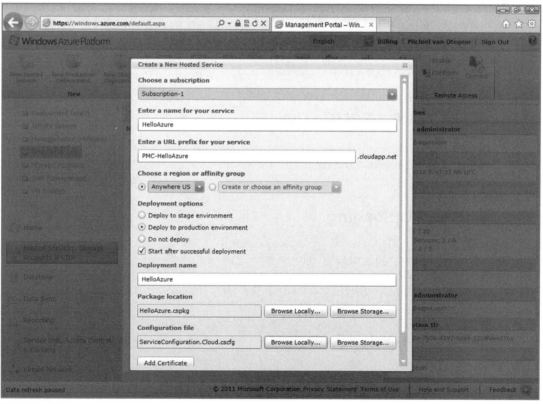

FIGURE 8-11

Setting Up Endpoints

When you run a role in the local development environment, the Compute Emulator automatically assigns it a port number so that it doesn't conflict with the default website already running on port 80. If you run a website only on one role, this isn't a problem. In a more elaborate environment, you may want to have full control over the port numbers, so you can statically configure the roles to communicate with one another. You also want to have full control when you use nonstandard port numbers to communicate between roles in the production environment. One reason to do this would be security because you can restrict access by port number.

If you go to the Endpoints tab, you can see the active endpoints. By default this is the single endpoint that runs on port 80 in the production environment but gets reassigned by the compute emulator. If you want no surprises in the compute emulator, you can pick another port, such as port 8080. You can set both a public port and a private port. The latter is optional, and if you set it, traffic on the public port is rerouted to the private port. The private port would also be where other roles access the role. Endpoints that should not be publically available must be marked as Internal with the drop-down in the Type column.

For a secure connection with SSL, you must select a certificate. Before you can do this, you need to add the certificate under the Certificates tab. You learn how to do this in Chapter 9. To enable a secure connection, you must change the protocol from http to https. TCP is also an accepted protocol that can be used for other forms of communication.

DEPLOYING YOUR APPLICATIONS

You can deploy an application in two ways. You can deploy it directly from Visual Studio, or you can package it and then upload and deploy it through the Management Portal. Both options are discussed next.

Packaging and Uploading

Deployment through packaging and uploading is most likely the case if the production environment is managed by a system administrator. This is usual in larger organizations because application development and deployment must be done according to some predefined process with different responsibilities assigned to different roles within the organization.

To deploy using a package, take the following steps:

1. In Visual Studio, right-click the Windows Azure project in the Solution Explorer and select Package.

2. In the dialog presented select the cloud service configuration, and set the build type; then click Package.

3. When the application is packaged, Windows Explorer opens and shows the package folder.

4. Open a browser and sign in to the Management Portal.

5. Go to Hosted Services ➪ Storage Accounts & CDN.

6. On the taskbar click New Hosted Service.

7. Enter the details of the hosted service to create, as shown in Figure 8-12. Under Deployment options, the default is Deploy to Stage Environment, which has been changed in Figure 8-12.

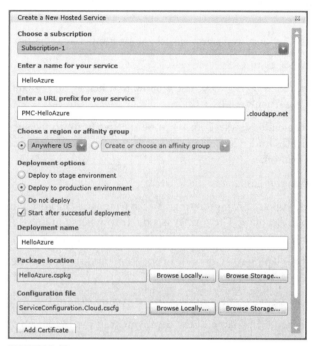

FIGURE 8-12

8. Browse for the package and configuration in the location opened in Step 3.

9. Click OK. This starts the deployment process, which can take a while.

After you deploy your application, it is available through the URL for which you entered the prefix. In Figure 8-12 this would be `http://PMC-HelloAzure.cloudapp.net/`. If you deploy to staging, your application gets an automatically assigned GUID as the URL prefix, so it is available under a URL such as `http://4ab5ac2001324585ba5a902f4242a98c.cloudapp.net/`. This URL can change any time you deploy to staging.

Deploying from Visual Studio

In smaller organizations and in test environments, deploying an application directly from Visual Studio is a good option. It's the easiest way to deploy, so if you don't need strict separation, it's the best option. Of course, it's also a good option for test environments in which the strict separation of roles is not needed.

To deploy directly from Visual Studio, you first need to ensure that Visual Studio is allowed to deploy. This is managed by a certificate, which is safer than a username and password. On your local machine you need the certificate with both the public and private key. In Windows Azure you need the certificate with the public. You can create a certificate the first time you publish, using the following steps.

1. In Visual Studio right-click the Windows Azure project in the Solution Explorer, and select Publish.

2. Click the Credentials drop-down list, and select <Add...>, opening a new dialog.

3. Click the drop-down list under 1, and select <Create...>.

4. Enter a name for the certificate, and click OK. Use a name that helps you remember that it's a publishing certificate for a particular subscription.

5. Follow the instructions in the dialog under 2 and 3 to tie the certificate to the subscription. You can manage the certificates under Management Certificates in the Hosted Services, Storage Accounts & CDN section.

6. Give the credentials a meaningful name, and click OK.

7. If you have not done so yet, you are prompted to go to the Management Portal and create a Hosted Service and a Storage Account. The former is similar to when you upload a package, but as shown in Figure 8-11, you need to indicate that you don't want to deploy.

8. Indicate whether you want to deploy to staging or production, and the storage account to use for publication.

9. As with packaging indicate the environment and build the configuration.

10. In the Publish label textbox, enter the name of the deployment in the Management Portal.

11. Click Publish to start the publication process, which will take a while.

When you publish the next time, all values are prefilled and Visual Studio detects that there is an existing deployment of the same project. If you confirm, Visual Studio removes the existing deployment and deploys the new version.

Deploying from Staging to Production

If you've done a deployment to Windows Azure staging, you can deploy to production easily using a virtual IP-swap. This means the IP addresses of the staging and production environment are switched. You can see this option on the Management Portal taskbar if you have a staging deployment and a production deployment for the same hosted service.

HANDLING CHANGES

As with all software, it is likely that over time you will make configuration changes and minor changes to the software. If you have a new build, you can do a new deployment using one of the techniques previously described. To do this with the least disruption, you can deploy in staging and then do a virtual IP-swap, so the redeployment of instances doesn't disrupt service. Alternatively, you can do an in-place upgrade by clicking the Upgrade icon on the Management Portal taskbar. This enables you to upload a new package and configuration.

If you just have to change the configuration, you have two options: upload a new service configuration or edit the existing configuration. The latter is only a good option if all you need is to increase or decrease the number of instances. Other than that tinkering with a configuration file is not a good idea. You should make changes to configuration settings used in the application in a file first, so you can easily check them and possibly even test them.

PROGRAMMATICALLY CONTROLLING YOUR SERVICE

By now, you may realize that Windows Azure is more than just a hosting environment. It's a dynamic environment in which you can make runtime changes to adapt to the needs of users. The Management Portal gives you the facilities to modify the configuration, but you can also do this programmatically.

Using the Services Runtime

The Services Runtime is the set of classes available to your application to retrieve information about the role and instance configuration. Through the Services Runtime you can also request a restart of an instance, in case something has gone wrong with the instance. You've already seen the `RoleEnvironment` class when you learned about the service configuration. However, the `RoleEnvironment` class is much more than your gateway to the service configuration. It is the starting point for all information about the roles and instances in your application. It contains several static properties:

➤   `CurrentRoleInstance`: The instance in which the code runs.

➤   `DeploymentId`: The unique identifier of the deployment. For the staging environment this corresponds with the URL at which the application is made available.

➤   `IsAvailable`: Indicates whether the instance runs in Windows Azure.

➤   `IsEmulated`: Indicates whether the instance runs in the compute emulator.

➤   `Roles`: The roles in the deployment.

The information you can get through these properties is mostly static, in the sense that you can't change these through the API. However, you can change them from the Management Portal and with the Service Management API discussed next. When that happens, you can use the `RoleEnvironmentChanging` and `RoleEnvironementChanged` events to take action based on those changes. Most likely, you want to update configuration settings you've read using the `GetConfigurationSettingValue` method. The other method that's important is `RequestRecycle`, with which you can restart an instance. This is handy when an unrecoverable exception occurs within your application. You can find the complete Services Runtime namespace reference at `http://bit.ly/serviceruntime`.

Understanding the Service Management API

The Service Management API is a REST API that enables you to do most of what you can do with the Management Portal. You've already had a taste of this when you learned about the REST API for Storage Tables, but you can do more. At the basic level you can create, update, and delete most entities in Windows Azure, such as affinity groups, storage accounts, and certificates. The API for hosted services is more elaborate and enables you to perform operations such as deploy, reboot role instances, and change a role configuration. The latter is particularly interesting considering that you can change the number of instances that way. This means that if you can detect the load of your application, you can increase or decrease the number of instances automatically.

 You can find the full reference of commands you can give at `http://bit.ly/servicemanagementapi`.

SUMMARY

In this chapter you learned to take the first steps into developing applications for Windows Azure. Assuming you already know how to develop .NET applications, you can now get and fire up Visual Studio and begin. That said, Visual Studio is by no means required. As long as you have the development environment and SDK for you language of choice, which can be Java or PHP, too, you're good to go.

Applications, also known as Hosted Services, can consist of one or more roles, with each role being run on one or more instances. To ensure availability, it's advisable to run a role on at least two instances. Because instances can fail, you should not store data that needs to be persisted locally. That data should be placed inside Azure Storage Tables.

After you develop an application, you can test it in the local development fabric and then deploy it to Windows Azure. You can deploy using Visual Studio or through the Management Portal, which also enables you to make configuration changes afterward, such as increasing or decreasing the number of instances your application runs on. You can also make these changes programmatically through the Service Management API.

Identity in Azure

WHAT'S IN THIS CHAPTER?

➤ Understanding a federated identity and claims-based identity

➤ Working with federation and claims with Windows Identity Foundation

➤ How to deploy and troubleshoot a WCF service on Windows Azure

Most applications need some way to identify users and to determine what a specific user may or may not do, and this is no different for applications running in Windows Azure, in fact it's more critical for many reasons. Windows Azure is unlike your typical server sitting in a data center under your control, in that applications are not part of your own network environment or domain. In your own network, you can fall back on the security at an infrastructure level, which is definitely not the case in Windows Azure, which is accessible from anywhere, so you need to compensate for this. Also, you can't rely on network credentials to authenticate users because that doesn't work over a firewall. Another aspect of the security picture is the increasing need for applications to interact. Put this all together, and you need a different strategy for identity.

IDENTITY IN THE CLOUD

Many applications (or services) need to uniquely identify the user—some for the purpose of giving you a personalized experience, and others to determine your access rights. Until a few years ago, you could be identified in two ways. The first was through credentials like a username and password unique to the application; the other was through your network credentials used across the applications in the local network. The latter is user-friendly; log on once and all applications know you. However, beyond the realm of your local network, your network credentials mean nothing. So on the Internet, applications tend to use a username and password. The last time I checked I had more than 100 accounts on various websites, and I probably forgot about quite a few. I doubt this is any different for other regular computer users. You need something better to manage your identity in the cloud.

With cloud computing the need for secure and flexible identity management is even more important. Cloud computing blurs the line between the local network and the Internet. Applications running in the cloud may conceptually be internal applications, with data that should be well guarded against falling into the wrong hands. In these cases the identity of the user and the user's access rights must be above all suspicion. Granting access based on just a username and password that is entered on a public accessible web page may not be secure enough. The security mechanism used by cloud applications should facilitate options that are more secure. On the other hand, it should also facilitate less-strict forms of identity. After all, an application hosted in the cloud could also be meant for public use.

Another aspect that impacts the way you need to think about security in the cloud is applications working together. A photo print service for instance could work together with your online photo album to make the prints you want. Instead of uploading the photos you want printed, you can grant the photo print service partial access to the online photo album. This means identity in the cloud also needs some way to provide other people or applications limited access to your data.

Understanding Federated Identity

You can solve many of the problems just discussed with *federated identity*. But before going into that deeper, you need a definition of what an (electronic) identity is. The problem is that if you talk to different people, you'll get different definitions, for instance:

➤ Username and password

➤ Some unique key identifying a user

➤ Authentication and authorization

➤ All data associated with a user account

For the purpose of this discussion, an identity is a set of attributes associated with a user or entity wanting access to some secure resource. Some of these attributes identify the user or entity uniquely (for example, security identifier, e-mail address, and so on), so the sum of the attributes is in essence unique.

A federated identity also qualifies as an identity but has some additional characteristics. First, it enables single sign-on across many applications, regardless of whether these applications share the same security domain. Second, the information making up your identity doesn't need to be stored in a single place, but rather in places where they make sense. In addition, applications get only the information they need and to which access is granted. This way an application doesn't simply have access to all information about a user. For instance, an application that only needs to know whether you're an adult won't get your date of birth, only an indicator telling the application you are in fact an adult. Both the distributed nature of a federated identity and that an application gets access to only what it needs means that privacy is handled better.

Because the attributes sent to an application can be filtered, there is no guarantee of uniqueness. However, this is also not always necessary. For instance, an application that helps you find a clothing store may need only your location and gender. Where a unique identifier is needed, that identifier can still be decoupled from your actual identity for privacy purposes.

How Does Identity Federation Work?

With identity federation an application does not authenticate the user. That job is left to an *Identity Provider (IdP)*, which as the name suggests provides you with an electronic identity after it has verified that you are who you say you are. The identity is passed to the application in a *token*, which contains the information the application needs and has been approved to get. The token is produced by a *Security Token Service (STS)*, which is often part of the IdP. As you'll see later, this isn't necessarily the case, which can make things confusing. This is also why you'll find that in some literature IdP and STS are used interchangeably. Here the term IP-STS indicates an STS that is also an IdP.

When an STS creates a token, it signs the token, so an application is certain it was issued by that STS. Most often a token is also encrypted, and in most cases you can assume it is; although it isn't necessary in all scenarios. To work together, the STS and the application must have a trust relationship. This is why an application (or service) using the STS is also called a *Relying Party (RP)*, which is the term used while discussing the theory. For Windows Azure, an RP is synonymous with a Hosted Service. In general terms you can think of an RP as one or more secured *resources* a client might want to access, such as a web page, a service, or a file.

Because the application in no longer authenticating users directly, the authentication process is more complex, as shown in the sequence diagram in Figure 9-1.

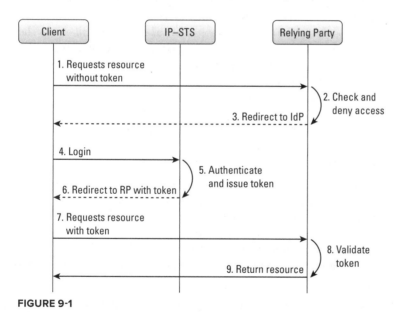

FIGURE 9-1

Redirection ensures that the client gets to the IP-STS and back to the RP after the client has acquired a token (refer to Figure 9-1). Steps 5 and 8 respectively deal with generating a token and validating the generated token. The first step consists of signing and possibly encrypting the token for additional security. The second step decrypts the token (if needed) and checks the signature to see if the token comes from a trusted STS. After that the RP determines how to check authorization, which is discussed later.

In generic terms, the process shown in Figure 9-1 is how federated identity works. There are, however, two flavors of the process: *active federation* and *passive federation*. With active federation the client plays an active role in the process, hence active federation. This means that the client sets up communication with the STS and sends a token request. This is possible with clients that support the protocols and encryption techniques used to make identity federation work. The problem is that web browsers are actually dumb in this respect; they know nothing more than (secure) HTTP, and as such can't request a token. To solve this, the user is sent to a login-page hosted on the IP-STS, so there is no need for the browser to request a token. The token is sent back as part of the response to the browser. A small piece of script then posts the token to the RP. To the browser the token is just some data sent back and forth.

A good example of passive federation is Microsoft LiveID. When you log in to a service requiring a LiveID, you're sent to `https://login.live.com`, which authenticates you. You can see what goes on under the covers using a network profiler such as Fiddler (`www.fiddler2.com`) or F12 Developer Tools built into Internet Explorer 9. You can also do this after you've built your own RP and STS later in this chapter.

Identity Federation and Network Credentials

A key aspect of a federated identity token is that it is signed. This is typically done using an X.509 certificate, but other mechanisms such as symmetric keys are also supported in most protocols. Basically, the RP needs to trust the issuer of the token and ensure the token is authentic. How the user was authenticated and where the STS is located is not relevant to the RP. This makes it easy to have an STS in a local network, only accessible to users on that network, and only accepting network credentials, which provides tokens for an RP in the cloud. Unless such an RP also accepts tokens from another STS, it is only accessible to users that are on the local network. This effectively extends the local network to include the RP and achieves single sign-on across application in the local network and the RP based on network credentials. Figure 9-2 shows how this works.

Identity Federation Beyond the Basics

Identity federation breaks down some of the barriers from the past, but it won't help much if an RP can work only with a single STS. If that is the case, you would just outsource authentication and add an additional layer of complexity in the process. Fortunately there is no limit to the number of STSs an RP can trust, and the RP must determine how to deal with identities from different STSs. For instance, you can allow users to authenticate using their Facebook or LinkedIn credentials. Whether you see these as different accounts, or allow the user to access the same account with both Facebook and LinkedIn, is up to you.

Because an RP trusts an STS doesn't say anything about the way the user was authenticated. The RP just trusts the STS and the token it gets from the RP. This opens the door to another option when dealing with multiple security domains, as shown in Figure 9-3. Instead of having the RP trust multiple STSs, the RP can trust a single STS. That STS can then trust other STSs to authenticate users. Because the STS federates only the identity, such an STS is also known as the Federation Provider or FP-STS.

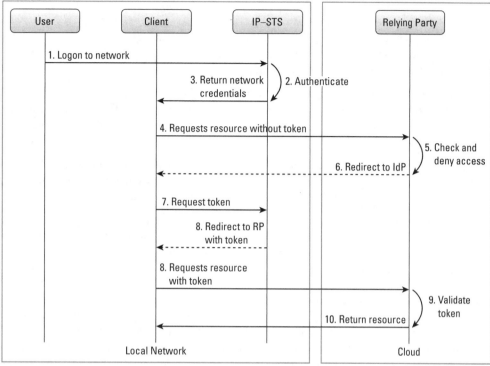

FIGURE 9-2

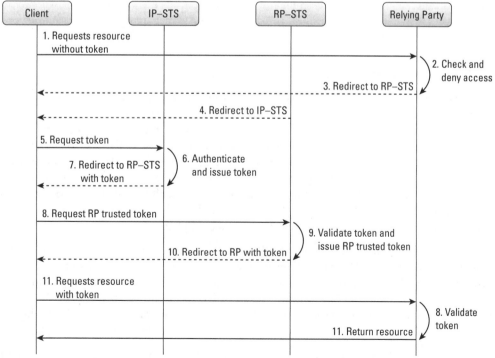

FIGURE 9-3

Cross-domain federation (refer to Figure 9-3) is key for collaboration and business-to-business scenarios. Consider for instance of two companies: `OfficeGiant.com` and `Laws'R'us`. `OfficeGiant .com` sells office supplies, and `Laws'R'us` is a big law firm with several departments. Within each department the office manager is responsible for buying office supplies as needed. With conventional security technologies there are several ways to solve this:

> ➤ **One account could be used for the entire company and the username and password shared among the office managers.** This is obviously not a good approach. There's no way to track who used the account, so fake or wrong orders are a possibility, especially if an office manager is disgruntled.

> ➤ **Each office manager could create an account and have it linked to the company.** This is better than the previous option, but from an administrative point of view, it not handy. Also, if the office manager left the company, who's going to disable the account?

> ➤ **The company could get a master account with the ability to create accounts for each office manager.** This is a good approach but still requires management of user accounts, which are not linked to local domain accounts. So if an office manager would leave the company, the account should be disabled.

With cross-domain federation `OfficeGiant.com` could accept the IP-STS at `Laws'R'us` as a trusted IdP for its FP-STS. The `OfficeGiant.com` FP-STS transforms the incoming token from the `Laws'R'us` IP-STS and can add information to the token telling the application that the user is actually from `Laws'R'us`. If the IP-STS at `Laws'R'us` uses the network credentials as previously shown in Figure 9-2, employees at `Laws'R'us` are logged in transparently with `OfficeGiant.com` with their network credentials. You can assume that the network credentials are managed much better than accounts on some external site, so when someone leaves the company, the account is quickly disabled. Also, whoever has access to `OfficeGiant.com` can be controlled by the `Laws'R'us` system administrator by adding or removing users from groups.

Understanding Claims

As stated earlier, identity federation isn't just about authentication; it is also about the information making up a user's identity. This information captured in *attributes* is sent to the RP in the token in the form of *claims*. A claim is basically a name-value pair with some piece of information about the user. This can be anything, such as an e-mail address, membership number, or role. The name of the value is often some unique identifier such as a URI, and if possible a standard value, such as `http://schemas.xmlsoap.org/ws/2005/05/identity/claims/emailaddress` for an e-mail address, so any application understands the meaning of that particular claim. Claim values can be values direct from some data store such as a birth date but also a derived value such as age. A typical STS can determine what goes into a token through rules applicable to an RP.

Claims are called such because they claim something about the user. The claims sent to an RP are (or should be) relevant to that RP, and for that RP the given values are what makes up the identity of the user. The STS where the claim originates is key in determining how truthful the claim is; providing truthfulness is relevant. For example, on an online forum my name might be Darth Vader and my real name is unknown. However, when I do my tax returns, Darth Vader can't do the job.

The RP needs my real name and Social Security number. What's more, the RP accepts only a token from an STS that it trusts to give my real name and Social Security number and has verified this. I can't just go around and give any Social Security number. This is no different from real life; your membership card for the local gym will suffice to get you into the gym, but a police officer will not accept it because the officer can't trust that the gym has verified your data. Your driver's license on the other hand is given out by an organization a police officer trusts.

Although you can still do role-based authorization using the standard role claim type, claims enable you to model security around much more than just role membership. Because claims can contain any type of value, they can tie into the business logic. For instance, when the age of the user is a claim value, you can do a check against the value in the business logic. Another example might be a bank-account number. There's no need to do a lookup in a database because it can be made part of the token. This flexibility makes the use of claims as the basis for authorization powerful and much more natural than role-based authorization.

Putting information such as a Social Security number or bank account number into a token may sound scary, but you can argue that it is much safer than putting them in an application database. An STS is likely to be much better secured because it deals only with personal data. An application with a lot of functionality can have vulnerabilities in all sorts of places. More important, a token needs to be trusted by an STS. A token from an untrusted STS will simply be discarded, so spoofing data is not possible unless you hijack the STS or get a hold of the private key of the signing certificate. A commercial STS such as Active Directory Federation Services (ADFS) 2.0 has several lines of defense to guard against such breaches and is rigorously tested.

Windows Identity Foundation Overview

With the theory firmly under your belt, you can now move to how you can work with identity federation and claims-based identity in your application. Several standards implement the theory in practice. For instance, the interactions discussed before may include the WS-MetadataExchange standard to retrieve a policy structured with the WS-Policy standard, an STS implementing the WS-Trust standard and formatting tokens with Security Assertion Markup Language (SAML), and the WS-Federation standard to tie the communication between client and service together. To make matters worse, this is not the only option.

You can imagine that implementing these standards and the cryptography needed yourself is a daunting task. Fortunately, Microsoft has done the heavy lifting for you. *Windows Identity Foundation (WIF)* is a framework for building applications using federated claims-based identity. It abstracts WS-Trust, WS-Federation, and SAML, and presents developers with an API on top of the .NET Framework. WIF works with .NET Framework 3.5 SP1 and up, and runs on Windows Server 2003 and up. This of course includes Windows Azure, which builds on Windows Server.

 WIF is not automatically installed when you install all the components needed to develop Windows Azure applications using the Web Platform Installer. See Chapter 8 for more information on setting up your development environment with WIF.

WIF is an important part of the Microsoft software stack moving forward. Applications such as Microsoft Office are being made claims-aware by integrating WIF. This is no surprise because federated claims-based identity is much better than other options, as discussed earlier in this chapter. For that reason it is a good idea to build your own applications using WIF, so you need to get acquainted with it.

> *In this book you learn about the basics of WIF. For more details you can read the excellent whitepaper "Microsoft Windows Identity Foundation (WIF) Whitepaper for Developers," which you can download from* `http://bit.ly/ wifwhitepaper`.

Understanding How WIF Integrates into .NET

With WIF you can build *claims-aware applications*, but you can also use it to build an STS. In both cases you have to deal with only the API and not with the underlying standards. If you build a relying party, you don't need to learn a lot of new stuff because WIF integrates with the existing .NET Framework user infrastructure provided by the `IPrincipal` and `IIdentity` interfaces. WIF defines several interfaces and classes that build on .NET Framework constructs, making WIF easy to use for .NET developers.

The Claim Class

WIF revolves around claims-based identity, so a key class is the `Claim` class, which corresponds to a single value of a particular claim type. The `Claim` class looks like the following code snippet.

Available for download on Wrox.com

```
public class Claim
{
    public virtual string ClaimType { get; }
    public virtual string Issuer { get; }
    public virtual string OriginalIssuer { get; }
    public virtual IDictionary<string, string> Properties { get; }
    public virtual IClaimsIdentity Subject { get; }
    public virtual string Value { get; }
    public virtual string ValueType { get; }

    public virtual Claim Copy();
    public virtual void SetSubject(IClaimsIdentity subject);
}
```

code snippet 01_Claim class.txt

The key properties on the `Claim` class are `ClaimType` and `Value`. The `ClaimType` is a unique string value such as a URI, as discussed earlier. This nice, low-level approach means you can easily define your own types. The value is also always a string, but the `ValueType` property may give a clue as to the actual data type. Several standard claims, such as e-mail, date of birth, and of course name, are available through the `ClaimTypes` class, which exposes claim types as public string constants. However, you can also define your own claims as you see fit.

A claim always has an issuer, which you can check with the `Issuer` property. For identity federation there may be multiple issuers in the chain, in which case the original issuer of the claim is in the `OriginalIssuer` property. Then the `Issuer` property contains the last STS in the chain. In `Properties` you can also find meta data about the claim, such as metadata harvested from a SAML token. In most cases you won't do anything with this metadata. Finally, the `Subject` property is the identity the claim belongs to, which is an object of type `IClaimsIdentity` discussed next.

The IClaimsIdentity Interface

WIF defines the `IClaimsIdentity` interface, which extends the `IIdentity` interface, so it can be used as an `IIdentity` replacement. WIF provides a default implementation of this interface with the `ClaimsIdentity` class. The `IClaimsIdentity` interface has the following signature:

```
public interface IClaimsIdentity : IIdentity
{
    ClaimCollection Claims { get; }
    IClaimsIdentity Actor { get; set; }
    string Label { get; set; }
    string NameClaimType { get; set; }
    string RoleClaimType { get; set; }
    SecurityToken BootstrapToken { get; set; }

    IClaimsIdentity Copy();
}
```

code snippet 02_IClaimsIdentity.txt

Most important in the preceding interface is the `Claims` property, which gives you access to the claims applicable to the user. What's interesting is that this is basically the only information available from a token. There is no username and no information about the roles the user is in. Any and all information is captured in claims, including username and roles, which should be specific claims. These claims need to be mapped to the `IIdentity.Name` property and the `IPrincipal.IsInRole` method. This is what the `NameClaimType` and `RoleClaimType` properties are for. They represent the claim types to search for on the claims collection for the username and roles. It is not mandatory for a claims identity to contain a username or roles. An identity is just a set of claims that the application can do checks on. It is up to the application to determine which claims must be available. The other three properties are mainly there for advanced scenarios. The `Label` property is there for convenience to keep different identities apart. The `Actor` property is used in delegation scenarios, and the `BootstrapToken` property contains the original security token for the application if WIF is configured for this.

The IClaimsPrincipal Interface

WIF also defines the `IClaimsPrincipal` interface to go with the `IClaimsIdentity`. This enables WIF to replace the active principal in context, which is `HttpContext.User` for

ASP.NET application, ServiceContext.User for WCF services, or Thread.CurrentPrincipal at a more basic level. The IClaimsPrincipal interface looks as follows:

```
public interface IClaimsPrincipal : IPrincipal
{
    ClaimsIdentityCollection Identities { get; }

    IClaimsPrincipal Copy();
}
```

code snippet 03_IClaimsPrincipal.txt

What stands out on the IClaimsPrincipal interface is that a principal can contain multiple identities. In the common case there is always a single identity, but there are scenarios in which multiple identities from different STSs could be requested to form a comprehensive identity. Such scenarios are not discussed in this book, but it is good to be aware of the reason the interface looks the way it does.

Checking for a Claim

The whole idea behind claims is that you can use logic to check for a certain claim—either to use that claim to perform some action, such as sending an e-mail to the e-mail address in the Email claim, or to authorize the user for some functionality. Basically what you need to do is loop all the claims associated with the identity until you find the right type and possibly value. Because this is somewhat inconvenient to code all the time, you can create extension methods, as shown in Listing 9-1.

LISTING 9-1: Extension Methods to Access Claims

```
public static class IClaimsIdentityExtensions
{
    // Get all values for the given claim type.
    public static IEnumerable<string> GetClaimValues(
        this IClaimsIdentity identity,
        string claimType)
    {
        return from c in identity.Claims
                where c.ClaimType == claimType
                select c.Value;
    }

    // Get the first value for the given claim type.
    public static string GetClaimValue(
        this IClaimsIdentity identity,
        string claimType)
    {

        IEnumerable<string> values = GetClaimValues(identity, claimType);
        if (values == null || values.Count() == 0) return string.Empty;
        return values.ElementAt(0);
```

```
        }

        public static bool ClaimHasValue(
            this IClaimsIdentity identity,
            string claimType,
            string value)
        {
            IEnumerable<string> values = GetClaimValues(identity, claimType);
            foreach(string s in values)
            {
                if(s.Equals(value, StringComparison.OrdinalIgnoreCase))
                    return true;
            }
            return false;
        }
    }
```

The main extension method in Listing 9-1 is `GetClaimValues`, which directly interacts with the `ClaimsCollection` of `IClaimsIdentity`. As you can see it is just a single LINQ statement, but the trouble is that it returns an `IEnumerable<string>` instead of a single value. That's because any claim can exist multiple times with different values. This is most likely for claims such as a role claim but could be so for many more. If functionally speaking you need only a single value and you can expect that there is only a single value, you can use the `GetClaimValue` method, which just gets the first value it encounters for the given claim type. You can use this to send e-mail for instance. Finally, the `ClaimHasValue` extension method loops all the claims of a particular type to check if the required value is among them, so you can easily authorize a user with an `if` or `switch` statement like in the following snippet.

```
if (identity.ClaimHasValue(ClaimTypes.Gender, "Male"))
{
    ShowMaleCatalog();
}
else
{
    ShowFemaleCatalog();
}
```

code snippet 04_CheckForClaim.txt

Before you can use the extension methods like in the preceding code, you need the `IClaimsIdentity`. Here again you must deal with the fact that there can be multiple. Luckily in the common case there is only one, so you can use the following code snippet to get the first identity of the principal.

```
IClaimsPrincipal principal = Thread.CurrentPrincipal as IClaimsPrincipal;
if (principal == null)
{
    throw new SecurityException("Couldn't get IClaimsPrincipal.");
}
IClaimsIdentity identity = principal.Identities[0];
```

code snippet 05_GetIClaimsIdentity.txt

You can combine this code with the extension methods in Listing 9-1 to create a helper class that enables you to perform checks with a single line of code.

 An alternative to the previous code is to use the ClaimsPrincipalPermission, *however, this is a more advanced technique and beyond the scope of this book. For more information, you can visit* http://bit.ly/claimscheck.

Understanding Federation Metadata

Up until now the focus has been on getting the principal, identity, and claims with code. But how do you actually know which claims you are going to get? Unfortunately, this is determined by the STS. That said, the STS publishes the claims it can produce at the default location /FederationMetadata/2007-06/FederationMetadata.xml, which looks like the XML is Listing 9-2.

LISTING 9-2: Example Federation Metadata

```xml
<?xml version="1.0" encoding="utf-8"?>
<EntityDescriptor
    ID="_9070250a-3132-496a-9e3f-cd24d189c6cc"
    entityID="http://exampleSTS.com/"
    xmlns="urn:oasis:names:tc:SAML:2.0:metadata">

  <ds:Signature xmlns:ds="http://www.w3.org/2000/09/xmldsig#">
    <!~DH omitted for brevity ~DH>
  </ds:Signature>

  <RoleDescriptor
      xsi:type="fed:SecurityTokenServiceType"
      protocolSupportEnumeration="http://docs.oasis-open.org/wsfed/
  federation/200706"
      xmlns:xsi="http://www.w3.org/2001/XMLSchema-instance"
      xmlns:fed="http://docs.oasis-open.org/wsfed/federation/200706">

    <KeyDescriptor use="signing">
      <KeyInfo xmlns="http://www.w3.org/2000/09/xmldsig#">
        <X509Data>
          <X509Certificate><!~DH omitted for brevity ~DH></X509Certificate>
        </X509Data>
      </KeyInfo>
    </KeyDescriptor>

    <ContactPerson contactType="administrative">
      <GivenName>contactName</GivenName>
    </ContactPerson>

    <fed:ClaimTypesOffered>
      <auth:ClaimType
        Uri="http://schemas.xmlsoap.org/ws/2005/05/identity/claims/name"
        Optional="true"
```

```
        xmlns:auth="http://docs.oasis-open.org/wsfed/authorization/200706">
        <auth:DisplayName>Name</auth:DisplayName>
        <auth:Description>The name of the subject.</auth:Description>
      </auth:ClaimType>
      <!~DH more claim types go here ~DH>
    </auth:ClaimType>
  </fed:ClaimTypesOffered>

  <fed:SecurityTokenServiceEndpoint>
    <EndpointReference xmlns="http://www.w3.org/2005/08/addressing">
      <Address> http://exampleSTS.com/</Address>
    </EndpointReference>
  </fed:SecurityTokenServiceEndpoint>

  <fed:PassiveRequestorEndpoint>
    <EndpointReference xmlns="http://www.w3.org/2005/08/addressing">
      <Address> http://exampleSTS.com/</Address>
    </EndpointReference>
  </fed:PassiveRequestorEndpoint>
</RoleDescriptor>
</EntityDescriptor>
```

In Listing 9-2 you see a lot of XML namespaces. Don't worry about understanding those. These are basically part of the plumbing. Also part of the plumbing—and in most cases taken care of for you—is the stuff in the `<ds:Signature>` element and the `<KeyDescriptor>` element. The latter of those contains the public key RPs needed to sign messages sent to the STS. The former is the signature of the Federation Metadata, so it can't be tampered with. Even different whitespace changes the signature, so you never want to touch a Federation Metadata with an editor after it has been signed.

The `<fed:SecurityTokenServiceEndpoint>` and `<fed:PassiveRequestorEndpoint>` tell RPs where to go to get a security token. In the latter case this is the URL of the STS login page the user is sent to when passive federation is used.

Most interesting for developers is the `<fed:ClaimTypesOffered>` element, which lists the claim types an RP can request from the STS. Important there is the URI of the claim type, which uniquely distinguishes it from any others. This is the value that you need to look for when searching for a particular claim. Also note the `optional` attribute. If this is set to `true`, it may or may not be in the security token, which could be significant. This is actually where the Federation Metadata of the STS and the RP should match up. An RP also publishes Federation Metadata but with less information. Most of what's in there should correspond with what's in the STS Federation Metadata, but instead of `<fed:ClaimTypesOffered>` the Federation Metadata of an RP contains `<fed:ClaimType sRequested>`, which looks as follows:

```
<fed:ClaimTypesRequested>
  <auth:ClaimType
      Uri="http://schemas.xmlsoap.org/ws/2005/05/identity/claims/name"
      Optional="true"
      xmlns:auth="http://docs.oasis-open.org/wsfed/authorization/200706" />
      <!~DH more claim types go here ~DH>
</fed:ClaimTypesRequested>
```

code snippet 06_ClaimsRequested.txt

`<fed:ClaimTypesRequested>` contains the same elements as `<fed:ClaimTypesOffered>`, which means you also see the `Optional` attribute returning. This is key because if a claim is optional for the STS and required by the RP, a token sent by the STS may not contain all claims required by the RP. The STS can change the set of claims an RP can request, and some products even enable the STS to differentiate between different RPs it serves. For this reason it is a good idea for an RP to periodically check the Federation Metadata to determine if all the claims it requires are still provided by the STS, and if not notify the application administrator.

WORKING WITH WINDOWS IDENTITY FOUNDATION

Now that you know about identity federation, claims, and WIF, it's time to put the theory into practice. Passive federation and active federation are discussed separately, starting with passive federation. Currently that is the most common scenario, and it is also a lot simpler to get working than active federation.

Creating a Claims-Aware Website

To start with passive federation in Windows Azure, you need to create an ASP.NET Web Role like you did in the last chapter and hook it up to an STS. The steps that follow walk you through the process.

1. Run Visual Studio as Administrator.

2. Create a new Windows Azure project named **WifPassiveFed**.

3. Add an ASP.NET Web Role.

4. Rename WebRole1 to **WebRoleRP** to indicate this is a relying party.

5. Set the endpoint of WebRoleRP to a fixed port, as shown in the previous chapter so that you can browse to `http://127.0.0.1:8080/` to access the RP.

6. In the Solution Explorer right-click the solution, and select Add ➪ New Web Site.

7. Select ASP.NET Security Token Service, and provide a location inside the current solution folder.

8. When the website has been added, expand the FederationMetadata folder until you see the `FederationMetadata.xml` file. Right-click the file, and select View in Browser.

9. Copy the URL in the browser.

10. Start the Windows Identity Foundation Federation Utility—FedUtil for short—to start a wizard that guides you in turning the application into a claims-aware application. You can find FedUtil in the WIF SDK folder or by typing **fed** in the Start menu.

 If you use Visual Studio Professional or higher, you can also right-click the WebRole in the Solution Explorer and select Add STS reference. If you do this, the web.config *in the next step presets to the web.config of the WebRole.*

11. FedUtil starts with a screen to select `web.config` and to set the URL under which the application is reachable. Select `web.config` of the website and set the Application URI field to reflect the URL from step 5, as shown in Figure 9-4.

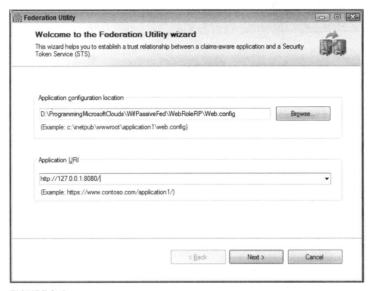

FIGURE 9-4

12. Click Next. You see a warning indicating that you are not using a secure connection. Although you should use a secure connection in production, you don't need to use one in development, so you can just ignore the warning and click Yes.

13. You are now presented with a screen to select the STS used to authenticate users. Select Use an Existing STS.

14. Paste the URL copied in step 9 into the textbox, and click Next. Ignore the warning you get.

15. Click Next, Next, and then Finish.

Understanding FedUtil

FedUtil sets up your website to use WIF, but what does it do exactly? First, it adds a website *WebRoleRP_STS* to the solution. This is a simple STS that just authenticates anyone. It doesn't require a password. (More about the STS later.)

 An STS that doesn't require a password isn't secure. You should use this only for development purposes. For production applications, use a tried and tested STS such as Active Directory Federation Services 2.0 or the Azure Access Control Service. The latter is discussed in Chapter 14.

The second thing FedUtil has done is change the `web.config` of WebRoleRP. The authentication mode has been set to none because authentication is handled by two HTTP modules configured in the `<system.webServer>` section. FedUtil also added an `appSettings` value indicating where to find the Federation Metadata file of the hosted service and has granted all users access to it by adding a `<location>` element. Finally, a new section was added with the name `<microsoft.identityModel>`. A sample of these changes is shown in Listing 9-3.

LISTING 9-3: Sample web.config Changes by FedUtil

```
<system.webServer>
  <modules runAllManagedModulesForAllRequests="true">
    <add name="WSFederationAuthenticationModule"
      type="Microsoft.IdentityModel.Web.WSFederationAuthenticationModule,
        Microsoft.IdentityModel, Version=3.5.0.0, Culture=neutral,
        PublicKeyToken=31bf3856ad364e35" preCondition="managedHandler" />
    <add name="SessionAuthenticationModule"
        type="Microsoft.IdentityModel.Web.SessionAuthenticationModule,
        Microsoft.IdentityModel, Version=3.5.0.0, Culture=neutral,
        PublicKeyToken=31bf3856ad364e35" preCondition="managedHandler" />
  </modules>
</system.webServer>
<appSettings>
  <add key="FederationMetadataLocation"
      value="D:\ WifWindowsAzure\WebRoleRP_STS\FederationMetadata\
2007-06\FederationMetadata.xml" />
</appSettings>
<microsoft.identityModel>
  <service>
    <audienceUris>
      <add value="http://127.0.0.1:81/" />
    </audienceUris>
    <federatedAuthentication>
      <wsFederation passiveRedirectEnabled="true"
                    issuer="http://localhost:8800/WebRoleRP_STS/"
                    realm="http://127.0.0.1:8080/"
                    requireHttps="false" />
      <cookieHandler requireSsl="false" />
    </federatedAuthentication>
    <applicationService>
      <claimTypeRequired>
        <!~DHFollowing are the claims offered by STS
            'http://localhost:8800/WebRoleRP_STS/'. Add or uncomment
            claims that you require by your application and then update
            the federation metadata of this application.~DH>
        <claimType
          type="http://schemas.xmlsoap.org/ws/2005/05/identity/claims/name"
          optional="true" />
        <claimType
          type="http://schemas.microsoft.com/ws/2008/06/identity/claims/role"
          optional="true" />
```

```
        </claimTypeRequired>
      </applicationService>
      <issuerNameRegistry type="Microsoft.IdentityModel.Tokens.➡
ConfigurationBasedIssuerNameRegistry, Microsoft.IdentityModel,➡
Version=3.5.0.0, Culture=neutral, PublicKeyToken=31bf3856ad364e35">
        <trustedIssuers>
          <add thumbprint="CC85FEF38933D30CA163F37C0D283B19144F9F98"
               name="http://localhost:8800/WebRoleRP_STS/" />
        </trustedIssuers>
      </issuerNameRegistry>
    </service>
  </microsoft.identityModel>
```

The `WSFederationAuthenticationModule` configured in Listing 9-3 handles incoming WS-Federation tokens to authenticate the user for the first time. If the user presents a valid token, this module processes the token and authenticates the user. Because a token must be posted to the application, this is not something that can happen for each request the user makes, and this is where the `SessionAuthenticationModule` comes in. For subsequent requests in the same session, its job is to create a `ClaimsPrincipal` object from session data and assign it to `HttpContext.User`. It does this based on a cookie that contains the token.

> *The modules configured by FedUtil are in the* `Microsoft.IdentityModel` *assembly. FedUtil does not add a reference to this assembly to the WebRole because it is not needed for any code, and it expects the assembly to be in the Global Assembly Cache.*

The `microsoft.IdentityModel` section tells WIF where to find the STS and for which domain (realm) it authenticates, the claim types provided by the STS and used in the hosted service, and finally the thumbprint of the certificate the STS uses to sign the token, so WIF can determine whether a token received from the STS is valid. This information is basically what FedUtil got from the Federation Metadata file of the STS.

Testing the Application

Now that all is in place, you can run the hosted service and see what happens. When you click Run, the Web Role will start and open in a browser window—no surprise there. However, instead of showing you the default page, you are automatically redirected to the STS created for you by FedUtil. The STS shows you the login page, so you can login to the STS itself, as is needed for passive federation. As mentioned earlier, the created STS is simple, so you don't need to enter a password. You can just enter any username, and press Submit.

When you log in, a token is created and posted back to the hosted service, but instead of seeing the home page, you see the exception in Figure 9-5.

The exception in Figure 9-5 is caused by the fact that the token transmitted to the hosted service is a piece of XML, and by default request validation in ASP.NET doesn't accept that because of

Cross-Site Scripting (XSS) attacks. You could solve this by disabling request validation completely, but because that poses a serious security risk it is definitely not recommended. The better option, and the only one discussed further in this book, is replacing the default `RequestValidator` class with one that can distinguish a token from other potentially harmful requests. This sounds complicated, but it isn't. You can actually find one in the Quick Start samples of the WIF SDK, but you can also roll your own in just a few lines of code, as shown in Listing 9-4.

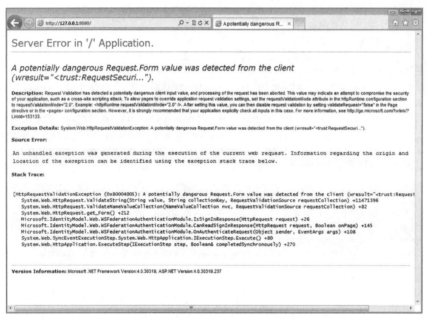

FIGURE 9-5

LISTING 9-4: RequestValidator Class Accepting a Federation Token

```csharp
using System;
using System.Web;
using System.Web.Util;
using Microsoft.IdentityModel.Protocols.WSFederation;

public class WifRequestValidator : RequestValidator
{
    protected override bool IsValidRequestString(
        HttpContext context,
        string value,
        RequestValidationSource requestValidationSource,
        string collectionKey,
        out int validationFailureIndex)
    {
```

```
validationFailureIndex = 0;

// Check for passive federation in form (HTTP POST) values
if (requestValidationSource == RequestValidationSource.Form)
{
    // Validate if being checked is WS-Federation response
    if(collectionKey.Equals(
                    WSFederationConstants.Parameters.Result))
    {
        // Try to construct a SignInResponseMessage from value
        var message =
        WSFederationMessage.CreateFromFormPost(context.Request)
            as SignInResponseMessage;
        if (message != null) return true;
    }
}

// Validation inconclusive, fall back on built-in method
return base.IsValidRequestString(
    context,
    value,
    requestValidationSource,
    collectionKey,
    out validationFailureIndex);
    }
}
```

The main method of the `RequestValidator` class is the `IsValidRequestString` method, which you need to override. It is called for each value in the request collection to validate that value. If any value is not safe, this results in the exception in Figure 9-5. At the end of Listing 9-4 the base method is called, so as long as you don't do anything stupid in the code before it, you can always fall back on the built-in validation. The purpose of the override in Listing 9-4 is to ensure that a security token posted to the hosted service is actually accepted as a valid request. This is done by checking the value of the field in the request collection that's used for passive federation. The key of this field is identified by the constant `WSFederationConstants.Parameters.Result`. From the value WIF should create a `SignInResponseMessage`, and only if this succeeds can the overridden validator indicate that the value is valid.

To use the `RequestValidator` in Listing 9-4, you must register it with the Http Runtime as the request validator of choice. To do this, you need to add (or change) the `httpRuntime` element in `web.config` as follows:

```
<httpRuntime requestValidationType="WebRoleRP.WifRequestValidator,WebRoleRP"/>
```

At this point the code does not yet compile because the code in Listing 9-4 requires a reference to the `Microsoft.IdentityModel` assembly. After you add the reference you can run the hosted service again. You should be logged into the application, and the username you entered is shown in the top-right corner, as shown in Figure 9-6.

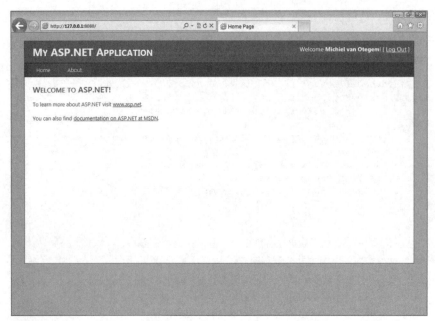

FIGURE 9-6

Extending the Local Development STS

The development STS produces two claims: a name claim and a role claim. The name claim corresponds to the username and is actually used as such in the ClaimsIdentity by default. The role claim indicates a role that the user is part of. As explained earlier, this handles the result of the IsInRole method, and a token can contain multiple role claims. The development STS isn't useful because the name claim is whatever you type as username, and there is only one fixed role. To make the STS useful for development purposes, it needs to be more flexible. The following are the steps to do that.

 The following steps assume that you're already familiar with Visual Studio. If you're not, please refer to http://bit.ly/learnvs

1. Add a new WebForm page named **FormsLogin.aspx** to the WebRoleRP_STS.

2. From the Toolbox drag a Login-control onto the page, and then save the page.

3. Open web.config and change Login.aspx to FormsLogin.aspx in the <authentication> element, so it looks like the following code snippet.

Available for
download on
Wrox.com

```
<authentication mode="Forms">
  <forms loginUrl="FormsLogin.aspx"
         protection="All"
```

```
                  timeout="30"
                  name=".ASPXAUTH"
                  path="/"
                  requireSSL="false"
                  slidingExpiration="true"
                  defaultUrl="default.aspx"
                  cookieless="UseDeviceProfile"
                  enableCrossAppRedirects="false" />
        </authentication>
```

code snippet 07_AuthenticationConfig.txt

4. Open CustomSecurityTokenService.cs in the App_Code folder.

5. Scroll all the way down to the GetOutputClaimsIdentity method.

6. Replace

```
        outputIdentity.Claims.Add(new Claim(ClaimTypes.Role, "Manager"));
```

with the following code snippet:

```
        // Add email claim with the member's email.
        var member = Membership.GetUser();
        outputIdentity.Claims.Add(new Claim(ClaimTypes.Email, member.Email));

        // Add a role claim for each role the member is in.

        foreach (var role in Roles.GetRolesForUser())
        {
            outputIdentity.Claims.Add(new Claim(ClaimTypes.Role, role));
        }
```

code snippet 08_AddClaimToToken.txt

7. Click Website ⇨ ASP.NET Configuration.

8. Click the Security link or tab.

9. Click Create user.

10. Enter the required information to create a new user, and click the Create User button.

11. Go to the Security tab again, and click Enable roles; then click Create or Manage roles.

12. Add two roles.

13. For each role add the user you created to that role.

    a. Click Manage on the role you want to add the user to.

    b. Find the user.

    c. Check the User Is In Role check box.

    d. Click Back.

When you run the solution now, you're presented with the login page you created, and you need to enter the username and password of the user you created. You are then authenticated with the application as before. The original unsecured login page that comes with the STS by default is now disabled and is replaced with ASP.NET Membership. The ASP.NET Roles functionality is now also enabled, and you can manage users as you would in any other ASP.NET application using Membership and Roles. This makes the STS much more suitable to test your application with. If you want it to be even more effective, you can add claims in the `GetOutputClaimsIdentity` method, which you can store in ASP.NET Profiles.

Alternatively, you can use the Thinktecture IdentityServer, which you can download from `http://identityserver.codeplex.com`, where you can also find installation instructions. Another option is using ADFS 2.0, which is a free add-on to Windows Server 2008 and up. If an STS is going to be deployed in the local production network, ADFS 2.0 is a likely candidate, so using it would get you closer to a live environment. The downside is the need for Active Directory and a Windows domain to get ADFS 2.0 working. On a Windows Vista/7 machine that will not work, so you need a development server or to use a virtual machine.

The previous exercise shows you that if you have an existing application using ASP.NET Membership and Roles, you can easily migrate it to WIF. All you need to do is add role claims to the token corresponding to the roles the user has in the application. Then you need to remove Membership and Roles from the application and hook the application up to the STS.

Using Claims Received from the STS

When you have an application you're developing hooked up to an STS, you can start using the claims that you receive. For debugging purposes it is always good to see which claims you are actually getting, and it is easy to list these. A good way to do this is to add a `GridView`-control to the Master Page, so the claims are visible at the bottom of each page, like this:

```
<h2>Claims</h2>
<asp:GridView runat="server" ID="claimsGrid" />
```

On the `Page_Load` method of the Master Page, you can then add the following code to fill the `GridView`-control with the claims received:

Available for download on Wrox.com

```
IClaimsPrincipal principal = Thread.CurrentPrincipal as IClaimsPrincipal;
if (principal != null)
{
    IClaimsIdentity identity = principal.Identities[0];
    claimsGrid.DataSource = identity.Claims;
    claimsGrid.DataBind();
}
```

code snippet 09_LoadClaimsInGridView.txt

When you now login through the STS, you see the page in Figure 9-7. Because of the way the `GridView`-control is defined, all claim properties are shown, so it gives a nice insight into what is actually in the token.

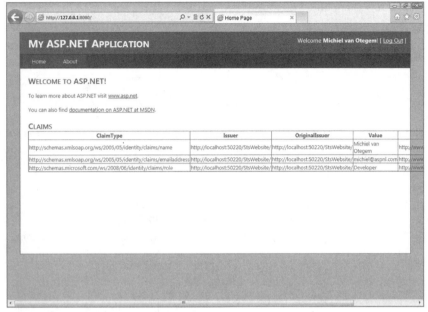

FIGURE 9-7

Armed with the knowledge of the claims you receive, you can use the `IClaimsIdentity` extension methods shown earlier in Listing 9-1 to use the claims in whichever way is suitable for your application.

Creating a Claims-Aware Web Service

By now you should be fairly familiar with WIF and the concepts around it. If you develop only web applications, then what you've learned so far may actually be all you need. Chances are that you will also be working with WCF web services at some point, and that's more complicated. The security bar is raised quite a bit higher for web services. This means that the quick-and-dirty solution of having FedUtil creating an STS will not work.

Creating Certificates

Because the security requirements are higher, you need a secure connection on both the web service and the STS. To host an application, including an STS, under SSL you need certificates. Certificates are also used for signing and encrypting tokens, and although you could do so with the same certificate used for a secure connection, it is good practice to separate these.

You don't need to understand the finer points of certificate signing and encryption, but a token is signed with the private key of a certificate and checked by the receiving party with the public key. Reversely, tokens are encrypted with the public key of a certificate and decrypted by the receiving party with the private key. Effectively, this means that the STS requires a certificate with a private key to sign tokens and needs the public key of the certificate the RP uses to decrypt the token. The RP needs the public key of the signing certificate, and a certificate with a private key for decryption.

If you choose to use separate signing and encryption certificates, you need the following certificates:

➤ SSL certificate for the STS

➤ SSL certificate for the RP

➤ Certificate used by the STS to sign tokens

➤ Certificate used by the STS to encrypt tokens and by the RP to decrypt tokens

To start, you can create these certificates locally for development purposes. Doing this right is somewhat of a hassle because you need to ensure the certificates are located in the right certificate store and the private key is accessible to IIS, which by default isn't the case.

For your development environment the Windows Azure SDK creates an SSL certificate for the address 127.0.0.1 when you run an HTTPS endpoint for the first time. This covers the SSL certificate needed for the RP. The WIF SDK already created a certificate called STSTestCert when you used the Visual Studio STS project template. That's the certificate used by default to sign tokens.

 FederationMetadata.xml *is signed and contains information about the signing certificate. If you want to change the signing certificate, you need to regenerate* FederationMetadata.xml. *This is also the case if you want to add more claim types. Shawn Cicoria has created an editor you can use, which you can download from* http://bit.ly/fedmetadatagen.

Creating the SSL Certificate

For development purposes you still need only an SSL certificate for the STS, which can run under localhost and an encryption certificate for the RP. You can give the latter certificate any name you want, but it makes sense to have the name reflect its purpose, for instance RpEncrypt. Use the following steps to create the certificates.

1. Open the Visual Studio command prompt or the Windows SDK command prompt as Administrator. If you use the Windows SDK command prompt, change directory to `c:\Program Files\Microsoft SDKs\Windows\v7.1\bin`.

2. Type `makecert -a sha256 -n CN=localhost -pe -r -sky exchange -ss My -sr LocalMachine`.

3. Repeat step 2, replacing `localhost` with `RpEncrypt`.

Allowing the Compute Emulator and IIS to Access the Private Key

The certificates are now created, but the Windows Azure Compute Emulator and IIS can't access the private key yet, and this necessary for everything to work. You can do this with the Microsoft Management Console (MMC).

1. Click the Start button, and type **mmc** and press enter.

2. Click File ➪ Add/Remove Snap-In.

3. Select the Certificates Snap-in and click Add.

4. Select Computer account.

5. Leave Local computer selected, and click Finish and then OK.

6. In the left pane, expand the tree until you see Console Root ⇨ Certificates (Local Computer) ⇨ Personal ⇨ Certificates. In the middle pane the certificate you created should be listed, as shown in Figure 9-8.

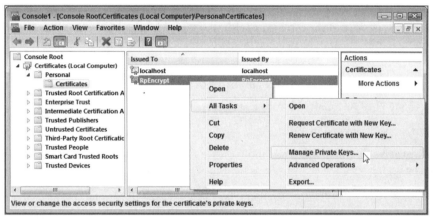

FIGURE 9-8

7. Right-click the RpEncrypt certificate, and select All Tasks ⇨ Manage Private Keys.

8. Click Add.

9. Enter **IIS_IUSRS** in the text area if you use Windows 7 or Windows 2008 R2; otherwise type **NETWORK SERVICE**, and click Check Names.

10. If all is well, the text you entered will change into a user account. Click OK, followed by OK again.

11. Repeat steps 7 through 10 for the localhost certificate.

Exporting the Certificates

The certificates are now created and have the right authorizations set. However, they are not in the right certificate store yet. The localhost certificate should also be in the Trusted Root section of the local computer, so when you hit localhost with a browser, you won't get any security warnings. You can do this by copying the certificate to the other store. For both the STS and the RP to work correctly with the encryption certificate, it needs to be in the Personal store of the current user with the private key and in the Trusted People store of the current user without the private key. The best way to do this is to export and import the certificate with the MMC. In the process you create a certificate file you need later.

1. Right click the RpEncrypt certificate, and select All Tasks ⇨ Export.

2. Click Next.

3. Select Yes, Export the Private Key, and click Next.

4. Click Next.

5. Type a password for the certificate (twice), and click Next.

6. Enter the filename and location, and click Next and then Finish.

7. Export again, this time without the private key.

Importing the Certificates

You now have a *.pfx file of the certificate with the private key and a *.cer file without the private key. You can now import the exported certificate to the Personal certificate store of the current user using MMC.

1. Add Certificates to the selected snap-ins.

2. Select My User Account.

3. Click Finish, followed by OK.

4. In the left pane, expand the tree until you see Console Root ⇨ Certificates - Current User ⇨ Personal.

5. Right-click the Personal folder, and select All Tasks ⇨ Import.

6. Click Next.

7. Change the file select filter to *.pfx so that you can select the certificate with the private key.

8. Click Next.

9. Enter the password and click Next.

10. Click Next and then Finish.

11. Repeat the import process for the *.cer certificate, and place it in Console Root ⇨ Certificates - Current User ⇨ Trusted People.

Creating a Local Development STS for WCF

WCF requires an STS to run under HTTPS. This means you need to host the STS under IIS or IIS Express because the web server built in to Visual Studio doesn't support HTTPS. For this reason it is a good idea to build the local development STS first when working with WCF, instead of having FedUtil generate one. To get the STS working under HTTPS, you first need to enable HTTPS for the Default Web Site in IIS.

1. Open the Internet Information Services (IIS) Manager by clicking the Start button and typing **iis and pressing enter.**

2. In the left pane, expand the tree to select Default Web Site.

3. In the right pane click Bindings.

4. Click Add.

5. In the Add Site Binding dialog, select https as type. This automatically switches the port to the HTTPS port 443.

6. From the SSL Certificate drop-down, select the localhost certificate, as shown in Figure 9-9.

7. Click OK to close the dialog and Close to finish.

8. Verify by typing **https://localhost** in the browser. It should show the IIS welcome screen.

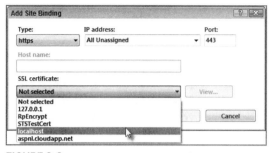

FIGURE 9-9

With localhost running under HTTPS, you can now add the STS to it. Because Visual Studio needs to add the project to IIS, you need to run it as Administrator.

1. Go to Start and find Visual Studio or Visual Web Developer. Right-click it, and select Run as Administrator.

2. Click File ➪ New Web Site.

3. Select Visual C# as the programming language.

4. Select WCF Security Token Service, and click the Browse button next to the Web location textbox.

5. In the left bar of the dialog, select Local IIS.

6. Select the Default Web Site folder in the tree on the right, and click the Create New Application button, which you can find on the right top of the screen, as you can see in Figure 9-10.

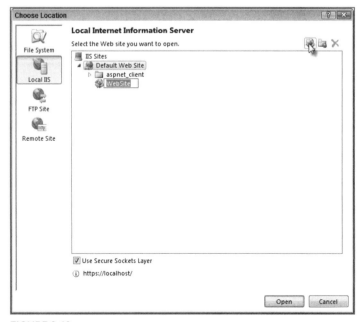

FIGURE 9-10

7. Name the new application **LocalSts** and check Use Secure Sockets Layer.

8. Click Open and then OK to create the STS.

You have now created the STS, but there is still some work to do. At this point the STS uses some default certificates for signing and encryption, but you created specific certificates for that purpose. Because you use these certificates in Windows Azure later, you must replace the default certificates with the ones you created. The certificates are controlled by two application-settings elements in `web.config`. Find the following configuration:

```
<appSettings>
  <add key="IssuerName" value="ActiveSTS"/>
  <add key="SigningCertificateName" value="STSTestCert"/>
  <add key="EncryptingCertificateName" value="CN=DefaultApplicationCertificate"/>
</appSettings>
```

and replace it with this:

```
<appSettings>
  <add key="IssuerName" value="ActiveSTS"/>
  <add key="SigningCertificateName" value="CN=StsSign"/>
  <add key="EncryptingCertificateName" value="CN=RpEncrypt"/>
</appSettings>
```

The last thing you need to do is ensure that the service meta data is requested over HTTPS. To do this you need to use the `mexHttpsBinding` instead of the `mexHttpBinding` for the meta data exchange endpoint and set `httpsGetEnabled` to `true` on the service meta data setting of the service behavior. These settings are highlighted in the (abbreviated) service model configuration in `web.config`.

```
<system.serviceModel>
  <services>
    <service name="Microsoft.IdentityModel.Protocols.WSTrust.➡
WSTrustServiceContract" behaviorConfiguration="ServiceBehavior">
      <!-~DHomitted for brevity~DH>
      <endpoint address="mex" binding="mexHttpsBinding"
                contract="IMetadataExchange" />
    </service>
  </services>
  <bindings>
    <!-~DHomitted for brevity~DH>
  </bindings>
  <behaviors>
    <serviceBehaviors>
      <behavior name="ServiceBehavior">
        <!-~DHomitted for brevity~DH>
        <serviceMetadata httpsGetEnabled="true" />
        <!-~DHomitted for brevity~DH>
      </behavior>
    </serviceBehaviors>
  </behaviors>
</system.serviceModel>
```

code snippet 10_ServiceModelConfiguration

You can't verify that the STS works, but you can open the web service in the browser, which should show you information about the `SecurityTokenService` Service.

Creating a Web Service and Client

When creating web services, you should first ensure that the service works. Therefore, you should first create the service and a client that talks to it before trying to secure it with WIF.

1. Start Visual Studio or Visual Web Developer as Administrator.

2. Create a new Windows Azure project named **WifActiveFed**.

3. Add a WCF Service Web Role.

4. Rename WCFServiceWebRole1 to **WcfWebRoleRP** to indicate you will be building a WCF relying party.

5. In the Solution Explorer double-click the WcfWebRoleRP role configuration to show the configuration properties.

6. Uncheck the HTTP endpoint check box under Launch Browser For, so the browser won't start when you run the service.

7. On the left select the Endpoints tab.

8. Change the port number of Endpoint1 to port 8080, so it can't collide with IIS, and click the Save button.

Getting all the parts working with WIF is a challenge, so for now you don't need to bother with the functionality. Just leave the default Service1 as it is and continue with creating a client project.

1. Start the web service without debugging with Ctrl+F5.

2. Start a new instance of Visual Studio or start Visual C# Express.

3. Create a new Console Application named WcfActiveFedClient.

4. In the Solution Explorer right-click the project, and select Add Service Reference.

5. In the address textbox enter the address of the web service, which is `http://127.0.0.1:8080/Service1.svc`, and click the Go button.

6. The dialog should now show you Service1. Click OK to add the reference to the project.

7. Put the code in the following snippet in the Main method:

```
while (true)
{
    Console.Write("Enter a value: ");
    var input = Console.ReadLine();
    if (string.IsNullOrEmpty(input)) break;
    int value;
    if (int.TryParse(input, out value))
    {
        var client = new ServiceReference1.Service1Client();
```

```
        Console.WriteLine(client.GetData(value));
    }
}
```

code snippet 11_LoopWebServiceCall.txt

8.   Save the file and run the client.

9.   Enter and integer value to test if the client works correctly with the service.

Connecting the Web Service to the STS

Now that you have the web service and client working, you can hook them up to the STS. This sounds easy because this is done with FedUtil. But there is more to it than that. First, you need to ensure the RP runs under a secure SSL connection, so all interaction between client, STS, and service is secure.

1.   In the Solution Explorer double-click the WcfWebRoleRP role configuration.

2.   Go to the Endpoints tab and click Add Endpoint.

3.   You can give any name to the endpoint, but it helps to give it a name that indicates what it is, such as **HttpsEndpoint**.

4.   Switch the protocol to HTTPS.

5.   Set the Public Port to 8443, so it doesn't interfere with SSL port 443 on IIS.

6.   For now you don't need to select a certificate, in which case the DevFabric uses the built-in certificate for IP 127.0.0.1, so the screen looks like Figure 9-11.

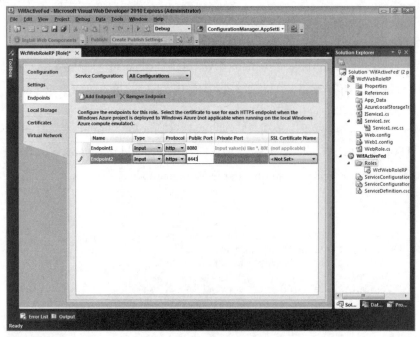

FIGURE 9-11

7. Go to the Configuration tab, and notice that the HTTPS endpoint check box is checked to launch it in the browser on startup. You can uncheck this, but for verification purposes it can be handy.

8. Save the configuration.

9. Verify that the service runs under SSL by pressing Ctrl+F5 to start without debugging.

10. When the browser opens, change the address to `https://127.0.0.1:8443/Service1.svc`. After ignoring the certificate warning, you should see the service page.

To avoid the certificate warning, you need to make the built-in DevFabric certificate trusted. You can do this using the MMC.

1. In the left pane of the MMC, fold open the tree until you see Console Root ⇨ Certificates (Local Computer) ⇨ Personal ⇨ Certificates.

2. Select the localhost certificate and copy it.

3. In the left pane, fold open the tree until you see Console Root ⇨ Certificates (Local Computer) ⇨ Trusted Root Certificates ⇨ Certificates.

4. Right-click the Certificates folder, and select Paste.

Now you're almost ready to fire up FedUtil. To do its job, FedUtil needs a configured endpoint in `web.config` to know which service it's going to secure. However, in .NET Framework 4.0 WCF services don't need an endpoint configuration because this is handled at machine level for default bindings. So before running FedUtil you need to add a temporary endpoint configuration.

1. Open `web.config` of WcfWebRoleRP.

2. Add the following endpoint configuration to the `<system.serviceModel>`.

Available for download on Wrox.com

```
<services>
  <service name="WcfWebRoleRP.Service1">
    <endpoint address=""
              binding="basicHttpBinding"
              contract="WcfWebRoleRP.IService1" />
  </service>
</services>
```

code snippet 12_EndpointConfig.txt

3. Save `web.config`.

4. Run FedUtil as administrator.

5. Point FedUtil to the `web.config` of the web service.

6. In the Application URI enter the URL of the application *as it will run in production*, so `https://[YourAppName].cloudapp.net`.

7. Click Next to show the screen with Application Information. This is different from passive federation because it shows the service(s) and contract(s) you can secure. This is the endpoint you added in set 2.

8. Click Next to show the STS selection screen. This time select Use an Existing STS.

9. In the textbox you need to enter the location of the FederationMetadata.xml file that FedUtil needs to configure the service. You can open the LocalSts project and browse the file to get the correct URL. The dialog should look like Figure 9-12.

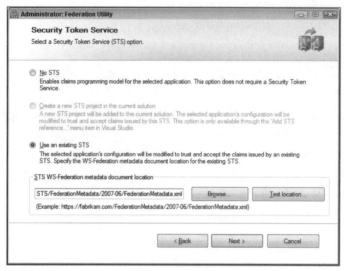

FIGURE 9-12

10. Click Next to show the dialog to set encryption. Select Enable encryption and then choose an existing certificate, which you can select with Select Certificate.

11. Select the RpEncrypt certificate as in Figure 9-13, and click OK.

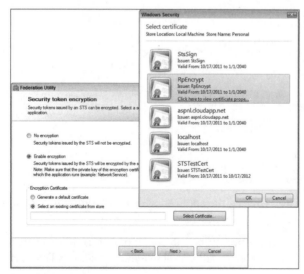

FIGURE 9-13

12. Click Next to show the claims offered by the STS.

13. Click Next again to show the summary, and click Finish.

Compared to passive federation, the changes FedUtil made to the `<Microsoft.identityModel>` section of the `web.config` are minor. It has set the audience URIs and some information about the STS in the `<issuerNameRegistry>` element. The most important difference is that the `<service>` element now contains a name attribute, with the name of the web service it applies to. This also explains why compared to Listing 9-3 this section contains so few elements. This information is now part of the `<system.serviceModel>` section, which has been modified extensively. The endpoint has been changed to a `ws2007FederationHttpBinding`, and a binding configuration has been added. This in itself doesn't have anything to do with WIF because this binding predates WIF. For this reason WIF works together with WCF through a behavior extension. This extension is added as the `federatedServiceHostConfiguration` behavior extension and then configured in the behaviors for the service it applies to. This is highlighted in the following configuration snippet:

```
<behaviors>
  <serviceBehaviors>
    <behavior>
      <federatedServiceHostConfiguration
          name="WcfWebRoleRP.Service1" />
      <serviceMetadata httpGetEnabled="true" />
      <serviceDebug includeExceptionDetailInFaults="false" />
      <serviceCredentials>
        <!~DHCertificate added by FedUtil.
            Subject='CN=RpEncrypt', Issuer='CN=RpEncrypt'.~DH>
        <serviceCertificate
            findValue="149A6F02DC3D60CC312CD009A188229303DC63FA"
            storeLocation="LocalMachine" storeName="My"
            x509FindType="FindByThumbprint" />
      </serviceCredentials>
    </behavior>
  </serviceBehaviors>
</behaviors>
<extensions>
  <behaviorExtensions>
    <add name="federatedServiceHostConfiguration"
        type="[omitted for brevity]" />
  </behaviorExtensions>
</extensions>
```

csode snippet 13_WifBehaviorConfig.txt

Apart from the highlighted elements, FedUtil has added a reference to the encryption certificate in the `<serviceCredentials>` element. To ensure that the web service can find the certificate, you need to add it to the WebRole configuration.

1. In the Solution Explorer double-click the WcfWebRoleRP role configuration.

2. Go to the Certificates tab, and click Add Certificate.

3. You can give any name to the certificate configuration, but it makes sense to give it the name of the certificate itself, in this case **RpEncrypt.**

4. Go to the Thumbprint column, and click the Ellipsis button to select the correct certificate.

5. Select the RpEncrypt certificate, and click OK.

6. Save the configuration.

With the binding configuration set by FedUtil, you'd expect that now everything would work fine, and all you'd have to do is update the service client to use the right binding. This unfortunately is not the case, so you still need to make some changes to the configuration. These changes exercise a little more control over the interaction between the client, STS, and service, which you need later. To achieve this you must replace the `ws2007FederationHttpBinding` with the custom binding in Listing 9-5. When you do this, don't forget to replace the highlighted Address with that of your application in production.

LISTING 9-5: Custom Binding for Identity Federation

```
<customBinding>
  <binding name="WifActiveFedBinding">
    <security authenticationMode="SecureConversation"
            messageSecurityVersion="WSSecurity11WSTrust13➡
WSSecureConversation13WSSecurityPolicy12BasicSecurityProfile10"
            requireSecurityContextCancellation="false">
        <secureConversationBootstrap
            authenticationMode="IssuedTokenOverTransport"
            messageSecurityVersion="WSSecurity11WSTrust13➡
WSSecureConversation13WSSecurityPolicy12BasicSecurityProfile10">
          <issuedTokenParameters>
            <additionalRequestParameters>
              <AppliesTo xmlns="http://schemas.xmlsoap.org/ws/2004/09/policy">
                <EndpointReference xmlns="http://www.w3.org/2005/08/addressing">
                  <Address>https://[YourAppName].cloudapp.net/</Address>
                </EndpointReference>
              </AppliesTo>
            </additionalRequestParameters>
            <claimTypeRequirements>
              <add claimType="http://schemas.xmlsoap.org/ws/2005/05/identity➡
/claims/name"
                    isOptional="true" />
              <add claimType="http://schemas.microsoft.com/ws/2008/06/identity➡
/claims/role"
                    isOptional="true" />
            </claimTypeRequirements>
            <issuerMetadata
                address="https://localhost/LocalSTS/Service.svc/mex" />
          </issuedTokenParameters>
        </secureConversationBootstrap>
    </security>
    <httpsTransport />
  </binding>
</customBinding>
<EntityDescriptor
```

After you've added the custom binding, you need to make some more minor modifications to the configuration. The following steps take you through these changes:

1. Open `web.config`.

2. Give the behavior added by FedUtil a name, for instance **`WifActiveFedBehavior`**.

3. Add the behavior configuration to the service configuration.

4. Tie the endpoint to the new custom binding called `WifActiveFedBinding` in Listing 9-5. To ensure the endpoint works regardless of the address, remove the URL FedUtil placed in the address property.

5. Add a meta data exchange endpoint to the service, and ensure it runs under SSL by setting the **`mexHttpsBinding`** instead of the `mexHttpBinding`.

6. To complement the meta data exchange binding over SSL, find the behavior of the serviceMetadata element, and rename `httpGetEnabled` to **`httpsGetEnabled`**.

After you take the preceding steps, the service configuration should look like the following snippet:

Available for download on Wrox.com

```
<service name="WcfWebRoleRP.Service1"
        behaviorConfiguration="WifActiveFedBehavior">
  <endpoint address=""
            binding="customBinding"
            contract="WcfWebRoleRP.IService1"
            bindingConfiguration="WifActiveFedBinding" />
  <endpoint address="mex"
            binding="mexHttpsBinding"
            contract="IMetadataExchange" />
</service>
```

code snippet 14_Modified WifiConfig.txt

The last thing you have to change is some WIF configuration. When WIF receives a token, it checks to see if the token actually applies to it. For this reason the STS adds information to the token, indicating the intended recipient. On the receiving end you must set for which URIs you accept tokens, which you do in the `<audienceUris>` element of the WIF service definition. Right now the only URI in there is the URI you entered in FedUtil, which is the URI of the production environment. To make it work on your local machine, you need to add the URI of the local service as highlighted in the following configuration.

Available for download on Wrox.com

```
<microsoft.identityModel>
  <service name="WcfWebRoleRP.Service1">
    <audienceUris>
      <add value="https://[YourAppName].cloudapp.net/" />
      <add value="https://127.0.0.1:8443/Service1.svc" />
    </audienceUris>
    <!~DHomitted for brevity~DH>
  </service>
</microsoft.identityModel>
```

code snippet 15_WifAudienceUriConfig.txt

In the preceding sample, the full URI to the service has been added instead of the root URI. This is a temporary work around because of an issue with the STS. This is discussed in more detail in the section "Deploying and Troubleshooting" later in the chapter.

Updating the Client

Now that the service has been meticulously tweaked, updating the client is easy. All you need to do is reconfigure the service reference to point to the right location. When you do this in Visual Studio, the service reference is automatically updated.

1. Make sure the latest service deploys by pressing Ctrl+F5 in the WifActiveFed solution.

2. Open the client project in Visual Studio of Visual C# Express.

3. In the Solution Explorer, open the Service References subfolder to reveal ServiceReference1.

4. Right-click ServiceReference1, and select Configure Service Reference.

5. In the address textbox change the address to the new secure URL
   https://127.0.0.1:8443/service1.svc and click OK.

After following the preceding steps, the client should run without any changes to the code or config and get a result. Be aware that the current STS configuration works based on your Windows identity as provided by the client to the STS. You can verify this by changing the code of the `GetData` service method to return the username of the logged on user.

```
IPrincipal principal = Thread.CurrentPrincipal;
Return string.Format("Hello {0}. You entered: {1}",
                     Principal.Identity.Name, value);
```

The fact that authentication works based on the Windows identity doesn't actually matter, even if you use an STS in production that utilizes another authentication method. This is because you've effectively outsourced the authentication method, so the service works regardless of which authentication type you use. You have to change only the binding to the STS and have the service accept the signing certificate of the STS. On the client, you also need to change the binding to supply another type of user credentials. This is discussed in Chapter 14 where you learn about the AppFabric Access Control Service.

DEPLOYING AND TROUBLESHOOTING

As you've seen so far, setting up a website with passive federation is a walk in the park compared to working with active federation. When it comes to deployment and troubleshooting, it's much the same. Because you have a user interface when working with a website, it's much easier to get to exceptions and trace them. Deploying and troubleshooting a WCF service on Windows Azure is a different matter. You can't just deploy, and debugging is also much harder, because you can't just throw in trace statements. For this reason the focus of this section is on getting the WCF service to work; although, some of it applies to the website as well.

Getting WIF to Work on Windows Azure

Although the Azure Compute emulator is quite good at emulating the Windows Azure environment, there are some key differences with the actual staging and production environments in Windows Azure. Also, the staging environment may be physically the same, but there are some subtle differences that are especially important when using WIF.

The key aspect of much of the trouble you can run into with WIF is that you don't have access to the file system of Windows Azure instances. As explained in the previous chapter, this is important to ensure scalability, but it does have some nasty side effects when it comes to WIF.

Working with Certificates

Before you deploy, you need to set up the environment properly. On top of what you learned in Chapter 8, you also need to install the needed certificates.

Up until now you've used certificates you created yourself. Although this works fine in development, there are some serious drawbacks when using these in a live environment. The problem is that your local machine is not a trusted issuer of certificates, so when your certificate is validated by a browser or other client, the least that can happen is that you get a security warning. Earlier you avoided this by making the certificates trusted and disabling certificate chain validation, and even then you may have had to ignore a warning here and there. This doesn't work in a in a live environment. You can't ask users to ignore the security warnings because that defeats the purpose of having them in the first place. And users definitely should not be asked to put certificates in the Trusted People store. For this reason you should get the needed certificates from a trusted root such as COMODO, GeoTrust, or VeriSign.

Working with certificates from a trusted root is also good practice for signing and encryption, but there the need is smaller. Normally, a certificate is checked including the chain back to the trusted root. This is to ensure that if the root is no longer trusted, certificates issued by that root are automatically invalidated.

With self-signed certificates the check back to the trusted root obviously doesn't work. However if you manage trust between an STS and an RP under your control, using a self-signed certificate is fine. In that case you don't need the check back to the trusted root.

In your development environment, you simulated the certificate chain by copying certificates to the Trusted Root and Trusted People folders. In Windows Azure you can't do this, so you need to disable the check. You can do so by adding the highlighted configuration to the following WIF service configuration.

Available for download on Wrox.com

```
<microsoft.identityModel>
  <service name="WcfWebRoleRP.Service1">
    <!~DHOmitted for brevity~DH>
    <certificateValidation certificateValidationMode="None" />
  </service>
</microsoft.identityModel>
```

code snippet 16_DisableCertChainValidation.txt

Installing Certificates

When you have the certificates, trusted or otherwise, you must install these in Windows Azure. Because you don't have access to the file system, and can't install them in the instance directly, Windows Azure provides you with an external certificate store. From there certificates are copied to any instance created. This does mean, however, that you have no control over the actual certificate store these certificates are installed in, so you can't go around and move a certificate to the Trusted Root, for instance. That said, the certificates are of course installed in a store accessible from your application.

To install certificates into Windows Azure, take the following steps:

1. Log on to `https://windows.azure.com`.

2. Select Hosted Services, Storage Accounts & CDN.

3. Select the Hosted Services folder to see your subscription with all the hosted services underneath in the middle section of the screen.

4. Right-click the Certificates folder of the hosted service you want to add a certificate to, and click Add Certificate.

5. Select the certificate file of the certificate you want to upload to Windows Azure. You can upload `*.pfx` files only.

6. Enter the certificate password, and click OK.

You should upload the certificate used to create a secure connection and the encryption certificate of the RP.

Installing the STS Certificate

When you installed the HTTPS and RP encryption certificates, you installed them with the private key. However, to check the STS signature of a token only the certificate itself is needed. Having the private key of the STS certificate actually doesn't make sense, and when making use of an STS that is not under your control, you don't even have the private key. This means you should, and in most cases can only, upload the certificate without the private key. The problem is that you can only upload a `*.pfx` file to Windows Azure, and by default this is a certificate with the private key. If you can obtain a `*.pfx` certificate without a private key from whoever manages the STS, you're fine. Otherwise you'll most likely get a `*.cer` file, which means you need to convert the certificate. Because you can export only a certificate without a private key from MMC as a `*.cer` file, you have the same problem with the certificate being used so far. Fortunately, you can convert a certificate with just a few lines of code. The method in Listing 9-6 shows you how.

LISTING 9-6: Method to Convert a Certificate to *.pfx

```
public void ConvertCert(string fullPath, string password)
{
    var dir = Path.GetDirectoryName(fullPath);
    var file = Path.GetFileNameWithoutExtension(fullPath);
    var cert = new X509Certificate(fullPath);
    var certBytes = cert.Export(X509ContentType.Pfx, password);
    File.WriteAllBytes(dir + @"\" + file + ".pfx", certBytes);
}
```

Configuring the SSL Certificate

In the development environment you used the DevFabric certificate for 127.0.0.1, which was automatically tied to the secure endpoint, because you didn't select a certificate. However, in the production environment you use an actual SSL certificate, which you installed a little earlier. You need to configure this certificate in the WebRole as well.

1. In the Solution Explorer double-click the WcfWebRoleRP configuration.

2. Select the Certificates tab.

3. Click Add Certificate.

4. Enter a name for the certificate. Although any name can suffice, it makes sense to give the certificate the name of domain it will secure, so use **[YourAppName].cloudapp.net**.

5. Go to the thumbprint textbox to enter the thumbprint of the certificate. You can do this in one of two ways:

    ➤ If you installed the certificate on your development machine, you can click the Ellipsis button to select the certificate.

    ➤ Otherwise you can double-click the certificate file from Windows Explorer and copy the thumbprint from the Details tab.

6. Save the configuration.

Deployment

You can deploy your application the same way as discussed in Chapter 8 but with one proviso: You need to ensure the `Microsoft.IdentityModel` assembly is copied along with your application. Because this assembly is not part of the .NET Framework, it is also not installed on Windows Azure. However, on your local machine it's in the Global Assembly Cache, so by default it will not be deployed. In the current WcfWebRoleRP the assembly isn't even referenced because it is used only in configuration. To ensure the assembly gets copied along with the project, take the following steps:

1. In WcfWebRoleRP reference `Microsoft.IdentityModel`.

    a. In the Solution Explorer right-click the References folder, and select Add Reference.

    b. Switch to the .NET tab.

    c. Select the `Microsoft.IdentityModel` assembly, and click OK.

2. In the References folder find the added assembly, and select it.

3. In the Properties window, set the Copy Local property to **True**.

As discussed previously, until you are ready to go to production, it makes sense to turn off custom errors in `web.config` so that it is easier to see configuration errors. And speaking of configuration, it makes sense to change the port numbers you set earlier in the WebRole configuration to use the default https and https ports, instead of 8080 and 8443.

Dealing with URI Issues

If you deploy your application to the staging environment, now it will run. Or at least it will not give any errors if you open the service page. The client you built will not yet work, even if you change the endpoint it points to at the endpoint in the staging environment. The problem is that contrary to the local development environment and the production environment, the staging environment URI is random. The staging URI looks something like this:

```
https://4ab5ac2001324585ba5a902f4242a98c.cloudapp.net/
```

This URL changes every time you deploy, and this causes a chicken-and-egg problem. Normally, you would just go into web.config and add another audience URI as you did earlier for the local development environment earlier. But when deployed, you can't change the web.config in the running instances. But if you add the URI to the `web.config`, you have to redeploy, which changes the URI again. The easiest way to solve this is adding **mode="Never"** to the <audienceUris> element, which disables the audience URI check altogether. For staging this may be acceptable, but it would be wise to alter it before going to production, which defeats the purpose of a staging environment somewhat. You wouldn't be able to do a virtual IP switch deployment to production in that case. If you don't need to deploy that way, you're in the clear. Another option is to modify the STS so the token it sends back actually uses a URI that is already in the <audienceUris> element. This will not work with a product such as ADFS 2.0, but with the local development STS this is not an issue. In the same manner you can also solve the problem discussed earlier that the local development STS uses the complete URI of the service instead of just the root URI.

1. In the LocalSts project open CustomSecurityTokenService.cs in the App_Code folder.

2. Find the `GetScope` method.

3. In the `GetScope` method there's a constructor to create the `scope` object. The first parameter is the URI to which the token will apply, and as you can see it takes the original URI. Replace that parameter with **"[YourAppName].cloudapp.net"**.

You can modify the last step to be a method that determines the correct URI based on a translation table, configuration, or whatever other solution you can think of. Now you can modify the client configuration to point to the correct URI. You can find the root URI in the Windows Azure Management Portal, as discussed in Chapter 8.

Scaling Up

As long as you work with one instance, chances are that everything will work just fine. But Windows Azure wasn't made to scale for nothing. Your application is hosted in an environment in which you can add instances as needed. This is possible because all instances share the same configuration and code. There's a catch though, and it has to do with the security session. In a load-balanced environment you need some way to ensure that it doesn't matter which instance a request hits. In ASP.NET this is done with a cookie, but with the default binding FedUtil uses it is not. That's an important reason why earlier you had to switch to the custom binding in Listing 9-5. On the <security> element of the binding `requreSecurityContextCancellation` property is set to false. You wouldn't think so from the name, but this actually switches WCF to cookie mode. Using cookies is only half the story though because cookies are encrypted. By default this is done using the machine key, a unique key for every instance, and the Windows Data Protection API, also known as DPAPI. Because the machine key is different on every instance, the cookie can be decrypted only on that instance. This means that the other instances in the load-balanced environment cannot decrypt the cookie and use it. This would cause the client to be sent back to the STS for a new token, after which a new cookie is set in place of the old one.

The best way to solve this problem is by using a certificate for the encryption instead of the machine key. You can do this with a custom `SessionSecurityTokenHandler`, and this works for both a website and a web service. The way you set it up is different though.

Setting Up Cookie Handling in a Website

To set up the `SessionSecurityTokenHandler` in a website, you need override the service configuration, and you can do this by hooking into the `ServiceConfigurationCreated` event of the `FederatedAuthentication` class. Listing 9-7 shows what the event handler should look like. It adds three cookies transforms, one to deflate the cookie so it is compressed, one to encrypt the cookie using the service certificate, and one to sign the cookie. You could, of course, use different certificates to encrypt and sign, but the service certificate is easily available.

Available for download on Wrox.com

LISTING 9-7: Replacing the SessionSecurityTokenHandler

```
void OnWifSvcConfigurationCreated(object sender,
        ServiceConfigurationCreatedEventArgs e)
{
    var certificate = e.ServiceConfiguration.ServiceCertificate);
    var transforms = new List<CookieTransforms>(
        new CookieTransform[] {
            new DeflateCookieTransform(),
            new RsaEncryptionCookieTransform(certificate),
            new RsaSignatureCookTransform(certificate) });
    var handler = new SessionSecurityTokenHandler(tranforms);
    e.ServiceConfiguration.SecurityTokenHandlers.AddOrReplace(handler);
}
```

To use the preceding event handler, you still need to wire it up. You do this in the `Application_Start` event handler in `global.asax`. The following line of code does the trick:

```
FederatedAuthentication.ServiceConfigurationCreated +=
    OnWifSvcConfigurationCreated;
```

Setting Up Cookie Handling in a WCF Service

To set up the `SessionSecurityTokenHandler` on a WCF service, you need to create a custom handler, which uses the same cookie transforms used for websites. When you create the new handler, you need to inherit from `SessionSecurityTokenHandler`. In the constructor, you need to hook up the cookie transforms. Listing 9-8 shows you how.

Available for download on Wrox.com

LISTING 9-8: RsaSessionSecurityHandler Constructor

```
public RsaSessionSecurityTokenHandler(X509Certificate2 certificate)
{
    var transforms = new List<CookieTransforms>(
        new CookieTransform[] {
```

```
        new DeflateCookieTransform(),
        new RsaEncryptionCookieTransform(certificate),
        new RsaSignatureCookTransform(certificate) });
    this.SetTransforms(transforms);
}
```

You also need to override the `ValidateToken` method to ensure that the incoming token is intended for the endpoint the request was sent to. This is needed because a cookie will be sent along with any request if the client thinks the cookie applies to the request being made. Listing 9-9 shows the overridden `ValidateToken` method. It basically checks the URI embedded in the token with the URI of the endpoint.

LISTING 9-9: RsaSessionSecurityHandler.ValidateToken method

```
public override ClaimsIdentityCollection ValidateToken(
    SessionSecurityToken token, string endpointId)
{
    // argument checks omitted for brevity

    Uri endpointUri;
    Uri tokenEndpointUri;
    bool endpointHasUri = Uri.TryCreate(endpointId,
                                        UriKind.Absolute,
                                        out endpointUri);
    bool tokenHasUri = Uri.TryCreate(token.EndpointId,
                                     UriKind.Absolute,
                                     out tokenEndpointUri);
    if (endpointHasUri && tokenHasUri)
    {
        if (endpointUri.Scheme != tokenEndpointUri.Scheme ||
            endpointUri.DnsSafeHost != tokenEndpointUri.DnsSafeHost ||
            endpointUri.AbsolutePath != tokenEndpointUri.AbsolutePath)
        {
            throw new SecurityTokenValidationException(
                "The incoming token is not scoped to the endpoint.");
        }
    }
    else if (String.Equals(endpointId, token.EndpointId,
                           StringComparison.Ordinal) == false)
    {
        throw new SecurityTokenValidationException(
            "The incoming token is not scoped to the endpoint.");
    }
    return this.ValidateToken(token);
}
```

To apply the `RsaessionSecurityTokenHandler` to the service, you need a service behavior. This is a class implementing the `IServiceBehavior` interface, which has three methods. You need to do some work only in the `Validate` method, which is shown in Listing 9-10. The `AddBindingParameters` and `ApplyDispatchBehavior` methods don't have to do anything, so you can leave those completely empty. (These should not throw a `NotImplementException`.)

LISTING 9-10: Validate Method for the RsaSessionServiceBehavior

```
public void Validate(ServiceDescription svcDescription,
                     ServiceHostBase svcHostBase)
{
    FederatedServiceCredentials.ConfigureServiceHost(
        svcHostBase,
        RoleEnvironment.GetConfigurationSettingValue("Deployment"));

    var behaviors = svcHostBase.Description.Behaviors;
    FederatedServiceCredentials credentials =
        behaviors.Find<FederatedServiceCredentials>();
    credentials.SecurityTokenHandlers.AddOrReplace(
        new RsaSessionSecurityTokenHandler(
            svcHostBase.Credentials.ServiceCertificate.Certificate));
}
```

The final piece of plumbing you need is a behavior extension so that you can make the behavior available in configuration. Listing 9-11 shows you the code for this extension.

LISTING 9-11: RsaSessionServiceBehaviorExtension

```
public class RsaSessionServiceBehaviorExtension :
    BehaviorExtensionElement
{
    public override Type BehaviorType
    {
        get { return typeof(RsaSessionServiceBehavior); }
    }

    protected override object CreateBehavior()
    {
        return new RsaSessionServiceBehavior();
    }
}
```

> The `RsaSessionSecurityHandler` *and the associate behavior and behavior extension classes are also available in the Identity Developer Training Kit, which you can download from* `http://bit.ly/identitytrainingkit`*.*

Hooking up the `RsaSessionServiceBehavior` is easy. In the `<system.serviceModel>` section you need to add it to add the behavior extension to the `<behaviorExtensions>` element inside the `<extensions>` element, as shown in the following code:

```
<extensions>
  <behaviorExtensions>
    <add name="RsaSessionServiceBehavior"
        type="WcfWebRoleRP.RsaSessionServiceBehaviorExtension,
            WcfWebRoleRP" />
```

```
    </behaviorExtensions>
  </extensions>
```

code snippet 17_RsaBheaviorConfig.txt

Next you need to add the behavior to the service behavior you defined for the web service, which is nothing more than adding the following:

```
<RsaSessionServiceBehavior />
```

With the behavior in place, you can redeploy your service and scale up to as many instances as you need.

Exposing the Correct WCF Meta Data

Your Windows Azure instances live behind a load balancer. When a client does a request, it hits the load balancer, and the load balancer routes the request to one of the instances. WCF is not aware that it is working behind a load balancer, so when you use the meta data exchange endpoint to get the service configuration, the meta data actually contains the internal address used behind the load balancer. This address is not reachable from outside the load balancer, so the meta data is incorrect. Up until now you had no problems because you altered the configuration manually. But after you deploy for production use, chances are your service is going to be used by other parties, so the meta data must be correct. To ensure the meta data requested actually contains the address of the service under which it is reachable from outside the load balancer, you need to tell WCF to use the host specified in the incoming request headers to construct the meta data address. You can do so by adding the following configuration to the `WifActiveFedBehavior` your created earlier.

Available for download on Wrox.com

```
<useRequestHeadersForMetadataAddress>
  <defaultPorts>
    <add scheme="http" port="80" />
    <add scheme="https" port="443" />
  </defaultPorts>
</useRequestHeadersForMetadataAddress>
```

code snippet 18_MetadataCorrectionConfig.txt

Diagnosing Issues

Diagnosing issues in a website is easy; you can turn off custom errors to show exceptions in the page and insert trace statements that you can show in the page. Also you can use full debugging support in Visual Web Developer Express to debug applications running on Windows Azure. One thing you can do to make this even easier is run the website outside of the Windows Azure DevFabric, so you can focus on Azure-specific issues when you do run in DevFabric.

With WCF services, you can also use debugging support, but where it concerns the binding and built-in behaviors, you can't diagnose anything. You just get a runtime exception and hope you can decipher what went wrong. To make it easier to diagnose issues, you can use diagnostics tracing that's built into the .NET Framework. .NET Framework and WIF components write trace information to the diagnostics system. Trace listeners can pick up the trace information and write it to a trace log. However, as mentioned several times already, you don't have access to the local file system of Windows Azure instances, so where do you leave the log information? The answer is Azure Table Storage because it runs separately from your Windows Azure instances.

When you create a project, an `AzureLocalStorageTraceListener` is automatically created. As the name implies this is a trace listener that writes trace information to local storage. Hence it doesn't work on a live deployment of Windows Azure. For most issues that's sufficient because if you've debugged the functionality of your application, what remains are configuration issues. Understanding what goes wrong in the development environment can help you resolve issues with the live environment. If you need to do diagnostics tracing in a live environment, you must use a trace listener that writes to your storage account. You can find one at `http://bit.ly/ SimpleAzureTraceListener`, and you can find more information on the whole diagnostics system in Windows Azure at `http://msdn.microsoft.com/en-us/library/gg433048.aspx`.

Getting the diagnostics working on your local machine just takes a few steps:

1. Open `web.config` of WcfWebRoleRP.

2. Comment out the existing `<system.diagnostics>` section.

3. Almost at the top of the configuration, there's a commented `<system.diagnostics>` section for Windows Azure; uncomment it. This enables diagnostics tracing for WCF.

4. You also need diagnostics tracing for WIF. To do this, add another source for the `Microsoft.IdentityModel` namespace, as follows:

```
<source name="Microsoft.IdentityModel" switchValue="Verbose">
  <listeners>
    <add name="AzureLocalStorage" />
  </listeners>
</source>
```

5. Open `WebRole.cs`.

6. After the three lines of code setting up `diagnosticsConfig`, add the following line of code:

```
DiagnosticMonitor.Start(
    "Microsoft.WindowsAzure.Plugins.Diagnostics.ConnectionString",
    diagnosticConfig);
```

7. Save and run the application on your local development environment.

After you've run the client, the service should have collected trace information. Now you need to get that information from the local table storage. For this you can use the Azure Storage Explorer that you can download from `http://azurestorageexplorer.codeplex.com`. After installation you can do the following to get to the trace files:

1. Start Azure Storage Explorer, which is in the Neudesic folder of the Start menu.

2. Click Add Account.

3. Check the check box Developer Storage, and click Add Storage Account.

4. In the left pane you now see all containers in your development storage environment. Select wad-tracefiles.

5. In the right pane a trace file should appear. Select it, and in the Blob section of the task bar, click Download.

6. Select a location to save the file to, and click OK.

7. Open the location you saved the file to in Windows Explorer, and double-click the file to open it in the WCF Service Trace Viewer.

SUMMARY

In this chapter, you have learned about identity federation and claims-based identity. These two mechanisms implemented in Windows Identity Foundation (WIF) enable you to outsource authentication to an Identity Provider. A Security Token Service can then create a token that is sent to the application, also called a Relying Party, which can use the information in the token to authorize the user.

Implementing passive federation for a website is straightforward and runs out-of-the-box when you hook up the website to an STS with FedUtil. For WCF service it is complex because the security bar is set a lot higher. You must create several certificates, for a secure connection, for encrypting the security token, and for signing the security token. You also need to implement a STS that runs under a secure connection. You can create a local development STS, but as an alternative you can use a product such as Active Directory Federation Services 2.0. When you have an STS running, you can create a WCF service and a client to use it. Getting those to operate requires you to tweak the binding configuration FedUtil inserts.

Getting the WCF service to run on the DevFabric environment is only half the work. If you want to deploy the application, you still must take care of issues surrounding certificates, sessions, and meta data, which is the result of the Windows Azure live environment being a highly scalable, load-balanced environment.

Finally, you have learned how to set up diagnostics so that you can easily track issues with WCF and WIF.

10

Leveraging Blob Storage

WHAT'S IN THIS CHAPTER?

➤ How blobs and Blob storage works

➤ How to program Blob storage

➤ How to create, list, and delete a container

➤ How to manage blobs

➤ How to manage access to blobs

Storage is important for applications, and understanding how to put information into storage and retrieve it is the backbone of applications. The Azure Storage System provides storage for all your cloud-based storage needs including tabular, blobs, and queues. This chapter explains how to leverage Blob storage to effectively store, retrieve, and manage your large binary files.

UNDERSTANDING BLOBS AND BLOB STORAGE

Binary Large Objects (blobs) have been in IT vocabulary for quite a while. Blobs are simply binary files and are commonly but not exclusively multimedia files; they can be any type of file from images, videos, audio, and to documents. Many of the files you may access on a day-to-day basis could be consider a blob. Consider the video you watch online, the file that contains the data viewed in Microsoft Excel, or even this book if you are reading it on a computer or mobile device. These files are large binary files that can be considered a blob. Microsoft SQL Server has supported the storage of them within a database for some time. With Azure Storage you now have a support to Blob storage in the cloud.

As part of its Storage services, Azure supports the storage and retrieval of large unstructured files using Blob storage. Therefore to understand blobs and Blob storage, you must have a basic understanding Azure Storage.

What Is Azure Storage?

Azure Storage is simple—it's storage in the cloud. In line with Azure's ability to host applications in the cloud, Azure Storage makes cloud data available as a service. Azure Storage provides the features and services to store and retrieve data in the cloud where it is available anywhere, anytime.

Four unique storage options are available in Azure Storage. Each one provides a solution for different application requirements. The four storage options are as follows:

➤ **Table storage:** Designed to store and retrieve structured data in row set form. The table itself does not define a singular data schema, but it may contain multiple schemas for different entities stored in the table. The entity schemas associated with the tables define the fields for a particular item. This is quite unlike a table schema seen in relational databases. Items saved to Table storage must correspond to one of the defined schemas. Table storage, unlike a relation database, does not support relations and indexing common to relational databases.

➤ **Blob storage:** Provides storage for large amounts of unstructured data such as documents, videos, images, or audio files as well as associated meta data. The primary emphasis is on the storage of the binary file and not the meta data storage. Blob storage can handle large files—up to one terabyte—and give support for random access read and writes It also provides version support (through snapshots), exclusive locks (leases), and streaming media.

➤ **Queues:** Provides reliable message routing between Azure applications and components of an Azure application. Queues are asynchronous, reliable, and durable. Each defined queue contains zero or more messages placed into and processed from the queue by one or more applications. When processed, the message is removed from the queue.

 Azure recently introduced a new form of queue mechanism in the Azure AppFabric range of products. For more information on both types of queues, please refer to Chapter 13.

➤ **Azure Drives:** Gives an application a mounted NTFS storage volume that appears as a local volume. Access to the mounted volume is via a mapped drive letter, which is configured via your Azure application. For example, a mounted drive may be associated with "Z:\drive." This local storage is persisted outside of an Azure role application and persists even during an Azure role recycle. Azure drives are actually based around Azure Blob storage via an implementation of a Page blob, which supports random reads and writes. The drive blob is formatted as a Virtual Hard Drive.

Understanding the Blob Hierarchy

Blob storage has a hierarchy of objects that define a resource URI and security. The hierarchy is a series of "containers" that have zero or more items. To understand how to leverage Blob storage, you must first understand how it uses these containers to define resource URIs and manage access. Figure 10-1 shows an example of the basic Blob storage container hierarchy starting with the Storage account, which is the top most container.

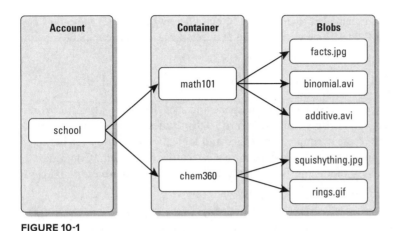

FIGURE 10-1

 Objects contained in Blob storage are uniquely addressable using a REST API. Each object has a universe resource identifier (URI), which uniquely identifies the object.

How Do Storage Accounts Work?

Storage accounts are associated with an Azure subscription and provide a security and access boundary separating the contained storage objects from other Storage account objects. The name given to a specific Storage account is also part of the root URI for the various entry points into the Azure Storage Service. Storage accounts are not specific for Blob storage; a single Storage account provides services for all storage types: Blobs, Tables, and Queues.

 Azure Storage Service is exposed using a REST API. Items contained in the Storage Service are identified using a URI. The base URI for Blob storage is `http://<accountName>.blob.core.windows.net`.

An Azure subscription can contain zero or more Storage accounts. These accounts are created and managed using the Azure Management Portal located at `https://windows.azure.com`. Creating a new Storage account provisions the required storage components in Azure and the required entry points to the services in DNS. These entry points are the resource URIs that access blobs stored in Blob storage. A new Storage account requires a unique account name, which becomes part of the resource URI. The account name must be unique from all other Storage account names, have a length of 3–24 characters, and use lowercase letters and numbers. As an example, Figure 10-1 uses a generic name of "school" for the account name, which will result in a Blob storage resource URI of `http://school.blob.core.windows.net`. This URL requests service from our Blob storage service.

The Storage account is also a security boundary. Each Storage account has two generated keys called Access Keys. These keys generate a signed Authorization header for use in the web request to validate and authorize the request. Without knowledge of the keys, a request is not signed and cannot be validated. Two keys are provided to allow one to be in use, whereas the second key can be regenerated resulting in no loss in service when changing access keys. Keys are managed from the Azure Management Portal.

How Do Containers Work?

Similar to the Storage account, containers provide namespace and security boundaries functionality to Blob storage and contain zero or more containers. Figure 10-1 includes two containers: math101 and chem260. Container names create a unique namespace and logical organization of contained blobs, and they give the appearance of a path-like structure similar to a file system. Containers also define the security for the contained blobs, but they exist only within a Storage account and cannot exist beyond the scope of the Storage account.

The Azure Management Portal does not provide an interface to create containers, therefore you create them programmatically with a name and optional meta data information. Containers cannot be nested; therefore, each container within a Storage account must be unique. Container names must follow the following guidelines:

➤ Start with a letter or number.

➤ Must be lowercase.

➤ Dashes are allowed, but must be preceded and followed by a letter or number.

➤ Must be 3–64 characters in length.

 Attempting to create a container with a name that does not follow the naming guidelines results in an Authentication Failure exception. Pay close attention to container names to avoid ambiguous error messages.

The container name is included as part of the resource URI. For example, in the container math101 displayed in Figure 10-1 the resource URI would be `http://school.blob.core.windows.net/math101`.

 Blob Storage accounts have a root container and you can place blobs there. A root container would be represented as a forward slash or `$root`. *Example:* `http://school.blob.core.windows.net/$root` *or* `http://school.blob.core.windows.net/`

Containers may have associated meta data stored as a name-value pair. Meta data is added and retrieved from Blob storage as header values in the web request and response. The name of the meta data item must start with `x-ms-meta-`. For this example use meta data to identify the primary responsible party for a container using a custom metadata tag such as `x-ms-meta-responsibleparty`.

Containers allow the controlling of access to the container as a whole and to its contained blobs. There are only two access scenarios in Blob storage:

➤ **Owner:** Are identified by the presence of a properly encrypted Authorization header value in the web request. By default, only the Owner can access Blob storage objects. Access can be changed to allow anonymous read access using the APIs.

➤ **Anonymous:.** This access does not require the Authorization header value. Table 10-1 shows two levels of anonymous access.

TABLE 10-1: Anonymous Access

ACCESS	PERMISSIONS
Full Public Read Access	Can view container and contained blob information; can enumerate blobs in the container.
Public Read Access for Blobs Only	Can view only blobs; cannot view container information or enumerate blobs

Basic access control is not granular. Either you have access to the Storage account Access Keys and can properly sign the Authorization header value in the web request or you are anonymous.

Blobs

Blobs themselves are unstructured text or binary files up to 1 terabyte in length depending on the blob type. Similar to containers blobs are created programmatically. The Azure Management Portal does not provide a user interface to create blobs. Blobs do not have a specific security setting; security is determined by the container. The type of blob, Block or Page (discussed later in this section), is determined at the time of creation and cannot be changed.

The blob name is used as part of the resource URI and must be unique within a container. It can contain any character and must have a length of 1 to 1,024 characters. Reserved URL characters in the name must be properly escaped. It is legal to include path separators such as the forward slash (/) as part of the blob name. As noted in the previous "Working with Containers" section, the storage schema is flat. There are no subcontainers to create a hierarchical path similar to a file system path. You can create a virtual path when you use the forward slash in the blob name. For example, consider the math101 container in the school Storage account. A blob named `additive.avi` would have a resource URI of `http://school.blob.core.windows.net/math101/additive.avi`.

If the blob were named `/videos/additive.avi`, the resource URL of the blob would be `http://school.blob.core.windows.net/math101/videos/additive.avi`.

Although it appears there is a nested hierarchy, that's not the case. The container remains math101, and the name of the blob is `/videos/additive.avi`, as shown in Figure 10-2.

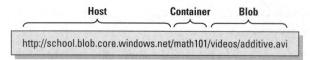

FIGURE 10-2

Like containers, blobs support associated meta data as name-value pairs. These are added and retrieved from Blob storage as header values associated with the web request and response. The name of the meta data must start with `x-ms-meta-`. For this example, consider meta data that identifies the content owner. This meta data field may be named `x-ms-meta-owner` and have a value of `Bob`.

Blobs have two means of support for managing concurrency: ETags and leases.

➤ **ETag:** This is an HTTP construct. Modification of a blob changes the value of the ETag. Applications can compare ETags to determine if the blob has been modified. The optional conditional headers `If-Match` and `If-None-Match` will compare the ETag with the header value to determine the appropriate response.

➤ **Leases:** These are a distributed system lock. Programmatically an application can obtain a lease on a blob. This is a 1-minute exclusive server-side lock on the blob. While the blob is locked, it cannot be edited by another user. Leases can be acquired, renewed, and released. There is also an option to release the lease but have it remain locked until the lease expires.

Block Blobs

Block blobs are commonly used for data such as videos and documents with each blob being a single piece of content. Block blobs support a maximum size of 200 GB. Uploading large files in an HTTP-based system can be problematic because they can cause timeouts, network issues, and can become corrupted; in fact, it's not uncommon to upload a large file only to have network connectivity issues and need to restart the upload. Block blobs avoid these common issues by managing smaller pieces of the complete file. Block blobs are composed of one or more uploaded blocks of different sizes, which are then committed to the system as a single blob (see Figure 10-3). The current maximum block size is 4 MB. To upload large blobs to Blob storage, the file is chunked

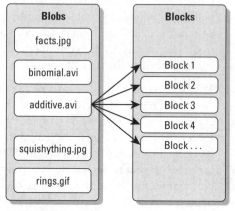

FIGURE 10-3

into multiple blocks, and each block is uploaded to Blob storage. When all the blocks are in Blob storage, the blocks are committed and the blob is available for use. Until the blocks are committed, the blob is not available.

The process of uploading blocks and ultimately committing multiple blocks is the responsibility of the programmer or application. You can upload files smaller than 64 MB as a single operation. You must partition files larger than 64 MB into blocks and commit them in Blob storage.

Page Blobs

Page blobs support random access read and writes in Blob storage. They allow the application to start a read or write operation at an offset location in the file. This means faster access to the data and does not require the application to re-upload a large file due to a write operation. Blob storage uses Page files to support Windows Azure Drives and logging operations.

Consider the difference between a common Block blob (image) and a Page blob (log file). When the image file is modified, the complete image file is manipulated and must be reloaded to Blob storage. Most image formats do not allow for an isolated byte change in the file. Log files are commonly sequential files where you target an isolated change based on an offset. There is little need to rewrite the complete file for a byte level change.

Page blobs consist of an array or indexed collection of pages. Each page is 512 bytes in size. The total size of a Page blob cannot exceed 1 terabyte and must be a multiple of 512 bytes. Applications can write to pages in the Page blob based on the 512 byte offset, and a single write request can write up to 4 MB of data. The Page blob can grow by adding pages. Unlike the Block blob, Page blobs do not require a commit request. Data written to a Page blob is immediately available at the end of the write request.

Currently, empty pages are not calculated in the charge model.

PROGRAMMING BLOB STORAGE

Armed with a basic understanding of Azure Storage and Blob storage, you can now leverage Blob storage as a cloud-based data store. This section focuses on how to programmatically work with Blob storage using the Windows Azure Storage Services REST APIs.

You can find the code download for this chapter at www.wrox.com. *To run the example code, you need an Azure subscription, a Storage account, and Visual Studio 2010. The example code demonstrates all the methods discussed in this section. You need to provide the Storage account name, access key, paths to your image, and videos to upload.*

Creating a Storage Account

Before you power up your favorite code editor and start programing the Blob storage, you need to create a Windows Azure Storage account. The Storage account is the top-level container that provides configuration and access to the Azure storage services. As mentioned previously, creating a Storage account generates the necessary namespaces in Azure as well as the required access keys needed to create and manage content.

To create a Storage account, you need to have an active Azure subscription. For more information on how to create one, see Chapter 8.

To create a Storage account for Windows Azure, follow these steps:

1. Log in to the Windows Azure Platform Management Portal. This is where you manage your Azure subscription.

2. Click the Hosted Services, Storage & CDN button located in the bottom left column, as shown in Figure 10-4.

3. To view any existing Storage accounts, click the Storage accounts link located in the left column, as shown in figure 10-5. Figure 10-5 displays a 3-Month Free Trial subscription, which is used in this chapter to create the Storage account.

FIGURE 10-4

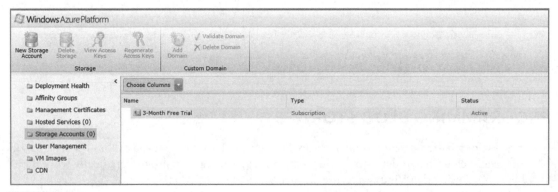

FIGURE 10-5

4. To create the new Storage account, click the New Storage Account ribbon button located at the top-left corner of the screen. This opens the Create a New Storage Account dialog box.

5. Enter your Storage account information, as shown in Figure 10-6. You must enter a value to complete the URL. This value is used later in the chapter as the Account Name value. The URL along with the service type (Table, Blob, or Queue) will be the entry point to the specific storage service. In this example the blob service endpoint is `school.blob.core.windows.net`. Next, select the Create or Choose an Affinity group radio button and then be sure to select "Create or choose an affinity group" from the drop down menu. Select Create a New Affinity Group item to open the Create a New Affinity Group dialog box show in 10-7.

 Affinity groups are used by Azure to attempt to colocate services together. For example, if you have a Web Role that consumes blobs from the Blob storage service, you can select the same affinity group, and Azure attempts to provision the services in the same datacenter or at least one in the same region, thereby reducing latency between services.

FIGURE 10-6

FIGURE 10-7

6. Enter an Affinity Group Name and select a Location. Click OK to exit the Create a New Affinity Group dialog box.

 Using affinity groups to colocate services does not guarantee Azure will provision the services in the same data center. Although this may occur, it only guarantees the same geographical region.

 You are not required to create a new affinity group to work with blobs. Selecting a region is acceptable.

7. After the affinity group has been created, click OK on the Create a New Storage Account dialog box to start the provisioning of the Storage account. The provisioning of the account takes a few minutes. During the provisioning process the Storage account page provides a status on the provisioning process. After the provisioning has completed, the Storage account is ready for use and has a status of Created. Figure 10-8 shows the provisioned Storage account.

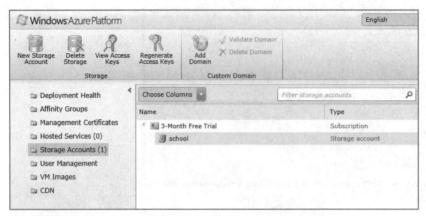

FIGURE 10-8

 Each Storage account provides two 256-byte access keys: primary and second-ary. These keys create the encrypted authorization header, which the Storage service uses to authenticate requests to the storage system. You can use either key to create an authorization header. Two are included so you can use one key while regenerating the other key and still maintain service.

8. Click the View Access Keys button, shown in Figure 10-8, to view the account's access keys. Figure 10-9 shows the dialog box. These keys are long, and you should use the Copy button located to the right of the key to copy it completely.

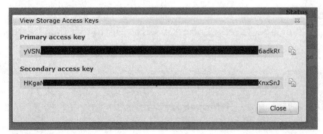

FIGURE 10-9

Overview of the Rest APIs

Windows Azure Storage Services provides REST APIs to access the item contained in Azure Storage. This API supports programmability via common HTTP methods for Blob, Table, and Queue storage. This chapter focuses on blob access using the REST APIs. You can find these APIs documented at http://msdn.microsoft.com/en-us/library/windowsazure/dd179355.aspx.

The Blob service REST API works on three basic types of objects:

➤ Blob service

➤ Container

➤ Blobs

By working with the Blob service using the REST API, an application can:

➤ Manage Blob service properties

➤ List containers

The REST API provides the following Container functionality:

➤ Create containers

➤ Manage container properties

➤ Manage container meta data

➤ Manage container access

➤ Delete containers

➤ List blobs

Finally, the REST API functionally for blobs includes the following:

➤ Create blobs

➤ Manage blob properties

➤ Manage blob meta data

➤ Lease a blob (enforcing exclusive access)

➤ Manage blob snapshots (accessing read-only prior versions)

➤ Copy blobs

➤ Delete blobs

REST APIs are web-based APIs and they require a request to the service endpoint using HTTP. REST APIs rely on the basic request methods defined in HTTP including PUT, GET, HEAD and DELETE. The URL of the request is a resource URI for a specific resource such as a container or blob. Some requests require additional action information, and those items can be included as a URI parameter, request header, or in the body of the request.

For example, to create a container named math101 in a Storage account named school, the URI would be http://school.blob.core.windows.net/math101. The request would also need to include a URI parameter named restype with a value of the container. The Blob service also requires a few headers in the requests. The headers required to create the container include the x-ms-date, x-ms-version, authorization, and content-length header. Finally the request is created using the PUT HTTP verb.

Many of the requests are similar in format, and most of the example code is repetitive. The example C# code provided with this chapter follows the same basic format:

1. Create a `HTTPWebRequest` object.

2. Set the request method (`GET`, `PUT`, `HEAD`, or `DELETE`).

3. Set the `x-ms-date` and `x-ms-version` headers.

4. Set any additional headers.

5. Create and set the Authorization header (see next section for more information).

6. Start the request.

7. Process the response.

The example code included with the chapter has abstracted some of the repetitive code into helper methods including `GetWebRequest`, `CreateSharedKeyLiteAuthorizationHeader`, `GetCanonicalizedHeaders`, and `GetCanonicalizedResourceString`. You should review these to understand some of the key pieces to formulating a web request with the proper headers and values. The example code does not handle exceptions outside of a basic try/catch block and does not provide parameter validation to minimize the amount of code. A production-ready application should include robust exception handling, logging, validation, and even retries of failed web requests.

 This chapter focuses on using the Rest API. There are other APIs including a managed object model API and various community projects that can be used to access Blob storage.

Creating the Authorization Header

Access to a container or blob is controlled by the container itself. Unless the container's access policy has been changed, only the Owner is allowed access. Recall from "How Do Containers Work" section that there are only two types of users with regard to access: Owner and anonymous. Blob storage uses a signed Authorization header value to authenticate an Owner. Blob storage supports two types of authentication schemes: Shared Key and Shared Key Lite. This chapter uses only Shared Key Lite because of its simplicity. For further understanding of the Shared Key authentication scheme, take a look at Authentication Schemes in the Azure API reference located at `http://msdn.microsoft.com/en-us/library/windowsazure/dd179428.aspx`.

When creating a request to Blob storage, the Authorization header value is one of the more challenging pieces. It must be constructed, converted to a byte array, encrypted, and finally encoded. Not following the rules to create the value will result in an Authentication Failure exception. The Authorization value is composed of a string calculated from key pieces of the request, including the HTTP method, the resource URI, the comp URI parameter (if available) and certain web request headers and values. These values in a certain well-defined order are concatenated into a string. The string is then converted to a byte array. This byte array is encrypted using the HMAC-SHA256 algorithm, and the hash is Base64 encoded.

Listing 10-1 contains the three custom methods used to create the Authorization header value for the chapter's sample code. The CreateSharedKeyLiteAuthorizationHeader method controls the creation of the value. It uses GetCanonicalizedHeaders method to filter out only headers that start with x-ms- and sorts the values. These values must be in alpha order before they are added to the signature string in a name:value\n format. The GetCanonicalizedResourceString method is responsible for creating the correctly formatted resource string. The sharedKey value is one of the two Storage account's access keys. It is converted to a byte array for the signing process. The result of the CreateSharedKeyLiteAuthorizationHeader method is added to each web request as the Authorization header value. Any web request that requires Owner access needs to include the Authorization value. The only exception is for container policies and Shared Access Signatures, which are discussed later in the "Managing Permissions" section.

LISTING 10-1: Creating the Shared Key Lite Authorization Value

```
private String CreateSharedKeyLiteAuthorizationHeader(string method,
                                WebHeaderCollection headers,
                                string accountName,
                                string encodedPath,
                                string container,
                                string contentType )
{

    byte[] sharedKey = Convert.FromBase64String("<YOUR ACCESS KEY>");

    string signature = "{0}\n{1}\n{2}\n{3}\n{4}{5}";

    string signatureString = String.Format(CultureInfo.InvariantCulture,
            signature,
            method.ToUpper(),      //Uppercase HTTP Method  - 0
            "",                    //Content-MD5 - 1
            contentType,           //Content-Type - 2
            "",                    //Date - 3
            GetCanonicalizedHeaders(headers), //Canonicalized Headers - 4
            GetCanonicalizedResourceString(accountName,
                                    encodedPath,
                                    container)
                                    //Canonicalized Resource - 5
            );

    byte[] signatureBytes = System.Text.Encoding.UTF8.GetBytes(signatureString);
    HMACSHA256 crypto = new HMACSHA256(sharedKey);
    byte[] hashedSignature = crypto.ComputeHash(signatureBytes);
    return System.Convert.ToBase64String(hashedSignature);
}

//Select only values staring with x-ms- and sort collection
private string GetCanonicalizedHeaders(WebHeaderCollection headers)
{
    String result = "";
    List<string> requiredHeaders = new List<string>();

    foreach (string header in headers)
```

continues

LISTING 10-1 *(continued)*

```
    {
        if (header.StartsWith("x-ms-"))
        {
            string tmpHeader = String.Format("{0}:{1}\n",
                                            header,
                                            headers.GetValues(header)[0]);
            if (!requiredHeaders.Contains(tmpHeader))
            { requiredHeaders.Add(tmpHeader); }
        }
    }
    requiredHeaders.Sort();

    requiredHeaders.ForEach((hdr) => result += hdr);

    return result;
}

//Create the correct resource string
private string GetCanonicalizedResourceString(string accountName,
                                            string encodedUriPath,
                                            string container)
{
    string containerParam = container == "" ? container : "?comp=" + container;
    return string.Format("/{0}/{1}{2}", accountName,
                        encodedUriPath, containerParam);
}
```

Creating the correct Authorization value can be frustrating if you don't know the intricacies of the process. Review Authentication Schemes in the Azure API reference located at http://msdn.microsoft .com/en-us/library/windowsazure/dd179428.aspx for more details of the process.

 An HTTP debugging tool such as Fiddler can help you quickly isolate issues with the Authorization value. Blob storage includes the string that it expected to be encoded and encrypted. Comparing the string to the string value before encoding and encryption can reveal any issues with concatenating the strings. Figure 10-10 displays a Fiddler capture of a failed request. A close review of the Raw response as shown in Figure 10-10 will review the values Blob storage expected in the encrypted Authentication header value.

WORKING WITH CONTAINERS

You saw earlier in the chapter that Storage accounts contain zero or more containers. There is no user interface provided in the Azure Management Portal to create or manage containers. You can create, modify, and delete containers using the Storage REST API. This section covers how to create a web request to create, modify, and delete containers in a Storage account.

Request Headers
PUT /chem140?restype=container HTTP/1.1
Cookies / Login
    Authorization: SharedKeyLite school:XWoV+o6DI+kdeTJ7TINSqsgDnYQdogE8E+Y2grUWChk=
Entity
    Content-Length: 0
Miscellaneous
    x-ms-date: Sat, 17 Mar 2012 23:33:35 GMT
    x-ms-meta-primaryowner: Meg
    x-ms-meta-topic: Chemistry
    x-ms-version: 2011-08-18
Transport
    Connection: Keep-Alive

Get SyntaxView | Transformer | Headers | TextView | ImageView | HexView | WebView | Auth | Caching | Cookies | Raw | JSON | XML

HTTP/1.1 403 Server failed to authenticate the request. Make sure the value of Authorization header is formed correctly including the signature.
Content-Length: 689
Content-Type: application/xml
Server: Microsoft-HTTPAPI/2.0
x-ms-request-id: ebcd721f-ab01-44af-b624-6e168c98242f
Date: Sat, 17 Mar 2012 23:33:49 GMT

<?xml version="1.0" encoding="utf-8"?><Error><Code>AuthenticationFailed</Code><Message>Server failed to authenticate the request. Make sure the value of Authorization header is formed correctly
RequestId:ebcd721f-ab01-44af-b624-6e168c98242f
Time:2012-03-17T23:33:49.6861616Z</Message><AuthenticationErrorDetail>The MAC signature found in the HTTP request 'XWoV+o6DI+kdeTJ7TINSqsgDnYQdogE8E+Y2grUWChk=' is not the same as any computed si

x-ms-date:Sat, 17 Mar 2012 23:33:35 GMT
x-ms-meta-primaryowner:Meg
x-ms-meta-topic:Chemistry
x-ms-version:2011-08-18
/school/chem140'.</AuthenticationErrorDetail></Error>

FIGURE 10-10

> The code included in the following sections is available in the chapter code on www.wrox.com. The code focuses on the specifics of a web request. Most common functionality, such as setting the x-ms-date value and formatting the Authorization value, has been refactored to helper functions.

Creating a Container

A newly created Storage account does not have any containers. To create a container the web request to the storage service must include the following:

- ➤ The request method must be PUT.
- ➤ Resource URI of the container.
- ➤ URI parameter restype with a value of container.
- ➤ ContentLength value.
- ➤ x-ms-date header.
- ➤ x-ms-version header.
- ➤ Authorization header.

Optionally, you can include custom meta data during the creation of a container. Listing 10-2 demonstrates how to create a web request to generate a container. The containerName must be a valid name and the meta data parameter passes custom meta data using a name-value pair. The meta data parameter is required in this code, but passing in an empty dictionary object is allowed.

LISTING 10-2: Creating a Blob Storage Container

```
private void CreateContainer(string containerName,
                        Dictionary<string, string> metadata )
{
   HttpWebRequest request = GetWebRequest("PUT",
                                    ROOT_URI + "/" +
```

continues

LISTING 10-2 *(continued)*

```
                                        containerName.ToLowerInvariant() +
                                        "?restype=container");

    //~DH~DH~DH Create Headers ~DH~DH~DH~DH-
    request.ContentLength = 0;

    // custom metadata x-ms-meta
    foreach (KeyValuePair<string, string> nvp in metadata)
    {   request.Headers.Add(nvp.Key, nvp.Value); }

    string encryptedHeader = CreateSharedKeyLiteAuthorizationHeader(
                    request.Method,
                    request.Headers,
                    STORAGE_ACCOUNT,
                    containerName.ToLowerInvariant(),
                    "",
                    "");

    request.Headers.Add("Authorization",
                        string.Format(CultureInfo.InvariantCulture,
                            "SharedKeyLite {0}:{1}",
                            STORAGE_ACCOUNT, encryptedHeader));

    //Process response
    try
    {
      using (HttpWebResponse response = request.GetResponse() as HttpWebResponse)
      {
        if (response.StatusCode == HttpStatusCode.Created)
        {
          Console.WriteLine("Created container: {0}",
                            containerName.ToLowerInvariant());
        }
      }
    }
    catch (WebException webEx)
    {
      Console.WriteLine("Error creating: {0}. {1}",
                        containerName.ToLowerInvariant(),
                        webEx.Message);
    }
  }
```

Successful creation of the container results in an HTTP status of `Created`. If the container already exists, an error is returned, which can be caught and handled. By default, the container permissions is set to Owner. To access the container a correctly signed Authorization header value must be supplied.

 PUT *requests require a* `ContentLength` *value. For a* PUT *request with no body use a value of* 0.

Container names that do not meet the name requirements will result in an error. The error is commonly an Authentication failed error, which is confusing.

Listing Containers

Containers within a Storage account can be listed. Web requests created to list containers must include the following:

➤ The request method must be GET.

➤ Resource URI for the Storage account.

➤ URI parameter comp with a value of list.

➤ x-ms-date header.

➤ x-ms-version header.

➤ Authorization header.

Optionally, you can use the include-metadata URI parameter to return container meta data. This adds a meta data section to the results and returns any custom meta data associated with the container. A request for listing containers may also include the prefix URI parameter, which you use to limit the results to containers that start with the provided prefix parameter value. Listing 10-3 includes the example code to list all containers within a Storage account. The code defines two requests: one that lists all containers and one that uses the prefix URI parameter to limit the results. Also, notice in the CreateSharedKeyLiteAuthorizationHeader method call the value of list is passed in. The comp parameter value is required when building the Authorization header value. When there is no comp parameter, an empty string is used in the Authorization header value.

A successful web response includes an HTTP status of OK with XML including the results, as shown of Listing 10-3.

LISTING 10-3: Creating a Blob Storage Container

```
private void ListContainers(bool includeMetadata)
{
  //List all containers
  HttpWebRequest request = GetWebRequest("GET",
                     ROOT_URI + "/?comp=list" +
                     (includeMetadata?"&include=metadata":""));

  //List only containers that start with math
  // HttpWebRequest request = GetWebRequest("GET",
                     ROOT_URI +
                     "/?comp=list&prefix=math" +
                     (includeMetadata?"&include=metadata":""));

  string encryptedHeader = CreateSharedKeyLiteAuthorizationHeader(
                  request.Method,
                  request.Headers,
```

continues

LISTING 10-3 *(continued)*

```
                            STORAGE_ACCOUNT,
                            "",
                            "list",
                            "");

request.Headers.Add("Authorization",
                    string.Format(CultureInfo.InvariantCulture,
                    "SharedKeyLite {0}:{1}",
                    STORAGE_ACCOUNT,
                    encryptedHeader));

//Process response
Console.WriteLine("Containers:");
using (HttpWebResponse response = request.GetResponse() as HttpWebResponse)
{
  if (response.StatusCode == HttpStatusCode.OK)
  {
    StreamReader rdr = new StreamReader(response.GetResponseStream());
    XElement root = XElement.Parse(rdr.ReadToEnd());

    foreach (XElement c in root.Element("Containers").Elements("Container"))
    {
      Console.WriteLine(c.Element("Name").Value);
      if (includeMetadata)
      {
        foreach (XElement meta in c.Element("Metadata").Elements())
        {
          Console.WriteLine("\tMetadata {0} = {1}",
                            meta.Name.ToString(), meta.Value); }
      }
    }
  }
 }
}
```

The resource URI for listing a container requires a forward slash before the parameter list.

Deleting a Container

Deleting a container requires a web request using the DELETE request method. The deletion process occurs in two steps: Containers are initially marked for delete, but this is a logical or "soft" delete. The container is not truly deleted until a garbage collection sweep occurs. During the time of the logical deletion and the sweep, you may receive an error if you attempt to create another container using the same container name. Web requests created to delete containers must include the following:

➤   The request method must be DELETE.

➤   Resource URI of the container.

➤ URI parameter `restype` with a value of "container."

➤ Authorization header value.

➤ `x-ms-date` header value.

➤ `x-ms-version`.

The result of a successful delete is an HTTP status of `Accepted`. Listing 10-4 includes example code to delete a container.

LISTING 10-4: Deleting Containers

```
private void DeleteContainer(string containerName)
{
  HttpWebRequest request = GetWebRequest("DELETE",
                      ROOT_URI + "/" +
                      containerName.ToLowerInvariant() +
                      "?restype=container");

  string encryptedHeader = CreateSharedKeyLiteAuthorizationHeader(
                      request.Method,
                      request.Headers,
                      STORAGE_ACCOUNT,
                      containerName.ToLowerInvariant(),
                      "",
                      "");

  request.Headers.Add("Authorization",
                      string.Format(CultureInfo.InvariantCulture,
                      "SharedKeyLite {0}:{1}",
                      STORAGE_ACCOUNT,
                      encryptedHeader));

  //Process results
  try
  {
    using (HttpWebResponse response = request.GetResponse() as HttpWebResponse)
    {
      if (response.StatusCode == HttpStatusCode.Accepted)
      {
        Console.WriteLine("Container {0} has been deleted", containerName);
      }
    }
  }
  catch (WebException webEx)
  {
    Console.WriteLine("Error deleting container: {0}. {1}",
                      containerName.ToLowerInvariant(),
                      webEx.Message);
  }
}
```

WORKING WITH BLOBS

Blobs are the core of Blob storage. Blobs can be created, modified, copied, and deleted. This section focuses on Block blobs. Page blobs are similar in most requests with the exception of the upload process.

Creating Blobs

There are two different approaches for creating a blob in a container, depending on the size of the blob.

➤ **Blobs less than 64 MB in size:** This involves making a simple single request to add a blob and passing just one binary stream.

➤ **Larger blobs:** Must be partitioned to manageable chunks, uploaded in multiple requests, and finally committed.

Web requests for uploading a small binary as a blob in a single request require the following:

➤ The request method must be PUT.

➤ Resource URI of the blob.

➤ Authorization header value.

➤ x-ms-blob-type header value.

➤ x-ms-date header value.

➤ x-ms-version header value.

Listing 10-5 includes an example that creates a Block blob using a single request. The PUT request can include optional meta data. Meta data can also be added or modified as a separate request. Pay close attention to the blobName. The blob name must be a valid name. An invalid name results in Authorization error, which can lead your troubleshooting effort down the wrong path. The x-ms-blob-type header defines the type of blob created, page or block, and is required. This code sets the content type of the blob. You use the content type value to create the Authorization header and it's therefore passed in as a parameter to the CreateSharedKeyLiteAuthorizationHeader method. The content type value is optional, but if you include it as a web request header, it must be included in the Authorization header, or you receive an authorization failure error. If successful the expected result is an HTTP status of Created.

LISTING 10-5: Creating a Blob - Single Request

```
private void PutBLockBlob_Single(string blobName,
                                 string contentType,
                                 string filePath,
                                 Dictionary<string, string> metadata)
{
  HttpWebRequest request = GetWebRequest("PUT",
                                ROOT_URI + "/" +
```

```
                                          blobName.ToLowerInvariant());

    //~DH~DH- Create Headers ~DH~DH~DH~DH
    request.Headers.Add("x-ms-blob-type", "BlockBlob");
    request.ContentType = contentType;

    // custom metadata x-ms-meta
    foreach (KeyValuePair<string, string> nvp in metadata)
    { request.Headers.Add(nvp.Key, nvp.Value); }

    string encryptedHeader = CreateSharedKeyLiteAuthorizationHeader(
                             request.Method,
                             request.Headers,
                             STORAGE_ACCOUNT,
                             blobName.ToLowerInvariant(),
                             "",
                             contentType);

    request.Headers.Add("Authorization",
                        string.Format(CultureInfo.InvariantCulture,
                        "SharedKeyLite {0}:{1}",
                        STORAGE_ACCOUNT,
                        encryptedHeader));

    using (Stream vid1 = File.OpenRead(filePath))
    {
      byte[] buffer = new byte[4096];
      while (true)
      {
        int bytesRead = vid1.Read(buffer, 0, buffer.Length);
        if (bytesRead == 0) break;
        request.GetRequestStream().Write(buffer, 0, bytesRead);
      }
    }

    //Process response
    using (HttpWebResponse response = request.GetResponse() as HttpWebResponse)
    {
      if (response.StatusCode == HttpStatusCode.Created)
      { Console.WriteLine("Blob: {0} created", blobName.ToLowerInvariant()); }
    }
}
```

Files greater than 64 MB in size must be partitioned into smaller files called *blocks*. Each block along with its id is uploaded to Blob storage as an uncommitted block. After all blocks have been uploaded to Blob storage, the blocks can be committed and composed into the actual blob. Partitioning the file into smaller blocks of content allows for parallel upload of data and the potential to restart the upload of the remaining blocks after an error instead of restarting the file upload again. Listing 10-6 is an example of partitioning a file into smaller blocks, uploading the blocks to Blob storage, and committing the blocks to create the blob.

Multiple web requests are required to upload large files as multiple blocks. Listing 10-5 contains all the requests in one single method. The nature of committing multiple blocks into a blob does not require that all the web requests happen in a single method. There is no requirement that all the blocks must be uploaded in order or at the same time. The only requirement is that all the blocks have been uploaded successfully before the final list of blocks is uploaded to commit the blocks to a blob.

 Uncommitted blocks exist in Blob storage for up to 1 week. If the blocks have not been committed within 1 week, the blocks will be garbage collected.

Two basic web request types are required to upload a multiblock blob. The type of web request is used to upload each block. There is one web request for each block. The web request to upload a block requires the following:

➤ The request method must be `PUT`.

➤ Resource URI of the blob.

➤ `comp` header value of `block`.

➤ URI parameter of `blockid` with a value of the unique ID.

➤ Authorization header.

➤ `ContentLength` value.

➤ `x-ms-date` header.

➤ `x-ms-version` header.

➤ Base64 encoded block array for the body.

The second web request type is used to commit the blocks as a single blob to Blob storage. This is done by posting an XML request that contains the order and id of blocks that creates the blob. This web request requires the following:

➤ The request method must be `PUT`.

➤ Resource URI of the blob.

➤ `comp` header value of `blocklist`.

➤ `x-ms-blob-content-type` with a value of the content type of the blob.

➤ URI parameter of `blockid` with a value of the unique ID.

➤ `x-ms-date` header.

➤ `x-ms-version`.

➤ Base64 encoded XML list for the body.

There are a few items to point out with the code in Listing 10-6:

➤ **The first section is dedicated to retrieving the file from the file system and parsing the file into blocks.** The maximum size for a block is 4 MBs. Blocks do not need to be the same size. The parsing routine stores the block content in a custom Block class. The content is stored as a byte array, and the ID is a string. Each block requires an ID that is scoped for the block and is a Base64, URL-encoded string. Block IDs do not have to be consecutive.

➤ **The second section creates a web request to upload each created block.** For simplicity, this code is run in a serial fashion. In a real implementation, parallel processing should improve the block upload timings. The example code does not check for exceptions or retries. If any block does not upload to Blob storage correctly, the blob cannot be created.

➤ **The final section creates a simple Xml representation of the BlockList.** This list contains the blocks that create the blob. This list is used in the final web request as the body of the request. The final web request PUTs the BlockList into Azure which then commits the appropriate blocks to the blob.

LISTING 10-6: Using Blocks to Upload a Large File

```
private void PutBlockBlob_MultipleBlocks(string blobName,
                                         string contentType,
                                         string filePath,
                                         Dictionary<string, string> metadata)
{
    List<Block> blocks = new List<Block>();

    //Get file content
    Byte[] fileAsBytes = File.ReadAllBytes(filePath);
    int maxAllowedBlockSize = 4000000;
    int targetBlockSize = maxAllowedBlockSize;
    int currentPos = 0;
    int len = fileAsBytes.Length;
    int currentBlockId = 0;

    //Create partition the byte[] into smaller blocks
    while (targetBlockSize == maxAllowedBlockSize)
    {
        if ((currentPos + targetBlockSize) > len)
            targetBlockSize = len - currentPos;
        byte[] blockContent = new byte[targetBlockSize];
        Array.Copy(fileAsBytes, currentPos, blockContent, 0, targetBlockSize);

        blocks.Add(new Block()
        {
            Id = Convert.ToBase64String(System.BitConverter.GetBytes(currentBlockId++)),
            BlockArray = blockContent
        });
        currentPos += targetBlockSize;
    }
    //Put each block into Blob storage
    blocks.ForEach((blk) =>
    {
        HttpWebRequest request = GetWebRequest("PUT",
                                               ROOT_URI +
                                               "/" + blobName.ToLowerInvariant() +
                                               "?comp=block&blockid=" + blk.Id);

        //~DH~DH- Create Headers ~DH~DH~DH~DH
        request.ContentLength = blk.BlockArray.Length;
```

continues

LISTING 10-6 *(continued)*

```
    string encryptedHeader = CreateSharedKeyLiteAuthorizationHeader(
                                request.Method,
                                request.Headers,
                                STORAGE_ACCOUNT,
                                blobName.ToLowerInvariant(),
                                "block",
                                "");

    request.Headers.Add("Authorization",
                        string.Format(CultureInfo.InvariantCulture,
                        "SharedKeyLite {0}:{1}",
                        STORAGE_ACCOUNT,
                        encryptedHeader));

    //getting the current block content
    request.GetRequestStream().Write(blk.BlockArray, 0, blk.BlockArray.Length);

    //Process response
    using (HttpWebResponse response = request.GetResponse() as HttpWebResponse)
    {
      if (response.StatusCode == HttpStatusCode.Created)
      {
        Console.WriteLine("Block: {0} created", blk.Id);
      }
    }
  }
);

  //Create the BlockList as XML
  XElement root = new XElement("BlockList");
  blocks.ForEach((blk) =>
      { root.Add(new XElement("Uncommitted", blk.Id)); }
  );

  //Put the block list into Blob stroage
  HttpWebRequest req = GetWebRequest("PUT",
                                ROOT_URI + "/" +
                                blobName.ToLowerInvariant() +
                                "?comp=blocklist");

//~DH~DH- Create Headers ~DH~DH~DH~DH
req.Headers.Add("x-ms-blob-content-type", contentType);

// custom metadata x-ms-meta
foreach (KeyValuePair<string, string> nvp in metadata)
{ req.Headers.Add(nvp.Key, nvp.Value); }

string encryptedHeader2 = CreateSharedKeyLiteAuthorizationHeader(
                                req.Method,
                                req.Headers,
```

```
                                    STORAGE_ACCOUNT,
                                    blobName.ToLowerInvariant(),
                                    "blocklist",
                                    "");

    req.Headers.Add("Authorization",
                    string.Format(CultureInfo.InvariantCulture,
                    "SharedKeyLite {0}:{1}",
                    STORAGE_ACCOUNT,
                    encryptedHeader2));

    //getting block list
    byte[] byteArray = Encoding.UTF8.GetBytes(root.ToString());
    req.GetRequestStream().Write(byteArray, 0, byteArray.Length);

    //Processing resposne
    using (HttpWebResponse response = req.GetResponse() as HttpWebResponse)
    {
     if (response.StatusCode == HttpStatusCode.Created)
       {
         Console.WriteLine("Blob: {0} created", blobName.ToLowerInvariant()
       }
     }
   }
 }
```

Retrieving Blobs

There are two ways to retrieve blobs from Blob storage, depending on what you need to do. The first way retrieves an XML list of the details of the blobs included in a container, and the second is to actually stream the blob out from storage, such as downloading the blob to a file system. Blobs are stored as binary files in Blob storage, and the latter approach retrieves this binary file stream.

Listing blobs is similar to listing containers. Web requests created to list blobs must include the following:

➤ The request method must be GET.

➤ Resource URI of the container.

➤ URI parameter comp with a value of list.

➤ Authorization header.

➤ x-ms-date header.

➤ x-ms-version header.

The web request to list blobs can also include a Prefix URL parameter to limit the results, and a parameter to determine what information is included in the results. The included URL parameter accepts values of snapshot, metadata, or uncommittedblobs. Listing 10-7 includes example code to list all blobs in a container. The comp parameter value is passed to the CreateSharedKeyLiteAuthorizationHeader method. Failure to pass the comp value into the custom CreateSharedKeyLiteAuthorizationHeader results in an authentication failure.

LISTING 10-7: Listing Blobs in a Container

```
private void ListBlobs(string containerName, bool includeMetadata)
{
    //Show all blobs
    HttpWebRequest request = GetWebRequest("GET",
                                ROOT_URI + "/" +
                                containerName.ToLowerInvariant() +
                                "?restype=container&comp=list" +
                                (includeMetadata?"&include=metadata":""));

    //show only blobs that start with instruments
    //HttpWebRequest request = GetWebRequest("GET",
                                ROOT_URI + "/" +
                                containerName.ToLowerInvariant() +
                                "?restype=container&comp=list&
                                Prefix=instruments" +
                                (includeMetadata ?
                                "&include=metadata" : ""));

    string encryptedHeader = CreateSharedKeyLiteAuthorizationHeader(
                                request.Method,
                                request.Headers,
                                STORAGE_ACCOUNT,
                                containerName.ToLowerInvariant(),
                                "list",
                                "");

    request.Headers.Add("Authorization",
                    string.Format(CultureInfo.InvariantCulture,
                    "SharedKeyLite {0}:{1}",
                    STORAGE_ACCOUNT,
                    encryptedHeader));

    Console.WriteLine("Blobs:");
    using (HttpWebResponse response = request.GetResponse() as HttpWebResponse)
    {
        if (response.StatusCode == HttpStatusCode.OK)
        {
            StreamReader rdr = new StreamReader(response.GetResponseStream());
            XElement root = XElement.Parse(rdr.ReadToEnd());

            foreach (XElement c in root.Element("Blobs").Elements("Blob"))
            {
                Console.WriteLine(c.Element("Name").Value);
                if (includeMetadata)
                {
                    foreach (XElement meta in c.Element("Metadata").Elements())
                    {
                        Console.WriteLine("\tMetadata {0} = {1}",
                                    meta.Name.ToString(),
                                    meta.Value);
                    }
                }
```

```
          }
        }
      }
    }
```

A successful listing results in an HTTP status of OK and a stream of XML with the results of the list request. The example code retrieves the XML and displays the blob name and meta data to the console.

Recall that the Blob service is REST enabled and that, in this model, a simple GET request is sufficient to retrieve the resource directly if the resource allows for unauthenticated access. This means, for example, that simply typing the address of a blob into a regular Internet browser will retrieve the blob and render it according to the browser's rendering rules for the file type. Programmatically, accessing the blob is a little more work. You need to programmatically create a web request using a GET request method and the blob's resource URI and retrieve the blob as a stream and save to a local file. The section that follows covers this latter scenario—generating a web request programmatically and retrieving a blob to a local file.

Web requests created to retrieve a single blob must include the following:

➤ The request method must be GET.

➤ Resource URI of the blob.

➤ Authorization header.

➤ x-ms-date header.

➤ x-ms-version header.

Listing 10-8 displays example code that downloads a blob and saves it to the file system. The majority of the code is simply for writing the response stream to the file.

LISTING 10-8: Downloading a Blob

```
private void GetBlob(string containerName, string blobName, string outputPath)
{
  HttpWebRequest request = GetWebRequest("GET",
                               ROOT_URI + "/" +
                               containerName.ToLowerInvariant() +
                               "/" +
                               blobName.ToLowerInvariant());

  string encryptedHeader = CreateSharedKeyLiteAuthorizationHeader(
                               request.Method,
                               request.Headers,
                               STORAGE_ACCOUNT,
                               containerName.ToLowerInvariant() + "/" +
                               blobName.ToLowerInvariant(),
                               "",
                               "");

  request.Headers.Add("Authorization",
```

continues

LISTING 10-8 *(continued)*

```
                        string.Format(CultureInfo.InvariantCulture,
                        "SharedKeyLite {0}:{1}",
                        STORAGE_ACCOUNT,
                        encryptedHeader));

    //Process response
    try
    {
      using (HttpWebResponse response = request.GetResponse() as HttpWebResponse)
      {
        if (response.StatusCode == HttpStatusCode.OK)
        {
          using (Stream strm = response.GetResponseStream())
          {
            using (Stream file = File.OpenWrite(outputPath))
            {
              byte[] buffer = new byte[8192];
              int len;
              while ((len = strm.Read(buffer, 0, buffer.Length)) > 0)
              { file.Write(buffer, 0, len); }
            }
          }

        Console.Write("Blob: {0} downloaded to: {1}",
                      containerName.ToLowerInvariant() + "/" +
                      blobName.ToLowerInvariant(), outputPath);
        }
      }
    }
    catch (WebException webEx)
    {
      Console.WriteLine("Error retrieving {0}. {1}",
                      containerName.ToLowerInvariant() + "/" +
                        blobName.ToLowerInvariant(), webEx.Message);
    }
  }
```

Copying Blobs

Blobs can be copied in a Storage account without the need to download the binary to a file system and upload the binary again. Copying a blob from one container to another also copies the binary and the meta data.

Web requests created to copy a blob must include the following:

➤   The request method must be PUT.

➤   Resource URI of the blob copy to location.

➤   Authorization header.

➤   Content Length value.

➤ `x-ms-copy-source` header.

➤ `x-ms-date` header.

➤ `x-ms-version` header.

Listing 10-9 shows example code used to copy a blob. The `CopyBlob` parameters define the location of the copy. The `x-ms-copy-source` header is the location of the blob to be copied. This value must include the Storage account name in the resource URI or the request will fail. In the example code provided, the `x-ms-copy-source` value is passed in as custom meta data and is appended as a web request header. The copy request can also add meta data during the copy. A successful copy results in an HTTP status of `Created`.

LISTING 10-9: Copying a Blob

```
private void CopyBlob(string containerName,
                      string blobName,
                      Dictionary<string, string> metadata)
{
  HttpWebRequest request =GetWebRequest("PUT",
                                        ROOT_URI + "/" +
                                        containerName.ToLowerInvariant() + "/" +
                                        blobName.ToLowerInvariant());

  //~DH~DH~DH Create Headers ~DH~DH~DH~DH-
  request.ContentLength = 0;

  // custom metadata x-ms-meta
  foreach (KeyValuePair<string, string> nvp in metadata)
  { request.Headers.Add(nvp.Key, nvp.Value); }

   //Format of passed in copy-source metadata
   //"x-ms-copy-source", "/<STORAGE_ACCOUNT>/<container>/<Blob path>");

   string encryptedHeader = CreateSharedKeyLiteAuthorizationHeader(
                            request.Method,
                            request.Headers,
                            STORAGE_ACCOUNT,
                            containerName.ToLowerInvariant() + "/" +
                            blobName.ToLowerInvariant(),
                            "",
                            "");

   request.Headers.Add("Authorization",
                       string.Format(CultureInfo.InvariantCulture,
                       "SharedKeyLite {0}:{1}",
                       STORAGE_ACCOUNT,
                       encryptedHeader));

  //Process response
  try
  {
```

continues

LISTING 10-9 *(continued)*

```
    using (HttpWebResponse response = request.GetResponse() as HttpWebResponse)
    {
      if (response.StatusCode == HttpStatusCode.Created)
      { Console.WriteLine("Blob has been copied"); }
    }
  }
  catch (WebException webEx)
  { Console.WriteLine("Error copying Blob. {0}", webEx.Message); }
}
```

Deleting Blobs

Deleting a blob is similar to deleting a container. You use the DELETE request method with the URI of the blob. Like containers, blobs are initially marked for deletion. This is a logical delete. The container is not truly deleted until a garbage collection sweep occurs. During the time of the logical deletion and the sweep, you may receive an error if you attempt to create another blob using the same container name. Any snapshots created from the blob must be deleted before the blob can be deleted.

Web requests created to delete containers must include the following:

➤ The request method must be DELETE.

➤ Resource URI of the blob.

➤ Authorization header.

➤ x-ms-date header.

➤ x-ms-version header.

The result of a successful delete is an HTTP status of Accepted. Listing 10-10 includes example code to delete a container.

LISTING 10-10: Deleting a Blob

```
private void DeleteBlob(string containerName, string blobName)
{
  HttpWebRequest request = GetWebRequest("DELETE",
                                    ROOT_URI + "/" +
                                    containerName.ToLowerInvariant() + "/" +
                                    blobName.ToLowerInvariant());

  string encryptedHeader = CreateSharedKeyLiteAuthorizationHeader(
                              request.Method,
                              request.Headers,
                              STORAGE_ACCOUNT,
                              containerName.ToLowerInvariant() + "/" +
                              blobName.ToLowerInvariant(),
                              "",
```

```
                                    "");

            request.Headers.Add("Authorization",
                            string.Format(CultureInfo.InvariantCulture,
                            "SharedKeyLite {0}:{1}",
                            STORAGE_ACCOUNT,
                            encryptedHeader));

                    //Process response
            try
            {
              using (HttpWebResponse response = request.GetResponse() as HttpWebResponse)
              {
                if (response.StatusCode == HttpStatusCode.Accepted)
                {
                  Console.WriteLine("{0} has been deleted",
                                    containerName.ToLowerInvariant() + "/" +
                                    blobName.ToLowerInvariant());
                }
              }
            }
            catch (WebException webEx)
            {
              Console.WriteLine("Error deleting {0}. {1}",
                                containerName.ToLowerInvariant() + "/" +
                                blobName.ToLowerInvariant(), webEx.Message);
            }
        }
```

Managing Permissions

It was mentioned previously in this chapter that security is associated with a container and not a blob. There is no blob-level security in Azure. Access policies are associated with the container, and to set different access policies on different blobs require different containers. The default access setting for a container is Owner. Owner is defined as anyone with access to the Storage account's access keys.

Two methods allow you to set anonymous access to containers and the contained blobs. Anonymous access is anyone without access to the Storage account's access keys. The first and simplest method is to modify the container's x-ms-blob-public-access header value. The second method is more challenging and too lengthy to cover in a single chapter. That method of access control is using Container Policies and Shared Access Signatures, which can provide more granular access control to users. It still applies only to containers and not to individual blobs. For more information on container policies and Shared Access Signatures, review the topics in the Azure SDK located at http://msdn.microsoft.com/en-us/library/windowsazure/ee393343.aspx.

Setting and managing the x-ms-blob-public-access header value allows the Owner to define one of three options:

➤ No public read access

➤ Public read access for blobs

➤ Full public read access

No public read access is the default Owner setting. Any request to access the container or contained blobs require a correctly signed Authorization header value. The signed Authorization header value is what determines who can be considered as the Owner. Public read access for blobs allows anonymous users to access blobs, blob properties, blob meta data, and block lists and page regions (used in Page blobs). With public read access for blobs set as the access policy on a container, users must know the correct URL to access the resource. Finally, full public read access allows anonymous users to access the same items as public read access for blobs and includes the access to list blobs in containers and view container properties and meta data. At no time can an anonymous user create a list of containers located in a Storage account.

To manage public access for a container, a web request must have the following:

➤ The request method must be PUT.

➤ Resource URI of the container.

➤ restype URI parameter set to container.

➤ comp URI parameter set to acl.

➤ Authorization header.

➤ ContentLength value.

➤ x-ms-date header.

➤ x-ms-version header.

➤ x-ms-blob-public-access header.

The x-ms-blob-public-access header value can be set to container for full public read access, or blob for public read access for blobs. To set remove public access to the container, you must exclude the x-ms-blob-public-access header in the web request. Listing 10-11 contains example code that sets the x-ms-blob-public-access header based on the parameter aclChoice, which is a custom enumeration used for the example.

LISTING 10-11: Setting Public Access on a Container

```
private void SetContainerACLs(string containerName, containerACLs aclChoice)
{
    HttpWebRequest request = GetWebRequest("PUT",
                                    ROOT_URI + "/" +
                                    containerName.ToLowerInvariant() +
                                    "?restype=container&comp=acl");

    //~DH~DH~DH~DH~DH Create Headers ~DH~DH~DH~DH~DH~DH~DH-
    request.ContentLength = 0;

    if(aclChoice == containerACLs.PublicContainer)
        request.Headers.Add("x-ms-blob-public-access", "container");
    else if(aclChoice == containerACLs.PublicBlob)
        request.Headers.Add("x-ms-blob-public-access", "blob");

    //no check necessary for owner.
```

```
        //By default not setting the x-ms-blob-public-access
        //header results in owner access.

        string encryptedHeader = CreateSharedKeyLiteAuthorizationHeader
                            (request.Method,
                             request.Headers,
                             STORAGE_ACCOUNT,
                             containerName.ToLowerInvariant(),
                              "acl",
                              "");

    request.Headers.Add("Authorization",
                        string.Format(CultureInfo.InvariantCulture,
                        "SharedKeyLite {0}:{1}",
                        STORAGE_ACCOUNT,
                        encryptedHeader));

    Console.WriteLine("Set ACLs for {0}", containerName.ToUpperInvariant());

    using (HttpWebResponse response = request.GetResponse() as HttpWebResponse)
    {
      if (response.StatusCode == HttpStatusCode.OK)
        Console.WriteLine("\tContainer ACLs set to {0}", aclChoice.ToString());
    }
  }
}
```

With the container's public access set to either container or blob access, anyomous users can access blobs by entering a URL into a browser. For example if the school Storage account has a blob located at URI `http://school.blob.core.windows.net/math101/additive.avi`, the user can copy this URL into Internet Explorer and view the video. If the container's access is set to container, an anonymous user could list the blobs in the container using a browser. For example if the container with a URI of `http://school.blob.core.windows.net/math101/additive.avi` has the container access set to container, the user may use the URL `http://school.blob.core.windows.net/math101/` to list blobs in the container.

Retrieving the container's access policy is a simple web request. To manage public access for a container, a web request must have the following:

➤ The request method must be GET or HEAD.

➤ Resource URI of the container.

➤ `restype` URI parameter set to `container`.

➤ `comp` URI parameter set to `acl`.

➤ Authorization header.

➤ `x-ms-date` header.

➤ `x-ms-version` header.

The result of a successful request is an HTTP status code of OK. The response is the `x-ms-blob-public-access` value for the container. Listing 10-12 contains example code to retrieve the public access settings for a container.

LISTING 10-12: Retrieving the ACLs for a Container

```
private void GetContainerACLs(string containerName)
{
  HttpWebRequest request = GetWebRequest("GET",
                              ROOT_URI + "/" +
                              containerName.ToLowerInvariant() +
                              "?restype=container&comp=acl");

  string encryptedHeader = CreateSharedKeyLiteAuthorizationHeader(
request.Method,
                          request.Headers,
                          STORAGE_ACCOUNT,
                          containerName.ToLowerInvariant(),
                          "acl",
                          "");

  request.Headers.Add("Authorization",
                      string.Format(CultureInfo.InvariantCulture,
                      "SharedKeyLite {0}:{1}",
                      STORAGE_ACCOUNT,
                      encryptedHeader));


  Console.WriteLine("ACLs for {0}",containerName.ToLowerInvariant());
  using (HttpWebResponse response = request.GetResponse() as HttpWebResponse)
  {
    if (response.StatusCode == HttpStatusCode.OK)
    {
      string accessHeader = response.Headers["x-ms-blob-public-access"];
          if (accessHeader == null)
        Console.WriteLine("Access is private to account holder");
      else
        Console.WriteLine(accessHeader);

      using (Stream strm = response.GetResponseStream())
      {
        StreamReader rdr = new StreamReader(response.GetResponseStream());
        string results = rdr.ReadToEnd();
        Console.WriteLine(results);
      }
    }
  }
}
```

SUMMARY

Azure Storage provides applications with a cloud-based storage solution. Developers can select from one of many storage options depending on application requirements. Blob storage provides the features and functionality to store and manage large unstructured files in the cloud using a REST API. The nature of the REST API allows access to Blob storage from any language or platform that can create a web request; you are not limited to only .NET languages. Using the REST APIs you can easily create, manage and secure large binary objects and make them available to users and applications with access to the web.

PART V
Programming Azure

11

SQL Azure

In this chapter you learn the fundamental differences between SQL Azure and SQL Server 2012, and how to create, manage, and use SQL Azure Databases from your applications.

SQL AZURE OVERVIEW

SQL Azure is a highly available, distributed relational Database-as-a-service built on SQL Server technologies. SQL Azure focuses on a *scale-out* approach of adding more small physical machines rather than a *scale-up* approach of adding larger and more powerful physical machines, as is typically done with SQL Server.

The Difference Between SQL Server and SQL Azure

Unlike SQL Server where your Databases are the only ones on your Database server, SQL Azure may use a single physical server to host Databases from many different customers. This difference in approach is fundamental—SQL Azure is inherently multitenant, and it needs to share physical resources among all clients of the service. This fact underlies many of the feature differences between SQL Server and SQL Azure; although, a tremendous overlap exists in functionality and compatibility between the two.

Comparing Architectures

SQL Azure is specifically intended to feel familiar to developers using SQL Server, because it takes a recognizable approach to communication, authentication, and development. In many cases, the difference between programming against SQL Azure and SQL Server is the value placed in the connection string. Using the Tabular Data Stream (TDS) protocol for communication, using SQL logins for authentication, and programming with Transact SQL (T-SQL) are familiar to any SQL Server developer.

It is helpful to understand the differences between the on-premises SQL Server and the cloud-based SQL Azure by comparing the communication architecture of each one side-by-side, as shown in Figure 11-1. For an on-premises SQL Server, you typically have your applications talking directly to SQL Server across your local area network using the TDS protocol over TCP/IP or via HTTP endpoints. This is different from how your on-premises applications communicate with SQL Azure. As you can see, your applications must now call out, possibly through your own network's firewalls, and reach the SQL Azure Gateway via the Internet, and they can use only TCP/IP.

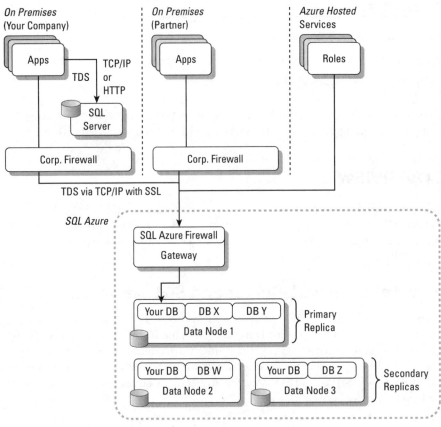

FIGURE 11-1

In addition, unlike for SQL Server, which can communicate on a configurable port without transport security, communication with SQL Azure must happen using SSL, and it must occur via port 1433. Furthermore, it is already at the Gateway that validation of your login occurs. SQL Azure, unlike SQL Server, supports only SQL Server Authentication (using a login and password, not Windows Integrated Security).

The Gateway is also where another firewall enters the picture—the SQL Azure Firewall. This firewall enforces IP-level security, catering only for IP addresses and address ranges that you explicitly define to be allowed access to your SQL Azure Server.

Once past the Gateway, a connection to the backend data node hosting your SQL Azure Database is made, using the Gateway as a proxy. Each backend data node runs a single instance of SQL Server containing its own Database, where this database is divided into partitions. Each partition contains a SQL Azure user Database (e.g., your database).

Aside from this single instance, each SQL Azure user Database is replicated a further two times, on two different backend data nodes. These replicas provide no load-balancing services to handle user queries—they are solely to provide SQL Azure's very high availability by enabling failover to one of the two replicas should the node hosting the primary node go down.

However, an element of load balancing does exist in this picture. If one backend node becomes overloaded by the workload of its shared tenants, then the underlying infrastructure (called the *SQL Azure Fabric*) may change the primary replicas of some users' Databases to one of the backup replicas found on a different backend node, converting this primary into a secondary replica for those Databases.

Beyond providing relational Database capabilities to your on-premises applications, observe how SQL Azure is well positioned to provide support for off-premises applications (like partners) and, more important, applications hosted within Windows Azure.

Aside from the architectural differences, numerous feature differences become apparent during development on, administration of, and licensing for SQL Azure that you should be aware of. The following sections explore the notable differences for these.

Development

In the spirit of maintaining a familiar feel, SQL Azure has a high degree of feature parity to SQL Server with respect to the needs of the developer. In terms of support for T-SQL grammar for Data Definition Language (DDL), Data Manipulation Language (DML), and general programmability, you can find a mixture of levels of support that vary between full parity with the SQL Server; to partial parity (where some options are omitted, or added uniquely to support SQL Azure); to data types, functions, operators, statements, procedures, and system tables/views that are flat-out not supported at all.

DDL Differences

DDL encompasses the features you need to define your Database schema and objects. For DDL, you can find near full-feature parity for DDL statements like Create/Alter/Drop affecting Database objects such as Tables, Views, Stored Procedures, Functions, Triggers, User Defined Types, and Indexes. There are some notable differences though, in that they generally lack support for some specific features that exist only in the on-premises versions of SQL Server. The following are a couple of stand-out differences:

➤ The Common Language Runtime (CLR) integration is not supported within SQL Azure, which means stored procedures, triggers, and user-defined functions written in a .NET language are not supported in SQL Azure. This limitation has its roots in the multitenant nature of SQL Azure, aiming to protect tenants from the accidental or intentional misuse of CLR objects by other tenants on the same server.

➤ Extended Stored Procedures, such as xp_sendmail, are not supported. This, too, is a limitation designed to ensure tenant isolation.

➤ Table partitioning (horizontal partitioning that spreads table/index data across multiple file groups within a single Database to improve performance on large datasets) is not supported.

➤ A clustered index is required on all SQL Azure tables. SQL Azure does not support heap tables, and INSERT operations will fail until a clustered index is created.

➤ Snapshot isolation is enabled and cannot be turned off at the Database level.

SQL Azure supports almost all the system data types found in SQL Server from numeric types such as int and real, date and time such as datetime, character strings such as char and nvarchar, and binary strings such as varbinary and image. It even supports some of the more specialized data types such as the spatial data types geography and geometry, hierarchyid, and xml. Although the XML data type is supported, typed XML and XML indexing are not.

 For a complete list of supported data types in SQL Azure, you should read this document on MSDN:

> http://msdn.microsoft.com/en-us/library/windowsazure/
> ee336233.aspx

Data types that are not supported include: CLR user-defined types and user-defined aggregates, and the FILESTREAM attribute on varbinary(max) typed columns is not supported.

DML Differences

Data Manipulation Language (DML) encompasses the features for performing *CRUD* (*create, read, update, delete*) operations against your Database data. The standard querying of tables and views accomplished using the SELECT clause, TOP, and the FROM statement, and optionally WHERE, ORDER BY, GROUP BY, or HAVING statements function exactly as they do in SQL Server. In addition, you can find support for the following:

➤ EXCEPT, INTERSECT, and UNION

➤ TOP

➤ Cursors

➤ Common Table Expressions

➤ FOR XML and FOR BROWSE

➤ *MARS (multiple active result sets)*

SQL Azure supports all the same Query, Table, and Join Hints as the on-premises SQL Server, with the exceptions of MAXDOP (which it always treats as 1) and PAGLOCK and REMOTE (neither of which it supports).

The largest difference to query support is that Full-Text search (for example, using CONTAINS, FREETEXT, and so on) is not supported by SQL Azure. Character-based searches with LIKE are supported.

For data modification, UPDATE, INSERT, DELETE, and MERGE are all fully supported, but BULK INSERT is not supported.

> *For more details on statements that are partially supported, and to see specifically which options are missing, check out* http://msdn.microsoft.com/en-us/library/ee336267.aspx.

Programmability

In terms of programmability, consider the T-SQL statements you typically use to define logic within stored procedures and functions. The following are all supported:

➤ IF. . .ELSE, BEGIN. . .END, DECLARE

➤ Exception handling with TRY. . .CATCH, as well as THROW, is fully supported.

➤ RAISERROR

➤ CAST and CONVERT

➤ Use of tempdb and creation of temporary tables

In addition, SQL Azure provides full support for all aggregate functions (AVG, MAX, and so on), all ranking functions (RANK, ROW_NUMBER, and so on) and all ODBC scalar functions, as well as most scalar functions found in SQL Server. Only the row set functions CONTAINSTABLE, FREETEXTTABLE, OPENDATASOURCE, OPENQUERY, OPENROWSET, and OPENXML are not supported.

> *For an exhaustive list of supported/unsupported functions, you should check out* http://msdn.microsoft.com/en-us/library/ee336248.aspx.

The feature most likely to catch you unaware as a developer is SQL Azure's transaction support. Local transactions that work with only the current Database (such as those using BEGIN_TRANSACTION. . .END, COMMIT, and ROLLBACK) are fully supported, but distributed transactions that span multiple Databases are not.

Naming Conventions

SQL Azure does not support the use of four-part names (`server.Databasename.schema.object`). Three-part names (`Databasename.schema.object`) are supported, but with the further restriction that `Databasename` must be the name of the current Database or tempdb. In other words, you cannot reach across to another SQL Azure Database, even one that may be under the same server (because SQL Azure reserves the right to move Databases between servers to balance its load).

Administration

Aside from the lack of physical server and application management and patching, hosting a relational Database in the cloud naturally introduces changes to how Database administration is performed. SQL Azure has quite a few changes from SQL Server that you should be aware of.

Deployment

The architecture of a SQL Azure deployment is logical, rather than physical. When you create a SQL Azure Database, what you actually manage are three logical entities: Subscription, Server, and Database (see Figure 11-2).

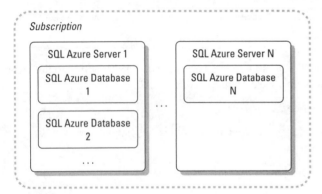

FIGURE 11-2

A Subscription encompasses all your Windows Azure platform services, such as hosted services, storage, caching, and SQL Azure, and provides the context under which use of these services is metered and billed.

Unlike a SQL Server, an Azure Server does not represent a physical or virtual machine running the Database services. In Azure, a Server is a logical grouping of Databases sharing a common datacenter region and firewall configuration. Databases grouped beneath a single Azure Server may run on different physical data nodes in the SQL Azure infrastructure.

A Database is a logical representation of the familiar SQL Server user Database. Recall from the introduction that in the SQL Azure topology your Database actually exists as a partition within a SQL Server Database instance. Each Database is created with a specific maximum size and edition. Currently, sizes and editions are available, as shown in Table 11-1, but the maximum database size is 150GB.

TABLE 11-1: SQL Azure Database Size Options

EDITION	MAX SIZE
Web	1GB
Web	5GB
Business	10GB
Business	20GB
Business	30GB
Business	40GB
Business	50GB
Business	100GB
Business	150GB

It used to be that the edition selected would restrict which sizes you could select, or switch between. For example, if you selected Web, then you could switch between only 1GB and 5GB Databases; switching a Web edition Database to a 10GB Business edition Database was not possible. This originally was designed to encourage you to commit to a certain maximum size (which presumably helped behind the scenes with resource allocation). Thankfully, as of the latest versions of SQL Azure, you can switch between sizes without restriction. You must ensure you never reach the configured maximum size because at that point you will receive errors when trying to create objects or insert or update data.

When a Server is created, a master Database is created along with it that is used to store metadata about the Server and the Databases it contains. This master Database cannot be deleted.

A single Server can manage 149 user-created Databases plus the required master Database for a total of 150 Databases. A Server can manage any mixture of Database editions and sizes. By default, a single Subscription can create up to six Servers. In addition, a Subscription defines a global quota across all Servers of 15 Business Edition Databases or 150 Web edition Databases.

 You can increase many of the quotas mentioned is this chapter by contacting Microsoft Windows Azure Platform Support. You can find the contact information for Microsoft Azure Support by visiting `https://mocp.microsoftonline .com/site/Support.aspx`*.*

Security and Access Control

Access to SQL Azure is controlled by two devices: a firewall and SQL logins. A SQL Azure Server enables you to specify Firewall rules allowing access from ranges of IP addresses, as well as from Windows Azure platform resources. When a SQL Azure Server is created, an administrative login referred to as the Server-level principal is also created. This login is conceptually equivalent to the "sa" account on SQL Server. SQL Azure does not support Windows Integrated authentication, so all logins are SQL Logins having a username and password.

At the Database level, SQL Azure security has a great deal of parity to an on-premises SQL Server. You create additional logins that enable connection to the Server, and associate those with Database users who have permissions within a specific Database. The T-SQL for access control–related statements, such as Create/Alter/Drop Login; Role, User or Grant/Revoke Database Permissions; Database Principal Permissions; and Type Permissions or changing entity ownership with Alter Authorization, is supported.

SQL Azure requires that all connections use Transport Layer Security (TLS) by allowing only connections that happen across SSL. Clients of SQL Azure should validate the Certificate provided by SQL Azure to prevent man-in-the-middle attacks when using SSL.

When it comes to encryption of data at rest, SQL Azure lacks a few of the features found in SQL Server. For example, SQL Azure does not support Transparent Data Encryption nor the Extensible/External Encryption Key Management features of SQL Server. If you need to encrypt portions of your data, you must implement your own solution for key management and for encrypting/decrypting data.

Availability

SQL Azure provides for high availability with an infrastructure delivering automatic replication across three replicas and automatic failover from the primary replica to one of the two backup replicas. However, this replication is specific to SQL Azure and is not to be confused with SQL Server Replication. In addition, SQL Azure does not provide support for Database mirroring or log shipping.

Backup and Restore

Backup and restore of production Databases is vital to any Database. Although SQL Azure provides the aforementioned replication to provide high availability, this protects you only against failures within the datacenter (such as hardware problems, data corruption, and so on). It does not protect your data against user errors.

With SQL Server, you would typically create a backup to the filesystem and restore from the same. With SQL Azure, this is not allowed because that filesystem for an SQL Azure data node represents a potentially shared resource across all the tenants who have Databases on that node. This translates to there being no support for BACKUP/RESTORE statements or attaching/detaching Databases; instead you must take an alternative approach, such as the following:

➤ **Database copy:** With SQL Azure you can run a CREATE DATABASE statement that creates a copy of a SQL Azure Database in another Database within the same or a different Server.

➤ **Data Tier Application Import/Export:** You can export entire SQL Azure Databases, schema, and data, as Data Tier Applications (BACPAC) and import from them as well via the Azure Portal.

➤ **Scripts:** You can use the Generate Scripts Wizard within SQL Server Management Studio to export schema and data from your SQL Azure Database to SQL script files, which you can run to re-create your Database.

➤ **Data Sync Services:** Enables you to run regular synchronizations between SQL Azure Databases or SQL Azure and SQL Server Databases.

➤ **SQL Server Integration Services:** You can use an instance of SSIS running on-premises against a SQL Azure Database.

➤ **Bulk copy:** Using the bcp utility or `SqlBulkCopy` class to bulk load data.

➤ **SQL Azure Migration Wizard:** Among other features, enables you to create backups of SQL Azure Database schema and data, or migrate between SQL Server and SQL Azure.

Backup to Azure Blob Storage via BACPAC is currently available in CTP form within the Azure Portal and is planned for a future release. That said, there is also a small community of third-party tools to help you with your SQL Azure Backup needs, such as SQL Azure Backup from Red Gate Software.

Diagnostics and Monitoring

Because SQL Azure instances are multitenant, many of the diagnostic and monitoring features you may have been accustomed to accessing as a system administrator really no longer apply and are not available. These include the SQL Server Utility (for holistic monitoring of resource utilization across servers), SQL Trace & Profiler, Extended Events (for example, ETW traces written to Event Log), the Data Collector, and many system tables. Instead, most diagnostic and health monitoring is performed by querying a small set of dynamic management views.

> *For a complete list of the supported system views, visit* `http://msdn.microsoft` `.com/en-us/library/ee336238.aspx`.

Administration Automation

Many of the features for automating administration are still available with SQL Azure, with the caveat that there is no direct remote access to the server. As a result, any automation tools must be run from on-premises or, for instance, from a Windows Azure-hosted role that targets SQL Azure. SQL Server PowerShell and SQL Agent (and Jobs), for example, do not run within SQL Azure but can run from remote machines that target your SQL Azure instance. Furthermore, SQL Azure does not support the use of Service Broker (which is often used in the absence of SQL Agent) or the Policy-Based Management available since SQL Server 2008.

Other Unsupported Features

Depending on your specific requirements of SQL Server, you may find additional features missing in the current release of SQL Azure, including the following:

➤ Master Data Services

➤ Change Data Capture and Data Auditing

➤ Resource Governor

➤ Data compression

➤ SQL Server Browser

Microsoft, as a cloud vendor, is continually improving the feature set of SQL Azure, often with the result of increasing feature parity, or at least offering multitenant-friendly alternatives, so it is worth keeping abreast of the latest release notes:

> http://msdn.microsoft.com/en-us/library/windowsazure/
> ff602419.aspx

Unique to SQL Azure—Support for Federations

As previously mentioned, table partitioning is not supported. However, similar performance gains for handling large data can be achieved with SQL Azure Federations, which effectively spreads your data across multiple SQL Azure Databases. This is a powerful feature update to SQL Azure that makes it easier to leverage SQL Azure's scalability.

Tooling

In general, working with SQL Azure enables you to leverage the tools familiar to you from working with SQL Server, such as SQL Server Management Studio (this includes the Express Edition, but requires 2008 R2 with Service Pack 1 and upward and Visual Studio 2010 with Service Pack 1).

Beyond these, SQL Azure provides some of its own additional web-based tooling for development and management in the Azure Management Portal and the Database Manager.

In addition, a preview of a cloud-based version of Reporting Services, called SQL Azure Reporting, provides report hosting and management as a service. Reports published here can be created with SQL Server Business Intelligence Development Studio or Report Designer and, when published, viewed directly within the web browser or via other formats such as Excel and PDF. These reports can report only on data sourced from SQL Azure Databases.

Licensing

Because SQL Azure is provided as a service, its licensing model is naturally quite different from SQL Server. In the latter, you buy licenses for servers or clients, whereas with SQL Azure you pay a monthly fee for the Databases that you use by the maximum size used, prorated by their usage in the month. For example, in the current pricing scheme, a single Database using 10GB costs $45.954 per month, and you would be charged that much if you had such a Database created for the whole month (and less than that for each day the Database was not created). In addition to size, you are also billed for the amount of data transferred out of the Azure datacenter.

Observe that there is a special pricing tier for web edition databases created with a MAXSIZE of 1 GB, when the actual space used is between 0 and 100 MB. In this case, you still create a 1GB database, but assuming you use less than 100 MB over the month, you pay half of the rate charged for a 1 GB database per month (for example, $4.995 instead of $9.99). In a similar fashion, databases with an actual space used in the 1-10 GB range, are billed for the first GB, with a lower cost per additional GB. Databases with actual space used between 10-50 GB are billed for the first 10 GB, with an even lower cost per additional GB. Finally, Databases with an actual space used between 50-150 GB are billed for the first 50 GB, with the lowest cost per additional GB.

Another substantial difference is that SQL Azure provides a service-level agreement (SLA), which defines a baseline 99.9 percent availability for your Databases over the course of a month, below which Microsoft issues credits applied to your next month's bill.

With the differences between SQL Azure and SQL Server under your belt, it is time to dive into creating and working with your first SQL Azure Database.

Getting Started with Your First SQL Azure Database

To create a SQL Azure Database, you need a Subscription for the Windows Azure platform. If you do not already have one, visit `www.microsoft.com/windowsazure/` and follow the instructions to set up one. At the time of this writing, there are offers that can help you start using SQL Azure for free.

The easiest way to create your first Database is by using the Azure Management Portal. Go to `http://windows.azure.com` and log in to the Azure Management Portal with the Windows Live ID associated with your Subscription. Now you are ready to begin by creating your first SQL Azure Server.

Creating Your First Server

Recall that a Server provides a logical grouping of Databases, the point to define the region in which Databases are hosted, and the administrative account used to access those Databases.

A Server is not a physical entity; it does not represent a VM or machine hosting your Databases. Databases defined under a common Server are often hosted by different physical machines.

To create your first Server, follow these steps:

1. Navigate to the Database area of the portal.

2. Click the Database button in the column of buttons found in the lower-left of the screen, as shown in Figure 11-3.

3. Select your subscription. To do this, click the node for your subscription found in the tree view on the upper-left of the screen (see Figure 11-4).

FIGURE 11-3

FIGURE 11-4

4. Create your SQL Azure Server by clicking the Create button found within the Server group on the Ribbon at the top of the screen, as shown in Figure 11-5.

FIGURE 11-5

5. You can create your Server using the wizard that appears. In the Create Server dialog, choose the Region in which your Database will be hosted (see Figure 11-6), and then create your server-level principal (aka Administrator login) by providing a login name and password (as shown in Figure 11-7).

Create Server

Create a new server

This wizard will guide you through the specific tasks to create your SQL Azure server and to prepare it for use.

Select a region where your SQL Azure server should be hosted.

Region: South Central US

< Previous   Next >   Cancel

FIGURE 11-6

6. Configure your Firewall Rules. Here you configure what IP address ranges are allowed to connect to your SQL Azure Server. If you want to grant access to services hosted in Windows Azure (such as service hosted in a Windows Azure Web Role), check the check box at the bottom of the screen, as shown in Figure 11-8.

Your newly created server appears in the list. You are now ready to create your first Database. For the server you just created, you already have one Database: the master Database. This Database is required per Server and cannot be dropped.

FIGURE 11-7

FIGURE 11-8

Creating Your SQL Azure Database

With a Server in place, you are now ready to create a new SQL Azure Database with the following steps:

1. Ensure you have your Server selected both in the tree-view and in the button bar at the top.

2. Click the Create button found within the Database group (see Figure 11-9).

FIGURE 11-9

3. In the Create Database dialog that appears, provide a name for your new Database and specify the Edition and Maximum Size, as shown in Figure 11-10.

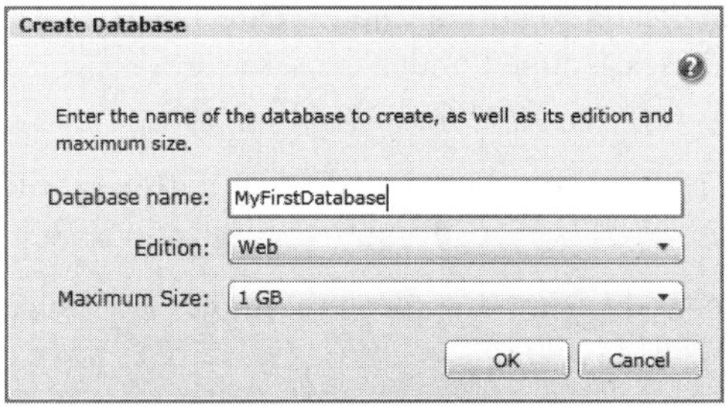

FIGURE 11-10

Your Database now appears beneath your Server in the tree-view. Congratulations, you have just created your first SQL Azure Database!

Understanding the Administrator Login

When you create a SQL Azure Server, you also create an administrator login. This account is a server-level principal that is a login to the Server. Whenever you create a Database beneath that server, a Database user is created and mapped to this login. The result is that your administrator user has permissions to manage all Databases, including the master, within the Server. In addition, this login has server-level permissions for creating and dropping Databases, as well as creating, altering, and dropping logins.

Naturally, this highly privileged login is not one you want to use for everyday access to your Database, because it is effectively the keys to your Database kingdom! Just as for SQL Server, SQL Azure enables you to create additional logins and new Database users with more appropriate permissions. The following section shows you how to accomplish this, as you explore how to program against SQL Azure.

PROGRAMMING DATABASES

In this section, you learn how to program against SQL Azure by using Transact-SQL run directly from your local SQL Server Management Studio, how to connect to it from the Excel client on your desktop, and how to access it from .Net applications (perhaps even hosted within Windows Azure) using the ADO.Net classes in the `System.Data.SqlClient` namespace or the Entity Framework.

Before we begin though, let's start with a quick note on what this section does not cover. This section is not intended to provide a complete treatment of T-SQL, `System.Data.SqlClient`, or the Entity Framework, as each of these topics easily fills books on its own. Instead, the focus is on the aspects of using these technologies that are specific to SQL Azure and to point you in the right direction to start. If you need a primer on any of the technologies mentioned, see the Additional Resources section at the end of the chapter.

Using SQL Server Management Studio

When you have created your initial Server in the Azure Portal, and have your administrator login at hand, you can use SQL Server Management Studio to author and execute T-SQL queries against the master Database or any of your user Databases grouped under the same Server. You can also use Object Explorer within SSMS to navigate your existing Database objects.

The easiest way to connect SSMS to SQL Azure is to first click the Connect button on the Object Explorer toolbar. From there you can create new SQL scripts using that connection. To begin:

1. Open SQL Server Management Studio, and ensure that Object Explorer is visible. (Press F8 or select View ➪ Object Explorer if it is not visible.)

2. From the Connect drop-down menu, select Database Engine.

3. In the Connect to Server dialog (see Figure 11-11), for the Server Name, enter the fully quali-fied DNS name of your server (for example, **myserver.Database.windows.net**, where **myserver** refers to your actual server name), for the Authentication type select SQL Server Authentication, and for the Login enter your administrator login.

> *You can also use other logins you've created, in addition to your administrator login, when connecting via SSMS. See the following section titled "Working with Logins and Users."*

4. Optionally, you can choose which Database to connect to. Click the Options ⇨ button, and then click the Connection Properties tab, as shown in Figure 11-12. In the Connect to Database combo box, type or select the Database with which you want to work.

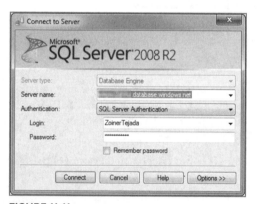

FIGURE 11-11

FIGURE 11-12

6. Click Connect. You should see Object Explorer list your Server, and if you expand it, the Database to which you are connected. If you expand the Database, you should see the Database objects it contains.

7. Now that you are connected, create a query by right-clicking your Database in Object Explorer and selecting New Query. A new document window appears enabling you to run T-SQL against the connected SQL Azure Database, as shown in Figure 11-13.

8. In this document window, enter your T-SQL, and click the Execute button on the toolbar to run your first query against SQL Azure.

The following sections examine the T-SQL syntax you can execute from SSMS or Database Manager for creating Database objects in SQL Azure. It also covers querying your SQL Azure Database from various clients beyond SQL Server Management Studio.

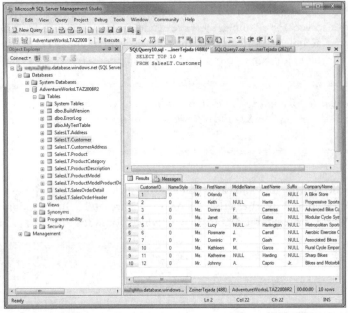

FIGURE 11-13

USER OPTIONS

SET statements enable you to configure various settings that apply to your current session with SQL Azure, such as when executing queries from SQL Server Management Studio. SQL Azure supports most of the SET statements provided by SQL Server, except for the following five SET statements:

➤ SET CONCAT_NULL_YIELDS_NULL: Has been deprecated even in SQL Server and is always ON for SQL Azure.

➤ SET OFFSETS: Has been deprecated in SQL Server and is not available in SQL Azure.

➤ SET QUERY_GOVERNOR_COST_LIMIT: The resource governor is not available in SQL Azure; therefore this setting is unsupported.

➤ SET ANSI_DEFAULTS: Not supported in SQL Azure.

➤ SET REMOTE_PROC_TRANSACTIONS: Distributed transactions are not supported by SQL Azure.

This trend is important to understand the availability of SQL Server features in SQL Azure. If the feature is deprecated in SQL Server, it's not likely to appear in SQL Azure.

DBCC commands, except for DBCC SHOW_STATISTICS, are not supported by SQL Azure.

The Database Manager Alternative

If you do not have SSMS available to you, you can use the Silverlight-based Database Manager available from the Azure Portal. This tool enables management functionality empowering you to create new Databases (Figure 11-14), deploy data-tier applications, extract a SQL Azure Database to a data-tier application, and drop a Database. It also enables you to see summary statistics about a selected Database; query tables and views; update records; execute stored procedures; and create and modify tables (Figure 11-15), views, and stored procedures.

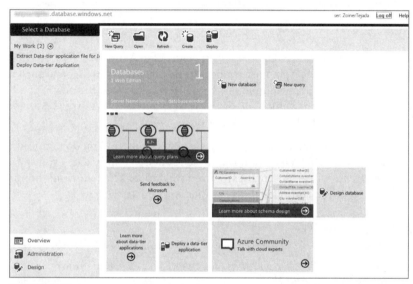

FIGURE 11-14

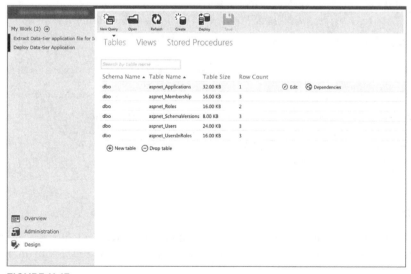

FIGURE 11-15

To get to Database Manager, click the Databases tab in the Azure Portal; then select a Server in the Subscriptions tree view. On the Ribbon, click the Manage button found within the Server group. In the prompt, log in with your Server Administrator credentials.

> *To use the Database Manager, the Firewall Rules configured for your SQL Azure Server must have the Allow Other Windows Azure Services to Access This Server check box checked.*

Creating Databases

After you create a Server, you can create a new Database using either the Azure Portal or SSMS. In this section, we will assume you use SSMS. You must connect to the master Database, and then use the CREATE DATABASE statement. This statement amounts to specifying the Database name, and optionally the EDITION (which can have the values web or business) and MAXSIZE (which specifies the max size as 1, 5, 10, 20, 30, 40, 50, 100, or 150 GB) options.

Collectively these two options define the maximum size of your new Database. You do not need to specify either option, in which case a 1GB web edition Database results, and in practice you specify only the MAXSIZE because the EDITION is set automatically from this value. The following shows how you can explicitly create a 1GB web edition Database called MyFirstDatabase.

```
CREATE DATABASE MyFirstDatabase
(MAXSIZE = 1 GB, EDITION = 'web');
```

> *You must be connected to the master Database using either the administrator login or a login that is a member of the dbmanager role to execute this statement.*
>
> *You can always change your Database's MAXSIZE or EDITION at a later date simply by executing the ALTER DATABASE statement. For example, to change MyFirstDatabase to a 10GB business edition, you would run the following:*
>
> ```
> ALTER DATABASE MyFirstDatabase
> MODIFY (MAXSIZE = 10 GB);
> ```

> *When your Database has reached MAXSIZE, you are prevented from inserting/ updating data or creating objects. Although you can still read and delete data/ objects, it can take up to 15 minutes before creation or update operations are allowed following these deletions.*

Working with Logins and Users

After creating your Database, one of the first things to consider doing is to create a login associated with just that Database. Why? Your administrator login is basically the keys to the kingdom; it grants access not just to a single Database, but also to every other Database including the master, as well as all-powerful permissions that, among other things, enable the creation, deletion, and management of Databases within the Server.

Creating a new login with access limited to only a single Database is a two-step process:

1. Create the login that enables connection to your SQL Azure Server.

2. Associate that login with a Database user created within the Database to which access is wanted.

Creating Logins

To create a login and give it a password, you need to execute the CREATE LOGIN statement from the context of a connection to the master Database. The following snippet shows how to create the login foobar with the password 'abc!1234'.

```
CREATE LOGIN foobar WITH PASSWORD = 'abc!1234'
```

Unlike SQL Server, which has a lot of options that could follow the WITH keyword, SQL Azure supports only specifying a string password.

Creating a User to Grant Database Access

Database access is granted to a login by creating a user from that login. A Database user must be created from within the context of a connection to the Database to which the user requires access. Therefore, when connecting via SSMS, you need to connect to the Database to which you want to grant access (and not master). Then you can use the CREATE USER statement. The syntax for creating the foobaruser from the previously created foobar login appears as follows.

```
CREATE USER foobaruser FROM LOGIN foobar
```

When a Database user is in place, you can configure permissions just as for an on-premises SQL Server, such as:

➤ Manage user membership in the built-in Database roles using the system stored procedures sp_addrolemember and sp_droprolemember.

➤ Grant/deny/revoke schema permissions and define schema ownership.

➤ Grant/deny/revoke permissions on Database objects.

Granting Database-Level Permissions

With both the login and user created, you can now connect with this login from SSMS or any other SQL Azure client application (for example, your own ASP.NET website, or WPF application). However, if you try to connect you'll find that this user has no access to Database objects—for example, no Database objects will be listed in Object Explorer, and simple T-SQL queries will indicate that the user does not have sufficient permissions. To enable access, you need to provide additional permissions, and the easiest way to accomplish that is by adding the Database user to the appropriate built-in Database role.

SQL Azure includes the following ten built-in Database roles:

➤ db_accessadmin

➤ db_backupoperator

➤ db_datareader

➤ db_datawriter

➤ db_ddladmin

➤ db_denydatareader

➤ db_denydatawriter

➤ db_owner

➤ db_securityadmin

➤ public

 For a detailed description of all the permissions assigned to the built-in Database roles, see http://msdn.microsoft.com/en-us/library/ms189612.aspx.

To add a Database user to a role, use the sp_addrolemember system stored procedure when you are connected to the master Database with an administrator account. For example, to grant a user the highest level of permissions at the Database level, you add the user to the db_owner Database role using the sp_addrolemember stored procedure. For the foobar Database user, this would appear as follows:

```
EXEC sp_addrolemember 'db_owner', 'foobaruser';
```

Naturally, you want to choose the role that most accurately restricts the actions the user needs to perform. Each role describes one or more Database permissions assigned to members of that role. If you want to assign permissions in a more granular fashion, you can use the GRANT statement. For example, to apply permissions equivalent to those assigned by adding the foobaruser to the db_owner role, you can give the user the CONTROL permission directly as follows:

```
GRANT CONTROL TO foobaruser WITH GRANT OPTION;
```

Granting Server-Level Permissions

If you want to grant a login the ability to create, alter, or drop logins, or if you want it to create or drop Databases, you need to grant server-level permissions to the user in the master Database associated with the login. Similar to Database-level permissions, you can assign server-level permissions by adding the Database user to the appropriate security roles:

➤ loginmanager: Required to create/alter/drop logins

➤ dbmanager: Required to create/drop Databases

To add a user to either of these roles, connect to the master Database and create in it a user for `foobar`, as shown previously. Then use the `sp_addrolemember` system stored procedure and specify the role and login name. For example, to add the `foobaruser` to the `dbmanager` role, you need to execute the following snippet.

```
EXEC sp_addrolemember 'dbmanager', 'foobaruser'
```

Creating Tables

Tables ultimately store the data managed by your Database in the form of rows and columns. To create a table in SQL Azure, you can follow syntax as simple as the following that defines the table name and name/datatype pair for each column.

```
CREATE TABLE table_name (column_name data_type, …)
```

However, for SQL Azure this is not enough to create a useable table. All tables in SQL Azure require a *clustered index*, which governs the physical sort order of rows in the table. You can define a clustered index in two ways within the CREATE TABLE statement: either by using the UNIQUE CLUSTERED keywords or by the PRIMARY KEY keyword. (By default SQL Azure creates a unique Clustered Index for primary key constraints.) In both cases, you need to indicate which columns participate in the clustered index for the row.

To create a table called `Products` having ID, Name, and Description columns, with a primary key consisting of just the ID column, you would execute the following T-SQL:

```
CREATE TABLE Products (ID int, [Name] varchar(255), [Description] varchar(max)
CONSTRAINT PK_Products_ID PRIMARY KEY (id))
```

Alternatively, to create the `Products` table with a unique clustered index constraint, you can execute the following:

```
CREATE TABLE Products (ID int, [Name] varchar(255),
[Description] varchar(max)
CONSTRAINT CI_Products_ID UNIQUE CLUSTERED (id))
```

Although SQL Azure enables you to create a table without a clustered index, it throws an exception as soon as you attempt to insert data. This is why the previous example includes creating the table with a primary key or clustered index constraint.

The CREATE TABLE statement includes a host of other options that enable you to specify column options (such as collation, nullability, default constraints, and identity) and column constraints (such as unique constraints or nonclustered indexes), as well as to define computed columns.

 For the complete syntax for creating a table, showing all supported and unsupported options, visit http://msdn.microsoft.com/en-us/library/ee336258.aspx.

One interesting column option is SPARSE columns, which starts to address the gap between the rigid table schemas required by SQL Azure, and the features offered by NO-SQL style storage such as Windows Azure Tables, which flexibly support jagged rows. *Jagged rows* do not necessarily have the same columns present across all rows. One benefit of jagged rows is that it minimizes the storage required for rows that do not have values for some columns. Columns marked as SPARSE have optimized storage for NULL values present in unused columns for a given row. For large or wide tables where the majority of columns tend to have null values, this can result in significantly decreased storage requirements. A SPARSE column for storing color can be defined on the Products table shown previously using the following statement.

```
CREATE TABLE Products (ID int, [Name] varchar(255),
[Description] varchar(max), [Color] varchar(100) SPARSE
CONSTRAINT PK_Products_ID PRIMARY KEY (id))
```

Creating Indexes

In the previous section on creating a table, you saw that tables in SQL Azure require a clustered index. You may wonder what exactly a clustered index is or why it is necessary to have one. This section briefly introduces the two major index types and shows how to use them in SQL Azure.

Why create indexes? In short, for improved query performance. Without any index on a table, finding the rows that satisfy a query requires a complete row by row search of all rows in the table. Like the index for this book, looking for a key value in an index involves significantly less work than scanning every page in the book, aka the entire table. In addition, you can use indexes to ensure that certain columns with rows have values unique across all rows in the table.

Every table created in SQL Azure can have two physical types of indexes:

➤ **Clustered index:** This type of index controls the physical sort order of rows in the table because it defines the order in which the rows are actually written to disk. There can be only one clustered index on a table because the data can be stored only in one order.

➤ **Nonclustered index:** This type of index is like an index that points to the clustered index. It builds an index of column values that point to entries in the clustered index. SQL Azure supports creating up to 999 nonclustered indexes on a table.

You can create a Unique constraint with either a nonclustered or clustered index to ensure that the key values are unique across all rows in the table. When you define a Primary Key on a table, you are in effect defining a unique constraint.

Creating a Clustered Index

You have already seen how to create a clustered index at table creation time, but what if you want to create a clustered index for a table that already exists (and does not already have a clustered index)? You can do this using the CREATE CLUSTERED INDEX statement. For example, assume you had not created the clustered index ID on the Products table shown previously. To create the clustered index, you would execute the following T-SQL, providing a name for the index (CI_Products_ID), the name of the table (Products), and the column on which to build the index and sort the table (ID).

```
CREATE CLUSTERED INDEX CI_Products_ID ON Products (ID)
```

Creating a Nonclustered Index

You can create additional nonclustered indexes to speed query performance on key values besides those used for the clustered index, at the expense of additional storage. To create a nonclustered index, you use the CREATE NONCLUSTERED INDEX statement. Assume, in the case of the Product's table, that you often need to query by the name of the product (in addition to the product ID already covered by the clustered index).

```
CREATE NONCLUSTERED INDEX NCI_Products_Name ON Products ([Name])
```

Creating a Unique Index

To create a unique index either in a clustered or non-clustered index, you specify the UNIQUE option within the CREATE...INDEX statement; you do this by including the UNIQUE keyword after CREATE. For example, assume you wanted to ensure that product names were also unique across all rows in the table. You could create a nonclustered index as follows that enforces this uniqueness.

```
CREATE UNIQUE NONCLUSTERED INDEX UNCI_Products_Name
ON Products ([Name])
```

Accessing SQL Azure from Applications

SQL Azure Databases are not typically created for use solely by SQL Server Management Studio, but rather to power applications. SQL Azure, because it is provided as a cloud-hosted service, enables access from two categories of client applications:

➤ **Access from on-premises applications:** Applications that exist on your local network, such as thick client Windows Presentation Foundation apps, intranet websites, or even those that feed into existing desktop productivity applications such as Excel. This category could also include access by other on-premises applications located at partner organizations or at branch offices outside of headquarters.

➤ **Access from Azure-hosted applications:** Websites/web services hosted in an Azure Web Role, computational services running in an Azure Worker Role, or even applications running within an Azure VM Role.

Supported Client Libraries

Applications communicate with SQL Azure using one of the many client libraries available. This communication with SQL Azure occurs via the Tabular Data Stream protocol version 7.3 or later. Clients utilizing earlier versions are not supported, nor are connections to SQL Azure via OLE DB. That said, many client libraries are supported:

➤ .NET Framework Data Provider for SQL Server (in other words, the classes in the System .Data.SqlClient namespace) included with the .NET 3.5 Service Pack 1 or later

➤ Entity Framework included with the .NET Framework 3.5 Service Pack 1 or later

➤ SQL Server 2008 or 2008 R2 Native Client ODBC driver

➤ SQL Server 2008 Driver for PHP, version 1.1 or later

➤ SQL Server JDBC Driver 3.0, with support for the SQL Azure Database

The following sections show how to use both System.Data.SqlClient classes and Entity Framework.

Accessing SQL Azure from Azure-Hosted Applications

In the following sections, you will see how to create a simple Web Role and use it to access a SQL Azure Database using either SQL Client or Entity Framework. After which you will probably agree, the experience is almost identical to using SQL Server and often amounts to simply a difference in the connection string used.

Creating the Sample Database

For the samples in the following sections, use the AdventureWorks LT for SQL Azure sample Database available from CodePlex. Follow these steps to create a sample database:

1. Ensure you have a SQL Azure Server set up. You deploy the AdventureWorks LT Database to your own server.

2. Download the ZIP file from `http://msftdbprodsamples.codeplex.com/releases/view/37304` and extract it to your local filesystem.

3. Open the command prompt, navigate into the `AW2008R2AZ\LT` subfolder of the extracted contents, and type the following command (replacing `<server>` with the name of your SQL Azure server, `<login>` with your SQL Azure administrator login, and `<password>` with the password):

   ```
   buildawltaz.cmd tcp:<server>.Database.windows.net <login>@<server> <password>
   ```

After a minute or two, you will have a new Database called AdventureWorksLTAZ2008R2 created within your SQL Azure Server. This Database contains a relatively simple schema and sample data that makes it easy to experiment with building clients, which you will do next.

 Ensure that the SQL Azure Firewall is configured with rules allowing access both from Windows Azure platform services (if you deploy a client built in the following to Azure), and for the external IP address of your development machine (when testing it locally).

Creating the Azure Host Project

Recall from above that you can create Windows Azure hosted services that communicate with SQL Azure, which can be Web Roles, Worker Roles, or VM Roles. All of these roles are written in standard .NET, so irrespective of which type of application you are building, the steps required to interact with SQL Azure are:

1. Create the host service project.

2. Add the appropriate assembly references for the desired client library (you will see specifically which assemblies in the sections that follow).

3. Add a connection string that points to your SQL Azure Database.

4. Use the client library (SQL Client or Entity Framework) API to interact with your SQL Azure Database.

Create the Web Role

In the following steps, you construct an MVC 3 Web Role hosted service project and configure it to use `System.Data.SqlClient` classes first and then, later, Entity Framework. Simply follow these steps:

1. Launch Visual Studio 2010.

2. From the menu select File ⇨ New Project.

3. From the list of Installed Templates on the left, select Cloud, and on the right select Windows Azure Project.

4. Name your project **AWOnline** and click OK, as shown in Figure 11-16.

FIGURE 11-16

5. In the New Windows Azure Project dialog, select ASP.NET MVC 3 Web Role from the left side, and click the right arrow (>) button to add it to your new cloud project, as shown in Figure 11-17, then click OK.

6. From the New ASP.NET MVC 3 Project dialog, leave the Empty template selected and the rest of the fields at their default values. Click OK.

This creates a new solution containing two projects: a cloud project that describes the configuration of the Web Role and an MVC Web Project where all your content goes. In addition, the assembly references needed for using either the `System.Data.SqlClient` classes (namely `System.Data.dll`) and Entity Framework (namely `EntityFramework.dll` and `System.Data.Entity.dll`) are also added.

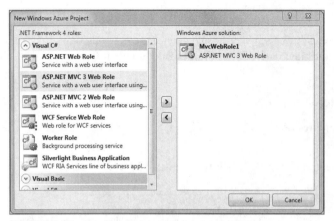

FIGURE 11-17

Access Using the System.Data.SqlClient Classes

The classes in the `System.Data.SqlClient` namespace provide the lowest level API for communicating with SQL Server and SQL Azure by using `SqlConnection` to connect to the server, `SqlDataReader` to process result rows in a forward-only fashion, `SqlCommand` to execute queries, and `DataSet` to retrieve data in batches. In the following steps, you will use these classes to query the Product table to provide a basic listing of products.

1. In Solution Explorer, expand the MvcWebRole1 project, right-click the Controllers folder, and select Add ➪ Controller.

2. In the Add Controller dialog, enter **ProductsController** for the Controller name.

3. In the template drop-down, select Controller with Empty Read/Write Actions (see Figure 11-18) and click Add.

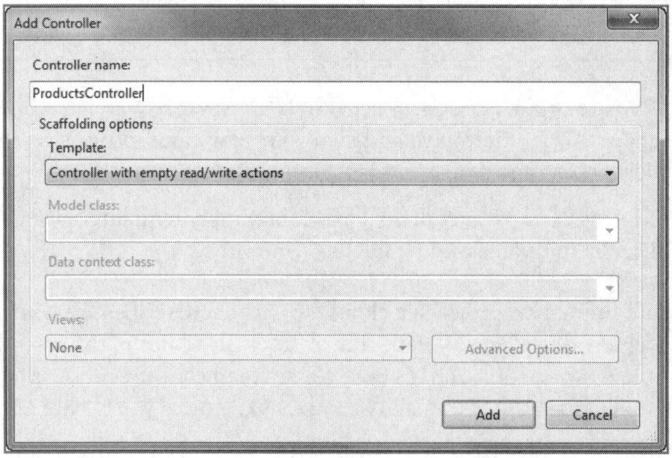

FIGURE 11-18

4. Navigate to the `Index()` controller action in `ProductsController.cs`. Just above it, define the global variable to hold the connection string retrieved from `web.config`. (You will add this connection string in a moment.)

5. Add a using statement for `System.Data.SqlClient` to the top of the file.

6. Update the contents of the `Index` method so that it appears as follows:

```
string connectionString =
    System.Configuration.ConfigurationManager.
    ConnectionStrings["AdventureWorks"].ConnectionString;

//
// GET: /Products/
public ActionResult Index()
{
    List<Tuple<string, decimal>> products =
new List<Tuple<string, decimal>>();

    using (SqlConnection sqlConnection =
        new SqlConnection(connectionString))
    {

        SqlCommand command =
          new SqlCommand("SELECT Name, ListPrice FROM SalesLT.Product");

        command.Connection = sqlConnection;

        sqlConnection.Open();

        SqlDataReader dataReader = command.ExecuteReader();

        while (dataReader.Read())
        {
            products.Add(new Tuple<string, decimal>(
              dataReader.GetString( dataReader.GetOrdinal("Name") ),
              dataReader.GetDecimal( dataReader.GetOrdinal("ListPrice") )
              ));
        }
    }

    return View(products);
}
```

You need to observe a few points about the previous snippet:

➤ The `SqlConnection` instance is created within a using block so that it automatically closes when the scope completes or if an exception occurs.

➤ The `SqlConnection` instance is opened and associated with the `SqlCommand` instance that defines an inline T-SQL Select statement.

➤ The results are read via a `SqlDataReader` and inserted into a simple Tuple data structure and added to the list of products for display by the view.

7. Right-click `Index()` and select Add View. Click Add in the dialog that appears to create an empty view in which you can render the list of products.

8. Replace the contents of this view CSHTML with the following code, which renders the products list in an HTML table using the Razor syntax of MVC 3:

```
@model List<Tuple<string, decimal>>

<h2>Products</h2>

<table>
<tr>
    <th>Product</th>
    <th>List Price</th>
</tr>

@foreach (var product in Model){
    <tr>
        <td>
            @product.Item1
        </td>
        <td>
            @product.Item2
        </td>
    </tr>
}
</table>
```

9. Add the connection string to your `web.config`. Open `web.config`, scroll down to the bottom, and within the `connectionStrings` element add the following (replacing your server name, login, and password):

```
<add name="AdventureWorks"
connectionString="data source=[ServerName].Database.windows.net;
initial catalog=AdventureWorksLTAZ2008R2;
user id=[Login];
password=[Password];
multipleactiveresultsets=True;
TrustServerCertificate=False;"/>
```

 You should always validate the server certificate of SQL Azure to prevent man-in-the-middle attacks. Doing this is easy with ADO.NET applications because it is just a matter of appending the following to the connection string used in `web.config`*:*

```
TrustServerCertificate=False
```

10. Run your solution! Press F5. In the browser window that appears, append `/Products` to the URL (for example, `http://127.0.0.2:81/Products`) to view the results retrieved from SQL Azure using the SqlClient library. Figure 11-19 shows an example of the output.

Products

Product	List Price
HL Road Frame - Black, 58	1431.5000
HL Road Frame - Red, 58	1431.5000
Sport - 100 Helmet, Red	34.9900
Sport - 100 Helmet, Black	34.9900
Mountain Bike Socks, M	9.5000
Mountain Bike Socks, L	9.5000

FIGURE 11-19

The steps shown in this section apply equally well to modifying data in SQL Azure using the `System.Data.SqlClient` *classes, either with inline SQL or via Stored Procedure calls. For examples of this, see* `http://msdn.microsoft.com/en-us/library/3btz0xwf.aspx`.

Access Using Entity Framework

If you prefer to work with SQL Azure Databases with strongly typed entities, rather than the more weakly typed approach taken by the `System.Data.SqlClient` classes, you can use the Entity Framework. If you are already familiar with the Entity Framework, working with SQL Azure is no different than working with SQL Server; the primary difference is the data source, which points to SQL Azure instead.

In the following steps, you will see how you can quickly use the Entity Framework combined with MVC 3 scaffolding to query the Products table.

1. Create the entity model. You will continue with the solution you have created so far. Within Solution Explorer, right-click MvcWebRole1, and choose Add ⇨ New Item. From the Installed Templates list on the left, choose the Data node, and on the right select the ADO.NET Entity Data Model item, as shown in Figure 11-20. Click Add.

FIGURE 11-20

2. In the wizard, on the Choose Model Contents screen, select Generate from Database, and click Next.

3. On the Choose Your Data Connection, click the New Connection button.

4. In the Connection Properties dialog that appears, enter the fully qualified DNS name of your SQL Azure Server in the Server Name field, select Use SQL Server authentication, and enter your login and password.

5. For the Database Name, you can either type the name of the Database (**AdventureWorksLTAZ2008R2**) or pick it from the drop-down. Figure 11-21 shows what a completed connection dialog should look like. Click OK.

6. On the Choose Your Data Connection screen, select the Yes, include the "sensitive data in the connection string" option (see Figure 11-22), and then click Next.

FIGURE 11-21

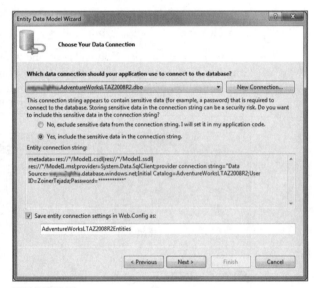

FIGURE 11-22

7. On the Choose Your Database Objects screen, expand the Tables node and select the Product table. Click Finish.

   The result of this is an Entity Framework model (which guides the generation of the .NET types, the structure of the actual Database objects, and how the types map to the entities) in the form of the file `Model1.edmx`, which is added to the website project, and the connection string named AdventureWorksLTAZ2008R2Entities added to `web.config`.

8. Before you move on, build your solution by going Build ➪ Build Solution to ensure the types generated by the Entity Framework are visible to the MVC Scaffolding Wizard you use in the next step.

9. Add an MVC controller that defines the action to query for the product list. Right-click the Controllers folder and select Add ➪ Controller.

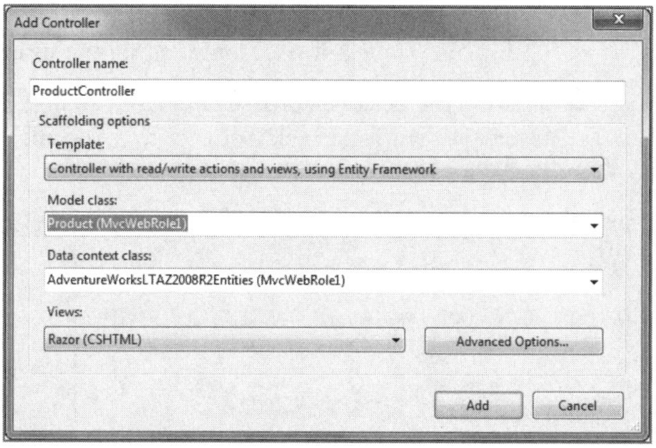

10. In the Add Controller dialog, for the controller name specify ProductController. (And ensure this is a different name from the name you used in earlier the `System.Data.SqlClient` example. In the Scaffolding options Template drop-down menu, select Controller with Read/Write Actions and View, Using Entity Framework. For the Model class drop-down, choose Product (MvcWebRole1) and for the Data context class drop-down, select AdventureWorksLTAZ2008R2Entities (MvcWebRole1), as shown in Figure 11-23. Click Add to complete the process and create the controller and related MVC views.

FIGURE 11-23

The Index action within the ProductController that was automatically created shows how the Entity Framework queries SQL Azure for the list of products:

```
public ViewResult Index()
{
    return View(db.Products.ToList());
}
```

The view that renders this list is `Index.cshtml`, found underneath the /Views/Product/ folder.

11. Re-run your solution; this time append /Product to the URL in the browser. You see the product list—this time generated using Entity Framework to query SQL Azure.

 Connections to SQL Azure may be closed due to excessive resource usage when idle for 30 minutes or when a failover occurs.

Accessing SQL Azure from On-Premises Applications

You can use many existing on-premises applications to communicate with SQL Azure, provided your Firewall configuration is correct. Microsoft Excel 2010 is a great example of this capability. In this section you see how to query the Product table from the AdventureWorks Database and view the results in an Excel spreadsheet.

1. Launch Excel 2010, and on the Ribbon, select the Data tab. From the Get External Data button, choose From Other Sources and then From SQL Server, as shown in Figure 11-24.

2. In the Connect to Database Server dialog, enter your SQL Azure Server's fully qualified domain name and your login, as shown in Figure 11-25.

3. From the Select Database and Table dialog, pick the AdventureWorks Database in the drop-down list, check Connect to a Specific Table, and select the Product table, as shown in Figure 11-26.

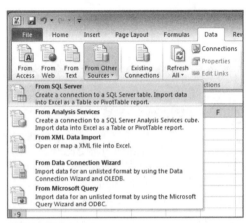

FIGURE 11-24

FIGURE 11-25

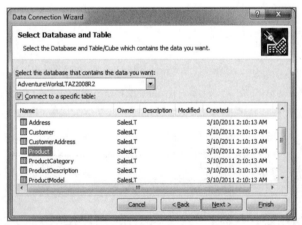

FIGURE 11-26

4. In the last dialog, as shown in Figure 11-27, you can optionally save the connection information to *.odc file, so you can reconnect easily later. Click Finish.

5. When the Import Data dialog appears (see Figure 11-28), choose how you want to view the data. In this case, select Table and click OK.

After a moment, the product list appears within the spreadsheet (see Figure 11-29) and you can perform whatever analysis you choose.

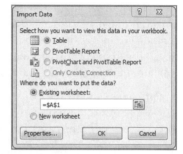

FIGURE 11-27

FIGURE 11-28

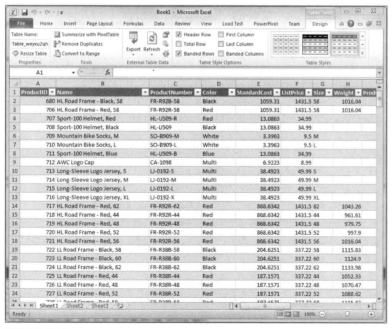

FIGURE 11-29

Working with Transactions

Transactions provide consistency when multiple operations (queries or modifications) happen on data at the same time, such as ensuring that all operations succeed or fail together as a unit.

Transactions in SQL Azure

Traditionally consistency is brought about by placing locks on the rows or tables involved in a query that prevent other concurrent operations from making changes until the operation completes—referred to as *pessimistic concurrency.*

SQL Azure takes a different approach; concurrent operations are allowed, and no locking takes place. Instead, if one operation makes a change to the data used by another operation, when the latter operation completes, it gets an error indicating that it was operating on stale data. This is the optimistic approach to concurrency used by SQL Azure. Grouping the individual steps of the operation into an atomic unit of work (that can fail or complete as a whole) is the transaction.

SQL Azure provides support for local transactions only. These are transactions created in T-SQL with BEGIN TRANSACTION, followed by ROLLBACK TRANSACTION (in the case of an error), and finally COMMIT TRANSACTION (in the case of a successful completion).

In other words, SQL Azure does not support distributed transactions. *Distributed transactions* are those that, for example, span multiple SQL Azure Databases or include other transaction-aware resources beyond the SQL Azure Database you connect to. If you are familiar with distributed transactions with SQL Server, this also means that SQL Azure does not provide support for resource managers such as the Microsoft Distributed Transaction Coordinator (MS DTC).

Transactions in SQL Azure default to running with READ_COMMITTED_SNAPSHOT as the isolation level. Because this setting cannot be changed at the Database level, it represents a fundamental shift in concurrency behavior. Your transactions must run with optimistic concurrency behavior (for example, an error is thrown when attempting an update to a stale record) instead of the pessimistic concurrency (for example, where records are locked) that was standard for SQL Server.

 For a background or refresher on the purpose and application of isolation levels, be sure to read:

    http://msdn.microsoft.com/en-us/library/ms173763.aspx

Consider that before starting a transaction with BEGIN TRANSACTION, you can set the isolation level to REPEATABLE READ as follows:

    SET TRANSACTION ISOLATION LEVEL REPEATABLE READ

Even in this case, you are still running with optimistic concurrency. You can re-create the pessimistic concurrency behavior of SQL Server on SQL Azure by using the WITH (READCOMMITTEDLOCK) hint for every table queried in every transaction.

Choosing SqlTransaction over TransactionScope

When programming against a SQL Azure Database using SQL Azure, you have the option to use a TransactionScope to wrap a block of code in a transaction. Be careful of this! The

`TransactionScope` class starts with a local transaction so long as you are working with only one connection to SQL Azure. However, if within this scope you add connections to another Database, if you nest connections to the same Database, if the ambient transaction is already a distributed transaction, or if you invoke another resource manager with a Database connection, you'll be working with a distributed transaction, and this will get you a runtime exception.

The safest way to avoid the problem of unexpected runtime exceptions caused by accidentally creating a distributed transaction is to use `SqlTransaction` explicitly instead of `TransactionScope`. The following snippet shows the pattern you should follow to use `SqlTransaction`. Even though you switched from `TransactionScope`, you still get the benefit of exceptions automatically causing the transaction to roll back and undo the work done by both commands. The difference is that commands do not automatically join an ambient transaction, even if there is one, and so you avoid accidentally enlisting in a distributed transaction.

```
using (SqlConnection sqlConnection =
  new SqlConnection(connectionString))
{
  sqlConnection.Open();

  using (SqlTransaction sqlTransaction =
    sqlConnection.BeginTransaction())
  {
  // Create your first command and execute it
    SqlCommand firstCommand = new SqlCommand("firstCommmand",
      sqlConnection, sqlTransaction);

    firstCommand.ExecuteNonQuery();

    // Create your second command and execute it
    SqlCommand secondCommand = new SqlCommand("secondCommmand",
      sqlConnection, sqlTransaction);
    secondCommand.ExecuteNonQuery();

    sqlTransaction.Commit();
  }
}
```

 Note that if you are doing simple, discreet operations, like in the sample MVC web application, `TransactionScope` *is going to be fine. You should, however, always keep an eye out for situations that implicitly enlist in a transaction and cause unexpected behavior.*

TROUBLESHOOTING

In this section, you will take a pragmatic approach to solving the issues typically faced when using SQL Azure, such as working with firewalls, dealing with connection loss, reducing latency, and estimating usage costs.

Working with Firewalls

If you have difficulty connecting to SQL Azure, you may want to check firewall configuration on both ends of the pipe in order to:

➤   Ensure local firewalls are configured to allow outbound TCP on port 1433.

➤   Ensure your external IP address is configured with access within a SQL Azure Firewall Rule. In some cases, your local IP address may not be the external address that presents in communications with SQL Azure. One way to find your external IP is to visit a public website such as http://whatismyipaddress.com that displays it. The SQL Azure Firewall dialog shows you your current address; albeit in rare cases this may not give you the correct address (in which case try a third party site as mentioned previously).

➤   If you only want to allow your IP address, specify the same IP address values in the "from" and "to" boxes.

➤   Remember to create a rule for each IP address or range you will use. For instance, if you create a rule allowing you access from your laptop at work, do not forget to add another rule containing your home IP address if you use your laptop from home.

When a Firewall Rule is not configured properly for your client, you should expect errors of the following form:

```
Cannot open server 'servername' requested by the login.
Client with IP address 'XXX.XXX.XXX.XXX' is not allowed to access the server.
To enable access, use the SQL Azure Portal or
run sp_set_firewall_rule on the master
Database to create a firewall rule for this
IP address or address range.
It may take up to five minutes for this change to
take effect.

Login failed for user 'ZoinerTejada'.
```

This typically means your IP address has changed since you last configured access in the SQL Azure Firewall.

The easiest way to correct this is to follow these steps:

1.   Return to the Azure Portal Databases page and select your Server in the tree-view.

2.   Click the Firewall Rules button to see the list of configured rules, as well as the buttons to Add, Update, or Delete them. This dialog also provides a check box for easily adding or removing the rule for access to your SQL Azure server from other Windows Azure services.

If you have examined all the preceding items and still have trouble connecting, consider that it can take up to 5 minutes before a SQL Azure Firewall configuration takes effect.

Failing that, you may want to verify that your login and password are both correct and that your login has permission to access the target SQL Azure Server.

Troubleshooting Connection Loss

The resources for SQL Azure are shared by multiple tenants. To provide a generally balanced experience for all tenants, you may experience intermittent or transient errors that disconnect you from your Database.

Various causes for disconnection relate to the way SQL Azure throttles usage, particularly when the system resources are limited. Limits include:

➤ Network problems

➤ Large number of locks

➤ Too many uncommitted transactions

➤ Locks blocking system calls

➤ Excessive transaction log storage consumption by a transaction

➤ Transactions that require too much space in TempDB

➤ Excessive memory consumption

➤ MAXSIZE of Database reached

➤ Connections idle for 30+ minutes

➤ Large number of login failures from a single IP

➤ When the primary Database replica has failed over to a backup replica

➤ Overloaded physical server

To address connection-loss issues, you should know how to diagnose the cause and take preventative measures in your application design.

Diagnosing the Cause of a Connection Loss

In many cases, the reason for connection loss is present in the exception text returned to your application (such as "the Database has reached its size quota") and may point you directly to the cause of the connection loss for which a solution is obvious (such as increase your MAXSIZE, or clean up your Database).

In other cases, you may need to understand more about the problem (such as when you have excessive locks or long-running queries). Here you have two options.

➤ You can examine the System Views for examining query performance:

 ➤ **Identify time-consuming queries:** sys.dm_exec_query_stats and sys.dm_exec_sql_text

 ➤ **Monitor for excessive locking:** sys.dm_tran_locks

 ➤ **Pinpoint inefficient query plans:** sys.dm_exec_query_stats

For examples of querying these views to troubleshoot query performance, visit http://msdn.microsoft.com/en-us/library/ff394114.aspx.

➤ You can try to stress test your application by gradually increasing the workload until you trigger the connection loss (which should provide you with the reason in the error text).

Taking Preventative Measures

The measures taken in the previous section are great tools after a problem has occurred, but ideally you should build your application to work around the connection loss when it happens.

The best approach to this is to build retry logic into your application that responds to these transient errors automatically. This can be quite an undertaking, when you consider you must first identify which errors are transient (for which a retry will ultimately repair the problem) and which are permanent.

In addition, your retry approach needs to factor in a back-off strategy. In many cases, the system just needs some additional time to be available again, and trying again directly after the initial transient error only results in the same error. Your solution instead needs to retry after waiting for a small period of time (say a few seconds) and gradually increase that wait (say to 10 seconds) if the transient error persists.

Fortunately, the Windows Azure AppFabric Customer Advisory Team has put together a library that encapsulates this robust retry logic for SQL Azure. You should check out the tutorial available at http://social.technet.microsoft.com/wiki/contents/articles/retry-logic-for-transient-failures-in-sql-azure.aspx that walks you through the setup and basic use of the retry library.

In rare cases, SQL Azure may be unavailable. You can always check the status of SQL Azure by visiting the Azure Health Status page at http://www.microsoft.com/windowsazure/support/status/servicedashboard.aspx.

Reducing Latency

If you move your SQL Server Database out of your local network to SQL Azure, your applications will experience greater network latency owing to the geographical distance introduced between your on-premises application and the cloud-hosted SQL Azure. This distance is the result of various factors including network congestion and available bandwidth (which is likely far less over the Internet than on your local network).

It may be obvious, but the best way to reduce latency of network requests between your application and SQL Azure is to minimize the distance between them. Practically speaking, this means you should host your application in Windows Azure (such as within a Web or Worker Role), and when you create your application's hosted service on Windows Azure, make sure the region you select is the same as the region for your SQL Azure Server. This reduces latency because communication happens across the much faster internal networks rather than across the Internet. In addition, this can result in a cost-savings on bandwidth because data transfer within a datacenter is not charged. You also have the added benefits that Windows Azure hosted services provide, for instance high availability of your website.

Calculating Usage

Although you can view metrics of your usage and accrued costs in web-page form by visiting the Microsoft Online Customer Portal (http://mocp.microsoftonline.com), you can also get a reasonably accurate estimate programmatically. You might want to do this to ensure that you have adequate capacity (for example, have selected the appropriate MAXSIZE for your Database) or to estimate accrued costs. You can calculate storage space use, billed edition/size use, and bandwidth use by querying specific system views.

Calculating Storage Usage

The following query provides the current amount of space used by your SQL Azure Database. You must be logged in to the Database you want to report on—and it cannot be the master Database.

```
SELECT SUM(reserved_page_count)*8.0/1024 as 'Size (MB)'
FROM sys.dm_db_partition_stats;
```

Calculating Database Edition Usage

To examine the cumulative usage for all the Databases within your SQL Azure Server by day, query the sys.Database_usage system view, as shown in the following snippet. Note that you must connect to the master Database with the administrator login.

```
SELECT *
FROM sys.Database_usage
```

Rows are returned by day (note the time zone is UTC), and as Table 11-2 shows, if you incurred charges for multiple editions (SKU), more than one row is returned for that day.

TABLE 11-2: Sample Database Usage Output

TIME	SKU	QUANTITY
2011-08-23 00:00:00.000	Web	3.000000
2011-08-23 00:00:00.000	Business	1.000000
2011-08-24 00:00:00.000	Web	3.000000

Given this, you can calculate your approximate usage costs for the month, for all Databases within the Server, using the following query.

```
SELECT sku,
    avg_size = AVG(quantity),
    estimate = CASE
        WHEN AVG(quantity) > 50
            THEN (125.874 + (AVG(quantity) - 50) * 0.999)
        WHEN AVG(quantity) > 10
            THEN (45.954 + (AVG(quantity) - 10) * 1.998)
        WHEN AVG(quantity) > 1
            THEN (9.99 + (AVG(quantity) - 1) * 3.996)
        WHEN AVG(quantity) > 0.5
            THEN (9.99)
        ELSE 4.995
        END
FROM sys.Database_usage
WHERE
        datepart(yy,[time]) = datepart(yy, getutcdate()) AND
        datepart(mm,[time]) = (datepart(mm, getutcdate()))
    GROUP BY sku
```

The key point to the previous query is how Database sizes are encoded in the quantity. If you have a single 1GB web edition Database using 1GB of space, its quantity shows up as 1. However, for a single 100 MB Database, the quantity has a value of 0.5. The query shown includes the prices available at the time of this writing: you may have to update these values as new pricing is announced.

You may notice that this estimate may underestimate costs in cases where you have a mixture of database sizes across the different price tiers, because the quantity field rolls up the total space used by day per SKU and provides no way to figure out the correct cost per additional gigabyte. This happens because it cannot be certain whether, for example, a quantity of 15 means:

➤ A single 15 GB database billed as 10 GB at $45.954 plus 5 additional GBs at $1.998 each, for a total of $55.944

➤ An 11 GB database ($45.954 + 1 x $1.998) and a 4 GB database ($9.99 + 3 x $3.996) billed for total of $69.93

The query shown would provide the estimate of $55.944 for a quantity of 15, so just be wary of this limitation.

Calculating Bandwidth Usage

You can view your bandwidth usage in KBs for an hourly time period by querying the sys.bandwidth_usage system view from the context of the master Database with the administrator login.

```
SELECT *
FROM sys.bandwidth_usage
```

This returns data similar to Table 11-3, with four rows for each Database in use for any single hour.

TABLE 11-3: Viewing Bandwidth Usage

TIME	DATABASE_NAME	DIRECTION	CLASS	TIME_PERIOD	QUANTITY
2011-11-23 02:00:00.000	MyDb	Ingress	Internal	Peak	7
2011-11-23 02:00:00.000	MyDb	Ingress	External	Peak	10
2011-11-23 02:00:00.000	MyDb	Egress	Internal	Peak	10
2011-11-23 02:00:00.000	MyDb	Egress	External	Peak	40

For the purposes of estimating your bill, you need to be concerned only with rows having the class
`'External'` (traffic leaving the Windows Azure datacenter) and Direction Egress (out from SQL
Azure) because ingress is free of charge (regardless of whether internal or external), and data egress
within the same subregion (as indicated by a Direction of Egress and Class of Internal) is also free
of charge. Therefore, to approximate your bandwidth costs for the month to date by Database, you
could use the following query.

```
SELECT Database_name,
   SUM (quantity/1048576) as 'GB Out',
   SUM (0.12 * (quantity/1048576)) as 'Bandwidth Costs'
FROM sys.bandwidth_usage
WHERE direction = 'Egress' and Class = 'External' AND
datepart(yy,[time]) = datepart(yy, getutcdate()) AND
datepart(mm,[time]) = datepart(mm, getutcdate())
GROUP BY Database_name
```

 *The previous query assumes your data transfer is $0.12 per GB (currently the fee
for Zone 1). You should adjust this amount to reflect the fees associated with the
region in which your SQL Azure server is hosted.*

SUMMARY

In this chapter, you saw how the cloud-based SQL Azure differs fundamentally from on-premises
SQL Server, yet ultimately provides a familiar experience for developing against a SQL Server-based
relational Database.

You saw how SQL Azure Databases are logically grouped underneath a SQL Azure Server for management reasons, as well as how to create SQL Azure Servers using the Windows Azure portal. You

also saw how to create SQL Azure Databases through the portal, as well as how to manage them using T-SQL executed from SQL Server Management Studio or the Database Manager.

In addition, you were exposed to some of the myriad ways applications can be built to target SQL Azure, and how you can troubleshoot connection issues, reduce latency, and calculate usage for your SQL Azure powered applications.

ADDITIONAL RESOURCES

SQL Resources

Viera, Robert. *Beginning Microsoft SQL Server 2008 Programming.* (Wrox)

SQL Server Database Design

http://msdn.microsoft.com/en-us/library/bb510424.aspx

Transact-SQL Reference

http://msdn.microsoft.com/en-us/library/bb510741.aspx

SQL Client Resources

SQL Server and ADO.NET

http://msdn.microsoft.com/en-us/library/kb9s9ks0.aspx

Entity Framework Resources

The ADO.NET Entity Framework Developer Center

http://msdn.microsoft.com/en-us/data/aa937723

12

An Azure Datamarket Overview

WHAT'S IN THIS CHAPTER

➤ Understanding Windows Azure Datamarket

➤ Creating and managing your Marketplace account

➤ Browsing and subscribing to published content

➤ Understanding and using Datamarket datasets

The amount of data available for applications is incredible—and unfortunately, it's locked behind corporate walls. If you can navigate the multitude of access methods to get to the data, that data is invariably presented in various formats. Accessing different data sources from different vendors—or even the same vendor—and then corralling and controlling that data can be a nightmare. But you can simplify data publishing and even consumption using a cloud-based solution that provides access to disparate data from multiple sources via a common format and access. Enter Azure Datamarket.

WHAT IS WINDOWS AZURE DATAMARKET?

Windows Azure Datamarket is a subset of the Windows Azure Marketplace wherein a single Marketplace account can purchase applications and data. Datamarket was the first area in the Azure Marketplace. Microsoft has since introduced Applications published to Datamarket, which is not limited to the .NET and Windows world. Currently located at `https://data-market.azure.com/`, the Marketplace gives users access to a store of applications and datasets for purchase. Figure 12-1 shows the Marketplace homepage.

Introduced as code-name Dallas, and based on common nonplatform-specific web technologies such as HTTP and AtomPub, Datamarket provides a single location where content owners can publish and sell content to the masses using a standardized publish/subscribe model, and which users can access from a wide variety of platforms and applications.

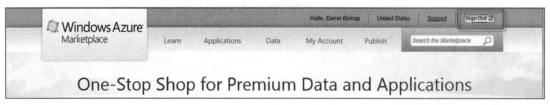

FIGURE 12-1

The benefits of Marketplace are as follows:

➤ **Organizations with vast amounts of content can use Marketplace to advertise and monetize their data to a large audience.** Using Marketplace, publishers do not need to invest in the logistics in creating a storefront, billing and account management. Marketplace takes care of the common functionality required to publish data, leaving publishers free from mundane storefront tasks so that they can concentrate on which data is exposed and how it is queried.

➤ **Consumers use Datamarket to find, subscribe, and browse using the published data within the terms of agreements.** Datamarket provides one-stop shopping for various datasets. It also gives consumers common tools to view and explore data as well as consume data in common (including Microsoft Excel) and custom applications. Marketplace provides the common account management, access controls, and billing to the datasets. From a consumer stand-point, using data from Marketplace ensures a consistent experience and makes it easier for users to work with more data as applications grow.

In summary, Marketplace provides not only data but also the common account, subscription, and billing management for applications. Datamarket provides the foundation for publishing and con-suming datasets via OData, basic authentication, and OAuth. This is data in the cloud, which means it's easy to publish, subscribe to, and work with premium content. This chapter focuses on how to locate, subscribe to, and consume data from Azure Datamarket.

Working with Datamarket

As mentioned before, you can consume data from Datamarket in many different ways—from the Service Explorer, which you learn about later in this section, to Microsoft Excel to custom applica-tions. Datamarket allows anyone to browse a list of published datasets. Before you can actually sub-scribe to and use a dataset , you must register with Marketplace and create a Marketplace account. The following sections walk you through how to do this.

 Browsing the available datasets in Datamarket does not require a Marketplace account; however, subscribing to Datamarket and using Datamarket data does.

Creating an Azure Marketplace Account

To start using Azure Data Market you must log in using a Windows Live account. If you don't have a Windows Live account, Marketplace has an option to create a Windows Live account during the sign-in process. If you don't have a Marketplace account associated with your Windows Live account, you are prompted for registration information. To sign into Marketplace, follow these steps:

1. Click the Sign In button located in the top-right corner of the Azure Marketplace homepage located at `https://datamarket.azure.com/`. Figure 12-2 shows the Marketplace homepage with the Sign In button. You are directed to the Registration page, as shown in Figure 12-3.

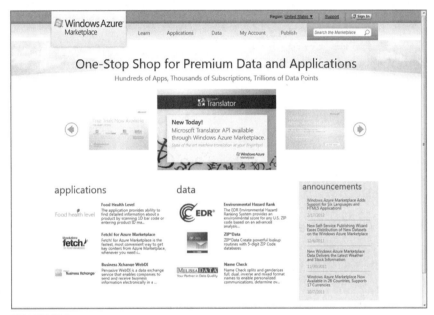

FIGURE 12-2

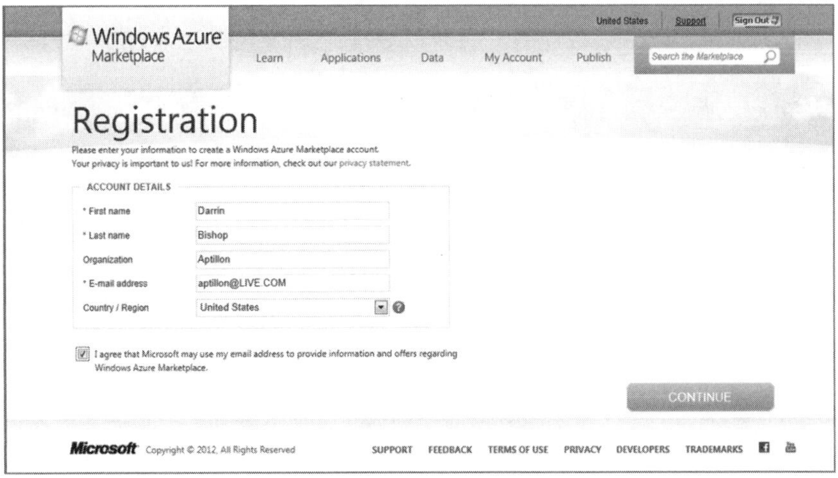

FIGURE 12-3

2. Provide registration information such as your first and last name as well as your e-mail address. Select the check box to agree with the Marketplace offers, and click the Continue button.

3. You must accept the Terms of Use agreement before you can register. Select the check box stating you do indeed agree to the terms of use, and click the Register button to complete your Marketplace registration. You can determine that you have successfully registered and signed in when you see your name located in the page header, as shown in Figure 12-4.

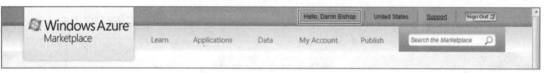

FIGURE 12-4

After you complete the registration process and have a Marketplace account, you can sign in and out as needed. You can use the My Account pages discussed in the Managing Your Account section to manage your account.

Browsing Available Datamarket Datasets

Marketplace enables you browse a listing of available published datasets by clicking the Data tab located at the top of the page. The Datamarket homepage enables you to browse, filter, or search for datasets that you may be interested in subscribing to.

Datamarket categorizes datasets by cost, category, and publisher:

➤ **Cost:** The three types of cost are Free, Paid, and Free Trial. Figure 12-5 shows a listing of Free datasets. Free trials are generally limited access for a specific time before transaction costs start to accrue. Specific details for each subscription is available before subscribing.

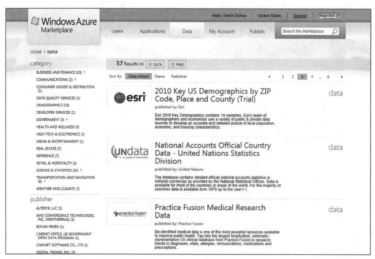

FIGURE 12-5

➤ **Categories:** These are generalized buckets of datasets. A single dataset may be included in multiple categories. Using these three filter categories, you can drill into the datasets to find exactly what you are looking for. The Marketplace also enables you to search for datasets, which can help limit the number of datasets you view at a time.

➤ **Published by:** If you know the content publisher's name, you can filter results by the specific publisher. For example Zillow, Inc. has many published datasources based on homes and mortgages. You can filter the datasets by the publisher Zillow, Inc.

Reviewing Dataset Details

Each published dataset provides an information page that includes details. Clicking on the title of the published content or the associated icon before the title in the search will refer you to the information page.

Figure 12-6 shows an example of an information page and shows information for the Stock Sonar-Sentiment Service of US Stocks dataset.

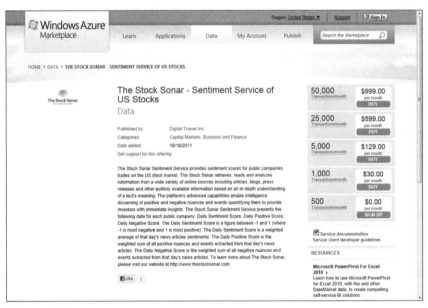

FIGURE 12-6

 Content publishers set how you can access the data, how much data access costs, and any licensing restrictions associated with the published data. Pay close attention to these details because they are different for each set of published content.

The information page includes the following:

➤ **Title:** This is the name of the dataset.

➤ **Description:** This is the content publisher's description of the dataset.

➤ **Dataset details:** This is found in the lower half of the information page. Some of the details are required and some are optional, with the content publisher determining what optional information is included.

> ➤ **Sample Images:** Many datasets provide examples of the data used in a custom application.

> ➤ **Details:** This tab provides key information about supported queries, query parameters (required and optional) as well as the fields returned from the query (refer to Figure 12-7). This is where you must look to determine if the dataset provides the data you require.

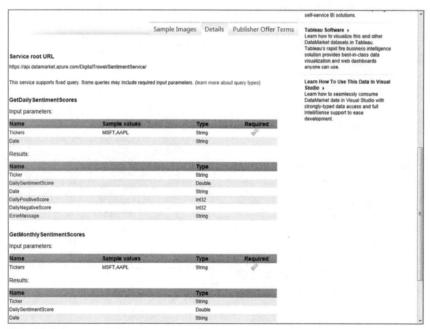

FIGURE 12-7

> ➤ **Publisher Offer Terms:** This includes the terms and agreements for using the content. You must agree to those terms in order to subscribe to and use the dataset.

 Pay close attention to the offer terms. The terms differ from dataset to dataset, and the terms might not support the access required for your application or use.

➤ **Cost:** This can be free or paid and is set by the content publisher. Some published datasets provide limited data access for free or as a trial. Many datasets have a tiered schedule. Refer to Figure 12-6 to see the transaction fee for the Stock Sonar-Sentiment Service of the US Stocks dataset listed in the right column. This dataset uses a tiered cost schedule, meaning that the first 500 transactions per month are free. If you need more than that, you must purchase an option that provides the correct amount of transactions per month.

> *A transaction is currently defined as one page of results with up to 100 results per page. Requesting multiple pages of results from a single query results in multiple transactions. Usage information can be viewed using the My Account pages, which are detailed in the Managing Your Account section.*

Subscribing to a Dataset

A subscription to the dataset is required before you can access or view the dataset. This includes both paid and free datasets. To subscribe to the dataset, follow these steps:

1. Click the Sign Up or Buy button located on the dataset's information page (see Figure 12-6). These buttons (see Figure 12-8) are located with the pricing schedule for a dataset. Datamarket confirms your subscription request by displaying a form containing information associated with the dataset including a link to the terms and cost of the subscription. Figure 12-9 displays the subscription page for www.zillow.com's MortgageInformationAPIs dataset, a free dataset that provides average mortgage rates and monthly mortgage payments.

FIGURE 12-8

2. You must agree to the publisher's terms and privacy agreement before the subscription request is finalized. Read the publisher's terms and agreements, and select the associated check box.

3. Click the Sign Up or Buy button to finish the request. You must repeat the subscription process for each data set you plan to access. When subscribing to a paid dataset, the confirmation page includes payment option information.

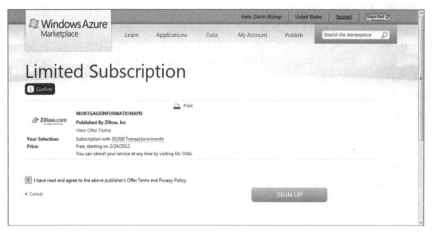

FIGURE 12-9

Working with the Service Explorer

Datamarket provides the Service Explorer interface to access subscribed data without creating a custom application. End users can use the Service Explorer tool to query and view data in many different formats including tabular, chart, or raw XML. This interface also enables export from Datamarket to various formats and import into existing applications.

You can access the Service Explorer by clicking the Explore This Dataset link (see Figure 12-10) located on the dataset's information page. This link is only available when you are signed into Marketplace and viewing the information page of a dataset you have subscribed to. Clicking the Explore This Dataset link opens the Service Explorer page.

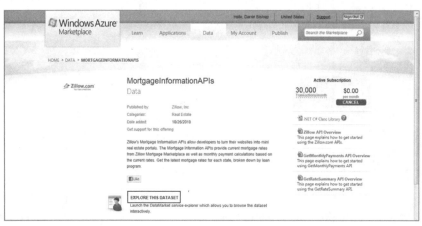

FIGURE 12-10

The Service Explorer provides a quick view into the data. As an example, Figure 12-11 shows the Service Explorer querying the MortgageInformationAPIs for the average mortgage rate for Illinois. This dataset queries and finds average mortgage rates and monthly mortgage payments. Users can select the query and any query parameters, and view the results in either tabular, chart, or XML format. Users can export results to file as XML or CSV, or format and open the results in Excel PowerPivot or Tableau. The Service Explorer is a useful tool that enables end users to quickly search and export data from subscribed datasets.

 Using Service Explorer incurs any agreed upon transaction fee for the subscription.

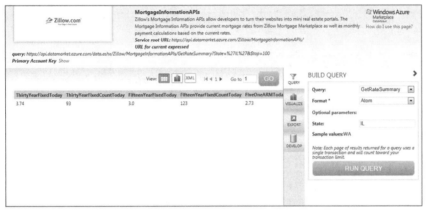

FIGURE 12-11

End users are not the only audience for Service Explorer. Developers commonly use Service Explorer as a quick way to explore and understand the available queries and data schema while creating an application or creating, or modifying a query.

The process behind Service Explorer involves the following steps:

1. Datasets are exposed as OData, which is a URL query format.

2. The Service Explorer provides a graphical interface that creates the URL search query posted to Datamarket.

3. These URL queries are posted to Datamarket to retrieve the results.

4. The posted query and its parameters display in the Service Explorer tool.

5. The results are displayed in the Service Explorer window.

The query displays above the results windows Applications that have a specific fixed query requirement; the Service Explorer can be used to create the URL query which can then be copied into the application code. You can use simple string manipulation such as `String.Format` to modify the URL parameters. The query created to display the average mortgage rate for Illinois is:

```
https://api.datamarket.azure.com/data.ashx/Zillow/MortgageInformationAPIs/GetRate
Summary?State=%27IL%27&$top=100.
```

The Service Explorer can also display the result set as XML. This is particularly useful for non-.NET developers who may not have a proxy to simplify development. Viewing the results of the query as XML allows the developer to see the schema of the results and aids in parsing the XML. Listing 12-1 displays the result for the preceding URL query in XML. This particular query is formatted as AtomPub.

LISTING 12-1: Results of a Query Viewed as XML

```xml
<feed xmlns:base="https://api.datamarket.azure.com/Data.ashx/Zillow/
MortgageInformationAPIs/GetRateSummary"
xmlns:d="http://schemas.microsoft.com/ado/2007/08/dataservices"
xmlns:m="http://schemas.microsoft.com/ado/2007/08/dataservices/metadata"
xmlns="http://www.w3.org/2005/Atom">
<title type="text" />
 <subtitle type="text">
    The GetRateSummary API returns the current rates per loan type from Zillow
Mortgage Marketplace. Current supported loan types are 30-year fixed, 15-year
fixed, and 5/1 ARM. Rates are computed from real quotes borrowers receive from
lenders just seconds before the rate data is returned. The GetRateSummary API
returns rates for a specific state if the optional state parameter is used
    </subtitle>
 <id>https://api.datamarket.azure.com/Data.ashx/Zillow/MortgageInformationAPIs/
GetRateSummary?State='IL'&amp;$top=100</id>
 <rights type="text"> Zillow, Inc., 2008</rights>
 <updated>2012-03-01T12:53:17Z</updated>
 <link rel="self" href="https://api.datamarket.azure.com/Data.ashx/➥
 Zillow/MortgageInformationAPIs/
GetRateSummary?State='IL'&amp;$top=100" />
 <entry>
  <id>https://api.datamarket.azure.com/Data.ashx/Zillow/MortgageInformationAPIs/
GetRateSummary?State='IL'&amp;$skip=0&amp;$top=1</id>
  <title type="text">RateSummaryEntity</title>
  <updated>2012-03-01T12:53:17Z</updated>
  <link rel="self" href="https://api.datamarket.azure.com/Data.ashx/Zillow/Mortgage➥
  InformationAPIs/
GetRateSummary?State='IL'&amp;$skip=0&amp;$top=1" />
  <content type="application/xml">
   <m:properties>
    <d:ThirtyYearFixedToday m:type="Edm.Double">3.8</d:ThirtyYearFixedToday>
    <d:ThirtyYearFixedCountToday m:type="Edm.Double">
      94
    </d:ThirtyYearFixedCountToday>

    <d:FifteenYearFixedToday m:type="Edm.Double">
```

```
    3.04</d:FifteenYearFixedToday>
  <d:FifteenYearFixedCountToday m:type="Edm.Double">
    87
  </d:FifteenYearFixedCountToday>
  <d:FiveOneARMToday m:type="Edm.Double">2.84</d:FiveOneARMToday>
  <d:FiveOneARMCountToday m:type="Edm.Double">28</d:FiveOneARMCountToday>
  <d:ThirtyYearFixedLastWeek m:type="Edm.Double">
    3.75
  </d:ThirtyYearFixedLastWeek>
  <d:ThirtyYearFixedCountLastWeek m:type="Edm.Double">
    5695
  </d:ThirtyYearFixedCountLastWeek>
  <d:FifteenYearFixedLastWeek m:type="Edm.Double">
    3.0
   </d:FifteenYearFixedLastWeek>
  <d:FifteenYearFixedCountLastWeek m:type="Edm.Double">
    4950
  </d:FifteenYearFixedCountLastWeek>
  <d:FiveOneARMLastWeek m:type="Edm.Double">2.59</d:FiveOneARMLastWeek>
  <d:FiveOneARMCountLastWeek m:type="Edm.Double">
    2928
  </d:FiveOneARMCountLastWeek>
 </m:properties>
  </content>
 </entry>
</feed>
```

Managing Your Account

Now that you have an account and have subscribed to one or more datasets, you'll need to know how to manage your account settings, which includes managing your account keys and datasets. You can manage your account from the My Account pages, which you access from the My Account link located in the top menu bar on the Windows Azure Marketplace interface. This page has links on the left side:

➤ **Account Information:** Clicking this displays the Account Details page, as shown in Figure 12-12. This page contains your contact information, customer ID, and primary account key. This key should be treated like a password and not provided to everyone. From this page you can edit your account information or view your billing history in the Microsoft Billing and Account Management pages. You cannot edit your primary account key or custom ID.

➤ **My Data:** Clicking this displays the My Data page, as shown in Figure 12-13, which includes a list of your subscribed datasets with details such as a transaction count for those subscriptions that are not free. From this page you can view the subscription information, cancel a subscription, open the Service Explorer, or view the accepted publisher terms. The My Data page is also where you monitor how many transactions are left in the billing cycle. Figure 12-13 shows five different datasets of which four have a transaction limit.

➤ **Account Keys:** Clicking this displays the Account Keys page, as shown in Figure 12-14, where you manage your Marketplace accounts. This is one place where you can find all your keys. From this page you may add new account keys, and edit or remove any additional account keys. You cannot remove the default key. These keys are used during the authentication process.

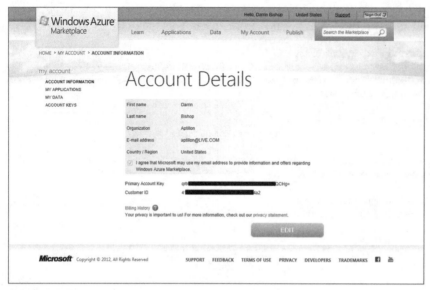

FIGURE 12-12

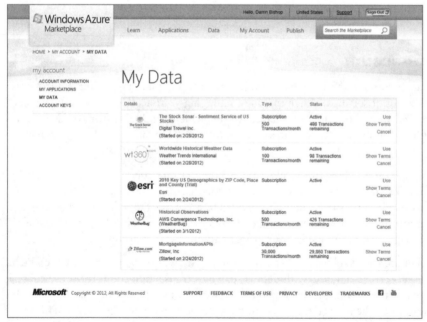

FIGURE 12-13

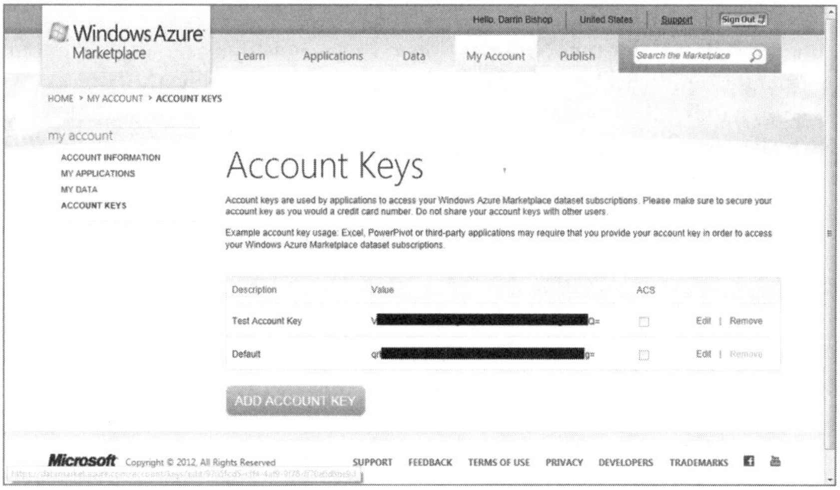

FIGURE 12-14

PROGRAMMING DATAMARKET

Datamarket data can be exported and used by many existing applications including Excel, PowerPivot, and Tablau (an end user business intelligence tool). Exporting data as XML or as a comma-separated value formatted file (.csv) opens up the number of applications that can use the data. All these tools work well to browse, filter, and explore the data to find some trend or data point.

What about consuming Datamarket data in a mashup or custom application? Datamarket is easily consumed by applications of all types, including .NET or other platforms. Datamarket data can also be consumed by forms-based, web-based, console-based, and mobile applications to meet the requirements of your business.

Datamarket Concepts

Datamarket helps to standardize how you can access various data potentially residing in different data stores in the cloud. Datamarket achieves this by using common well-known schemas and protocols such as OAuth, OData, AtomPub, JSON, and HTTPS. Using these common schemas and protocols allows standardized access to data by .NET applications and non-.NET applications alike.

This section covers core concepts that you will need to know to programmatically work with Datamarket datasets.

OData and WCF Data Services

OData stands for *Open Data Protocol*, which defines a common access method to data using standard web technologies. This access method adds, edits, deletes, and queries data abstracted from the storage mechanism. Building on common web-based technologies such as AtomPub, JSON, HTTP, and XML, data stores supporting OData can be accessed from any application that can create and process a simple web request. For more information on OData, visit www.odata.org/.

Datamarket data is served up using WCF Data Services, which is a .NET framework supporting the creation and consumption of OData. For the .NET developer, this means that you have the main plumbing required to generate a query to Datamarket and make the results easily available as class entities. There is no need to hand-code web requests, create OData queries, or parse XML results into entity objects. WCF Data Services provides this functionality. For more information on WCF Data Services, go to `http://msdn.microsoft.com/en-us/data/bb931106`.

 WCF Data Services provides much of the common plumbing for an OData request. The proxy objects created on the client side require a .NET language. Developers not working in a .NET language can still use web requests and other OData frameworks to query and retrieve data from Datamarket.

Authentication

Datamarket supports two authentication scenarios at this time: Basic Authentication and OAuth. This chapter focuses only on Basic Authentication but understanding the difference between the two scenarios is important for a developer consuming Datamarket datasets.

Basic Authentication is simply passing a user's credentials along with the web request. As the name implies, it is one the most basic methods to authenticate a user. In the .NET world it is simple to create a NetworkCredential and attach it to the request. Although simplicity is the key with Basic Authentication, it does have its detractors. Basic Authentication uses a single account to control access. There is no management of users; it is all or nothing because everyone uses the single key for access. All transactions incurred with Basic Authentication are assigned to the owner of the key.

OAuth is a token-based authentication system that is increasingly in use because of the network of available social applications. Datamarket can use OAuth to authenticate users, but compared to Basic Authentication, it's a bit more challenging to implement. Using OAuth in your application to authenticate to Datamarket requires you to register the application with Marketplace. For more information on OAuth and Datamarket, go to `http://msdn.microsoft.com/en-us/library/windowsazure/gg193416.aspx`.

Query Types

Accessing data involves creating and submitting queries to Datamarket. Content providers determine the queries that are allowed for the dataset. The Details tab located on the dataset's information page (refer to Figure 12-7) includes the supported types of queries. Figure 12-15 shows the supported queries for the Stock Sonar - Sentiment Service of US Stocks dataset.

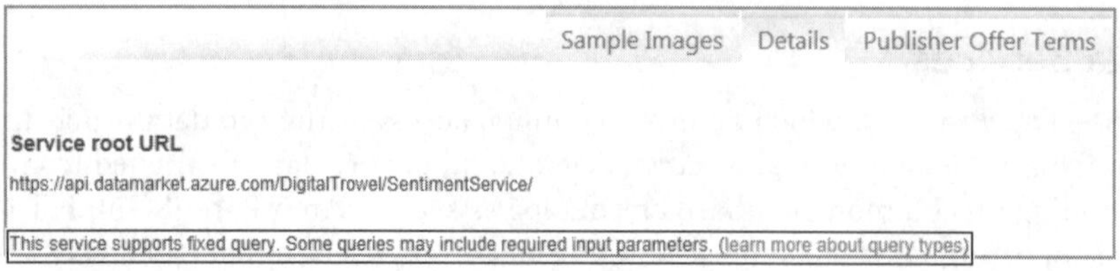

Sample Images   Details   Publisher Offer Terms

Service root URL

https://api.datamarket.azure.com/DigitalTrowel/SentimentService/

This service supports fixed query. Some queries may include required input parameters. (learn more about query types)

FIGURE 12-15

Datasets in Datamarket supports two types of queries: Fixed and Flexible. Each dataset may support both types of queries:

➤ **Fixed queries:** These are the most common query types and are predefined queries that generally have required and optional parameters. Predefined queries create a limit on how you can access the data; the query creates a "box" around the data. Fixed queries are supported in .NET with a provided proxy class available from the dataset's detail page. You can use this proxy to simplify the code required to access the dataset. The provided proxy for a Fixed query uses WCD Data Services internally to access the dataset. This chapter includes an example using a fixed query.

➤ **Flexible queries:** Are just that—flexible. Currently there are far fewer datasets that provide Flexible queries. Flexible queries remove the artificial box that Fixed query creates and allows more access to the dataset. Flexible queries support the name/value pair convention for parameters via the URL and support most of the available OData query options. For a current list of supported OData query options, see the Supported OData located at `http://msdn.microsoft.com/en-us/library/windowsazure/gg312156.aspx`. Flexible queries are supported in .NET by adding a .NET Service Reference to the project.

Building a Fixed Query Datamarket Application

This section covers how simple it is to create an application that uses a Fixed query to retrieve data from a Datamarket dataset. This application queries and retrieves data from the Zillow MortgageInformationAPIs available from Datamarket. The MortgageInformationAPIs dataset provides two fixed queries to retrieve data from the dataset. This application shown in Figure 12-16 uses the `GetRateSummary` query to retrieve average mortgage rates. To create the application, follow these steps:

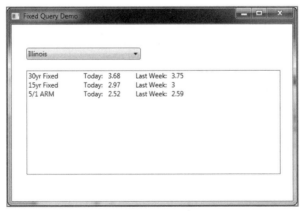

FIGURE 12-16

> *To complete the demo application you must create a Marketplace account and subscribe to the Zillow MortgageInformationAPIs. The first section of this chapter discusses how to create a Marketplace account and subscribe to datasets.*

1. **Locate and open the starter project for the Fixed Query application.** The project is named `Wiley.Datamarket.MortgageRates` and is available in the code download for Chapter 12 (search `www.wrox.com` using the book ISBN). The starter project is a WPF application and includes most of the code and markup not directly associated with the accessing Datamarket.

> *The completed project minus the account keys is available with the chapter content.*

2. **Download the proxy.** Fixed queries are supported by a predefined proxy supplied from Datamarket. You must downloaded the proxy (shown in this step) and add it to the project (shown in the next step). The link to download the proxy is located on the dataset's information page. To access the link you must be logged into the Marketplace with an account that has a subscription to the MortgageInformationAPIs dataset. Figure 12-17 shows the .NET C# Class Library link. Click the link and download the proxy to your computer.

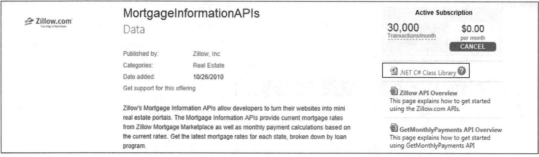

FIGURE 12-17

3. **Add the proxy class to the project.** Right-click the project name in the Solution Explorer pane, click Add, and then click Existing Item. Navigate to the downloaded `MortgageInformationApiContainer` `.cs` file, and click Add. Figure 12-18 shows the proxy class added to the project.

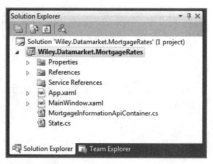

FIGURE 12-18

If you review the `MortgageInformationApiContainer`, *you can see a small amount of code for the specifics of the two queries:* `GetRateSummary` *and* `GetMonthlyPayments`. *These methods create and return a* `DataServiceQuery`. *When executed the* `DataServiceQuery` *retrieves the data from the data service in DataMarket.*

4. **Include an assembly reference.** The proxy requires a reference to the `System.Data.Services.Client` assembly. To include this assembly reference in the project, right-click the project name in Solution Explorer. Then select Add Reference. Select the .NET tab from the Add Reference Dialog box, and select `System.Data.Services.Client`. Then click OK. Figure 12-19 shows the Solution Explorer with the `System.Data.Services.Client` reference.

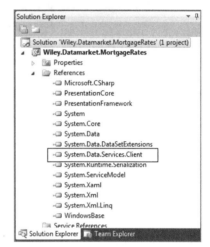

Now you're set to query and display data retrieved from Zillow's MortgageInformationAPIs dataset.

FIGURE 12-19

5. **Add the using statement.** You do this by right-clicking `MainWindow.xaml` in the Solution Explorer and clicking View Code to open the `MainWindow.xaml` .cs file. Add the following `Using` statement to the list of existing `Using` statements:

```
Using Zillow;
```

6. **Create a results collection.** You need to create an `ObservableCollection`-based property to contain the results. The user interface uses data binding to display `RateSummeryEntity` objects returned from Datamarket. Add the code in Listing 12-2 to the `MainWindows.xaml` .cs file below the comment `//TODO: Add Rates collection` (see the bold code).

LISTING 12-2: The Completed MainWindow Constructor

```
private ObservableCollection<RateSummaryEntity> _rates;
public ObservableCollection<RateSummaryEntity> Rates
{
   get { return _rates; }
}

public MainWindow()
{
  InitializeComponent();

  //TODO: Initial _rates collection
```

continues

LISTING 12-2 *(continued)*

```
_rates = new ObservableCollection<RateSummaryEntity>();
this.DataContext = this;
LoadStates();
cboState.SelectedIndex = 0;
}
```

With the results collection defined and initialized, the next step is to create a method to query the dataset and populate the results collection with the result.

7.   **Query the dataset by creating a method named GetStateMortgageAvg.** This method accepts a string parameter of a state abbreviation. Listing 12-3 shows the completed method.

LISTING 12-3: The GetStateMortgageAvg Method

```
private void GetStateMortgageAvg(string stateAbbreviation)
{
  Rates.Clear();
  MortgageInformationApiContainer mortgageClient =
        new MortgageInformationApiContainer(
                                new Uri(
            "https://api.datamarket.azure.com/Zillow/MortgageInformationAPIs"));

  NetworkCredential credentials = new NetworkCredential();
  credentials.UserName = "[Your Email Account]";
  credentials.Password = "[Your Marketplace Key]";

  mortgageClient.Credentials = credentials;
  //Catch Average selection
  string stateAbr = stateAbbreviation == "AV" ? "" : stateAbbreviation;

  var results = mortgageClient.GetRateSummary(stateAbr);

  foreach (RateSummaryEntity rates in results)
  {
   Rates.Add(rates);
  }
}
```

 To run this application, include your Marketplace e-mail address and the Marketplace key. You can find the key on the My Accounts pages in Azure Marketplace.

8.   **Complete the ComboBox event handler.** You do this by adding a final line of code to the application, which is the call to GetStateMortgageAvg method from the existing cboState_ SelectionChanged event handler. This event handler is called when a user selects a state. Listing 12-4 contains the completed cboState_SelectionChanged event handler.

LISTING 12-4: The Completed cboState_SelectionChanged Event Handler

```
private void cboState_SelectionChanged(object sender, SelectionChangedEventArgs e)
{
 ComboBox s = sender as ComboBox;
 State selectedState = s.SelectedItem as State;

 //TODO: Call GetStateMortgageAvg Function
 GetStateMortgageAvg(selectedState.Abbreviation);
}
```

The Fixed Query application is now complete. You can build and run the application by pressing F5 in Visual Studio. The application initially calls into GetStateMortgageAvg with the AV abbreviation. This queries the dataset for mortgage rates based on an average of all states. It is in this method that the proxy is used to connect to Datamarket and query the dataset. Notice that a network credential is associated with the request in the GetStateMortgageAgg method. See Figure 12-20.

When you select a state from the drop-down control, the application calls GetStateMortgageAvg passing in the associated state abbreviation. Figure 12-21 displays the current averages for the State of Illinois.

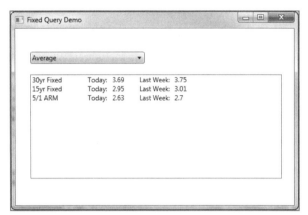

FIGURE 12-20

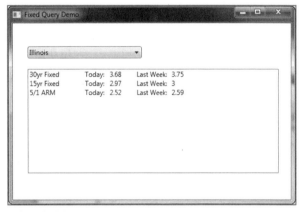

FIGURE 12-21

Building a Flexible Query Datamarket Application

This section shows how simple it is to create an application that uses a Flexible query to retrieve data from a Datamarket dataset. This application queries and retrieves data from the WeatherBug Historical Observations available from Datamarket. This dataset provides a limited number of monthly transactions for free and supports Flexible queries. The Historical Observations supports Flexible queries to query WeatherBug stations and historical weather observations. The Flexible query application, as shown in Figure 12-22, uses a Flexible query to return a list of weather stations located within a specific ZIP code. Selecting a specific weather station generates another query to retrieve a set of historical weather observations generated from the selected station.

> *To complete the demonstration application, you need to create a Marketplace account and subscribe to the WeatherBug Historical Observations. Refer to the first section of this chapter to create a Marketplace account and subscribe to datasets.*

1. **Open the starter project.** Locate and open the starter project for the Fixed Query application. The project is named `Wiley.DataMarket.WeatherBug` and is available in the code download for Chapter 12 (search `www.wrox.com` using the book ISBN). The starter project is a WPF application and includes most of the code and markup not directly associated with the accessing Datamarket.

> *The completed project minus the account keys is available with the chapter content.*

2. **Add the WeatherBug Historical Observation service reference to the project.** Flexible queries are supported by a .NET service reference. Adding the service reference creates the proxies to access the dataset using WCF Data Services from the client. To add the service reference to the project, right-click the project name in the Solution Explorer, and select Add Service Reference. Enter the URL to the service reference in the Address list box. You can find the URL address to the service reference on the information page for the dataset or in the Service Explorer. Enter `https://api.datamarket.azure.com/WeatherBug/HistoricalObservations/` into the Address list box, and click Go. After you locate the service, enter a Namespace value of **WeatherBugSvc**. Figure 12-23 shows the Add Service Reference dialog. Click OK to add the service reference to the project.

Flexible Query

Station

Lincoln Land Community College

Station Information

Lincoln Land Community College
Springfield, IL 62703

High Temp	High Temp	Low Temp	Wind Gust	Monthly Rain	Yearly Rain
12/27/2010 12:00:00 AM	22.039	12.815	13.592	0.32	40.35
12/26/2010 12:00:00 AM	29.577	21.086	24.333	0.32	40.35
12/25/2010 12:00:00 AM	28.455	25.361	24.114	0.32	40.35
12/24/2010 12:00:00 AM	30.251	27.831	15.565	0.32	40.35
12/23/2010 12:00:00 AM	36.044	25.917	11.619	0.32	40.35
12/22/2010 12:00:00 AM	31.6	21.643	28.279	0.32	40.35
12/21/2010 12:00:00 AM	42.46	32.165	18.195	0.32	40.35
12/20/2010 12:00:00 AM	36.777	28.675	26.745	0.32	40.35
12/19/2010 12:00:00 AM	25.428	22.825	6.706	0.32	40.35

FIGURE 12-22

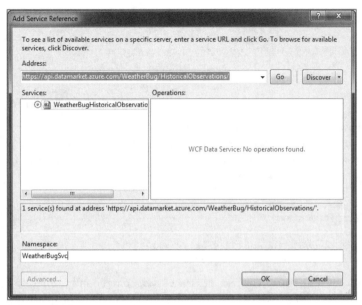

FIGURE 12-23

3. **Set credential values.** You do so by right-clicking `MainWindow.xaml` in the Solution Explorer and clicking View Code to open `MainWindow.xaml.cs`. Locate the `_userId` and `_pwd` variables under the class declaration. Enter the Live ID e-mail and account key associated with your Marketplace account.

4. **Create the StationList ObservableCollection property.** The `StationList` `ObservableCollection` property contains the list of weather stations retrieved from the dataset. The `Statlist` type is defined and added to the project by the service reference. The user interface databinds to this collection to populate the Station ComboBox. Listing 12-5 includes the complete `StationList` property. Add this property below the class level variables in the `MainWindow` class.

LISTING 12-5: **StationList Property Code**

```
public ObservableCollection<Statlist> StationList
{
  get;
  private set;
}
```

5. **Create the StationObservations ObservableCollection property.** The `StationObservations` `ObservableCollection` property contains the list of weather observations retrieved from the dataset. The `HistHilo` type is defined and added to the project by the service reference. The user interface data binds to this collection to populate the grid displaying the station's observations. Listing 12-6 includes the complete `StationObservations` property. Add this property below the `StationList ObservableCollection` property created in step 4.

LISTING 12-6: StationObservations Property Code

```
public ObservableCollection<HistHilo> StationObservations
{
  get;
  private set;
}
```

6. **Initialize the ObserableCollections.** The two properties are backed by an `ObserableCollection`. The properties must be initialized before use. Locate the `MainWindow` constructor and initialize the two properties by adding the code in Listing 12-7 after the `DataContext` is set.

LISTING 12-7: Initializing Properties

```
StationList = new ObservableCollection<Statlist>();
StationObservations = new ObservableCollection<HistHilo>();
```

7. **Populate the Station ComboBox.** The user interface uses a databound ComboBox to display a list of weather stations retrieved from the dataset. This requires a query against the Datamarket dataset. The query filters the retrieved weather stations located in a specific ZIP code. The skeleton `GetWeatherStation` method exists in the starter project. Listing 12-8 shows the completed `GetWeatherStation` method.

LISTING 12-8: Retrieving Weather Stations

```
private void GetWeatherStations()
{
  StationList.Clear();

  WeatherBugSvc.WeatherBugHistoricalObservationsContainer svc =
   new WeatherBugSvc.WeatherBugHistoricalObservationsContainer(
   new Uri(_svcRootUrl));

  svc.Credentials = new NetworkCredential(_userId, _pwd);

  //Query for stations that have the value of _zipCode.
  //Order by station name
  IEnumerable<Statlist> stations = svc.Statlist
      .Where((station) => station.Zip_Code == _zipCode.ToString())
      .OrderBy((station) => station.Station_Name);

  //execute the query and add each result station to the
  //StationList collection
  stations.ToList().ForEach((station) => StationList.Add(station));
}
```

Simply creating the query does not immediately execute the query. This query is not executed until the results are requested. In the GetWeatherStations *method the results are requested when the stations variable is converted to a list using* stations.ToList(). *At this time the query is sent to Datamarket and processed. The results are added to the* StationList ObservableCollection, *which is bound to the user interface.*

Listing 12-9 shows the complete MainWindow constructor with the GetWeatherStations method call.

LISTING 12-9: Completed MainWindows Constructor

```
public MainWindow()
{
  InitializeComponent();
  this.DataContext = this;

  StationList = new ObservableCollection<Statlist>();
  StationObservations = new ObservableCollection<HistHilo>();
  GetWeatherStations();
}
```

At this time the application should compile and populate the ComboBox with weather stations.

8.   **Populate the Observation Grid.** After you select a station from the ComboBox, the application can retrieve a collection of observations made from the selected station. This involves another query to the dataset and another transaction. The GetStationHiLos method exists in the starter project and is responsible for retrieving the station observations.

Listing 12-10 includes the complete GetStationHiLos method. Use Listing 12-10 to complete the GetStationHiLos method.

LISTING 12-10: The Completed GetStationHiLos Method

```
private void GetStationHiLos(string stationId)
{
 StationObservations.Clear();

 WeatherBugSvc.WeatherBugHistoricalObservationsContainer svc = new
          WeatherBugSvc.WeatherBugHistoricalObservationsContainer(
                                          new Uri(_svcRootUrl));
 svc.Credentials = new NetworkCredential(_userId, _pwd);

 IEnumerable<HistHilo> observations = svc.HistHilo
              .Where((hilo) => hilo.Station_ID == stationId)
              .OrderByDescending((hilo) => hilo.Observation_Date);
```

continues

LISTING 12-10 *(continued)*

```
        observations.ToList().ForEach((hilo) => StationObservations.Add(hilo));
    }
```

The `GetStationHiLos` method is similar to the `GetWeatherStation` method. This method filters the `HistHilo` collection for items that have a matching `Station_ID` value and places those items in the `StationObservations` property, which is databound to the user interface. The query returns a collection of `HistHilo` entity objects. The `HistHilo` entity class was created when the service reference was added to the project.

The `GetStationHiLos` method should be called when the selected station changes. This requires a transaction for each change of station. To keep the user-interface grid in sync with the currently selected station, the ComboBox's `SelectionChanged` event is used. The completed `cboStation_SelectionChanged` method is shown in Listing 12-11. Two method calls were added. The first `SetStationDetails` is called to populate the selected station name and location in the user interface. Then the `GetStationHiLos` is called to retrieve the stations' observations.

LISTING 12-11: The Completed SelectionChanged Event

```
private void cboStation_SelectionChanged(object sender,
                                SelectionChangedEventArgs e)
{
    ClearStationDetails();
    ComboBox c = sender as ComboBox;
    Statlist stationItem = c.SelectedItem as Statlist;
    SetStationDetails(stationItem);
    GetStationHiLos(stationItem.Station_ID);
}
```

The Flexible query application is now complete. Build and run the application by pressing F5 in Visual Studio. The application initially retrieves the stations for the ZIP code. Selecting a specific station from the ComboBox generates a query to Datamarket for the observable collections for the station. The complete code for example shows the simplicity of accessing data from Datamarket using a Flexible query as most of the common plumbing has been created by the addition of the service reference.

SUMMARY

The amount of data available to the user and developer is massive. The various access methods, authentication requirements, account management, and billing processes make it difficult for an organization to efficiently consume the available data. Simply finding the right data source can be problematic.

Datamarket simplifies the overhead of working with many different data sources. It does so by creating a consistent experience when you work with cloud data regardless of who owns the content or how the content is stored. Using open web technologies allows a reach beyond the Microsoft .NET tools. For those using .NET languages, integrating the data into an application is even easier with the support provided by service references and proxies.

Organizations that have premium content should look to Datamarket in order to reduce the amount of overhead of maintain the account management billing as well as a storefront. Datamarket enables content publishers to focus on content and not plumbing.

13

Service Bus

WHAT'S IN THIS CHAPTER?

➤ Understanding the Service Bus

➤ Programming Service Bus brokered messaging

➤ Selecting between REST and managed clients

➤ Choosing between Service Bus Brokered Messaging and
   Windows Azure Queues

An important component of any cloud architecture is the means by which the various components communicate. This chapter examines the September 2011 Release of the Service Bus, a cloud-hosted platform designed to enable on-premises to on-premises, cloud-hosted to cloud-hosted, and hybrid on-premises to cloud-hosted communication scenarios.

WHAT IS SERVICE BUS?

The Windows Azure Service Bus represents a rich collection of cloud-hosted services that enables both brokered and relayed communication scenarios. This section introduces the major features Service Bus provides.

Understanding Service Bus Brokered Messaging

Service Bus brokered messaging takes the basic concept of a hosted queue and extends it to provide support for:

➤ **Publish-subscribe messaging:** This is where one sender can broadcast messages to multiple interested recipients.

➤ **Temporal decoupling:** This is where recipients do not need to be online when senders transmit.

➤ **Load leveling:** A situation in which a spike of sent messages does not overwhelm recipients who see a constant stream of messages.

These features enable message-driven communication between managed and REST clients, both on-premises and cloud-hosted, so long as the Service Bus is accessible from the clients by TCP or outbound HTTP. Clients can be written in .NET using the Service Bus managed library communicating via TCP/IP utilizing the Service Bus client protocol. Alternatively, clients can communicate across HTTP from any platform that supports the REST style of communication.

At its core, Service Bus brokered messaging relies on three primary components: queues, topics, and subscriptions.

➤ **Queue:** Provides the simplest offering of the traditional first-in-first-out queue, albeit with many enhancements you see later in the chapter. Senders can send messages to a queue and receivers can receive messages from that queue.

➤ **Topic:** A form of queue to which senders send messages, but with a twist. Messages sent to the topic are then broadcast to subscriptions and consumers receive their messages from a subscription instead of the topic.

➤ **Subscriptions:** Subscriptions are like virtual queues or views (in the relational database sense) that are overlaid above the topic. Receivers pull messages from subscriptions. Subscriptions enable filtering, which means that even though all messages are sent to a topic, not all messages are ultimately seen by a consumer of the subscription, as some may be filtered out.

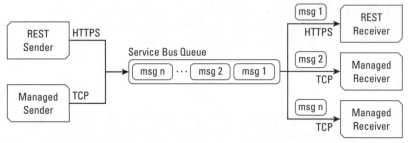

FIGURE 13-1

Figure 13-1 shows a single Service Bus queue that has two senders adding messages to the queue. The same queue also has three receivers pulling messages from it. Observe, as implied in the diagram, that queues support REST and managed clients simultaneously. The same is also true for topics and subscriptions.

In the default case, each subscription receives every message sent to the topic, and in this case functions similarly to a queue, except messages are sent to a topic and received from a subscription.

Subscriptions offer richer functionality than simply multicasting to multiple receivers across multiple subscriptions, however, because they support filters, actions, and rules.

➤ **Filter:** Enables the subscription to look at properties of a message sent to the topic to decide if the message should be made available by the subscription to its consumers

➤ **Action:** Adds, removes, or alters message properties and values

➤ **Rule:** A container describing an action and filter pair

For example, for a given topic with two subscriptions and one receiver for each subscription, when a producer sends a message to the topic, the message is received separately by both receivers from their respective subscription—unless there is a rule in place that defines a filter. Figure 13-2 demonstrates this scenario, where receiver A gets only the one message from subscription A that matches the filter condition. Receiver B gets all the messages sent to the topic from subscription B because no filter is configured.

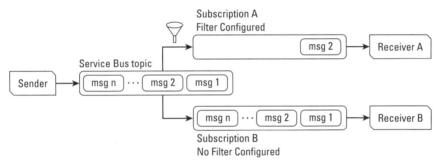

FIGURE 13-2

Each rule specifies a filter, an action, or both. A rule can be defined as just a filter, with no explicit action defined, to select which messages a subscription receives. A rule can also define a filter to determine when to apply an action that manipulates message properties and values (for example, messages that match the filter have their properties altered according to the action).

Rules enable you to create subscriptions that funnel messages to different consumers. For example, you could create a subscription that accepts only high-priority messages (such as paying customers) and are processed by a near real-time consumer, whereas all other messages (such as those from demo customers) get consumed by a scheduled process. You accomplish this by having a rule with a filter that examines whatever message property you deem contains the priority flag. Those that match go to the high-priority subscription and those that do not go to the normal-priority subscription.

By leveraging topics and subscriptions, you can plug in additional subscriptions to the topic at any time. For example, if at some point you need to add a consumer that logs details about messages for auditing purposes without affecting the regular processing of messages, you would simply create a new subscription for this, leaving the other subscriptions unaffected.

Understanding Service Bus Relayed Messaging

The Service Bus Relayed Messaging feature set enables bidirectional communication between message senders (clients) and listeners (services) via a cloud-hosted service referred to as a *relay service*. In this scenario, clients and services may be hosted on-premises, in Azure roles or in some combination of the two. Senders may be implemented with WCF or with any platform supporting REST communication, whereas listeners are traditionally implemented as WCF services. Listeners and senders can communicate over TCP and HTTP/S.

The relay is designed so communication between senders and listeners can easily traverse network boundaries and firewalls. Communication between sender and listener that ordinarily traverses the cloud-hosted relay can "upgrade" to direct communication between sender and listener, for example, when the sender and listeners are on the same network (see Figure 13-3). In addition, the relay provides features for event-distribution to large numbers of listeners, and a naming registry that quickly updates to list the registered service endpoints of listeners.

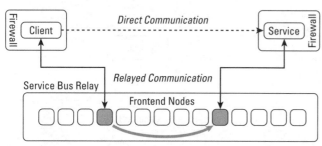

FIGURE 13-3

The key difference between Relayed and Brokered Messaging is that the former requires both client and server to be online at the same time to exchange messages.

> *The relayed messaging feature set of Service Bus is covered in the book* Professional WCF 4: Windows Communication Foundation with .NET 4, *published by Wrox. We will not repeat that content here, and instead focus on the large swath of newer features released with Service Bus Brokered Messaging.*

Other Features

If you explore the Service Bus APIs or documentation, you may find references to Service Bus Message Buffers. This functionality was designed to provide a transient, in-memory buffer for decoupled communication in a style similar to queues. Message Buffers have been superseded by the brokered messaging functionality and are maintained for backward compatibility only (in other words unlikely to receive future enhancements). For new solutions, you should use the Brokered Messaging features of queues, topics, and subscriptions.

PROGRAMMING SERVICE BUS BROKERED MESSAGING

Service Bus Brokered Messaging can be programmed using both a managed library and directly from REST clients. This section demonstrates how to leverage the Service Bus first from the managed world and later from a REST client.

Understanding Prerequisites

Before you can write your first line of code against a queue, you need to create a Service Namespace for your Service Bus. You can think of a *Service Namespace* as an application boundary for all Service Bus resources your application might use and as the moniker under which usage charges accrue. The important results of creating a Service Namespace are the namespace and a shared secret key that you will need for access to Service Bus services.

To create a Service Namespace, follow these steps:

1. Log in to the Azure Management Portal (at `http://windows.azure.com`) with your Windows Live ID.

2. Click the Service Bus, Access Control & Caching tab in the lower left of the screen (see Figure 13-4). The Service Bus, Access Control & Caching screen should load with the AppFabric node selected in the tree on the left.

3. Click the { } New button at the top left of the screen to display the Create a New Service Namespace dialog.

4. For the purposes in this chapter, you must have only the Service Bus item checked. Fill in a value for your Namespace, choose a Country/Region from the drop-down, and ensure the Subscription selected is the subscription under which you want the Service Namespace created.

FIGURE 13-4

 You do not need to select a connection pack for the demos you follow in this chapter; just leave it set to 0 Connections. For production use of the relay, you need to use a Connection Pack that gets you a discounted rate, but because your demos will not make use of the relay, there is no reason to commit to any connection pack.

5. Continue by clicking Create Namespace, as shown in Figure 13-5.

6. In the Properties tab on the right, scroll down until you can see the Default Key property. Click View. This displays a dialog showing the Default Issuer (which is "owner") and the Default Key (which is a base 64 encoded sequence of characters). The Default Issuer is your username, and the Default Key is your password to your Service Namespace. You need these values if you attempt to run the sample code that follows, and anytime you make use of the Service Bus Brokered Messaging features.

A few minutes later, you should see your new Namespace listed under the Service Bus category (the node underneath AppFabric in the tree) with a status of Active, as shown in Figure 13-6.

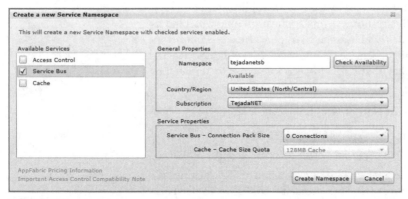

FIGURE 13-5

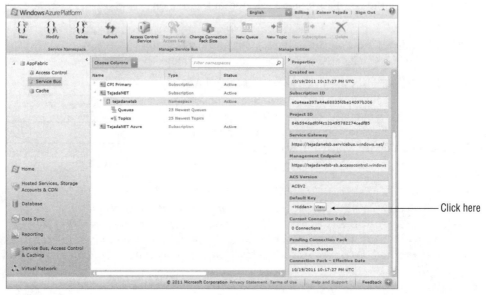

Click here

FIGURE 13-6

In addition to providing you with these important credentials, you can also use the Azure Management Portal to examine useful runtime information about existing queues, topics, and subscriptions. For example, the Portal provides the message count and storage sizes in MB of queues and the storage size in MB of topics. Currently, it does not provide the message counts for subscriptions. You can also use the Portal to create new queues, topics, and subscriptions with your service namespace.

Building a Managed Queue Client

You should build a managed client when your code to send or receive messages runs within a .NET process or if the code has access to the .NET framework. So what does it take to build a managed queue client? This section shows how to create a queue in your Service Namespace and send messages to it. You also see how to receive messages from it. For all the samples in this chapter you can start with the Console project that Visual Studio 2010 provides, or, more simply, just use LINQPad to run the code provided as shown in the text. Either way, you need to add a reference to the `Microsoft.ServiceBus.dll` assembly that is available with the Windows Azure AppFabric SDK version 1.5. This assembly contains all the classes you need to interact with Service Bus Brokered Messaging. You will also likely want to add using or import statements for the namespaces `Microsoft.ServiceBus` and `Microsoft.ServiceBus.Messaging`.

 You can download the latest Windows Azure SDKs, including those for Service Bus, from `http://www.microsoft.com/windowsazure/sdk/`.

Building a Namespace

To build a build a Namespace, follow these steps:

1. You need the credentials to your Namespace that you acquired from the management portal. The Service Bus authenticates clients by requiring them to present a token acquired from Access Control Service (ACS), and ACS authenticates the clients with a service namespace, issuer name, and issuer key.

2. When you create a Service Namespace in the management portal, ACS is configured for you to issue this token. Therefore, the first order of business is to handle acquiring the token from ACS, which you can accomplish by instantiating a `TokenProvider` as shown in the following code. A `TokenProvider`, such as the `SharedSecretTokenProvider` used here, handles acquiring and renewing tokens from ACS automatically.

 The sample code `Dump()` *has an extension method that functions identically to* `Console.WriteLine()` *when you run it within LINQpad. It simply prints out the string version of the object that precedes it to the output window. If you are re-typing this code in Visual Studio, instead of opening the provided sample project, just use* `Console.WriteLine()` *instead and pass it the object you want to output.*

Available for download on Wrox.com

```
string issuerName = "owner";
string issuerKey = "<INSERT YOUR ISSUER KEY>";
string serviceNamespace = "<INSERT YOUR SERVICE NAMESPACE>";
string queueName = "PrimaryQueue";

TokenProvider tokenProvider = TokenProvider.
```

```
CreateSharedSecretTokenProvider(
            issuerName, issuerKey);
```

3. Create a Queue programmatically. The functionality for creating a queue, deleting existing queues, and checking for existence is exposed through a `NamespaceManager` as shown in the following code:

```
Uri serviceUri = ServiceBusEnvironment.CreateServiceUri("sb",
        serviceNamespace, string.Empty);

NamespaceManager namespaceManager =
        new NamespaceManager(serviceUri, tokenProvider);

"Checking if queue already exists...".Dump();
if (namespaceManager.QueueExists(queueName))
{
        "Deleting queue...".Dump();
        namespaceManager.DeleteQueue(queueName);
}

"Creating queue...".Dump();
QueueDescription queueDescription =
        namespaceManager.CreateQueue(queueName);
```

The constructor of a `NamespaceManager` requires the URI to your service namespace (in the form `sb://<serviceNamespace>.servicebus.windows.net/`), which you can easily construct using the `CreateServiceUri` static method of the `ServiceBusEnvironment` class. Although this is just a simple URI that you could create by hand, it is recommended that you use this method instead of building the string to protect your code in case the service URI format changes in the future.

This example constructs the `namespaceManager` and uses it to ensure that you start from a clean slate, deleting the queue if it happens to exist from a previous demo run so you do not get an error when re-creating an existing queue. You make the call to create the queue through `namespace Manager.CreateQueue()`, passing it the wanted name of the queue. The name of the queue can be a path of any depth (for example, `top/left/center/myqueue`), so long as it less than 290 characters. The call to `CreateQueue` returns a `QueueDescription` object that provides all the properties describing the queue, all of which are simply the default values at this point. One property of interest to you is the `queueDescription.Path`, which contains that `queueName` you provided.

Sending Messages to the Queue

Now you're ready to start sending messages to the queue. You do this by acquiring a `QueueClient` from a `MessagingFactory` instance. You can use a `QueueClient` to send or receive messages from queue. Note that creating a `QueueClient` results in you also opening a persistent TCP connection to the queue.

```
//Create the queue client and use it to send messages to the queue
MessagingFactory messagingFactory =
        MessagingFactory.Create(serviceUri, tokenProvider);
```

```
QueueClient queueClient =
        messagingFactory.CreateQueueClient(queueDescription.Path);
for (int i = 0; i < 5; i++)
{
        BrokeredMessage msg =
          new BrokeredMessage(string.Format("Message #{0:00}", i));
        msg.MessageId = i.ToString();

        queueClient.Send(msg);
        string.Format("Sent message with ID: {0} and Body: {1}",
                msg.MessageId, msg.GetBody<string>()).Dump();
}
```

code snippet Simple Queue Producer.linq

Messages are represented by the `BrokeredMessage` class which allows you, among other things, to specify various message properties and content for the body (which must be serializable) of the message. In this example, you create a message with a body containing the string text `Message #xx` (passing that formatted string into the `BrokeredMessage` constructor) and a `MessageId` property with the value of the counter. To enqueue the message, you call the `Send` method of the `QueueClient` and pass it the `BrokeredMessage` instance.

When your loop completes, you'll have sent all five messages and should wait for your consumers to run their code to retrieve messages before cleaning up the queue.

```
"Messages sent. Ensure consumer is running.".Dump();
Thread.Sleep(120000);

//Cleanup sample
queueClient.Close();

//Deletes queue and any messages within
namespaceManager.DeleteQueue(queueName);
"Deleted queue.".Dump();

"Finished.".Dump();
```

code snippet Simple Queue Producer.linq

The output of this should look as follows:

```
Checking if queue already exists...
Deleting queue...
Creating queue...
Sent message with ID: 0 and Body: Message #00
Sent message with ID: 1 and Body: Message #01
Sent message with ID: 2 and Body: Message #02
Sent message with ID: 3 and Body: Message #03
Sent message with ID: 4 and Body: Message #04
Messages sent. Ensure consumer is running.
Deleted queue.
Finished.
```

Building Code to Read Messages

Now that you have your queue created and a producer sending messages to it, you can build the code to read the messages from the Queue. This follows almost the same setup steps as before (get the credentials and create the `TokenProvider`, `serviceUri`), but this time you use the `Receive()` operation on the `QueueClient`. Your call to `Receive` indicates a long poll (where the server holds off responding immediately if there is no data ready yet), which waits for up to 10 seconds for a message. The reason you put the call to `Receive` within the condition of the `while` is to handle the case where the 10 seconds passes and no message data is returned. In this case, a `null` value is returned.

**Available for
download on
Wrox.com**

```
string issuerName = "owner";
string issuerKey = "<INSERT YOUR ISSUER KEY>";
string serviceNamespace = "<INSERT YOUR SERVICE NAMESPACE>";
string queueName = "PrimaryQueue";

TokenProvider tokenProvider =  TokenProvider.
      CreateSharedSecretTokenProvider(issuerName, issuerKey);
Uri serviceUri = ServiceBusEnvironment.CreateServiceUri(
      "sb", serviceNamespace, string.Empty);

MessagingFactory messagingFactory = MessagingFactory.Create(
      serviceUri, tokenProvider);

//Create a consumer in PeekLock receive mode
QueueClient queueClient = messagingFactory.CreateQueueClient(
      queueName, ReceiveMode.PeekLock);

BrokeredMessage msg;
while ((msg = queueClient.Receive(TimeSpan.FromSeconds(10))) != null)
{
      string.Format("Received message with ID: {0} and Body: {1}",
      msg.MessageId, msg.GetBody<string>()).Dump();
      //must call msg.Complete() to delete peek-locked
      //message from queue
      msg.Complete();
}
"Finished.".Dump();
```

code snippet Simple Queue Consumer.linq

Following are a few things worth observing in the previous code.

➤ You create the `QueueClient` via the `MessagingFactory` instance with a `ReceiveMode` of `PeekLock`. This mode temporarily removes the received message from the queue for a configured interval, which is 60 seconds by default.

➤ The peek-lock approach to message retrieval provides *at-least-once* delivery behavior (where the message is guaranteed to be received by at least one consumer) because if a consumer retrieves a message and then fails, the message, at some point, is made available to another consumer of the queue.

➤ The call to `msg.Complete()` actually deletes the message and prevents it from reappearing in the queue.

The output running the previous code (after the producer code finishes sending but has not yet deleted the queue) follows:

```
Received message with ID: 0 and Body: Message #00
Received message with ID: 1 and Body: Message #01
Received message with ID: 2 and Body: Message #02
Received message with ID: 3 and Body: Message #03
Received message with ID: 4 and Body: Message #04
Finished.
```

You can also retrieve messages from the queue using the `ReceiveAndDelete` mode instead of `PeekLock`. In this case, the message is retrieved and deleted from the queue in a single, atomic operation. The change alters the `ReceiveMode` specified in the call to `CreateQueueClient` and omits the call to `msg.Complete()`.

```
QueueClient queueClient = messagingFactory.CreateQueueClient(
    queueName, ReceiveMode.ReceiveAndDelete);

BrokeredMessage msg;
while ((msg = queueClient.Receive(TimeSpan.FromSeconds(10))) != null)
{
    string.Format("Received message with ID: {0} and Body: {1}",
        msg.MessageId, msg.GetBody<string>()).Dump();
    //no need to call msg.Complete(), message already deleted
}
```

code snippet Simple Queue Consumer.linq

 Instead of using `QueueClient`, *you can use instances of* `MessageReceiver` *to consume messages and* `MessageSender` *to send messages. You create both from the* `messagingFactory`, *using* `CreateMessageReceiver` *or* `CreateMessageSender` *respectively, and you use them in the same way as the* `QueueClient`. *You might choose to use* `MessageSender` *or* `MessageReceiver` *when the object you need is going to be used for sending or receiving exclusively.*

Programming Topics and Subscriptions

Now that you understand how to program against queues, learning to program against their fuller featured cousins, topics and subscriptions, is an incremental step. For new projects, you can start with topics and subscriptions instead of queues because doing so leaves you well positioned to add additional "taps" into the topic in the form of a subscription without first needing to migrate from a queue-based implementation.

This section assumes the following constants for code snippets.

```
string issuerName = "owner";
string issuerKey = "<INSERT YOUR ISSUER KEY>";
string serviceNamespace = "<INSERT YOUR SERVICE NAMESPACE>";
string topicName = "PrimaryTopic";
string auditSubscriptionName = "AuditSubscription";
string regularSubscriptionName = "RegularSubscription";
```

code snippet Simple Topic Producer.linq

Now, you can dive into the details.

Creating a Topic

The pattern for creating a topic is nearly identical to that for creating a queue. With your authenticated `NamespaceManager` in hand, you simply call `CreateTopic`, passing in a path for the topic, where the path is subject to the same restrictions as a queue path (max length of 290 characters and must be URI-friendly).

```
TokenProvider tokenProvider = TokenProvider.
    CreateSharedSecretTokenProvider(issuerName, issuerKey);
Uri serviceUri = ServiceBusEnvironment.CreateServiceUri(
    "sb", serviceNamespace, string.Empty);

//Create topic
NamespaceManager namespaceManager = new NamespaceManager(
    serviceUri, tokenProvider);

if (namespaceManager.TopicExists(topicName))
{
    namespaceManager.DeleteTopic(topicName);
}
TopicDescription topicDescription = namespaceManager.
                            CreateTopic(topicName);
```

code snippet Simple Topic Producer.linq

Creating a Subscription

After you create a topic, creating a subscription is as easy calling `CreateSubscription` with the topic path and the name you want for the subscription. The name of a subscription is not a path; it must be a single segment and less than 50 characters.

```
SubscriptionDescription auditingSubscription =
            namespaceManager.CreateSubscription(
                    topicDescription.Path,
                    auditSubscriptionName);
```

code snippet Simple Topic Producer.linq

Sending Messages to a Topic

Sending messages to a topic is just like sending a message to a queue. You must first create a `TopicClient` instance from a `MessagingFactory` instance and then call the topic client's `Send` method.

```
//Create the topic client and use it to send messages to the topic
MessagingFactory messagingFactory =
    MessagingFactory.Create(serviceUri, tokenProvider);
TopicClient topicClient =
    messagingFactory.CreateTopicClient(topicDescription.Path);
for (int i = 0; i < 5; i++)
{
    BrokeredMessage msg = new BrokeredMessage(
```

```
              string.Format("Message #{0:00}", i));
    msg.MessageId = i.ToString();

    topicClient.Send(msg);
    string.Format("Sent message with ID: {0} and Body: {1}",
        msg.MessageId, msg.GetBody<string>()).Dump();
}
```

code snippet Simple Topic Producer.linq

Receiving Messages from a Subscription

Messages can be received from a subscription using either a receive-and-delete or peek-lock/complete receive mode. The approach is to create a `SubscriptionClient` instance for the topic path and subscription name, specifying the receive mode in the call to `CreateSubscriptionClient`. With a `SubscriptionClient` instance in hand, you call `Receive`. This example calls `Receive` with a timeout of 10 seconds. `Receive` returns a `null` `BrokeredMessage` if the timeout expires. If you use the peek-lock receive mode, you must call `Complete` on the `BrokeredMessage` instance to remove it from the subscription. Otherwise, it reappears after the configured lock duration and the same message would be processed multiple times.

```
SubscriptionClient auditingSubscriptionClient =
            messagingFactory.CreateSubscriptionClient(
                topicName, auditSubscriptionName,
                ReceiveMode.ReceiveAndDelete);

SubscriptionClient regularSubscriptionClient =
            messagingFactory.CreateSubscriptionClient(
                topicName, regularSubscriptionName,
                ReceiveMode.PeekLock);
BrokeredMessage msg;
while (
    (msg = auditingSubscription.Receive(TimeSpan.FromSeconds(10))) != null
)
{
        //…process msg …
}


while (
    (msg = regularSubscription.Receive(TimeSpan.FromSeconds(10))) != null
)
{
        //…process msg …
        msg.Complete();
}
```

code snippet Simple Topic Consumer.linq

 In the Simple Topic Consumer example, observe that messages will be pulled from the auditingSubscription *first, and only when there are no more messages will the* regularSubscription *be processed.*

Subscription Rules, Filters, and Actions

Subscriptions support rules, which can define filters (that evaluate an expression typically containing message properties for a match) and actions (that can modify message properties). When a filter is matched for a subscription, the subscription contains the message; otherwise the message is ignored by the subscription.

Service Bus brokered messaging supports filters and actions that use a SQL-92–based syntax to define expressions. When programming with the managed library, you can create a filter that matches any message by providing an instance of the `TrueFilter` class, or no message with an instance of the `FalseFilter` class. Behind the scenes these create `SqlFilters` that contain the SQL expressions $1 = 1$ and $1 = 0$ respectively.

You can also create more advanced expressions using the `SqlFilter` class. For example, use `messageSource LIKE 'A%'` to match messages that have a message property called `MessageSource` whose value starts with `A`.

 An explanation of the complete supported syntax for SQL Filter Expressions and Actions is beyond the scope of this chapter, so be sure to check out the resources section at the end of this chapter for links to the appropriate documentation.

Available for download on Wrox.com

```
SubscriptionDescription auditingSubscription =
        namespaceManager.CreateSubscription(
            topicDescription.Path,
            auditSubscriptionName,
            new TrueFilter());

SubscriptionDescription regularSubscription =
        namespaceManager.CreateSubscription(
            topicDescription.Path,
            regularSubscriptionName,
            new SqlFilter("MessageSource LIKE 'A%'"));
```

code snippet Filtered Subscriptions Producer.linq

Observe that the previous snippet uses an overload of `CreateSubscription` that takes the path, subscription name and filter.

 The snippet shows the use of both a `TrueFilter` and a SQL Filter expression specified at the creation time of a subscription. `MessageSource` is a custom property— one that would be added to the `BrokeredMessage` instance's Properties collection at send time. If you need to access the fixed properties of the `BrokeredMessage` instance, such as to access the `ContentType` property, you need to prefix the property name with sys, for example `sys.ContentType LIKE 'XML%'`.

The Service Bus provides one more type of Filter, which `enables` efficient matching on the complete value of a message property—in the `CorrelationId BrokeredMessage` property. For example, you could treat all high-priority messages differently by using a `CorrelationFilter`, as shown in the following snippet. This subscription would receive all messages that have a value of `"VIP"` in the `message.CorrelationId` field.

```
string priorityCorrelationValue = "VIP";
SubscriptionDescription prioritySubscription =
        namespaceManager.CreateSubscription(
            topicDescription.Path,
            prioritySubscriptionName,
            new CorrelationFilter(priorityCorrelationValue));
```

code snippet Filtered Subscriptions Producer.linq

If you need to modify message properties as part of making a message available through a subscription, you need to define an action. To define an action you must create a rule and apply it to the subscription at subscription creation time. Within the rule you specify the filter that determines if the action is applied to the message, and also specify the `SqlRuleAction` that can add, modify, or remove message properties. The following snippet creates a rule that applies to messages having a `messageSource` (a custom property we added) that starts with `A` (such as `Affiliate`), and when true add a new message property called `IsAffiliate` with a value of `true`.

```
RuleDescription sourceStartsWithARule = new RuleDescription()
{
        Name = "sourceStartsWithA",
        Filter = new SqlFilter("MessageSource LIKE 'A%'"),
        Action = new SqlRuleAction("SET IsAffiliate = TRUE")
};

SubscriptionDescription regularSubscription =
        namespaceManager.CreateSubscription(
            topicDescription.Path,
            regularSubscriptionName,
            sourceStartsWithARule);
```

code snippet Filtered Subscriptions Producer.linq

To send custom message properties or correlation values with a message, you simply set the corresponding property on the `BrokeredMessage` instance. The following snippet shows how to add a custom property to the `Properties` collection, as well as setting a `CorrelationId`.

```
for (int i = 0; i < 5; i++)
{
        //Create messages having differing properties
        //and correlation values
        BrokeredMessage msg = new BrokeredMessage(
                string.Format("Message #{0:00}", i));
                msg.MessageId = i.ToString();
                msg.Properties["MessageSource"] =
                    ( i == 2 || i == 3) ? "Affiliate" : "Public";
        msg.CorrelationId = (i == 4) ? "VIP" : null;
        topicClient.Send(msg);
}
```

code snippet Filtered Subscriptions Producer.linq

Async Programming

So far you've seen the synchronous ways to interact with the Service Bus. The managed library for Brokered Messaging offers versions of those operations that follow the standard .NET Asynchronous Programming Model. Use the async approach to program against the Service Bus for high-throughput scenarios, or within in WPF or Windows Forms applications. The following snippet provides an example of how to receive messages asynchronously from a subscription and process them within a callback.

```
AsyncCallback cb = null;
cb = (result) =>
{
        try
        {
                BrokeredMessage msg =
                    regularSubscription.EndReceive(result);
                //msg may be null if no messages received before timeout
                if (msg != null)
                {
                        //…do something with msg …
                        regularSubscription.BeginReceive(
                                            TimeSpan.FromSeconds(10),
                                            cb,
                                            regularSubscription);
                }
                else
                {
                        //no more messages to process
                        //…stop polling or call BeginReceive again …
                }
        }
        catch (Exception ex)
        {
                //handle exception
        }
};

//Invokes callback when either a message is received
//OR wait timeout expires
regularSubscription.BeginReceive(
                        TimeSpan.FromSeconds(10),
                        cb,
                        regularSubscription);
```

code snippet Async Topic Consumers.linq

Building a REST Client

REST clients are able to perform the same core functionality available to managed clients for interacting with Service Bus Brokered Messaging, particularly for sending to queues or topics and receiving from queues or subscriptions (as well as applying any rules, filters, or actions defined) and managing the creation or deletion of such messaging entities.

In this section, you follow the same process for working with a filtered subscription as was shown previously with the managed client using the managed API, but instead you see how these steps can be accomplished with a simple REST client. Along the way you see highlighted notable differences between the two APIs.

Authenticating

Building a REST client forces you take on the complexity of authenticating with ACS to acquire the SWT token (basically a string passcode that is sent in the request headers) that you must present with all calls to the Service Bus. In addition, you are responsible for renewing the token when necessary (something the managed library otherwise handles for you) as shown in the following code:

Available for download on Wrox.com

```
static string GetServiceBusTokenFromACS(string serviceNamespace,
string serviceIdentityUsername, string serviceIdentityPassword)
{
    string acsHostName = "accesscontrol.windows.net";

    WebClient client = new WebClient();
    client.BaseAddress = string.Format(
        "https://{0}-sb.{1}", serviceNamespace,
        acsHostName);

    string realm = string.Format(
        "http://{0}.servicebus.windows.net/",
        serviceNamespace);

    NameValueCollection values = new NameValueCollection()
    {
        {"wrap_name", serviceIdentityUsername},
        {"wrap_password", serviceIdentityPassword},
        {"wrap_scope", realm}
    };

    byte[] responseBytes =
        client.UploadValues("WRAPv0.9/", "POST", values);

    string response = Encoding.UTF8.GetString(responseBytes);

    string token = "WRAP access_token=\"" +
        Uri.UnescapeDataString(response
        .Split('&')
        .Single(value => value.StartsWith("wrap_access_token=",
            StringComparison.OrdinalIgnoreCase))
        .Split('=')[1]) +
        "\"";

    return token;
}
```

code snippet REST APIs.linq

Creating a Queue

Before you can communicate across the Service Bus by sending or receiving messages, you need to create a messaging entity such as a queue or topic. This shows how to create a queue, and then next, a topic. You can create a queue when you know you do not need the additional features offered by subscriptions—namely filters and actions. With the code to acquire a token from ACS in hand, creating a queue is straightforward and demonstrates a pattern all the REST management APIs follow. First, you craft the URI to the Service Namespace:

```
string uriToNamespace =
        string.Format(
          "https://{0}.servicebus.windows.net/",
          serviceNamespace);
```

code snippet REST APIs.linq

You then use this URI, along with the queue path you want for the new queue, and the token previously acquired from ACS as inputs to the queue creation method.

```
static string CreateQueue(string uriToNamespace,
        string queuePath, string token)
{
        string queueUri = uriToNamespace + queuePath;

        WebClient wc = new WebClient();
        wc.Headers[HttpRequestHeader.Authorization] = token;

        string queueDescription =
        @"<entry xmlns=""http://www.w3.org/2005/Atom"">
        <title type=""text"">" + queuePath + @"</title>
        <content type=""application/xml"">
                <QueueDescription
xmlns:i=""http://www.w3.org/2001/XMLSchema-instance""
xmlns=""http://schemas.microsoft.com/netservices/
2010/10/servicebus/connect"" />
        </content>
        </entry>";

        byte[] response = wc.UploadData(
                        queueUri,
                        "PUT",
                        Encoding.UTF8.GetBytes(queueDescription));

        return Encoding.UTF8.GetString(response);
}
```

code snippet REST APIs.linq

In the previous code, notice the pattern:

➤ You craft a full URI to the messaging entity, in this case, the Queue.

➤ You include your token in the Authorization header of the request.

➤ You build an ATOM payload. For a queue, this consists of an entry whose Title is the queuepath and whose content is a QueueDescription.

➤ You then UTF8 encode the payload and perform either a REST POST, PUT, or DELETE against the full URI of the messaging entity. In the case of creating a queue, you need to perform a PUT. Some operations require performing a GET, for which your code looks as follows. (Observe that you use wc.DownloadString in place of UploadData.)

```
static string GetQueues(string uriToNamespace, string token)
{
```

```
        string queuesUri = uriToNamespace + "/$Resources/Queues";
        WebClient wc = new WebClient();
        wc.Headers[HttpRequestHeader.Authorization] = token;
        return wc.DownloadString(rulesUri);
    }
```

code snippet REST APIs.linq

Table 13-1 presents a summary of the parameters for all REST operations. Use this table in lieu of repeating the same basic code for the other operations shown in this section.

TABLE 13-1: Creating a Queue

PARAMETER	DESCRIPTION
Entity URI	uriNamespace + queuePath
Header	Authorization: token
Payload	QueueDescription
Verb	PUT
Response	QueueDescription

An example of Queue Description payload follows:

```
"<entry xmlns=""http://www.w3.org/2005/Atom"">
        <title type=""text"">" + queuePath + "</title>
        <content type=""application/xml"">
                <QueueDescription
                    xmlns:i=""http://www.w3.org/2001/XMLSchema-instance""
                    xmlns=""http://schemas.microsoft.com/netservices/
2010/10/servicebus/connect"" />
        </content>
</entry>"
```

The response to a successful creation operation, just as in the managed case, is QueueDescription. The response instance provides value for all properties of a QueueDescription. For values not supplied by the client, the server-side default values are applied to the queue and included in the response.

Creating a Topic

You generally want to create a topic when you send messages across the Service Bus because it gives you the flexibility to plug in additional subscriptions (with differing rules) at any point later. If you start with a queue and find you need a filter or want to modify message properties with an action, you must delete the queue and replace it with a topic and one or more subscriptions. This also means you need to adjust any code written that sends a message to a topic and that which receives messages to receive from a subscription. The approach for creating a topic is almost identical to creating a queue, except that you need to submit a TopicDescription instead of a QueueDescription, as shown in Table 13-2.

TABLE 13-2: Creating a Topic

PARAMETER	DESCRIPTION
Entity URI	uriNamespace + topicPath
Header	Authorization: token
Payload	Topic Description
Verb	PUT
Response	Topic Description

A `TopicDescription` has the following format:

```
"<entry xmlns=""http://www.w3.org/2005/Atom"">
<title type=""text"">" + topicPath + "</title>
<content type=""application/xml"">
        <TopicDescription
            xmlns:i=""http://www.w3.org/2001/XMLSchema-instance""
            xmlns=""http://schemas.microsoft.com/
netservices/2010/10/servicebus/connect"" />
</content>
</entry>"
```

Creating a Subscription

You create a subscription to receive messages sent to a topic and to define filters and actions. Creating a subscription is also similar to creating a queue or topic, as shown in Table 13-3. Rules for a subscription are created separately, as you see in the next section.

TABLE 13-3: Creating a Subscription

PARAMETER	DESCRIPTION
Entity URI	uriNamespace + topicPath + "/Subscriptions/" + subscriptionName
Header	Authorization: token
Payload	SubscriptionDescription
Verb	PUT
Response	SubscriptionDescription

The payload for creating a subscription is a `SubscriptionDescription`:

```
"<entry xmlns=""http://www.w3.org/2005/Atom"">
<title type=""text"">" + subscriptionName + "</title>
<content type=""application/xml"">
        <SubscriptionDescription
            xmlns:i=""http://www.w3.org/2001/XMLSchema-instance""
            xmlns=""http://schemas.microsoft.com/
```

```
netservices/2010/10/servicebus/connect"" />

</content>
</entry>"
```

Creating Rules

With a Subscription in place, you define Rules to filter out messages from appearing in the sub-scription, alter properties of the message, or both. Unlike the experience with the managed client library, when using REST, rules are created in a separate call from the one creating the subscrip-tion. In the following code , the `ruleText` for a trivial rule could be 1 = 1, which is equivalent to a `TrueFilter`, or you could provide a more complex rule such as `MessageSource LIKE 'A%'` to evaluate message properties, as shown in Table 13-4.

TABLE 13-4: Creating a Rule

PARAMETER	DESCRIPTION
Entity URI:	uriNamespace + topicPath + "/Subscriptions/" + subscription-Name + "/Rules/" + ruleName
Header:	Authorization: token
Payload:	RuleDescription
Verb:	PUT
Response:	RuleDescription

The `RuleDescription` payload takes the following form:

```
"<entry xmlns=""http://www.w3.org/2005/Atom"">
<content type=""application/xml"">
      <RuleDescription
          xmlns:i=""http://www.w3.org/2001/XMLSchema-instance""
          xmlns=""http://schemas.microsoft.com/
netservices/2010/10/servicebus/connect"" />
      <Filter i:type=""SqlFilter"">
            <SqlExpression>" + ruleText + "</SqlExpression>
            <CompatibilityLevel>20</CompatibilityLevel>
      </Filter>
      <Action i:type=""EmptyRuleAction"" />
      </RuleDescription>
</content>
</entry>";
```

Sending Messages to Queues and Topics

You send messages to a queue or topic for the eventual consumption by a receiver reading from the queue or from the subscription created on the topic. Sending messages to queues or topics is simply a POST to the messages segment of the entity path combined with a timeout (specified in seconds) in the query string, as shown in Table 13-5. Message Properties, as used by the `BrokeredMessage` type, appear within the Header. The body can take any form so long as it serializes to a UTF 8 encoded byte array.

TABLE 13-5: Sending Messages to a Queue or Topic

PARAMETER	DESCRIPTION

Entity URI	Queue
	`uriNamespace + queuePath + "/messages?timeout=60"`
	Topic
	`uriNamespace + topicPath + "/messages?timeout=60"`

Header	`Authorization: tokenMessage Properties`
Payload	`Message body`
Verb	`POST`
Response	N/A

When providing string values in message properties, you must quote the value. Otherwise, you receive an HTTP 400 error from the Service Bus when sending the message because it tries to parse the value as a bool, integer, or float and fails. In .NET, such a value would appear as:

```
wc.Headers[headerName] = "\"" + headerValue + "\"";
```

The payload of a message sent to a queue can be as simple as `"Hello world."`

Receiving Messages from Queues and Subscriptions

Rules enable you to define actions (which can alter message properties) and filters (which control the availability of messages) on a subscription. Messages can be received from queues or subscriptions using either receive-and-delete or peek-lock/complete approaches. The calling pattern, as shown in Table 13-6, is the same in both cases.

TABLE 13-6: Receiving Messages from a Queue or Subscription

PARAMETER	DESCRIPTION

Entity URI	Queue
	`uriNamespace + queuePath + "/messages/head?timeout=60"`
	Subscription
	`uriNamespace + topicPath + "/Subscriptions/" + subscriptionName + "/messages/head?timeout=60"`

PARAMETER	DESCRIPTION
Header	`Authorization: token` `Message Properties`
Payload	Empty byte array
Verb	Receive and Delete - `DELETE` Peek Lock - `DELETE`

Response	Headers:
	`BrokeredProperties`
	`Message Properties`
	Body:
	`Message body`

An example value of `BrokeredProperties` follows (observe the JSON format used):

```
{"DeliveryCount":1,
"LockToken":"6dc54ba3-6c5b-4ae4-b25f-b457586282b3",
"LockedUntilUtc":"Thu, 20 Oct 2011 17:40:29 GMT",
"MessageId":"18d2c9e585d840f690ab276bf71ed98c",
"SequenceNumber":1,
"TimeToLive":922337203685.47754}
```

When performing a peek-lock receive, you must capture the values of the lock token (aka lock Id) and message ID returned in the `BrokeredProperties` header found within the response headers to complete the receive operation later. The value of this header is a JSON formatted dictionary. Refer back to Table 13-6 for a sample. Table 13-7 shows how to complete a peek-locked message and actually delete it from the queue or subscription.

TABLE 13-7: Completing a Peek Locked Message in a Queue or Subscription

PARAMETER	DESCRIPTION

Entity URI	Queue
	`uriNamespace + queuePath + "/messages/" + messageId + "/" + lockId`
	Subscription
	`uriNamespace + topicPath + "/Subscriptions/" + subscriptionName + "/messages/" + messageId + "/" + lockId`

Header	`Authorization: token`
Payload	Empty byte array
Verb	`DELETE`
Response	N/A

Deleting Queues, Topics, Subscriptions, and Rules

You are billed for the existence of messaging entities such as queues, topics, and subscriptions. It is common sense to clean up resources you do not use or no longer apply (such as a rule). The approach used to delete any entity is to perform a DELETE operation against the entity URI, providing the token in the authorization header and an empty byte array as the payload, as Table 13-8 summarizes.

TABLE 13-8: Deleting a Queue, Topic, Subscription, or Rule

PARAMETER	DESCRIPTION

Entity URI	Queue
	`uriNamespace + queuePath`
	Topic
	`uriNamespace + topicPath`
	Subscription
	`uriNamespace + topicPath + "/Subscriptions/" + subscriptionName`
	Rule
	`uriNamespace + topicPath + "/Subscriptions/" + subscriptionName + "/Rules/" + ruleName`

Header	`Authorization: token`
Payload	Empty byte array
Verb	`DELETE`
Response	N/A

Getting Queues, Topics, Subscriptions, and Rules

You can also request information about existing queues, topics, subscriptions (see Table 13-9) and rules using REST (see Table 13-10). You would do this to see what setting you used previously during the entity creation or to see what default values have been applied.

TABLE 13-9: Getting a List of Queue, Topic, or Subscription Descriptions

PARAMETER	DESCRIPTION

Entity URI	Queues
	`uriToNamespace + "/$Resources/Queues"`
	Topic
	`uriToNamespace + "/$Resources/Topics"`
	Subscription
	`uriNamespace + topicPath + "/Subscriptions/"`

PARAMETER	DESCRIPTION
Header	`Authorization: token`
Payload	Empty byte array
Verb	`GET`
Response	An ATOM feed containing a collection of the requested descriptions.

When requesting subscription descriptions, you must specify the topic path, which returns the subscriptions to that topic.

TABLE 13-10: Getting Descriptions for All Rules on a Subscription

PARAMETER	DESCRIPTION
Entity URI	`uriNamespace + topicPath + "/Subscriptions/" + subscriptionName + "/Rules/" + ruleName`
Header	`Authorization: token`
Payload	Empty byte array
Verb	`GET`
Response	ATOM feed containing collection of `RuleDescription` elements (which contain Filter and Action subelements) for each rule applied to the subscription

Advanced Features

Service Bus brokered messaging offers many more features, which are not shown in the previous code samples. This section mentions them and refers you to the resources at the end of the chapter as well as the source code included with the book for details. Each feature serves to show that there is much more to messaging with Service Bus Brokered Messaging than sending and receiving messages, and that it helps you solve tough problems such as building a request/response messaging pattern across queues or automatically dealing with poisonous messages that repeatedly crash the receiver, or even optimizing communication by batching requests.

Sessions

Queues and subscriptions provide support for grouping messages into a session. Effectively this enables you to receive multiple messages related by a `Session ID` (specified at send time) in order, regardless of other messages that might have also been sent to the queue or topic in-between. The `MessageSession` class provides this functionality and is created from either a `QueueClient` or `SubscriptionClient` via the `AcceptMessageSession` method. This method can take a parameter indicating a wanted Session ID to process, or no parameter at all to process messages from the next session. These are referred to as named and nameless sessions respectively.

➤ **Named sessions:** Can be used in support of a request and response messaging pattern, whereby messages forming a Response are sent back to the requestor who accepts messages for a specific Session ID. The requestor, when originally sending the request message, would have specified a `ReplyToSessionId` on the `BrokeredMessage` instance.

➤ **Nameless session:** Can be used to group multiple messages together, or to assist in sending a large message that has been split up into multiple smaller messages, that must be received for correct re-assembly by the recipient.

Finally, sessions have a durable property for maintaining Session State that that you can use independent of the messages within the session, or to collect statistics about the session.

Transactions

The Service Bus provides support for `Complete` (of a peek-locked message) and for `Send` as part of local transactions such as those created within a `TransactionScope`. This enables you, for example, to delete a peek-locked message from a queue and send a message to another queue as a single atomic operation. If either step fails, the peek-locked message is not completed, and the other message is never sent. Neither receive in peek-lock nor receive-and-delete participate within a local transaction, which means, for example, that you cannot rollback a receive operation (as if the message were never acquired) if a subsequent send operation in the same transaction fails.

Dead Lettering

Dead lettering is the process to remove a message from the active queue or subscription into a special subqueue, called a *dead letter queue*, which is designed to capture messages that cannot be processed. The Service Bus enables you to automatically dead letter a message if its Time-To-Live (TTL) expires, if it's received more than a certain number of times, or if the message encounters an exception when a filter expression is being evaluated for it. You can also manually dead letter messages via the `BrokeredMessage` instance's `DeadLetter` method.

Deferred Message Processing

You can opt to defer the processing of a received message and control when that happens in your application by calling `Defer` on a `BrokeredMessage` instance. A deferred message is not available to other clients of a queue or subscription and must be retrieved by using its message sequence number (which needs to be captured and stored by the application upon initial retrieval, for later use).

Duplicate Detection

In scenarios in which processing duplicate messages is unwanted, you can set the `MessageId` of sent messages to some unique value and rely on the Service Bus to ensure that no message with that `MessageId` reappears within a configurable window of time. (The default is 10 minutes.)

Batching and Message Prefetch

By default, the Service Bus enables client-side batching for asynchronous `Send` and `Complete` requests made with the managed client library. With this enabled, the client holds back on sending messages for small amounts of time, up to a maximum batch size, in order to send multiple messages or multiple `Complete` requests in a single request.

When receiving a message, you can use prefetching to return not only the next message, but also multiple messages in a single request (which will contain multiple messages). These prefetched messages are returned to `Receive` calls from a local cache and have a lock on them that expires (such that they again become available in the queue) after an interval of 60 seconds if they have not been received by the client who cached them.

Choosing Between Managed and REST Service Bus Clients

In many cases, choosing between using the Service Bus managed client and the REST API is decided by the platform on which you build your clients (for example, you are forced to build REST if the clients are not built with .NET such as mobile phone clients). However, if both are still options there are other factors to consider; in this section you receive practical guidance to aid your selection.

Considerations for Choosing the Service Bus Client Protocol

The performance is lower for REST clients when compared to managed clients because the Service Bus Client Protocol maintains an open TCP connection to the Service Bus (while the `MessagingFactory` is open), whereas each HTTP request must open a new connection. This is an expensive operation that cannot be avoided for REST clients.

In addition, the Service Bus client protocol provides client-side batching on asynchronous send or complete and message prefetching (both introduced previously). These can significantly improve throughput by minimizing the number of round trips that need to be made for managed clients but is not available to REST clients.

Finally, if you need to support sessions, for reasons such as chunking large messages, you must use the managed client because sessionful receivers are not currently supported by the REST API.

Considerations for Choosing REST

One feature that may drive you to use the REST API is a high number of senders and receivers. Service Bus queues, topics, or subscriptions can support a maximum of 100 concurrent clients each. Therefore, if you have the potential for more connections, the REST APIs that open a connection make the request and close immediately, representing the best approach to maximize your use of concurrent connections.

Connectivity may also cause you to use REST. For most firewall-protected networks, outbound HTTP is usually allowed, but TCP may be blocked on port 9354—the port used by the Service Bus Client Protocol. In this case, you either must open that port or switch to using a REST client.

Best Practices

The following section discusses best practices that achieve better performance and reliability with Service Bus Brokered Messaging.

Optimizing Service Side Performance

One key to understanding how to achieve the best performance with Service Bus is to understand how messages are processed and where they are stored internally. A single queue stores its data within a single database, and all messaging operations are handled by that single database instance. A topic and all its subscriptions are stored within the single database, and all messaging operations across the topic and the subscriptions are handled by the same node. Each node can handle several thousand messages per second, but an upper bound to the throughput exists, which implies the following:

➤ Use multiple queues or topics if you require throughput higher than approximately 2,000 messages/sec.

➤ Expect a lower throughput receiving subscriptions from a single topic as you increase the number of subscriptions because the throughput that the node can provide is effectively divided among the topic and all its subscriptions.

Optimizing Client-Side Performance

On the client side, when using the Service Bus Client Protocol, recall that each messaging factory shares a single open connection irrespective of the number of queue, topic, or subscription clients created from it. To increase throughput, you should do the following:

➤ Create multiple `MessagingFactory` instances, and create your clients from those.

➤ Reuse clients created from your `MessagingFactory` instance across multiple requests, and close only the `MessagingFactory` instance when done so that you incur only the expense of opening the connection to the Service Bus once (when you create the `MessagingFactory` instance).

➤ Always use the asynchronous methods when invoking Service Bus operations using the Service Bus Client Protocol. You must do this to leverage client-side batching of `Send` and `Complete` requests.

➤ Enable message prefetch for your `Receive` operations, especially if you already use peek-lock receives. Doing so increases receive throughput for your client. Message prefetching works for both peek-lock and receive-and-delete modes, but you should carefully consider if your system can afford to lose messages retrieved in a batch by a receiver that crashes under the latter scenario.

IMPROVING RELIABILITY

There are a handful of transient errors (`ServerBusyException`, `MessagingCommunicationException`, and in some cases `TimeoutException`), that, if handled with the original operation retried, may succeed on a subsequent attempt. For these types of errors, you should leverage a retry framework. For this, Microsoft has provided the Transient Fault Handling Framework, which you can download from the MSDN Code Gallery at `http://code.msdn.microsoft .com/Transient-Fault-Handling-b209151f`. For a Service Bus Brokered Messaging specific approach using this framework, see the Windows Azure Customer Advisory Team's implementation at `http://windowsazurecat .com/2011/09/best-practices-leveraging-windows-azure-service- bus-brokered-messaging-api/`.

Comparing Service Bus Brokered Messaging to Azure Queues

Fundamentally, Windows Azure Storage queues and Service Bus Brokered Messaging provide the same core queuing functionality. If your solution requires only the basics, either may suffice. Scenarios beyond the basics, however, can likely benefit from the richer feature-set provided by the Service Bus. The following are the key differences:

> **Message and queue size limits are a first consideration for many scenarios.** Azure Queues support a payload of 64KB, in comparison with Service Bus that supports payloads up to 256KB and provides support for messages of any size by chunking messages into "streams" created by using sessions. Although Service Bus queues can be created in sizes of 1GB to 5GB, Azure Queues individually are limited only by the 100TB limit that applies to the entire storage account.

> **Depending on your scenario, the length of time a message can remain within the queue might be important.** Messages within the Service Bus are durable and have no upper limit on their TTL, whereas within Azure Queues their TTL is limited to 7 days. That said, messages in the Azure Queue can be added with a visibility timeout (such that the message becomes visible at a later time) and support clients extending their lease on a dequeued message.

> **One other basic difference that might affect your management scenarios involves queue depth.** The message count returned by management requests is approximate in Azure Queues but exact for Service Bus Queues and Subscriptions.

> **Your scenario might need more than basic queuing functionality.** Only the Service Bus provides support for brokered messaging functionality such as publish/subscribe (for example, sending to a single topic read though multiple filtered subscriptions), altering of message properties, ordered sessions, both peek-lock and receive-delete receive methods, support for transactions with peek-locked messages and session state, message deduplication, and automatic message dead-lettering.

> **The final factor is cost.** Pricing between Azure queues and Service Bus queues is comparable, except on three dimensions. First, in Service Bus Queues you don't pay for storage of your messages, unlike for Azure queues where you will pay $0.14 per GB per month. Second, Service Bus queues require ACS, and so you will be paying $1.99 per 100,000 ACS token transactions—something not used or needed by Azure queues. Third, on Azure queues you will pay for all operations such as creating a queue, deleting a queue, sending and receiving messages, but in Service Bus Queues you pay only for sending and receiving messages at $0.01 per 10,000 messages.

 For a very detailed comparison of Azure Queues and Service Bus Brokered Messaging, see this article on MSDN: `http://msdn.microsoft.com/en-us/library/hh767287(VS.103).aspx.`

Service Bus Billing and Quotas

Now that you have an understanding of using Service Bus Brokered Messaging, the following section looks at the Service Bus quotas and how your usage is measured and ultimately billed.

As of this writing, Service Bus Brokered Messaging is free of charge in production but introduces two meters you can use today to measure your consumption using the Microsoft Online Customer Portal. When pricing comes into effect, it will revolve around these meters.

The two meters are Relay Hours and Messages:

➤   **Relay Hours:** Measures the amount of time you have an established connection to the Service Bus Relay. Billed at $0.10 per 100 relay hours.

➤   **Messages:** This refers to messages received from a queue or subscription (irrespective if an actual message were available and returned) as well as messages sent to a queue or topic. The current rate is $0.01 per 10,000 messages.

In addition, multipliers exist on these meters based on message size or storage used. Although Service Bus supports message sizes up to 256KB, costs for messages above 64KB in size and the number of message operations are multiplied for each additional 64KB sent or received.

Table 13-11 lists the Quotas enforced for features in Service Bus Brokered Messaging.

TABLE 13-11: Service Bus Brokered Messaging Quotas

ITEM	QUOTA LIMIT
Max messages exchanged	5,000,000,000
Queue or Topic Size	5GB
Concurrent TCP (non-REST) Connections to Queue, Topic, or Subscription	100
Number of Topics or Queues per Namespace	10,000
Message Size	256KB
Message Header Size	64KB
Number of Subscriptions per Topic	2,000
Number of SQL Filters per Topic	2,000
Number of Correlation Filters per Topic	100,000

SUMMARY

In this chapter you had an overview of the major features of the Service Bus: Relay and Brokered Messaging. You then dove into Brokered Messaging and its constituent components, queues, topics, subscriptions, and rules, learning how to leverage them from managed clients using the Service Bus Client Protocol and the managed SDK, as well as by interacting with the REST API.

Along the way, you considered some of the additional features such as Sessions and Batching that make the managed scenario quite robust. You also received some guidance on how to choose between the managed and REST APIs for scenarios in which either is an option, as well as how the Service Bus feature set compares to that of the similar Windows Azure Queues.

The coverage concluded with the best practices you should follow to optimize your Service Bus performance and reliability, and understanding what quotas and billing metrics are in place with this release.

Take the knowledge you gained and start connecting your components—happy messaging!

OTHER RESOURCES

Windows Azure CAT (Customer Advisory Team) website: `http://www.windowsazurecat.com/`

SQL Syntax for Filter Expressions: `http://msdn.microsoft.com/en-us/library/microsoft.servicebus.messaging.sqlfilter.sqlexpression.aspx`

SQL Syntax for SQL Rule Actions: `http://msdn.microsoft.com/en-us/library/microsoft.servicebus.messaging.sqlruleaction.sqlexpression.aspx`

Service Bus Resources on MSDN: `http://msdn.microsoft.com/en-us/library/ee732537.aspx`

14

AppFabric: Access Control Service

WHAT'S IN THIS CHAPTER?

➤ Using the Access Control Service to secure web applications with Windows Live ID and Google ID

➤ Integrating the Access Control Service log on page into your application

➤ Setting up single sign-on from the local network to the cloud

Security is one of the key aspects of cloud computing. Often, cloud applications run in the public space, so managing who has access is crucial. Also, business applications that run in the cloud should be as accessible as if they were running in the local network. The Access Control Service helps you with these scenarios.

WHAT IS THE ACCESS CONTROL SERVICE?

In Chapter 9, "Identity in Azure," you learned about identity federation with Windows Identity Foundation (WIF); you built your own Security Token Service (STS) to provide tokens for authentication and authorization with websites and web services with a trust relationship on that STS. Because of the importance of the STS, building your own STS may not be the best idea from a security perspective. Most of the time, you should rely on a battle-tested STS, such as Active Directory Federation Services (ADFS) 2.0. For Windows Azure the *Access Control Service (ACS)* is the STS of choice. Not just because it is part of the Windows Azure suite of services, but also because it supports several ways to authenticate and several protocols. In addition, ACS is a cloud-based solution, so new features are added more quickly than with traditional software packages.

Access Control Service Architecture

The key to the flexibility of ACS lies in its architecture. ACS acts as a universal adapter, supporting multiple identity providers, authentication and authorization protocols, and token formats. Contrary to the STS you built in Chapter 9, ACS is not an Identity Provider (IdP). As shown in the architecture in Figure 14-1, ACS relies on external services such as Windows Live ID (default), Facebook, and ADFS 2.0 to identify users. The latter option makes it possible to integrate with the Active Directory of your local network, so users can use their network credentials to access applications (relying parties) connected to ACS. These applications don't necessarily need to be hosted inside Windows Azure. Any relying party that trusts ACS and is accessible to the user will work.

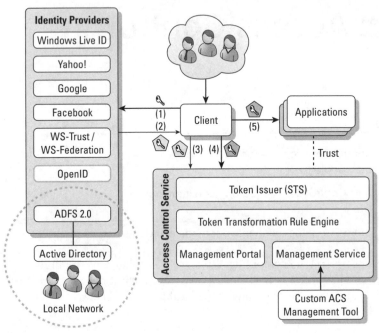

FIGURE 14-1

ACS basically consists of four components (refer to Figure 14.1):

➤ The STS issues tokens for use with applications that trust ACS.

➤ The STS uses the Token Transformation Rule Engine to transform an incoming token from an identity provider to an ACS token trusted by the relying parties.

➤ The rules in the Rule Engine determine which information is passed in the token and may add additional claims.

➤ The Rule Engine can be managed either through the Management Portal or through a custom application using the Management API.

The Management Portal and Management API also manage configuration of identity providers within ACS, as well as the trust relationship between ACS and relying parties that accept tokens from ACS.

Access Control Service Fundamentals

ACS is a cloud service, so you must share it with others. As with the Service Bus discussed in Chapter 13, you define a Service Namespace to create your own ACS environment. You can create multiple namespaces if you have environments you want to keep separated. This can be useful to separate test and production environments, different groups of applications, different groups of users, and so on.

Identity Providers

Within a Service Namespace you can configure multiple identity providers and multiple relying parties. You can also configure which identity providers are valid for which relying parties. Windows Live ID is configured as an identity provider out-of-the-box, and Google or Yahoo are available preconfigured, so you can add these easily. If you want to use Facebook, you first must create a Facebook application, so that's a little more work. With the Management Portal you can add any identity provider using WS-Federation, such as ADFS 2.0. With ADFS 2.0 you can authenticate using a Windows account, which you can do with a username and password, but also with a client certificate or smartcard, enabling multifactor authentication. The Management Service also enables you to add OpenID 2.0–based identity providers.

One of the major advantages of ACS reliance on external identity providers is that it is up to ACS to stay up to date when the identity provider changes its protocol. When Facebook changed its protocol, applications that used ACS were shielded from those changes and continued to work as if nothing had happened.

The limited number of identity providers (currently) supported may seem a major restriction, but because ACS supports both WS-Federation and OpenID, it is perfectly acceptable to create your own authentication mechanism. You can also construct a protocol bridge to another authentication mechanism, as shown in Figure 14-2. Such a protocol bridge isn't hard to construct if you use the Visual Studio template for a STS, as discussed in Chapter 9, although you must tighten the security of the code you get from the template.

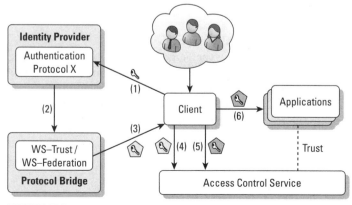

FIGURE 14-2

Service Identities and Management Service Accounts

Not all identity providers lend themselves well to doing service-to-service communication without user interaction. For this purpose ACS also provides a concept known as a *Service Identity*. This is an identity you define within ACS, so ACS is the identity provider. A service can then authenticate with ACS using a username-password combination, X.509 certificate, or symmetric key. How to use this is discussed in more detail in the section "Working with Service Identities."

The Management Service of ACS is accessed in a similar fashion as you would access services using a Service Identity. Accounts for the Management Service have exactly the same properties, but these accounts apply only to the Management Service.

Supported Protocols

To authorize users with applications, ACS defaults to WS-Trust and WS-Federation, but ACS also supports *OAuth Web Resource Authorization Protocol* (*OAuth WRAP*) and *OAuth*. OAuth is an open standard that enables users to hand out tokens for authorization to data hosted by a service provider (application). OAuth tokens can authorize for parts of the data and with limited access rights. An example is a token that grants a photo print service access to a selection of pictures on a site such as Flickr or Picasa. OAuth 2.0 is the current version of the standard, but although OAuth WRAP is deprecated, ACS supports it for backward compatibility with existing applications.

Available Token Formats

The following are the token formats ACS supports:

➤ **Security Assertion Markup Language (SAML) 1.1:** SAML is an XML format and standard governed by the Organization for the Advancement of Structures Information Standards (OASIS). SAML 1.1 is supported by WIF and is used in Chapter 9.

➤ **SAML 2.0:** The most recent version of the SAML token format.

➤ **Simple Web Token (SWT):** This is basically a string of key-value pairs with a signature; although it also contains information about the issuer, the application the token applies to, and when the token expires. The simplicity of SWT makes it easier to use this format with applications not natively supporting a token format.

Rules and Rule Groups

What goes into a token sent to a relying party is governed by rules. These rules can look at the incoming claims and determine which claims are placed in the outgoing token. Rules are grouped in rule groups. All rules in a rule group are executed if a token is created for a relying party for which the rule group is enabled. You can create multiple rule groups, and you can enable multiple rule groups to a relying party. Also, a rule group can apply to multiple relying parties. A rule is scope for a particular identity provider, so whether the rule fires depends on whether it applies to the identity provider used by the user.

GETTING STARTED WITH THE ACCESS CONTROL SERVICE

Now that you understand what the Access Control Service is, and how it is structured, you can start to work with it. That means setting up ACS and setting up applications to make use of the tokens ACS provides.

Creating a Service Namespace

The first thing you need to do is set up a Service Namespace, as shown in the following steps. You do this from the Management Portal under Service Bus, Access Control & Caching.

1. Select Access Control in the submenu.

2. In the taskbar click New, showing the dialog to create a Service Namespace, preconfigured to create a Service Namespace for Access Control.

3. Enter a meaningful namespace name that's still available. The URL for the Service Namespace is based on what you choose. The values in Figure 14-3 create a Service Namespace with the following URL: `https://pmc-accesscontrol.accesscontrol.windows.net`.

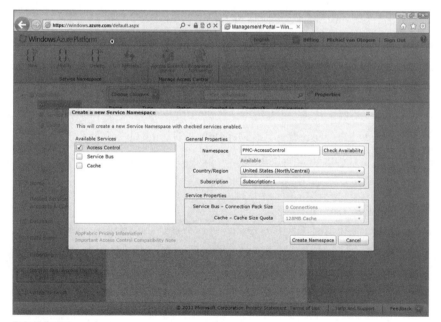

FIGURE 14-3

4. Choose the data center location under Country/Region.

5. If you have more than one subscription, select the subscription the Service Namespace applies to.

6. Click Create Namespace.

After the Service Namespace is created, you can select it in the Management Portal, and click Access Control Service in the Manage Access Control section of the taskbar. This redirects you to the aforementioned URL. You can also go to the URL directly and log in with Windows Live ID, if you're not already logged in.

Securing a Web Application

After you create a Service Namespace, you can start with enabling applications to accept authentication through ACS. For applications using WIF, this doesn't differ much from what you learned in Chapter 9, although ACS works differently than an STS you create. You need to create a web application.

1. Create a new Windows Azure project in Visual Studio called **AcsPassiveRP**.

2. Add an ASP.NET Web Role and name it **WebRoleRP**.

3. Configure the Web Role to be hosted under SSL on port 8443.

The preceding steps should be familiar to you from Chapter 9. Now you need to hook up the application to ACS. You need to ensure the application accepts tokens from ACS.

1. Go to the Access Control Service Management Portal.

2. From the menu select Application Integration.

3. From the Endpoint Reference section, copy the URL for the WS-Federation Metadata.

4. Start the Windows Identity Foundation Utility (FedUtil) as you learned in Chapter 9.

5. Select the `web.config` of the Web Role, set the Application URI, and click Next.

6. Using an existing STS, paste the ACS Metadata URL, and click Next.

7. The default ACS certificate is self-signed, so keep chain validation disabled, and click Next.

8. At this point there is no encryption, so click Next.

9. Finish by clicking Next and Finish.

10. Start the project with Ctrl+F5. This results in the error shown in Figure 14-4.

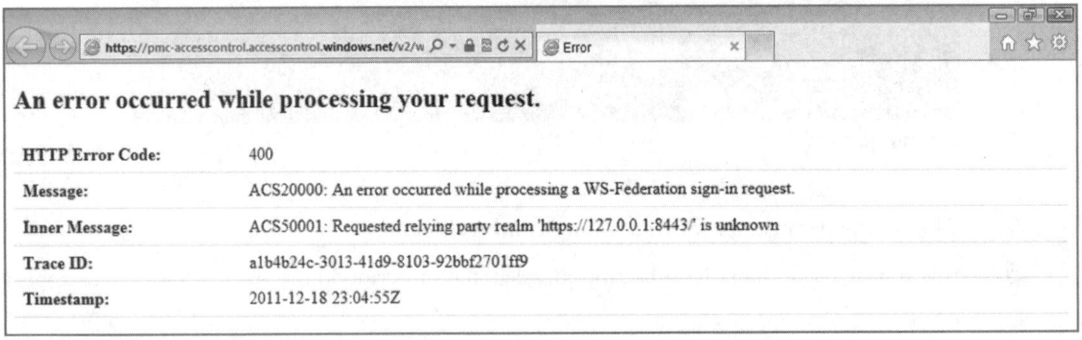

	https://pmc-accesscontrol.accesscontrol.**windows.net**/v2/w 🔎 ▾ 🔒 🖹 🖒 ✕ Error ✕

An error occurred while processing your request.

HTTP Error Code:	400
Message:	ACS20000: An error occurred while processing a WS-Federation sign-in request.
Inner Message:	ACS50001: Requested relying party realm 'https://127.0.0.1:8443/' is unknown
Trace ID:	a1b4b24c-3013-41d9-8103-92bbf2701ff9
Timestamp:	2011-12-18 23:04:55Z

FIGURE 14-4

The error in Figure 14-4 happens because the application hasn't been configured yet as a relying party in ACS. ACS issues tokens only to applications it knows about, so other people can't use your ACS and run up the costs. There is also a security aspect to this. If a token sent to an application contains information about the user only some applications should know about, then sending tokens to any application asking for one would result in a security breach. The following steps register the application with ACS.

1. Go to the Access Control Service Management Portal.

2. From the menu select Relying Party Applications.

3. Click Add.

4. Enter a display name for the relying party, for example **AcsPassiveRP**.

5. Under Realm enter the base URL, which is **https://127.0.0.1.8443/**.

6. Enter the same URL under Return URL.

7. Keep the remaining settings as they are and click Save.

> *Using the Federation Metadata from the application is much easier when you want to hook up an application to ACS. However, ACS can access only public IP addresses, so it can't reach your local system. This, of course, is different after you deploy to Windows Azure.*

If you run the application now, you will be asked to log in with your Windows Live ID, unless you're still logged into your ACS Management Portal because then you're already logged in. If you want to check if you need to log in, start a private browsing session in your browser.

After logging in, you will receive another error from ACS, which is shown in Figure 14-5. That's because although a rule group has been created for the relying party, it contains no rules. Therefore, the generated token will be empty, and that's not allowed. To solve this, you must add rules to the rule group.

1. From the menu select Rule groups.

2. Click the link of the rule group created for AcsPassiveRP.

3. Click Generate.

4. In the screen presented, click the Generate button.

Now when you run the application you will no longer get an error from ACS. Instead, you will get the dangerous request exception you also received in Chapter 9. You must add the `WifRequestValidator` discussed in Chapter 9 to solve this issue. After you do that, you're logged into the website, which indicates this in the top right. However, on closer inspection you'll note there is no username. The problem is that Windows Live ID actually doesn't give you a name claim, which is what WIF uses as the username, by default. You can solve this in two ways:

➤ Modify WIF to use another claim type for the username.

➤ Modify the generated rule to transform the incoming claim type to the name claim type.

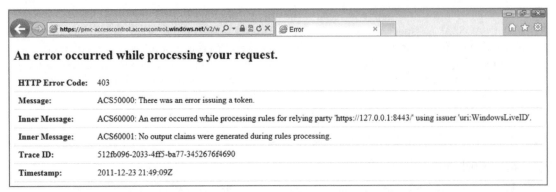

FIGURE 14-5

The latter makes more sense because if you ever switch to another STS, the name claim might be available again. Also, using rules you can unify identifiers coming in from different identity providers because these are likely to differ.

To modify the generated rule, follow these steps:

1. From the menu, select Rule groups.

2. Click the link of the rule group created for AcsPassiveRP.

3. Click the nameidentifier rule.

4. Keep the If section of the claim rule the same. For the Output claim, select **http://schemas .xmlsoap.org/ws/2005/05/identity/claims/name** in the Then section, which is the name claim type used by WIF.

5. Set the description to indicate that nameidentifier is transformed to name.

6. Click Save.

Now when you log in again through ACS you'll find an identifier behind the Welcome message. Because Windows Live ID uses your e-mail address as the login name, you may have expected that to be in the nameidentifier claim. As you can see in Figure 14-6, that is not the case. The only thing you get is some unique identifier of the user. You can use that identifier to store information in your application about the user. If you require information beyond the unique identifier, you must store that in your own database. This includes any authorizations you may want to give the user.

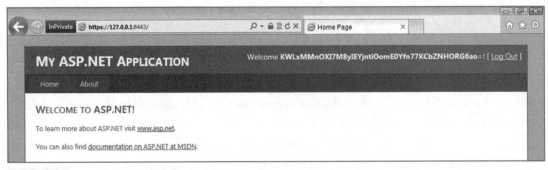

FIGURE 14-6

Because the nameidentifier claim is not a name, you can't use it for display purposes. If you intend to have a username displayed coming from data within the application, it is better not to transform the claim as shown here. That way you can fill in the name value yourself.

 In the preceding section, SAML 1.1 is the token format used because it is the default in WIF. It is beyond the scope of this book to discuss using the Simple Web Token (SWT) format, because SWT is used far less than SAML.

Configuring Additional Identity Providers

Authenticating users through Windows Live ID, which is the default for ACS, may work fine for your application; it probably beats building your own functionality to log in, recover a forgotten password, and so on. The downside, of course, is that your users require a Windows Live ID, and you can safely assume that not all users have one or are inclined to get one. However, if you add Google and Yahoo! as identity providers, you'll cover a lot more people, and your users can choose which provider they use. If they don't have an account with any of these providers, they can create one with the provider they trust the most. Adding these providers is easy.

1. Go to the Access Control Service Management Portal.

2. Select Identity Providers from the menu. You see Windows Live ID already configured.

3. Click Add. This shows a list of all the identity providers you can add.

4. Under the preconfigured providers select Google (or Yahoo!) and click Next.

5. You are now presented with the configuration screen for the chosen provider, which looks like Figure 14-7 and is the same for Google and Yahoo! Everything is already good to go, so you can just click Save.

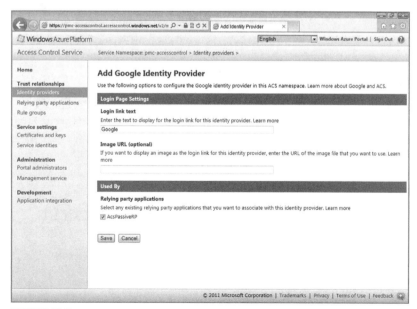

FIGURE 14-7

In the section "Federating from a Local Network with ADFS 2.0" later in this chapter, you learn how to add an identity provider that is not preconfigured.

As you can see in Figure 14-7, you can change the text of the login link and set an image to be shown with the login link. What you enter there is used on the page the user sees when an application sends the user to ACS to log in. There the user can select the login method by clicking the appropriate link. This page is also known as the *home realm discovery* page. The *home realm* is the network where you come from or where you log in. This name is misleading for Google or Yahoo! because you are not on the network of one of those companies (unless you happen to work there).

As you can also see in Figure 14-7, you can also select which relying parties the identity provider applies to. By default, all configured relying parties are selected. A reason why you may want to change this could be that you have an application that should be accessible only to users in your own network through ADFS, whereas other applications must be available for users outside the company. Because you can differentiate between identity providers, there is no need to set up a separate Service Namespace for this scenario.

Because the current rule group works only with Windows Live ID, you still need to add a rule for Google.

1. From the menu, select Rule Groups.

2. Click the link of the rule group created for AcsPassiveRP.

3. Click the Generate link, which shows the Generate Rules page with Google selected and Windows Live ID not selected because there is already a rule for it.

4. Click the Generate button, which results in the screen shown in Figure 14-8.

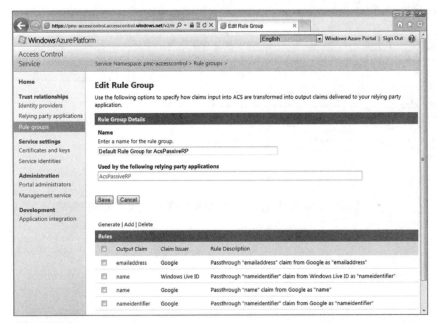

FIGURE 14-8

Google provides ACS with more information about the user than Windows Live ID. In addition to the nameidentifier claim, you also get the name and e-mail address of the user. This ties back to the earlier comments about whether it's a good idea to transform the nameidentifier claim that Windows Live ID provides to a name claim.

Because there are now two identity providers configured in ACS for your application, you are not sent to Windows Live ID directly when you start the application. Instead, you are sent to the home realm discovery page, which is shown in Figure 14-9. From the home realm discovery page, you can choose how you want to log in. If you now choose Google, you can log in with any Google account. After you're authenticated, and you have given Google permission to share your information with your ACS Service Namespace, you're logged in to the application and your name is shown in the Welcome message.

FIGURE 14-9

CUSTOMIZING THE ACCESS CONTROL SERVICE

The Access Control Service (ACS) is more than just a gateway that provides users with the ability to log on using identity providers such as Windows Live ID, Google ID, and so on. It is a platform that supports many access control scenarios through the different protocols it supports. It also provides extensibility points you can use to customize and manage how ACS works for you.

Enhancing the Login Experience

Up until now the login experience was quite simple. When you start the sample application, you are immediately sent to ACS because all pages are secured. WIF crafts the correct login link from configuration, which was built with FedUtil. When you reach ACS, it either shows you the home realm discovery page, or sends you to the identity provider if only one is configured. This works fine but doesn't work as well if your users come into a page that's public, and if you have pages that contain both public and personalized content. Also, the home realm discovery page hosted by ACS is functional, but it doesn't shine in the design department.

ACS provides two login options, which you can find in the ACS Management Portal by following these steps:

1. Go to the ACS Management Portal.

2. On the menu select Application integration.

3. Click Login Pages to reveal a list with all configured relying parties.

4. Select the application for which you want to change the login experience, in this case AcsPassiveRP.

You are now presented with information for both login options, which are discussed in more detail in the next two sections.

Linking to the Login Page

The first option you have is to link to ACS yourself. This doesn't make the graphical design any better, but it does give you more control over what happens when a user logs in. To embed it in the application, take the following steps.

1. Copy the link from the Login Page Integration page of the relying party.

2. In Visual Studio, open `Site.master`.

3. Find the `<AnonymousTemplate>` in the `<asp:LoginView>` control.

4. Add `&wctx=rm%3d0%26id%3dpassive%26ru%3d%252f` to the end of the link.

5. Replace the existing link with the link copied from ACS.

6. Open `web.config`.

7. Find the `<authorization>` section and delete it or turn it into a comment.

8. Run the application. Instead of sending you straight to the home realm discovery page, you see the home page.

9. Click the Login link to initiate the login process.

10. Finish the login process to see the home page in logged in state.

Step 4 is crucial. The link provided by ACS is missing information for WIF to recognize the response from ACS as a sign in response. Adding a properly formatted `wctx` parameter to the querystring fixes that. The `wctx` parameter sends context information in the request to ACS (or any other STS) that gets passed around and back to the requestor, so the requestor can give itself information on how to process the response to its own request. The string in step 4 is URL-encoded and contains three name-value pairs:

➤ `rm=0`

➤ `id=passive`

➤ `ru=/`

The first two help WIF identify the passive federation response. The third, which actually has a double URL encoding because the value is a forward slash, indicates which page to go to after the sign-in has been processed. Because the steps currently have this code, it redirects you to the home page. If you want to redirect to another page, all you need to do is add the path, keeping in mind that you must replace a forward slash with `%252f`. Also, don't forget to encode the URL and querystring you want to send along.

 A more complex but more elegant way to manipulate the `wctx` *parameter is through the* `Context` *property of the* `SignInRequestMessage` *object. You can do this in the* `RedirectingToIdentityProvider` *event of the* `WSFederationAuthenticationModule,` *which you can hook up to a handler in the* `Application_Start` *event handler in* `global.asax.`

Hosting a Custom Login Page

Because the default home realm discovery page doesn't look nice, and likely doesn't fit the design of your application, you may want to provide your own. ACS provides you with a JSON feed to accomplish this. The JSON feed contains an entry for each configured identity provider available for the relying party. Each entry contains the values listed in Table 14-1.

TABLE 14-1: ACS Home Realm Discovery JSON Feed Values

NAME	DESCRIPTION
Name	The display name of the identity provider as configured in the ACS Management Portal.
LoginUrl	The URL to login with the identity provider.
LogoutUrl	The URL to logout with the identity provider. Only works with Windows Live ID and ADFS 2.0.
ImageUrl	URL of the image to display for the identity provider as configured in the ACS Management Portal.
EmailAddressSuffixes	E-mail address suffixes associated with the identity provider. Only suffixes for ADFS 2.0 identity providers can be configured.

The most important value in Table 14-1 is the login URL. As you saw in the previous paragraph, it needs to be tweaked to ensure WIF recognizes the sign in response. Also a slight mistake can actually make ACS return an error. If you use the default URL or use the example login provided in the ACS Management Portal, logging in to the relying party doesn't work. You can fix this by altering the parameters sent to ACS to get the JSON feed. Table 14-2 shows the URL parameters you can use to alter the login URL.

TABLE 14-2: Parameters for the Home Realm Discovery JSON Feed

NAME	DESCRIPTION
`protocol`	Protocol the relying party uses for authentication through ACS. Currently only the value `wsfederation` is accepted.
`realm`	Realm configured in ACS for the relying party.
`version`	Version of the feed. Must have the value `1.0`.
`reply_to`	Optional parameter to indicate where ACS should return to after authenticating at the identity provider.
`context`	Optional parameter with context information that can be passed back to the relying party in the token.
`callback`	Optional parameter indicating the JavaScript function to call when the JSON feed is returned. The feed is passed to the function as an argument.

From Table 14-2, the `context` parameter is what you need to use to get a login URL that works with WIF. Its value should be exactly the same as the `wctx` parameter you used earlier.

 When you use the `reply_to` *parameter to specify the return URL, you will likely get an ACS error—and not the desired effect. You can configure the return URL in the* `context` *parameter as shown earlier with the* `wctx` *parameter.*

To create a working self-hosted login page, take the following steps:

1. Download the example login page from the Login Page Integration page of the relying party.

2. In Visual Studio, add a new HTML page to `AcsPassiveRP`.

3. Copy the contents from the downloaded login page into the page added in the previous step.

4. Add the following to the body tag: `style="background-color: Red"`.

5. Find the last `<script>` element in the page. The element should have a `src` attribute with a URL that points to your ACS Service Namespace.

6. In the `src` attribute, find the context parameter. After the equals character (=), paste the following: `rm%3d0%26id%3dpassive%26ru%3d%252f`.

7. Save the page and then open `Site.master`.

8. Find the `<AnonymousTemplate>` in the `<asp:LoginView>` control.

9. Replace the existing link with a link to the page added in step 2, and then save the file.

When you run the application and click the Login link, you see the login page you just added to the application. It looks the same as the page hosted in ACS, except that the background is now bright red. That, of course, is only so you can see that you are actually viewing the page you added instead of the ACS hosted page. You can modify the design of the page as you see fit and integrate it into an application to align with the technology you use (for example: ASP.NET MVC, PHP). You can find more samples to integrate with ACS in the Codeplex site setup for ACS 2.0 samples and documentation at `http://acs.codeplex.com/`. There you can also find samples to use for other protocols.

Working with Service Identities

If you want to secure web services with ACS, you can't use any of the external identity providers. You need to authenticate with ACS directly. This is what Service Identities are for. A Service Identity is a credential that a client can use to request a token to access a web service. This works using active federation, as discussed in Chapter 9, and works with the same types of bindings using the WS-Federation protocol. As discussed earlier, ACS also supports other protocols, for which you can find samples and documentation at `http://acs.codeplex.com/`. However, if you use .NET, why would you deviate from what you already know and the standard supported by Windows Identity Foundation?

Creating a Relying Party Service

Creating a WCF service in Windows Azure is similar to what you learned in Chapter 9. However, because the STS is already there, you don't need to create it. Also, you can take a few shortcuts to speed up the process. The first thing you need to do is create a service. It makes sense to run it only under HTTPS, so instead of first going through the motions to make a basic service and connect the client, you can set it up under HTTPS directly.

1. Create a new cloud project called `AcsActiveRP`.

2. Add a WCF Service Web Role to the solution and call it `WcfWebRoleRP`.

3. Open the `WcfWebRoleRP` configuration and go to Endpoints.

4. Change the protocol of Endpoint1 to https and set the public port to port 8443.

5. Save the configuration.

6. Open `Web.config`.

7. Find the `<serviceMetadata>` element and change the `httpGetEnabled` attribute to `httpsGetEnabled`.

8. In the same behavior add the configuration to use the request headers for the meta data as you learned in Chapter 9 with the following XML:

```
<useRequestHeadersForMetadataAddress>
  <defaultPorts>
    <add scheme="https" port="8443" />
  </defaultPorts>
</useRequestHeadersForMetadataAddress>
```

code snippet 01_MetadataRequestHeadersConfig.txt

9. Because you're not going to expose the service on HTTP first, you need to add a binding and a service endpoint configuration that uses HTTPS. The following configuration takes care of that:

```
<bindings>
  <basicHttpBinding>
    <binding name="myBinding">
      <security mode="Transport">
        <transport clientCredentialType="None" />
      </security>
    </binding>
  </basicHttpBinding>
</bindings>
<services>
  <service name="WcfWebRoleRP.Service1">
    <endpoint address=""
              binding="basicHttpBinding"
              bindingConfiguration="myBinding"
              contract="WcfWebRoleRP.IService1" />
  </service>
</services>
```

code snippet 02_HttpsBasicHttpEndpointConfig.txt

10. Deploy the service and ensure you can access the WSDL through `https://127.0.0.1:8443/service1.svc?wsdl`.

After you create the service, you can hook it up to ACS. This is a two-step process. First, use FedUtil to set the appropriate configuration on the server, and then register the relying party with ACS. As you've learned in Chapter 9, the devil is in the details when it comes to using WIF, and to ensure you do it correctly follow these steps.

1. Open the ACS Management Portal and select Application integration from the menu.

2. Copy the WS-Federation Metadata URL.

3. Start FedUtil.

4. Select `web.config` of `AcsActiveRP`.

5. Set the Application URI to `https://127.0.0.1:8443/Service1.svc`.

> `Service1` *is spelled with a capital letter. This value is used in the audience URI configuration, which needs to match exactly with the audience URI in the token.*

6. Click Next and click Next again in the next dialog.

7. Select Use an Existing STS and then paste the URL you copied in step 2.

8. Click Next and click Next again in the next dialog.

9. Select Enable Encryption, and select the `RpEncrypt` certificate from Chapter 9 as the certificate to use.

10. Click Next, followed by Next and Finish.

At this point the configuration is nearly correct. There are just two issues you need to correct:

➤ The `ws2007FederationHttpBinding` is now configured for Message security, and as such it doesn't take into account that the service is running under HTTPS. You can solve this by changing

```
<security mode="Message">
```

to

```
<security mode="TransportWithMessageCredential">
```

➤ The endpoint is configured with an absolute address, even though the following is also configured:

```
<serviceHostingEnvironment multipleSiteBindingsEnabled="true" />
```

This setting requires all addresses to be relative. The easiest way to solve this is to remove the address altogether from the endpoint. The endpoint is already provided at a specific address because of the `Service1.svc` file in the root of the application.

With these issues resolved, there is one more thing you need to do: ensure the WSDL is accessible. To do this, add the following configuration to enable the Metadata Exchange endpoint:

```
<endpoint address="mex"
          binding="mexHttpsBinding"
          contract="IMetadataExchange" />
```

code snippet 03_MetadataExchangeConfig.txt

> *Don't forget to remove the Metadata Exchange endpoint when you deploy an application to production, unless you want third parties to read the WSDL. Otherwise, it is wiser to save the WSDL file and provide it separately.*

Configuring ACS

With the service done it's time to shift your attention to ACS. There you need to configure the relying party and the Service Identity. Start with the former.

1. Log in to the ACS Management portal.

2. On the menu select Service Identities.

3. Click Add.

4. Enter the name `AcsServiceIdentity`.

5. Select Password from the drop-down under Type.

6. Enter a password in the Password textbox that appears.

7. Click Save.

In step 5, the credential type of choice is Password, which translates to a username and password combination when you call the service. If you prefer stronger security, you can also use Symmetric Key or an X.509 certificate. With the former you just specify the key, without a username. With the latter you use a certificate in ACS for which you have the certificate with private key installed on the service side. Of these options using an X.509 certificate is by far the most secure because it is much harder to copy around certificates than simple strings. If you elect to use a certificate, you are prompted to upload the .cer file of the certificate you want to use. You learn how to deal with this in the client later.

> *You can add multiple credentials to a Service Identity. This means you can use different authentication mechanisms side by side. Multiple credentials of the same type (for example, different passwords) are also supported.*

After setting up the Service Identity, you can set up the relying party. This is just like setting up a relying party for passive federation. The user interface is geared toward passive federation, but don't let that fool you. It just means that you can skip some information because, for instance, a return URL is not used for active federation. The following steps take you through the process.

1. Log in to the ACS Management portal.

2. On the menu select Relying Party Applications.

3. Click Add.

4. Enter a name for the relying party. It makes sense to name it the same as the application, in this case `AcsActiveRP`.

5. Under Realm enter the service address.

6. From the drop-down under Token Encryption Policy, select Require Encryption.

7. The application works with a Service Identity, so deselect all the identity providers to avoid confusion.

8. Under Token Encryption browse for the `RpEncrypt.cer` file, which corresponds with the `RpEncrypt` certificate you selected with FedUtil earlier.

9. Click Save.

The relying party configuration is now done, but there are no rules yet in the rule group. Without at least one rule, a valid token can't be created when the client requests a token. A service identity doesn't have a lot of information associated with it, so the rule can be a simple Passthrough rule. A Passthrough rule, as the name suggests, passes through all claims coming from the issuer. Creating one is easy.

1. From the menu select Rule Groups.

2. Select the rule group created for `AcsActiveRP`.

3. Click Add.

4. Under Input Claim Issuer, select Access Control Service.

5. Ensure that the remainder of the options in the If section are on Any and on Pass Through in the Then section.

6. Click Save. Notice that the name of the created rule is Passthrough.

Creating the Client

With the service ready and ACS configured, the last step is to create a client that uses the service. First, you need to set up the service proxy by adding a service reference to the service you created.

1. Start Visual C# and create a new Console Application named **AcsActiveClient**.

2. Right-click the project and select Add Service Reference.

3. With the service running in the development fabric, enter the URL to the meta data of the service, which is `https://127.0.0.01:8443/Service1.svc?wsdl`.

4. Click OK.

When the service proxy is created, the configuration contains the necessary binding configuration. This configuration defaults to using a symmetric key for authentication. Previously you created a Service Identity with a password, so you need to change this. Fortunately, the ACS Federation Metadata not only contains the endpoint of the default authentication method, but also the alternative methods. Visual Studio adds all the alternative bindings, and as comments shows how you should change the custom binding to use one of the other methods. All you need to do is change to the correct method.

1. Open `app.config`.

2. Find the `<issuer>` element in the custom binding. It's just above a commented section starting with `<alternativeIssuedTokenParameters>`.

3. Comment out the `<issuer>` element, by selecting it entirely and typing **Ctrl+K** followed by **Ctrl+C**.

4. Now copy the third `<issuer>` element in the commented section. The address attribute value should end with `/v2/wstrust/13/username`.

5. Paste the copied element under the `<issuer>` element you commented out in step 3.

The last thing you need is the code to call the service, which is almost the same code you used in the chapter to call a service with the same signature. The difference is that now you can't use your Windows identity, so you should provide a username and password. Listing 14-1 shows the modified code, which you should add to the `Main` method of `Program.cs`. The bolded lines show you the added lines, which provide the username and password.

LISTING 14-1: Loop Calling the Service on User Input

```
while (true)
{
    Console.Write("Enter a value: ");
    var input = Console.ReadLine();
    if (string.IsNullOrEmpty(input)) break;
    int value;
    if (int.TryParse(input, out value))
    {
        var client = new ServiceReference1.Service1Client();
        client.ClientCredentials.UserName.UserName = "AcsServiceIdentity";
        client.ClientCredentials.UserName.Password = "Password";
        Console.WriteLine(client.GetData(value));
    }
}
```

If you run the client now, you should be able to call the service. The initial response may take a while, and sometimes the first call even times out. Don't be alarmed, just try again. If you get any other exception than a timeout, check the error message to see what's wrong. In the inner exception you will find an ACS error code and description.

Refining the Service

In Chapter 9, several modifications were made to the service up front to provide proper cookie handling in a load balanced environment such as Windows Azure. At this point the configuration is just a deafult `ws2007FederationHttpBinding`, so the changes needed for the load balanced environment haven't been made yet. To get that operational, you need to modify the binding to be like the binding used in Chapter 9, and you need to set up `SessionSecurityTokenHandler`. Fortunately, changing the binding to the custom binding used in Chapter 9 has no effect on the client configuration. Everything will work fine.

Because it doesn't make sense to repeat the exercise from Chapter 9, the steps are not discussed here. The code download for Chapter 14, however, does contain a sample with the modified binding and `SessionSecurityTokenHandler`.

Authenticating with a Client Certificate

Client certificates are an effective way of authentication. Certificates are tried and tested, and can use a large encryption key for optimal security. Because you need to explicitly install a certificate on both the client and the identity provider, in this case ACS, the chances of a security breach are much lower than with a username and password. With the latter a malicious programmer can just try username and password combinations. With certificates this isn't quite so easy.

Setting up client authentication with ACS is fairly simple. In essence you need to create a certificate, upload it to ACS, and modify your application to use the certificate. With the following steps, you create a certificate and upload it to ACS.

1. Open the Visual Studio command prompt or the Windows SDK command prompt as Administrator. If you use the Windows SDK command prompt, change the directory to `c:\Program Files\Microsoft SDKs\Windows\v7.1\bin`.

2. Type `makecert -a sha256 -n CN=AcsServiceIdentity -pe -r -sky exchange -ss My -sr LocalCurrentUser`.

3. After the certificate is created, export the certificate without the private key, as you learned in Chapter 9.

4. Open the ACS Management Portal and navigate to Service Identities.

5. Click `AcsServiceIdentity`.

6. Click Add.

7. Select X.509 Certificate from the Type drop-down, and upload the certificate file you created in step 3.

8. Click Save.

With ACS all set, you need to modify the configuration of your client to use the certificate. This consists of two steps:

➤ Modifying the issuer like you did before

➤ Specifying the certificate to use

The first step is needed because ACS provides a different endpoint for each authentication type. Each authentication type uses a slightly different protocol configuration, so if you point the client to another endpoint, you also need to modify the protocol binding slightly. The following steps take care of that for certificate authentication.

1. Open `app.config` of `AcsActiveClient`.

2. Now replace the `<issuer>` element with the fourth alternative option, which ends in `/v2/wstrust/13/certificate`.

3. Add the following code to the `<system.serviceModel>` section:

```
<behaviors>
  <endpointBehaviors>
    <behavior name="ClientCredentialsBehavior">
```

Available for download on Wrox.com

```
<clientCredentials>
  <clientCertificate
      storeLocation="CurrentUser"
      storeName="My"
      x509FindType="FindByThumbprint"
      findValue=""/>
  </clientCredentials>
 </behavior>
</endpointBehaviors>
</behaviors>
```

code snippet 04_ClientCertificateBehaviorConfig.txt

4. Open the certificate file you created and go to the Details tab.

5. Scroll down to the Thumbprint property and select it, as shown in Figure 14-10 (without the leading space).

6. Copy the thumbprint and paste it into the behavior configuration as the value for the `find-Value` attribute.

7. Find the endpoint configuration and add `behaviorConfiguration="ClientCredentials Behavior"` to the element, so it looks like this configuration:

```
<endpoint address="https://127.0.0.1:8443/Service1.svc"
         binding="customBinding"
         bindingConfiguration="WS2007FederationHttpBinding_IService1"
         behaviorConfiguration="ClientCredentialsBehavior"
         contract="ServiceReference1.IService1"
         name="WS2007FederationHttpBinding_IService1" />
```

code snippet 05_CertificateBehaviorEndpointConfig.txt

8. Save `app.config`.

9. Open `Program.cs` and remove the highlighted lines of code in Listing 14-1.

10. Save `Program.cs` and run the application.

Strictly speaking, step 9 is superfluous. The binding uses a certificate and the certificate to use is in the configuration. The username and password specified are just ignored because they are not used with the configured protocol.

Federating from a Local Network with ADFS 2.0

One of the great things about the way identity federation works is that the security token service and the relying party don't necessarily need to contact each other. As long as the client can reach both, it can get a token from the

FIGURE 14-10

STS and present it to the relying party. The trust relationship between the STS and the relying party ensures the token is accepted. This has two advantages:

➤   You can use your network credentials to sign in to an application running in Windows Azure.

➤   An STS in the local network is much less likely to be compromised.

This scenario was already briefly covered in Chapter 9 and shown in Figure 9-3, so before you actually learn how to set this up, you may want to reread that section.

The main ingredient for this scenario is Active Directory Federation Services 2.0 (ADFS), which acts as the STS in the local network. ADFS 2.0 is a free add-on for Windows Server 2008 and up.

Installing ADFS 2.0

To install ADFS 2.0 you need an Active Directory domain running on Windows Server 2008 or higher. For a domain you need to enable the Active Directory Domain Services (ADDS) role of Windows Server.

> *Setting up a Windows Server 2008 machine and installing ADDS is beyond the scope of this book, but you can find ADDS setup instructions at* `http://bit.ly/ installadwin2008`. *Be sure to pick a domain name that doesn't collide with online domains. You can ensure this by using the* `.local` *suffix. It's also a good idea to use a meaningful domain name, for instance* `azuredemo.local`.

Users with a domain account can use their credentials for authentication to acquire a token from ADFS 2.0. They can do so from outside the domain, providing they have access to the ADFS 2.0 server, in which case they are prompted for their credentials. If users are logged into the local domain, because their computer is tied to the domain and they work in the local network, they get a single sign-on (SSO) experience because the browser uses the credentials used to log on to the computer transparently.

> *ADFS 2.0 doesn't require you to authenticate using a Windows domain account. You can actually set up other identity providers as you would in ACS. You still need to set up an Active Directory domain, but you would bypass it.*

After you set up the domain, you can install ADFS 2.0. ADFS 2.0 requires Internet Information Server, Windows Identity Foundation, Windows PowerShell, and several hotfixes. The installer checks for the prerequisites and installs these automatically if possible. Otherwise, you must install them manually. You can download the free ADFS 2.0 installer from `http://bit.ly/adfs2rtw`. You must take the following steps to perform a simple ADFS 2.0 installation:

1.   Start the downloaded installer.

2.   Click Next.

3. Accept the license agreement and click Next.

4. Select Federation Server and click Next.

5. Click Next and Finish so the Microsoft Management Console for ADFS 2.0 is started automatically.

6. Click the AD FS 2.0 Federation Service Configuration Wizard.

7. Select Create a new Federation Service and click Next.

8. Select New Federation Server Farm and click Next.

9. The settings for SSL should already correspond with the SSL certificate used in the server, so click Next.

10. Select the account that runs the ADFS 2.0 service. It is good practice to create a dedicated account for this like `ADFSservice`.

11. Enter the password of the service account and click Next.

12. Click Next and then Close.

With the previous steps, you install a single ADFS 2.0 service. There are however several different topologies. Which topology is best depends on your network setup, whether the service is available on a public address, and what your security level needs to be.

It is beyond the scope of this book to discuss the different topologies, but you can find more information in the ADFS 2.0 section of TechNet, and more specifically on the pages discussing the possible deployment topologies. You can find the latter at `http://bit.ly/ADFS2Topo`.

Adding ADFS 2.0 as Identity Provider

When you've installed ADFS 2.0 in your domain, you can add it as an identity provider for your ACS Service Namespace. If you use ADFS 2.0 to extend the reach of local network credentials to federate across the network boundary (and firewall), it is most likely that the ADFS 2.0 service is only available from the local network. Of course, it is not a requirement. However, if you plan to expose ADFS 2.0 to the outside world, you (or the system administrator) should be aware of the design considerations that go with that. The aforementioned section of TechNet and the link to deployment topologies are required reading in that case. If you expose ADFS 2.0 to the outside world, ACS can reach the federation meta data file. Otherwise, you need to store it locally and upload it to ACS, as is done in the following configuration steps.

1. Browse to the federation meta data file of ADFS. You can find it at `https://[hostname]/federationmetadata/2007-6/federationmetadata.xml`.

2. Save the federation meta data file locally.

3. Open the ACS Management Portal.

4. From the menu select Identity providers.

5. Click Add.

6. ADFS 2.0 is a WS-Federation identity provider, so click Next.

7. Enter a name for the identity provider used in the Management Portal.

8. Under WS-Federation meta data browse for the meta data file you saved in step 2.

9. Enter the text to be shown on the login page under Login link text.

10. Under e-mail domain names enter the e-mail suffix used when you installed ADFS.

11. From the menu select Rule groups.

12. Select the default rule group for AcsPassiveRP.

13. Click Generate.

14. Ensure only ADFS is selected and click Generate.

When you check the rules that are part of the default rule group, there are quite a few now; you need to page through the list of rules to see all of them. Through the federation meta data, ADFS 2.0 exposes all the claim types it is capable of producing, including any custom claim types you may have configured. However, by default ADFS 2.0 does not send any claim to the relying party unless it has been configured to send specific claims. The claim types listed in the federation meta data are claim types that ADFS 2.0 could expose based on the data you could store about users in Active Directory.

Because ADFS 2.0 publishes so many possible claim types, it makes sense to actually create a separate rule group for it. That way you can more easily keep it apart from other identity providers.

Making ACS an ADFS Relying Party

That ACS has read the federation meta data and configured ADFS 2.0 as an identity provider is only half the process. ADFS 2.0 won't issue a token unless it knows the relying party, in this case ACS. To make ACS a known relying party, take the following steps:

1. Open the ADFS 2.0 Management Console.

2. In the left pane navigate to AD FS 2.0 ⇨ Trust Relationships ⇨ Relying Party Trusts.

3. In the Actions pane on the right, select Add Relying Party Trust.

4. Click Start.

5. In the active textbox enter the URL of the Service Namespace: `https://YourServiceNamespace.accesscontrol.windows.net/` and click Next.

6. Enter a friendly display name, and click Next.

7. Keep the setting that permits all users access, and click Next.

8. Click Next again to confirm, and then click Close.

9. Click Add Rule.

10. From the drop-down select Pass Through or Filter an Incoming Claim, and click Next.

11. Enter Name as the Claim rule name.

12. Select Name as the Incoming claim type from the drop-down.

13. Keep the remainder of the settings, and click Finish.

14. Click OK to close the rule dialog.

After completing the previous steps, everything should work. You can test this with the `AcsPassiveRP` project you created earlier.

1. Start the application.

2. Click the login link.

3. Under "Sign in using your e-mail address," enter a valid e-mail address for the ADFS domain. If you followed the installation instructions earlier, `administrator@azuredemo.local` should work.

4. After clicking Submit, a Windows Security dialog displays. Enter the username with the domain name, as follows: **`azuredemo.local\administrator`**.

5. Also enter the password, and click OK.

These steps should log you in and show the website with the username including the NETBIOS domain name, which is AZUREDEMO in this case.

 If the previous steps don't work, you may need to clear the cookies in your browser.

Modifying the Token with Rule Groups

Earlier in the chapter you learned how to adjust a token to transform an incoming claim to another, so you could use it as the username. Depending on the identity provider, you can get few or quite a few claims, and you can pass these through or create new claims based on them. It does not matter how many claims you receive; you can create as many derivative claims as you like.

The Anatomy of a Rule

Rule groups are all about rules. A rule group is just a container of rules, making it easier to manage rules. You already created some simple rules, so you probably have some idea of how they work. Basically, a rule is an if-statement. It adds a claim to a token if certain conditions are met. These conditions are tested against an incoming claim. The conditions consist of three parts:

➤ The issuer of the claim

➤ The type of the claim

➤ The value of the claim

If all these conditions are met, the Then portion of the rule is executed and a claim is added to the token sent to the relying party. The issuer of the incoming claim can be either of the configured identity providers or the ACS itself. The latter is the case with a Service Identity, but also when the rule acts on a result of another claim rule. This implies that rule processing actually happens in two steps, as shown in Figure 14-11.

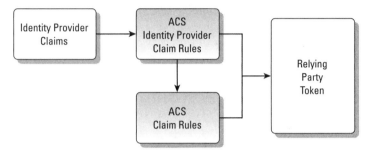

FIGURE 14-11

The input claim type determines which name-value pair is evaluated. Unless you are passing through everything that comes in, you must specify a specific type. For preconfigured identity providers, ACS knows which types it can receive, and you can select those types from the drop-down. You can also specify it manually in the textbox, but this doesn't make sense for identity providers with known claim types. If you connected an identity provider using the Federation Metadata file, like you learned with ADFS, the claim types are also known up front because these are specified in the Federation Metadata.

The claim value is a string that is checked if you specify one. Otherwise, the existence of the type is enough for the Then portion of the rule to be executed. This most often is used in pass-through scenarios.

In the Then portion of a rule, you again must specify the claim type and the claim value. You can pass through both from the If portion, or just the type or the value. Of course, you can also define a completely new type and value. You can either specify the type manually or select the type from the drop-down. The drop-down consists of all the known types in ACS, either because they are preconfigured or coming from one of the preconfigured identity providers, or because you imported Federation Metadata from an identity provider or relying party.

Dealing with User Data

ACS does not provide any options to save data about users that you could use in rules to generate a token with additional user information. In contrast, ADFS has the option to configure Attribute Stores that hold data about the user, and by default Active Directory is configured as one. In ADFS, you can then specify rules that use the data in the attribute store. Because ACS doesn't provide that, it makes sense to manage user data in the relying parties. The downside, of course, is that you must do that on all relying parties individually, unless you can let them share Azure Storage or a SQL Azure database. However, because ACS uses rule groups, you could create a rule group per user and use a single incoming claim to generate all the outgoing claims you need. For a small number of users, you can manage this with the ACS Management Portal, but for a larger user base, this becomes unmanageable. With the Management Service API, you can automate that management for values that users provide (for example, e-mail, phone number, or favorite pet), and provide a more appropriate user interface for user administrators to do this.

 Discussing the Management Service API is beyond the scope of this book, but the ACS Samples you can download for http://acs.codeplex.com/ *provide many samples and a common library that does all the heavy lifting.*

SUMMARY

In this chapter you learned that the Access Control Service is a ready-to-go Security Token Service that supports protocols such as WS-Federation, OpenID, and OAuth. It also enables you to use different identity providers, such as Windows Live ID, Facebook, and WS-Federation identity providers such as ADFS. Because ACS supports WS-Federation, it works well with Windows Identity Foundation, so it is easy to set up a relying party like you learned in Chapter 9. In addition you learned how you can customize the login experience of users, so the page presented to them is not a plain ACS page but a page that fits well with the user interface design of your application.

You also learned that for active federation relying parties you can use service identities, identities you define in ACS, and which clients can authenticate using a symmetric key, username and password, or certificate.

A key scenario for ACS is authenticating users that access business applications hosted in the cloud from the local network of their organization. You learned how to set up this using Active Directory Federation Services 2.0, which hooks into the Active Directory of an organization. The same also works if the local identity provider is not ADFS but uses the WS-Federation protocol.

15

Azure Connect

WHAT'S IN THIS CHAPTER?

➤ Defining Windows Azure Connect

➤ Exploring Windows Azure Connect versus Service Bus

➤ Understanding Windows Azure Connect fundamentals

➤ Setting up Windows Azure Connect

➤ Troubleshooting Windows Azure Connect

In cloud computing, many developers and their corresponding applications and infrastructure may not move to the cloud overnight, if at all. There may be a number of factors including security, latency, business requirements, functionality, or performance requirements that may require an on-premises deployment. However, these developers may still benefit from the Azure Cloud by finding a way to bridge their on-premises and cloud components. To connect to on-premises resources or applications, Windows Azure provides the Windows Azure Connect technology that makes connecting the Azure cloud to an on-premises resource as easy as a simple configuration. Without Azure Connect, you need to create and maintain secure connections, authentication, authorization, and troubleshooting between Azure and your on-premises resource, which takes valuable developer and IT professional time.

WHAT IS AZURE CONNECT?

One of the major blockers in moving to the cloud has been the capability to support a hybrid model between private clouds and public clouds. There may be instances of workloads that cannot move from on-premises servers to a public cloud infrastructure because of a myriad of reasons ranging from technology to policy and compliance reasons. To help remove this blocker, the Microsoft Azure team introduced Azure Connect. *Azure Connect* is similar to an on-demand virtual private network that connects your Azure instances to your on-premises computers. Azure Connect enables you to connect public and private clouds without having to worry about setting up complex infrastructure including IPSec, IP addresses, and other complexities. Azure Connect also enables location transparency; you do not need to know which Azure cluster you connect to: The software does all the location awareness, negotiation, and setup of the infrastructure layer. For example, you can use Azure Connect to connect to a local file share, a SharePoint Server, and a local SQL Server, or even join an Azure instance to your AD domain.

One fundamental piece of Azure is that it operates at the network layer, so applications do not need to be modified or coded to the network layer. Instead, developers can use logical names and addresses to access their resources, and Azure Connect can make sure the calls get to the appropriate resource, whether in the public or private cloud.

WINDOWS AZURE CONNECT VERSUS SERVICE BUS

You may wonder how Azure Connect compares to the Azure Service Bus, discussed in Chapter 13. Remember that the Azure Service Bus is at the application level and relays messages at the application level between application endpoints. These endpoints could exist on-premises, in the public cloud, or in both places. The Azure Service Bus requires a developer to write the service, configure the endpoint, and then run the endpoint to make sure that the service is available.

How the Azure Service Bus Works

Azure Service Bus provides a relay service that allows an on-premises client to connect to another service via this intermediary. Both the on-premises client and the Azure cloud client connect to the relay service through an outbound port, and then both create a bidirectional endpoint that they can communicate using a particular common address created by the relay service. Then, when one client needs to talk to the other client, it calls the outbound connection, which passes to the relay, which passes to the other service. The following are some things to remember about the Service Bus:

➤ **No client location or direct connection needed:** Neither the client nor the server needs to know where the other is located nor do they need a direct connection to each other.

➤ **The client doesn't need to be open to a firewall:** The on-premises client does not need any ports opened in the firewall because the bidirectional socket that the client creates with the relay service can traverse different network topologies.

➤ **The Service Bus operates at the application layer:** This enables you to secure your connections using transport security, message security, or both.

➤ **Multiple listeners are allowed:** The Service Bus allows for multiple listeners on a single endpoint. An example of this is if you need to multicast your message to multiple subscribers listening on a single Service Bus endpoint. You may want your application to notify multiple subscribers that something has changed. With multiple listeners on a single endpoint, you can deliver the message once, and the Service Bus relays the message to the multiple listeners on your behalf.

➤ **The Service Bus is a durable messaging infrastructure:** Transient failures of any part of the delivery of the messages between clients will be retried. The Service Bus ensures the messages are delivered whenever the message receiver is back online.

How Azure Connect Works

In contrast to Azure Service Bus, Azure Connect works at the network layer rather than the application layer. This means that Azure Connect is less focused on application constructs, such as setting up application level transports and message queuing, but instead focuses on setting up the networking pipeline between the different endpoints. Rather than forcing you to set up a VPN between your on-premises instances and your Azure roles, Azure Connect makes this setup as easy as installing software on your on-premises servers and making a small configuration change to your Azure role instance. In addition, Azure communicates over IPv6 between Azure and your on-premises servers using IPSec. Some things to remember when working with Azure Connect:

➤ **Azure Connect works at the network layer:** Because Azure Connect works at the network layer, it does not provide durable messaging like Service Bus. Your application would need to realize that the call or function failed and try the call again.

➤ **Azure Connect does not allow for communication between Azure role instances:** Instead Azure Connect targets private and public cloud integration scenarios. So, if you want to connect two applications running in two separate Azure roles instances, you must use the Service Bus as your communication layer.

➤ **Azure Connect does not require application changes:** This is in contrast to the Service Bus, which does require application changes. This means you can to connect directly to applications such as file shares, SQL Server, or SharePoint without writing a Service Bus endpoint. Accessing these applications are exactly the same as accessing them as you would on your corporate network. Azure Connect handles all the protocol and security negotiation on behalf of the caller.

➤ **Azure Connect is not as rich in security:** The Service Bus has a much richer security model through the use of the Windows Azure Access Control Services (ACS). Using ACS, you can authentication and authorize users using a variety of sources including Active Directory, OAuth sources, or custom authentication mechanisms. With Azure Connect, you will be limited to the configured network policy you create in the Azure portal, which defines which Azure roles and which local endpoints connect together. From there, authentication can be based on your local AD groups and users.

➤ **Azure Connect provides more control options:** You can remotely connect, administer, and debug your Azure role instances. You can use existing tools such as network or application monitoring tools or remote PowerShell using Azure Connect.

Which Technology Should You Choose?

Which technology you choose to use depends on what you want to achieve. If you make mostly minimal changes to your existing on-premises infrastructure and do not want to write a Service Bus frontend to your existing applications, Azure Connect is a good option to explore. If you want the ultimate flexibility in the services you expose and how your users access and authenticate against those services, the Service Bus can provide the most flexible approach, but the flexibility comes at the price of needing to write custom code and maintain that code over time.

WINDOWS AZURE CONNECT FUNDAMENTALS

Looking at the core architecture for Windows Azure Connect, Azure Connect is made up of three key components:

➤ **Name Service:** Provides name resolution so that the Azure and on-premises machines can locate each other through logical names that are translated to IPv6 addresses.

➤ **Relay Service:** Allows the connectivity between the on-premises machines and the hosted Azure machines.

➤ **Client Installation:** There is a client component that needs to be installed on the on-premises machines that configures and connects the on-premises machine to the relay server.

If you drill deeper into the networking fundamentals, each connected machine has a routable IPv6 address even if the machine has only an IPv4 address. One of the requirements of Azure Connect is having IPv6 enabled even if you do not use IPv6 as your main network addressing mechanism. The Azure Connect client agent sets up the virtual network adapter for Azure Connect, and there are no changes to the existing networks because all the changes Azure Connect makes are additive to your existing network stack and implementation.

The reason Azure Connect uses IPv6 is because of the larger address space, its native support for IPSec, and the better routing performance compared to IPv4. The IPv6 traffic is encapsulated over IPv4 using the SSTP SSL VPN protocol. All the connectivity of Azure Connect can work as long as your network has the capability to route traffic through the outbound HTTPS port. This allows Azure Connect to work through firewalls and NAT devices.

In addition, DNS name resolution for connected resources are based on the machine names through the name server. For local, non-connected resources, the on-premises machines continue to use their local DNS for name resolution. The Azure instances always use the Connect Name Service for all name resolution. Developers do not need to change code that uses logical names rather than networking addresses in their applications.

Finally, all communication between the resources is secured via an end-to-end certificate-based IPSec tunnel. The tunnel is scope to the Azure Connect virtual network. In addition, the Azure Connect agent automates the management of the IPSec certificates so that the IT administrator or developer does not need to configure or deploy these certificates. The authorization follows the network policy that you configure through the Azure Connect portal. IPSec also operates in the Encapsulating Security Payload (ESP) mode, which uses AES encryption and SHA-2 to ensure integrity of the payloads. To enable troubleshooting, the `ping` command and protocol ICMP is exempt from the IPSec policy rules.

Network Policy Model

To authenticate and authorize your machines in Azure Connect, your local machines need to be organized into Endpoint Groups. You can name these groups whatever you like, such as SQL Servers or Directory Servers or whatever logically makes sense. Within an Endpoint Group, you have computers, and a computer can be only in a single group at a time. Newly-activated computers are, by default, unassigned and require you to explicitly add them to an Endpoint Group.

Azure roles can be connected to the Endpoint Group, which allows connectivity between the role instances and the local computers in the group. Azure Connect does not control or connect Azure roles together. It only controls and connects Azure roles to local computers. This lack of connectivity between Azure roles is intentional because the Azure runtime controls this connectivity, and Azure Connect should not interfere with this capability.

In addition, you can connect Endpoint Groups to other Endpoint Groups. This allows connectivity between local computers within each group. Connectivity between Endpoint Groups is not transitive in that if Group A is connect to Group B and Group B is connected to Group C, Group A cannot connect to Group C without an explicit connection. You can also set a single Endpoint Group as interconnected, which allows connectivity between local computers within the group. Figure 15-1 shows the Network Policy management in the Windows Azure Portal.

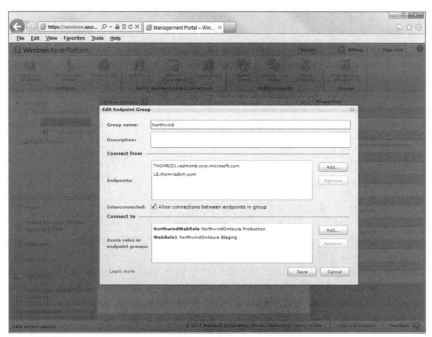

FIGURE 15-1

The Azure Role Architecture

In order to make use of your Azure Role, you can make some architectural and configuration changes using Azure Connect.

1. You need to enable your Web or Worker role to include the Azure Connect plug-in as part of your Service Definition file.

2. For a VM role, you need to install the Connect agent in your VHD image using the Azure Connect VM install package. The Azure Connect agent then automatically starts up with your Azure role instances.

3. When provisioned, you need to make sure that the Activation Token is part of your configuration settings for your Azure role. The Activation Token is a unique per-subscription token that you obtain from the Azure Connect administration portal.

4. You can also manage your Active Directory domain joined settings and connectivity options. For connectivity options, you can make Azure Connect wait for connectivity before enabling the Azure Role. If connectivity to the resource is not available, the Azure Role instance remains in the initializing state until the Connect Agent is initialized and connectivity is established. If the Azure Role instance is domain-joined, the Azure Role instance waits until the instance has been successfully joined to the domain. This is a powerful feature but should be used with care because if something goes wrong, your role instances will be blocked from starting.

Azure Connect Client Agent

As part of your Azure Connect deployment, you need to install the Azure Connect agent on your on-premises machines. This agent can be installed either through a web-based or standalone package install. If you use the web-based install, your per-subscription activation token is embedded in the URL, so there you do not need to enter that information. If you use the stand-alone package, you must provide your activation token either through the install or embedded in an unattended setup package. Whichever way you install the agent, you need to make sure that TCP 443 outbound port is open.

After install, the agent creates a Tray icon and also has a client UI that you can use to interact with the agent. Through this UI, you can view the activation state and connectivity status and also refresh your network policy, as shown in Figure 15-2.

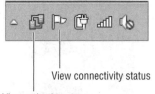

View connectivity status

View activation state

FIGURE 15-2

The agent sets up the virtual network adapter, connects to the relay service, and gets an IPv6 routable address. The agent also configures the IPSec policy based on the network policy you configured in the Azure Connect administration portal. The agent enrolls for a certification for IPSec for authentication purposes. The policy rules are kept in sync with the Azure Connect service, and the certificates are automatically renewed by the agent before they expire. The agent also installs the DNS name service provider for name resolution using the Azure Connect name service.

One caveat is that you can install only one copy of the Azure Connect agent and have only one activation token enabled for that agent. If you want to use a different subscription and activation token, you must uninstall the Azure Connect agent on your on-premises instance and reinstall using the new activation token.

If you are domain-joining your Azure instances to your on-premises AD deployment, you need to install the Azure Connect agent on a Domain Controller (DC) and a DNS server. You must have at least one DC with the agent software on it, and it is recommended that you install the agent on a Global Catalog server.

SETTING UP WINDOWS AZURE CONNECT

To set up Windows Azure Connect, you need to do some on-premises and Azure role instance configuration and meet some system requirements. This section steps you through both the configuration and requirements.

System Requirements

Windows Azure Connect has some specific system requirements especially for your on-premises computers. In particular, you need to run the following:

➤   Windows Vista, Windows 7, Windows Server 2008, or Windows Server 2008 R2.

➤   Windows Azure SDK.

➤   Windows Azure Tools for Visual Studio release 1.3. These tools enable you to configure and deploy your Azure instances that connect using Windows Azure Connect.

Requesting Access to the Azure Connect CTP

At the time of this writing, Azure Connect is in Community Technical Preview (CTP). You need to request access to the CTP through the Windows Azure portal. During the CTP period, Azure Connect is free of charge and has no service-level agreement (SLA). The pricing and SLA will change when Azure Connect is released, so be prepared to possibly pay for the service and understand what will and will not be covered by the Azure Connect SLA.

Enabling and Configuring Azure Connect for Azure Roles

Before you work with Azure Connect, you need to retrieve your Activation Token, as shown in Figure 15-3. This token will be used in the configuration for your Azure role.

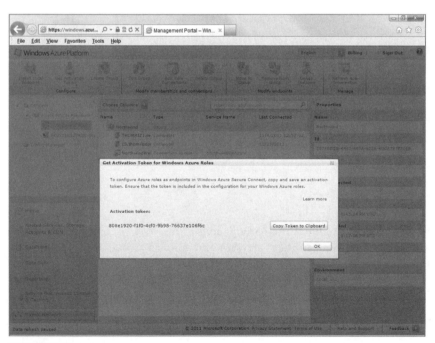

FIGURE 15-3

When you have the Activation Token, you can create an Azure project in Visual Studio. Bring up the properties for the role you are creating and you can activate Azure Connect by checking the Activate Windows Azure Connect check box under the Virtual Network tab, as shown in Figure 15-4. You need to paste your Activation Token in the dialog box so that Azure knows which subscription to connect to.

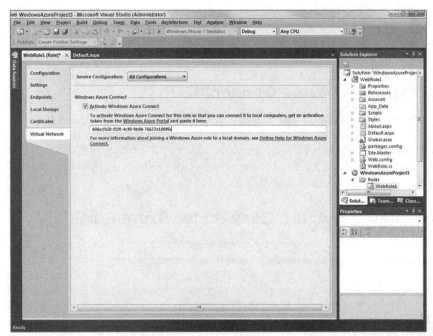

FIGURE 15-4

Although you don't need to use the visual interface to configure Azure Connect, it does make it easier. And you can perform the steps that Visual Studio does on your behalf. What Visual Studio does is modify your `ServiceDefinition.csdef` to add an import directive for the Azure Connect plug-in as shown here.

```
<Imports>
    <Import moduleName="Connect" />
</Imports>
```

In the `ServiceConfiguration.cscfg` file, Visual Studio adds to the `<ConfigurationSettings>` section of the activation token that you pasted, as shown in the following code in addition to other Azure Connect plug-ins.

```
<Setting name="Microsoft.WindowsAzure.Plugins.Connect.ActivationToken"
value="" />
<Setting name="Microsoft.WindowsAzure.Plugins.Connect.Refresh" value="" />
<Setting name="Microsoft.WindowsAzure.Plugins.Connect.Diagnostics"
value="" />
<Setting name="Microsoft.WindowsAzure.Plugins.Connect.WaitForConnectivity"
```

```
value="" />
<Setting name="Microsoft.WindowsAzure.Plugins.Connect.Upgrade" value="" />
<Setting name="Microsoft.WindowsAzure.Plugins.Connect.EnableDomainJoin"
value="" />
<Setting name="Microsoft.WindowsAzure.Plugins.Connect.DomainFQDN"
value="" />
<Setting name="Microsoft.WindowsAzure.Plugins.Connect.DomainControllerFQDN"
value="" />
<Setting name="Microsoft.WindowsAzure.Plugins.Connect.DomainAccountName"
value="" />
<Setting name="Microsoft.WindowsAzure.Plugins.Connect.DomainPassword"
value="" />
<Setting name="Microsoft.WindowsAzure.Plugins.Connect.DomainOU" value="" />
<Setting name="Microsoft.WindowsAzure.Plugins.Connect.DNSServers"
value="" />
<Setting name="Microsoft.WindowsAzure.Plugins.Connect.Administrators"
value="" />
<Setting name="Microsoft.WindowsAzure.Plugins.Connect.DomainSiteName"
value="" />
```

After you set up these settings in your role, you can continue to develop your role as you normally would. When finished, you can publish the role to Azure. When the role is in a ready state in Azure, you should see the Azure Connect enabled roles you published in the Azure Connect portal, as shown in Figure 15-5.

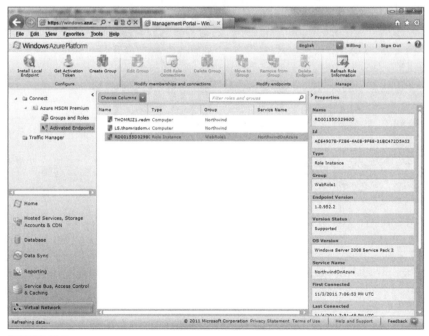

FIGURE 15-5

Enabling and Configuring Azure Connect for a VM Role

Enabling a VM role is different than enabling an Azure role. You need to download and install the Azure Connect software on your VM image from `http://waconnect.blob.core.windows.net/client/latest/x64/wacendpointpackagefull.exe`. When installed, you need to manually edit your `ServiceConfiguration.csfg` file to provide your Azure Connect token.

Enabling and Configuring Your Local Machines

To set up your local machines with Azure Connect, you need to install the Azure Connect agent. This software is available from the Azure Connect portal in the Ribbon as Install Local Endpoint. Your Activation Token is automatically appended to a URL for downloading the client, as shown in Figure 15-6, and the setup automatically configures your activation token for you.

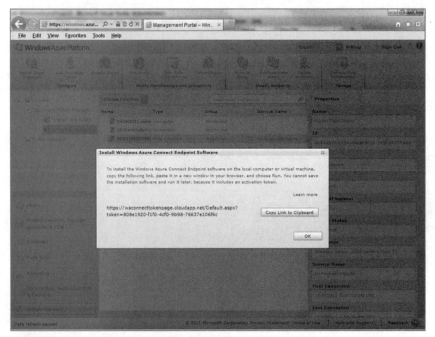

FIGURE 15-6

The setup screen, as shown in Figure 15-7, allows you to select the language you want to install for the client. The setup then installs the client on your machine. If successful, you should see a Taskbar icon, as shown in Figure 15-8.

FIGURE 15-7

After the client is installed, it auto-configures and connects to the Azure Connect service. When connected, your local machine appears in the Azure Connect portal as an activated endpoint, as shown in Figure 15-9.

FIGURE 15-8

From here, you can configure the network connectivity for your Azure Connect to set the policies for your local machines to connect your Azure role instances.

FIGURE 15-9

Configure Your Network Connectivity Policy

To configure your network policies, you need to perform two steps: Create an endpoint group, and add machines to your machine endpoint group from your local and Azure role instances.

You interconnect your endpoints if you have multiple local machines that need to communicate to each other through the service. For example, if you have multiple developers who are in different geographies, you can use Azure Connect to allow their local machines to access the Azure service in addition to each other's development machines.

Although connectivity to Azure roles may make sense, you may wonder why you may need to connect to other Endpoint Groups. Connecting Endpoint Groups is useful if you break your local machines into different endpoint groups. For example, you may create an endpoint group that contains your local development machines and a separate endpoint group for all your databases.

To create an endpoint group, in the Azure Connect portal, follow these steps:

1. Click the Create Group button. This displays the UI, as shown in Figure 15-10.

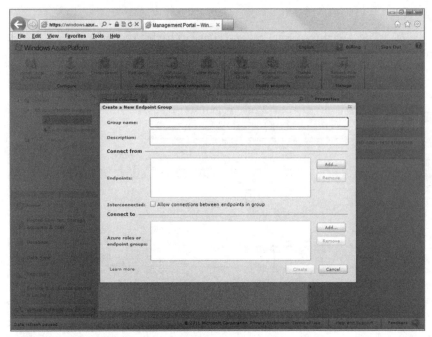

FIGURE 15-10

2. As part of the UI, you can name your group, put in a description, and then select the local machines you want to add to the group as endpoints. If you see no endpoints in the UI, that means that your local machines using the connect agent did not successfully connect and activate.

3. As part of the endpoint UI, you can also check the Allow Connections Between Endpoints in Group option, which allows you to connect your local machines together using Azure Connect.

4. After setting your endpoints, you can set the Azure roles or other Endpoint Groups to connect your endpoint with. To connect your development endpoint group to your database endpoint group, you add one to the other's endpoint group list and then connectivity will work.

5. When done, you can manually refresh the local connect agent to download the latest network connectivity policy by right-clicking the Azure Connect tray icon and selecting Refresh. By default, the client refreshes the policy every 5 minutes.

6. Azure also enables you to select the region for your relay to be hosted so that you can pick a relay geographically close to your deployment. Your three options for regions are the USA, Europe, or Asia. You should choose the region where the majority of your endpoints will be if you span across multiple regions.

7. Azure also allows you to use a certificate-based endpoint activation for local endpoints. This is different than the token-based endpoint activation and requires you to have an X509 certificate installed on your local endpoint. Then, in the Azure Connect management portal, you can upload that certificate, and Azure Connect activates only machines that have the same certificate installed.

Testing Connectivity to SQL Server

One of the most common scenarios for Azure Connect is to use it to connect your Azure instances to a locally installed SQL Server. Because Azure Connect utilizes low-level connectivity, you can use local names to connect to your SQL Server instances. The web application, as shown in Figure 15-11, runs in Azure and connects to a local SQL Server.

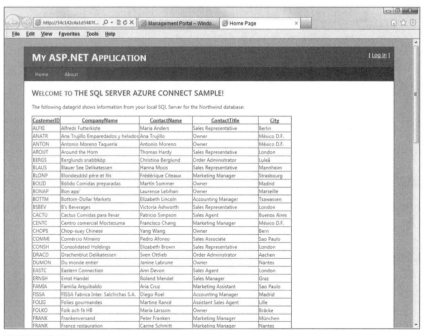

FIGURE 15-11

To connect your local SQL Server to your role instance, you need to perform a number of steps to make sure that the network infrastructure for SQL Server supports the calls and also that your local SQL instance and your Azure role instance connect through the Azure Connect network policy. Now you walk through these steps, outlined in in the following sections, to see how you can connect the two together.

Configuring SQL Server

The first step to configure your SQL Server instance involves making sure that both the security credentials can be passed to SQL Server from your Azure role instance and also the port and protocol that Azure uses will be accepted by your SQL Server:

1. Right-click your SQL Server name and select Properties. You want to make sure that security works by enabling both SQL Server and Windows Authentication in your SQL Server instance. You do not need to do this if you domain-join your Azure role instance using Azure Connect, which is covered later in this chapter, because domain credentials can be passed in this scenario to SQL Server. Figure 15-12 shows how you set the security properties for SQL Server in SQL Server Management Studio.

2. In the same dialog box, under the Connections section, you select the Allow Remote Connections to This Server check box. You want to ensure remote connections are enabled for your SQL Server instance so you need to check this box to allow remote connections to SQL Server.

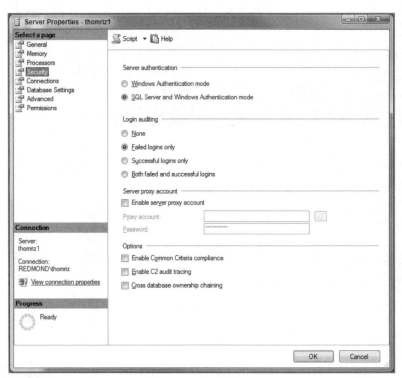

FIGURE 15-12

3. When this is complete, go to the SQL Server Configuration Manager and make sure that the TCP/IP protocol is enabled for your server. You can find the SQL Server Configuration Manager in your Programs list under the Microsoft SQL Server folder and then under Configuration Tools. When there, you must expand the SQL Server Network Configuration section and select the Protocols section for your SQL Server instance. Make sure that TCP/IP is enabled, as shown in Figure 15-13.

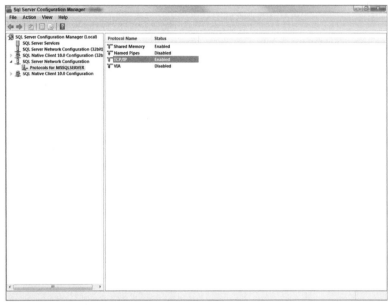

FIGURE 15-13

4. Double-click the TCP/IP protocol, and make sure that port 1433 is enabled under the IP All section. You can see this in Figure 15-14.

5. Make sure to restart your SQL Server service so that the changes can be applied.

Configuring Firewall Rules

The next step is to configure your firewall to allow inbound connections on port 1433. This section shows how to use Windows Firewall, but if you use a different firewall technology, you should follow the steps for your firewall provider.

1. To launch the firewall settings, in the Control Panel, click Windows Firewall.

2. Click Advanced Settings and then click Inbound Rules. Click New Rule and select the Rule Type as Port, as shown in Figure 15-15.

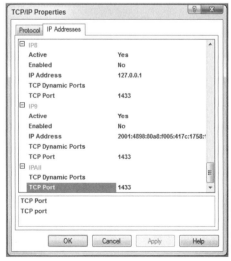

FIGURE 15-14

3. Select Protocols and Ports and then TCP and specify the local port to 1433, as shown in Figure 15-16.

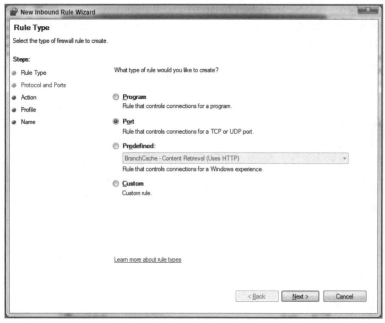

FIGURE 15-15

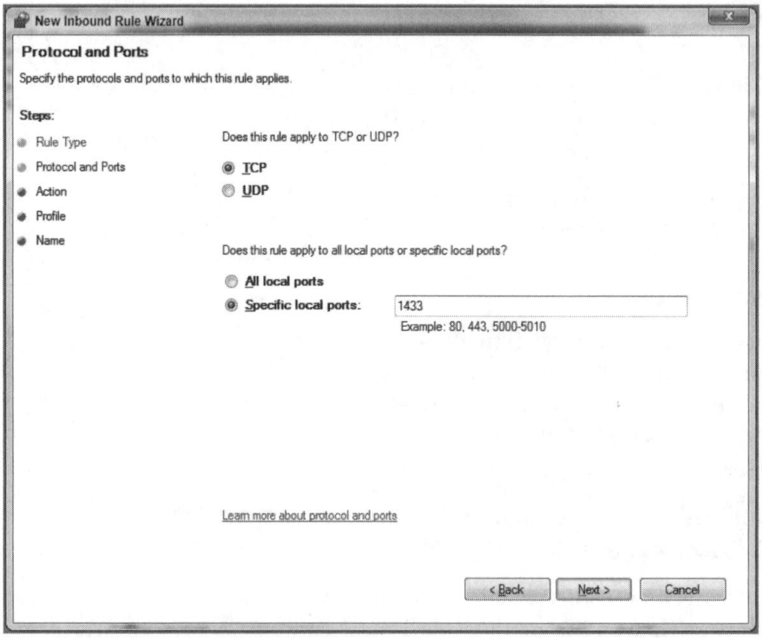

FIGURE 15-16

4. Click Next twice to keep the default settings for the Action and Profile sections, and then enter a name for your new rule, such as **SQL Server 1433 Port**.

5. Click Finish to complete the creation of this firewall rule.

Installing the Connect Agent on SQL Server

In the next phase, make sure to install the Azure Connect agent on your SQL Server machine through the Azure Connect portal. You can do this by using the Install Local Endpoint button from the menu for your Azure Connect subscription.

Creating Your Azure Role Instance

The next phase is to create your cloud project inside of Visual Studio that connects to your local SQL Server instance.

1. In Visual Studio, click New Project, and under the Cloud template select the Windows Azure Project, as shown in Figure 15-17.

FIGURE 15-17

2. Create an ASP.NET Web Role as your Azure solution, and click OK.

3. Open `Default.aspx` in design mode, and drag and drop a GridView control on the page.

4. Create a new datasource using the GridView tasks, and configure the datasource to be your local instance of your SQL Server. You can use local naming instances to connect to your SQL Server, as shown in Figure 15-18.

5. When finished, you can connect your Azure role instance to Azure Connect by putting your Azure Connect Activation Token into the configuration for your project. First, go to the Azure Connect portal and copy your Activation Token to the clipboard by clicking the Get Activation Token button on the Azure Connect menu. This brings up a dialog box, as shown in Figure 15-19.

6. Go back to Visual Studio, and select your web role, such as WebRole1.

7. Right-click and select Properties to bring up the Property dialog box.

8. Select the Virtual Network tab and then click Activate Windows Azure Connect, and paste your token into the token textbox, as shown in Figure 15-20.

FIGURE 15-18

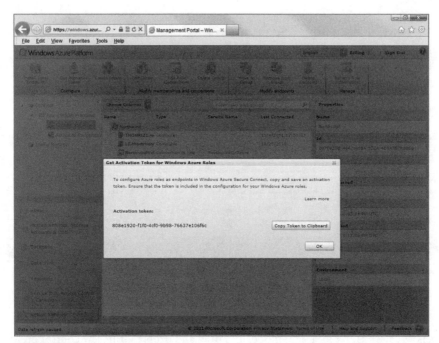

FIGURE 15-19

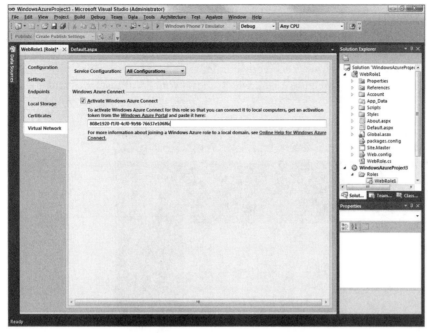

FIGURE 15-20

Your project is ready to be published, so you can now use the automated publishing tools in VS to compile and upload your project to Azure, as shown in Figure 15-21.

FIGURE 15-21

Creating Endpoint Groups

When your role is successfully deployed and initialized, you need to add it to an endpoint group. In the Azure Connect portal, create a new Endpoint Group to connect your local SQL Server to your Azure role instance. If your instances are all correctly configured and network connectivity works, you should see a dialog box similar to Figure 15-22 which shows your local instances and your Azure role instance.

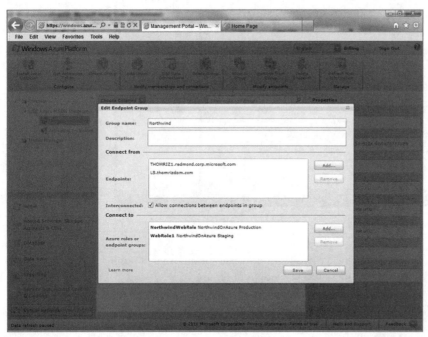

FIGURE 15-22

That's it! You can now connect your Azure role instance ASP.NET application and see data from your local SQL Server.

Troubleshooting Tips

If you find that you can't connect the Azure role instance to your SQL Server, you can try the following troubleshooting tips to get it to connect.

➤ **Make sure the Azure Connect agent is connected on your local machine.** You can do this via the Azure Connect icon in your taskbar. It displays the status of the agent, as shown in Figure 15-23.

➤ **Check the edge traversal option.** When you create your firewall rule, there may be times in which the traffic is still blocked because there is an edge device between Azure and your local instance, such as a firewall or NAT device. By default, when you create your SQL Server firewall inbound rule, edge traversal is blocked. Try changing this setting to Enabled by looking at the Advanced settings for your inbound rule.

➤ **Create firewall rules to block IPv4 traffic.** When domain-joined, there may be times when your connection to SQL Server times out because the SQL client software attempts to connect over IPv4 by default rather than IPv6. This won't happen with non-domain-joined machines because the Azure Connect service always returns back an IPv6 address. However, with a domain joined Azure Connect instance, Azure Connect uses your local DNS, which may return IPv4 addresses. Therefore, the SQL client software attempts to connect over IPv4 first, which won't work, and then attempts IPv6. Depending on the timeout for your application, this could cause application issues. The simplest way to fix this problem is to create a firewall rule that blocks IPv4 traffic to the SQL Server port 1433. You can do this through the Windows Firewall UI or the following `netsh` command, customized with your IPv4 range, which also creates a Windows Firewall rule.

```
netsh advfirewall firewall add rule name="BlockSQLIPv4" dir=out
action=block protocol=tcp remoteport=1433 remoteip=(on-premises IPv4
range)
```

FIGURE 15-23

Building a Domain-Joined Configuration

There may be times when you want to domain-join your Windows Azure instance to your local instances. This is convenient if you want to extend your network and security boundary to include your Windows Azure deployment. The benefit is that the Azure instances are trusted by your on-premises instances so that authentication is seamless whether a user accesses an on-premises resource or accesses an Azure-based resource. Domain-joining is useful if you want to determine which users and groups have access to your application, want to apply AD policies to your Azure machines, and want to manage your Azure instance like you manage your on-premises instances because your Azure instance appears on your network with your policies and management tools.

Because the steps are complex and more IT-oriented, you must use the following overview to configure your domain-joined instances, which is outside the scope for this book: `http://blogs.msdn .com/b/windows_azure_connect_team_blog/archive/2010/12/10/domain-joining-windows-azure-roles.aspx`.

TROUBLESHOOTING WINDOWS AZURE CONNECT

When dealing with hybrid solutions that span networks, firewalls, and applications, you will have some issues and need to troubleshoot those issues at some point. Azure Connect attempts to make the setup, deployment, and running of your interconnected application easy, but in the cases in which you run into issues, Azure Connect also provides some troubleshooting tools to help you figure out where the errors could be. This section steps you through some of the tools and techniques you can use to troubleshoot your Azure Connect deployments.

1. Always check the Azure Connect agent diagnostics. These diagnostics help you understand where potential issues may lie—IPSec certificate issues, IPv6 errors, or anything in between.

2. Have Azure Connect generate diagnostic logs for you in your Azure role instance. This does require you to enable remote desktop to your Azure role instance.

3. When you have RDP set up, RDP into the Azure role instance, and in a command prompt that has administrative privileges, run the following command:

   ```
   %programfiles%\Windows Azure Connect\Endpoint\diagnose.exe /collectlogs
   ```

   This generates a `diagnostics.cab` file in your Logs subdirectory.

4. If you open the cab file, you can find many logs, whether firewall rules, IPSec, or other information. You can parse through these logs to see if you can solve your problem.

If you have connectivity issues, you can do a couple things to make sure that you have network connectivity:

➤ Make sure to check that you have IPv6 enabled on your local network adapter on your local instance.

➤ Make sure you have the outbound port 443 enabled to allow connectivity.

➤ Allow IPv6 ping communications in your firewall by running the following command line:

   ```
   netsh advfirewall firewall add rule name="Pingv6" dir=in action=allow
   enable=yes protocol=icmpv6
   ```

➤ Make sure you have any proxy settings configured correctly. You can also try removing the proxy to see if connectivity works.

SUMMARY

In this chapter, you learned about Windows Azure Connect and how you can use Azure Connect to bring together your Azure and on-premises instances to build a single solution that ties both together. Azure Connect makes it easy to set up and maintain secure network connectivity between your instances and also enables you to join your Azure instances to your local Active Directory domains.

16

Azure Diagnostics and Debugging

WHAT'S IN THIS CHAPTER?

➤ Defining Windows Azure Diagnostics

➤ Comparing local debugging to cloud debugging

➤ What is Intellitrace?

➤ How to use profiling

➤ How to use Windows Azure Diagnostics

➤ How to view your logs

➤ Working with Windows Azure MMC

Whenever you write an application, you debug or diagnose it. The reasons for this are numerous—from bugs to performance issues to testing changes in your algorithms or code. Windows Azure provides both debugging and diagnostic capabilities, and you can use both together to get to the root cause of any issues that arise in your application. In addition, Visual Studio provides rich tools so that your debugging does not need to happen against the live instance of your service; you can debug against an emulated environment, which makes the debugging process available anytime and anywhere.

WHAT IS WINDOWS AZURE DIAGNOSTICS?

Windows Azure Diagnostics enables you to collect data about your Azure application so that you can use that data to debug, troubleshoot, measure performance, or perform other development tasks. You can run Windows Azure Diagnostics locally or remotely and configure it separately from your Azure application. This flexibility enables you to work with diagnostics without changing your Azure application. In addition, you can transfer Windows Azure Diagnostics either on a schedule or on-demand to a Windows Azure storage account, which allows you to persist and build a data warehouse of performance metrics over time.

Windows Azure Diagnostics enables you to collect a number of different logs including the Windows Azure logs, IIS logs, and Windows Azure Diagnostics infrastructure logs, in addition to other sources, such as the Windows Event log and crash dumps. Beyond logs, you can also use tracing and debugging to help you understand where issues may occur in your code. Optionally, you can also leverage performance counters to understand the health of your Azure application. These performance counters can either be built-in or custom performance counters that you create.

LOCAL VERSUS CLOUD DEBUGGING

For debugging you have your choice to either debug:

➤ Locally on your development environment using the emulated Azure environment

➤ Using the remote desktop and the remote debugger to debug your running Azure worker role instances

Although both have their merits, debugging is easier against your local instance while leveraging diagnostics as a viable alternative to an attached debugger for your production Azure instances running in the cloud.

Your local debugging session may not uncover all your issues because it is fundamentally different from running your code in the cloud. For example, your network or machine utilization is different locally versus running in the Microsoft datacenter. Therefore, if your application fails because of an overloaded network or starvation for resources, you may not find those issues when performing a local debugging session.

Because debugging is based on the built-in Visual Studio debugger, you do not need to perform special steps to start debugging except setting a breakpoint and starting your application with debugging enabled.

USING INTELLITRACE

Intellitrace is a feature of Visual Studio 2010 Ultimate that enables you to debug your applications by showing you events that occurred during the running of your application and the context surrounding those events. You can configure Intellitrace for the events to collect and allow for the collection of additional data, such as parameters and return values.

Configuring Intellitrace is easy with Azure. Check the Enable Intellitrace for .NET 4 Roles box that turns on Intellitrace for your Azure deployment, as shown in Figure 16-1.

When enabled, you need to deploy your solution for Azure. When initialized, you can view the Intellitrace logs from your Azure instance, as shown in Figure 16-2.

FIGURE 16-1

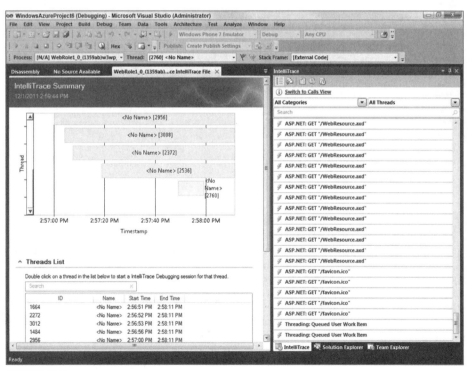

FIGURE 16-2

Using the Intellitrace logs, you can track down both the events and calls that happened in your instance and look back in time to understand what went wrong. Intellitrace is a little bit like the movie *Back to the Future* in that you can go back in time and understand the events that lead to the current situation, the variables and threads involved, and the state of the machine at the time. You should not use Intellitrace on production instances of your Azure application because it will slow performance.

USING PROFILING

Beside Intellitrace, you can also use profiling to debug your applications. One restriction is that you can use only Intellitrace or profiling but not both at the same time. Many times you should first use Intellitrace to look for any exceptions in your application and try to fix those exceptions. Then, you can enable profiling, which can help you identify the most time-consuming areas in your code.

With Azure profiling, you can activate the following settings, as shown in Figure 16-3.

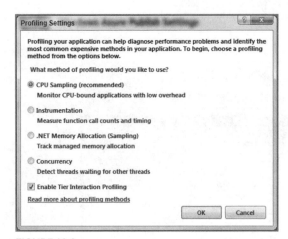

FIGURE 16-3

➤ **CPU Sampling:** With this option, you can collect different methods including CPU sampling, instrumentation, .NET memory allocation, and concurrency. You can use CPU sampling to track down any CPU spikes (such as runaway code). Sampling has a low impact on your application.

➤ **Instrumentation:** This collects information about the entry, exit, and time in a function. This enables you to detect functions that take a long time to execute or take a long time to get or receive data.

➤ **.NET Memory Allocation:** This lets you know if you're utilizing memory in an efficient way, if you're allocating too much memory, or if you're not destroying objects correctly.

➤ **Concurrency:** This collects process and thread execution data, which enables you to identify resource contention and deadlocking in a multithreaded application. You can determine if other code in your application is blocking and therefore starving your code of CPU or resources. You can use only one collection method at once, such as CPU sampling or instrumentation. If you need to collect using different methods, you must change your profile settings and redeploy your Azure instance.

➤ **Enable Tier Interaction Profiling:** If you use ADO.NET in your application, this allows you to understand the execution times for your synchronous ADO.NET calls. For example, you can track elapsed time either in the process or in the queries, the number of queries, or the query command text.

After you deploy your Azure instance and initialize it, you can have Visual Studio download the profiling data and view the profiling reports. From there, you can troubleshoot your application to understand where the biggest demands of resources or time take place. Figure 16-4 shows a profiling report against an Azure instance.

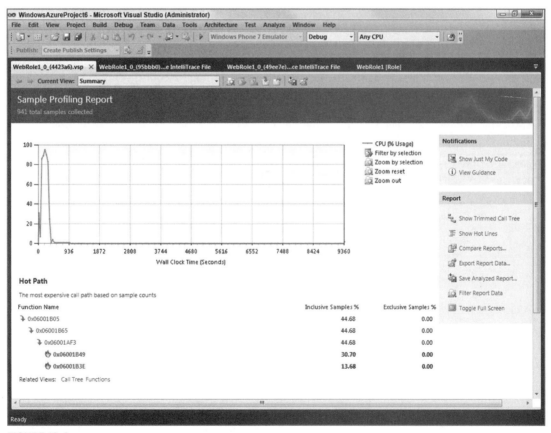

FIGURE 16-4

USING WINDOWS AZURE DIAGNOSTICS

When you work with your Azure applications, there are times when you want to collect diagnostics about your application for debugging or troubleshooting purposes. By allowing you to collect diagnostic information and persisting that information, Azure ensures that your application runs at the optimal configuration over time without forcing an intrusive process.

Configuring Azure Diagnostics

To configure Azure Diagnostics, you need to import the Azure Diagnostics module into your service model. This is as simple as adding an `Import` element to your `ServiceDefinition.csdef file`, as shown in the following code:

```
<?xml version="1.0" encoding="utf-8"?>
<ServiceDefinition name="MyHostedService" xmlns="http://schemas.microsoft.com/
ServiceHosting/2008/10/ServiceDefinition">
  <WebRole name="WebRole1">
    <Imports>
      <Import moduleName="Diagnostics" />
    </Imports>
  </WebRole>
</ServiceDefinition>
```

If you persist your diagnostic information to your Azure Storage account, you must also specify a connection string in your `ServiceConfiguration.cscfg` file so that Azure knows how to export the diagnostic log and store it in Azure storage. The XML for the connection string is shown in the following code block. It shows how to use the storage emulator for storage and then shows passing in an account name and key to store the log in an Azure storage account.

```
<?xml version="1.0" encoding="utf-8"?>
<ServiceConfiguration serviceName="AzureService" xmlns="http://schemas.microsoft.
com
/ServiceHosting/2008/10/ServiceConfiguration" osFamily="1" osVersion="*">
  <Role name="WebRole1">
    <Instances count="1" />
    <ConfigurationSettings>
      <Setting name="Microsoft.WindowsAzure.Plugins.Diagnostics.ConnectionString"
 value="UseDevelopmentStorage=true" />
    </ConfigurationSettings>
  </Role>
</ServiceConfiguration>

<ConfigurationSettings>
    <Setting name="Microsoft.WindowsAzure.Plugins.Diagnostics.ConnectionString"
    value="DefaultEndpointsProtocol=https;AccountName=AccountName;
AccountKey=AccountKey"/>
</ConfigurationSettings>
```

Be default, Azure does not collect all available diagnostics data so that it can save system resources. Table 16-1 shows which diagnostics data is collected and how that data is formatted.

TABLE 16-1: Azure Diagnostic Collection

DATA SOURCE	DEFAULT COLLECTION	FORMAT
Windows Azure Logs	Yes	Table
IIS Logs	Yes	Blob
Infrastructure Logs	Yes	Table
Event Logs	No	Table
Failed request logs	No	Blob
Performance Counters	No	Table
Crash Dumps	No	Blob
Custom Logs	No	Blob

To add the logs not collected by default, you need to perform different procedures based on the type of log. The next sections step through collecting each of the different nondefault logs.

Collecting IIS Failed Requests

To collect IIS failed requests, you need to modify the `web.config` for your web role in Azure. You must add code to the `system.webServer` section to include the providers you want to track, such as Authentication, CGI, Security, and so on. In addition, you can configure the HTTP status codes that you want for collection. The following code shows how to modify the `system.webServer` section to turn on the IIS failed request collection.

```
<tracing>
    <traceFailedRequests>
        <add path="*">
            <traceAreas>
                <add provider="ASP" verbosity="Verbose" />
                <add provider="ASPNET" areas="Infrastructure,Module,Page,
                 AppServices" verbosity="Verbose" />
                <add provider="ISAPI Extension" verbosity="Verbose" />
                <add provider="WWW Server"
                    areas="Authentication,
                           Security,
                           Filter,
                           StaticFile,
                           CGI,
                           Compression,
                           Cache,
                           RequestNotifications,
                           Module"
                        verbosity="Verbose" />
            </traceAreas>
            <failureDefinitions statusCodes="400-599" />
        </add>
    </traceFailedRequests>
</tracing>
```

Collecting Windows Event Log and Crash Dumps

To collect the event log information, you need to write a bit of code after you deploy your Azure instance with the diagnostic monitoring enabled. To do this, you want to make sure your code references the `Microsoft.WindowsAzure.Diagnostics.dll` file. Then, you write code in your `OnStart` method for your role to configure the diagnostics module and add in your Windows Event Log datasource, such as System or Application. The following code shows you how to configure the Application event log. You cannot access the Security event log because of the locked down permissions that your Azure service accounts runs under.

```
using Microsoft.WindowsAzure.Diagnostics;
var diags = DiagnosticMonitor.GetDefaultInitialConfiguration();
diags.WindowsEventLog.DataSources.Add("Application!*");
//Set the timeframe for collection
diags.WindowsEventLog.ScheduledTransferPeriod = TimeSpan.FromMinutes(1);
//Restart the Diagnostic monitor with changes
DiagnosticMonitor.Start(
"Microsoft.WindowsAzure.Plugins.Diagnostics.ConnectionString", diags);
```

A couple caveats exist when working with event log collection:

➤ **Unless you use filtered events, you collect all events into the log, both your own applications as well as the system.** The preceding sample would dump all events in the Application log. Azure will charge you for the storage and transactions.

➤ **The log can list a lot of events, so you must make sure to limit the amount of events.** To filter events, use an XPath expression to specify the filter. The easiest way to get the XPath expression is to use the local event viewer on your dev machine, filter for the event you want in the viewer, and then switch to the XML view of the event viewer custom view creator, as shown in Figure 16-5. From there, you can get the XPath expression, such as `Application!*[System[Provider[@Name='HttpEvent']]]`.

FIGURE 16-5

➤ **To collect crash dumps, you need to enable the collection of crash dumps through the API.** A value of false collects a partial crash dump, and true collects a full crash dump. In addition to using `EnableCollection`, you can also use `EnableCollectionToDirectory` method, which enables you to pass a string that is the directory to write the logs to.

```
//Put true for complete crash dump collection
Microsoft.WindowsAzure.Diagnostics.CrashDumps.EnableCollection(false);
```

Adding Tracing

Azure also enables you to use tracing as a means to monitor the execution of your code. You can use three classes: `System.Diagnostics.Trace`, `System.Diagnostics.Debug`, and `System.Diagnostics.TraceSource` to trace your application. To do so, you initialize the trace listener. If you use Visual Studio, this step is done for you, but if you use a different tool, the following code shows how to configure the trace listener in your `web.config` or `app.config` file.

```
<system.diagnostics>
    <trace>
        <listeners>
            <add type=
"Microsoft.WindowsAzure.Diagnostics.DiagnosticMonitorTraceListener,
            Microsoft.WindowsAzure.Diagnostics,
            Version=1.0.0.0,
            Culture=neutral,
            PublicKeyToken=31bf3856ad364e35"
            name="AzureDiagnostics">
            <filter type="" />
        </add>
        </listeners>
    </trace>
</system.diagnostics>
```

When enabled, you can use `Trace` statements to write out to the trace log. For example, if you want to write out a statement to the trace log, you can use `Trace.WriteLine` to add a new text line to the trace log.

Using Performance Monitors

In addition to using diagnostics and tracing, you can also use the performance monitor to track the performance of key counters in your Azure applications. As with the other methods, you must modify your `OnStart` method in your web role to enable your performance counter monitoring. As with event logs, you must specify the path to your performance counters. For example, if you want to collect the % Processor Time, the path would be `\Processor(_Total)\% Processor Time`, or if you want to collect the available memory, you use `\Memory\Available MBytes`. The easiest way to figure out these paths is to use performance monitor to view these counters and construct their paths from the user interface navigation.

When you have your path, you can configure Azure Diagnostics to start collecting your performance counters similar to the way you did for the other diagnostic technologies, as shown in the following code:

```
using Microsoft.WindowsAzure.Diagnostics;
var diags = DiagnosticMonitor.GetDefaultInitialConfiguration();
```

```
diags.PerformanceCounters.DataSources.Add(new PerformanceCounterConfiguration()
    {
        CounterSpecifier = @"\Processor(_Total)\% Processor Time",
        SampleRate = TimeSpan.FromSeconds(5)
    });
diags.PerformanceCounters.ScheduledTransferPeriod = TimeSpan.FromSeconds(1d);
diags.PerformanceCounters.BufferQuotaInMB = 512;
//Set the timeframe for collection
diags.WindowsEventLog.ScheduledTransferPeriod = TimeSpan.FromMinutes(1);
//Restart the Diagnostic monitor with changes
DiagnosticMonitor.Start("
Microsoft.WindowsAzure.Plugins.Diagnostics.ConnectionString", diags);
```

VIEWING YOUR LOGS

Viewing your logs is straightforward whether you use the local debugging environment or your
Azure Storage Account using Visual Studio. In the Server Explorer in Visual Studio, you can open
either your local storage environment or the Azure Storage environment to view both your blobs
and your tables. Make sure that you enable your Azure Storage account by using the Properties
dialog for your Web Role in Visual Studio and provide the account and key for your Azure Storage
account, as shown in Figure 16-6.

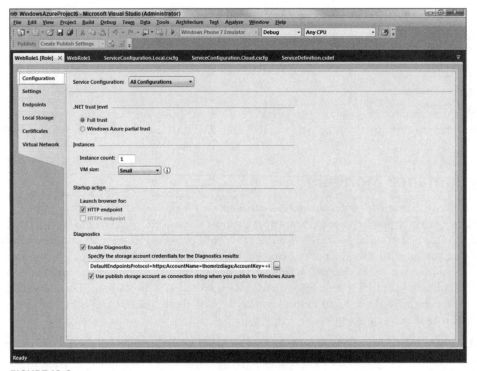

FIGURE 16-6

You also must configure Azure to ship the logs over to your storage account by modifying the WebRole.cs under the OnStart() method, as shown earlier in the chapter. After you make all these changes, you can deploy your solution to Azure and start viewing your logs in Visual Studio, as shown in Figure 16-7.

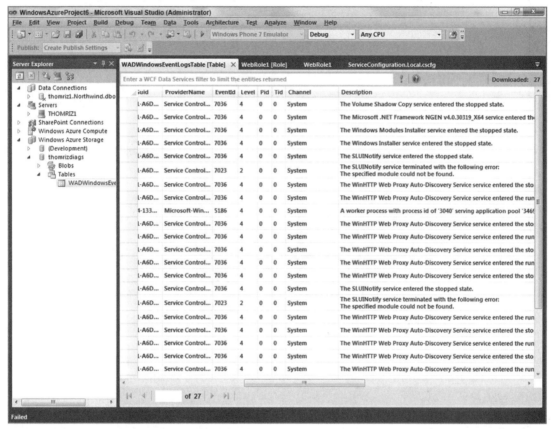

FIGURE 16-7

WINDOWS AZURE MMC

When working with diagnostics, try to leverage as many tools as you can to quickly configure and deploy your diagnostic settings and code. Visual Studio provides a number of tools (such as Intellitrace, discussed earlier in the chapter) but there are also third-party tools that you should consider. Windows Azure MMC is a tool that enables you to monitor and manage your Azure deployment. You can upload, deploy, or upgrade your Azure instances. You can also configure the diagnostics for Azure, which may be faster than writing all the configuration code. You can find the MMC tool at http://wapmmc.codeplex.com/. Figure 16-8 shows the Windows Azure MMC interface.

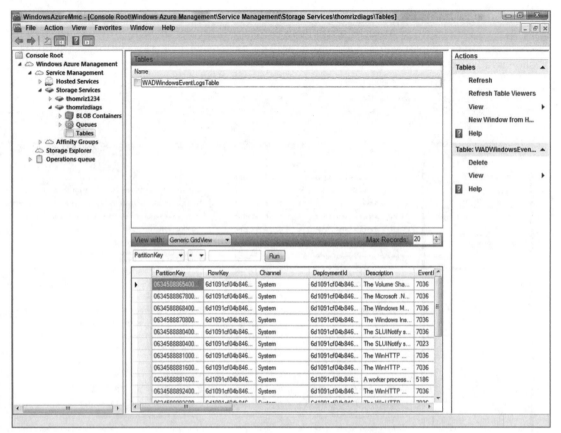

FIGURE 16-8

SUMMARY

In this chapter, you learned how to monitor and debug your Azure applications. By leveraging technologies such as Intellitrace, profiling, and diagnostics, you can ensure that your Azure applications run in a scalable manner, and if you do encounter errors, you can figure out those errors more quickly.

17

When to Use Azure Versus Office 365

WHAT'S IN THIS CHAPTER?

➤ The flexibility of each service

➤ Azure and Office 365 identity federation

➤ How each service handles identity federation

➤ The productivity features each service offers

➤ Understanding cross-platform considerations

➤ What you can expect with the service-level agreement

➤ The development tools you can use with each service

Both Microsoft Azure and Office 365 are Microsoft cloud-based service offerings that cater toward different business needs. Microsoft Azure essentially provides IaaS and PaaS service offerings, which makes it a broader cloud platform. Office 365 is basically a SaaS offering which provides features such as collaboration, messaging, and communication. The sections in this chapter cover various facets of each service, so you know how to use each appropriately. Figure 17-1 illustrates how the two services differ.

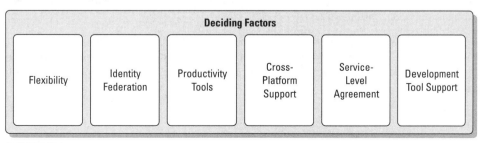

FIGURE 17-1

WHICH SERVICE IS MORE FLEXIBLE?

Microsoft Azure enables businesses to develop, deploy, and scale cloud-based solutions with different agility needs. With Azure you get the flexibility to choose the technology on which to build solutions (for example, PHP, ASP.NET, and so on) and you can also easily scale your solutions both up and down based on your needs (for example, using different number of worker roles at different times).

With Office 365 you get relatively less flexibility to choose technology—all the offered services are based on Microsoft Products and Technologies. Also, Office 365 services are streamlined to suit specific needs such as messaging, collaboration, and communication. Microsoft enables limited customization for most of its Office 365 service offerings, so if you look forward to building or migrating existing solutions to the cloud, Azure provides broader options. On the other hand, if the majority of your business requirements are met by SharePoint Online, Exchange Online, and Lync Online services, you may opt for them rather than reinventing the wheel and developing features already provided by these services. For more details on the Office 365 service offerings, visit `www.microsoft.com/download/en/details.aspx?id=13602`.

Although Azure and Office 365 offers different degree of flexibility, there is no reason not to integrate them—they don't need to be mutually exclusive. In fact there are numerous scenarios where a business might actually require features from both Azure and Office 365. For example, consider a scenario where your business stores customer support tickets on SQL Azure but you need to manage these tickets through a corporate portal based on SharePoint Online. By using Business Connectivity Services—a feature of SharePoint Online, you can perform CRUD (Create/Edit/Update/Delete) operations on relevant tables in SQL Azure using SharePoint Online.

HOW DOES EACH SERVICE HANDLE IDENTITY FEDERATION?

Identity federation is an authentication mechanism that enables organizations to perform single sign on and cross-domain sign in using an authentication mechanism of choice. Identity federation is quite common these days, and most businesses want it as part of their basic service offering. Microsoft Azure provides identity federation through its Access Control Service (ACS) feature. When customers subscribe to the Microsoft Azure service, ACS is available at no additional charge. With ACS, users can authenticate using their Live, Facebook, Yahoo, and Gmail accounts without doing any development to authenticate against these providers; Azure has already done the hard work behind the scenes. Office 365 also supports identity federation by using Active Directory Federation Services (ADFS) on-premise. However, ADFS requires you to set up and maintain this on the on-premise server, which means you carry the extra cost of hardware, software, and performing maintenance and upgrades.

You also need to ensure that ADFS and Active Directory and Domain Controller are all properly licensed on-premises. Licensing can also quickly get complicated depending on the size of organization and usage of particular features. You must not take this lightly; at the end of the day, it's licensing that legitimizes the use of these products.

WHAT PRODUCTIVITY TOOLS DOES EACH OFFER?

Productivity tools help users to perform their day-to-day tasks with the least amount of effort. Microsoft is famous for its productivity tools. The Microsoft Office suite is a good example of this; it brings applications, such as Word and Excel, to the end users and is one of the most commonly used tools on the market today.

Microsoft Office 365 supports the latest version of Microsoft Office suite (included as part of its Enterprise subscription plans). For example, if a business chooses to adopt Office 365, there is an almost flat learning curve when using Microsoft Office suite. Microsoft Azure does not offer the Microsoft Office suite when you subscribe to its services. That does not mean that you cannot use it with Microsoft Azure; for example, if you choose to implement a custom content management solution, you can store Office documents on Azure. However, the overall experience is much different from Office 365. Azure does not provide advance features such as document co-authoring, online viewing, and editing of documents. Similarly, features such as document check-in, versioning, and so on are also absent.

HOW DOES EACH HANDLE CROSS-PLATFORM SUPPORT?

Cross-platform support is another important area of consideration for many organizations as they evaluate cloud-based platforms. For the most part, cloud-based services are consumed using web browsers, which enable border platform support. For example, most websites eventually render on a browser as HTML regardless of the technology used to build these websites. This makes it much easier to target a wide user base with different operating systems and browsers. Because you can build and deploy a wide range of solutions using Microsoft Azure, the nature of those solutions determines what features you offer; many features may not be available or fully functional across all the platforms. With Office 365, only certain features work with Microsoft Windows; others have more limited functionality depending on the user choice of a browser. Also, tools, such as SharePoint Workspace, SharePoint Designer, and the like are only supported on Microsoft Windows.

HOW DO SERVICE-LEVEL AGREEMENTS WORK?

For legal and operational purposes, a vendor must provide a *service-level agreement* (*SLA*) to define its operational commitment to a business that will consume its cloud services. Much like most IaaS and PaaS offerings, Microsoft Azure provides 99.9 percent availability as part of its SLA for most of its services at the platform level. However, because these offerings by definition require custom development, the final availability depends on the specific solution you develop and deploy, so you need to plan and test for this explicitly.

Office 365 also provides 99.9 percent availability as part of its SLA. Because it's a SaaS offering, the degree of customizations to its services are limited in scope. For example, SharePoint Online only supports deployment of its custom server-side solutions in the form of Sandboxed Solutions. Exchange Online and Lync Online do not enable custom server-side solutions at all. For small businesses with limited resources to develop, deploy, and manage custom solutions, Office 365 is a great option because it offers services with baked-in communication, messaging, and collaboration features; Microsoft takes care of feature availability as part of standard SLA.

WHAT DEVELOPMENT TOOLS DO AZURE AND OFFICE 365 SUPPORT?

Developers can expect to enjoy great tool support and powerful API programming tools with both Microsoft Azure and Office 365.

Microsoft Azure provides developers the following:

➤ **The platform to build and deploy applications from scratch.** This includes a variety of technologies including PHP, .NET, and Java.

➤ **SDKs for a variety of technologies.** Microsoft did a remarkable job with this.

➤ **A seamless development experience.** Developers who are already familiar with Visual Studio will notice that after the SDK is installed, Azure templates become available immediately and relevant emulators, for example, compute, storage and so on, are installed on local workstation. This allows developers to test and debug their solutions locally without the need to connect to Azure Platform.

➤ **SQL Azure allows developers to work with a database engine in a similar way they use on-premise SQL Server.** Again, developers can leverage all their existing knowledge and skillset related to the database programming because there are only slight differences between the SQL Azure and SQL Server from the developer's prospective.

➤ **Azure provides reliable and secure messaging relay functionality in the form of Server Bus.** Developers can utilize Service Bus to build applications that are decoupled and highly scalable.

➤ **By using Azure Connect, developers can build applications that can be hosted in hybrid environments.** For example, you can host custom solution on Azure and connect to SQL Server, which resides on-premises. Also, using Azure Connect, developers can perform remote debugging by connecting to applications hosted on Azure using a local machine. This aids developers in debugging and troubleshooting hosted applications in the real time rather than using emulators on the local machine.

The Office 365 development is slightly different because it is essentially a combination of many different services. There is no single Office 365 SDK that developers can download. You can't start building the solutions for all the Office 365 services. For example, Exchange Online development requires you to install the Exchange Managed API, which then enables developers to connect and program against Exchange API; the same is true for Lync Online. SharePoint Online templates do get installed as part of Visual Studio installation, so there is no need to install them separately.

COMPARISON OF AZURE AND OFFICE 365

Although, conducting a holistic comparison between Azure and Office 365 is beyond the scope of this chapter, Table 17-1 provides a side by side comparison of Azure and Office 365.

TABLE 17-1: Comparison of Azure and Office 365

FACTOR	AZURE	OFFICE 365
Flexibility	More flexible, but requires more resources.	Limited flexibility.
Identity Federation	Provided by ACS with no maintenance required on-premises.	Provided by ADFS, but need to be maintained on-premises.
Productivity Tools	Office suite is only available through custom content management; advanced features are not available.	Office suite is available as part of its service offering.
Cross-Platform Support	The nature of your solution determines which features are supported cross-platform.	Certain features work only with Microsoft Windows operating system. Others have limited functionality based on the browser.
Service-Level Agreement	Provides 99.9 percent availability at the platform level. You must ensure service availability for custom solutions.	Offers 99.9 percent availability, It's a SaaS offering and customization is limited in scope.
Development Tools Support	You have a seamless development experience with a platform SDK to develop, test, debug and deploy custom solutions.	There is no single Office 365 SDK available to developers. Extra effort is required to ensure development platform is ready for Office 365 development.

SUMMARY

This chapter covers factors that help you determine when it's best to use Microsoft Azure and when it's best to use Office 365. Although each factor plays a different role in the decision-making process, you should carefully consider each factor with equal importance. Flexibility of the cloud platform and SLAs are critical for businesses because they impact the operations and future vision. Productivity tools and cross-platform support impacts end users as they perform day-to-day operations. Finally, development tools support for cloud-based services is important for developers who build custom solutions and customize existing services to meet their business needs.

INDEX